ALSO BY ROBERT KAGAN

The Jungle Grows Back: America and Our Imperiled World

The World America Made

The Return of History and the End of Dreams

Dangerous Nation: America's Foreign Policy from Its
Earliest Days to the Dawn of the Twentieth Century

Of Paradise and Power: America and Europe in the New World Order

Present Dangers: Crisis and Opportunity in
America's Foreign and Defense Policy

A Twilight Struggle: American Power and Nicaragua

THE GHOST AT
THE FEAST

THE GHOST AT THE FEAST

America and the Collapse of World Order,
1900–1941

ROBERT KAGAN

ALFRED A. KNOPF   NEW YORK 2023

THIS IS A BORZOI BOOK
PUBLISHED BY ALFRED A. KNOPF

Copyright © 2023 by Robert Kagan

All rights reserved. Published in the United States by Alfred A. Knopf,
a division of Penguin Random House LLC, New York, and distributed
in Canada by Penguin Random House Canada Limited, Toronto.

www.aaknopf.com

Knopf, Borzoi Books, and the colophon are registered
trademarks of Penguin Random House LLC.

Library of Congress Cataloging-in-Publication Data
Names: Kagan, Robert, author.
Title: The ghost at the feast: America and the collapse
of world order, 1900–1941 / Robert Kagan.
Other titles: America and the collapse of world order, 1900–1941
Description: First edition. | New York: Alfred A. Knopf, 2023. | "This is a Borzoi
book published by Alfred A. Knopf." | Includes bibliographical references and index.
Identifiers: LCCN 2022005163 (print) | LCCN 2022005164 (ebook) |
ISBN 9780307262943 (hardcover) | ISBN 9780593535196 (ebook)
Subjects: LCSH: United States—Foreign relations—
20th century. | World politics—1900–1945.
Classification: LCC E744 .K146 2022 (print) | LCC E744 (ebook) |
DDC 327.73009/04—dc23/eng/20220222
LC record available at https://lccn.loc.gov/2022005163
LC ebook record available at https://lccn.loc.gov/2022005164

Jacket image: The Spanish-American War, destruction of the battleship *Maine,*
Havana harbor, Feb. 15, 1898. Everett Collection / Bridgeman Images
Jacket design by Kelly Blair
Maps by Mapping Specialists Ltd.

Manufactured in the United States of America
First Edition

For Leni and David

The ghastly suspicion that the American people would not honour the signature of their own delegates was never mentioned between us: It became the ghost at all our feasts.

—Harold Nicolson[1]

CONTENTS

THE GHOST AT THE FEAST

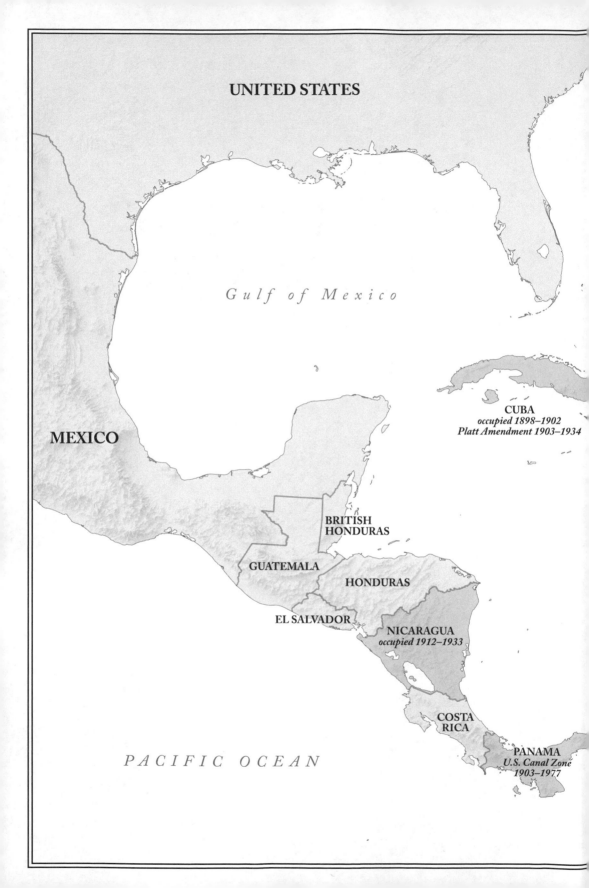

UNITED STATES

Gulf of Mexico

MEXICO

CUBA
occupied 1898–1902
Platt Amendment 1903–1934

BRITISH
HONDURAS

GUATEMALA

HONDURAS

EL SALVADOR

NICARAGUA
occupied 1912–1933

COSTA
RICA

PANAMA
U.S. Canal Zone
1903–1977

PACIFIC OCEAN

ATLANTIC OCEAN

BAHAMAS

HAITI
*occupied
1915–1934*

DOMINICAN
REPUBLIC
occupied 1915–1924

U.S. VIRGIN ISLANDS
purchased from Denmark, 1917

PUERTO RICO
acquired from Spain, 1898

JAMAICA

Caribbean Sea

VENEZUELA

COLOMBIA

Europe on the Eve of World War I, 1914

Allies
Central Powers
Neutrals

Baltic Sea

RUSSIA

AUSTRIA-HUNGARY

ROMANIA

Black Sea

SERBIA

BULGARIA

ALBANIA

OTTOMAN EMPIRE

GREECE

Mediterranean Sea

German-controlled Territory at the end of 1916, "Brussels to Baghdad"

Allies
Central Powers
German-controlled
Neutrals

RUSSIA

Black Sea

ROMANIA

BULGARIA

OTTOMAN EMPIRE

GREECE

Baghdad

Mediterranean Sea

Europe After 1919, The Versailles Settlement

New or restored countries

FINLAND

ESTONIA

LATVIA

LITHUANIA

RUSSIA

POLAND

CZECHOSLOVAKIA

HUNGARY

ROMANIA

YUGOSLAVIA

BULGARIA

ALBANIA

OTTOMAN EMPIRE

GREECE

Baltic Sea

Black Sea

Mediterranean Sea

DENMARK

North
Sea

Ceded
to Denmark

• Hamburg

Weser River

NETHERLANDS

Berlin •

Ruhr River

GERMANY

BELGIUM

Rhine River

Ceded
to Belgium

Demilitarized
Zone
1919–1936

LUXEMBOURG

Main River

SAAR

Returned
to France

FRANCE

Danube River

Munich •

SWITZERLAND

Germany After World War I

SWEDEN

Baltic Sea

LITHUANIA

Ceded
to Lithuania

Danzig

DANZIG

East
Prussia

Polish
Corridor

Ceded
to Poland

Oder River

Warsaw

POLAND

Prague

Ceded
to Poland

Ceded
to Czechoslovakia

CZECHOSLOVAKIA

Vienna

AUSTRIA

HUNGARY

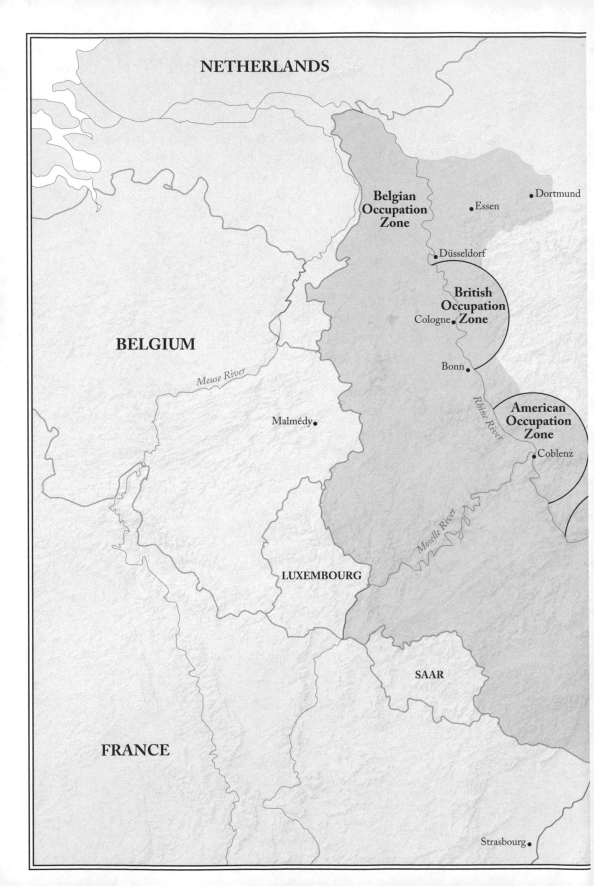

GERMANY

**French
Occupation
Zone**

•Frankfurt

Mainz•

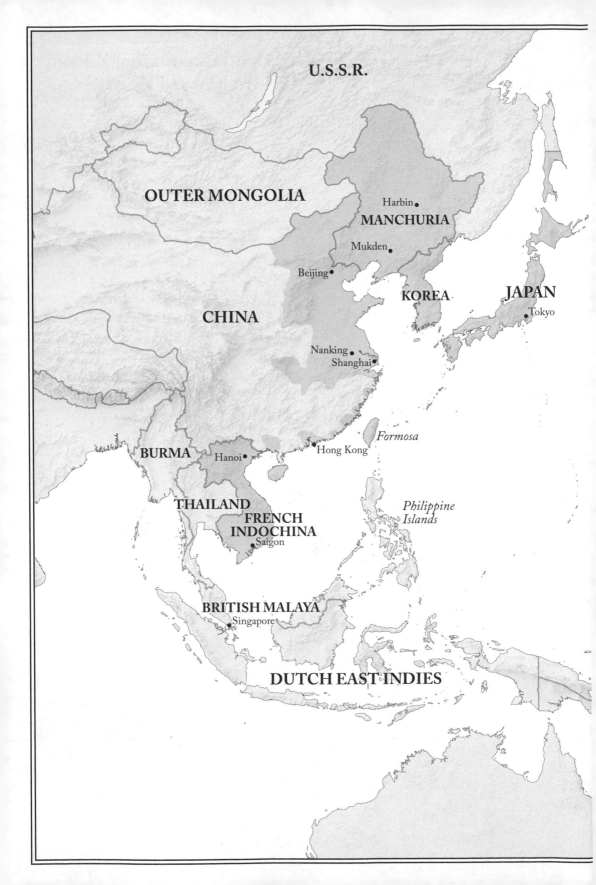

Territory under Japanese control,
December 7, 1941

Area Under Japanese Control, August 1942

Territory under Japanese control

CANADA

U.S.

*Hawaiian
Islands*

NEW
ZEALAND

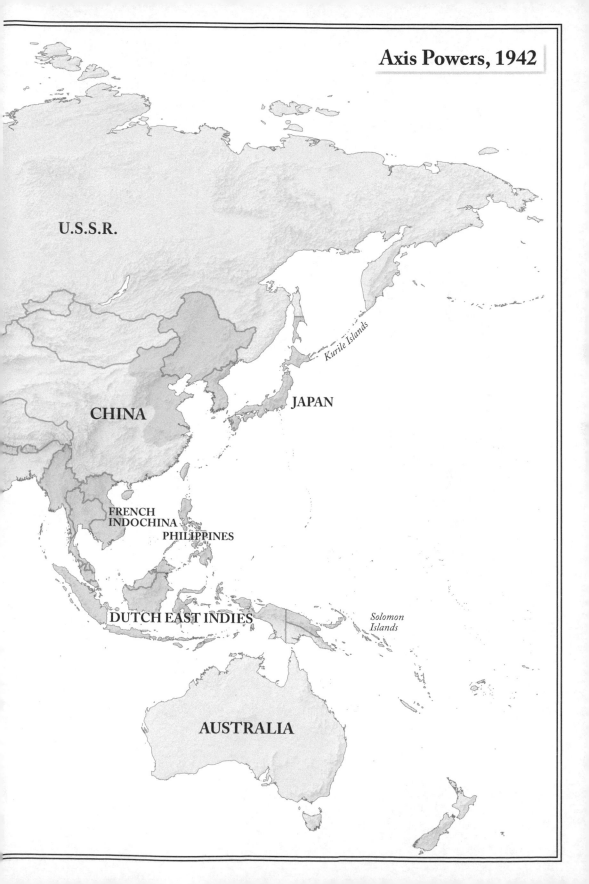

Axis Powers, 1942

U.S.S.R.

CHINA

JAPAN

Kurile Islands

FRENCH
INDOCHINA

PHILIPPINES

DUTCH EAST INDIES

*Solomon
Islands*

AUSTRALIA

Introduction

She sails upon a summer sea . . . safe from attack, safe even from menace, she hears from afar the warring cries of European races and faiths, as the gods of Epicurus listened to the murmurs of the unhappy earth spread out beneath their golden dwellings . . .

—James Bryce, 1888[1]

POWER CHANGES everything. The United States at the end of the nineteenth century was in many respects the same country it had been a century earlier. Its system of government was shaped by the same Constitution, albeit modified by the Civil War. Its guiding principles were still based on those articulated in the Declaration of Independence, which Americans revered if not always practiced. America's favorable geography was the same, although American dominance of the North American continent was more complete. Yet America's power relative to that of other nations in the world—measured in wealth, land and resources, population, and potential military capability—had grown so great as to change completely the way the rest of the world viewed the United States. It also changed the way Americans viewed themselves, though less completely. William McKinley declared the era of isolation over. But most Americans were not much interested in change and, at the end of the nineteenth century, still held to old ideas about themselves. They still saw their nation standing apart from the rest of the world, different and also superior, and by and large they liked it that way.

This perception was understandable. America did stand apart, even in 1900, a virtual distant island in geopolitical terms, on a huge continent surrounded on two sides by vast oceans, thousands of miles from all the other great powers of the world. Americans' physical location had long given them unique advantages and a unique perspective. First and foremost, it had given them both wealth and a remarkable degree of economic independence. The United States by 1900 had grown into the world's largest and most dynamic economy. Some of this success was due to the particular American style of capitalism, the open and highly mobile nature of its society, compared to the more rigid and inhibiting traditions and class structures of Europe. American patent and commercial laws fostered invention, innovation, entrepreneurship, and investment, both domestic and foreign. But modern economists judge that the biggest factor behind America's breathtaking economic growth in the last decades of the nineteenth century was simply the availability of abundant natural resources. Americans led the world in the production of copper, coal, zinc, iron ore, lead, and other valuable minerals. They produced half the world's oil and a third of its pig iron, silver, and gold.[2] They had raced ahead of the British in the production of steel and coal, the two greatest measures of economic power at the time, as well as in industrial manufacturing. They produced more than half of the world's cotton and corn.[3] They were also largely self-sufficient. Although Americans traded with the other large economies, they did not depend on that trade in the way that the other top economies, Britain and Germany, did. They had the land and resources to feed themselves. Their homegrown businesses produced the goods they needed and wanted, and the large population was rich enough to buy more than 90 percent of domestic production. The other advanced economies depended on access to foreign markets and foreign sources of supply, and these requirements shaped their foreign policies. Americans believed that they did not have to rely on anyone but themselves, and they were mostly right.[4]

This relative economic self-sufficiency complemented a historically unique geopolitical independence. Of the large, industrializing nations of the world—Britain, France, Germany, Austria-Hungary, Italy, and Japan—the United States was the only one surrounded only by much smaller, weaker powers and by oceans. The European great powers all lived on top of each other and therefore in a constant state of insecurity. The Asian powers, either the formerly great, like China, or the aspiring to be great, like Japan, competed for control of land and resources with each other and also with the British, French, Russian, and, more recently, German empires. Only Americans did not live in a highly contested strategic environment. This was not due simply to fortune or to the allegedly "free security" afforded by Britain's Royal Navy. Americans had once shared the continent with the powerful empires of Britain, France, Spain, and

Russia, but over the course of a century they had driven or bought them out and compelled their acceptance of U.S. hegemony through stubbornness, belligerence, and occasional aggression. The task had been made easier by enduring geopolitical facts, however. The other great powers' main concerns were generally closer to home, thousands of miles from the New World. Thus Americans at the end of the nineteenth century found themselves enjoying a level of security that others could never share, or even comprehend. On the eve of World War I the British ambassador, Cecil Arthur Spring Rice, had to explain to his puzzled colleagues that Americans lived on a continent that was "remote, unconquerable, huge, without hostile neighbors." They therefore enjoyed an "unvexed tranquility," free from the "contentions and animosities" that were part of the everyday existence of Europeans.[5]

These unique circumstances had an impact not only on America's foreign policies but on American society and governance. The other powers had no choice but to spend large portions of their national incomes arming themselves for the constant possibility of war. Russia's peacetime army numbered almost 2,000,000 at the turn of the century; Germany had 600,000 men under arms; France had 575,000; Austria-Hungary, a second-rank power, had 360,000; and even the British, who lived on an island and relied almost entirely on their navy, had over 200,000 men in their standing army. The United States inhabited a territory almost as vast as Russia's, and had the world's third-largest population, yet its regular army at the end of the nineteenth century numbered only in the tens of thousands, a "corporal's guard," as Theodore Roosevelt called it, barely sufficient to deal with Native American tribes on the western plains, the U.S. Army's main post–Civil War mission.[6] Yet it seemed adequate for the nation's defense because, as British intelligence officers judged at the time, whatever the size of the American army, "a land war on the American Continent would be perhaps the most hazardous military enterprise that we could possibly be driven to engage in."[7]

Americans had recently invested more in their naval forces. In the early 1880s their navy had been no bigger than that of Chile, and they had launched a sizable peacetime naval buildup—but again they built less and spent less than the leading naval powers. The "New Navy" consisted of a handful of armored cruisers and eventually 7 modern battleships. By comparison, in 1901 Britain's Royal Navy had 50 battleships cruising the oceans, France had 28, Germany had 21, and even Italy had 15. Like the army, the U.S. Navy was small in proportion to the nation's wealth and size, even though it had to operate in two vast oceans and the Caribbean

and protect thousands of miles of coastline. Had there been any real
challenge from another great naval power, the American fleet would have
been dangerously inadequate. But in the world as it was configured, the
other powers were reluctant to expose themselves to their neighbors by
sending their fleets thousands of miles away to take on the United States.
Even in the age of steam, distances still mattered. Americans enjoyed
far greater security than other great powers, therefore, even though they
spent barely 1 percent of their national income on defense, a small fraction of what the great powers of the day spent.[8]

Low defense costs meant Americans could spend their money elsewhere and keep taxes relatively low. It also meant less need for strong
central government, less military bureaucracy, and less need for speedy
and efficient decision-making. Americans had less need to take foreign
policy very seriously, and generally they didn't. Henry Cabot Lodge,
who wished it were otherwise, admitted that "our relations with foreign
nations" filled "but a slight place in American politics" and most of the
time excited "only a languid interest."[9] The political parties saw foreign
policy problems as chiefly opportunities to score points, while Congress
saw foreign policy chiefly as a constitutional struggle with the executive.

British officials liked to tease their American colleagues that the United
States was most fortunate "in being untroubled by any foreign policy."[10]
But as James Bryce, the British historian and long-serving ambassador to
the United States, observed, this was a luxury Americans seemingly could
afford. The great powers of Europe had no choice but to maintain their
systems of government "in full efficiency for war as well as for peace."
But Americans could tolerate "the want of unity and vigour in the conduct of affairs by executive and legislature" because they lived in a world
of their own and sailed "upon a summer sea."[11]

The United States also stood apart ideologically. It was a young, democratic republic in a world still dominated by ancient hereditary monarchies and aristocracies. At the turn of the century, Russia was ruled
by Nicholas II, latest in the line of Romanov tsars going back to 1613;
Wilhelm II, of the eight-hundred-year-old House of Hohenzollern, was
emperor of Germany and king of Prussia; Franz Joseph I, a descendant
of the eight-centuries-old House of Habsburg, was emperor of Austria,
king of Hungary, and king of Bohemia; Abdul Hamid II, the Sublime
Khan and thirty-fourth Ottoman sultan, ruled in Turkey; the Empress
Dowager Cixi, former concubine of the Xianfeng Emperor of the Qing
dynasty, ruled as regent in China; the Emperor Meiji was the 122nd
emperor of Japan; Italy, a constitutional monarchy, was ruled by King

Umberto I and then by his son Victor Emmanuel III, of the thousand-year-old House of Savoy. In this world, the United States, a little over a century in existence, remained a revolutionary upstart. The kaiser could still appeal to the other crowned heads of Europe to show the American democratic "rascals" that "Europe's kings really stand together," as he did in the lead-up to the Spanish-American War in 1898.[12] The kaiser's grandmother agreed. Queen Victoria was in her sixty-third year on the British throne. Her father was born ten years before the American Revolution. Her grandfather was George III.

The United States was not only governed differently; it was not even a "nation" in the way that the other great powers were. Americans shared neither common blood nor an ancient rootedness in the soil. All they shared, at least in theory, was a common allegiance to their written Constitution and a theoretical fidelity to the principles of the Declaration of Independence. This universalistic, ideological nationalism had been revolutionary when it first erupted on the scene in the late eighteenth century, and it remained revolutionary a century later. It would continue to shape Americans' choices in foreign policy.

And Americans had choices. That, too, set them apart from most great powers. In Europe the leaders of a rising Germany worried about encirclement because Germany was, in fact, surrounded by great powers that had banded against it in the past and might do so again in the future. Germans believed that they had to build a large navy if their growth as a nation was not to be blocked by British naval and commercial dominance, and that they needed overseas colonies if they were to assume the place of a "world power" alongside the other great empires. France and Russia engaged in imperial competition with Britain and other powers because they feared the consequences of falling behind. Germany's rising power also scared them, and they built up their armies to deter it and preserve their influence in the face of an exploding German economy and population. The British had to respond constantly to the encroachments of all these other powers when they threatened access to India and other vital components of the empire. In Asia, Japan and China were locked in competition with each other and with the British and other European empires. Great-power rivalries, old and new, tended to determine and constrain the foreign policy choices of the other strong nations in the world. They did what they had to do to survive and flourish.

For Americans, the question was less what they had to do than what they wanted to do, or what they felt they should do. At the end of the nineteenth century, Americans could choose one of two paths in the world. One was to confine themselves chiefly to matters within their own borders, or at most within their own hemisphere, and to focus on improving their own society. This approach, mislabeled then and later as "isolationism," had a long tradition. Washington had laid down his "great rule" in his Farewell Address in 1796, to have with foreign powers "as little political connexion as possible." Jefferson in his inaugural address in 1801 called for "Peace, commerce, and honest friendship with all nations—entangling alliances with none." As the German émigré politician Carl Schurz put it, in "our compact continental stronghold we are substantially unassailable . . . we can hardly get into a war unless it be of our own seeking."[13]

Since the United States did not have to act out of necessity, many argued, what was the justification for any foreign action? Why put at hazard America's remarkably beneficial circumstances? And what right did the United States have to involve itself in the affairs of others? Because every overseas action seemed optional, moral and ideological questions loomed larger for Americans than for other nations acting out of perceived necessity. Those Americans who argued for rigid fidelity to Washington's "great rule" believed the only motives for an active foreign policy were greed, unseemly ambition, a desire for domination, or even a desire for conflict, or what many in the late nineteenth century called "jingoism." To pursue further expansion, for financial gain or for glory, as all the other powers of the world did, was, for many Americans, a sign of bad character. As Grover Cleveland's secretary of state, Walter Q. Gresham, put it in 1894, a strong nation like the United States had to be "conscious of an impulse to rush into difficulties" that did not concern it "except in a highly imaginary way."[14] Those who favored restraint also warned against the stronger central government, the large federal expenditures, and the "imperial," anti-democratic mentality that a more vigorous foreign policy would require.[15]

Americans were also plagued by fears of the different races and ethnicities that came to their shores as immigrants and refugees. Many among the shrinking white Anglo-Saxon Protestant majority feared the effects of an active foreign policy on the nation's complexion. Some were already unhappy at the way immigrant groups had grasped the foreign policy tiller. By the late nineteenth century, Irish Americans, German Americans, Italian Americans, Jews, and Catholics had begun to have a significant impact on relations with Britain, Russia, Germany, and other nations. In addition, many of the activist foreign policies pushed by "expansionists"—usually in Republican administrations—entailed the acquisition of various islands with large non-white populations, such as Hawaii or assorted islands in the Caribbean. White supremacists in the South and even many northern liberals objected to adding more darker-skinned people to an increasingly non–Anglo-Saxon Protestant population. As Gresham put it, if Americans did not "stay at home and attend to their own business," they would "go to hell as fast as possible."[16]

But were Americans capable of staying home? Was abstention from the world consistent with American universal principles or with the American character as a people? By 1900 an increasing number of leading Americans thought the answer to those questions was no.

In fact, for all their professed desire to remain aloof from the world, Americans had never been very good at minding their own business. They may have wanted to be left alone but they had never left anyone else in their vicinity alone. They had expanded territorially, commercially, and ideologically almost continually since before the nation was even founded. Although the United States did not need foreign trade to flourish, Americans regarded trade as both normal and desirable, and as a critical right of sovereignty. As John Adams once observed, their "love of commerce, with its conveniences and pleasures," was as "unalterable as their natures." Americans had fought a war against the world's strongest empire in 1812 largely over their neutral rights to trade, refusing to cooperate with the British embargo against Napoleon's France.[17] Even in their state of "isolation" in the nineteenth century, Americans were quick to express their opinions about the behavior of other states, cheering for liberal revolutions in Spain, Greece, Italy, and Hungary and, of course, in the Western Hemisphere, condemning tsarist persecution of Jews, British persecution of the Irish, standing up, rhetorically, for the rights of the Chinese against their imperial oppressors. Americans had never been shy about judging others against their own standards.

Nor had Americans ever been shy about their ambitions. Even as a weak, vulnerable, and barely unified string of states along the Atlantic Seaboard, the founding generation's leaders had spoken of their new republic as a "Hercules in a cradle," the "embryo of a great empire." Washington himself had foreseen the day when, thanks to the "increase of population and resources," the United States would be able to "bid defiance to any power on earth."[18] A second generation of leaders, buoyed by the heady experience of fighting the British to a draw in the War of 1812, envisioned the United States as the leader of an entire hemisphere of republics. This "American system," as Henry Clay had called it in the 1810s, would marshal the powers of the New World, with the United

States at its head, to defy the Old. Territorial ambition persisted well into the nineteenth century, as many Americans looked north in anticipation of eventually taking all of Canada, while others looked south in the expectation of planting an American flag in Mexico City.

Americans talked a great deal about peace, but they had never been a tranquil or pacific people. Nor was the "historic American propensity toward violence," as the historian Russell Weigley called it, limited to "Jacksonians" of Scotch-Irish stock.[19] Jefferson and John Quincy Adams were no less expansionist than Andrew Jackson, and no less willing to employ force when necessary to achieve their objectives. From the Massachusetts Puritans' massacre of the Pequot in the 1630s to the Trail of Tears two centuries later, Americans of all backgrounds had taken the lands they coveted, forcefully and usually in violation of treaties they had negotiated with the inhabitants. The French and Spanish pushed out of Florida and Louisiana in the early nineteenth century warned of Americans' "warlike" nature.[20] America itself had been forged in war, first in the Revolution and then in the war to end slavery and preserve the Union. The Civil War had left 600,000 dead and another 470,000 wounded in "a conflict of peculiarly intense destructiveness, of peculiarly unrestrained military means deployed in pursuit of notably absolute objectives."[21] In 1900, northerners still remembered the war as a glorious moral crusade, and the South celebrated it as a noble "lost cause." Americans from both sides lionized their military heroes, built statues to them, threw annual celebrations in their honor, and elected them to high office.

The illusion of American restraint in foreign policy emerged during the long struggle between the North and South over slavery, when Americans turned their expansiveness, ambition, and belligerence inward against themselves. The internal conflict produced westward and southward expansion as the North and South raced each other to acquire new lands and new states. The ten years of Reconstruction after the war also focused the nation's attentions inward. But it was not long before old ambitions returned and people like William Henry Seward and James G. Blaine again dreamed, like the founders, of the United States becoming "the great power of the earth."

By the end of the nineteenth century, with such dreams largely fulfilled, some Americans insisted that, under the new circumstances, Washington's dictum was no longer relevant. It may have been wise counsel for the weak nation that the young republic had been, but not for the strong nation it had become. President Benjamin Harrison argued that "we are great enough and rich enough to reach forward to grander conceptions" than those entertained by "our statesmen in the past."[22]

The unanswered question, however, was what did "great" mean? With the continent conquered and all but invulnerable to foreign attack, few Americans at the dawn of the twentieth century yearned for more territory or for any other tangible acquisitions. The economy boomed in the late 1890s, such that Americans now needed less from the world beyond their greatly expanded borders than at any time in their history. For many Americans, greatness was to be measured not by wealth or territory but by such intangible factors as morality, principle, honor, and responsibility. They believed the United States should assume new responsibilities commensurate with its new power.

At the turn of the century, the political home for this way of thinking was the Republican Party—"the party of progress that fought slavery standing across the pathway of modern civilization," as Henry Cabot Lodge liked to describe it. Republicans sought to replicate that great moral victory on a larger stage. Resistance to this expansive and moralistic view of America's role in the world came chiefly from Democrats. The party still dominated by the South remained the defender of states' rights, small government, and, therefore, what traditionally accompanied them: a restrained foreign policy. As was so often the case in the United States, therefore, foreign policy became yet another area of partisan division, along with the tariff and the role of the federal government. To those, like Gresham, who argued that the United States had no business involving itself in the affairs of other nations, Lodge responded that "the proposition that it is none of our business is precisely what the South said about slavery." He and Roosevelt constantly drew comparisons between events in their own time and the Civil War struggle. Every Democratic president they opposed was "another Buchanan," every great foreign policy challenge was a "second crusade."[23]

For most of the three decades after the Civil War the evenly balanced parties tended to cancel each other out and produce stasis in both domestic and foreign policy.[24] The United States was like a crewed boat in which one side was rowing in one direction and the other side was rowing in the other, with the result that the boat went nowhere. The stalemate ended when the balance of political power shifted decisively in the Republicans' favor. The Democrats lost 113 seats in the House in the congressional elections of 1894, and in the 1896 presidential contest, William McKinley defeated the populist William Jennings Bryan by a substantial margin.

Republicans, with their more expansive and moralistic views of foreign policy, were in charge.

By the end of the nineteenth century, various forms of "internationalism" had gained adherents across the political, ideological, and social spectrum, from Republicans like Roosevelt and Lodge to Democrats like Bryan, religious leaders like Lyman Abbott and Josiah Strong and academics like Stanford's David Starr Jordan, Princeton's Woodrow Wilson, and Harvard's Charles W. Eliot.[25] Nor were internationalist views confined to the "elite." The populist Bryan, accepting the Democratic nomination in 1900, envisioned the United States "solving the problems of civilization," "a republic gradually but surely becoming the supreme moral factor in the world's progress and the accepted arbiter of the world's disputes."[26] Even the Boy Orator of the Platte saw a historic international role for the United States. These "internationalists" differed on many issues, sometimes violently. Their ranks included both proponents and opponents of retaining the Philippines after the Spanish-American War, for instance. But they agreed that the United States could no longer stand apart from the rest of the world. Many Americans understood that the world was shifting around them, creating both new opportunities and new dangers. Technological revolutions in transportation and communications—the wireless telegraph, transoceanic cables, and ocean-going steamships—eliminated the time and distance that had separated peoples, cultures, and civilizations since the dawn of history. Some hoped they would also erase the social and cultural boundaries that had long divided nations and caused the wars between them. The political scientist Paul Reinsch asserted that the transmission of news in a single day, "from Buenos Aires to Tokyo, from Cape Town to San Francisco," could produce a "psychological unity of the world."[27] McKinley, in his last speech before being assassinated in 1901, set forth the increasingly common view that "God and man have linked the nations together. . . . Isolation is no longer possible or desirable. . . . The period of exclusiveness is past."[28]

While most expected the new technologies to bring unity and comity among peoples, some worried about increasing competition. Technology brought armies and navies closer together, too. New battleships projected unprecedented power over thousands of miles and diminished the strategic protection of oceans and distances. The increasingly interdependent global economy forced the great powers into more intense competition for land and markets.

The United States, some feared, would increasingly be drawn into this global fracas. While Americans depended less on international trade at the end of the century than before, the rest of the world depended more than ever on access to American goods and consumers.[29] By the end of the nineteenth century, the British population was so dependent on the importation of American foodstuffs that one British official worried that "we should be face to face with famine" if the supply was ever cut off. European finance ministers were "beginning to recognize more and more the influence of American commercial policy upon their revenues."[30] By the turn of the century, the United States had joined Britain as the world's banker. Foreign companies became increasingly dependent on American finance, a reversal of the flow of investment in the mid-nineteenth century. As John Hay observed in 1902, the "debtor nation" had become the "chief creditor nation." The "financial center of the world, which required thousands of years to journey from the Euphrates to the Thames and Seine, seems passing to the Hudson between daybreak and dark."[31] The world's increasing dependence on the American economy meant that the United States would be a critical factor in any war between great powers, should the peace break down.

It also made for a certain resentment and hostility. The "Americanization of the World," as the British journalist W. T. Stead called it, was not welcome everywhere. The United States "loomed so gigantic on the horizon of industrial and diplomatic competition," one contemporary observed," that "talk of European combination to oppose her advance was in the air."[32] Some of the hostility was cultural. Many Europeans did not want their societies polluted by the invasion of America's crass capitalist individualism. After a tour of the United States, Prince Albert of Belgium remarked, "Alas, you will eat us all up."[33] While many across Europe decried Americans' frenetic acquisitiveness, however, the British political leader Lord Rosebery suggested that if Britons hoped to keep up, they would do well to "inoculate" themselves "with some of the nervous energy of Americans."[34]

To many Germans, the United States looked like a dangerous competitor and a potential obstacle to Germany's growth and rise as a world power. German industrialists demanded tariff barriers against American goods and yearned for a new Bismarck to rise up and save Europe from "the American peril."[35] The kaiser tried to convince the British to link arms against the new threat from across the Atlantic. It was only a matter of time, he warned, before the Americans, "swollen by prosperity and pride and unweighted by any of the responsibilities which enforce caution on other States, would inevitably come into collision . . . with the present Mistress of the Seas."[36]

The British had other ideas. The alliance they sought was with their Anglo-Saxon "cousins." Indeed, it was out of concern for Germany's growing power, as well as the pressure exerted on British interests by both Russia and France, that the British increasingly looked to the United States to lighten the Royal Navy's burden in East Asia and the Pacific. The British were not alone in seeing the influential Americans as useful partners in their own struggles. The Japanese reached out, hoping the United States might back them in their competition with Russia. The French would have been delighted to have the United States on their side as a balance against Germany. Even the kaiser sometimes thought he could turn the Americans into an asset in his dealings with the other European powers. Whether as a friend or a foe, the United States could no longer be ignored.

Nor could Americans themselves ignore the imperial competition that increasingly shaped international affairs at the end of the nineteenth century, the struggle among the European powers for control in parts of Africa and the Middle East, and in Asia, where they competed for spheres of influence in a weak and prostrate Chinese empire. How long before this global competition brought them "into contact with American interests"? Lodge asked. What was to keep the European empires from carving up the Western Hemisphere too?[37] By the mid-1880s, American officials were becoming concerned about German ambitions in particular. As Cleveland's secretary of state Thomas F. Bayard put it, the Germans were entertaining "schemes of distant annexation & civilization in many quarters of the globe," including the Western Hemisphere.[38]

Such concerns partly explained the increasing prickliness and occasional belligerence Americans showed in response to relatively minor European encroachments in the Western Hemisphere. In 1895, even the normally cautious and restrained Cleveland practically threatened war when Britain at first refused to submit a long-simmering border disagreement with Venezuela to arbitration. Cleveland's action was partly a response to political pressure from Republicans, who accused him of weakness in defending the Monroe Doctrine, and from Irish constituents who hated the British. But it also revealed his own administration's increasing concern that America's tranquil cruise on the "summer sea" was in danger of coming to an end.

No Americans in these years called for global imperial expansion. Even the more aggressive internationalists like Roosevelt and Lodge limited their goals to defense of the Western Hemisphere. They and others wanted to build a canal across the Central American isthmus linking the Atlantic and Pacific coasts, a desire Americans had harbored since completion of the Suez Canal in 1869. Like most Republicans since the days of Seward and Blaine, they wanted to acquire bases in the Caribbean—the Danish West Indies, in particular—to control and defend the approaches to an eventual canal. Like many American administrations of all parties going back to the 1840s, they also wanted to annex Hawaii to the United States, to protect the approaches to the Pacific Coast from attack, to protect the planned canal, and to promote commerce with Asia. Their aim was not to enter the United States into the global great-power competition but to shield the United States from that competition. Lodge did not want the United States to "entangle itself in the questions of Europe or Asia."[39] He had no interest in "a widely extended system of colonization." He and Roosevelt wanted control of "the outworks" of America's defenses, nothing more.[40] Lodge and Roosevelt did worry about whether the American character was up to the challenge of a more competitive world in which it would be harder for the United States to hide behind two oceans. A common theory of the day, recently popularized by Brooks Adams, was that great civilizations fell because they became decadent and "effete," too enamored of luxury and comfort, too lacking in the "barbarian" virtues necessary to preserve their civilization. There was much talk about what Alfred Thayer Mahan called the "masculine combative virtues," which presumably were being lost in all the money-making. The great jurist Oliver Wendell Holmes, Jr., worried that Americans in their "snug, over-safe corner of the world" worshiped only "the man of wealth."[41] The United States had to be more than a "successful national shop," Lodge insisted.[42]

"Responsibility" was an increasingly common theme of the late-nineteenth-century American discourse about foreign policy. Most internationalists believed the United States had a role to play in preserving peace and advancing civilization, even if this meant abandoning Washington's great rule. The present international order, characterized by a general peace and a relatively open trading system, and dominated by the liberalizing governments of Britain and France, was so well suited to American interests that it was only right that a newly powerful United States take some share of the burden of supporting it. John Hay thus imagined the United States joining Great Britain, Russia, and Germany "in a grand design to stabilize the existing distribution of power, and call a halt to the race for commerce and armaments."[43] Americans did take a leading role in the arbitration movement on both sides of the Atlantic. When McKinley urged Congress to ratify the first arbitration agreement, with Britain, he declared it a "duty to mankind" for the sake of "advancing civilization."[44] (Congress, naturally, rejected it.) McKinley authorized the negotiation of more than a dozen treaties of reciprocity, abandoning his earlier support for high tariffs, on the theory that "good trade insures good will."[45] When Russia's Tsar Nicholas II called the world's great powers together at The Hague in the spring of 1899 to discuss mechanisms for peace and limits on armaments, McKinley sent a distinguished bipartisan American delegation with detailed instructions to establish an international court of arbitration. The Republican Elihu Root hoped the gradual creation of international rules and institutions would eventually bring a lasting peace among the "civilized nations"— a " 'Parliament of man, and Federation of the world.' "[46]

Beyond helping establish the international mechanisms for preserving the peace, many Americans also wanted their nation to take a larger part in advancing and protecting the rights of other peoples and helping to alleviate human suffering. Such impulses had roots in the religious and progressive reform movements of the nineteenth century. The influx of immigrants and refugees over the course of the century added to the pressures on American officials to condemn repression and persecution in the new arrivals' homelands. Irish Americans influenced American policy toward Britain in solidarity with their oppressed brethren back home. Jewish refugees from Russia and parts of eastern and central Europe remained interested in the fate of those still trapped under anti-Semitic despotisms. As governor of the state of New York and later as president, Roosevelt repeatedly denounced Russian pogroms and official anti-Semitism. In 1902 John Hay filed a protest with Romania for tolerating and encouraging anti-Semitism and similar "wrongs repugnant to the moral sense of liberal modern peoples."[47]

By 1900, there were twice as many American missionaries serving overseas as all the missionaries of Europe combined.[48] Their goal was not only conversion but the provision of aid and education to better people's lives. Josiah Strong, one of the leaders of the Social Gospel movement, preached the motto "The whole world a neighborhood and every man a neighbor."[49] By the 1890s, Americans were engaging in famine relief in Russia and India, sending money and grain through the American Red Cross, saving thousands from starvation.

The greatest show of humanitarianism came in response to the genocidal slaughter of Armenians in Turkey beginning in 1894. The mass butchery of Christians by their Muslim overlords, sensationally reported in American newspapers, pained and angered readers. Nationwide appeals led by John D. Rockefeller, Jacob Schiff, and other prominent Americans raised hundreds of thousands of dollars for relief (the equivalent of $10 million today). Clara Barton took her Red Cross team out of the country for the first time to help the victims in Turkey. Americans even debated whether the United States should intervene with force to help end the horrors. Josiah Strong, William Lloyd Garrison, Julia Ward Howe, and other prominent rights advocates signed a petition calling for immediate U.S. intervention, and the Cleveland administration dispatched two naval cruisers to Turkish waters, ostensibly for the purpose of rescuing American missionaries but also as an expression of American concern.[50] For many, that was not enough. Church groups asked why their Christian leaders could not "force the Government to remove the swords from the hands of Islam?"[51] Many blamed the European powers, chiefly Britain and Germany, for allowing the massacres. Lodge commented that British financial interests did not care "how many Armenians are butchered." American progressives like the feminist leader Charlotte Perkins Gilman pleaded for some nation to take the lead and "usher in the new age of global consciousness."[52]

This was the America that greeted the new century, a nation divided along numerous fault lines and with aspirations and concerns pulling in different directions. It was a nation unsure about the role it wanted to play in the world, if any. Americans were the beneficiaries of a world system they had no responsibility for maintaining. Many preferred to continue sailing on the summer sea and avoid being sucked into what seemed an ever more competitive, conflictual, and militarized international environment. But many also were eager to see the United States taking a share of international responsibility, working with others to preserve the peace and advance civilization. The story of American foreign policy in the first four decades of the twentieth century is about the effort to do both—"to adjust the nation to its new position without sacrificing the principles developed in the past," as one contemporary put it.[53] As the nineteenth century came to a close, Americans had no grand international plan and no clear direction.

CHAPTER ONE

A Tale of Two Wars

Now, we have fought a righteous war . . . and that is rare in history . . . but by the grace of that war we set Cuba free, and we joined her to those three or four free nations that exist on this earth; and we started out to set those poor Filipinos free too, and why, why, why that most righteous purpose of ours has apparently miscarried I suppose I never shall know.

—*Mark Twain*[1]

THE WAR with Spain that began in April 1898 is generally regarded as a great turning point in the history of American foreign policy, the moment when the United States became a "great power," a "world power," an "imperial" power. The great majority of Americans who supported the war, however, had no such ambitions. Intervention in Cuba did not seem to them a great deviation from their previous path. Cuba was an old issue, almost as old as the nation itself. Thomas Jefferson, John Quincy Adams, and other American statesmen of the early republic saw Cuba as a natural appendage of the growing country and assumed the island would eventually fall "like ripe fruit" into American hands. In the 1850s, southerners tried to purchase Cuba from Spain and make it the heart of a new slave empire in the Caribbean. During the long Cuban rebellion of the 1860s and '70s, known as the Ten Years' War, the U.S. government winked as private American citizens, many of them naturalized Cubans, lent financial and military support to rebels fighting to liberate the island from Spanish colonial rule. In 1873 the United States almost went to war when Spanish forces captured a retired Confederate warship, the *Virginius,* running guns to Cuba. When the Spanish executed the American captain and dozens of passengers, the Grant administration assembled the Atlantic fleet in the waters around Florida. Eventually, the Spanish government apologized, and Grant was not eager to go to war with the decrepit, outgunned American fleet of the time. The memory of the *Virginius* lingered in the popular imagination, however.[2] Failed Cuban rebellions in 1879, 1883, 1892, and 1893 ensured that the struggle made news with some regularity.

The fighting that erupted in Cuba in 1895 caught Americans' attention because it was especially brutal and destructive. This time the rebels, seeking to shake the pillars of Spanish colonial rule, went after the island's economy, burning plantations and factories and driving thousands out of work. The Spanish government, with little money and too few troops to crush the rebellion, responded with measures as harsh as they were ultimately unproductive. A new general, Valeriano Weyler, inaugurated a counterinsurgency strategy aimed at isolating the rebels from the rural population.[3] Farmers and their families were driven from their homes and herded into fortified towns and "reconcentration" camps with only what they could carry on their backs. Anyone found outside the camps was presumed a subversive and arrested or shot. Spanish soldiers scoured the countryside, burning villages and fields, destroying food stocks, slaughtering livestock, and razing homes. Eventually Weyler decreed a halt to all sugar production to prevent producers from paying bribes to the rebels. The Cuban economy ground to a halt.

The worst was yet to come. By the end of 1896, as the Cleveland administration was ending, Weyler's reconcentration policies created a humanitarian catastrophe. The influx of some 300,000 displaced persons into the designated towns and makeshift camps overwhelmed municipal authorities and camp operators who lacked the food, supplies, medicine, sanitation, and manpower to care for them. Thousands lived on daily rice rations meant to feed hundreds. Cubans began to starve and succumb to disease.[4] Hospitals were overwhelmed, lacking adequate staff, beds, and medicines. In the cities, bodies lay unburied in the streets; small children with bloated stomachs died searching garbage heaps for food. Over the course of a year at least 300,000 Cubans died—about one-fifth of the island's population—and the deaths continued to mount.[5]

Most Americans were on the rebels' side from the beginning. From early 1896 on, Congress was flooded with petitions from peace groups, church groups, labor unions, and farmers' associations calling for aid to the rebels and recognition of Cuban independence.[6] When reports arrived of the mass starvation and disease, the popular outcry matched the response to the Armenian genocide two years before. Cuba was "our Armenia," the editors at the *San Francisco Examiner* insisted.[7] Even the conservative *New York Times* wrote that the "civilized world" had an interest in preventing such inhuman behavior "in Cuba as well as in Armenia."[8] Many Americans insisted that the United States must not "share the blood-guiltiness of Europe."[9]

Some hoped the United States could end the suffering by mediating between Spain and the Cubans, but many were prepared to use force if diplomacy failed. The newspapers of William Randolph Hearst and Joseph Pulitzer competed for readers by stirring up outrage with lurid and sometimes fanciful stories of Spanish barbarity, but the call for intervention also came from religious publications with an even broader circulation than the "yellow press."[10] The Christian theologian and editor Lyman Abbott saw it as a necessary act of Christian charity, "the answer of America to the question of its own conscience: Am I my brother's keeper?"[11] The suffragist and social activist Elizabeth Cady Stanton observed, "Though I hate war *per se*, . . . I would like to see Spain . . . swept from the face of the earth."[12] An editorial in *The Evangelist* proclaimed that if it was the "will of Almighty God" that only war could sweep away "the last trace of this inhumanity of man to man," then "let it come!"[13] William Jennings Bryan, the choice of six million voters in the 1896 election and the closest thing to a pacifist ever chosen to lead a major national party, led the cry for intervention. War was "a terrible thing," he declared, but sometimes it was necessary when "reason and diplomacy" have failed. "Humanity" demanded that the United States act.[14]

The popular response to the humanitarian catastrophe in Cuba did not fit the usual stereotypes. The foreign policy or establishment "elite" generally opposed intervention.[15] The business community and its influential supporters in Congress worried that war would stall the economic recovery that had begun to gather steam at the end of 1896.[16] The big investors in Cuban mines and plantations relied on the Spanish colonial authorities to protect their investments and rightly feared what the rebels would do to their investments if they won.[17] President Cleveland himself regarded the rebels as "the most inhuman and barbarous cutthroats in the world."[18] The most enthusiastic support for intervention came from the "Bryan sections of the country," from the populists and progressives who tended to view the Cuban conflict as a class war, akin to the struggle between workers and government-backed plutocrats in the United States. To them it made perfect sense that the Cleveland administration, which had ordered the U.S. Army to kill striking railroad employees during the Pullman strike in 1894, was now supporting the Spanish government as it killed farmers and workers in Cuba.[19]

In his last two years in office Cleveland maintained strict neutrality as the conflict exploded, coolly ignoring the pro-Cuban resolutions emanating from Congress. He was aware of the breadth and depth of popular sentiment, however. In his last days as president, he urged the Spanish government to get control of the situation, warning that American patience was not infinite and that if Spain did not either bring the war to an end or stop its brutal policies, America's desire to remain neutral in the conflict could be "superseded by higher obligations."[20] His secretary of state, Richard Olney, advised the Spanish government to make good on its promises of reform and grant Cuba some form of autonomy; he offered to help mediate. When Spanish officials refused, insisting that talks could only begin after the rebels surrendered, Cleveland privately predicted that the United States would be at war within two years.[21]

This was the last thing the new president, William McKinley, wanted when he entered the White House in 1897. The long-serving member of Congress and, most recently, governor of Ohio had never taken a great interest in foreign policy except on matters of trade and had said little about it during his campaign. His overriding concern was the U.S. economy. He had run as the "advance agent of prosperity," and, luckily for him, the economy had already begun to take off when he took office. In 1897 the stock market rose, business investment increased, farm prices climbed, farm exports rose, and iron and steel production reached new heights.[22] War was a big risk to what still seemed a fragile recovery.[23] In his inaugural address, McKinley said pointedly that "wars should never be entered upon until every agency of peace has failed."[24]

As the full magnitude of the humanitarian disaster among the *reconcentrados* began to unfold in 1897, however, McKinley found himself drifting toward conflict.[25] He implored the Spanish government "in the name of common humanity" to change its tactics and relieve the island's misery. He would have been content if the Spanish had simply put down the rebellion—like Cleveland, he had little sympathy for the Cuban rebel leaders and no interest in Cuban independence—but it was becoming clear that Spain simply lacked the capacity to end the war.[26] The problem was compounded by the fact that the Madrid government also did not believe it could survive politically if it made any concessions either to the rebels or to the United States. Although a liberal government was temporarily in power, even Spanish liberals did not believe they could be seen giving away the "jewel in the crown" of the declining empire without a fight. As the American minister reported, they preferred "the chances of war, with the certain loss of Cuba, to the overthrow of the Dynasty."[27]

This left McKinley with two options: step back and let the war continue indefinitely, with all that entailed in terms of ongoing death and suffering; or step in and compel an end to the conflict. After several diplomatic go-rounds, in which Madrid yielded tactically but not on the main point of offering the Cubans a clear path to autonomy, McKinley decided he had no choice but to intervene.[28] Two events increased public pressure for action. The first was the tragic explosion of the *Maine* in Havana harbor, which killed 260 American seamen on board and was widely if erroneously attributed to Spanish agents. The other was an insulting letter to Madrid from the Spanish ambassador, which was leaked to the Hearst press. McKinley insisted he would not go to war over either of these incidents—the Civil War veteran told friends he had already "seen the dead piled up" in one war and believed he had an obligation to resist pressure for an "avenging blow"[29]—but he was pushed into declaring war sooner than he might have preferred.[30]

On April 11, 1898, to thunderous applause in the House chamber, McKinley declared that "in the name of humanity, in the name of civilization, in behalf of endangered American interests which give us the right and the duty to speak and to act, the war in Cuba must stop." In phrases redolent of the North's justification for war with the South, he declared that it did not matter that the horrors were occurring "in another country, belonging to another nation." It was, he insisted, "specially our duty, for it is right at our door."[31] In articulating a moral obligation to relieve suffering so close to American shores, the president at that moment spoke for the overwhelming majority of Americans—Republicans and Democrats, progressives, populists, labor leaders, and, at the very end, even conservatives and most businessmen.

Modern historians have tended to treat the American decision for war with a certain cartoonish condescension—Americans were "mad for war," "lashed to fury," falling "over each other . . . with a whoop and a holler" through "the cellar door of imperialism in a drunken fit of idealism."[32] Some argue that Americans were suffering from a mass "hysteria" brought on by some "psychic crisis," that they went to war to relieve pent-up emotions, to distract themselves from economic difficulties or status anxieties, to resolve the North-South conflict, or to prove their manhood.[33]

Yet Americans did not actually rush to war, and in the end it was not mass "hysteria" but a shift among conservative and moderate opinion that tilted the United States toward intervention. The turning point for many conservatives was not the sinking of the *Maine* but a speech on the Senate floor by the Vermont Republican Redfield Proctor. A successful businessman and former governor known for moderate views and for his close relationship with the president, Proctor traveled to Cuba in early March 1898 to see things for himself. He went "with a strong conviction that the picture had been overdrawn" by the yellow press, but what he saw changed his mind: thousands living in huts unfit for human habitation, "little children . . . walking about with arms and chest terribly emaciated, eyes swollen, and abdomen bloated to three times the normal size," hundreds of women and children in a Havana hospital "lying on the floors in an indescribable state of emaciation and disease."[34] What moved him to support intervention, he said, was "the spectacle of a million and a half of people, the entire native population of Cuba, struggling for freedom and deliverance from the worst misgovernment of which I ever had knowledge."[35] After Proctor's speech, even the nation's more conservative newspapers came around to the view that the situation in Cuba was "intolerable," and that it was America's "plain duty" to intervene.[36]

On April 25, the United States Congress authorized McKinley to use force. The war was over in ten weeks. Although there was hard fighting on land, the war began and ended with dramatic and decisive naval battles. On May 1, 1898, Commodore George Dewey, commanding the U.S. Asiatic Squadron, defeated a Spanish squadron at Manila Bay in a few hours with virtually no American losses. Two months later, on July 3, two American squadrons defeated a Spanish squadron in the battle of Santiago Bay. With both its fleets destroyed and the Spanish coast vulnerable to American attack, the Madrid government sued for peace. American losses were not insignificant for such a short war—385 men died in battle and another 2,000 died from disease, mostly contracted in poorly equipped training camps in Florida—but for a nation that could still remember losing that many soldiers in one hour of fighting during the Civil War, it felt like a low-cost affair.

John Hay called it a "splendid little war," therefore, but not only because it was won so handily. It was also "splendid" because it had been fought for "the highest of motives."[37] Although it is impossible to measure how many lives were saved by American intervention, a reasonable guess would put the number in the tens of thousands.[38] Nor did the humanitarian crisis end with the war. The Cuban population was in a desperate condition. Disease and famine were rampant. Municipal services, from medical care to sanitation, were nonexistent. Cities had been left "full of sick and starving people, the streets littered with dead horses and dogs," stinking of human waste, while the island's interior, according to American military observers, had become "almost a wilderness."[39] The U.S. Army worked to address the continuing humanitarian crisis in its role as an occupying force. Army distribution centers provided food to 20,000 Havana residents, and over the course of 1899 the army distributed more than five million daily rations to the Cuban population across the island.[40] Army sanitation teams cleaned up the major cities—those tasked with cleaning up Havana, which they found almost unimaginably filthy and disease-ridden, took great satisfaction in making it "cleaner than any other city had ever been up to that time."[41] Army medical officers joined Cuban doctors to treat the sick. A Cuban physician, Carlos Finlay, working with the U.S. Army's Walter Reed and other American doctors, identified the mosquito responsible for transmitting yellow fever and began the long fight against a disease that had killed more than seven hundred people every year in Havana alone.[42] Like the Union army in the South, veterans of which were now in charge of the occupation, U.S. forces carried out sweeping reforms in the way Cuba was governed. Influenced by progressive ideas, they overhauled the court system, penal institutions, health and sanitation services, and the operation of municipal governments. They even instituted an eight-hour workday, which had yet to be enacted in the United States. They built hundreds of new schools, and Harvard University's president, Charles W. Eliot, raised funds to bring more than a thousand Cuban teachers to Cambridge for training.[43] Few Americans doubted the good that had been accomplished. Massachusetts senator George Frisbie Hoar, who would soon become a leading "anti-imperialist" over the question of the Philippines, called the intervention in Cuba "the most honorable single war in history," one that Americans began "for the single and sole purpose that three or four hundred thousand human beings within ninety miles of our shores" should not be "deliberately starved to death."[44]

The intervention in Cuba would many decades later be described as an example of American "imperialism," but that was not how Americans saw it, either at the time or even in the decades that followed. Prominent anti-imperialists of the day, like the philosopher William James, believed that war had been the product of "perfectly honest humanitarianism, and an absolutely disinterested desire on the part of our people to set the Cubans free."[45] Mark Twain, among the most coruscating critics of American foreign policy in general, and of American imperialism in particular, had not opposed the intervention in Cuba. On the contrary, he believed that in Cuba the United States had "occupied the highest moral position ever taken by a nation since the Almighty made the earth."[46] Even the anti-imperialist and antiwar standard-bearer of the 1910s and 1920s, Wisconsin senator Robert M. La Follette, never included Cuba in his list of America's sins. "When we did 'intervene' in Cuba," he recalled, "it was to help a people struggling for liberty."[47]

Where the anti-imperialists objected was to the unanticipated acquisition of the Philippines. In fact, the Philippines had never been part of anyone's plan prior to May 1898.[48] No one prior to the war saw the Philippines as a prize, either in itself or as a base for future imperial expansion, nor even as a stepping-stone to the China market. The battle plan that Commodore Dewey carried out, and which took him to Manila Bay to face the Spanish fleet on May 1, had not been formulated by Roosevelt and Lodge but by obscure naval planners at the U.S. Naval War College several years earlier. It was part of contingency planning for a theoretical conflict with Spain, and the attack on the Spanish base at Manila was intended as a harassing maneuver, not as the precursor to imperial expansion. The idea was to engage Spain's Pacific fleet, chiefly to prevent it from attacking American commerce or the California coast or from sailing off to join the main Spanish fleet in the Caribbean.[49] In the most optimistic scenario, the planners had hoped that if the Asiatic Squadron could defeat the Spanish fleet at Manila, the port city could be traded back to Spain as part of the bargaining for Cuban independence. The latest version of these plans, updated in 1895, directed the Asiatic Squadron to "go and show itself in the neighborhood of the Philippines . . . for the purpose of further engaging the attention of the Spanish navy."[50] Although there is a common myth that attacking Manila was somehow Theodore Roosevelt's idea, his only role was to urge Dewey to prepare to carry out the existing plans.[51] In the last days before the official declaration of war, it was not Roosevelt but his superiors, Secretary of the Navy John D. Long and President McKinley himself, who gave the decisive orders for Dewey to move on Manila. On April 25, the day Congress passed the resolution, Dewey left Hong Kong—he was ordered to do so by the neutral British—and arrived at Manila Bay five days later. In the early morning of May 1, he launched his attack. By noon his ships had destroyed the entire Spanish Pacific fleet. Suddenly and quite unexpectedly, just eleven days after Congress declared war and long before the battle for Cuba was to start,

American guns had Manila in range; the port city was under assault by Filipino rebel forces and was ready to fall.[52]

McKinley later allegedly remarked, "If Old Dewey had just sailed away when he smashed that Spanish fleet, what a lot of trouble he would have saved us!"[53] That was either a bit of humor or disingenuousness.[54] As McKinley well knew, Dewey could not return his little fleet to Hong Kong, or sail to Singapore or Nagasaki. These were the closest ports, but they were controlled by neutral Britain and neutral Japan. The closest American base was seven thousand miles away in California (Hawaii at the time offered only a coaling station). Manila was therefore the only readily available port, but Dewey did not believe he could safely station his fleet in Manila Bay so long as the city and its battery of guns remained in Spanish hands. After Dewey's unexpected naval victory, the Spanish dispatched a force to reinforce its garrison at Manila. To secure Dewey's position, McKinley ordered American troops across the Pacific to take and hold Manila. They left California in late May and arrived in the Philippines in early June under explicit orders not to "conquer an extensive territory" but to establish a garrison "to command the harbor of Manila" and make it safe for Dewey's fleet.[55] As McKinley later explained, Manila "became a question from which we could not escape."[56]

The decision to send troops to hold Manila was a big one, and it certainly indicated McKinley's willingness to expand the American operation beyond what had been envisioned by military planners. Yet McKinley still had no broad plans for taking all or even part of the Philippines.[57] His administration had not prepared for this contingency.[58]

McKinley's decision ultimately to hold the Philippines came about partly through a process of elimination.[59] All the alternatives seemed to McKinley and his advisers either impracticable, contrary to American interests, or immoral.

After what the Spaniards had done in Cuba, the idea of returning the Filipinos to Spanish rule was repugnant to many Americans and McKinley knew he would face "a great storm of criticism" if he did so.[60] American military officials in Manila reported that the Filipinos would never accept return to Spanish rule without a fight, in any case, nor could Spain win such a fight. Any attempt to return the islands to Spain would simply produce civil war, anarchy, and eventual intervention by other powers.[61]

Another option was to hand the islands off to some other power. But most of the other powers weren't interested. Lodge recommended trading all but the island of Luzon to Britain in exchange for Jamaica, the

Bahamas, and the Danish West Indies, but the British were desperately trying to offload burdens in East Asia to the United States, not to acquire new ones. The Japanese and the Russians preferred to see the Philippines in American hands rather than passed to their imperial competitors. Tokyo's ambassador told American officials that the Japanese government would be "highly gratified if the United States would occupy the Islands."[62]

The only great power eager for some or all of the Philippines was Germany, but this was not an attractive option. Just a few months before, in early 1898, German forces had seized control of the Chinese port of Kiaochow in supposed retaliation for the murder of two German soldiers, prompting alarm in all the capitals and setting off a scramble for territory and spheres of influence in the weak Chinese empire. Britain took Weihaiwei and Hong Kong; France took Indochina; Russia advanced into Manchuria and took Port Arthur. The following month the German chancellor proclaimed Germany's "demand" for a "place in the sun" in a speech supporting Germany's new naval buildup. Kaiser Wilhelm II, declaring an end to Germany's "over cautious policy" in East Asia, promised to demonstrate "through the use of sternness and if necessary the most brutal ruthlessness" that the "German Emperor cannot be trifled with."[63] Just a few weeks before Dewey's victory, German gunships assembled off the coast of Haiti to demand an indemnity for the imprisonment of a German citizen. To Americans, it seemed that Germany had its eyes on "every beachhead in Latin America and every atoll in the South Pacific."[64] Those concerns only grew when, just after Dewey's victory, a potent German naval force arrived in the waters of Manila Bay, commanded by the same officer who had taken Kiaochow.[65]

There was another obvious option, of course: Give the Philippines to the Filipinos, just as Cuba was nominally returned to the Cubans. McKinley rejected this idea for a number of reasons. The first was a widely shared conviction, among some leading Filipinos as well as many Americans, Europeans, and Japanese, that the islands could not "remain one year a peaceful united Archipelago under an independent native government" without some protection and supervision by an outside great power.[66] Much of this judgment was based on racial prejudices: Americans and other whites, but also the Japanese, viewed the darker-skinned native Filipino population as inherently incapable of self-government without a long period of "tutelage" by a "civilized" power. Americans with experience in the region argued there was no actual Filipino "nation," only a "collection of different peoples," some twenty-four tribes living on more than seven thousand islands. Establishing "a peaceful united Archipelago under an independent native government" seemed impossible in the near term.[67] Spain, which had ruled the Philippines since Magellan discovered the islands in the sixteenth century, had done nothing to prepare the Filipinos for self-government, since it had never been Spain's intention to set them free. Anglo-American Protestants generally felt that any people subjected to centuries of Spanish and Catholic rule would necessarily need time to recover from centuries of superstition and Catholic cruelty. As Elihu Root expressed the common view, the Spanish had left their colonial subjects "wholly ignorant of the art of self-government."[68]

Even in the unlikely event a stable Filipino government could be established, moreover, outside observers warned, it "would not be strong enough to protect itself against foreign aggression."[69] It would only be a matter of time before either Germany intervened or the competing powers began struggling for control.[70] This was a concern shared by the Filipino leader, Emilio Aguinaldo. McKinley declared he had no intention of flinging the Philippines, like "a golden apple of discord, among the rival powers."[71]

Another option was to make the Philippines an American protectorate. This was Aguinaldo's preferred option. He hoped that the United States would protect the Philippines from external threat while allowing the Filipinos complete independence in governing themselves. But McKinley and his advisers regarded the idea as problematic. If, as they expected, the Filipinos proved not ready to govern themselves and the islands became chronically unstable, the other powers would demand that the United States either restore stability or let them intervene to protect their interests. Germany, they feared, would likely seize any opportunity to get its share of the spoils, as it had recently in China.

In the end, therefore, McKinley decided that the only "responsible" course was to hold on to the islands, for the interests of everyone, including the Filipinos. "We could not give them back to Spain," he later explained. "We could not give them . . . to any European power for we should have a war on our hands in fifteen minutes." So "there was nothing left for us to do but to take them all, and to educate the Filipinos, and uplift and civilize and Christianize them, and by God's grace do the very best we could by them, as our fellow-men for whom Christ also died."[72] Any other course of action would dishonorably shirk obligations the United States took on when it went to war. One observer later wrote that this was "a sincere and characteristic American point of view."[73]

Characteristically, it was a point of view riddled with racist assumptions. McKinley's instructions to the military occupation authorities in December 1898 had more than a faint echo of American policy toward Native Americans in the time of Jefferson. The "mission of the United States," he declared, was "benevolent assimilation." American authorities would help them become more like Americans. Both the Filipinos and the Cubans were victims of centuries of Spanish Catholic rule. They would teach them English, Americanize the Catholic Church, and train them to respect individual rights and the rule of law.[74] The powerful American Protestant churches embraced the chance to convert a native population benighted for centuries by Spanish Catholic "superstition." Many Americans regarded America's task to fill the deficiencies left by the Spanish and put the Filipinos on the road to Anglo-Saxon-style government and society. This was what Rudyard Kipling meant when he urged Americans to "take up the white man's burden" in the Philippines. Americans had not set out on that mission when they went to war with Spain, but once in possession of the Philippines, it became a justification for not letting them go, at least not right away. Indeed, most officials involved doubted this benevolent mission could be accomplished any time soon. Taft told McKinley that "our little brown brothers" would need "fifty or one hundred years" in order "to develop anything resembling Anglo-Saxon political principles and skills."[75]

Americans had other motives that were more obviously selfish. One was nationalist pride. The battle of Manila Bay was the first naval triumph over a foreign power since the battle of Lake Erie in 1813, and Dewey's triumph produced an explosion of patriotism, the first truly national celebration since the Civil War. The late spring and summer of 1898 was a campaign season, and politicians on the stump found their audiences adamant that "where the flag goes up it must never come down."[76] Dewey received a hero's welcome, cheered and feted across the nation, and immediately became mentioned as a presidential candidate.

Some insisted there were economic and strategic benefits to retaining the islands, though few had noticed these benefits before the war. The United States, in fact, did very little trade with the Philippines. Nor was the archipelago geographically well situated to serve as a stepping-stone to the China market. Manila was 1,100 miles south of Shanghai and 1,800 miles south of Beijing, the two places where most American trade with China—such as it was—was conducted.[77] As for their strategic value, there would be none unless the United States decided to build fortifications and augment the Pacific fleet both to protect them and project power from them. Otherwise, they would be a vulnerable strategic liability, or as Roosevelt would soon describe them, a "heel of Achilles." The most potent arguments for keeping the Philippines, however, were intangible. Having "freed" the Filipinos from their Spanish masters, many believed, the United States had incurred an obligation to help them. Whitelaw Reid, the prominent Republican, former ambassador to France, editor of the *New York Tribune,* and member of the peace commission that negotiated the treaty with Spain, put it this way: "Having broken down the power in control of them, we could not honorably desert them."[78] Woodrow Wilson expressed a common view when he argued that the United States had fought "to give Cuba self-government" and it was on Americans' "conscience" to do no less for the Philippines.[79] Even anti-imperialists like Charles Eliot argued that the United States had "incurred obligations" to the Filipinos.[80]

For Lodge and Roosevelt, the argument over the Philippines was above all a test of the national character. Although they were not "imperialists" in the sense of seeking to expand American colonial holdings, they shared a certain admiration for the "imperialist instinct" of the British and others—a constancy and seriousness of purpose that they feared Americans lacked. Before the war they had sought to inspire in Americans an "imperialist elan" without the imperialism. Now, faced with the choice of supporting the acquisition of the Philippines or watching the American people shrink from the challenge, they pushed ahead vigorously.[81] For Roosevelt the question was whether modern Americans still had the courage and gumption of their forefathers. They had "conquered the West, but we are a feeble folk and we cannot hold the Philippines." The question was whether Americans were prepared to play "the part of a great nation."[82]

As always there was a partisan dimension to such arguments. McKinley and other Republican politicians combined appeals to responsibility and patriotism in a politically potent mix. In his campaign tour of the Midwest the president provoked raucous cheering when he spoke of America's "moral obligation" to "keep the flag flying" over the Philippines.[83] A Republican administration had intervened to help the Cuban people and brought military glory to the nation, after a Democratic administration had shrunk from the task. America's liberation of the Cubans, and acceptance of responsibility for the Filipinos, seemed enough of a winning issue that it featured prominently in the 1900 Republican national campaign.

—

A vocal minority in the United States fought against America's new imperial venture. An Anti-Imperialist League formed in Boston, funded by Andrew Carnegie, and made up of a who's who of prominent intellectuals: the philosophers John Dewey and William James; Stanford's president, David Starr Jordan; the authors Mark Twain and William Dean Howells, and retired elected officials, including the two ex-presidents Grover Cleveland and Benjamin Harrison. The original target of the anti-imperialists was the annexation of Hawaii, which President McKinley pressed through Congress in the summer of 1898 and which they saw as "but the entering wedge" that would "cleave a way open for empire."[84] They did not oppose the Cuban intervention, but the acquisition of the Philippines a few months later seemed to fulfill this prophecy.

The arguments of the anti-imperialists varied. They hammered away at the "bad business proposition," the empty promise of economic or strategic gain, and at the idea that the United States, which had never sought the Philippines, now had a responsibility to the Filipinos. As the former secretary of state William Day put it, just because Americans had "done good in one place," by which he meant Cuba, "we were not therefore compelled to rush over the whole civilized world, six thousand miles away from home."[85]

More potent was the moral case against imperialism. What gave Americans the right to "sow our ideals, plant our order, impose our God" on another people? William James asked.[86] He could not believe that "in the twinkling of an eye," the United States could "puke up its ancient soul," and "without a hint of squeamishness."[87] "There must be two Americas," Mark Twain commented: "one that sets the captive free, and one that takes a once-captive's new freedom away from him."[88] Americans had "fought a righteous war" and "set Cuba free," Twain wrote, but in the Philippines "that most righteous purpose" had "miscarried."[89]

Racial fears and prejudices played a part, too. Congressman Champ Clark, a Democrat from Missouri who would later become the party's leader in the House, warned that if the Philippines were kept, it was only a matter of time before Americans would see "almond-eyed, brown-skinned United States Senators." Whether or not Filipinos were "fit to govern themselves," he declared, they were "not fit to govern us!"[90] Such arguments prompted those in favor of retaining the Philippines to promise that under no circumstances would the Filipinos be granted citizenship. Some even suggested that the principles of the Declaration of Independence did not apply to "backward" non-white peoples.[91]

In the end, neither the appeal to American anti-imperialist principles nor the appeal to white fear and xenophobia had much effect on the McKinley administration or on the public. Among the anti-imperialists' biggest handicaps was that they were trying to undo a fait accompli. Perhaps it was a mistake to take the Philippines, but it was no simple matter to decide what to do with them now that they had been taken. Not even the anti-imperialists suggested returning them to Spain, and even those who favored granting the Filipinos independence believed the United States should make the islands a protectorate.[92] As Secretary of State John Hay put it, "I think our good friends are wiser when they abuse us for what we do, than when they try to say what ought to be done."[93]

Another problem for the anti-imperialists was the political dominance of the Republican Party and the weakness of the Democrats. In the 1898 midterm elections, McKinley's Republicans held on to their majority in the House and picked up enough seats to gain a dominant majority in the Senate, 50–25, a strong showing for an incumbent party in a midterm election. The election was not a referendum on the Philippines, but McKinley's decision to take the islands had made it a party issue, and party regulars had no difficulty supporting it. The Senate's vote to ratify the Treaty of Paris was close, but that was no measure of its popularity, since throughout this period the Senate rejected almost every treaty submitted to it.[94] Woodrow Wilson's perception, as he later wrote, was that the American people were "uncritically approving" of the acquisition, and even those less happy with the decision didn't disagree. "You and I don't want the Philippines," McKinley's navy secretary, John Davis Long, wrote a friend, "but it's no use disguising the fact that an overwhelming majority of the people do."[95]

The McKinley administration's biggest problems were on the ground, and this was true in both Cuba and the Philippines. How to govern peoples who may have been grateful for their "liberation" but were not grateful for the American rule that followed and which seemed to many to make a mockery of Americans' good intentions? In the case of Cuba, the war had been fought under the banner of *Cuba Libre,* and Congress had explicitly ruled out making Cuba a colony or annexing it to the United States. Congress had promised to "leave the government of the Island to its people," and that aim was widely shared by the American public.[96] Even McKinley, who had little faith in the Cuban people, and even less in the rebel leaders, would not buck the prevailing sentiment. "Free Cuba," he insisted, had to be made a "reality, not a name."[97]

Most American officials who dealt with the Cuban people and their leaders, in fact, did not believe they were ready for self-government. As with the Philippine question, racism played a big part in this judgment. The Cuban population in 1899 was about two-thirds white Spanish *criollos,* with the remaining third divided between blacks and people of mixed race. Some Americans, reflecting their own prejudices and fears, worried that immediate independence would unleash a race war and could not imagine turning Cuba over to the blacks and mixed-race people who had played such a big part in the rebellion. American officials preferred dealing with "the better sort," namely the more prosperous whites, but they were still "dagos" in American eyes and therefore unready to take charge. Most U.S. officials serving in Cuba agreed that the island's people were "no more fit for self-government than gun-powder is for hell."[98]

Congress was growing restive, however, and the McKinley administration searched for some way to grant Cuba independence without risking the upheaval that officials feared. The answer was the Platt Amendment. The United States would essentially make Cuba a protectorate. It would withdraw its forces and turn over governance of Cuba to an elected government. But it would also reserve the right to send troops back, if necessary, to preserve "Cuban independence" and maintain a "stable Government" capable of protecting "life, property, and individual liberty." American officials hoped it wouldn't be necessary. The United States would establish naval bases on the island to protect Cuba and also America's expanding interests in the Caribbean, including the planned transisthmian canal. An amendment to this effect sponsored by Connecticut senator Orville H. Platt was approved in the Senate by a substantial margin and signed into law by McKinley in the spring of 1901.[99]

Outraged Cuban leaders at first refused to enshrine a North American right of intervention in the new nation's founding document. But the American secretary of war, Elihu Root, warned that the American people would not take kindly to "ingratitude" for their "expenditure of blood and treasure" to free Cuba from Spain.[100] In June 1901 Cuba's constituent assembly adopted the new constitution, including the terms of the Platt Amendment. In December that year a new Cuban president was elected. Six months later, on May 20, 1902, General Leonard Wood officially transferred authority, and American flags came down all across Cuba.

—

American policy tried to make good on the administration's promise to help the Filipinos, too. A local police force was reestablished. A secular public education system was erected for the first time. The army distributed schoolbooks, paid teachers' salaries, and helped support 1,000 schools and 100,000 students. It revised tax codes to create a more hospitable environment for trade and development. It reconfigured lighting and water systems, rebuilt roads and bridges, overhauled the sanitation system, instituted vaccination programs, and built health clinics. American officials ranged through the streets of Manila as if they were progressives cleaning up Chicago, "poking into slaughterhouses, marketplaces, dispensaries, and hospitals, and clearing up garbage and filth."[101]

McKinley's policy of "benevolent assimilation" was paternalistic, but it did set a standard of behavior for Americans. McKinley insisted that there would be "no exploitation of any of the islands" by American businesses, and, unlike in Cuba, for the most part there wasn't. Of course, unlike in Cuba, American businesses were not interested in the Philippines—very few sought to invest in the islands or own property there—which made it easier to keep the administration of the islands "free of an exploitative taint."[102]

As in Cuba, Americans assumed the local Filipino population would be grateful to the United States for liberating them from Spanish imperial control, even if it was to be replaced by American control. This proved a serious misjudgment. In early 1899 a full-blown armed rebellion erupted, led by Aguinaldo and fueled by Filipino desires for independence and by bitter feelings of betrayal. This reaction ought to have been predictable. Aguinaldo and his colleagues had assumed that, like Cuba, they would soon acquire at least nominal independence and were outraged when they discovered that the Americans had no such intention. The irony was that Aguinaldo would have been more content with a Platt Amendment than the Cubans were, so long as Filipinos could govern themselves.

The further irony was that one reason the United States did not quickly grant the Filipinos independence was that no one at the outset of the war had anticipated taking the Philippines at all. There had been no Filipino junta lobbying in the United States, no equivalent of the *Cuba Libre* rallying cry, no self-denying congressional resolutions like the Teller Amendment. Although most Americans believed in eventual Filipino self-government, they were prepared to rule the Philippines as a colony until that time arrived—something they would not have accepted in Cuba. Aguinaldo and his fellow Filipinos had expected better of the

Americans, and so when it became clear that American forces were not leaving or handing over power, they turned to war as their best chance. They assumed the Americans had no stomach for the fight. McKinley and his advisers were stunned when war broke out in the Philippines. Although American ground forces were nominally superior, officials in the War Department feared that the rebel force would "take to the interior of the country" and that American troops would become bogged down in "a prolonged Indian-fighting style of campaign."[103] That was exactly what happened.

American commanders in the field were slow to respond to the guerrilla-style tactics. The commander of American occupying forces in the Philippines, General Elwell S. Otis, wanted to help Filipinos, not kill them. The best answer to the rebellion, he believed, was effective colonial and native government—municipal services, fair taxation, and a reliable and unbiased system of laws.[104] General Otis did not believe he needed large numbers of combat troops for what was largely a civilian effort, but it turned out that this strategy required even more troops than a purely military mission.[105] The Filipino civilian officials who cooperated with the Americans became targets of assassination by the rebels, and most had to play a double game of appearing friendly while the Americans were around, then aiding the guerrillas when the Americans were gone. The only answer to this was to keep American troops in or near villages to protect them.[106] The lack of a steady American presence in and around the towns also deprived the military of useful intelligence. Guerrilla fighters typically engaged in battle, then hid their weapons and melted into the population. Without established networks of informants and knowledge of the local scene, American soldiers could not tell an *amigo* from an *insurrecto*.[107] Instead of winning Filipino public support, therefore, Otis's strategy was losing it. As one officer put it, "This business of fighting and civilizing and educating at the same time doesn't mix very well. Peace is needed first."[108] Journalists reported in the summer of 1899 that the situation was "blacker now than it has been since the beginning of the war." Headlines in American papers read, in various ways, "Otis Has Seriously Blundered. Many More Troops Needed at Once."[109] That summer Elihu Root, recently named secretary of war, overruled Otis, preferring to "err on the safe side in sending too many troops than too few."[110] The number of American forces rose from 30,000 to 60,000, then to 70,000, and continued to increase. Still, the fighting continued. In April 1900, Theodore Roosevelt announced that "the insurrection in the Philippine Islands has been overcome," but that proved wildly premature.[111] When General

Arthur MacArthur, Jr., took over command from Otis that spring, the guerrillas were launching attacks with a thousand men at a time, ambushing American patrols and inflicting significant casualties.[112]

The Filipinos' strategy was to wait the Americans out. By escalating the fighting, even without major victories, they aimed to convince the American people that the war was pointless. American troops could see that the rebels hoped disillusionment with the war would help defeat McKinley and put the anti-imperialist Bryan in the White House. As one officer put it, "The Filipinos just now are keeping things stirred up as much as they can, in the hopes that the 'anti-expansionists' will win out."[113]

With the McKinley administration bogged down in a war for which it had not prepared, the anti-imperialists did have another chance to influence U.S. public opinion. Americans of all political and ideological persuasions were indeed unhappy with the unexpected war.[114] Some developed sympathy for Aguinaldo and the Filipinos fighting for independence, especially as the war dragged on with no end in sight. As the New York *World* asked, "Is it not plain that the whole policy of pacification by force of arms is as impracticable as it is un-American?"[115]

The McKinley administration remained determined to defeat the rebellion, however, and a majority of Americans seemed to agree. At least that was how Roosevelt and other Republicans read the public mood. The war might no longer be popular, but its opponents were even less so. The anti-imperialists did themselves no favors. They sent antiwar literature to the troops in the field, which rubbed many people, including the troops, the wrong way. They warned that America was becoming a militarist empire and that the army was about to take control of the U.S. government, an idea "so ludicrous," one contemporary observer noted, "as to make it quite impossible for Americans to take it seriously."[116] Defenders of the war accused the anti-imperialists of treason. They might just as well "send rifles, Maxim guns and ammunition to the Filipinos," the New *York Times* editorialized, for at least that would be "more openly and frankly treasonable."[117] Roosevelt barnstormed around the nation asking audiences to stamp their feet in outrage at the anti-imperialists' slanders against brave American soldiers who were making the "ultimate sacrifice for their country." He invited veterans to join him onstage and called to the audience: "Behold your tyrants!"[118] Even the soldiers fighting in the Philippines accused the anti-imperialists of offering aid and comfort to the insurgency.[119] The prevailing view in the United States seemed to be that, whatever else might be true, the guerrillas should be defeated.

The war certainly did nothing to dent McKinley's popularity. The

1900 election returned him to the White House by an even larger margin than his decisive victory four years earlier, and Republicans again added to their majorities in both houses of Congress—this despite the fact that the Democrats had made imperialism a central focus of their campaign. At stake, they argued, was "the very existence of the Republic and the destruction of our free institution." At their national convention a giant flag descended from the rafters bearing the words "The Flag of the Republic forever, of an Empire never."[120] But they did not campaign as if they meant it. Even in their platform they did not propose granting independence to the Philippines until "a stable form of government" was in place, which was not very different from McKinley's policy.[121] Nor was Bryan the ideal anti-imperialist candidate. In 1898 he had led the call for war with Spain. In 1899 he had advised Democrats to support ratification of the treaty with Spain granting the Philippines to the United States. Even anti-imperialist newspapers referred to the "bogus anti-imperialism of Colonel Bryan."[122] In the end, many leading anti-imperialists did not vote for him.[123]

Woodrow Wilson nonetheless exaggerated when he later wrote that Americans were "uncritically approving" of the acquisition of the Philippines.[124] Bryan may not have run hard against it, but Republicans had not run hard for it, either. Many sensed that while the public was not ready to abandon the Philippines to a rebel victory, there was also no enthusiasm for the war.[125] McKinley had all along worried that the public mood would sour "when the difficulties, expense and loss of life which it entailed, became more manifest."[126]

The costs did rise, including the moral costs. With McKinley safely re-elected, General MacArthur notified his commanders of a "new and more stringent policy" aimed at destroying the insurgents' networks of supply and communication and their support from the towns. From the end of 1900 through the summer of 1901, the army conducted increasingly large and effective operations against insurgent forces in over half of the Philippine provinces. Better intelligence and the use of mobile mounted forces, combined with the purging of municipal governments of suspected rebel sympathizers, left the insurgents increasingly isolated and on the run.

American brutality also increased. American forces began taking "punitive" measures against both insurgents and suspected supporters, destroying crops and property, without much concern for who actually owned them. More than one Civil War veteran compared the army's tactics to Sherman's devastation of the South.[127] They moved civilians into "protected zones" to separate them from insurgents, drawing comparisons with Weyler's *reconcentrado* policies in Cuba.[128] MacArthur and many of his commanders started treating captured insurgents as not part of a "regular organized force" and therefore "not entitled to privileges of prisoners of war."[129] Captured prisoners were sometimes subjected to "the water cure," in which large amounts of water were forced down the prisoner's throat, simulating drowning and producing a painfully swollen stomach, which was then punched repeatedly until the prisoner gave in.

The most brutal American actions followed the "Balangiga Massacre" of September 1901, in which Filipino villagers, angered at mistreatment by the American occupying force, rose up and killed forty-eight Americans, leaving only a handful of survivors. U.S. Army patrols and offshore naval gunboats were ordered to "make a desert of Balangiga."[130] The local commander on the island of Samar, where Balanginga was located, claimed he was told by his commanding officer to turn the interior of the island into a "howling wilderness." Although he apparently refused to obey orders to shoot every captured insurgent over the age of ten, the U.S. Army devastated the land and killed many Filipinos both as retaliation and to deter further attacks on American forces.

Back in the United States reports of the Balangiga massacre and the army's response sparked an outcry and led to congressional investigations. The American commander was excoriated in the press as the "Butcher of Samar."[131] The administration at first tried to deflect the criticism, with now-president Roosevelt arguing that in war there were always atrocities and that even American soldiers were not immune from savage instincts. Officials testified that the atrocities were often acts of revenge for atrocities committed by the Filipinos.[132] The fact was, however, that many American soldiers simply regarded the Filipinos as savages. Racism was rampant. Some soldiers asserted unashamedly that the Philippines wouldn't be pacified until the "niggers" were "killed off like the Indians" and "every nigger" was blown "into a nigger heaven."[133] The Roosevelt administration was gradually forced to back down, and Roosevelt stated that "no provocation however great can be accepted as an excuse for misuse of the necessary severity of war, and above all not for torture of any kind or shape."[134] Still, he praised "the bravery of American soldiers" who were fighting "for the triumph of civilization over the black chaos of savagery and barbarism."[135]

Although Roosevelt worried about the public reaction to American atrocities, and the anti-imperialists hoped it would turn the American people against Roosevelt's policies in the Philippines, the revelations did not have much effect on public support for the war, especially once American efforts seemed to be succeeding. The first few months of 1901 saw the surrender of several rebel leaders, including Aguinaldo himself. Civilian Filipinos, wearied by the seemingly endless war, urged the remaining insurgents to come in from the jungle. Although there would be much fighting through 1902, including the worst defeat of American forces in the entire war, the insurgency was winding down. On July 4, 1902, President Roosevelt announced the end of formal hostilities—this time with greater accuracy.

The anti-imperialists, baffled and outraged by the lack of public outcry, "concocted conspiracies" to explain the inexplicable, insisting that "a few ambitious men in Washington" were "leading the nation on this new and dangerous course" against the wishes of the people.[136] But William James acknowledged that, despite everything, the public had endorsed that course. Americans, it seemed, were no better but also "no worse than the best of men have ever been," that "angelic impulses and predatory lusts divide our heart exactly as they divide the hearts of other countries. . . . We are not superhuman."[137]

Most Americans did not share the philosopher's disillusionment. Woodrow Wilson, lecturing in the fall of 1903, did not dwell on the problems of American occupation of the Philippines but only on the responsibilities he believed the United States had rightly assumed. "We kept faith with Cuba," he insisted, "and we mean, with God's help, to keep faith also with the people of the Philippines Islands, by serving them . . . without . . . a selfish end."[138] Root did not see how anyone could object to "the external forces of civilization" stepping in to "replace brutal and oppressive government" with "ordered liberty and individual freedom."[139]

Most Americans probably took a more mixed view. Prior to accepting the job as governor general of the islands, William Howard Taft told Roosevelt that he had opposed taking the Philippines. It was "contrary to our traditions," and it would be a "burden" at a time "when we had quite enough to do at home." Yet "now that we were there we were under the most sacred duty to give [the Filipinos] a good form of government . . . so that they might be developed into a self-governing people."[140]

In both Cuba and the Philippines American intervention left a complex legacy. In the eyes of most Americans at the time and for the next two decades, the intervention in Cuba was something to take pride in. Roosevelt boasted in his autobiography, "We made the promise to give Cuba independence; and we kept the promise. . . . Then we left the island, turning the government over to its own people."[141] Even anti-imperialists did not dispute this. Neither they nor other Americans were troubled by the Platt Amendment. Nor were they troubled by American investors buying up banana, coconut, and sugar plantations or American corporations building railroads, developing mines, taking charge of utilities, and marketing fruit and produce. By 1905, as many as 13,000 Americans held title to Cuban land worth as much as $50 million.[142] The war that the American business community had so strenuously opposed turned out to be good for business.

But Cubans also reaped benefits. The flood of American investment breathed life into the devastated economy. A reduction of the U.S. tariff on Cuban sugar, which President Roosevelt forced through a reluctant Congress, spurred a large infusion of investment and modern technology into that vital Cuban industry. Sugar production soared, doubling every decade until the global market crashed in the late 1920s. The sugar boom also stimulated a long period of higher wages and rising standards of living for the average Cuban.[143] In time, a new Cuban entrepreneurial class emerged to compete with foreign businesses, and Cubans began to take a greater share in their own economy.[144] The expansion of economic and educational opportunities in turn produced "an extremely rapid rate of social mobilization" and a vastly increased "politicization" of the Cuban population. Even when American troops were sent to re-occupy Cuba following a tumultuous 1906 presidential election season, and remained until 1909, the Cuban presidential elections of 1908 were openly contested and drew 71 percent of the eligible population to the polls.[145] They were, as one historian notes, "probably the fairest in Cuban history."[146] Most Americans continued to believe that the war for Cuba was, as Mark Twain put it, a "righteous war." Not until the 1920s and '30s and the disillusionments of that era would some Americans start to look at the intervention through a different and less celebratory lens.

The same could not be said of the Philippines, where the costs of the war, in both material and moral terms, were significantly higher and less justifiable even in the eyes of those who had supported the acquisition. Americans lost 4,200 men in three years of fighting the insurgency. More than 20,000 Filipino combatants were killed, and as many as 200,000 Filipino civilians died from violence, famine, or disease.[147] Roosevelt, who supported and praised the American effort from beginning to end and was untroubled by moral qualms, nevertheless as president quickly came to regard the islands as a strategic vulnerability, especially with the rise of

Japanese power and evident signs of Japanese expansionism. In general he considered it "a very hard problem" for the United States given its "needs and ideas" and the evident unwillingness of the American people to spend the money necessary to ensure the islands' defense.[148] He worried how long the American public would support involvement in what he saw as an "unremunerative and indeed expensive duty" that, in his view and in the view of many others, was of more benefit to the Filipinos than to the United States.[149]

Despite Roosevelt's fears and the anti-imperialists' hopes, however, the American public never turned against the overall policy. There were no mass calls for withdrawing American forces from the Philippines. The Republican Party and its leaders were not punished at the polls for leading the country into an unexpected war and incurring the burden of managing the distant islands with its alien, brown-skinned people. In 1904 the Democrats nominated Judge Alton Parker, a prominent anti-imperialist, as their presidential candidate, but anti-imperialism once again made little headway with the public. Roosevelt, campaigning against the anti-imperialists with gusto, won in a landslide. The anti-imperialists were left grumbling about the "sinister powers" that had seduced Americans into betraying their "most sacred principles and traditions."[150] But as Stuart Creighton Miller has observed, the anti-imperialists' imputation of the war to a small band of "sinister" actors was an evasion of the fact, even more disturbing from their point of view, that the American public did not share their horror at what had happened.[151]

Perhaps it was because many Americans could still recall the loss of almost 8,000 men in three days of fighting at Gettysburg, and the loss of half that many in three years of fighting did not seem unacceptably high.[152] Most Americans gave little thought to the losses suffered by the Filipinos. Perhaps, too, it was because the war ended in an American victory, which washed away memories of both American losses and American misdeeds (which most of the public had never been very troubled about anyway).

Americans may also have been satisfied with the general conduct of the United States in a project that was billed as an unavoidable and honorable act of responsibility toward the Filipinos. Even later critics acknowledged that American policies were "well-intended, and not exploitative."[153] The U.S. administration quickly granted the Filipinos a significant degree of local autonomy as well as a broad array of civil rights. Former rebel leaders became mayors and governors. Political parties demanding the islands' independence emerged and attracted a mass following.[154] In the end, the Philippines wound up very much as an American protectorate like Cuba under the Platt Amendment. After 1907, the Filipinos enjoyed substantial autonomy.

Some might ask whether the United States could have gotten to the same outcome without a war, by simply turning the Philippines over to Aguinaldo and his supporters at the outset. But the American public was not looking backwards. In fact, for the most part, once the war was over, Americans stopped thinking about the Philippines altogether. As one Cleveland newspaper commented at the time, "The islands might all have sunk into the sea and few Americans would have known the difference."[155] They barely noticed over the subsequent decades that the United States still held the islands and deployed thousands of American troops in the Philippines. Those troops did not depart until 1946, when the Filipinos finally achieved full independence.[156] As one contemporary observer put it, after all the emotion expended in arguing over imperialism, "we concluded to forget it."[157]

CHAPTER TWO

Empire Without "Imperialism"; Imperialism Without "Empire"

Since the days of the Holy Alliance it is doubtful that any government has thus declared its mission to reform the moral shortcomings of foreign nations.

—a British diplomat[1]

THE SPANISH-AMERICAN War was not the turning point in American foreign policy that many have imagined. After all, Americans had taken foreign territory before, including by force, and had ruled other, alien peoples before, often against their will. What was novel was the acquisition of a large, heavily populated territory beyond the seas that they had no intention of ever admitting into the Union. But this unplanned, unintended, and ultimately unwanted consequence of the war over Cuba did not prove a harbinger of future overseas expansion and colonial acquisition. McKinley and others might assert that the United States had suddenly become a "world power,"[2] but as one contemporary later observed, for the majority of Americans, "world power" had never been "clearly announced on the programme."[3] Whatever being a "world power" meant, most Americans were not interested. They had favored war with Spain in the spring of 1898 for a specific and limited purpose—to free Cuba from the grip of Spanish rule and end a humanitarian crisis—and they had endorsed keeping the Philippines as a matter of both nationalist pride and as a civilized, Christian responsibility. Americans in 1900 had acquired an empire, but it would be inaccurate to call them imperialists.

Certainly, the world's great imperial powers did not regard the United States as a member of the "imperial club."[4] As imperial acquisitions went, the Philippines was small beer. In 1900 the British Empire stretched across more than 11 million square miles, with colonies on every continent, and with a colonial population of more than 350 million subjects. In the last quarter of the nineteenth century alone it had expanded by 4,750,000 square miles and brought an additional 90 million people under British rule. More important, the empire was what had made Britain a world power and was integral to what it meant to be British. Possession of India alone had made Britain the dominant power from the Persian Gulf to the South China Sea.[5] India's vast population had provided troops for use in China, Persia, Ethiopia, Afghanistan, Egypt, Burma, and Africa.[6] In the First World War, over a million Indian soldiers would serve the British cause, with another million coming from Australia, Canada, and the rest of the dominions.[7] "As long as we rule India we are the greatest power in the world," Lord Curzon once observed. "If we lose it we shall drop straight away to a third rate power."[8]

The empire was also a vital part of British economic success. By the early twentieth century, Britain had become the world's leading exporter of manufactured goods—exports made up as much as 25 percent of gross national product—and much of this trade was carried out within the empire, with Canada and Australia, as well as with India, which alone took almost a fifth of British exports.[9] The vast trade was transported on seas kept open by the Royal Navy using the critical bases around the world that the empire provided. Without the empire, the British statesman Joseph Chamberlain claimed, "half at least of our population would be starved."[10] Nor was it just the material aspects. Without the empire, Chamberlain also observed, it "would not be the England we love."[11]

Empire was not as vital to France, but it was still important. At the turn of the century France controlled 6 million square miles of foreign territory in North Africa, sub-Saharan Africa, the Caribbean, and Southeast Asia, with a population outside of France of over 50 million subjects.[12] The French were less dependent on exports—they made up 12 percent of the economy—but Algeria alone took 60 percent of all of the goods France sold overseas.[13] On the eve of the Great War, some 700,000 French citizens lived abroad in the colonies, 500,000 of them in Algeria. Algeria itself, with a population of 5 million, was designated as a department of France, its administration overseen by the French interior minister.[14]

Many French leaders regarded the empire as vital for addressing their most acute strategic disadvantage: stagnant population growth. Following their disastrous defeat at the hands of Bismarck's Prussia in 1871 and facing the growing power of a unified Germany over the subsequent decades, French leaders had looked to a growing empire to balance the scales—"To save a small France there must be a greater France."[15] They hoped that in the next war their *Force Noire,* an army of African colonial subjects, would supplement the declining population of fighting-age men.[16] As Prime Minister Jules Ferry put it, "Marseilles and Toulon" would be "defended quite as much in the China Seas as in the Mediterranean.[17]

The American experience with empire was different. Only a tiny percentage of Americans had any relationship at all with the distant colony. A few thousand soldiers were deployed to maintain peace; a few hundred missionaries did their work; the American governing authority employed a couple of hundred civilians—that was the extent of it. Two-way trade was small. British observers, like Edward Grey, believed the "experience of Empire in the Philippines" was "too limited" to have "affected the consciousness" of Americans.[18]

The fact that Americans were not "imperialists" did not make them virtuous. Americans' lack of interest in empire did not mean they lacked greed or ambition. Although their liberal ideology suggested that ruling other peoples was immoral, they had managed to skirt around this problem at various times in their history when they deemed it necessary to acquire new lands inhabited by alien peoples.[19] But by the end of the nineteenth century they simply had no need of overseas empire to fulfill either material or intangible needs. Their vast continental domain supplied almost all their physical wants. Their already-inflated sense of their importance came from feelings of ideological and moral superiority, not from empire. Americans had believed they were better than everyone else when they were a tiny, weak, and vulnerable republic. They did not need colonies to make themselves feel the equal of Britain or any other power.

Had Americans genuinely sought an imperial vocation after 1898, they certainly were in a strong position to pursue it. They could have built fortified bases in the Philippines (and on the island of Guam, also acquired from Spain) and stationed a substantial portion of their fleet in the Pacific both to defend their new holdings and to join the great-power competition for territory and influence in China.

But the United States did none of these things. Although Roosevelt regarded the Philippines as a "heel of Achilles," vulnerable to Japan and Germany and any other great power prepared to move aggressively, Americans chose to let their new possessions dangle unprotected. When Congress rejected plans for the Philippines' defense, even Lodge welcomed the decision as a "wise" step.[20] The United States never did build a major fortified naval base west of Hawaii prior to the Second World War. Nor did Americans raise an objection when Germany took control of the island chains that straddled the main sea route from Hawaii to the Philippines, the Marshalls, Marianas, and Carolines.[21] As for Hawaii itself, after annexing the islands in 1898, the United States did nothing to make them useful for extending U.S. power in the Pacific. The attractive harbor at the mouth of the Pearl River was not even dredged until after 1908, and the first large ship did not enter Pearl Harbor until 1911.[22] Roosevelt continued to keep the main fighting fleet in the Atlantic, chiefly to guard against a possible German grab in the Caribbean. His successor, William Howard Taft, also kept the main battle fleet in the Atlantic, with the understanding that "when we need it in the [Far] East we will send it all there."[23] As for the Pacific, in 1910 the American naval presence still amounted to just three cruisers and a half-dozen gunboats patrolling the Yangtze River to protect American missionaries.[24]

Americans' failure to build on the acquisition of the Philippines reflected both a lack of ambition and a paucity of perceived interests in that part of the world. Although there was always much excited talk about the "China market," actual business interest in those markets was tepid. The overwhelming majority of American businessmen were more interested in the massive home market. Unlike Britain, the United States did not have an "export economy."[25] In 1910 exports made up just over one-twentieth of the nation's gross domestic product, compared to a quarter of Britain's. Even as the United States became the world's leading industrial producer, surpassing Britain by 1913, Americans still exported less than 7 percent of their manufactured goods. Andrew Carnegie said it was "bad days for us" when his companies had to sell abroad.[26]

To the extent that American businesses were interested in foreign markets, moreover, they looked to Europe and Canada. American exports to China in 1900 were 1.1 percent of total exports and would not rise by more than a point or two in the decades that followed.[27] This amounted to .0005 percent of America's GDP.[28] As the United States shifted increasingly toward the export of high-priced manufactured goods, the markets for such products could be found almost exclusively among the advanced industrial nations that had the money to pay for them and the infrastructure to use them.[29]

The primary push for an "open door" policy actually came not from businesses but from American diplomats and officials in Washington who hoped to use private economic investments to increase U.S. political influence in Asia and Latin America. "Dollar diplomacy" was not about using diplomacy to help private American companies earn more dollars; it was about using the companies and their dollars to help further U.S. diplomacy. In both Asia and Latin America, American officials constantly complained that businessmen showed little initiative and were lackadaisical in the competition with other foreign traders. Americans were so little concerned about expanding empire, even an informal commercial empire, that they refused to build a sizable merchant fleet. By contrast, Japan's merchant fleet expanded rapidly at the end of the nineteenth century, in keeping with Tokyo's growing ambitions to play a larger political and commercial role in East Asia. In 1900 the tonnage of Japanese merchant ships was 50 percent higher than that of the United States.[30]

The United States also did not keep pace with the other powers in naval construction. When the Royal Navy launched the first Dreadnought-type battleship in 1906, the size, speed, and range of its guns made all other battleships obsolete, but when Roosevelt sought authorization to build four Dreadnoughts, Congress declined.[31] By the time Taft took over in 1909, the Anglo-German naval race threatened to leave the American battle fleet outmoded and vulnerable. But Congress would not support more than one of the new big-gun battleships per year. By 1914, congressional authorizers had revived the nineteenth-century notion of building ships for "coast and harbor defense." On the eve of the great European conflict, American naval strategy was thus focused not on global expansion but on snuggling safely behind the two oceans.[32]

The American minister to China, earnestly trying to uphold the "open door," lamented the pitiful lack of American power in the region. "If we had a fleet of battleships ploughing the Pacific; if we had a foreign policy, persistent and consistent in its nature, and supported by the 'big stick'; if the necessity of market conditions once came home to the American people in such a way as to make them support a national policy in the Far East that insured the 'open door' and equal opportunities, the attitude of the nations towards us might be very different. As it is, we are comparatively helpless."[33]

Secretary of State John Hay's famous "open door" notes in 1899 and 1900, calling on the other powers to allow all nations to trade freely in China and to preserve that nation's "territorial integrity," had stirred enormous pride in the United States. But the pride was in America's superior morality, not in its superior power.[34] The notes committed the United States to nothing, and that, to Americans, was their great virtue. Even when the United States had a golden opportunity to put force behind the notes—when McKinley dispatched over two thousand troops to Beijing in 1900 to rescue the besieged American delegation during the Boxer uprising—Americans did not seize the opportunity to establish a strong presence on the ground in China.

Germany, by contrast, had not hesitated when presented with a like opportunity: When two German missionaries were killed by Chinese peasants in 1897, the Germans promptly seized the Chinese port of Kiaochow and demanded a ninety-nine-year lease. Kaiser Wilhelm II proclaimed that hundreds of thousands of Chinese would "tremble when they feel the mailed fist of the German Reich pushing down on their necks."[35] The other European empires quickly took their own concessions from the Chinese in compensation. The Americans did not.

The other powers, therefore, after a brief moment of apprehension during the war with Spain, quickly came to recognize Americans' lack of geopolitical ambition. The British were frustrated that the United States was not more ambitious, especially in the Far East, where Britain at the turn of the century desperately needed allies. Kipling's poem "The White Man's Burden," written in 1899, was mostly a plea to reluctant Americans to fill the vacuum left by a retreating Britain. But Roosevelt, as much as he loved Kipling, frankly told British officials that Asia was "the very place where America could least help you."[36]

Far from viewing the powerful United States as a threat, even after the war with Spain, every one of the world's powers was eager to make mutually beneficial arrangements with Washington. The British sought a triple alliance with Japan and the United States in Asia, which would have greatly strengthened the Americans' hand in preserving an "open door" in China. The Germans invited the United States to help protect the "open door" in Morocco against French efforts to control that market. The French would have been delighted to have the United States as an ally to balance Germany. Such alliances would have augmented American influence even if the United States did not increase its navy or build new bases abroad. But the Americans would not align with anyone. Most foreign powers knew enough not to ask, and those that asked were politely rebuffed.[37]

Little wonder that even after America's victory over Spain and its acquisition of an empire, most of the other great powers still did not view the United States as a true "world power." It had a massive, vigorous, imposing economy that could not be ignored. It was obviously capable of rousing itself and fighting a war. It was unmistakably jealous and even belligerent when it perceived itself to be challenged in the Western Hemisphere. But as for the big global game the rest of the powers were engaged in—in Europe, Asia, Africa, and the Middle East—the United States was not a player and did not appear to want to be. British diplomats concluded that the United States simply was not "a major factor in world politics beyond the western hemisphere."[38]

In the Western Hemisphere it was a different story, but even there it was not a simple one. Americans had never been shy about their desire to be the dominant power in the hemisphere. Hamilton had aspired to make the United States "ascendant in the system of American affairs . . . the arbiter of Europe in America."[39] A century later, Henry Cabot Lodge admitted that the United States might not have much of a foreign policy "outside of the Americas," but within the hemisphere "we had a very definite one." It was that the United States had to be "supreme."[40]

Lodge's statement actually revealed how little most Americans were interested in the region itself. Being "supreme" meant keeping other great powers out, nothing more. Americans no longer needed or coveted territory south of the border, as they had throughout much of the nineteenth century. The region held little attraction as a market or a source of resources, with the exception of Mexican oil, Cuban sugar, and Caribbean and Central American fruit. What Americans cared about most was the transisthmian canal, getting the land for it, building it, and then defending it. The primary purpose of the canal was to link America's coastlines and make it easier for American merchants on the East Coast to sell to markets on the West Coast (access to Asian markets was a distant second). Indeed, the United States may have been the only power in history that needed a small strip of foreign territory just to unite itself with itself.[41] Otherwise, the region was of interest to Americans only when other great powers threatened to become involved.

The paradox was that, while American presidents would have been happy if they never had to think about the region at all, problems in the Western Hemisphere absorbed most of their limited attention to foreign policy. In the first three decades of the twentieth century U.S. troops were almost constantly deployed in a region most Americans did not care about.

The common explanation for this consistent American involvement—economic imperialism or "dollar diplomacy"—is inadequate. American trade with the region was minuscule compared to overall U.S. trade. It was also minuscule compared to European trade with the region. Of the $500 million worth of goods South Americans imported in 1905, only $63 million, or 12.6 percent, came from the United States, despite its proximity. Most of the rest came from distant Europe. Multiple steamship lines linked Europe to South America, but not a single American line ran south of the Caribbean.[42] There were a few notable exceptions to American indifference. Minor C. Keith built a railroad linking Costa Rica's capital with the Caribbean port of Limón, then planted a banana crop to ship on it, and eventually merged his company with another to form the United Fruit Company, whose operations soon spread and gained a vast influence throughout Central America.[43] But between 1898 and 1906—a period often cited as the heyday of economic imperialism in the region—U.S. imports from Central America made up just 1 percent of the worldwide total; exports made up a little over 1 percent.[44] American investments in Central America in 1914 amounted to under 3 percent of all U.S foreign investment, down a half percentage point from 1897.[45]

A better explanation for the frequency of American interventions was the region's chronic instability and the great disparity of wealth and power between the United States and its poorer, weaker southern neighbors. American hegemony in such circumstances was hard to avoid. The Central American republics and Caribbean island nations, in particular, were plagued with shaky dictatorships, frequent revolutions, and cross-border aggressions.[46] American naval forces were constantly called upon to protect citizens caught in the crossfire of local conflicts or who ran afoul of local rulers.[47] The United States was also frequently invited to intervene by local governments and by their internal and external enemies.[48] American officials ignored and rebuffed most of these requests, and usually regretted those occasions when they did not.

What the United States rarely ignored, however, were pleas for protection against the great powers of Europe. Americans for decades offered support to Cubans fighting against Spain. They bridled when the Royal Navy imposed British will on Nicaraguans and Hondurans. When Britain and Venezuela confronted one another in 1895 in a minor dispute over the precise location of the border between Venezuela and British Guyana, Grover Cleveland threatened to go to war. When seven years later Venezuela became embroiled in another dispute over unpaid debts with both Britain and Germany, Theodore Roosevelt hinted again at military action to force the two European powers to back down. These bellicose responses had little to do with any great concern for Latin and Caribbean peoples, or even with American investments.[49] Presidents and their advisers simply feared letting any European power gain or regain a foothold in the hemisphere that might challenge American strategic dominance.

These fears may have been exaggerated, and were sometimes driven by domestic politics, but they were not irrational.[50] At the turn of the century the Europeans were aggressively competing for colonies and territories all across the globe, carving out new spheres of economic and political control wherever possible, and seizing on the misbehavior of the locals to take what they wanted. The British had sent troops to Egypt in 1882 over non-payment of debt, and those troops were still there two decades later. The United States was not looking for confrontations with the great powers of Europe—the whole point of American supremacy in the hemisphere was to avoid it. But the region's instability continually threatened to bring the Europeans in. Venezuela was not paying its debts; chaos in Haiti, the Dominican Republic, and Central America threatened foreign lives and property; and the great powers were unlikely to stand idly by and do nothing. Nor did Roosevelt and other Americans expect them to. "We do not guarantee any state against punishment if it misconducts itself," Roosevelt declared in 1901. But then, when Europeans did act—when German and British warships bombarded two Venezuelan forts and sank a handful of Venezuelan vessels—Americans were appalled at the brazen "violation" of the Monroe Doctrine and Roosevelt worried about further European encroachments.[51] Such concerns grew as the transisthmian canal came closer to completion.[52] Roosevelt told Congress in 1902 that the United States was going to have to take a "far greater interest than hitherto in what happens throughout the West Indies, Central America, and the adjacent coasts and waters."[53]

It seemed clear to Roosevelt and others that if the United States was going to say "Hands off" to the European powers, then the United States would have to take responsibility for keeping order in the region.[54] Indeed, British officials suggested it would be "a great gain to civilization" if the United States could prevent "these constantly recurring difficulties between European powers and certain States in South America."[55] As Elihu Root saw it, the United States had to "assume an attitude of protection and regulation in regard to all these little states in the neighborhood of the Caribbean."[56]

This approach came to be known as the Roosevelt Corollary to the Monroe Doctrine, and it constituted a revolutionary shift in American policy in the Caribbean with vast if, for the moment, unseen implications. In his 1904 annual message to Congress Roosevelt declared that Americans' one aspiration in the hemisphere was "to see the neighboring countries stable, orderly, and prosperous." Countries that "conduct[ed] themselves well," that acted "with reasonable efficiency and decency in social and political matters," that kept good order and paid their debts, would face no "interference from the United States." But those guilty of "chronic wrongdoing," or which revealed "an impotence" that resulted in the "general loosening of the ties of civilized society," might "ultimately require intervention by some civilized nation." In the Western Hemisphere the task of exercising "international police power" fell to the United States. It would interfere only as a "last resort," and only in "flagrant cases of such wrongdoing or impotence" which either violated American rights or "invited foreign aggression." But Roosevelt concluded portentously with what he called this "truism," that nations which wanted to preserve their independence had "the responsibility of making good use of it."

This was an extraordinary assertion of American rights and responsibilities and transformed whatever meaning the Monroe Doctrine had once had. Privately, Roosevelt made clear that his corollary was not intended to create "de facto colonies" or even "protectorates," the very idea of which he said he regarded "with repugnance."[57] Yet while Roosevelt himself might wish to do "as little as possible"—he sent troops to the region only twice in his seven and a half years as president—to declare the United States responsible not only for addressing "wrongdoing," but for fostering progress and prosperity, and for preserving "decency in social and political matters" and the "ties of civilized society," and in a region so burdened by political and economic difficulties, opened the door to constant intervention and involvement in the internal affairs of neighboring countries.[58] As Root summarized the new approach to the nations of the hemisphere: "First. We do not want to take them for ourselves. Second. We do not want any foreign nations to take them for themselves. Third. We want to help them."[59] Perhaps ironically, it was that third point that potentially made all the difference, for it helped produce the recurrent interventions that characterized American policy in the first three decades of the twentieth century.

Root may have been among the few American officials who actually cared about the region and its people.[60] A decade before Wilson talked about teaching South Americans to elect good men, it was Root who professed the desire to help the peoples of the hemisphere "acquire capacity for self-government," to lift them "up out of the discord and turmoil of continual revolution into a general public sense of justice and determination to maintain order."[61] The United States would benefit materially, but "underlying all the materialism and the hard practical sense of the American people," Root insisted, there was "a certain idealism," a "missionary calling to spread through the length and breadth of the world the blessings of justice and liberty and of the institutions which we believe make for human happiness and human progress."[62]

The first test of Roosevelt's new "corollary" came in the Dominican Republic. The Dominican government had defaulted on its debt, of which the biggest holders were French and Belgian citizens. France and other powers had already sent warships to the island, in response to the murder of a French citizen and to protect lives and property during a series of revolutions. With the Dominican Republic "drifting into chaos," Roosevelt ordered American forces in. The United States took control of the customs house, the main source of income for the government, and made sure that revenues were appropriately parceled out between the government and its international creditors. Once Roosevelt approved the plan, he hoped Dominicans would "behave" and make further actions unnecessary.[63]

The results at first seemed positive, and not just for the Dominicans but for the whole region. Foreign investors (mostly non-American), newly confident that the United States would guarantee their loans, poured more money into Latin government coffers. Central American and Caribbean governments began settling with their creditors, which made their bonds more attractive. The immediate result was an unprecedented rally in the market for Latin bonds.[64] The peaceful resolution of the Dominican crisis seemed to offer a solution to the American conundrum—how to maintain peace, keep the Europeans out, and benefit the native population, all without excessive U.S. intervention. Root hoped it would become "but a part of a great policy," and Roosevelt's successors in the Taft and Wilson administrations continually looked to both the Dominican affair and the Platt Amendment in Cuba as models of effective policy.[65]

Root also looked to other methods for keeping the peace in Central America. The five somewhat artificially constructed "republics" had been attacking and subverting each other with regularity ever since the end of Spanish rule. To bring about "tranquility" among them, the lawyerly Root looked to the application of "treaty law."[66] In 1907, in what seemed a triumph of diplomacy, Root, working closely with Mexico so as to avoid the appearance of North American dictation, helped the five governments establish a Central American Court of Justice. They agreed to compulsory arbitration of disputes, promised not to aid rebels in neighboring states or recognize governments that seized power by unconstitutional means, and agreed to a ten-year treaty of peace and amity.[67] When the Second Hague Peace Conference was held in 1907, Root insisted that the Latin nations be invited—the first time they had ever been asked to join the company of the European great powers. An effective international legal order with the full participation of the Latin states, he hoped, would shield them from intervention and abuse by the Europeans—further lessening the need for a heavy North American hand in the hemisphere.[68]

Root's hopes of bringing stability and prosperity to the Caribbean Basin with a light touch soon ran into trouble, however. Within a year, the Central American treaty broke down, and war erupted again.[69] In the Dominican Republic, the government eventually fell to insurrection and economic difficulty, leading to U.S. interventions in 1912, 1914, and 1916. Most disappointing of all was Cuba, which fell back into disorder in 1906 when its first elected president, who had ruled capably since the end of the American occupation, tried to ensure his re-election through fraud and intimidation. The opposition protested and threatened rebellion, and both sides called, somewhat ironically, for U.S. intervention under the terms of the Platt Amendment. Roosevelt and Root were very reluctant to send troops back to Cuba. When they finally decided to reoccupy Cuba, they regarded it as a failure of their policy.[70]

These failures revealed the inherent difficulties of establishing a stable peace in the region. But they also revealed some inherent problems with American policy. Root had hoped the Platt Amendment would make intervention unnecessary, for he assumed Cubans would prefer to settle their own differences. Instead, it had the opposite effect. Opposition leaders launched rebellions precisely to provoke U.S. intervention, hoping the result would be a fairer, U.S.-supervised election that they could win. The occupation of Cuba from 1906 to 1909 was followed by the landing of troops in 1912 under President Taft, another intervention in 1917 under President Wilson, and then a string of U.S. interventions into the early 1930s.

Root might be appalled, and Roosevelt could denounce the Cubans' "revolutionary habit," but they were playing the game according to rules the United States had set.[71] Throughout the region, the constant looming prospect of North American intervention did open space for opposition politics, and it tended to prevent any party or individual from consolidating power in a dictatorship.[72] But it also made frequent North American intervention, both armed and unarmed, all but inevitable. As the historian Lester Langley observes, Caribbean political leaders simply "acclimated themselves to the realities of American power." They learned how to manipulate American sentiments to their own advantage.[73]

Successive administrations searched for ways to break the cycle, but without success. Once again applying the tactics of "dollar diplomacy," the Taft administration tried to decrease U.S. military involvement by increasing private commercial activity.[74] "True stability" was "best established not by military, but by economic and social forces," Taft's secretary of state, Philander Knox, declared.[75] Although criticized by Democrats for using "diplomatic influence to advance the interests of American investors," Taft officials saw themselves as doing the opposite. They believed they were "using Wall Street to serve our national interest and to benefit other countries."[76] But dollar diplomacy fared no better than Root's earlier efforts. The struggles in these small societies were more about personal power and wealth than about the success of the national economy.[77] In the interest of stability, the United States in several of these countries took away everyone's weapons and established a supposedly depoliticized national guard to keep order, only to the see the national guard become the personal tool of the next caudillo.[78]

The United States also had a hard time following its own rules, especially when local leaders openly defied American preferences. The most brazen of these was Nicaragua's José Santos Zelaya, who had ruled the country since 1893, supported rebel groups in El Salvador and other neighboring countries, interfered in Costa Rica's elections, expropriated foreign properties, flirted with Germany (including offering an alternate canal route across Nicaragua), and discussed an alliance with Japan. When a revolt erupted against Zelaya in 1909, therefore, Taft officials wished the rebels well—notwithstanding Washington's policy against recognizing unconstitutional seizures of power. Although American officials neither instigated nor funded the rebellion (some American businessmen may have, however), everyone knew the United States wanted Zelaya gone. When Zelaya's forces captured and executed two American citizens serving with the rebel army, Secretary of State Knox denounced the dictator as "a blot on the history of Nicaragua" and praised his opponents as representing "the will of a majority of the Nicaraguan people."[79] Such was the power of the United States that Zelaya promptly resigned. The Taft administration helped install a new president, Adolfo Díaz, and took control of Nicaragua's finances.[80] Then Zelaya's Liberal Party launched a rebellion, and Díaz requested U.S. forces to protect "all the inhabitants of the Republic."[81] The Taft administration reluctantly sent first 100, than another 350, and finally up to 2,000 marines, claiming it had a "moral mandate" under the 1907 Washington Conventions to preserve the "peace of Central America," which was "seriously menaced by the present uprising."[82] The intervention proved bloody: the marines lost seven dead and more wounded and inflicted far greater casualties on Liberal forces. Díaz held on to power, but mostly because the Taft administration left 100 marines behind in Managua to serve as a legation guard and symbol of the U.S. commitment to oppose further rebellions. They would remain in Nicaragua for another thirteen years. They did bring stability, right up until the marines left and the next revolution immediately erupted.

The lesson was hard to ignore. As one historian observes, "Where American policy succeeded it did so not by dollars but by bullets."[83] Root at times despaired that bringing stability to the region seemed to require "a long period of armed intervention." That was something "that we cannot undertake."[84] Among other things, Root was troubled by the fact that the peoples of the region "hate us." They "think we despise them and try to bully them."[85] In the summer of 1906 he took his wife and family on a four-month cruise of South America, stopping at every capital and giving speeches in the hope of establishing a "new rapprochement . . . between the United States and South America."[86] "We know the mistakes we have made," he told Latin audiences, while professing America's lack of base motives.[87] "We wish for . . . no territory except our own; for no sovereignty except the sovereignty over ourselves," but only "to help all friends to a common prosperity and a common growth, that we may all become greater and stronger together."[88]

Root was undoubtedly sincere, but American policy did not always live up to these lofty ambitions. It was hard for America's hemispheric neighbors to forget those occasions where the United States had acted purely out of self-interest. Roosevelt's "taking" of Panama to build the canal was the most blatant instance. In 1902 one of many Panamanian revolutions against Colombian rule erupted. American naval forces, instead of helping the Colombians put it down, as they had in the past, this time facilitated the rebels' efforts. Roosevelt seized the opportunity to take the land he wanted for the canal by striking a quick deal with the new Panamanian government, much to the displeasure of the Colombian government.[89] There was scarcely an American alive who did not approve of Roosevelt's accomplishment, yet many blushed at his manner of accomplishing it.[90] Roosevelt himself betrayed a guilty conscience.[91]

—

When Woodrow Wilson was elected in 1912, many expected a dramatic change in U.S. policy toward the hemisphere. Democratic critics had long assailed the interventionism and dollar diplomacy of the Roosevelt and Taft years, and, on the stump, Wilson promised that his administration would "think of the progress of mankind rather than of the progress of this or that investment."[92] As president, he hoped to forge a "spiritual union" of the hemisphere through "sympathy and understanding" and "upon terms of equality and honor."[93]

Yet in a very short time Wilson managed just the opposite, intervening more frequently and with greater force than either of his two Republican predecessors. His secretary of state, William Jennings Bryan, who tended to refer to the Latin republics as "our political children," employed the same financial and legal tools as his predecessors, prompting one senator to remark that Taft's "dollar" diplomacy looked like a mere "30 cents" next to Bryan's.[94]

In Haiti, where seven presidents had been either assassinated or violently overthrown in just four years since 1911, and an eighth was dragged into the streets by an angry mob and literally torn to pieces in the summer of 1915, Wilson decided he had no choice but to act and prevent "the most sordid chaos."[95] Admiral William Caperton landed with several hundred marines, defeated a small rebel army, and appointed a new president. American officials drew up a new treaty with Haiti giving the United States control of its finances and customs houses, the administration of its sanitation and public works, and a new U.S.-trained and -led constabulary force. The marines would remain in Haiti for another nineteen years.[96]

In the Dominican Republic, rocked by a succession of assassinations, presidents seeking to extend their terms, and rebellions aimed at their ouster, Bryan publicly warned that "no more revolutions will be permitted." In 1916, Admiral Caperton again arrived with two thousand marines to put down the latest revolt. A U.S. military government ruled until 1924. As Wilson's biographer, Arthur Link, later put it, thus did the "idealistic President who talked movingly of Pan-American brotherhood and of the equality of nations great and small . . . [become] in fact the most extraordinary interventionist in Latin America in the history of the United States."[97]

Wilson was only following the general course Roosevelt had laid out in 1904 and which Root and his successors had tried and failed to implement ever since. Like them, he argued that the opening of the canal "made it increasingly important" that governments in the vicinity should have "fairly decent rulers," thereby avoiding the kind of "friction" that had led to the "Venezuela affair." He told a bemused British official that he intended to "teach the South American Republics to elect good men!"—a Wilsonian version of Root's earlier hopes.[98]

The British found American behavior in the hemisphere bewildering. It was not just the moralism that seemed to infuse American policies. It was also Americans' impatience, intolerance, and general unsteadiness in the day-to-day management of their "empire." The British knew all about the problems of managing an empire. They grappled almost constantly with rebellions large and small. As one British historian has quipped, the "sun never set on [the empire's] crises."[99] But the British generally took the difficulties of imperial management in stride. They did not have inordinately high expectations for those in their charge. Lord Cromer, who served as controller-general in Egypt, once remarked, "It will probably never be possible to make a Western purse out of an Eastern sow's ear."[100] They also had no difficulty using massive force against recalcitrant colonials. After the Sepoy Rebellion in 1857, the British stationed half their army in India.[101] Under British rule, "violence against natives was habitual, not just instrumental" and derived from Britons' belief in their right and even their vocation to rule non-white peoples.[102] Americans were at least as prone to feelings of white supremacy, but they bridled at the suggestion that they were ruling anyone. And partly as a consequence, they were never as tolerant either of the messiness, the cost, or the disappointing outcomes of their efforts. They intervened with the expectation of departing quickly, only to find themselves staying for years, just like the British in Egypt.[103]

Nowhere was the gap between American aspirations and their achievements greater than in Mexico. Beginning in the Taft administration, Mexico became for several years the biggest issue of American foreign policy and the focus of much ideological and partisan debate. To a significant degree, American intervention in Mexico was the beginning of the end of American efforts to spread the "blessings of liberty" and the institutions of "human progress" south of the border.

In 1910, the decades-long rule of Mexican president Porfirio Díaz had begun to crumble after the seventy-seven-year-old dictator returned himself to power in the latest of many fraudulent elections. By the end of 1911, however, Díaz lost control and fled the country. The revolutionary leader Francisco Madero—his followers called him the "Apostle of Democracy"—was then elected president in the "freest election in Mexican history."[104] The Taft administration recognized the new government immediately, but Madero's hold on power was fragile and in February 1913, one month before Woodrow Wilson took office, Madero was deposed and murdered in a coup by his own army commander, Victoriano Huerta.

Wilson faced the question of whether to recognize Huerta as the new Mexican president. Britain and the European powers had quickly done so, hoping that Huerta would bring stability and fearing that holding back recognition would only lead to a new round of violence.[105] But most Americans found the idea of recognizing the murderous Huerta objectionable. Wilson declared he would not recognize "a government of butchers," and he soon looked for some way to replace Huerta with a legitimate government.[106] He and other Americans were encouraged when forces led by Venustiano Carranza and Pancho Villa launched a rebellion with the stated aim of restoring the revolution and Madero's constitutional order. When Huerta responded by dissolving the Mexican Congress, arresting its Constitutionalist members, and assuming dictatorial power, Wilson became even more determined to drive him from power.

To Wilson, the confrontation with Huerta was about more than solving a crisis in a neighboring country. His top advisers urged him to pursue a policy "on a fundamental moral basis," as the United States had once done in Cuba, and "to blaze the way for a new and better code of morals than the world has yet seen."[107] Wilson needed little urging. He had supported the intervention in Cuba and had even broken with many Democrats in supporting the retention of the Philippines. He shared Roosevelt's belief in America's need to accept responsibilities commensurate with its power, and in the case of Mexico, he regarded the United States as the only "responsible" power on the scene.[108] The British, who were concerned only with defending their oil interests, continued to view the Americans with amazement. "Since the days of the Holy Alliance," one British official remarked, "it is doubtful that any government has thus declared its mission to reform the moral shortcomings of foreign nations."[109]

After Huerta rejected an ultimatum to step aside, Wilson notified Britain and the other powers that he considered it his "duty" to "employ such means as may be necessary" to remove him.[110] He soon found a pretext. On April 9, 1914, Mexican troops detained some American sailors who had landed unannounced at Tampico to purchase fuel. While the two countries haggled over the proper form of a Mexican apology, Wilson ordered the entire North Atlantic battleship fleet to Tampico, called a joint session of Congress, and requested authorization to "use the armed forces of the United States in such ways and to such an extent as may be necessary to obtain from General Huerta and his adherents the fullest recognition of the rights and dignity of the United States."[111] While the press puzzled over Wilson's decision to go to war over a point of honor— Andrew Carnegie likened it to "the fabled war of the two kings to decide which end of the egg should first be broken"—Wilson's real plan was to blockade both coasts of Mexico, seize Tampico and Veracruz, which Huerta controlled, and then perhaps send an expeditionary force from Veracruz to Mexico City to force Huerta from office.[112] His plans changed when he learned of a German arms shipment heading for Huerta's forces at Veracruz. At Wilson's orders, 1,000 U.S. marines landed at Veracruz, where they were immediately met by 800 Mexican troops, supported by young cadets from the nearby Mexican naval academy. The Atlantic fleet soon arrived with another 3,000 U.S. forces. The fighting was fierce, and when it ended the next morning, 126 Mexican troops had been killed and another 195 had been wounded. American losses were 19 dead and 71 wounded. It was by far the most serious battle American forces had engaged in since the Philippine war over a decade before.

Wilson was shaken. The "death of American sailors and marines owing to an order of his seemed to affect him like an ailment."[113] He had not expected the Mexicans to put up resistance, but the Constitutionalists and the Huertistas united in indignant nationalist fury.[114] Mobs across the country looted and destroyed American consulates, burned American flags, and imprisoned American officials and private citizens. Carranza commented that "even if a biblical apostle occupied the White House, Mexico could expect no good from the United States."[115]

Despite the bloodshed at Veracruz, and the lack of a willing partner in Mexico, Wilson pressed ahead. He would not stop, he said, until he could be assured that "the great and crying wrongs" the Mexican people had suffered were being addressed.[116] He even came to embrace some of the more radical Mexican demands for land reform, including the confiscation and dismantling of large estates.[117] "A landless people," he told the British, would "always furnish the inflammable material for a revolution."[118] Indeed, the Mexican Revolution increasingly seemed to him a modern replay of the French Revolution, and no less "profound" in its historical significance.[119] Huerta represented the old regime, "the aristocrats," "the vested interests," "the men who have exploited that rich country for their own selfish purposes."[120] Wilson was for "the submerged eighty-five percent of the people of that Republic."[121] The revolution provided "a wonderful opportunity" to show the world that the United States was "not only human but humane; that we are actuated by no other motives than the betterment of the conditions of our unfortunate neighbor, and by the sincere desire to advance the cause of human liberty."[122]

As so often in American politics, the debate over Mexico had a domestic angle. Wilson claimed to see in Mexico the same forces of wealth, privilege, and power arrayed against the revolution as were arrayed against the economic reforms he was trying to carry out at home.[123] Having seen how "material interests threaten constitutional freedom in the United States," he argued, Americans could only sympathize with Latin Americans fighting the same powerful interests in their own countries.[124] Wilson's Republican opponents also saw parallels. Wilson favored "a scheme of reform in the interests of the Mexican peons," Root cracked, but the "reformatory methods" of Carranza and Pancho Villa appeared to be "to kill the owner and take the land."[125] Most American Catholics, and the Catholic Church itself, were furious with Wilson for backing the Mexican revolutionaries, who, like their French antecedents, sought to destroy the power of the Mexican Catholic Church, which had long been allied with Díaz and the landowning aristocracy. When Constitutionalist forces desecrated churches and physically abused priests and nuns, American Catholics blamed Wilson and looked to punish him at the ballot box. Lodge professed to believe that the United States would have been better off leaving Huerta in power, for he at least could have done "sufficient throat cutting to restore peace."[126]

Remarkably enough, Huerta finally gave up and fled the country in 1914. Wilson had succeeded, albeit at a higher cost than he anticipated. Now the problem was replacing Huerta. The obvious choice was Carranza, but Wilson and his advisers had come to distrust him. The rebel leader, Pancho Villa, had always chafed under Carranza's leadership and now turned against him.[127] Wilson, to the astonishment of many, threw his support to Villa.

This turned out to be a mistake.[128] Before Villa became a famous revolutionary, he was known to have murdered at least four people and committed multiple acts of arson, robbery, kidnapping, and rape.[129] During the revolution, as self-anointed governor of Chihuahua, Villa made himself a Robin Hood, confiscating the property of the rich and passing it out to the poor, which even the American socialist journalist John Reed called "the socialism of a dictator."[130] One of his deputies had carried out the mass murder of three hundred prisoners locked in a corral.[131] Wilson acknowledged that Villa might be "a crude and cruel barbarian in many ways," but he was "the only man . . . looking out for the welfare of his country" and could become "the greatest Mexican of his generation."[132] When an incredulous Root asked the president if he really felt he could "trust Villa," Wilson replied, "Oh yes, he's a changed man."[133]

A few months later, however, Wilson abandoned Villa and threw American support to Carranza. This prompted one of the more bizarre episodes in the tumultuous history of Mexican-American relations. Villa, furious at Wilson's betrayal, began attacking American citizens in Mexico.[134] Then in March 1916, over one thousand *Villistas* crossed the border and descended on Columbus, New Mexico, setting fire to the town and raping and looting until the 13th U.S. Cavalry Regiment arrived. The attack resulted in the death of nineteen Americans and several dozen of Villa's men.

Wilson's closest advisers begged him to take military action against Villa, partly to protect American security but mostly because they feared a failure to act would cost him the 1916 election. Wilson resisted at first. "In a republic like ours, the man on horseback is always an idol," he lamented, no doubt thinking of his Rough Rider predecessor.[135] His greatest concern, he claimed, was for "poor Mexico, with its pitiful men, women, and children, fighting to gain a foothold in their own land!"[136] Yet with political pressures at home growing, on March 15 he finally ordered General John Pershing into Mexico with over 6,000 men as part of a "punitive expedition" to capture Villa.

Unfortunately for Wilson, the wily Villa was nowhere to be found. Wilson's military advisers soon began to worry about the mission. Not only was it undignified for the U.S. Army "to be hunting for one man in a foreign country," it seemed only a matter of time before the Mexican government had had enough.[137] Meanwhile, as Pershing pushed deeper into Mexico his lengthening supply lines grew indefensible. In the summer Carranza ordered his army to attack Pershing's troops if they headed in any direction other than due north. In mid-June, fighting erupted in the town of Carrizal, killing thirty Mexicans and fourteen Americans.[138] Wilson prepared for a full-scale military operation to clear northern Mexico of all armed bands, while 15,000 heavily armed Mexican troops moved northward to a base opposite Nacho, Arizona.[139]

Wilson was "infinitely sad" at the course of events and was also taking a political pounding in an election year.[140] His Republican opponent, Charles Evans Hughes, attacked him for intervening in Mexico "for an ignoble purpose," and then for retreating without accomplishing anything except destroying "the only government Mexico had." In the process he had subjected Americans to a "profound sense of humiliation."[141] Wilson refused to confirm the criticism by withdrawing Pershing in advance of the election, but once the election was over Pershing led his troops back across the border. Villa was still at large. Carranza was president, and would remain so until 1920, when he was replaced by a new group of military leaders, who took and held power for the next fifteen years.

The Mexican affair displayed the paradoxical, self-contradictory, and often self-defeating nature of American policy in the hemisphere. Wilson had no doubt been sincere in his desire to "aid and befriend Mexico" and not "coerce her." He privately complained that he was "the only man who really believed down in his heart that a people had the right to do anything with their government that they damned pleased to do, and that it was nobody else's business what they did with it."[142] But this was a striking and particularly American form of self-delusion. In a speech he prepared for delivery in the event of war, Wilson wrote that it was contrary to American principles "to dictate to another people what their government shall be."[143] When Secretary of State Robert Lansing read the draft, he put a question mark next to that sentence and scribbled in the margin "Haiti S Domingo Nicaragua Panama."[144]

Were these problems and failures avoidable? It is easy to make such an assessment in retrospect, but American policymakers throughout this period faced a genuine dilemma: how to shape an order in the hemisphere that would provide stability, lessening the prospect of European intervention and reducing the need for American intervention. They had assumed that the best way to do this, and also the most humane and honorable way, was to improve the well-being of the peoples of the hemisphere, both economically and politically, and to give them a chance to enjoy peace and security. Their motives combined self-interest and a genuine desire to do good.

The problem was that while the United States aimed to quell revolution in Latin America, Washington's preferred solution—stable, democratic, constitutional government—was even more revolutionary than the region's revolutions, which, after all, had been occurring ever since independence from Spain. Latin and Caribbean politics, like that of most peoples at all times, tended to revolve around strong individuals and clans who competed in winner-take-all struggles for power. Frequent rebellions and political instability retarded economic development. Where a single ruler managed to hold power for an extended period, as with Díaz in Mexico or Zelaya in Nicaragua, the economy might improve but the benefits were not widely shared. The poor and political opponents generally suffered from repression, which eventually led to revolution and began the cycle all over again. This confirmed the Americans in their belief that true stability and progress required democracy and constitutional government, but this prescription, whether right or wrong, proved hard to export without imposing it by force.

To later critics, the expressions of benevolence uttered by the likes of Roosevelt, Root, and Wilson were mere façades for imperialism. They weren't, but for those on the receiving end of American policy it didn't make that much difference. The North Americans spoke often of "Pan-Americanism," but for many in the region, "Pan-Americanism" was a synonym for North American hegemony. The fact of that hegemony was inescapable, regardless of what it was called and of Americans' intentions. As Lansing observed, "The primacy of one nation," based on its "superior physical might," was simply "out of harmony with the principle of the equality of nations which underlies Pan-Americanism, however just or altruistic the primate may be."[145]

One option was simply to walk away and let events in the region take their course. Root eventually came close to believing this might be the best policy for the United States, though he never managed to put it into practice while in office. Wilson on several occasions claimed he wanted to pursue such a course in Mexico, insisting that "if the Mexicans want to raise hell, let them raise hell. We have got nothing to do with it. It is their government, it is their hell."[146] But he, too, was unable to hold to a policy of strict non-interference—not in Mexico, or in Nicaragua, Haiti, or the Dominican Republic.

For all the crises and interventions, what was notable about the decade and a half following the war with Spain was the relative equanimity with which Americans greeted their enlarged role on the world scene. Foreign policy remained of little interest to most Americans, yet all four administrations, from McKinley to Roosevelt to Taft to Wilson, were fundamentally more internationalist in outlook than their nineteenth-century predecessors. There was, to be sure, as one contemporary observer put it, "a distinct disinclination" for further expansion after the liberation and occupation of Cuba, the acquisition and four-year war in the Philippines, and the other territorial acquisitions in Hawaii, Guam, and Puerto Rico.[147] The interventions in Cuba, Panama, the Dominican Republic, Nicaragua, and Haiti had spurred some debate and aroused some opposition. Yet there was no great "anti-imperialist" backlash—

anti-imperialism as a national movement died quickly after the Philippine war ended, despite the increased pace of American intervention in the Western Hemisphere. Nor was there a demand for retrenchment or a return to a pre-1898 international posture. When given a choice at the ballot box, Americans consistently chose the more internationalist of the two candidates. They had re-elected McKinley in 1900, at the height of the Philippine conflict, by an even greater margin than in 1896. In 1904, they elected Roosevelt, the very embodiment of muscular foreign policy, even if as president he was more cautious than many expected. Then in 1908 they elected Roosevelt's handpicked successor, William Howard Taft, whose résumé included stints as governor-general of the Philippines, provisional governor of Cuba, and secretary of war. The wild three-way election of 1912 pitted three leading internationalists against one another—Taft, Roosevelt, and Wilson—with Americans choosing, albeit unwittingly, the one who would become the most ambitious internationalist of all.[148]

The internationalists were not yet proposing a very challenging agenda, of course. After the war with Spain, they did not advance policies likely to get the United States into a war. Roosevelt throughout his seven-plus years as president steered clear of confrontations and, with rare exceptions, worked to soothe the ruffled feathers of other great powers when confrontations loomed. Partly this was because he knew the American public did not relish further military interventions. But he also believed American interests were, with few exceptions, best served by peace with and among the great powers. Even when the public was in a belligerent mood—for instance, when Californians threatened to provoke a confrontation with Japan over immigration—Roosevelt did all he could to restrain the public and prevent a crisis. When he left office, he boasted that "there was no nation in the world with whom a war cloud threatened . . . or from whom we had anything to fear."[149] Henry Stimson, looking back on this period from the perspective of the late 1940s, observed that the "age of Theodore Roosevelt, for all of its moral battles, had been a time of hope, not fear, and confidence, not worry."[150] Even the internationalist Wilson believed he would spend the great majority of his time on domestic affairs and thought it would be ironic if instead he was forced to focus his attention on the world.

CHAPTER THREE

Collapse of the Nineteenth-Century World Order

What are we going to do with the influence and power of this great nation?

—Woodrow Wilson, July 1914[1]

THEN AMERICANS suddenly confronted the challenge of a world order collapsing around them. From 1900 onward, tensions in Europe rose steadily, as German power grew and Britain, in response, increasingly made common cause with its former competitors and sometime adversaries, France and Russia. In Asia, an expansionist Russia ran headlong into an expansionist Japan, both seeking control of territory nominally owned by the weak Chinese empire, and thereby also butting up against British interests. Americans were happy not to be part of any of this, but some wondered how much longer they would be able to remain aloof.

Internationalists, in fact, saw in the growing instability around the world a new mission for the United States, as a mediating force in the search for peace. In the year before war broke out in Europe, there were almost as many peace organizations in the United States as in the rest of the world combined.[2] Many of the members of these groups were straightforward pacifists, inspired by religious conviction, by a secular enlightenment utopianism, or by a populist worldview that saw in war a plot by the wealthy to profit at the expense of the common man. The question of how to establish a permanent peace was the subject of endless treatises by academic historians, legal theorists, and political scientists.

Practitioners and statesmen also took it seriously. Roosevelt and Root were heroes of the peace movement in both the United States and in Europe.[3] As secretary of state, Root negotiated limited arbitration accords with twenty-four countries.[4] The Central American Court of Justice, established at his initiative in 1907, was hailed as a model for an eventual World Court.[5] Upon his retirement in 1909 the New York Peace Society held a great banquet in his honor.[6] As for Roosevelt, despite the modern cartoonish depiction of him as a "war lover," his contemporaries regarded him as an indispensable leader in the cause of international peace, and for good reason.[7] Although he personally relished combat and had contempt for anyone who would not go to war for "justice" and "righteousness," he also continued the efforts of previous administrations to support new international institutions aimed at preserving the peace.[8] Although a skeptic of arbitration agreements, he supported the new international tribunal at The Hague.[9] When the new court seemed in danger of becoming irrelevant due to the European powers' refusal to submit their disputes to it, European advocates sought Roosevelt's help. He promptly directed Hay to find some matter to submit to the court (it was a disputed claim with Mexico) and then persuaded Venezuela and its foreign creditors to submit their dispute, as well. Andrew Carnegie hailed him, and "peacemakers everywhere blessed Roosevelt for breathing life into the almost defunct institution."[10] Roosevelt was the only American president of the era—indeed, he was the only world leader of the era— who managed to bring warring powers to the negotiating table and broker a peaceful settlement between them, when in 1905 he mediated an end to the war between Russia and Japan, earning the Nobel Peace Prize and the applause of his fellow citizens. That same year he worked more discreetly behind the scenes to prevent conflict between Germany and France over Morocco. After Roosevelt left the White House, the New York Peace Society suggested him as the first "World President" of a new global government.[11] One activist wanted to give him the title "Theodorus Pacificator Maximus."[12]

An American president could play such a role, some believed, because the United States was different from the great powers of Europe. Precisely because it was not a member of the "imperial club," was not engaged in the scramble for territory in Africa, Central Asia, the Near East, or China, and was not part of the European system of alliances and arms races, it could act as "the supreme moral factor in the world's progress," the "sought-for arbitrator of the disputes of the nations," the "active dispenser of international justice."[13]

Many also believed that America's diverse ethnic population gave it a unique perspective. Roosevelt loved to boast of his variegated heritage, which gave him a special understanding. "The Englishman thinks of the German as an alien by race and innate disposition," he observed. But "I know better, for I have some English and some German blood in me, not to speak of other strains." If in Europe the Slav seemed destined to clash with the Teuton, "here in America the descendants of Slavonic immigrants become men precisely like ourselves."[14] Some saw the United States as "the world in miniature," the "prefiguration" of an eventual "United States of the world."[15]

The notion that the United States had a special role to play was typical American self-flattery. But others around the world did not entirely disagree. They could see that Americans behaved as selfishly as any other people and were capable of the same brutality as most. Americans' record with the Native Americans and the enslavement of millions of Africans, their demand for supremacy in the Western Hemisphere, their self-serving high tariffs, all undermined Americans' constant claims of exceptional moral character. No more than other peoples were Americans inclined to self-denial.

Yet the United States was different if only because of its unique material and geographical advantages. Without any great interest in Europe, except as a market for American products, without any interest in the partitioning of Africa, or the competition for influence in the Near East, or the "great game" in Central Asia, or even the fight over spheres of influence in China, the United States did enjoy, by comparison with the other great powers, a reputation for disinterested neutrality on the main disputes roiling the world in the early twentieth century. Other nations sought out the United States, sometimes hoping to sway its power and influence to their side, but also to solicit its help as mediator—as the Japanese and Russians did in settling their war, and as the Germans and French did in their dispute over Morocco.[16] "How I envy you the independence of your country," one foreign diplomat exclaimed when Roosevelt was negotiating between France and Germany. "[It] enables you to speak with such boldness and freedom to both [sides] . . . as neither of them can suspect you of any hostility and both are anxious to secure your cooperation and if possible support."[17]

This was a pleasant situation for a nation to be in. For internationalists the idea of America acting as neutral arbiter of the world's disputes achieved their ambitions in the least costly way possible. It gave the United States the prominent role and responsibility in world affairs that befitted its growing power and moral standing, without violating Washington's "great rule." Successful mediation required absolute neutrality among the warring parties and therefore permitted no alliances or close entanglements with the other great powers. It allowed the United States to shoulder its share of responsibility for maintaining world order, to act as a mature power in the interests of upholding civilization, but it did not require the use of force. To be the world's neutral arbiter required only a disinterested and benevolent leadership of the kind that Americans felt themselves uniquely capable of providing. The United States was becoming a world power, Henry Cabot Lodge argued, but a "world power in the finer sense," one whose "active participation and beneficent influence" would be "recognized and desired by other nations in those great questions which concerned the welfare and happiness of all mankind."[18]

To wield benevolent influence without wielding power or risking war was a great dream, but it was an easier dream to have when the world was so advantageously configured. The world order in which Americans grew prosperous and powerful had rested on a specific set of international conditions: a rough balance of power on the European continent; the absence of rising great powers outside Europe; and a satisfied naval superpower, Britain, which presided almost unchallenged over the oceans and the world's trading routes. Those had been the conditions during the decades when the United States recovered from the trauma and devastation of the Civil War and began its ascent to the pinnacle of the world economy. The happy circumstances that allowed Americans to imagine themselves a "world power in the finer sense" were in fact dependent on others exercising power in the traditional sense.

No power had played a greater role in shaping America's beneficial environment than Great Britain. This was not because the British provided the United States "free security." Americans, and good fortune, had provided their own security. The vast territory and enormous population of the United States, the two oceans, the weak neighbors on its borders, the moderately sized U.S. Navy, and the belligerent American spirit had long since made the United States an uninviting target for attack or conquest by the distant great powers. It was true that the existence of a generally benevolent Royal Navy allowed Americans to save themselves the expense of building a larger navy to protect their coastlines and the approaches to a canal, but Americans certainly had the means to build such a navy had they thought it necessary.

What Britain and the Royal Navy had provided, however, was the underlying security structure for a worldwide trading, finance, and communications system from which the United States benefited more than anyone. British naval power made it possible for the revolutions in transportation, communication, and commerce to knit the world's economies together, facilitating foreign investment, the interpenetration of markets, the relatively free exchange of goods and comparatively easy transfers of money, all of which characterized the modern international economic order that significantly raised the standard of living for all those who took part in it. The British had not created and sustained this order out of the goodness of their hearts. As a commercial and industrial nation situated on a small island in inhospitable seas, Britain depended on imports to survive and on exports to make it wealthy enough to afford its dominant navy. The British had a profound interest in secure trading routes and relatively open markets, therefore, and the byproduct of British empire was an extraordinarily liberal economic order unique in history.

The United States was both a beneficiary of this order but also its heir apparent. Ordinarily this might have led to tensions between the dominant power and its challenger, and such tensions did exist. Yet, for a variety of reasons, the British chose not to treat the United States as a threat. By the first decade of the twentieth century, the prospect of a war between the two Anglo-Saxon powers was practically nil (despite what U.S. naval planners, eyeing their budget, sometimes liked to claim). This was due less to American policies, for there had always been plenty of anti-British sentiment in the United States, than to the fundamental judgment made by British strategists that war with the United States was not merely unnecessary but unthinkable.

This strategic calculation was a great gift to the United States, for it meant that the United States could avoid the classic problem of all rising powers in history—how to achieve power and pursue commensurate ambitions without clashing with the existing order. At the moment when Germany, by contrast, was confronting all the dangers that rising powers normally faced, the United States was sailing ahead unhindered. The Germans might well have asked why the United States was allowed to expand and establish its vast sphere of influence in the Western Hemisphere, to increase the size of its navy, to make war on Spain and take away the jewel in its imperial crown, and to pursue an expanding commerce, sometimes at Britain's expense, while still enjoying peaceful relations with London. Yet it was Germany that Britons increasingly regarded as their number one enemy.

It was not that the United States posed no possible threat to British interests. In theory, it did. Canada was vulnerable, and the British still had important colonies and large investments in the Western Hemisphere, where it did more trade than the United States.[19] America's hegemonic demands, as in the case of Venezuela, came more at Britain's expense than at anyone else's. Yet the British accommodated and acquiesced. They simply "chose to regard their exclusion from the Caribbean as of no great moment."[20] Some of this was triage—the British couldn't take on everyone, and they chose to resist Germany, and keep a wary eye on the Russians and French, while accommodating the United States and Japan. Some of it was simply a rational perception of the threats Britain faced. It was very clear that Americans were largely content with their position in the world and did not seek to expand at Britain's expense where it really mattered. They did not compete with Britain in Africa, the Middle East, South Asia, and East Asia. In these vital areas, Britain's competitors were Russia, France, and lately Germany, and it was against those threats that the British actually hoped to enlist American help.

It was certainly easier for Britons to accommodate America's growing power because of what seemed to be their many affinities. Leading British statesmen believed a common language, a common culture, and a common liberal worldview bound the two nations together in a way that transcended normal strategic considerations.[21] The Americans were a "powerful and generous nation," the British colonial secretary, Joseph Chamberlain, declared. "They speak our language, they are bred of our race. Their laws, their literature, their standpoint upon every question are the same as ours; their feeling, their interest in the cause of humanity and the peaceful development of the world are identical to ours."[22] It was possible, as the First Lord of the Admiralty put it, to have "faith" in the "innate justice of the American people."[23]

Most of these British officials would have been shocked to learn how little these feelings were reciprocated on the other side of the Atlantic. The people whom Britons still called their "cousins" did not consider themselves part of the family. Early-twentieth-century America was composed of many different ethnic groups, and two of the largest, the Irish and German Americans, tended to Anglophobia. Nor had even the blue-bloods of Anglo-Saxon stock forgotten the Revolution, the War of 1812, or the shaky stance of the British during the Civil War. In 1895 Henry Cabot Lodge was still complaining that Britain had "always opposed, thwarted, and sought to injure us."[24] His view softened when the British took the Americans' side in their war with Spain, in contrast to the other European monarchies, which sided with the Spanish crown.[25] But even then, the majority of Americans felt no great affection for the British.

More importantly, perhaps, most Americans had little sense that the international order from which they benefited owed anything to Britain, or even that there was an international order. They were more inclined to believe that the happy circumstances in which their nation was rising were simply the result of inevitable human progress, divine favor, fortuitous geography, and their own virtuous behavior.

Few Americans showed much concern, therefore, when events around the world began to raise doubts about whether British global dominance could last. The world order established by British power in the nineteenth century was, like all world orders, the product of a unique confluence of circumstances—a Europe in which great rival powers were precariously balanced against one another; an East Asia where the old hegemon, China, was prostrate, and the future hegemon, Japan, was weak and in self-imposed isolation; and thus a world where a rapidly industrializing Britain could enjoy overwhelming and virtually unchallenged economic and naval superiority.[26] As the historian Paul Kennedy has observed, from the end of the Napoleonic Wars until the late nineteenth century, the British Empire "existed in a power-political vacuum."[27] This exceptional situation could not last, however, and by the turn of the century Britain's primacy was being challenged from all directions. The French pushed against the British in eastern Africa, near strategically vital Egypt and the Suez Canal, and the two nations nearly went to war in 1898. In Southeast Asia the two empires had carved out neighboring spheres in Indochina, as well as in China proper. The challenge from Russia was even greater. Imperial Russia was contesting for primacy in the decaying Ottoman Empire, challenging Britain for influence in Istanbul and along the Bosporus. It pressed hard in Central Asia, driving into Afghanistan and threatening the defenses of India, the heart of the British Empire. It pushed across Siberia to the Far East, searching for a port on the Pacific and for control of Manchuria, which nominally belonged to China, where the British believed they had important interests. Meanwhile, Japan was rising as a formidable power in the Far East, the first Asian power to do so in two centuries. These challenges alone had forced Britain to depart from its long-cherished policy of "splendid isolation." In 1902 Britain formed an alliance with Japan, partly as a bulwark against Russia and partly as insurance against Japanese encroachment against British holdings in the Far East. In 1904 the British formed an "entente" with France, which aimed in part at settling differences and avoiding further dangerous clashes between the competing empires.

Increasingly, it was Germany that became the greatest concern for

British officials. In the decade and a half since Kaiser Wilhelm II had taken the throne and fired Otto von Bismarck, Germany had grown ever more dissatisfied with the existing configuration of power in Europe and in the world. Unlike Bismarck, for whom the achievement of a unified Germany in 1871 had been the culmination of long-held dreams and ambitions and satisfied the nation's requirements, Wilhelm and the men around him saw German unification as but the starting point for further expansion. At the very least they believed Germany's newfound power, both economic and military, should elevate it to a higher status in the world, as an equal to Great Britain, with a concomitant increase in global influence and an expanding colonial empire—a "place in the sun." This ambition was accompanied by fear and anxiety that Germany would be hemmed in and encircled by hostile powers, with France to the west, Russia to the east, and the British hovering over all and controlling the sea and trade routes to everywhere. To escape the vise which Germans feared might close around them, the kaiser sought to pursue *Weltmacht,* or "world power," a more assertive approach in foreign affairs.

Germany's ambitions unnerved its European neighbors. In 1894, France and Russia concluded a military alliance, thereby fulfilling German fears of encirclement. Then came Germany's decision in the late 1890s to build a navy capable of challenging British supremacy on the high seas. The plan of Admiral Alfred von Tirpitz to build a new fleet of thirty-six battleships thoroughly alarmed British leaders who saw the buildup as a threat to their two most vital interests: defense of the empire and defense of the British Isles. Germany, meanwhile, grabbed Shantung from the Chinese, sought island outposts in the southwest Pacific, and demanded territories in southern Africa abutting British colonies. It also built a massive, highly trained, and well-equipped army in the heart of Europe, thus threatening the continental balance of power on which British security had long rested. By 1907, partly in response to growing concerns about German power and intentions, Britain joined France and Russia in a "triple entente." This was a diplomatic revolution for all three, who had long regarded each other as competitors and sometime adversaries. With Germany in turn allying itself ever more firmly with Austria-Hungary as a check on growing Russian power in the Balkans, Europe was divided into two heavily armed camps. The multipolar balance that had provided a modicum of stability following the Treaty of Vienna in 1815 was gone. So too was Britain's pivotal position as the arbiter of the European peace.

As Europe grew more unsettled and prone to conflict, Americans were loath to take sides. One reason was ethnic politics. There were enough immigrants from all parts of Europe to encourage neutrality. Roosevelt often expressed pride in his German blood and admiration for German culture and advancement. Like most educated Americans he was still inclined to think of Germany as the land of Goethe and Mozart; unlike many Americans Roosevelt also admired the strength, efficiency, and élan of the Prussian military. Although at times he worried about Germans' evident interest in gaining a foothold in the Western Hemisphere, throughout his presidency Roosevelt worked to keep on good terms with the kaiser. He pooh-poohed British fears of rising German power and told them not to worry about the German naval buildup, to the point where British officials sometimes regarded him as pro-German.[28] The kaiser did indeed refer to Roosevelt as "my friend"—a rare usage for the German ruler—and felt comfortable turning to him during the first Moroccan crisis in the hope that he might use his influence in London to detach Britain from France.[29] Roosevelt considered the kaiser "jumpy" and erratic, but was reluctant to regard him as dangerous.[30] In general he saw it as his mission to bring about a rapprochement between the two powers.

His most dramatic effort came in the Moroccan crisis in 1905, when Germany and France nearly came to blows over that North African kingdom. The dispute nominally concerned France's domination of the Moroccan economy and Berlin's desire to open the country to German political and economic influence. But everyone saw it as part of a broader clash between a nervous France and an increasingly assertive Germany. With the primary goal of keeping the peace in Europe, Roosevelt maneuvered between the two powers, alternately delighting the kaiser and undermining him, supporting German demands for an international conference (against British wishes), but taking France's side in the final settlement. It was the most significant diplomatic intervention by a president in European politics in American history, and it reflected both concern about the possibility of war and Roosevelt's personal desire to play a grand role on the world stage. Yet it was a sign of prevailing attitudes among the American public that he had to keep his efforts mostly hidden from view. Even the idea of sending a delegate to the conference at Algeciras sparked opposition in Congress, with members insisting that it was the "settled policy of this Government since its foundation to abstain from taking part in such political controversies between European nations."[31] Roosevelt kept his distance for the remainder of his presidency.

Europe was not the only place where the old order was breaking down. In Asia the rise of Japan, along with the weakening of Britain, presented new and more immediate problems for the United States.

At the turn of the century Americans had welcomed the rise of Japan.[32] The nation's political and social evolution in the Meiji era seemed promising, as the Japanese explicitly sought to copy Western ways in everything from politics to dress. Japanese troops fought side-by-side with Americans and Britons in the Boxer uprising and earned Roosevelt's admiration for their martial skills and bravery—"What extraordinary soldiers those little Japs are!" he exclaimed with the racial condescension typical of white Americans.[33] Mahan treated the Japanese as honorary "Teutons" in what he posited as the great struggle of the era between Teuton and Slav. At the turn of the century the big threat was thought to be Russia, and when in 1904 Japan scored early military victories against the tsar's forces, including a devastating surprise attack on the Russian fleet at Port Arthur, Roosevelt was delighted.[34] Oscar Straus, hostile to Russia because of its anti-Semitic practices, expressed a common view when he declared that "Japan is certainly battling on the side of civilization." Roosevelt agreed: "The Japs have played our game because they have played the game of civilized mankind."[35]

That perspective changed quickly after Japan's extraordinary triumph over Russia, however. The first victory by an Asian over a European power in the modern era led to fears of a "yellow peril." Japanese immigrants settling on the West Coast, and in Canada and Australia, met increasing racial hostility. Labor unions protested the influx of Japanese workers willing to toil for low wages and live in what the locals regarded as subhuman conditions; parents in California protested the increasing numbers of Japanese students crowding into their children's classrooms; while others worried more generally that this seemingly endless "stream of Japanese immigration" would soon lead to the "complete Orientalization of the Pacific Coast." American military planners noted the Japanese skill at "concealing their motives and objects" and their tendency to belligerence. They seemed "very much disposed to attack anybody," observed Lodge, who now worried about rumored Japanese activities in Mexico.[36] Roosevelt wondered whether Japan's ascent into the ranks of the civilized great powers was turning out to be such a blessing. With its deeply rooted samurai traditions, Japan increasingly appeared to be "of a different type from our civilizations." Maybe beneath their top hats the

Japanese viewed all Europeans and Americans as "white devils" to be "treated politely" only until they could be beaten one by one.[37] Roosevelt worried the Japanese might "get the 'big head'" after all their military triumphs and "enter into a general career of insolence and aggression."[38]

If so, however, that was not a fight that Roosevelt or his successors wanted. Japan had proved itself "a most formidable military power," he noted, as well as "very proud, very warlike, very sensitive."[39] It was probably best to treat the Japanese "with scrupulous courtesy and friendliness" so that they could have "no excuse for bearing malice toward us."[40] Roosevelt tried his best to tamp down anti-Japanese eruptions on the West Coast, with mixed results. In foreign policy he pursued a policy of accommodation and retreat. He acceded to Japan's territorial claims on the Asian continent, and although some worried about Japanese penetration of southern Manchuria at China's expense, he insisted the United States had no interests there worth fighting for.[41] If the Japanese did get the "big head," he wanted to steer them toward the Asian mainland and away from the indefensible Philippines, Hawaii, and the vulnerable Pacific Coast. So long as the Japanese had their eyes on Manchuria and China, he reasoned, their "natural enemy" would be Russia, not America.[42]

Roosevelt did take precautions. He ordered up a new war plan for Japan—Plan "Orange." He urged fortification of Subic Bay in the Philippines to serve as a Far Eastern outpost for the navy (which Congress rejected).[43] His acceleration of American battleship production—he wanted four new ships per year (which Congress also rejected)—was chiefly a response to the Anglo-German naval race, but battleships had a role in the Pacific as well. In 1908 he sent his "Great White Fleet" to anchor in Tokyo Bay and Yokohama, believing this display of American might would help "maintain peace."[44] As he told Germany's Admiral von Tirpitz, "I thought it a good thing that the Japanese should know that there were fleets of the white races which were totally different from the fleet of poor Rodjestvensky."[45]

Through the first two decades of the twentieth century, successive American administrations, though they often complained about Japan's policies, particularly in China, raised no serious challenge to Japan's expanding empire and spheres of influence.[46] Roosevelt, Taft, and Wilson struck agreements in public and in private recognizing Japan's burgeoning colonial empire, as well as its special prerogatives in lands it did not formally control, including in Korea and territories that were nominally part of China.

There was a tension in American policy that persisted throughout these decades, however. Americans had a special solicitude for China. The Celestial Kingdom had long held a place in the American imagination, less because of the potential 400-million-person market than for spiritual and political reasons. American missionaries helped shape the image of the Chinese as a people in need of saving, and Americans in general flattered themselves that, unlike the European imperial powers, they had sought nothing from the Chinese but the opportunity to help them. John Hay's "Open Door" notes, calling on the great powers to respect China's sovereignty and "territorial integrity" and to allow free and equal access to the Chinese market, put American policy on a higher moral plane, as defenders rather than despoilers of the Chinese—or so Americans believed.[47] As Japan's policies over the following decade increasingly aimed at bringing much if not all of China under its sway, therefore, many leading Americans felt some obligation to offer some assistance.

Some, but not too much. For all the goodwill Americans felt toward China, and for all the hostility they sometimes felt toward Japan— William Howard Taft once commented that "a Jap . . . would be glad to aggrandize himself at the expense of anybody"[48]—nevertheless, successive American governments did little to protect the Chinese or stand in Japan's way. What some have called America's "open door imperialism" in China never went far beyond words.[49] Hay once noted to Roosevelt that his famous notes had "accomplished a good deal" in East Asia "without the expense of a single commitment or promise."[50] Certainly the latter part was true. Americans extolled the "Open Door" and insisted that Japan do so, too, but beyond the rhetoric American policy was restrained. Roosevelt said the "open door" was an "excellent thing," but he knew it would be slammed shut whenever a powerful nation "willing to run the risk of war" wished to do so.[51] The Americans were not willing to run the risk of war, either to defend China or to prop the door open. As Philander C. Knox, Taft's secretary of state, put it, Americans were content to "stand consistently by our principles even though we fail in getting them generally adopted."[52]

As the contours of world affairs changed around them, Americans did their best to stay out of it. They were not seized with any sense of impending crisis. If Europe was heading toward conflict, Americans were unaware of it. Roosevelt after leaving the presidency set off on a yearlong African safari where he focused on wild beasts (he killed more than five hundred), followed by his near-fatal trip down the Amazon, followed by his failed return to politics as the leader of the Progressive Party in 1912. His successors in the Taft administration were preoccupied with Latin American issues, and to a lesser extent with China, and made it clear to all concerned that Europe's problems were Europe's, not America's.[53] When Wilson entered the White House, he did the same. To the extent that he took time away from his ambitious domestic agenda to focus on foreign policy, it was to immerse himself in the long crisis with Mexico. Before August 1914, he "gave scant attention to European affairs."[54] His secretary of state, William Jennings Bryan, when not also mired in Mexican and Caribbean affairs, devoted his energies to arbitration agreements and eventually negotiated "cooling off" agreements with some thirty nations around the world—none of which included the great powers of Europe.[55]

Many of those who did pay attention had grown accustomed to think of Europe as a fount of progress, not as a cauldron of atavistic conflict. From the late nineteenth century onward, American progressives had traveled to the continent to search out models for how the state, society, and the economy could be organized to serve the public good. They believed they saw fellow travelers among the socialists of France and Belgium and the social democrats of Germany.[56] Indeed, they regarded the United States as having fallen behind Europe in the march of social progress. Where once America had taught democracy to the Europeans, today it was Americans who were going to school in Europe. "Why has the tortoise Europe outdistanced the hare?" asked one of *The New Republic*'s founders.[57]

Americans took an optimistic view, therefore, even as crises in Europe began to multiply. The trend of the world was toward "international unity," Secretary of State Knox argued. As late as December 1913, President Wilson spoke of a "growing cordiality and sense of community of interests among nations" that was producing "an age of settled peace."[58] Such hopeful statements, coming at a time of growing international disruption, may have been partly a failure of understanding and partly a bit of wishful thinking, but, in either case, they did not suggest a prominent role for the United States.

Americans could be forgiven for not seeing more clearly what the real global trends were. As an astute British observer put it in 1907, the international situation was characterized by "unrest and incertitude . . . fierce contrasts . . . irreconcilable extremes . . . perplexing contradictions." The "old order" was gone, but a new order had "not yet established itself."[59]

There was evidence enough to support a hopeful view. Between 1899 and 1903, twenty governments signed arbitration agreements, and in 1904 alone, another twenty-six agreements were inked, prompting the French foreign minister, Théophile Delcassé, to declare a revolution in world affairs.[60] If one believed in treaties and institutions, one could easily imagine that a stable peace lay just over the horizon.

Only in fleeting moments did Roosevelt, and few others, recognize that the changes occurring in the world might pose challenges to America's general posture of aloofness. In an exchange with the German ambassador in 1912 Roosevelt commented that "as long as England succeeds in keeping up the balance of power in Europe, not only in principle but in reality, well and good." Were Britain unable to do so, however, Roosevelt believed the United States "would be obliged to step in, at least temporarily, in order to re-establish the balance of power in Europe." The fact was, he said, that the United States, "owing to our strength and geographical situation," was becoming "more and more the balance of power of the whole globe."[61] Two years earlier, accepting his peace prize in Norway in 1910, he had laid out a vague blueprint for a "League of Peace," a consortium of the great powers charged with maintaining world peace and enforcing the decisions of the International Court.[62] The United States would of course have played a prominent role in any such league. But that was just dreamy speculation. Even Roosevelt did not yet see a pressing need for such an institution and such a level of American involvement.

In fact, by 1912 the sequence of events that would lead to world war had already begun. Germany was the catalyst. German leaders felt surrounded by enemies, a situation that, as the historian A. J. P. Taylor observed, had come about "solely" as a result of Germany's own policies.[63] Wilhelm II's policies since the late nineteenth century had transformed an international situation in which all the great powers eyed each other with varying degrees of suspicion to one in which Germany had become the principal concern of all the other great powers except Austria-Hungary, now its lone ally. Prior to this "revolution in European affairs," Germany had "enjoyed greater security than at any time since the Crimean war."[64] Now it faced a heavily armed and hostile France in the west and in the east a hostile Russia that, like Germany, was building up its armed forces and undertaking significant military reforms to improve its war-fighting abilities. At a meeting between the kaiser and his military advisers in December 1912, the chief of the German General Staff, Helmut von Moltke, warned that Germany's "enemies" were arming at a faster pace than Germany. War had become "unavoidable," he told the kaiser, "and the sooner the better."[65]

German strategy called for a two-front war, necessary in light of the Franco-Russian military alliance. The specific war plan, devised by the chief of the General Staff, Alfred von Schlieffen, in 1906, required the rapid defeat of France so that the full weight of German power could then be turned on the supposedly more formidable and more numerous Russian enemy. A quick victory in the west was essential because otherwise in a long war of attrition the combined forces of France and Russia would eventually wear Germany down. As Schlieffen put it, "complete annihilation" of France's capacity to make war had to be accomplished before France's allies could come to her assistance.[66] In fact, if Germany didn't defeat France in six weeks, it would lose.[67]

That German leaders were willing to risk the fate of the nation on a single battle said much about their state of mind. By 1914, top German officials had become convinced that an "iron ring" of containment had been formed by Russia, France, and Britain and was designed to strangle the young, rising Germany in its crib.[68] Moltke believed time was not on Germany's side.[69] In two or three years Russia would have built its force up to the point where Germany could not prevail in a war. Therefore, Germany needed to "wage preventive war in order to beat the enemy while we still have some chance of winning."[70] As Moltke put it, this meant orienting German policy toward "the early provocation of war."[71]

The opportunity came after Serbian nationalists assassinated Austria's Archduke Franz Ferdinand in Sarajevo. Even before the assassination, German officials had been urging Austria to take a hard line in the Balkans, even if it meant provoking war with Russia. After the assassination they urged Austria to move against Serbia quickly. As the German ambassador in Vienna told an Austrian official, "It would have been better to attack yesterday than today; and better to attack today than tomorrow."[72] The kaiser sent a personal message to the Austrian foreign minister, warning him that action against Serbia was expected and that "it would not be understood in Germany if we allowed the opportunity to pass without striking a blow."[73] Most critical of all, the Germans assured Austrian leaders of Germany's unconditional support for any decision the Austrians might make, including, of course, war. This message, delivered on July 4, would later become known as the "blank check."

The Austrian government delivered an ultimatum to Serbia, but things did not proceed as the Germans expected. The Serb government shocked everyone by essentially agreeing to the humiliating terms; Russia immediately offered to engage in talks with Austria to address the crisis; and Britain's foreign secretary, Edward Grey, in a separate initiative, proposed a four-power conference, to include France, Italy, and Germany, in order to find some formula to "prevent complications."[74]

The kaiser now hesitated, and not for the last time. When he read Serbia's surprisingly conciliatory response to the Austrian ultimatum, he decided that "every reason for war is removed."[75] But it was too late. The Austrian government, responding to weeks of pressure and assurances from Germany, was now determined to punish Serbia.[76] It rejected the Russian and British offers to talk, and about an hour after the kaiser appeared to decide that war was no longer necessary, Austria declared war on Serbia.

The next day, Tsar Nicholas II approved the partial mobilization of Russian forces, but he also wrote his "Cousin Willie" in Berlin seeking to avoid war.[77] At about the same time, a telegram was on its way from the kaiser reporting that he was trying to get Austria to reach an understanding with Russia.[78] But the Germans had begun a partial mobilization of their own forces, which prompted the Russian military high command to insist on full mobilization, lest the frontiers of the Russian Empire in Europe be left exposed to a German attack. The next day, July 30, the tsar signed the order for full mobilization.

The German government, then and later, would make much of the fact that Russia had mobilized first, insisting it showed that Russia, not Germany, had started the war. In fact, the German government had gone to some lengths to ensure that Russia would appear to be the aggressor and instigator of the war. The German military had already planned to mobilize for war on August 1, regardless of what Russia did. The conciliatory note sent by Wilhelm to Nicholas on July 28 had been engineered by the German chancellor, Theobald von Bethmann Hollweg, to provide evidence, once war began, that the kaiser had wanted peace but had been rebuffed by the tsar.[79] As the German historian Annika Mombauer notes, "It was only a stroke of luck that Russia's general mobilization was announced in time to make Germany's own military measures *appear* as a reaction to Russia's."[80] A high-ranking military official in the kaiser's cabinet wrote in his diary after the outbreak of the war: "The government has succeeded very well in making us appear as the attacked."[81]

On August 1, Germany declared war on Russia. On August 2, Germany presented Belgium with an ultimatum demanding that German troops be granted free passage across the country into northern France. The next day King Albert notified Germany of Belgium's refusal to allow passage. That day Germany declared war on France, and on the morning of August 4 German forces entered Belgium on their way to northern France and eventually Paris.

The only remaining question concerned Great Britain. The German government, and especially the kaiser, hoped and expected Britain would stay out of the war. It was a reasonable judgment, based on British statements and actions throughout the July Crisis, and indeed in the years prior. Grey worked hard to avoid provoking Germany and to avoid any action that might pull Britain into a war.[82] On July 29 the kaiser's younger brother, Prince Henry, spoke to his cousin, King George V, and reported back to Berlin that the king had said, "We shall try all we can to keep out of this and shall remain neutral." Whether or not George V actually said that, the kaiser was satisfied: "I have the word of a King, and that is good enough for me."[83]

In fact, the British government was divided. Grey, Winston Churchill, and others wanted to come to France's aid. Grey told the American ambassador, "The issue for us is that, if Germany wins, she will dominate France; the independence of Belgium, Holland, Denmark, and perhaps Norway and Sweden, will be a mere shadow; their separate existence as nations will be a fiction; all their harbors will be at Germany's disposal; she will dominate the whole of Western Europe, and this will make our position quite impossible. We could not exist as a first-class State under such circumstances."[84] But others in the cabinet felt differently. Many Britons, including those in positions of influence, thought it absurd to fight on behalf of Serbia and Russia.[85] A majority of the British people and their government also had no desire to defend France. Publicly, David Lloyd George, chancellor of the Exchequer, said that "there could be no question of our taking part in any war in the first instance."[86] Grey had to tell the French ambassador on July 29 that if "Germany became involved and France became involved, we had not made up our minds what we should do; it was a case that we should have to consider."[87]

It was the German invasion of Belgium that more than anything tilted the scales in favor of intervention. German conquest of the lowlands directly across the English Channel posed a strategic risk to Britain, but it was more than that. Britain was signatory to a treaty dating back to 1839 that guaranteed the small nation's neutrality, as were France and Germany. Bismarck had long ago warned against violating the agreement on Belgium, precisely because he feared the unfavorable reaction it would cause throughout Europe. This proved prescient. The German invasion of Belgium, and the stalwart if ultimately doomed resistance put up by the Belgian people, had a significant impact on British public opinion. As the historian Max Hastings explains, "The perceived martyrdom of King Albert and his people rallied to the cause of war millions of British people who hitherto opposed it." The unprovoked attack on a small neutral nation by the vast German war machine provided the British people some "moral certainty amid a sea of Balkan and European confusions."[88] It also swung the internal debate in the cabinet in favor of intervention. Britain, like all great powers, was not always a stickler for the law when it came to its own needs, but the principles at stake in Belgium seemed to many important enough to defend, even at the risk of war. What would happen to the world order, and particularly the European order, if such a treaty could be violated and a small peaceful nation invaded with impunity? And what would it mean for Britain? In his dramatic speech to the House of Commons on August 3, Grey argued that if the British people did nothing, not only would "the whole of the West of Europe opposite us" fall under the "domination of a single power," something the British had for centuries sought to prevent. But in addition, "we should . . . sacrifice our respect and good name and reputation before the world."[89]

German officials were shocked to discover that the British were, after all, willing to go to war simply because the German army had to pass through Belgium on the way to France. Britain had no formal agreement to come to France's defense, and indeed, it was well known that the majority of the cabinet members opposed entry into the war on those grounds. Nevertheless, that day Britain declared war on Germany, and the world war—the Great War, as contemporaries called it—had begun.

CHAPTER FOUR

The European War and American Neutrality

We have no right to count on the good-will of Americans. . . .
[W]e wrongly suppose [that] because they talk our language, they
are an Anglo-Saxon people. As a matter of fact they are a foreign
nation, or rather several foreign nations. None of these nations is par-
ticularly friendly to us, and those of them who are of our race have
very particular reasons for disliking us. It would be wiser to bear this
in mind and to treat the American people not as cousins, still less as
brothers . . . but as English-speaking foreigners . . .

—Cecil Arthur Spring Rice, British ambassador
to the United States[1]

We definitely have to be neutral, since otherwise our mixed popula-
tions would wage war on each other.

—Woodrow Wilson, September 1914[2]

THE ERUPTION of war in Europe in August 1914 struck most Americans "like lightning out of a clear sky."[3] The response was more one of
fascination and excitement than fear. The lightning had struck far away.
On the night of August 4 as many as 400,000 people packed into Times
Square to read the bulletins regularly posted on the three sides of the
Times Building, the red-lettered sheets relaying the latest news from
Europe. For the next few weeks, daily full-page headlines reported each
dramatic turn of events: German forces racing through Belgium into
northern France, driving the French and the British backward; reports of
German atrocities; the destruction of the historic town of Louvain and

its ancient library; General Paul von Hindenburg's crushing defeat of the Russian Second Army at Tannenberg. In less than a month, German forces were within eight miles of Paris. But then in mid-September the German drive in the west halted at the Marne in a battle that produced a combined half-million casualties in a single week of fighting.[4]

As to the distant war's impact on Americans' daily lives, the newspapers focused on three matters in the first weeks: the fate of tens of thousands of American tourists trapped in Europe; the reactions of the many citizens and visitors in the United States who were born in the countries now at war; and the effect of the war on the American economy. The *Chicago Daily Tribune* ran stories of wealthy Chicagoans arriving in London with only the change in their pockets; of hundreds of German Americans crowding the consulate in Chicago to register for German military service; of "two thousand excited Poles" burning a picture of the Russian tsar on Milwaukee Avenue; and of congressional passage of a one-billion-dollar emergency currency issue to stave off a banking panic. The *St. Louis Post-Dispatch* reported that the market for hogs was soaring and editorialized about "the amazing opportunities for foreign trade" that the war had suddenly opened. The *New York Times* reported that two dozen French chefs had vanished from the city's restaurants and hotels, presumably to enlist in the armed forces of their home country, leaving the restaurateurs and hoteliers in a panic.[5] None of these reports suggested that the war might affect American security or its broader interests. Even the renowned strategist Alfred Thayer Mahan, in an August 3 interview reprinted in papers across the country, talked only of Germany's threat to Britain. He said nothing about the war's possible impact on the United States.[6]

The early actions of the Wilson administration and Congress reflected domestic priorities. Officials spent the bulk of their time helping stranded Americans get home, preventing bank runs, figuring out how to get crops to overseas markets, and trying to prevent clashes among ethnic groups in the United States. The only official American response to the war was a declaration of neutrality and Wilson's offer of America's "good offices" as an impartial mediator. Wilson told reporters on August 3 that if Americans maintained their "self-possession" and "nobody loses his head," they could get through the crisis and actually "help the rest of the world." Mostly, however, he assured Americans that the economic dislocations the war was causing would soon be remedied.[7]

For most Americans the issues at stake in the European conflict—who did what to whom, when, and why—were matters of curiosity and debate but not much more. The origins of the war were confusing, and the belligerents did their best to sway American public opinion to their side.[8] But Americans' attitudes toward the belligerents depended as much on ethnicity, geographical location, and social class as on documents and reports. Most of the eastern establishment, living and working in the northeast corridor between Washington, New York, and Boston, believed that Germany had started the war, had violated solemn treaties, and was bent on conquest. This included political and thought leaders like Roosevelt, Taft, Root, and Lodge, the editors of the influential eastern newspapers, eastern bankers, financiers, and leading lawyers, the presidents and leading professors of the top eastern colleges. To this elite group, the war was a straightforward struggle between the democracies (except Russia) on one side and autocracy and "Prussian militarism" on the other. They feared a German victory would mean "the unspeakable tyranny of militarism for generations to come," that Britain and the Allies were fighting for nothing less than the "cause of civilization."[9] Lodge, trapped on vacation in London at the war's outbreak, believed Great Britain, France, and Belgium were fighting "the battle of freedom and democracy against militarism and autocracy, the battle of the public against the law of the sword and for the right of small nations to exist."[10] Roosevelt privately condemned the "Prussianized Germany" that had acted "in a spirit of entirely brutal selfishness," rejecting "any theory of international morality," and that could "never escape blame for starting the war." If the Germans managed to defeat Britain, he feared, they would "invade the United States within five years."[11] Walter Lippmann, editor of the recently launched progressive journal *The New Republic,* agreed that if Germany won the war, the whole world would have to "arm against her—the U.S. included, for Germany quite seriously intends to dominate the World."

Since the major eastern newspapers generally reflected this pro-Allied perspective, it was easy for members of the eastern elite like Elihu Root to believe that the whole country was as "radically and unalterably opposed to German militarism" as he was.[12] That was not the case, however. In that "great part of America . . . on the other side of the Allegheny Mountains," as William Jennings Bryan liked to call it, few cared who was to blame for the war.[13] A poll of newspaper editors in the Midwest revealed that 80 percent did not prefer one side over the other.[14] Germany was unpopular, but so were the Allies. Most Americans saw little to choose in what William Randolph Hearst's editorials called a "war of kings" brought on by "homicidal maniacs."[15] The overwhelming majority of Americans in all sections of the country believed the best role for the United States in the present war was no role at all. Neutrality was such a natural posture that the Wilson administration drafted its proclamation of neutrality the moment war was declared, even before Germany invaded Belgium, before France declared war, and before the British decided to intervene.

Wilson's main concern was not the European belligerents but his own divided nation. Privately, he worried that if the United States did not remain neutral, "our mixed populations would wage war on each other."[16] He was not alone in this fear. The authorities in cities like New York and Chicago worried about civil unrest from clashing ethnic groups. When a small crowd in Times Square began singing "La Marseillaise" in the first week of the war, the police stepped in to break it up.[17] Passions were such that Wilson approved a presidential message asking movie audiences to "refrain" from "expressing either approval or disapproval" of the newsreels.[18] It was fear of ethnic strife that led Wilson to release a statement urging Americans to be "impartial in thought, as well as action," to put a "curb" on their "sentiments," to be careful what they said "in public meetings," what they wrote in newspapers and magazines, said in the streets, and even what ministers said in their pulpits.[19] He was not asking Americans to have no feelings about these matters as much as he was asking them to keep those thoughts to themselves.

Ethnic politics dominated American policy at the outset of the war. The United States in 1914 was no longer an Anglo-Saxon nation. Although a majority was still of English, Scottish, and Welsh stock, the 1910 census counted 90,000,000 Americans, of whom 2,500,000 had been born in Germany and 1,670,000 had been born in parts of the Austro-Hungarian Empire; another 1,600,000 were from various parts of the Russian Empire, many of them Poles and Jews, 1,350,000 were from Ireland, 1,340,000 were from Italy, and 1,250,000 were from the Nordic countries—altogether 10,000,000 Americans had been born in Europe. Tens of millions more had parents or grandparents who had emigrated from the European continent in recent decades.

Three of these ethnic groups played a critical role in shaping American policy toward the European war, and all three opposed the Allies. For American Jews, for instance, Russia in 1914 remained the focus of evil in the world. The tsarist government had official anti-Semitic laws and policies and a long history of pogroms that had killed tens of thousands and driven hundreds of thousands more from their homes. American Jews had long successfully pressed Washington officials to protest Russia's anti-Semitic policies. They helped tilt American policy toward the Japanese during the Russo-Japanese War, with Jewish bankers and financiers like Oscar Straus providing loans to Japan and blocking financing for Russia. When the European war broke out, the banker Jacob Schiff spoke for most Jews when he said the United States should not be helping an alliance that included in its ranks a "detestable and inhuman" Russian government that had murdered its own subjects.[20] Some of the most influential American Jews, like Schiff, Paul Warburg, and August Heckscher, had been born in Germany, still had relatives there, and were pro-German throughout the period of American neutrality.[21]

More influential still were the Irish Americans, whose sympathy for their kin back home and hostility to the English oppressor had long made for rocky relations between Washington and London. By the early twentieth century as many as five million Americans had been born in Ireland or had Irish-born parents. Many more were of Irish ancestry. Heavily concentrated in the Northeast, Irish Americans exercised an influence on American politics "out of all proportion to their numbers," for they were active, engaged, and also, as the beleaguered British ambassador observed, "the best politicians in the country."[22] Henry Cabot Lodge, from heavily Irish Massachusetts, had made a career of attacking Britain—"*th' bould Fenian,*" Mr. Dooley humorously called him.[23] Roosevelt never displayed partiality toward Britain in public.[24] The Irish naturally saw the European war as a golden opportunity, and in early August thousands of Irish Americans cheered the German kaiser at an open-air gathering in New York.[25] As one Irish American activist put it, "Liberty for Ireland" could only be won "through the triumphs of Germany-Austria."[26]

Even more important than the Irish Americans in this war were the German Americans. Fully 20 percent of Americans in 1914 were of German ancestry, more than any other ethnic group except Anglo-Saxons.[27] Ethnic Germans made up as much as 40 percent of the populations of Milwaukee, Detroit, Cleveland, and Cincinnati, 60 percent in Omaha, and substantial percentages in Chicago, St. Louis, and Kansas City. Politicians in states like Missouri, Wisconsin, Nebraska, and Ohio tended to be of German descent or took care to reflect the wishes of this well-educated, well-off, self-confident constituency.

Prior to the war German Americans had only occasionally involved themselves in foreign policy as an ethnic group.[28] But by the first decade of the twentieth century, German Americans had carved out a distinct identity within American society. When war broke out in Europe, they marched down main streets proudly singing "Deutschland über Alles" and "Die Wacht am Rhein," German-language newspapers sold pictures of the kaiser, "Iron Cross" watches, and "souvenir spoons" of General Hindenburg. German American families raised money for German war relief and promoted the sale of German war bonds. In a neutral United States, they saw no contradiction between devoting "our strength, our labor and our loyalty to the new fatherland" while devoting "our hearts to the old!"[29] The senator from Wisconsin, Robert M. La Follette, who represented a large and powerful German constituency, called for fusing "our respective fatherland traditions into mutual respect and sympathy."[30]

German Americans felt beleaguered after war broke out, but they did not shrink from the fight. They staged demonstrations against the major newspapers in New York and Chicago and bombarded them with complaints about one-sided coverage.[31] They boycotted cinemas in St. Louis, Milwaukee, and Chicago for showing pro-British newsreels. They attacked university faculty members whom they deemed pro-British, accusing Harvard's Eliot of being a British "partisan" and "dangerous demagogue."[32] The American German Catholic and German Lutheran churches, as well as the heavily German Socialist Party, all took part in defending the fatherland from British-inspired slander. They also formed alliances with other sympathetic groups, particularly the Irish Americans, a pillar of Wilson's Democratic Party. The two ethnic groups had joined in the fight against Prohibition. Now they linked arms to ensure that the Wilson administration pursued a "strict" neutrality that did not favor the British.[33]

American policy toward the European war can't be understood without an awareness that sizable portions of the American population had a complex mix of loyalties. A more homogeneous people would have had an easier time deciding what course to take. A less democratic government could have more easily ignored dissenting views. But politicians who depended on winning majorities of their constituents every two, four, and six years could not ignore the fact that their constituencies were deeply divided. Wilson knew he could never satisfy all sides in the American debate. He predicted when war broke out that he would be criticized from all directions, that the "various racial groups" would try to "lead us now one way and then another." There was nothing to do but "sit steady in the boat and bow our heads to meet the storm."[34]

Wilson's Republican opponents, Lodge and Roosevelt, faced the same problems. Although they privately favored the Allies, blamed Germany for starting the war, and even excoriated Wilson, privately, for not pro-testing Germany's invasion of Belgium, nevertheless they stood four-square behind neutrality in all their public statements in the first months of the war.[35] Americans had a "national duty" to observe a "strict neu-trality" that did not "benefit one belligerent and injure another," Lodge declared.[36] Roosevelt even went out of his way to praise the "stern, virile, and masterful" qualities of the German people, as well as the brilliance of the German General Staff in planning and executing the offensive.[37] In an essay published less than three weeks into the war, he wrote that he was "not taking sides one way or the other," and that it was "not neces-sary for us to try to assess or apportion the blame."[38] Both men privately admitted that their stance was all about politics, and particularly ethnic politics.[39] What they forgave in their own behavior, however, they did not forgive in Wilson.

In fact, Wilson privately shared his Republican opponents' views on the European conflict. He was appalled at Germany's invasion of Bel-gium, at reports of German atrocities and the destruction of Louvain. He feared a German victory would "change the course of our civiliza-tion."[40] The British ambassador came away from a meeting with Wil-son convinced that "at the right moment," England could "depend on an understanding heart here."[41] But Wilson was also a politician, and like Roosevelt and Lodge he had to consider the effect of his statements and actions on a variegated and divided American public.[42]

Unlike Roosevelt and Lodge, Wilson was also president. His state-ments and decisions had consequences. A wrong move or flippant com-ment could lead to war. Wilson also believed that, as president, he "had no right to permit his own passionate feelings to govern his public acts."[43] He had to consider what a majority of Americans wanted and to pursue America's rights and interests as most Americans understood them. And what the overwhelming majority of Americans wanted was to stay out of the European conflict.[44]

That seemed easy enough at first. Throughout the first few months of the European war, no one believed there was any real danger of the United States being dragged into it. Nor did anyone, including Roose-velt, even hint that the United States *should* intervene.[45] The only debate in the United States in 1914 concerned the nature of American neutrality, whether the United States was or should be helping one side more than the other, or whether it should pursue the "strict" neutrality that German and Irish Americans demanded.

These were complex matters, especially in this kind of war. The laws and traditions of neutrality had grown up over the course of the seventeenth, eighteenth, and nineteenth centuries to govern the behavior of nations generally fighting limited wars for limited ends. But there was nothing limited about this war.[46] Both sides quickly came to see it as a life-and-death struggle and would use every weapon at hand. Given that over the course of the war both sides would make use of poison gas, aerial bombing, and, in the German case, forced labor, despite having banned these weapons and practices, it was no surprise that neither side was inclined to respect neutral rights if doing so threatened their very survival.

This set up an inevitable clash between Britain and the United States. To compensate for its weakness on land, British strategy toward a European rival—whether Napoleon's France or Imperial Germany—had always been to use its naval dominance to control the supply routes to the European continent and starve the adversary into submission. In 1812, Americans' refusal to accede to aspects of the blockade had led to war. After the outbreak of the European conflict in 1914, many Americans believed the British were pursuing much the same course, and possibly leading to the same result.[47]

Although the American economy was relatively self-sufficient, it was more entangled with the economies of Europe than most Americans realized. Important industries depended on access to European markets and were therefore directly affected by the European crisis. A contraction in European credit markets in 1913, caused in part by fears of war, had sent the American economy into a deep recession by sharply reducing European purchases of American goods. By the summer of 1914 American factories in industries ranging from steel to shoemaking were operating at under 50 percent capacity. A high percentage of workers were unemployed.[48] When European bourses closed their doors in late July 1914, and Europe's central banks and private investors sold their American securities for cash and gold, the New York Stock Exchange was forced to close, too. Treasury Secretary William G. McAdoo had to step in with almost $400 million in "emergency currency" to steady the American banking system.[49] The outbreak of war in the first week of August shut down all transatlantic shipping. American raw materials, grain, meat, and manufactured goods slated for export piled up in warehouses and ports.[50] Trade with Europe for the month of August dropped by $58 million compared to the previous year.[51]

Some regions of the country were hit particularly hard. Cotton remained the pillar of the southern economy, for instance, and the 1914 harvest had produced one of the largest cotton crops in memory. But the biggest overseas market for cotton was Europe, and so the bales piled up in warehouses, cotton prices plummeted, and heavily indebted southern growers faced bankruptcy.[52] Midwestern grain producers faced similar problems as unsold wheat and corn piled up on farms and docks.[53] The federal treasury also suffered. Two-fifths of the nation's revenue came from customs receipts, and over the 1915 fiscal year the treasury stood to lose $100 million ($2.5 billion in 2020 dollars), which was one-tenth of the national budget. Wilson had to seek a $100 million tax increase to make up the shortfall, not exactly a popular measure with midterm elections approaching in November.[54] The way the transatlantic trading system normally worked, moreover, the United States ran a substantial trade deficit through the first half of the year, when Americans imported far more than they exported, and then balance was restored in the second half of the year after the harvest and the export of wheat, other grains, cotton, and tobacco. The war had disrupted this cycle. In August 1914 Americans owed British creditors approximately $250 million for imports in the first half of the year. If that debt could not be paid by the sale of exports, it would have to be paid in cash. Where would it come from? The deep recession in the United States threatened to turn into a depression.

Whatever Americans felt about neutrality, therefore, or about the British, it was clear that the well-being of significant portions of the economy lay in the hands of the Royal Navy. On August 3, a day before Britain entered the war, U.S. officials told the *New York Times* that "all our plans" depended on Britain entering the war, clearing the Atlantic, and making it possible to ship "our big grain crop."[55] When Britain did join the war the next day, American officials hailed the decision not primarily because they cared about German aggression but because it meant the seas would soon be reopened to merchant traffic.[56] Indeed, within a week the Royal Navy had mostly cleared the Atlantic—Tirpitz's High Seas Fleet, built at such great expense over the previous fifteen years, returned to the shelter of home ports—and the U.S. economic crisis began to abate.

Indeed, the U.S. economy not only recovered but entered into a long period of unprecedented growth, thanks to the war and Allied purchases. Grain exports soon rose to their highest levels in history. British orders for 100,000 tons of steel revived the flagging steel industry, and by mid-

November 1914 plants in Indiana and South Chicago were rehiring thousands of workers laid off the previous spring. New England shoe manufacturers began running factories night and day to fill Allied orders for over two million pairs of boots, while leather companies operated at 125 percent capacity compared to 40 percent before the war. Overall exports doubled in September, and by October goods were being shipped out of the port of New York at a record pace of $20 million per week. The effects rippled across the country. Markets from Chicago to California reported a "Western Business Boom." From August through October, Allied war purchases turned what had been a monthly trade deficit of $20 million into a monthly trade surplus of $60 million.[57]

British and American bankers, meanwhile, worked together to restore financial ties disrupted by the outbreak of war. They established mutual credits in New York and London to facilitate British purchases of grain and other goods and to help American merchants pay off their debts. In October a British delegation traveled to Washington and met with McAdoo to discuss the reopening of the London and New York stock exchanges. They also addressed the cotton problem, which British officials knew was a serious political issue for Wilson.[58] The southern cotton states were Democratic strongholds. Although cotton was legitimately contraband—it was used for soldiers' uniforms and as an ingredient in explosives—in late October British foreign secretary Edward Grey, over the objections of the Admiralty, declared that U.S. cotton shipments to Germany would not be banned for the time being. Over the next six months huge shipments of cotton made their way to Germany, thereby relieving the immediate cotton emergency.[59] British officials also proposed to buy and store much of the cotton crop so that American growers could be paid quickly.[60]

The ease with which British and American merchants, financiers, and government officials managed these problems reflected the long-standing ties between the British and American financial communities. While some leading American bankers and financiers, like Jacob Schiff and Felix Warburg, had closer ties with the German banks (run by their relatives), most American banks had closer ties with the British financial community. The most prestigious banking house in the United States, J. P. Morgan and Company, became the British government's commercial agent in the United States and would serve as broker between the Allied governments and American businesses for the duration of the war. Morgan bankers not only facilitated financial transactions but kept their British counterparts constantly informed about American political developments.[61]

These economic and political ties and understandings made a sham of American neutrality, but not because the Wilson administration's policies violated traditional rules. Robert Lansing, then counselor at the State Department, made sincere efforts to ensure that the United States complied strictly with the laws of neutrality as they then existed. But even the strictest observance could not compensate for the naturally unequal status of economic relations between the United States and the belligerents. One of the core principles of traditional neutrality laws, often misunderstood or ignored by critics, was that restrictions applied only to governments. Private citizens and companies could trade, make loans, and even sell weapons and other contraband items to belligerents to the extent that they were able. Even if the Wilson administration pursued "strict" neutrality as a matter of government policy, therefore, nothing prevented private companies from doing more business with the British than with the Germans.

The Germans contributed to this natural imbalance by their indifference to American concerns. Narrowly focused on the military campaign, counting on a quick victory with the Schlieffen Plan, and not nearly as dependent on American trade as the British, the Germans did not consider the salient political reality, which the British well understood, that the more Americans traded with them, the more the American government would be favorably inclined to cooperate with them. The German government did not even bother to promote the American cotton trade, even though Germany was a big market for American growers, nor did the Germans promote the trade in grains, foodstuffs, dyes, and fertilizers, all of which would have given Americans a greater stake in the German-American relationship.[62] Instead, the Germans in the early months sat by as the already close Anglo-American commercial and financial bonds strengthened. This failure also reflected the nature of German society and political economy. Britons and Americans naturally understood the close interplay between politics and economics in their freewheeling democratic capitalist systems—the British, for instance, instantly recognized the importance to Wilson of keeping the southern cotton growers happy. The Germans were less adept at the manipulation of American politics in part because they were less experienced with accommodating constituent demands in their own system.

All this had implications for American neutrality policies. The Wilson

administration did at first try to stop American private banks from lending to the Allies. When France asked the Morgan bank to float a large
loan in the United States in August 1914, the Wilson administration initially blocked it, arguing that while technically legal, such private loans
were "inconsistent with the true spirit of neutrality."[63] But it immediately
became apparent that if the Allies could not borrow dollars from American banks, they would not have the dollars to buy American goods. The
wartime economic boom would end as quickly as it began. After a few
weeks, Wilson lifted the ban and permitted American banks to provide
short-term "credits" (not "loans"). Soon millions of dollars of private
"credits" were flowing to the Allies.[64] Exports to Europe soared from
$500 million to $3.5 billion annually over the next three years.[65] Trade
with Germany, meanwhile, including the trade in arms and munitions,
slowed to a trickle.

German Americans and others did not understand how this stagger-
ingly lopsided trade could possibly conform to any conception of neutrality. Wilson even wondered himself sometimes, especially as he came
under sustained attack from his German and Irish American constituents.[66] He and the Democrats paid a price at the ballot box. Although
the Democrats kept control of Congress in the November 1914 elections,
they lost 61 seats in the House, and Bryan and other political analysts
believed Wilson's neutrality policies had cost "a good many votes" in
German American communities.[67]

Critics then and later believed that Wilson could have done more to
force Britain to loosen the blockade and allow more goods and even
weapons to go to Germany. He refused to press London harder, they
alleged, because in his heart he favored the Allies. According to this view,
his pro-British policies eventually drove Germany to take actions that led
America into war.

It was certainly true that Wilson favored the Allies, and especially the
British, at least in 1914. In private he argued that they were "fighting our
fight." He refused to "place obstacles" in their way or to take "any action
to embarrass England when she [was] fighting for her life and the life of
the world."[68] Had it not been for the pressure from German American
and Irish American politicians, as well as from southern representatives
of the cotton industry, he would probably have done even less to resist the
British blockade in the early months of the war.[69]

But Wilson's unwillingness to play hardball with London in 1914 and
1915 had less to do with his personal feelings than with his perception
of America's interests in these difficult circumstances. Yes, he could have

threatened a trade war to convince London to ease the blockade, but was such a war in America's interests? By the end of 1914 Allied war orders had become the "salvation of American business." American workers were streaming back to the factories after a year of layoffs. Had Wilson cut off this lucrative trade, just as he was pushing a $100 million tax increase through a reluctant Congress, there would have been "an instant storm."[70] But beyond the politics, Wilson believed that disrupting economic relations with Britain over what he regarded as annoying but tolerable violations of American neutral rights would be folly.[71]

He also doubted that the British would back down if challenged. Although Foreign Secretary Grey was bending over backwards to keep the Americans happy, there were limits to what he could do. Most Britons had no sympathy for American businessmen's complaints about lost profits, or for Wilson's political predicament, when they were sending hundreds of thousands of their sons, husbands, and fathers to fight and die in Belgium and France.[72] The Admiralty, which was not without influence, wanted to tighten the blockade, not loosen it, and insisted that successful prosecution of the war required it. Britain still enjoyed substantial naval superiority and could, if necessary, have handled a confrontation with the smaller U.S. Atlantic fleet while keeping the Germans in check. In the view of the American ambassador in London, Walter Hines Page, the British would risk "a serious quarrel or even war with us rather than yield."[73] The British simply had too much at stake. As Spring Rice put it to Wilson, "We each wish to defend our rights. But I am sure you will remember that the rights we are defending are our existence."[74]

The fact was, both sides knew that, even with the blockade in place, British policies were benefitting the United States enormously. Thanks to Allied war purchases, American per capita income during the period of neutrality rose by an astonishing 25 percent.[75] Neither the British nor Wilson believed the Americans would jeopardize that for a more generous interpretation of neutral rights or to do Germany a favor.

Wilson might have taken another course had he believed that the legal but objectively pro-British tilt of American policies would lead to war with Germany. But at the time, neither Wilson nor anyone else in a position of responsibility thought the United States could be dragged into the European conflict against its will.[76] "Look abroad upon the troubled world," he told a Jackson Day audience in January 1915. "Only America at peace!" In this mood of optimism, and sure of America's invulnerability to the intensifying war across the ocean, Wilson began thinking ahead to his role, as the nation's president, in mediating an eventual peace. It was only a matter of time, he believed, before the warring nations turned to the United States and said, "You were right and we were wrong. You kept your heads when we lost ours. You tried to keep the scale from tipping, and we threw the whole weight of arms in one side of the scale. Now, in your self-possession, in your coolness, in your strength, may we not turn to you for counsel and assistance?"[77]

Wilson was hardly the only American with such lofty ambitions for international peacemaking. Lodge, too, looked forward to "the right moment" when the United States could wield its influence on behalf of "a peace that will be lasting."[78] And arguably no public figure had given more thought to the role the United States should play at this moment in history than former president Theodore Roosevelt. In a series of essays published beginning in the fall of 1914, Roosevelt broached the idea of an international "League" to support and sustain the peace after the present war had ended.[79]

Wilson was not ready to make any such commitments. When Britain's Grey suggested to Wilson's emissary and closest adviser, Colonel Edward M. House, the idea of a "League for the preservation of peace" after the war, the colonel rebuffed him, noting that it was "not only the unwritten law of our country but also our fixed policy not to become involved in European affairs."[80] Wilson was content to stick with his vague offer of mediation. There was no need for grand and controversial commitments. In January 1915, the war in Europe was stalemated; American trade was flowing; Americans were prospering. Wilson and most political leaders in both parties were content with where the United States stood in relation to the war.

American complacency was understandable. The Germans themselves had certainly given no thought to fighting the United States prior to the outbreak of the war.[81] Neither the Schlieffen Plan nor Tirpitz's naval strategy accounted for the United States. As German chancellor Bethmann Hollweg summed up the thinking: the United States posed no threat "because of its lack of military forces."[82] As for America's well-known economic power, which in a long war would play a critical role, the Germans hadn't thought about that either, because the war was only supposed to last six weeks.

Things had not gone as planned, however. The Belgians' unexpectedly stiff resistance had slowed the German advance, the British had entered the war and landed troops, much to the Germans' surprise and chagrin, and the Allied victory at the Marne in mid-September produced a stalemate. The whole point of the Schlieffen Plan had been to avoid precisely that. After less than a month of fighting, military officials like Moltke knew that Germany had failed in its only chance for a decisive victory and would now be forced into the two-front war of attrition Germans had always dreaded. In November, General Erich von Falkenhayn, who replaced the broken Moltke as chief of staff, told the chancellor that as long as Russia, France, and England stayed in the war and held together, Germany would "run the danger of slowly exhausting ourselves."[83]

It was the United States, however, that suddenly emerged as a key player when the Schlieffen Plan failed to deliver the promised quick victory. Once the war became a long struggle of attrition, America's central role in the global economy, as provider of goods and financing, became critical to all the belligerents. Britain and France would rely on the United States for the duration of the war, for food, munitions, and the other sinews of war, including, eventually, massive loans to keep their economies afloat in the midst of total mobilization. The Germans would need the United States, too. By early 1915 Germans already faced food shortages due to the cutoff of imports from the United States, Latin America, and other neutral nations. But the real problem for Germany was that so long as Britain could count on an unlimited American supply of goods and money, it could stay in the war indefinitely. Germany could never win except through a most generous peace settlement that the British were unlikely to offer. Once the Schlieffen Plan failed, therefore, cutting Britain off from the United States became Germany's only hope of victory.

Even that would not have affected the Americans' situation, however, had another unexpected element not come into play—a new and untested weapon, the submarine, or U-boat—which changed the entire nature of the war, especially for Americans. The Germans had begun the war without the weaponry necessary for a long campaign of commerce-raiding. Tirpitz's High Seas Fleet had been designed to take on the British fleet in the North Sea, not to disrupt transatlantic trade.[84] In the fall of 1914, however, while the High Seas Fleet was being bottled up in its own ports, some enterprising U-boat captains managed to sneak through British defenses and sink a handful of British vessels. Tirpitz, seeing a possible salvation for his otherwise failed naval strategy, seized on the U-boat as Germany's miracle weapon, one that could bring the British to their knees.[85] In late November he told an American journalist that he planned to establish a submarine blockade around Britain. England wanted to starve Germany, he said. "We can play the same game."[86]

The turn to submarine warfare was a desperate move, however, and the Germans knew it. At the beginning of the war Germany had only twenty-one U-boats in operation, only nine of which were capable of traveling any distance from the German coast.[87] Both the Foreign Office and the chancellor worried that the benefits of submarine warfare were not worth the risk of bringing the United States into the war.[88] But advocates of the submarine campaign, including the head of the Admiralty, insisted that the U-boats could strike a decisive blow at England's lifeline long before the United States could bring any real force to bear. With its tiny army three thousand miles away, they argued that the United States could not hurt Germany any worse than it already was doing by supplying and financing the British war effort. German leaders also believed the Americans would not fight. They assumed the large German American population would be loyal to the fatherland and that any move toward war would produce a civil conflict—which was indeed among Wilson's chief concerns.[89] The German public, meanwhile, was demanding strong action. By March 1915 American munitions sold to Britain and France were just coming into use on the battlefield, and to Germans, who were not receiving American arms, it seemed that every father, brother, and son was being "killed by an American rifle, bullet, or shell."[90] A cartoon in one newspaper showed Uncle Sam receiving a bag of money from the figure of Death—the headline read "Neutral America."[91] To the German public, as much as to German military officials, the submarine was the magic weapon that could end the war. The public thus demanded that submarine commanders, now national heroes, be allowed to operate without restrictions on what they sank and how they sank it.[92] After some internal debate, the kaiser and his advisers approved the new strategy and unleashed the submarine as a new weapon of naval warfare.[93]

On February 4, 1915, the German government announced that henceforth "all the waters surrounding Great Britain and Ireland, including the whole of the English Channels" were a war zone. Enemy merchant vessels would be sunk without warning. The vessels of neutral nations would also be "exposed to danger" because British ships had begun flying neutral flags, including those of the United States. The Germans further warned that merchant vessels would be sunk even when it was not possible "to save their crews and passengers." This was a typically frank German admission that submarine warfare would have to violate the normal rules of commerce raiding, which included giving passengers and crew safe passage before sinking their vessel. Submarines were too small and vulnerable to follow those rules without unacceptable risks to their crews.[94] If others claimed this was immoral, the average German did not regard it as any more immoral than the mines Britain had laid in the North Sea in violation of international law.

The German announcement of unrestricted submarine warfare in February 1915 suddenly confronted Wilson with dangerous choices. Just weeks earlier he had ridiculed Republican calls for "preparedness," insisting that the European war "cannot touch us." Clearly that was no longer the case.

Wilson responded to the German announcement after a long week of deliberation. He objected to Germany's proposed campaign as a violation of the laws of naval warfare and "an indefensible violation of neutral rights." He warned that if German sub commanders sank American vessels or took the lives of American citizens on the high seas, the United States would hold Germany to "strict accountability" and take any steps necessary to "safeguard American lives and property and to secure to American citizens the full enjoyment of their acknowledged rights on the high seas." This was a firm statement, which the Germans initially read as an ultimatum threatening war. Bethmann in particular urged caution, at first. But Wilson's actions soon convinced both the Germans and the British that Wilson would go to great lengths to avoid war.

Near the end of March, a German submarine torpedoed and sank the *Falaba,* a British cargo and passenger ship, resulting in the death of over one hundred passengers and crew, including one American citizen. Lansing drafted a note to Germany condemning this violation of "international morality," but Secretary Bryan feared escalating the matter and persuaded Wilson to hold off.[95] The next day, a German aircraft dropped bombs on an American freighter in the North Sea. Again, Wilson did not react.[96]

Instead, he looked to the British to help him solve his problems with Germany. To show evenhandedness, he sent notes to both London and Berlin suggesting that they negotiate restrictions on the use of submarines, mines, and neutral flags. To appease the kaiser, Bryan suggested that Britain relax its blockade to allow U.S. shipments of food to Germany.

Unfortunately for Wilson, the British, like the Germans, were in no mood for compromise. The Foreign Office was actually delighted at the Germans' February announcement, which British officials hoped would soon force the United States into the war.[97] The German move emboldened the Admiralty to demand even stricter observance of the embargo, and in early March, the British issued a new Order in Council declaring that *all* neutral trade, both contraband and non-contraband, would be subject to blockade. Americans were furious, but Wilson felt helpless. In Berlin Ambassador James W. Gerard expressed his belief that the Germans would not hesitate to "go to war against us."[98] Ambassador Page reported similar concerns from London. Both sides were "seeing red," Wilson believed, listening not to reason but to "necessity" as they saw it.[99]

Both sides were also not listening to Wilson, whose evident eagerness for peace convinced the British and Germans alike that the United States would take no strong action, no matter what they did. Ambassador Johann Heinrich von Bernstorff reported from Washington that U.S. policy was "dominated by the sole idea of becoming enmeshed in no complications whatever.[100] (The kaiser, who liked to express his views by writing in the margins of cables and memos, wrote on this one, "Peace at any price.")[101] Wilson's passivity affected the internal debate in both Britain and Berlin. If Wilson intended to do nothing, even after Americans were killed in sub attacks, then Grey could not argue in London that it was too risky to tighten the blockade and Bethmann could hardly claim to his colleagues in Berlin that the submarine campaign was too risky.[102] Thus Britain took a more aggressive tack with the embargo and, at the end of April, the German naval command sent out new orders instructing the U-boats to attack all "transports, merchant ships, warships," including the vessels of neutrals. They were specifically told to attack without warning and to make no undue efforts to save passengers and crew.[103] U-boat captains immediately began searching the waters for rich targets. The British hoped they would find them and force the United States into the war on the side of the Allies.

The richest target of all was RMS *Lusitania.* The jewel in the crown of the Cunard Line and the largest passenger ship then sailing between New York and London, with over 1,200 passengers and a crew of more than 700, the *Lusitania* was also a known smuggler of contraband. When it set sail from New York Harbor in the first week of May, the ship carried in its hold millions of rounds of U.S.-made rifle ammunition. The German government made no secret of the fact that the *Lusitania* was a target. The day before it sailed from New York, the German ambassador posted an advertisement in the *Times,* right next to the announcement of the ship's sailing, reminding passengers of the risks of traveling in war zones. The massive ocean liner set sail anyway with its full complement of passengers. Despite the explicit warnings, apparently none of the passengers, nor the ship's captain, nor the executives of the Cunard Line believed that the Germans would sink an ocean liner with 2,000 civilians aboard.

On the afternoon of May 7, Captain Walther Schwieger, the experienced commander of U20, spotted the *Lusitania* off the southern coast of Ireland. The silhouette of the four giant smokestacks was unmistakable. As the ship passed directly in front of him, Schwieger fired one torpedo into the starboard bow just behind the bridge. A huge explosion followed, and the great ship began to sink. Within eighteen minutes it was gone from sight. Remarkably, 761 passengers and crew managed to survive. The remaining 1,198 people on board died, including 270 women and 94 children, many of them infants, most of whom drowned or froze in the frigid waters. Among those who lost their lives were 124 Americans.[104]

CHAPTER FIVE

Schrechlichkeit *and the Submarine War*

In God's name, how could any nation calling itself civilized purpose so horrible a thing?

—Woodrow Wilson[1]

AMERICANS WOULD long remember exactly where they were when they first learned of the *Lusitania*'s sinking.[2] They were shocked, horrified, and angered. Editorial pages referred to the Germans as "wild beasts," "outside the pale of civilization," and engaged in "savagery carried to its ultimate perfection."[3] "Modern history affords no other example of a great nation running amuck and calling it military necessity," the New York *World* thundered. "Does Germany want more war?"[4]

Some Americans who had already been in the pro-Allied camp believed the time had now come for the United States to enter the war on the side of the Allies. Elihu Root, who until the sinking had favored American neutrality, now believed the United States had a "duty" to uphold the principles of "humanity and civilization upon which our government was founded."[5] Roosevelt, in a private letter, said he would not tolerate any delay in "asserting in a most emphatic way all our rights."[6]

Some of Wilson's top advisers agreed that the sinking was a turning point. The United States had "come to a parting of the ways," House argued, "when she must determine whether she stands for civilized or uncivilized warfare." Americans could no longer remain "neutral spectators." If the nation failed to respond, it would earn the world's contempt and lose any chance of acting as the great arbiter of a European peace.[7] Robert Lansing agreed that there was no longer any question about the

United States eventually joining the war. The only task now was to prepare the American public for the moment "when we will have to cast aside
our neutrality and become one of the champions of democracy."[8] House
predicted that "we shall be at war with Germany within a month."[9]

Angry as most Americans were, however, there was less appetite for
war than House and Lansing imagined. Within Wilson's own cabinet,
opponents of retaliation and intervention included not only Secretary
of State Bryan but also Navy Secretary Josephus Daniels, Labor Secretary William B. Wilson, and Postmaster General Albert S. Burleson, all
of whom spoke for important constituencies in the Democratic Party.
In Congress, the Democratic Speaker of the House, Champ Clark, and
the majority leader, Claude Kitchin, remained dead set against intervention. German, Irish, and Jewish groups protested against any move in
favor of Britain and against Germany. The Democratic chairman of the
Senate Foreign Relations Committee, William J. Stone of Missouri, did
not understand why the United States should go to war when "a British
ship, flying the British flag" had been sunk following an "official warning
by the German Government."[10] The word from other leading members
in Congress was that neither the Democratic-controlled House nor the
Democratic-controlled Senate would support a declaration of war.[11]

Most Republicans were also wary. Former president Taft condemned
the "ruthless spirit of inhumanity which led to this tragedy" and hoped
Germany would eventually receive the punishment it deserved, but he
also hoped Wilson would "save us from war."[12] Days after the sinking,
he wrote the president that it was premature for the United States to join
the Allies. War was a "dreadful thing" and would exact such a great cost
in lives and treasure that every effort should be made to avoid it, consistent, that is, "with the dignity and honor of this country."[13] Publicly, Taft
called for caution and warned against letting the nation be driven by the
passions of the moment.[14]

Those passions were already subsiding. As one observer noted,
although Americans received the news of the sinking with "stunned
amazement that such bold savagery and ferocity could mark the public
policy of any great nation," there was "no stampede" for war.[15] Roosevelt heard from his Progressive Party contacts in the Midwest that the
outrage had "died down as suddenly as it had risen."[16] A Democratic
congressman from Indiana, after canvassing his constituents in the weeks
following the sinking, found that they were chiefly worried that Wilson
might rush the nation into war.[17] Out of a thousand editors polled across
the nation, less than 1 percent favored intervention. The vast majority

agreed that "we must protect our citizens, but we must find some other way than war."[18]

Wilson was not going to rush Americans into war. He was as outraged and horrified by the sinking as anyone. When Joseph Tumulty first related the terrible details, he saw tears in the president's eyes, and Wilson had exclaimed, "In God's name, how could any nation calling itself civilized purpose so horrible a thing?"[19] But horror and outrage were not a policy, and Wilson saw clearly that the public had no interest in war.[20] He continued to fear that intervention would tear the country apart, and it was not just the German, Irish, and Jewish Americans he worried about. He believed even the general public might turn against him once Americans began fighting and dying. As they "pored over the casualty lists" and witnessed the "horrors and bloody aftermath" of a decision to intervene, he worried they would soon be asking, "Why did Wilson move so fast in this matter? Why didn't he try peaceably to settle this question with Germany?"[21]

Wilson, for all his famed aloofness, was in this case certainly more attuned to the public mood than his critics. Lodge and Roosevelt would later excoriate Wilson for not seizing on the *Lusitania* disaster to lead the people to war, insisting that "he would have had behind him the enthusiastic support of the whole American people."[22] But that was not what keen observers saw at the time. Ambassador Spring Rice took no pleasure in reporting to London that despite the *Lusitania* sinking, Americans still wanted peace—perhaps not "at any price but . . . at a very considerable price."[23]

Wilson himself did not believe the American people wanted peace at *any* price. While they opposed entering the war at the moment, he believed there was a limit to what they would tolerate. They wanted peace, but they wanted peace with honor. He called it their "double wish." They wanted "to maintain a firm front in respect of what we demand of Germany and yet do nothing that might by any possibility involve us in the war."[24] Wilson learned this the hard way when he commented, three days after the sinking, that there was "such a thing as a man being too proud to fight."[25] To political enemies like Roosevelt, the phrase proved what they had always believed, that Wilson was a coward and put no value in the nation's honor. Wilson knew immediately that he had blundered.[26] As Tumulty later observed, his "gift for making striking and quotable phrases" occasionally got him into trouble.[27]

Wilson, in fact, was not too proud to fight. After the *Lusitania* sinking, he was determined to take a hard line with Berlin, even at the risk of war. This was not because he wanted war but because he believed it was the only way to deter Germany from taking further actions that the American people would find intolerable. Wilson knew that his passivity in the weeks before the sinking had only emboldened Germany. This time he meant to present Berlin with a real ultimatum. In a note to the Germans on May 13, six days after the sinking, Wilson not only demanded an apology and reparations, but also called for a complete end to submarine warfare. There simply was no way to use that weapon, he insisted, "without an inevitable violation of many sacred principles of justice and humanity."[28] Everyone understood that Wilson, while seeking "all honorable means to avert war," would accept war if the Germans refused to make the necessary concessions.[29]

In pursuing this course, Wilson had to overrule his secretary of state. Bryan opposed any action that could possibly lead to war and was prepared to accept national dishonor if that was the price of peace.[30] He wanted to submit the *Lusitania* affair to arbitration to give both sides time for "cooling off"; he wanted to warn Americans against traveling on belligerent vessels, even on passenger ships; and he wanted to pressure Great Britain to ease the blockade. Bryan even assured German and Austrian diplomats that the president's note did not mean what it appeared to mean and that the United States was eager to avoid any crisis.

Wilson considered but rejected Bryan's advice. Any appearance of backing down in the face of "threat and danger," he told Bryan, "would only make matters worse."[31] Any concessions would show "uneasiness and hedging" and "weaken our whole position fatally."[32] To counteract Bryan's backchannel messages to the Central Powers, Wilson leaked to the press that he considered the "conditions now prevailing in the marine war zone [were] rapidly becoming intolerable."[33] Bryan promptly resigned and attacked Wilson publicly for reckless belligerence.[34]

Bryan's resignation was widely taken as a sign that Wilson had decided to go to war, but Wilson, though happy to be rid of Bryan, still hoped for a diplomatic solution and was prepared to make concessions to get it. In a second note on June 9, after the Germans were not forthcoming in response to his first, Wilson asked only that they acknowledge their mistake and promise not to repeat it. When the Germans again failed to respond adequately, he sent a third note on July 21, this time dropping his demand that Germany cease all submarine warfare. He now insisted only that U-boat captains follow the rules of cruiser warfare. In return, he suggested he would pressure Britain to modify the blockade. He even hinted at future German-American cooperation against Britain. After all, he wrote, both nations were "contending for the same great object"—"freedom of the seas."[35]

He did end his third note by warning that continued acts by German commanders, when they "affect American citizens," would be regarded as deliberately unfriendly—a statement that was read in Berlin as a new ultimatum. This sent Kaiser Wilhelm into a fury—"Immeasurably impudent!" "Commands!" "Unheard of!" "a direct threat!" he wrote in the margins.[36] But it was clear to Ambassador Bernstorff that Wilson, although prepared to go to war if given no other choice, very much wanted to avoid war. The ambassador advised that if Berlin would agree to a policy of not sinking any more passenger ships without warning, the president would tolerate other kinds of actions.[37]

The German government now had to decide whether or not to seek accommodation with Wilson by putting back at least some of the restrictions on the U-boats. For the next twenty months the debate in Berlin would go back and forth. On one side were the top naval officials, Tirpitz and others, who insisted that the submarine was the key to bringing the British to their knees and that what Wilson did or did not do in response was irrelevant. On the other side, Bethmann and the Foreign Office argued that it would be a disaster to provoke the United States into joining the war. For much of this period, Bethmann enjoyed the support of General Falkenhayn, the chief of the General Staff, who agreed that turning neutral America against Germany could be fatal to the German position on the continent, especially if it led the other neutrals also to turn against Germany. With the general on his side, Bethmann prevailed in the early rounds. In the first week of June, the kaiser sent new orders to the fleet advising that attacks on neutral ships, and especially on "large passenger ships," were to be avoided "at any cost." No large liner, "not even an enemy one," should be sunk until further notice.[38] After Wilson's third note in July, Ambassador Bernstorff urged Berlin to make this official policy, and the kaiser was ready to agree. But then, on August 19, the commander of U-boat U24 fired a torpedo at the SS *Arabic,* an ocean liner of the British White Star Lines. The ship sank in eleven minutes and of the 423 passengers and crew over 30 perished, including three Americans.

House now advised expelling the German ambassador and calling a joint session of Congress. Wilson refused to take these steps toward war.[39] However, worried that the public would consider him "too easy" if he did not take firm action, he warned Berlin that he would sever relations if evidence revealed that Germany had acted in a "deliberately unfriendly" manner.[40] Bethmann and the Foreign Office once again pleaded with their colleagues and the kaiser to rein in the submarines; and again Falkenhayn agreed that it would be "irresponsible" to bring the United States into the war.[41] In late August, therefore, the German government officially promised that U-boat captains would abide by the laws of cruiser warfare and not attack passenger ships.[42] In order to ensure against future incidents involving the United States, the chief of the Admiralty Staff a month later further restricted submarine activities around the British Isles. For a time, the submarine campaign, which had been launched to such fanfare in Germany, was effectively suspended.[43]

It was a political victory for Wilson—the *New York Evening Post* ran his picture on the front page, over the headline "This is the man, who, without rattling a sword, without mobilizing a corporal's guard of soldiers or lifting the anchor of a warship, won for civilization the greatest diplomatic victory of generations." But privately Wilson was pessimistic. The *Arabic* sinking had shown what he already knew to be true: given the nature of submarine warfare, even when the Germans tried to accommodate his demands, such incidents, whether accidental or deliberate, were inevitable.

This was Bethmann's fear, too. As he wrote in an angry note to a senior naval official following the *Arabic* sinking, so long as submarine warfare in any form continued, it would ultimately depend on "the attitude of a single submarine commander whether America will or will not declare war."[44] He knew Germany would never completely renounce use of the "wonder weapon," but, like Wilson, Bethmann hoped to pursue two barely compatible goals: keeping the United States out of the war while insisting on Germany's right to employ the submarine as a tool of warfare.[45]

The United States and Germany would remain formally at peace for almost two years after the sinking of the *Lusitania,* but the sinking changed the nature of the relationship. Henceforth, the possibility of conflict was ever present. Wilson would have to wind his way through a narrow passage between the constant danger of war, on one side, and the prospect of national humiliation, on the other. Worse still, his fate was not in his own hands but dependent on the actions of the British and the Germans, both of whom seemed determined to do whatever they deemed necessary to avoid defeat.

The sinking of the *Lusitania* also had a profound and lasting effect on American attitudes toward Germany and the German people, which over time would harden and make the avoidance of war even more difficult. Americans were shocked not only at the sinking but at the German public's response to the sinking. The whole German nation seemed to rejoice. "With joyful pride we contemplate this latest deed of our Navy," exclaimed one editorial in a German paper. Ambassador Gerard reported hearing that "in parts of Germany school children were given a holiday to celebrate the sinking."[46]

The Germans had a term for such actions: *Schrechlichkeit,* which Americans translated as "frightfulness." It meant the deliberate attempt to instill terror in the enemy, and especially among civilians. The sinking of the *Lusitania* was an example of *Schrechlichkeit,* and it was clear that a great many Germans had no moral qualms about the deliberate sinking of an ocean liner filled with hundreds of women and children who had no knowledge of what might be in the ship's hold.

Americans were themselves capable of great brutality, of course, including against innocent civilians, as they had proved during their own "total war" between 1861 and 1865. But the deliberate sinking of an ocean liner with two thousand civilians abroad struck most Americans as beyond the pale. It raised questions about the German people's very humanity and planted seeds that would later grow into an almost blind hatred of "the Hun" as a monster that had to be destroyed.[47]

Modern accounts of World War I have drained the conflict of moral content—the war is treated as an opera bouffe, in which all the powers stand equally condemned for "sleepwalking" into conflict. But for the participants at the time, on both sides, and including the Americans, the war was very much a battle over morality and ideology, a struggle between right and wrong, good and evil. For the Belgians and the French, who were fighting for their land and homes, it was not a "war of dubious morality but a struggle for basic freedoms." Many in France saw it as a continuation of the struggle begun in 1789 for the rights of man, a renewal of the revolution against arbitrary rule, a fight not just for "home and hearth," but for "the awakening of liberty."[48] The famous French sociologist Emile Durkheim charged the Germans with destroying the "humanitarian morality of the Christianized west" in a Nietzschean drive for world dominance.[49] The British also believed they were fighting to uphold "the public law of Europe," against "the arbitrary will of a strong and overmastering Power" that aimed to "crush the independence and the autonomy of the Free States of Europe." A German victory would mean the "triumph of force over law, and brutality over freedom."

Britain was fighting "to protect against brute force the principles of civilization and the liberties of Europe."[50]

Critics after the war would ridicule these justifications as self-serving Allied and American propaganda, as no doubt they were in part. Yet even Germans agreed that the war was a moral and ideological struggle, pitting the Western democracies' idea of "civilization" and what the Germans considered their own unique *Kultur*.[51] According to the German economist Johann Plenge, Germany's "self-assertion" in 1914 had given birth to a "new idea" for all humanity, "the idea of German organization, the people's cooperative of national socialism." The German "ideas of 1914" rejected "liberalism and individualism" in favor of the distinctly German values of "duty, order, and justice."[52] Germans believed their "semi-constitutional system" was "immeasurably superior to that of the western democracies."[53] While Western liberals exalted their "universal rights of man," many Germans saw only a society of selfish individualists. Great Britain was a nation of "shopkeepers," who thought of nothing but their money and their comforts. Germany, on the other hand, was a land of selfless "heroes," who subordinated themselves to the "central will of government."[54] This superior system made Germany, and the German people, the rightful inheritors of the future and ensured their triumph over the commercialism of the liberal states, with their "all-powerful tyranny of individualism."[55]

This was not merely a belief of the German elites. On the eve of Britain's entry into the war, German men and women in the street stoned the British embassy shouting, "Death to the English pedlar nation!" German newspapers cheered the bombing of civilians in London, "the heart of the money world . . . which pumps the life-blood into the arteries of the brutal huckster nation."[56] So pervasive was this belief in the selfishness, greed, and lack of courage of the Anglo-Saxons that German military leaders based some of their most fateful decisions on it—first their conviction that the British would never enter the war merely to protect Belgium's neutrality, and later their belief that the nation of shopkeepers would quickly succumb to the submarines' destruction of their trade.[57]

As for the Allies' charge of German "militarism," German political leaders, scholars, and intellectuals did not regard it as an insult. They embraced it. The central role of the military in German society and culture was unique even in the militarized Europe of the early twentieth century. Bismarck had used the Prussian army to unify Germany by "blood and iron," which had given the military "a positive halo of national heroism" and made it in some respects the embodiment of German national identity. In the decade preceding the Great War, the military had become at once a unifying national institution, the key to Germany's status as a great world power, and the exemplar of Germany's celebrated virtues of collective discipline, efficiency, and technological prowess. The military ethos was embraced throughout German society. The kaiser appeared only in uniform. His civilian chancellor went before the Reichstag in uniform. Upward mobility in German society required participation in some aspect of military life—it had become "synonymous with manhood and with citizenship."[58]

With the military held in such high esteem, and with the army, under Bismarck's constitution, reporting directly and exclusively to the kaiser, "military necessity" served as a principal guide to policy.[59] In the deadly competition among nations, a nation had to do what was necessary to win without being hampered by international laws or moral norms. This was certainly the case in war, but to the German military mind all periods of peace were merely times of preparation for the next possible war. Therefore, "military necessity" had to be a governing principle at all times. This set Germany apart even from the other imperial powers of the day. From the late 1890s onward, the great powers had begun to try to codify international rules that could make war slightly more humane, to protect civilian populations from bombardment and enslavement by conquering powers. There were modest accomplishments along these lines at the Second Hague Conference of 1907. The Germans, although signatories to the conventions, resisted or ignored them. As one historian has noted, no other power, not even Russia, was "so distant from the emerging international norms."[60]

This was certainly the way British, French, Belgians, and other targets of German power viewed the Germans. Just days after the *Lusitania* sinking, the British government released the "Bryce Report," an account of the atrocities committed by German forces in Belgium and France in the first weeks of the war. Assembled by an investigative team led by the well-known historian and former ambassador to the United States, James Bryce, the report was dismissed by some at the time and later as propaganda. The German government and a host of German intellectuals did their best to discredit it. But while the report contained exaggerations and even some fabrications, the main body of facts, as confirmed by historians over the course of the next century, was stark enough. German troops, often with the knowledge and sometimes at the direction of their commanding officers, carried out numerous mass executions of civilians. Angered at the unexpectedly strong resistance of the Belgian army, and at what they mistakenly believed, or pretended to believe, were organized attacks by armed civilians, the Germans acted with deliberate ruthlessness to discourage such opposition.[61] In one Belgian town, 384 men ranging in age from thirteen to eighty-four were lined up at a church and shot. In another town, 612 men, women, and children were shot.[62] In the historic town of Louvain, after a surprise counterattack on German forces by the Belgian army, the furious local commander ordered the execution of more than 200 civilians and the deportation of some 1,600 men, women, and children to serve as forced labor in Germany. The rest of the 42,000 inhabitants were driven from the town while the Germans burned everything, including Louvain's historic ancient library. A German officer told an American diplomat, "We shall wipe [Louvain] out, not one stone will stand upon another! Not one, I tell you. We will teach them to respect Germans. For generations people will come here to see what we have done."[63] All told, the Germans executed some 6,500 civilians in Belgium and France in the first three months of the war.[64]

The German military also broke ground in the use of new weapons, including those that had been specifically outlawed by the Hague conventions. In the third week of the war German lighter-than-air ships, called zeppelins, dropped bombs on the Belgian city of Antwerp, killing people in their beds and in the streets. The casualties were low but the bombing struck terror among civilians who had never before experienced aerial bombardment. In January 1915, the zeppelins brought the war to English homes, dropping high-explosive bombs on coastal towns, and then in May, a couple of weeks after the *Lusitania* sinking, dropping hundreds of incendiary bombs and setting several London neighborhoods on fire. The casualties were again minor—one attack killed a dozen, another claimed the lives of seven, including four children—but many around the world were aghast. The bombing of undefended cities had been banned by agreement of the powers, including Germany, just seven years earlier. American editorialists wondered whether these zeppelin attacks showed "the madness of despair or just plain everyday madness" and asked, "What can Germany hope to gain by these wanton attacks on undefended places and this slaughter of innocents?" Wilson sent word to the American ambassador in Berlin that the German bombing with its "terror and the destruction of innocent lives" was making a "fatal" impression on the American public.[65]

April 1915 also saw the first use of poison gas in modern warfare, when German troops opened canisters containing 150 tons of chlorine gas and let the wind blow it across the lines against French troops at Ypres. The first reaction of the German commander on the scene was that "the task of poisoning the enemy as if they were rats went against the grain with me as it would with any decent sentient soldier." But if it would produce victory, then "all inner doubts had to be silenced." Reports of the agonizing deaths of Allied forces, of men "wriggling and writhing . . . their faces black . . . tearing at their throats," spread more horror—and more outrage.[66]

In May, as well, came the first reports of the genocide and mass deportation of Turkey's Armenian population by Turkish and Kurdish forces; between a half-million and a million men, women, and children were killed by Germany's new ally in the war. The killings went on for months, the British and French governments charged Turkey with "crimes against humanity," while American anger was directed at Germany, which many assumed could have pressed the Turks to desist if Berlin had so desired.[67]

Germans did not try to cloak their actions under any false moralities. They spoke with "ruthless objectivity" and unapologetically "appealed to the right of might."[68] On the day of the invasion of Belgium, Bethmann told the Reichstag that the attack was indeed "contrary to international law" but that "this wrong—I speak openly—that we are committing" would be made right once Germany's military objectives had been reached.[69] In a 1912 best-selling book, the retired general Friedrich von Bernhardi wrote that legal disputes among nations would be decided "by the measure of strength, war, which always decides biologically, and therefore fairly."[70] Such statements were part of a worldview that saw war and the violent struggle among nations not only as unavoidable but as an essential spur to human progress. As von Moltke put it, and many Germans across the political and social spectrum agreed, the German Reich could not "fulfill its role in civilization . . . without conflicts, as time and again opposition has to be overcome; this can only be done by way of war."[71]

Some in the West, admirers of German culture and intellectual prowess, of its music, its poets, and its philosophers, wanted to separate German *Kultur* from the "Prussian militarism" that, in their view, had hijacked the nation. Many American progressives had pursued postgraduate education at German universities in the 1880s and 1890s or had visited to study German institutions of social welfare that far outstripped those of the backward United States. Some were troubled by the German state's power—the police surveillance of political meetings, the monitoring of foreigners, the banning of books, the omnipresence of the military—but that did not stop them from also seeing a certain superior virtue in the German system.[72] Randolph Bourne, the progressive intellectual and writer, who would later pen a famous condemnation of the American progressives who embraced war with Germany, contrasted the order, civic-mindedness, and beauty of German cities with America's "endless chaos of straggling towns." While German society might be "undemocratic in political form," he saw it as "ultrademocratic" in giving the citizens "what they really wanted."[73]

For most American progressives, however, Germany's behavior in 1914 and after caused "acute bewilderment and dismay." Many decided that there must be two Germanys, one liberal, progressive, and peace-loving, and the other reactionary and militaristic. The war had come, they wanted to believe, because the dominant caste of militarist Prussian Junkers triumphed over the peaceful urban liberals and intellectuals.[74] This analysis fell apart when German intellectuals themselves indignantly rejected the idea of the two Germanys. In a famous public letter, an "Appeal to the World of Culture!" signed in October 1914 by ninety-three leading German artists and intellectuals and including "the cream of the German university establishment," the signatories not only denied German responsibility for the war and the charges of atrocities in Belgium. They also rejected the notion that the West's "war against our so-called militarism" was not also "a war against our culture." Without "German militarism," they insisted, "German culture would long since have been erased from the earth. . . . The German army and the German people are one."[75]

For American progressives, this response compounded an already deep disillusionment that went well beyond Germany. They had believed the world was steadily marching toward a more rational future, but now Europe, the supposed heart of Western civilization, had succumbed to the forces of "unreason." The German people had gone mad with atavistic nationalist passions.[76] The editors of *The New Republic,* looking back on this moment a year later, noted what a turning point it had been in their understanding of humanity. They had "thought of democracy, universal suffrage, equal rights, social legislation as benevolent diseases" that were spreading naturally from nation to nation across Europe. Great social and economic forces were driving history forward, "along a straight line of democratic progress" with all nations heading "in the same direction."[77] Many had believed, as Lewis Mumford later recalled, that in the new age of interconnected economies and technological miracles "certain kinds of cruelty and violence could never occur on a large scale again." The war and its brutal conduct struck them "like a baleful meteor from outer space."[78] It threw the whole idea of progress into question. During the war most Americans saw the Germans as the villains and enemies of progress. After the war, the blame for destroying the hope of progress would be cast more widely.

As the war took on moral and ideological significance for an increasing number of Americans, some began to wonder about the German Americans in their midst. Their behavior was troubling to many. Although it was only natural that the more Americans condemned Germany, the more German Americans came to Germany's defense, nevertheless, German American expressions of loyalty to the fatherland drove a deeper wedge between them and much of the rest of the country. Many Americans were appalled when German-language papers in Missouri argued that Germany had every right to sink the *Lusitania*.[79] They were outraged when the head of the German Red Cross in America commented about those who perished on the ship, "Anybody can commit suicide if he wants to," and outraged further when the National German-American Alliance suggested that American policies bore "part of the blame" for the sinking."[80] German American leaders exhorted ethnic Germans to celebrate their "Germanism"—those who ran away from it were "not worthy to be spat upon"—to remain "a united race of brothers" and to fight against their ideological enemies in the United States just as German soldiers were fighting them in Europe. "Instead of creeping around in gum-shoes," insisted German-born Congressman Richard Bartholdt of Missouri, German Americans had "to put on jack-boots."[81]

Professor Hugo Münsterberg, a pioneering psychologist who had moved to the United States to accept a post at Harvard in 1897 and had never returned home, argued that Americans themselves would benefit from being more German. The Anglo-Saxon exaltation of the individual had produced "carelessness and recklessness," had sapped "moral life, making education superficial and shallow, emptying the churches and filling the dance halls and saloons, undermining the family life and driving mankind to a senseless chase for wealth and luxury and more pleasure." He praised Germans' conviction that the individual was made to serve the state, not the other way around, that the state was the "bearer of the national culture." This instilled "thoroughness and discipline . . . and loyalty."[82] Münsterberg's Harvard colleague Albert Bushnell Hart, eminent historian, progressive, friend of Roosevelt, Anglophile, and, like so many of his generation, a scholar who had studied in Germany, condemned this exaltation of German *Kultur.* In the United States, he argued, "we look upon the State as the servant of the community; the Germans look upon it as a God-given master."[83] Hart condemned the effort to convince German Americans to "adhere together in a race group." Such a "theory of race relations," he warned, would do "immense harm to the republic."[84]

Some German Americans felt the same way. The twenty-three-year-old Reinhold Niebuhr, serving in his first assignment as minister at the Bethel German Evangelical Church in Detroit, was appalled at how "German" his parishioners had become since the start of the war. In the fall of 1915, just a few months after the sinking of the *Lusitania,* he saw among his flock "a resurgent wave of German pride," with "raw feelings of loyalty to the Fatherland" re-emerging after "decades of submersion." By November, he wrote a friend, "the German propaganda" had become "so hysterical among many of our ministers" that he found himself turning into "a violent American patriot." He was shocked to find that there was "no real interest in the welfare of this country and no genuine patriotism." Months later, in one of his first published articles, entitled "The Failure of German-Americanism," Niebuhr criticized his fellow German Americans' refusal to embrace American principles, "their constant attempts to belittle every American virtue and magnify every American evil." Little wonder, he wrote, that the rest of America looked on German Americans with "suspicions of disloyalty."[85]

For Wilson and his top advisers, it was more than a suspicion. Since the *Lusitania* sinking, Secret Service agents had been keeping an eye on German officials and agents suspected of engaging in various improper activities in the United States. At the end of July, they picked up a large briefcase full of documents that the German commercial attaché, Heinrich F. Albert, accidentally left on a New York train. The "Albert Papers" revealed the full extent of German espionage.

Albert had arrived in the United States in August 1914 and taken charge of what was known as the Secret War Council, based in New York. Key members included the German military attaché, Franz von Papen, the naval attaché, Karl Boy-Ed, and Bernhard Dernburg, nominally head of the German Red Cross. The council managed German propaganda, maintained close contact with the German American community, sold German war bonds, and engaged in legal trade. But it also organized all the clandestine activities in the United States from 1914 to 1917.

Although mostly amateurish and ineffective through the first months of the war, operations intensified in the spring of 1915. German agents purchased a large Connecticut munitions plant in order to prevent its output from reaching the Allies. They attempted to corner the market for "certain chemical works" and stir up resentment in Texas over the drop in cotton exports to Germany.[86] Explosions in ammunition factories and on board transport vessels increased dramatically during the period from May 1915 to October 1915.[87] German agents also worked closely with Irish revolutionaries and Irish American leaders like Jeremiah O'Leary, who offered to help sabotage munitions production in the United States in return for Germany providing weapons to the Irish uprising planned for 1916.[88]

Some of the more surprising revelations concerned the activities of a German naval intelligence officer, Commander Franz von Rintelen. Supplied with hundreds of thousands of dollars by the German government, Rintelen quickly organized an ultimately unsuccessful plot to destroy the Welland Canal in Canada, which linked the Great Lakes and the St. Lawrence Seaway; he set up a phony company to purchase gunpowder, which he then destroyed; he tried unsuccessfully to buy the DuPont gunpowder factory. Working with a German agent who had settled in the United States two decades earlier, and who now ran a chemicals business in New Jersey, Rintelen invented a time-delayed incendiary device, known as the "pencil" or "cigar" bomb. He hired Irish American dock workers to plant the devices on merchant ships bound for Britain and which exploded en route. He paid German steamship employees and local gangsters to manufacture bombs and plant them in New York Harbor. He created a labor organization, the Labor's National Peace Council, which led strikes and slowdowns in munitions factories. Most spectacularly, and to Wilson most outrageously, he met with Victoriano Huerta in a Manhattan hotel and organized the delivery of $12 million to Mexican counterrevolutionaries fighting President Carranza in the hope of embroiling the United States in war there. In a reckless moment, Rintelen revealed his role as a German secret agent to an American woman, Anne L. Seward, who happened to be the great-niece of the former secretary of state William H. Seward and a family friend of the Lansings. She immediately reported what Rintelen had told her.[89]

Coming within days of the discovery of the Albert Papers, the additional revelations about the "Rintelen Affair" shocked Wilson. The country, he now feared, was "honeycombed with German intrigue and infested with German spies."[90] The president still did not want war with Germany, but he ordered the leaking of the Albert Papers to the press, if only, as House put it, so that the public could "see things as those of us that know the true conditions have long seen them." In the middle of August the New York *World* launched a weeklong series of sensational exposés of Germany's role in sponsoring propaganda in the United States.[91] Roosevelt, noting the "recent exposures," said it was now clear that "the hyphenated American" posed an "active" threat, and that while most ethnic Germans were "just plain Americans like the rest of us," there was a large group of "professional" German Americans who "preached and practiced what comes perilously near to treason against the United States."[92]

Many German Americans refused to be cowed, however. When an Anglo-French delegation arrived in New York in mid-September seeking a $500 million loan from American bankers, German Americans and their congressional representatives launched a nationwide campaign to block the loan. The president of the German-American National Alliance sent a telegram to every branch in the country warning of a conspiracy by the "Money Trust" and the "Anglo-American finance combine." Senator La Follette declared that "with our manufacturing interests extending enormous credits to the Allies, with our money interests committed to keeping the bonds of the allied Governments good," the United States was "underwriting the success of the cause of the Allies." Neutrality was a sham and the American people were being duped by "Morgan and Schwab."[93]

The *New York Times* and other eastern papers pushed back against "our pro-German friends," insisting that most of the commerce with the Allies was not directly war-related and the U.S. economy depended on "our very large and growing exports of foodstuffs and manufactures." If the loan deal failed, the result would be a "trade depression," with overstocked markets, falling prices, falling wages, the shutting down of mills and factories, and massive layoffs. The proposed loan was thus "directly in our own interest," the *Times* argued. The New York *World* charged that opponents were a "thoroughly systematized movement organized and promoted by the German-American, Hungarian-American, Austro-American, and pro-German Irish-American agitators."[94]

Wilson and his advisers favored the loan, though less out of sympathy for the Allies, who were in fact in desperate financial shape, than out of concern for the American economy.[95] Lansing warned of "restriction of outputs, industrial depression, idle capital and idle labor, numerous failures, financial demoralization, and general unrest and suffering among the laboring classes." As Treasury Secretary McAdoo put it, "To maintain our prosperity, we must finance it."[96] The organized German American opposition to a policy that Wilson regarded as in the national interest only hardened his feelings against the "hyphenates." In the weeks after the *Lusitania* sinking, German Americans began denouncing Wilson's diplomacy as unneutral and hostile to Germany. In response to Wilson's third note, which German Americans, like the kaiser, found insulting and threatening, they called Wilson an autocrat, a "political bankrupt," and a "dupe of the Wall Street Pirates." A mass demonstration in Madison Square Garden at the end of June brought together German American and Irish American leaders and organizations and members of Congress, all condemning Wilson's policies. William Jennings Bryan spoke to thunderous applause.[97] Wilson and his advisers were furious at the German American attacks, which they regarded as inspired by the German government and its propaganda apparatus in the United States.

The contrast with Anglo-American cooperation continued to be stark. At the time of the loan decision, the administration had just gone through another intense round of negotiations with the British on the continually vexing problem of cotton. The British public was furious at American inaction following the *Lusitania* sinking, and the government had been ready to place a new ban on cotton shipments to Germany. Panicked southern cotton growers demanded that Wilson retaliate.[98] But once again British officials came to the rescue. Working with the Federal Reserve bank presidents in New York and Alabama, British officials agreed that as soon as the cotton ban went into effect, British treasury agents would go into the cotton exchanges in Liverpool, New York, and New Orleans and start buying until the price stabilized.[99] Presumably, southern growers and their representatives wouldn't care whether cotton shipments were banned or not, so long as they got their money. Wilson agreed and hoped that the public would see that "we were getting the best we could out of a bad situation."[100]

With the British once again cooperating to ease his political problems, Wilson approved the loan to the Allies.[101] Not only did the health of large sectors of the American economy continue to depend on Allied purchases, but after the sinking of the *Arabic* and the revelations of the Albert and Rintelen affairs, German-American relations were at their most brittle. The possibility of a confrontation was greater than at any time since the outbreak of the war. It hardly seemed the time for a crisis in Anglo-American relations as well.[102]

CHAPTER SIX

"He Kept Us Out of War"

*Those are the shadows proper for Shadow Lawn; the shadows of deeds
that were never done; the shadows of lofty words that were followed by
no action; the shadows of the tortured dead.*

—Theodore Roosevelt[1]

WITH THE risk of war increasing, Wilson turned to the question he had
earlier scorned: whether the United States was actually prepared to fight
if war could not be avoided. "Preparedness" was a political as well as
practical question, and it became more heated after the *Lusitania* sinking.
The National Security League, founded in December 1914 and financed
by Cornelius Vanderbilt and Simon Guggenheim, had made little headway until the *Lusitania* went down, at which point it attracted a substantial following. Now it counted in its ranks such pillars of the New York
and Washington establishments as Joseph Choate and Henry Stimson.
League chapters spread across the country; hundreds of thousands of
pieces of literature were distributed.[2] Supporters even helped engineer the
production and release of a full-length silent film in the summer of 1915,
The Battle Cry of Peace, depicting "an imaginary invasion of America
through New York City."[3]

Although the concerns of many preparedness advocates were
genuine—former secretary of war Stimson was aghast at the "fantastic
weakness of the American Army," which could send no more than 24,000
men into battle and with less than two days' worth of ammunition[4]—
still the preparedness movement remained overwhelmingly Republican.
At the end of August Roosevelt spoke at a newly established camp in
Plattsburgh, New York, where the still-active General Leonard Wood,
co-founder of the National Security League, was providing basic military

training to 1,400 bankers, lawyers, doctors, and merchants in what came to be known as the "Business Men's Regiment." Roosevelt took the occasion to denounce the "professional pacifists" and the "peace-at-any-price men," and it was clear that his real target was Wilson. While acknowledging that Americans should normally stand by the president in times of crisis, for instance, Roosevelt insisted they had no obligation to support a president who was not "loyal to the honor and the interests of the land."[5]

Worried that Roosevelt could make "preparedness" a major issue in the coming campaign, Tumulty urged Wilson to jump on the bandwagon.[6] Others offered the same advice, and not just on political grounds. Even Wilson's closest adviser, House, worried that the president had not grasped "the gravity of our unprepared position." War had grown more likely, he believed, in part because the Germans regarded the United States as "impotent."[7] James Gerard, the U.S. ambassador in Berlin, similarly warned that since the sinking of the *Lusitania,* the German people had become convinced that Americans "could be slapped, insulted and murdered with absolute impunity." He also warned that Germans harbored a "deep-seated hatred of America" and that if the Germans managed to win the war, "we are next on the list."[8] These were the kinds of intemperate exaggerations for which the excitable Gerard became known, but his warning rang true to Wilson and others. On the same day that Wilson sent his third *Lusitania* note to Berlin, he also sent messages to his secretaries of war and navy asking for proposals to increase U.S. military power on land and sea.

Wilson's concerns about Germany fused with his concerns about German Americans. He had received a typically overheated cable from Ambassador Gerard, reporting a conversation in which the deputy foreign minister, Arthur Zimmermann, had commented matter-of-factly that there were "500,000 trained Germans in America" ready to join the Irish and start "a revolution to upset our present Government!!!"[9] Wilson, shaken by the recent revelations of German espionage and sabotage, asked House about the possibility of a German American uprising in the event of a war.[10]

Although Wilson since the outbreak of war had tried to keep a lid on ethnic animosities, now, out of a combination of anger and concern, he began lashing out against "hyphenated" Americans with their "alien sympathies."[11] In making the case for preparedness, he even warned that the "gravest threats" to American security were at home and urged Congress to pass legislation to go after the "creatures of passion, disloyalty, and anarchy." This would later become the Espionage and Sedition Act.[12]

Wilson's attacks offended many German Americans, and undoubtedly frightened many, too. But it received enthusiastic support from many members of Congress who shared his fears of German American subversion.[13]

Wilson announced his preparedness program in his annual address to Congress in December 1915. He proposed nearly doubling the standing army to over 200,000 soldiers. More controversially, he proposed creating a reserve force of 400,000 citizen-soldiers to be called the "Continental Army." He called for a five-year naval construction program costing $500 million, an immense figure at a time when total defense spending was $430 million.[14] The program would produce ten additional dreadnought-type battleships, six battle cruisers, ten scout cruisers, fifty destroyers, and sixty-seven submarines, giving the United States by 1921 what Wilson called "incomparably the greatest navy in the world." Although he claimed to have "no thought of any immediate or particular danger arising out of our relations with other nations," his program called for the largest peacetime military buildup in American history.[15]

Wilson's proposal produced the biggest political crisis of his presidency up to that point.[16] Although Congress was generally sympathetic, the usual jealousy of congressional prerogatives combined with the usual partisan opposition to make passage difficult. The leading preparedness advocates happened to be Wilson's bitterest opponents, and they recalled how the president had ridiculed them back in December. Wilson had "evidently come to the conclusion" that there were "votes in it," Lodge sneered as Wilson joined the preparedness crusade.[17] At the other end of the Republican spectrum, midwestern and western progressives like La Follette from Wisconsin, George Norris of Nebraska, and Hiram Johnson of California opposed any increased spending on armaments. Other Republicans were prepared to support Wilson's program but without enthusiasm.

Wilson's bigger problem, however, was in his own party. Most Democrats had long opposed increases in military spending.[18] They had opposed Roosevelt's and Taft's requests for more battleships. They had enthusiastically rallied around Wilson when he opposed preparedness at the end of 1914. Now that their president was reversing himself, many Democrats were willing to hold their noses and support their party leader, but a substantial minority refused.[19] For these and other "peace progressives," Wilson's new stance was apostasy. They regarded the struggle against war (and arms) as inseparable from the struggle against the trusts and the bankers.[20] Only weapons makers and financiers benefited from war—the "great and influential lobby" of "millionaire magi" who profited while the average man fought and died.[21] Peace progressives had formed their own "anti-preparedness" movement, gathering the support of unions, urban reformers, muckraking journalists, feminists, socialists, and pacifists.[22] The pacifist anthem "I Didn't Raise My Boy to Be a Soldier" played on radios across the country.

The peace progressives were devastated by Wilson's about-face, for they had thought the president was one of them.[23] Progressive editorialists demanded to know "Who is threatening invasion?" "Who is coveting our territory?"[24] The Socialist leader, Eugene V. Debs, warned that Wilson's military program would "transform the American nation into the most powerful and odious military despotism on the face of the earth."[25] Bryan called it "a challenge to the spirit of Christianity."[26]

Breaking with these progressives carried risks for Wilson. They were critical allies in helping him pass historic reform legislation, lowering tariffs, promoting labor interests, creating the Federal Trade Commission and the Federal Reserve system. They had been a bulwark against his Republican and conservative opponents. To alienate them risked losing his strongest base of support. Bryan remained a major political force in the party and was already threatening to oppose Wilson's renomination.[27]

Wilson nevertheless went against them, and he brought his considerable talents as a popular orator to the task. Facing an uphill battle in Congress on his preparedness proposals, he decided to speak directly to the American people and "summon" their support.[28] In a remarkable weeklong, whistle-stop campaign in the winter of 1915–1916, Wilson traveled through the heartland of pacifism and non-interventionism and into the nation's largest concentration of German Americans, giving several speeches a day, usually without a text, in great convention halls and off the back of his train, in Pittsburgh, Cleveland, Milwaukee, Chicago, Des Moines, Topeka, Kansas City, St. Louis, and many smaller towns in between.[29]

Reversing his earlier assurances that the war was a matter of indifference to Americans, Wilson now argued that the world was "on fire," with "tinder everywhere," and that Americans deluded themselves if they imagined that the United States could remain untouched by the sparks and embers.[30] In a thinly veiled assault on the peace progressives, he said it amazed him to "hear men speak as if America stood alone in the world and could follow her own life as she pleased." Such people were undoubtedly "of high motive" but they suffered from a dangerous "provincialism." They believed the "contents of their own mind to be the contents of the mind of the world." As he told Jane Addams, realism required understanding that peace was kept by force, not by goodwill.[31]

Wilson admitted that he had changed his mind about preparedness, but insisted it was because the facts had changed. Because of the Germans' turn to submarine warfare, the United States could be drawn into the conflict at any time. The danger was "infinite and constant." So far, he had been able to deliver what he believed Americans wanted: peace with honor, albeit against "very great and sometimes unfair odds." But now he had to say frankly that the time might come "at any moment" when he could no longer "preserve both the honor and the peace of the United States." He was "ready to yield everything" to avoid war, but he could not "consent to any abridgement of the rights of American citizens in any respect." To retreat would only invite greater demands, until "the whole fine fabric of international law" was torn apart.[32]

The speeches predictably did not go over well with opponents. Bryan now openly threatened to oppose Wilson at the Democratic convention in June 1916 if he discovered that the president was trying "to drag this nation into this war."[33] Majority Leader Claude Kitchin accused Wilson of sounding "a little too war alarming in his speeches," and even—the ultimate insult—of sounding "too much like Roosevelt."[34] Roosevelt himself responded sourly. He would not believe a syllable of what Wilson was saying and described the president's "elocution" as that of a "Byzantine logothete," sending newspaper editors scurrying for their dictionaries.[35]

Wilson's tour was a success with the public, however. The crowds even in predominantly German American cities showed the president "a remarkable reverence, a hero worship that was almost affection itself."[36] In St. Louis, where a large German American population might have given him a cold hearing, journalists reported that a crowd of nearly 200,000 came out to cheer him. Through his stirring speeches, the editors of *The New Republic* believed, he had "checked his enemies, reassured his friends, disarmed many of his critics, and resumed control of the situation."[37]

Despite the smashing success of his whistle-stop tour, Wilson did not get everything he wanted from Congress. The "Continental Army" stood no chance of passage.[38] Congress instead increased the National Guard to 450,000 and the regular army to 175,000, short of the War Department's recommendation. Preparedness advocates were outraged—Roosevelt called the bill "unpatriotic," and the secretary of war resigned—but Wilson probably squeezed all he could out of Congress when it came to ground forces.[39]

The naval program fared better. It was always easier for Congress to spend on the navy than on the army, and enthusiasm for a bigger navy ran high after the battle of Jutland at the end of May, the one great confrontation between the Royal Navy and the German High Seas Fleet.[40] Although the House, led by Clark and Kitchin, tried to scale back Wilson's program, the Senate actually sought to augment and accelerate it. At the end of June 1916, a bipartisan proposal to complete the administration's five-year plan in three years passed the Senate by a vote of 71–8. Over the next year four dreadnoughts would be laid down, along with four battle cruisers, four light cruisers, twenty destroyers, and thirty submarines. Wilson was immensely pleased, while Kitchin mourned that the United States had become "the most militaristic naval nation on earth."[41]

Wilson's stern language again convinced many that he was preparing for war, but again, and unbeknownst to most Americans, he was working furiously to keep relations with Germany from exploding. Intelligence reports suggested that the ongoing debate inside the German government was tilting toward a return to unrestricted submarine warfare.[42] House reported from Berlin that General Falkenhayn, hitherto Bethmann's key ally in opposition, had shifted his position and now favored a return to unrestricted submarine warfare.[43] Bethmann still insisted that the military leadership was playing "a game of dice with Germany's existence at stake," that a return to unrestricted submarine warfare would result "in the condemnation of the entire world" and "a kind of crusade against Germany . . . the mad dog among nations." It could spell doom—*Finis Germaniae.* It should be done only if Germany's position was so desperate that there was no other choice.[44] Kaiser Wilhelm could not make a decision, which left things as they were for the moment. But the chancellor feared it was only a matter of time before the military commanders, lacking any other strategy for winning the war, convinced the kaiser that the submarine was the only thing standing between German victory and defeat. As it was, the navy greatly intensified the permitted warfare against enemy vessels, which, given the difficulty of distinguishing one nation's ships from another's, was bound to lead to new incidents.[45] Sure enough, on March 24, 1916, a German U-boat operating in the English Channel torpedoed a French passenger ferry, the *Sussex,* with 325 civilians on board, killing dozens and injuring others, including four Americans. Over the course of the next week, another four ships were torpedoed, all of them unarmed.

Lansing and House thought this was the moment to break relations. But again, Wilson hesitated. House lamented that the president seemed unaware "that one of the main points of criticism against him is that he talks boldly. But acts weakly."[46] Bernstorff reported to Berlin on April 5 that the American public's "affection for peace" and refusal to be "disturbed in making money" was carrying the day.[47] This caused Bethmann to relax. He told the Reichstag that the submarine campaign would continue.[48]

But American public opinion was shifting fast, and Wilson shifted with it. When the Germans implausibly (and erroneously) claimed that the *Sussex* had not been torpedoed but had hit a British mine, even pacifists were outraged. The New York *Evening Post,* normally a voice of caution, expressed exasperation. "We have had something too much of all this, ever since the day of the monstrous crime of May 7, 1915; the time has come for making an end of it."[49] At a meeting of Wilson's cabinet there was, for the first time, broad agreement that Germany had to be given some kind of ultimatum.[50] At a Jefferson Day dinner on April 13, 1916, Wilson asked the assembled Democrats if they were "ready to go in. . . . Are you ready for the test? Have you courage to go in?" The audience responded resoundingly, "Yes!"[51]

The president had earlier asked Lansing to draft a note warning Germany that the United States would break relations if submarine attacks on merchant ships did not stop, but he had hesitated to send it. Now he did. On April 19, 1916, the note was dispatched to Berlin and at the same time Wilson took the extraordinary step of calling a joint session of Congress to announce that German actions left him no choice but to sever relations unless the Berlin government immediately abandoned "its present methods of warfare against passenger and freight carrying vessels." Americans owed it to a "due regard for our own rights as a nation, to our sense of duty as a representative of the rights of neutrals the world over, and to a just conception of the rights of mankind to take this stand now with the utmost solemnity and firmness."[52]

The speech was one step away from a declaration of war, and had Germany not responded in a conciliatory fashion, Wilson might well have sought a declaration in April 1916 instead of a year later. Worried German American organizations and church groups flooded congressional offices with telegrams and petitions calling for peace, which only prompted accusations that they were disloyally undermining their president at a moment of crisis.[53] The German ambassador sent Berlin a sharp warning that another sinking like that of the *Sussex* "would necessarily force the United States into war."[54]

The German government panicked, and Bethmann, suddenly finding little resistance from the military command, managed to engineer a complete, if temporary, capitulation. Germany agreed to return to the earlier constraints on attacking merchant vessels and reaffirmed its earlier agreement not to target passenger vessels at all. In fact, angry naval officials, tired of the restrictions, stopped the submarine campaign altogether to await further developments, including the completion of an expanded sub fleet, which was then under construction. In a note to Wilson on May 4, what became known as the "Sussex Pledge," Germany agreed that ships would "not be sunk without warning and without saving human lives." In return Germany expected the United States would "now demand and insist" that Britain observe international law. If the United States failed to do so, then Germany reserved the right once again to lift all restrictions on its submarine warfare.[55]

The Sussex Pledge was the most important victory yet for Wilson in the months since the beginning of the submarine campaign. Paying little attention to the German warning at the end, most American observers saw only that the president had forced the Germans to back down. The pledge silenced hardline critics and pacifists alike. One month before the Democratic National Convention, and six months before the presidential election, Wilson could claim to have preserved peace with honor—just as he had promised.

Wilson could not have positioned himself better for the coming electoral contest. He had forced the Germans to back down; he had taken dramatic steps toward improving the nation's military preparedness; he had warned against "hyphenate" treason at home and German treachery abroad. In short, he had practically cornered the market on hawkishness, leaving Roosevelt or any Republican little room for complaint. The only direction Roosevelt could go would be to call for intervention. And that was a trap. Wilson had good reason to believe that the American people still wanted to stay out of the war. Having established his hawkish credentials, he planned to run on a simple, carefully balanced theme: peace with honor. The slogan of the campaign—"He kept us out of war"—had the virtue of being true but made no promises about the future. Wilson would do his best to keep the United States out of the war, but he warned that the days of America's "splendid isolation" were over and that this was the "last war" of its kind that the United States would be able to keep out of. In the future, Americans would have to lend not only their "moral influence" but the nation's "physical force" to preventing aggression.[56]

Most of the party faithful only heard half of this message, the part about staying out of the war. Although the carefully orchestrated party convention in St. Louis was supposed to praise Wilson for both keeping the peace *and* standing up for Americans' rights, the keynote speaker, New York governor Martin Glynn, veered from the script into straight pacifism. Urged on by the throng of convention delegates, he began to recount all the occasions in history when the United States had refused to go to war *despite* the violation of its rights. Each time he mentioned a case where American rights and sovereignty had been challenged, the crowd roared: "What did we do?! What did we do?!" and Glynn roared back: "We didn't go to war!"[57] The highlight of the convention came when William Jennings Bryan, who had broken with the president almost exactly a year earlier, returned to the fold to give his endorsement. He thanked God that "we have a President who has kept—who will keep—us out of war."[58]

In the general election campaign, the Democrats played the peace theme for all it was worth, knowing that the Republicans and their nominee, Charles Evans Hughes, had no effective response. If the Republicans accused Wilson of weakness, it implied they wanted a more aggressive policy, which the Democrats claimed meant war.[59] The Democratic message was simple: "If you want war, vote for Hughes. If you want peace with honor and continued prosperity, vote for Wilson."[60] The pacific theme appealed not only to Democrats but also to a good number of Republicans, especially across the Midwest, in the prairie states, and westward to the Pacific, where most Republican progressives were no less ardent for peace than the St. Louis Democrats.

These Republican progressives carried a lot of weight. They were a key swing vote in the election. They had followed Roosevelt out of the Republican Party in 1912 and were now looking for a new home. Both parties wooed them, but Wilson needed them more. Republicans had a clear electoral advantage going into the 1916 elections. They had won the presidency in every election save one since 1896, and their 1912 loss had been a fluke. Wilson's 41 percent of the vote in that three-way race was not going to keep him in the White House in a two-way race in 1916.

Wilson's domestic platform reflected this political imperative, for it moved away from the Democratic Party's traditional conservatism and embraced a number of proposals that Roosevelt had run on in 1912—an eight-hour day and six-day workweek, a prohibition on child labor, and a minimum wage.[61] In an early sign of his new tack, he named Louis Brandeis, the scourge of Wall Street and big business and conservative government generally, to the Supreme Court.[62] "I am a progressive," Wilson declared. "I do not spell it with a capital P, but I think my pace is just as fast as those who do."[63]

The Republicans played the same game. The party had tilted in a conservative direction under Taft in 1912, but party strategists knew they had to lean in a progressive direction to win back Roosevelt's followers. Hughes's moderately progressive record as governor of New York was too progressive for Taft, not progressive enough for Roosevelt, and therefore presumably just right for pulling the two wings of the party back together. The Republican platform was not dramatically different from the Democrats'. It called for government control of public utilities, pensions for the elderly, protections for labor, and legislation to help women and children. Hughes declared on the stump, "I would not be here if I did not think of the Republican Party as a liberal party."[64]

The struggle for the progressive vote had a foreign policy dimension, too, but here Wilson had the advantage. No one ought to have been in a better position to lead the progressives back into the Republican fold than Roosevelt, the great standard-bearer of the Bull Moose party, who four years earlier had stood before the wildly cheering throng and declared, "We stand at Armageddon, and we battle for the Lord!" But in 1916, the one issue that mattered most to Roosevelt—getting the United States into the war—was the one issue on which progressives would not follow him.[65] And he knew it.[66] Roosevelt was not only out of step with progressives on the war; he was out of step with many Republicans. Party strategists agreed with Taft that their best hope in the election was to be "conservative in the matter of war" and rebut any charge that they favored a "jingo policy."[67] Not only was this necessary to win Republican progressives, but it was where most Republicans actually stood. The evidence was everywhere—from Henry Ford's surprising success running as a pacifist in midwestern Republican primaries, to the great number of Republicans who would have voted to prohibit Americans from sailing on belligerent vessels if given the chance, to Republicans' lukewarm support for preparedness. That issue re-emerged in the fight over the party's platform at the Republican convention in Chicago. Roosevelt wanted Lodge and William Borah to ensure that the platform included a call for universal military service, an increase in the Regular Army to 250,000, and a navy "second to none." But they found little support for more "preparedness" among Chicago Republicans.[68]

The Republican nominee, meanwhile, was nearly the opposite of Roosevelt in both thought and temperament. Charles Evans Hughes, plucked from his seat on the Supreme Court, was a judicious and moderate man whose great political virtue in 1916 was that he had expressed no opinions on the war, or, for that matter, on almost anything having to do with foreign policy.[69] Hughes endorsed preparedness and criticized Wilson for doing too little too late. But, like Wilson, he promised to keep the country at peace. When asked what he would have done after the sinking of the *Lusitania,* he ducked.[70] Roosevelt fumed that the party was evidently hoping to "beat Wilson by keeping as neutral as he is as regards international duty."[71] In private, he started referring to Hughes as "Wilson with whiskers."[72]

While Hughes did his best to avoid bellicose comments, Roosevelt himself became the biggest obstacle to Republican efforts to look like a party of peace. Everyone in the nation knew where Roosevelt stood. Although he never openly called for war, people knew what he and Lodge meant when they insisted the question was not "whether we have kept the peace . . . but whether we have kept the faith," or when they proclaimed that there were things "more precious than life, comfort, safety, money-making, [and] prosperity."[73] Democrats insisted that whatever Hughes might say, the *real* Republicans were bent on war.[74] A full-page ad published in newspapers on November 4 proclaimed "Roosevelt says we should hang our heads in shame because we are not at war with Germany in behalf of Belgium!" Again, the choice was clear: "Wilson and Peace with Honor" or "Hughes with Roosevelt and War."[75]

Taft from the start worried that Roosevelt would be a "danger in the campaign," and he was right.[76] Roosevelt refused to be silenced.[77] In May he launched himself on a speaking tour of the Midwest, just as Wilson had done. There, in the heart of "ruralism, pacifism, and German-Americanism," he denounced pacifists, criticized "the short-sighted and uninformed and ease-loving people generally," and beseeched his audiences "to elect an American president and not a viceroy of the German emperor."[78] His tour ended one week before the Republican Party's convention, and it was not a success. Roosevelt knew that in speaking out he had killed any chance of winning the party's nomination. But he did more than kill his own chances.[79] His stance hurt the party with both progressives and the one constituency that ought to have been most solidly in the Republican camp, the German Americans.

Republican Party leaders did all they could to accommodate German American sentiment. The party's platform called for "a straight and honest neutrality between the belligerents," as opposed to Wilson's "sham neutrality."[80] Ohio governor Warren G. Harding vouched for German Americans' loyalty—it was "not surprising" that "their hearts" were with the land of their birth in "a life and death struggle."[81] Hughes did his best to woo the German American vote, even meeting with some prominent and outspoken Irish American and German American activists widely suspected of receiving funding from Berlin, including Jeremiah O'Leary, who was indeed secretly working with the German government.[82]

Since Wilson had little hope of winning over German Americans, the Democrats turned the tables and patriotically lambasted the Republicans for surrendering their "integrity" to win over "conspirators" who were actively trying to advance the interests of a foreign power to the "detriment of our country."[83] The New York *World* flatly called Hughes "the German candidate" and warned that a Republican victory would prove that "the German vote, and through the German vote the German Government," held the "balance of power in American politics."[84] Wilson ran on a platform of "true Americanism." He would not "fear the displeasure of that small alien element which puts loyalty to any foreign power before loyalty to the United States."[85]

Despite this, Hughes's effort to woo German Americans was undermined by Roosevelt, who just as loudly as Wilson attacked German Americans for disloyalty and "moral treason." The result was that Democrats were able to have it both ways. In most regions of the country, they portrayed Hughes as the candidate of the kaiser. But in places with high concentrations of German Americans, they portrayed Roosevelt as the true voice of the party.[86] Roosevelt for the second straight election proved to be Wilson's most useful adversary.

In the last days of the campaign Lodge tried to stir up voters by accusing Wilson, accurately, of having contemplated offering to refer the *Lusitania* matter to arbitration. Wilson shot back that Lodge was playing politics "with the loss of the lives of American citizens."[87] An enraged Roosevelt in New York two days later threw away his prepared remarks and let loose. Mocking the name of Wilson's new summer estate on the Jersey shore, Shadow Lawn, the former president sneered, "There should be shadows enough at Shadow Lawn, the shadows of men, women and children who have risen from the ooze of the ocean bottom and from graves in foreign lands; the shadows of the helpless whom Mr. Wilson did not dare protect lest he might have to face danger; the shadows of babies grasping pitifully as they sank under the waves, the shadows of women outraged and slain by bandits. . . . Those are the shadows proper for Shadow Lawn; the shadows of deeds that were never done; the shadows of lofty words that were followed by no action; the shadows of the tortured dead."[88]

Roosevelt's bravura performance brought cheers in the friendly confines of Manhattan's Cooper Union, but most of the rest of the country was either unmoved or even more convinced that a vote for the Republicans would be a vote for war.

The 1916 election was among the closest in history. Wilson won the electoral college 277 to 254. His winning margin in California, with 13 electoral votes, was less than 4,000 out of a million votes cast. Hughes held the Republican strongholds in the Northeast and industrial Midwest, while Wilson swept the Democratic South and most everything west of the Mississippi. But there was broad agreement that the issue of war and peace had played a critical role, especially in the Midwest, the prairie states, and the Far West. A bitter Taft believed the loss was "due to the emotional votes of the women, to the extreme speeches of Roosevelt, and to the besotted comfort of the western farmers."[89] "The Kansas farmers' motto was, 'I don't care a dern what happens so long as it doesn't happen to me,'" he complained, and that sentiment "prevailed throughout the jack rabbit states."[90] Lodge also believed the deciding votes were cast by midwestern and western progressives, including Republicans, who "went over to Wilson on the one cry that he kept us out of war."[91] Roosevelt heard directly from Senator Hiram Johnson that "in California one large factor in the vote for Wilson was the 'he kept us out of war' cry, especially affecting the women."[92] Wilson may even have attracted just enough German Americans to win the critical state of Ohio.[93] Roosevelt despaired for the country. "This is yellow, my friend!" he wrote to William Allen White. "Plain yellow!"[94]

Wilson ran a brilliant re-election campaign, satisfying disparate and in some cases opposing factions of the electorate. He ran on a peace platform without appearing weak. He ran as someone who could face down Germany without appearing belligerent. He did so, moreover, while managing an often unruly and rebellious Congress, compromising when necessary but also using his power and skills as president to bring his own party into line. It helped a great deal that his party controlled both houses and that his supporters in Congress were able to keep unhelpful legislation from coming to a vote. The Republicans, despite enjoying key electoral advantages, were left sniping and attacking in ways that only strengthened Wilson's position with the voters. It was a rare feat in the annals of presidential politics.

CHAPTER SEVEN

The Path to War

" 'If there is any alternative, for God's sake, let's take it,' he exclaimed. Well I couldn't see any, and I told him so."

—Frank Cobb, editor of the New York *World*[1]

WILSON HAD no time to savor his electoral triumph. Three weeks before the election, a note from Berlin warned that German patience was running out. The kaiser threatened a return to unrestricted submarine warfare if the United States did not put more pressure on the British either to end the blockade or negotiate a satisfactory peace.[2]

Wilson had seen this coming for months.[3] Throughout the summer and fall of 1916 he received reports that Bethmann was losing in his struggle with the navy and that the Germans were only waiting until after the American election to resume all-out warfare against the Atlantic trade. The Germans had favored Wilson's re-election, on the theory that any Republican successor would be less committed to peace, less willing to accommodate German concerns, and less likely to put pressure on the British.[4] The emperor, believing that Wilson was desperately "seeking a ladder for re-election," had offered him the "ladder of peace."[5] But Wilhelm and his advisers grew nervous in the fall as Wilson's electoral prospects seemed in doubt. The October note, House believed, was meant to force Wilson to take action against Britain while he was still in office.[6] Wilson could not possibly have taken such action before the election, however, and even afterwards he had little chance of forcing a change in British policy drastic enough to satisfy Germany in so short a time.

Wilson was finally facing the situation he had dreaded and successfully avoided for nineteen months. If Germany rescinded the Sussex Pledge, Wilson believed he would have no choice but to carry out his threat to break relations, which likely meant war. Yet the 1916 election had demonstrated more clearly than ever that the great majority of Americans still opposed war. Worst of all, the choice was increasingly out of his hands. Although he had run on the slogan "He kept us out of war," privately he admitted, "I can't keep the country out of war. . . . Any little German lieutenant can put us into war at any time by some calculated outrage."[7]

By the end of 1916, therefore, Wilson came to believe that there was only one escape from the terrible dilemma—and that was to bring the European war itself to an end, before the United States could be dragged in. Finding a way to achieve peace in Europe became Wilson's overriding concern, even his obsession.

Wilson and House had been trying on and off to bring the two sides together for almost two years, but they had repeatedly run up against the realities of the European war. Since the German conquest of Belgium, Luxembourg, and significant parts of northwest France in the first weeks of the conflict, the Allies had been unwilling to contemplate peace talks until the Germans were driven back. If negotiations began while the Germans held all these territories—and their later acquisitions in the east, Ukraine, Poland, and the Baltics—then the Allies would be bartering their own territory and Belgium for a settlement. Even if Germany could be persuaded to give up Belgium and all its other gains, the Allies had no interest in restoring the status quo ante. Returning to the Europe that existed in July 1914 would leave Germany in the same powerful position, with no guarantee that it would not simply rearm and resume the war to complete the continental conquest it had failed to achieve in 1914. France and Russia, in particular, refused to take that risk. They wanted security against another German attack. They also wanted revenge and repayment for the losses they had suffered. The French insisted on the return of Alsace and Lorraine, lost to Germany in 1871. The Russians wanted control of Constantinople and the Turkish straits. Both would have preferred the breakup of both the German and Austro-Hungarian empires.

British ambitions were more modest. They would be satisfied with the independence of Belgium and a return to something much like the status quo ante, although with at least some kind of guarantee against another war, preferably involving the Americans. The British people, however, were so outraged at Germany, both for starting the war and for the tactics used during the war, that a peaceful settlement that left Germany intact and unharmed was hard for many to swallow. The British government was also at pains to show solidarity with France. French officials worried constantly that Britain would abandon them to face the Germans alone. The British worried that those fears might lead France to make a separate peace, leaving Britain to face the Germans alone. In September 1914 the Allies had signed a pact promising to stick together to the end, and Britain had promised to support French war aims. This left less room for negotiation with Berlin. Before there could be any talk of peace, Germany had to be defeated or at least driven back substantially. Yet in two years of fighting, the Allies had not been able to score any significant military victories or push the Germans back on either the eastern or the western fronts. In early 1916 the British were training and mobilizing a new and much larger force to throw into the fight. Neither London nor Paris had any interest in peace talks before seeing what this new force would accomplish.[8]

House and Wilson's offers to mediate had been unwelcome in London, therefore, but they did put the British in a bind. Given Britain's dependence on the United States, and the hope that the Americans might ultimately enter the war, Grey did not want to appear intransigent. The British knew from intelligence that the Germans were constantly urging Wilson to seek peace, with Ambassador Bernstorff hinting at all sorts of possible German concessions, including the restoration of Belgium's independence. British officials believed it was all a disingenuous ruse— why, Grey asked, would Germany give up Belgium for nothing in return? But House professed to take the offers seriously, keeping the onus on the British.[9] All Grey could do was parry American inquiries and try to throw the ball back in Berlin's court.

Neither side was actually interested in Wilson's mediation. What the British wanted was American intervention.[10] Grey told House that if the United States would commit to entering the war, Britain "would yield to almost any demand" Wilson might make, including peace talks with Germany.[11] But the point for Grey was to get the United States into the war.

The Germans, despite their ambassador's frequent hints, were even less interested in actual American mediation. With control of Belgium, much of France, and large swaths of territory in the east, they had a strong hand. They didn't need Wilson, whom the kaiser regarded as hopelessly pro-Allied, getting in the way.[12] As far as Berlin was concerned, Wilson's only role was to get the Allies to the table and then bow out. Germany would handle the rest.[13] Bernstorff's instructions were to deflect American offers of mediation and hope that the British would refuse Wilson's offer. Indeed, he was specifically instructed by Deputy Foreign Minister Gottlieb von Jagow to "prevent President Wilson from approaching us with a positive proposal." Both sides looked to jolly Wilson along while blaming the other side's intransigence. For much of 1915, Grey had the easier time of it. The sinking of the *Lusitania,* growing anti-German sentiment in the United States, and the long, tense negotiations over submarine warfare that continued into the spring of 1916 focused Wilson's attention on Germany and relieved the pressure on London.

That changed dramatically after the Sussex Pledge. Although the Germans had effectively suspended submarine warfare after April 1916, Wilson knew it was only temporary. If he could not deliver the British to the negotiating table, the Germans would resume the attacks, and he would be forced to take the country to war. Wilson, therefore, turned his full attention to getting British agreement to mediation.

Grey had from the beginning suggested a quid pro quo—the British would accept mediation and peace talks if the Americans agreed to help preserve the peace and join a league of great powers after the war. Although House had initially dismissed the idea when Grey first broached it back in early 1915—before the submarine war began—Wilson was now growing desperate. If agreeing to join some as-yet-undetermined international organization for peace in the future was the price for avoiding being dragged into the present war, Wilson was prepared to make that trade.

At the end of May 1916, therefore, Wilson agreed to speak at a meeting of former president Taft's League to Enforce Peace, a recently formed group dedicated to the creation of such an international organization. Sharing the dais with Lodge, who took the occasion to argue for a league that would "put force behind international peace,"[14] the president announced that the United States was "willing to become a partner" in a "universal association of nations" that would act "in concert" to protect the rights of nations, to "maintain the inviolate security of the highway of the seas," and to "prevent any war" begun without warning, in violation of treaties, or without "full submission . . . to the opinion of the world." He offered no specifics and avoided the question of how and when the United States might be called upon to use force. The truth was, he had not given the matter much detailed thought, as he all but admitted. He had no plan in mind, he said, but for the moment wished only to "avow a creed."[15]

Wilson had been led to believe by House that in return for such a public commitment, however vague, Grey would accept American mediation and peace talks. Privately, Wilson let it be known that if Britain refused, the American public was "apt to be alienated from Great Britain in a very significant degree in the immediate future."[16] Spring Rice translated the thinly veiled threat: "The President is ready to help us make peace. If we refuse . . . we shall be made to feel the weight of American displeasure."[17]

Wilson's May 1916 offer had put Grey and the British in a corner. Although the foreign secretary had often hinted at such a deal, he had never made any commitment to House.[18] The last thing he wanted was to risk alienating the American president. Yet in the summer of 1916 the British public, his colleagues in the government, and the French were all opposed to peace talks—the French ambassador informed the State Department that "anyone trying at this time to bring about peace would be considered a friend of Germany."[19] Even Grey himself did not think the time was right for talks. He had therefore sent word to Wilson that his proposal was premature. Wilson and House were furious. "We have given them everything and they ever demand more," House complained.[20] The British wanted the United States "to sacrifice hundreds of thousands of lives and billions of treasure" on European soil. He condemned the "utter selfishness of their outlook."[21]

For Wilson, Grey's refusal to accept mediation in the summer of 1916, coming on the heels of the Sussex Pledge, made Britain, not Germany, the intransigent party. It was time to "get down to hard pan," he told House. Either Britain made a "decided move for peace," or he would start demanding British respect for American neutral rights "with the same plain speaking and firmness" that he had used with Germany.[22]

Wilson was not about to open a trade war with America's biggest customer, but in the summer of 1916 he began putting rhetorical distance between the United States and Britain. He took to depicting the European struggle not as a struggle over "civilization," but as meaningless and absurd, with both sides venal and foolish, and equally unworthy of American sympathy. At campaign stops he asked audiences, with feigned bemusement, "Have you ever heard what started the present war? If you have, I wish you would publish it, because nobody else has."[23] This of course had not been his perspective on the war earlier, and it would not be his perspective later, when he decided the United States had no choice but to intervene.[24] His anti-British sentiments beginning in the summer of 1916 were driven by fear and anger that British intransigence would drag the United States into a war the American people did not want.

An anti-British stance was generally good politics in the United States, and especially during the second half of 1916. The public mood, which had turned sharply against Germany in the summer and early fall of

1915, had more recently turned against Britain. The Sussex Pledge cast Germany in a favorable light, while the British tightened their blockade and added a new "blacklist" of American firms allegedly engaged in covert and illegal supply of Germany.

Anti-British sentiment had then exploded following the abortive uprising of Irish nationalists in April 1916. The "Easter Rising" enjoyed great support in the United States. The uprising itself was funded largely by contributions from Irish Americans. Sir Roger Casement, the distinguished Irish-born former British diplomat and famed human rights advocate, had traveled to the United States to meet Irish American leaders and prominent politicians like Roosevelt.[25] When British forces crushed the poorly planned effort, and then executed Sir Roger and others for treason, anti-British outrage erupted in the United States.[26] Congress gave the president powers to retaliate against the British blockade. Hughes, campaigning for the German American vote, criticized Wilson for not standing up to the British blockade and promised not to put up with "blacklists" or any "improper interference with American commerce."[27] Democratic leaders begged Tumulty to put a "little more 'punch'" in Wilson's speeches to show that the president was not simply a slave to England.[28]

With the shift in attitudes toward Britain in the summer of 1916 came a more general shift in attitudes toward the war. The initial effect of the *Lusitania* sinking had been to stir many Americans against Germany, but the delayed effect was to make many Americans wary of taking a strong stand against Germany. It was one thing to support Britain's fight for "civilization" when there was no risk of the United States being pulled into the war. But once it became clear that supporting Britain could well result in war with Germany, that was another matter. As the *New Republic* noted, many Americans began to re-examine some of the "old phrases" about how Britain was "fighting our fight" against Germany's assault on "civilization." Perhaps the rights and wrongs were not so clear-cut, perhaps the Germans were not solely to blame, perhaps the British had acted not for noble motives but out of selfishness. As the possibility of the United States being pulled into the war grew, the European struggle looked less and less like "a clean-cut fight between right and wrong, between democracy and absolutism, between public faith and international lawlessness."[29] Wilson himself seemed to have made that mental and psychological journey. From once believing the British were "fighting our fight" against the "wild beasts" of German militarism, he now began to describe the war as nothing more than "a drunken brawl in a public house."[30]

Wilson's rhetorical shift caused agonized outrage among Britons and their sympathizers in the United States. The president "wholly failed to grasp . . . the cause for which we and our Allies are fighting," British leaders complained.[31] Roosevelt and Lodge were, of course, appalled at Wilson's sudden about-face, but so were Wilson's own advisers. Ambassador Walter Page, visiting the president during a leave from his duties in London, was shocked to hear him say that the war was only a matter of "England's having the earth and of Germany wanting it." Of course, Wilson admitted to Page, Germany's system was "directly opposed to everything American." But it seemed to Page that he did not think this "carried any very great moral reprehensibility." Overall, Wilson showed "a great deal of toleration for Germany; and he was, during the whole morning that I talked with him, complaining of England."[32] Lansing was beside himself, writing in his diary that the president did not seem "to grasp the full significance of this war or the principles at issue. . . . That German imperialistic ambitions threaten free institutions everywhere apparently has not sunk very deeply into his mind. For six months I have talked about the struggle between Autocracy and Democracy, but do not see that I have made any great impression."[33]

Many Britons, including top government officials, believed Wilson might now be actively colluding with the Germans.[34] In September 1916 British intelligence intercepted a cable from Ambassador Gerard in Berlin reporting that Germany was "anxious to make peace" and proposing that Wilson offer his "good offices," which Germany would then accept "in general terms." But the Germans asked that their proposal be handled with the utmost secrecy—the idea for talks had to appear as the "spontaneous act of the President."[35] An uncharitable reader might see collusion between the two governments, with the aim of trapping the Allies into a bad agreement. The decrypted cable was passed to the then minister of war, David Lloyd George.[36] With the cable literally in his pocket, Lloyd George publicly lashed out at Wilson.

For two years, he told an American reporter, the British people had been fighting a brutal war against unfair odds. For two years the British soldier had been "beaten like a dog," had been forced to "take refuge in a trench," but had nevertheless fought on. And in all that time, while Germany was "remaking the map of Europe" and thousands of British citizens were being "battered, bombed, and gassed," those "neutrals of the highest purposes" had shed no tears but had "watched the early rounds of the unequal contest dry eyed." Now that Britain was finally ready to fight back, Lloyd George complained, the American president was calling for a halt. But the British people were not about to accept an unjust and insecure peace just to help Wilson with his political problems. The Germans had begun the war seeking a "finish fight with England," Lloyd George proclaimed. Britain intended to oblige them. "The fight must be to the finish—to a knockout."[37] Lloyd George's rallying cry had a political purpose: to help him supplant H. H. Asquith as prime minister, which he did in December 1916. But there could be no doubt that Lloyd George also expressed the defiant mood of much of the British public. Lloyd George's comments, which were republished in six hundred newspapers across the United States, summed up British frustration and anger at the prospect that Wilson might now "butt in for the purpose of stopping the European war."[38]

Grey worried about Lloyd George's intemperate attack on Wilson. An angry American president could do a great deal of damage to Britain if he chose. The British government had done some analyses in late 1916 to determine the extent of British and French dependence on the United States, and the conclusions were troubling. The United States was obviously "an absolutely irreplaceable source of supply" of food and munitions. But the bigger problem was Britain's near-total dependence on American loans.[39] John Maynard Keynes, then serving in the Treasury, warned that Britain would soon rely on American creditors for 80 percent of the funds necessary to purchase vital imports. Wilson need only discourage American banks from lending to destroy Britain's capacity to continue the war.[40] Spring Rice warned that Wilson would do exactly that if he believed it was the only way to keep the United States out of the war—and he would have the great majority of Americans solidly behind him. It was a mistake to "count too much on their goodwill."[41]

These warnings were on the mark. Wilson took no action before the election, but as soon as it was over, he moved to punish the British by signaling disapproval of further private loans from American banks.[42] He then worked swiftly to force the two sides to the table. Immediately after his re-election he began drafting a "peace note" to the belligerents calling on them to state their terms as a preliminary to beginning negotiations. House warned that the Allies would consider this "an unfriendly act," and he urged the president to "sit tight and await further developments." But Wilson would not wait. He feared the United States would soon "inevitably drift into war with Germany upon the submarine issue."[43] The two men wrestled over the draft. Wilson began his by declaring, once again, that the European struggle was about nothing, that its "causes and objects" were "obscure." House, baffled yet again at what he regarded as the president's obtuseness, advised replacing the offensive phrase with a clause indicating that Wilson "sympathized" with the Allies' view of the war. House seemed to believe, as would many future historians, that Wilson's overriding desire was to gain eternal fame as the great peacemaker, and so he tried to make the president understand that the Allies would never accept him as mediator if he continued to offend them.[44]

But House did not understand Wilson's purposes as well as he thought he did, perhaps because he could not admit that Wilson's views of the war were so different from his own, at least in December 1916. The British ambassador, less blinded by his own passions and prejudices, understood Wilson better. While the American president might want to play a "great part as peace maker," he wrote London, that was *not* the "main reason" for his actions. His overriding objective—indeed, at this time his only objective—was to keep the United States out of the war while avoiding national dishonor and personal humiliation. If the Germans made good on their threat to resume all-out submarine warfare, Spring Rice pointed out, Wilson would be forced to choose between "war or ignominious surrender." He was desperate to broker a peace before that happened and therefore had little patience for British objections and did not, at this moment at least, "sympathize" with the Allies. His peace note was not aimed at cajoling the British. He was prepared, Spring Rice warned, to "force us to accept" mediation, if necessary. What was more, Wilson was prepared to seek peace "quite irrespective of terms."[45] He did not at this moment care how the war ended, so long as it ended before the United States was dragged into it. After sending the peace note to the belligerents, Wilson told Lippmann, "We've got to stop [the war] before we're pulled in."[46]

In theory, the time seemed ripe to end the fighting and seek some kind of settlement to the war. By the end of 1916, after two years of the most horrific destruction modern Europe had ever known, the war had settled into what seemed a permanent stalemate. The Germans had launched a massive offensive in the west in the early part of the year, attempting to bleed French forces to death at Verdun, the almost mythic strategic and psychological linchpin of French resistance since the days of Attila. The battle had lasted ten months, costing the French and German armies nearly a million dead. It ended in December with the French still in control of the Verdun citadel. The Allies, meanwhile, had launched an offensive at the Somme, which lasted five months, left more than a million dead and wounded, and ended in November with Allied forces having driven the Germans back only a few miles. The mass carnage and utter futility of these offensives convinced many observers, including a growing number of Britons, that an Allied victory was either impossible or not worth the monstrous cost necessary to achieve it. Meanwhile, the fall of Bucharest to German forces at the beginning of December, combined with German victories against Russia and the disastrous British failure in the Gallipoli campaign over the previous year, as well as Germany's continuing control of parts of France and Belgium in the west, seemed to most observers to leave Germany firmly in control of the heart of central Europe, with no prospect that the Germans could be dislodged by force. By January 1917, much of the British public was turning against the war, and French morale was flagging. As for the Americans, they saw only the futility of further fighting. As Britain's Grey later recalled, Wilson's "whole policy" in these weeks "was founded on the assumption that the war was a stalemate, and that the most useful role of the United States was to promote an honourable end without a crushing victory."[47]

Events were moving fast, however. Before Wilson had even completed the draft of his peace note, the German government had already decided to bring matters to a head. On December 12 Bethmann had presented a peace proposal of his own. Delivered to the United States and other neutral powers for conveyance to the Allies, the note contained no specific terms but simply proposed opening talks to settle the war. If the Allies declined, then the war would continue and they alone would bear responsibility.

Although triumphal in tone—German forces had just conquered Bucharest and the note spoke of "further successes" to come—it was, for Bethmann, a last desperate attempt to resist the overwhelming domestic pressure to unleash the submarines. After months of struggle, the chancellor was losing his battle with the navy. Public pressure, the waning influence of the kaiser, and the growing strength of the military all pushed toward a decision to rescind the Sussex Pledge and resume unrestricted warfare, even if it meant bringing the United States into the war. The note's lack of any specifics reflected the fact that the kaiser and his high command had agreed on terms which Bethmann knew would be unacceptable to the Allies and offensive to Wilson.[48]

The Allies immediately signaled their rejection. The French premier denounced the German note as "a clumsy snare" and a "ruse"; the Russian Duma voted unanimously against entering any talks; and though the British made no immediate response, the new prime minister, Lloyd

George, had already pledged to fight until the "knockout," and they were not going to accept a proposal that France and Russia had rejected.

Wilson welcomed the German note—it was at least a step in the right direction—but it complicated his plans.[49] If he now went ahead and sent his own peace note, it would only seem to confirm British and French suspicions that he was colluding with Germany. But if he did not send his note and the Allies rejected the German offer (Wilson could not quite admit to himself that they already had done so),[50] then all hope of an early settlement would vanish. Wilson decided he had to send his own note immediately, even if it meant appearing pro-German.

On December 18, therefore, he delivered his own peace note to the belligerents, denying that it had anything to do with the German note and asking that it be judged "entirely on its own merits." His proposal by this point had become quite modest. He did not call for talks or offer mediation. He only asked both sides to state the terms they would be willing to accept. He himself was "indifferent" as to the terms of a final settlement. However, he did point out "the fact" that both sides' stated goals were "virtually the same." Both, he claimed, said they wanted to protect the rights of small states against aggression and to safeguard all nations' independence, territorial integrity, and political and commercial freedom. Both sides wanted to be made secure against attack, and both were ready to consider "the formation of a league of nations to insure peace and justice throughout the world."

The United States, Wilson declared, was "as vitally and directly interested" in these matters as the powers at war, for its interests, and those of other neutrals, had been "most seriously affected." The president insisted he was not proposing peace but was merely proposing that "soundings be taken" so that neutral and belligerent nations alike would know "how near the haven of peace may be for which all mankind longs with an intense and increasing longing." The American people were "ready, and even eager" to help in the search for a settlement, he claimed. But he accompanied his note with a warning, instructing his ambassadors that he wanted "the impression clearly conveyed that it would be very hard for the Government of the United States to understand a negative reply."[51]

The Allies' unofficial reaction was quite negative. Despite Wilson's denials, British and French officials regarded his December peace note not only as a "pro-German document," but, when viewed in conjunction with Wilson's decision to discourage loans to the Allies, as part of a "preconceived plan" promoted by "German interests, for the purpose of achieving German ends through American intervention."[52] Even those who did not see Wilson as a witting or unwitting pawn of the Germans were appalled at his claim that the two sides were fighting for the same ends. The American ambassador learned that "the King wept while he expressed his surprise and depression" at reading Wilson's message.[53]

In the United States, the reaction was more positive. Most editors across the country supported the president's efforts to achieve peace and were not at all put off by the equation of the two sides' war aims. Pro-Democratic newspapers like the New York *World* praised Wilson for reminding everyone, at home and abroad, that the United States had its own interests to protect and that its "standing in court" was not to be ignored. The more fervent supporters of the Allies in the United States were predictably unhappy.[54] Even the generally pro-Wilson *New York Times* complained that the president was "on unsafe ground" in claiming that the two sides sought the same objects in the war when in fact their goals were "about as dissimilar as could well be imagined."[55] Roosevelt, more blunt as always, said the equation of the two sides was "profoundly immoral and misleading," not to mention "wickedly false."[56]

The president's top advisers agreed. Lansing, like House, remained astounded that the president simply did not "grasp the full significance of the war," that it was a "struggle between Autocracy and Democracy" and that "German imperialistic ambitions" threatened "free institutions everywhere."[57] He was so upset that in an act of outright insubordination he decided without consulting Wilson to give a statement to the press explaining that the real import of the president's peace note was that the United States was "drawing nearer the verge of war" and therefore needed to know "exactly what each belligerent seeks in order that we may regulate our conduct in the future." Since it was inconceivable that the United States would enter the war on the side of the Germans, Lansing's statement was taken to mean—as he surely intended—that Wilson's note was but a prelude to breaking relations with Germany and entering the war on the Allies' side. This was the opposite of Wilson's intent, and the president was so furious that he contemplated firing his secretary of state on the spot. Instead, he had Lansing go out to the press a few hours later and issue what one press wag called "an explanation of his explanation." Lansing declared that he had not meant "to intimate that the Government was considering any change in its policy of neutrality."[58]

The day after Wilson dispatched his peace note, Lloyd George rose in the House of Commons, ostensibly to respond to Bethmann's peace offer but really to respond to Wilson. Acknowledging that it might be "difficult for those who were fortunate enough to live thousands of miles away to understand" what it was like to live next to an "arrogant, threatening, bullying" power like Germany, he made clear that Britain would not talk peace until Germany was defeated and its "Prussian military" regime was overthrown. And to drive home his point he quoted from Abraham Lincoln's speech to a war-weary nation in the summer of 1864: "We accepted this war for an object, and a worthy object, and the war will end when that object is attained. Under God I hope it will never end until that time."[59] Ten days later the Allies together formally rejected the German offer, insisting that unless the Germans made clear what their terms for a settlement were, there was nothing to respond to.

Wilson's peace note required more delicate handling. Lord Robert Cecil, the British under-secretary of state for foreign affairs, and a strong supporter of a League of Nations, warned against a "contemptuous rejection," noting that Wilson had the power, if he chose, to shut down the Allies' ability to fight.[60] After protesting "in the most friendly manner" Wilson's equation of the two sides' aims in the war, therefore, the Allies went on to do what Germany had refused to do: They stated their terms. These were the unconditional restoration of Belgium, Serbia, and Montenegro, all currently occupied by German forces, with reparations to be paid to each; the evacuation of German troops from France, Russia, and Romania, also with reparations; the return of territories taken in the past from the Allies "by force or against the will of their populations," a reference to Alsace and Lorraine; and "the liberation of Italians, of Slavs, of Roumanians, and of Tcheco Slovaques from foreign domination," a reference suggesting the breakup of the Austro-Hungarian Empire.[61] As for Germany, the Allies denied that they desired "the extermination of the German peoples." Their aim was only to "liberate Europe from the brutal covetousness of Prussian militarism."

These were maximalist goals, certain to be rejected by Berlin. Yet the Allied response went a long way toward repairing the breach between Wilson and Britain that had opened so wide over the previous year. The Allies' terms were neither surprising nor, in Wilson's view, unreasonable. In fact, American and Allied perceptions of the war were now fairly well aligned. Indeed, Wilson's favorable reaction to the Allies' maximalist terms validated the concerns of Kaiser Wilhelm and other German officials that the American president could never be trusted to see Germany's point of view on these matters. Despite Wilson's efforts to appear neutral, the Germans remained convinced that the United States was too entangled with the Allies economically and simply had too much of its money "in Entente business," as one Reichstag member put it, to be an

honest broker.[62] The German response, meanwhile, delivered days earlier, was from Wilson's point of view unsatisfactory. Still unwilling to
reveal German war aims, Bethmann did finally reveal his government's
unwillingness to let Wilson's participate in any peace talks. At about the
same time, Ambassador Gerard reported from Berlin, on "very good
authority," that the Germans only intended to use a peace conference
to split France and Russia off from the British and then "finish England
by submarines." Then, later, Germany could "take the scalps of Japan,
Russia, and France separately."[63] Wilson, now more annoyed with Berlin
than with London, asked House to pass word that "the time to accomplish something" had arrived, if, that is, the Germans "really and truly"
wanted peace. Did the Germans want him to help? Wilson demanded to
know, because he "genuinely" wanted to help and had put himself "in a
position to help without favour to either side."[64] The answer in Berlin,
however, was no. "I won't go to any conference!" Kaiser Wilhelm insisted
to his aides. "Certainly not under his chairmanship!"[65]

Wilson was still not ready to take no for an answer, however. When
House in early January 1917 discussed possible preparations for the war
he assumed would come soon, Wilson replied: "There will be no war.
This country does not intend to become involved in this war. We are the
only one of the great white nations that is free from war to-day, and it
would be a crime against civilization for us to go in."[66]

Instead, Wilson made his most dramatic appeal yet to the warring
powers. On January 22, 1917, speaking to a Senate chamber filled to the
rafters, with visitors leaning "forward in their seats to avoid missing a
phrase," Wilson delivered a thirty-minute speech that the *New York Times*
called "one of the most startling declarations of policy ever enunciated in
the history of the United States."[67] Part of it laid out the kind of peace
Wilson sought for Europe, one founded on respect for the "equality of
rights" of all nations, on the principle "that governments derive all their
just powers from the consent of the governed" and that peoples could not
be handed "about from sovereignty to sovereignty as if they were property." Such principles were not only dear to Americans but essential to
any lasting peace. Peace required stability, and there could be no stability
where there was no "sense of justice, of freedom, of right" and where the
peoples' will was in "rebellion." These were all noble-sounding principles,
and the speech was, as one historian has put it, at once "splendid, grandiose, and vague."[68]

The phrase for which the speech would become famous, although
most Americans at the time paid little attention to it, was his call for a

"peace without victory." In explaining what he meant, he said that "only a peace between equals" could last. Victory would mean "peace forced upon the loser, a victor's terms imposed upon the vanquished." It would be accepted "in humiliation, under duress, at an intolerable sacrifice, and would leave a sting, a resentment, a bitter memory upon which terms of peace would rest, not permanently, but only as upon quicksand." A "lasting peace" required "the right state of mind" and the "right feeling between nations."

Wilson's call for a "peace without victory" would later loom large in connection with the Versailles Treaty. But Wilson's purposes in 1917 were quite different than they would be two years later. In January 1917 he was trying to keep the United States out of the war, and the settlement he proposed, a "peace without victory," seemed to him the only plausible way to achieve his goal in the circumstances of military stalemate that then existed.

In the winter of 1916–1917 victory by either side seemed unlikely, and victory by the Allies seemed especially unlikely. For most of the war, Americans sympathetic to the Allies had assumed they would eventually prevail. In 1916 they had celebrated France's heroic stand at Verdun and cheered the minimal gains at the Somme. Even as late as November, the *New Republic*'s editors believed Germany was "on the defensive everywhere." Then suddenly it was the Allies that were in trouble and it was Germany that had achieved a seemingly unassailable dominance on the continent.[69]

Wilson was a careful reader of the small progressive journal, which had endorsed his re-election, and during these critical weeks when he was desperately trying to keep the United States out of the war the *New Republic*'s editorials and essays painted a bleak picture of the Allies' situation.[70] Germany had succeeded in establishing its "*Mitteleuropa,*" Walter Lippmann wrote. "German efficiency," "German organizing ability," and "the incontestable superiority of German methods" had produced an "empire" that extended from "the Baltic to Persia." Lloyd George's talk of a "knockout" was both irrational and irresponsible. Even a return to the prewar status quo was impossible. "Central Europe exists," and the only question was whether the Allies could "face facts" or, out of "vanity" and "stubbornness," try to ignore them.[71]

Facing facts meant giving serious consideration to Bethmann's recent proposal to begin peace talks. Given the strength of Germany's position, it seemed to the editors a "liberal offer." Bethmann was giving the Allies a choice. They could continue fighting for a "dictated" peace, the kind that a victor imposed on a vanquished foe, and that resulted from a "knock-out." Or they could accept the reality of Germany's unassailable position as the dominant power in central Europe. The editors believed that the Allies would be making a "grave mistake" if they refused to accept Bethmann's offer to negotiate simply because they would not let go of the "vain hope of a peace dictated to an utterly beaten and humiliated enemy." To abandon that hope "would be a gain rather than a loss."[72] What the Germans were proposing, Lippmann argued, was a "peace without victory," and since the Allies had no real chance of defeating or even dislodging Germany, a "peace without victory" was the best they could hope for. Making a virtue out of necessity, Lippmann argued that a "peace without victory" was also the most stable and the most likely to last, since an all-out triumph would only tempt the victor to crush the vanquished and leave the defeated nursing bitter hopes for revenge.[73]

There was no question that Lippmann's editorial influenced Wilson's thinking, or at least gave him the arguments he needed to support his attempts to bring about a peace.[74] In his January 22 address to Congress, Wilson implored both sides to "face realities" and give up fantasies about total victory. To encourage the British to accept peace talks, he returned to Grey's quid quo pro. Any peace settlement, he declared, would have to be "followed by some definite concert of power" to serve as "guarantor." No "covenant of cooperative peace" would be powerful enough "to keep the future safe against war" without the participation of the United States. The American people, he said, were prepared to "add their authority and their power" to that of other nations in order to "guarantee peace and justice throughout the world." Indeed, he declared it was "inconceivable that the people of the United States should play no part in that great enterprise."

The reactions to Wilson's speech on each side of the Atlantic could hardly have been more different. The British and French were once again angry and saddened at Wilson's call for a "peace without victory." The new foreign secretary, Arthur Balfour, called it a "dangerous fallacy" to imagine that a new international order could be built with a powerful Germany dominating the heart of Europe, or even on a "reversion to the *status quo ante bellum.*"[75] France's Georges Clemenceau, when he read the address, observed simply, "The moral side of the war has escaped President Wilson."[76] Few in Europe paid attention to Wilson's promise to bring the United States into a postwar "concert of power" to guarantee the peace, since to the British and French, the peace he had in mind looked a lot like a German victory.

In the United States, on the other hand, Wilson's offer to take part in a postwar "concert of power" was the only part of the speech that attracted attention, and the reaction was not especially favorable. Republicans and Democrats alike lashed Wilson for abandoning Washington's "great rule" and leading Americans into "the storm center of European politics." William Borah, the Republican senator from Idaho, accused the president of "moral treason" for proposing to grant other powers authority "to make war upon the United States."[77] Henry Cabot Lodge, who had once coined the term "league of nations," now joined Borah in criticizing Wilson for dragging the United States "into the field of European politics" where it had "no national or legal concern."[78] Most Americans did not care what kind of peace came to Europe. They just didn't want to commit to preserving it. For once, Wilson had jumped far ahead of American public opinion. He did so out of desperation, as the best and perhaps only way of bringing the war to an end in time to keep the United States out of it.

The whole discussion quickly became moot. The Germans had already made their decision. On January 9, 1917, two weeks before Wilson's dramatic speech, the kaiser had issued an imperial decree ordering the resumption of unrestricted submarine warfare beginning on February 1. Instructions sent to U-boat captains directed that they were to target all ships—military and civilian, armed and unarmed, enemy and neutral, and specifically including "passenger liners." All were to be treated as "enemy ships" and sunk without warning.[79]

The German decision had been coming for months. Chancellor Bethmann had worked to the point of physical and emotional exhaustion trying to head it off, but he had gradually lost influence. With the war dragging on with no end in sight, and with the United States continuing to provide supplies to the Allies, many Germans decided it was past time to unleash the "wonder weapon" that would bring England to its knees.[80] Bethmann's political opponents accused him of kowtowing to Wilson and opposing the one action that could win the war. By the end of 1916, moreover, civilians like Bethmann had begun to lose influence to Generals Paul von Hindenburg and Erich Ludendorff, the heroes of the eastern front who enjoyed overwhelming public support and whose military judgments the kaiser felt in no position to question.[81]

The two generals had in turn accepted the claims of the navy chief of staff, Admiral Henning von Holtzendorff, that the war could be won by a return to unrestricted submarine warfare and indeed could only be won that way. Holtzendorff guaranteed that if the submarines were allowed to operate unhindered, they could sink enough tonnage to starve Britain into submission. England, he promised, "would be forced to her knees within six months." The campaign had to begin immediately, however, partly so that Britain would be cut off from food supplies before the summer harvest and partly to cut the American supplies flowing to Britain and France as they launched their expected spring offensive.

The German military was no longer deterred by the risk of bringing the United States into the war. "From a military point of view," the navy minister commented, the United States was "as nothing." Few Americans would fight, the Germans believed. Those who did would have to be trained, but at the moment there were not enough officers in the small American army to train them. Once an army was assembled, it would have to be transported across the ocean, but the United States had too few transport ships and those it did have would make for good "hunting."[82] The admiral promised that the war would be won "before a single American has set foot on the continent."[83]

Some officials disagreed. The German treasury minister warned—presciently as it turned out—that unleashing the submarines might actually lead to an *increase* in American supplies to Britain. So far the Americans had left it to the British to protect and ensure the passage of supplies across the Atlantic, he noted, but once they entered the war they would also bring their own vast resources to the task of securing and increasing transatlantic shipping.[84] Military officials also took little account of psychological issues, particularly what effect America's entry into the conflict might have on Allied morale.[85] Nor did they calculate how the weight of American economic power might tilt the scales. As in 1914, the belief in a rapid victory, this time using submarines, prevented the Germans from thinking about the possible long-term costs of bringing the United States into the war.

German leaders also ignored the analysis of German diplomats. Ambassador Bernstorff in Washington and Chancellor Bethmann in Berlin believed Wilson was desperate to avoid bringing the United States into the war and would do almost anything to prevent it. They also believed he had no interest in the details of a peace settlement, that he did not care about where Europe's borders were drawn or who wound up with what, other than the independence of Belgium. He also favored certain principles, such as "freedom of the seas," which could work to Germany's advantage.[86] And there was always the chance that the Allies would balk at peace talks, in which case an angry Wilson would be more inclined to tolerate the return to unrestricted submarine warfare.[87]

These suggestions fell on deaf ears, however. The German leadership had stopped making careful and subtle calculations and had succumbed to a certain fatalism. Bethmann had all along suggested that the return to unrestricted submarine warfare would be a monumental "roll of the dice," a *Vabanque-spiel,* an "all-or-nothing gamble," the outcome of which would determine Germany's very existence as a great power.[88] Ludendorff had no confidence in the navy's assurances that England would be brought to its knees before the Americans could enter the war in a meaningful fashion. Although the U-boat fleet had expanded and was sinking more tonnage, it had not yet shown the capacity to shut down the transatlantic trade altogether. Even Admiral Holtzendorff admitted that his proposal was only the least bad of many bad options. But continuing along the current path meant "certain destruction."[89] Hindenburg's predecessor, Falkenhayn, who had long resisted the return to unrestricted sub warfare, finally concluded that there was "no choice" but to go forward "to a good or bitter end whether we wish it or not."[90] Hindenburg himself argued only that "things cannot be worse than they are now" and that the war had to be "brought to an end by the use of all means as soon as possible."[91] The pressures of public opinion played a role, too. Ambassador Gerard reported in mid-January that "the public feeling for the resumption of reckless submarine warfare" was so great that the officials he spoke to did not "see how any government can withstand it."[92]

CHAPTER EIGHT

America Declares War

We will not choose the path of submission and suffer the most sacred rights of our nation and our people to be ignored or violated.

—Woodrow Wilson[1]

THE GERMAN announcement on January 31 that it would resume "ruthless" submarine warfare hit Wilson hard. Although he had long anticipated that this day might come, it was still an "astounding surprise."[2] He felt "as if the world had suddenly reversed itself; that after going from east to west, it had begun to go from west to east, and that he could not get his balance." House, when he visited the president the next day, found him "sad and depressed, deeply disappointed in the sudden and unwarranted action of the German Government."[3] As Spring Rice explained, after Wilson had "done everything possible to put a stop to the war, in order to prevent the war reaching this country," he now faced the choice he had worked so hard to avoid, between "an ignominious surrender or a rupture of relations with Germany."[4]

Wilson was still not ready to give up. Lansing recorded that while the president was "deeply incensed at Germany's insolent notice," nothing "could induce him to break off relations unless he was convinced that, viewed from every angle, it was the wisest thing to do."[5] To House, Wilson "reiterated his belief that it would be a crime for this Government to involve itself in the war to such an extent as to make it impossible to save Europe afterward."[6] On several occasions he expressed the view that America should stay out of the war in order to ensure the continued global dominance of "white civilization."[7] In private conversation with House, the president admitted that Germany was "a madman that should be curbed," but when House asked if it was fair to let the Allies "do the curbing" alone, Wilson "noticeably winced." He "still held to his determination not to become involved if it were humanly possible to do otherwise."[8]

Some steps he could not avoid. Wilson had pledged to break relations if Germany resumed unrestricted submarine warfare, and on February 3 he went before a joint session of Congress to make the announcement.[9] Even as he declared that American "dignity and honor" required severing official ties, however, he would not regard German actions as hostile until the Germans actually attacked American ships.[10] He denied requests from American shippers to be escorted or armed by the government. He ordered the secretary of war not to station forces or make any move that could be read in Germany as preparation for war.[11] Bernstorff reported to Berlin that Wilson planned "to wait and see what we do" and expressed confidence that he would not declare war unless German submarines started sinking American ships.[12]

Wilson's approach, as usual, reflected the national mood. Spring Rice reported that within a couple of weeks of the German announcement, the public's "moral indignation" had again faded to "indifference," just as had happened after the *Lusitania* sinking, and he warned that it would be "extremely unwise to count with any certainty on the United States entering the war."[13] At mass rallies in New York, Washington, Philadelphia, Chicago, and Toledo, Socialist and Socialist Labor party leaders, church groups, women's organizations, and other peace activists joined with German and Irish Americans to demand peace and rail against those who plotted to drag the United States into war. It was "not OUR war," Bryan insisted. Even if Germany did sink American ships, he did not want to see "one single mother's son" sent across the ocean "to march under the banner of any European monarch or die on European soil, in the settlement of European quarrels."[14] Others denounced the "munitions makers, capitalists, American Admirals, Generals, Captains, and so-called metropolitan newspapers" that were all "leagued together" to push the United States into war.[15] Minnesota Republican Charles Lindbergh, father of the soon-to-be-famous aviator, warned that the "money trust" had brought the United States "to the very verge of war" and implored Americans not to "plunge this Nation into the maelstrom of hell . . . for the sake of vainglory."[16] Many demanded a national referendum so that the people, not Congress, could decide the question of war or peace.

It was hard to pin down exactly where the American public stood after Germany's January 31 announcement. As in the past, interventionist sentiment was highest in the East and diminished as one traveled west beyond the Alleghenies.[17] The *Milwaukee Sentinel* complained of a "Boston brand of Americanism" that protested "the Belgian deportations" but was "as meek as Moses" when "Mother England" hijacked American cargoes and opened American mail.[18] One Illinois editor suggested that while most Americans supported Wilson's decision to break relations with Germany, the "overwhelming majority" still desired "most earnestly to avoid war," *if* it could be done "honorably." If Germany sank American ships, he believed, most would approve "necessary measures" to protect American rights on the high seas, "even by the use of force." If force did turn out to be necessary, however, Americans opposed joining the Allies in the fight. They wanted no "entangling military alliances." Fully "nine-tenths of the people," moreover, would oppose sending American soldiers to fight in Europe.[19] In Congress, a resolution supporting the break with Germany passed easily, but many in both House and Senate opposed further actions that might lead to war.

Wilson had said he would respond to an "overt act" against American ships, but he soon found that, even absent an "overt act," the renewed submarine warfare was damaging the American economy. Although Germany had not yet "committed murder," Spring Rice reported, the "threat of murder" was having a big impact. Merchant vessels refused to cross the Atlantic and, just as in the first days of the war, goods piled up on the wharves, cotton and wheat prices fell, and the Midwest had difficulty getting its meat and grain to the British market. After just two weeks, Anglo-American trade fell by 75 percent.[20] The *New York Times* reported on February 15 that the entire economy "would soon feel the disastrous effects unless the government took measures to encourage American ship owners to venture into the war zones with some hope of survival."[21]

To address the crisis, Wilson decided to ask Congress for broad authority to arm merchant ships and take other measures that might be necessary. Even though American ships had not yet been sunk, he told Congress, "our commerce has suffered." In theory, the new policy of "armed neutrality" was supposed to avoid war with Germany.[22] In practice, however, there proved to be little distinction between "armed neutrality" and outright belligerency. German U-boat captains had to assume that armed American merchant ships might fire on them, and the American merchant ship captains had to assume that they might be preemptively torpedoed. It was only a matter of time before an incident turned armed neutrality into armed conflict.

Wilson began to lose hope of keeping the United States out of the war. His February 26 statement to Congress ended on an incongruous note. It was not "material interests" alone that guided his actions, he insisted. His "main thought," and what gave his proposed policy "dignity and weight," was the need to protect "fundamental human rights" and, above all, "the right to life itself." He spoke not only of American rights but also of those "rights of humanity without which there is no civilization."[23]

Those who had followed Wilson closely since the start of the war should have recognized the significance of this latest shift in his rhetoric. Since the Sussex Pledge, Wilson had said little about "civilization" but had talked instead about the war's absurdity. Now the old pro-Allies phrases returned. The president, as always a faithful reader of the *New Republic,* could not have missed the series of editorials following the Germans' January 31 announcement. Lippmann and his fellow editors, who had been calling for "peace without victory," suddenly reversed themselves and began making the case for entering the war on the side of the Allies. Instead of arguing that the war was unwinnable by either side and that the Allies should accept a compromise peace, now they argued that the United States had a profound interest in a British and French victory, and that it should do whatever was necessary to make that victory possible.[24] Not only America's "own existence," but "the world's order" was at stake. Americans were part of "one great . . . Atlantic community," Lippmann wrote. It was time for Americans to prove that they were ready, "now, as well as in the theoretical future, to defend the western world."[25]

Such statements showed that the impressions formed about Germany and the Germans after the sinking of the *Lusitania* had never really dissipated, even during the months when Wilson sought to preserve peace. The conviction that Germany under its present government represented a threat not only to American trade but to "civilization," to the "Atlantic community," and to democracy itself quickly became the context within which German actions would henceforth be viewed.

This conviction was only reinforced by the next bizarre development. The day before Wilson went to Congress to seek authority for armed neutrality, he learned of a telegram that the German foreign minister, Arthur Zimmermann, had sent to his ambassador in Mexico in January, and which had been intercepted and decrypted by British intelligence. The telegram explained that Germany was about to resume unrestricted submarine warfare and that while it was hoped the United States would remain neutral, if not the ambassador was to offer an alliance between Germany and Mexico. In return for making war on the United States, Mexico would receive "generous financial support" as well as the opportunity to reconquer Mexican territory lost to the United States in 1848, namely Texas, New Mexico, and Arizona. The Mexicans were also urged to invite Japan to join the alliance against the United States.

As Lansing read the translated version to Wilson, the president several times exclaimed "Good Lord." To the president, the telegram was remarkable less for the proposed alliance with Mexico than for what it revealed about the Germans' state of mind, even in January while he was still desperately searching for peace. Despite his herculean and politically risky efforts, it now seemed that Berlin had not been serious. As he told a visiting group of peace activists a few days later, "If you knew what I know at this present moment . . . you would not ask me to attempt further peace dealings with Germany."[26] Wilson did not mention the telegram in his speech on February 26, but he ordered its release on February 28, and the sensational news was blared across the front pages of the nation's papers on March 1: **"GERMANY SEEKS AN ALLIANCE AGAINST US; ASKS JAPAN AND MEXICO TO JOIN HER,"** read the full-page headline in the *New York Times;* **"BOLD GERMAN SCHEME REVEALED FOR WAR AGAINST UNITED STATES"** read the headline of the *Union Times* in South Carolina.

Wilson's next moves indicated the shift not only in his own thinking but in his reading of the public mood. His Armed Ship Bill passed overwhelmingly in the House and would have in the Senate as well had not a group of eleven senators, led by La Follette and Senate Foreign Relations Committee chairman William Stone, successfully filibustered and killed the bill. Wilson then took the rather extraordinary step of publicly denouncing the "little group of willful men" who, representing "no opinion but their own," had "rendered the great government of the United States helpless and contemptible." He then bypassed Congress and authorized arming of ships on his own authority. The always-observant Spring Rice speculated that Wilson would not have risked appealing "to the country against their representatives" had he not discerned that public sentiment was "growing stronger and stronger" against Germany.[27]

The Zimmermann telegram did not produce a "war hysteria," as some in the 1920s and 1930s would later claim. Its impact was more subtle. It put anti-interventionists, and German Americans, on the defensive.[28] Prominent German American spokesmen at first denounced it as a blatant "fabrication" perpetrated by the British, only to be contradicted by Zimmermann himself, who immediately confirmed its authenticity.[29] German Americans felt compelled to proclaim their loyalty and denounce the German government for this "foolish and unpardonable blunder."[30] They also warned, presciently, that when war did come, things would likely become "very unpleasant" for German Americans.[31] The country remained divided—Roosevelt fumed he would skin Wilson alive if the president didn't declare war, while the Socialist Party leader, Eugene V. Debs, declared that he preferred to be shot as a traitor than "go to war for Wall Street"[32]—but there was no doubt that opinion had shifted.

Wilson was now moving more deliberately toward intervention. Within days of the Zimmermann telegram's release, Wilson explained that there were forces "lying outside our own life as a nation and over which we had no control" that were pulling the United States "more and more irresistibly into their own current and influence." Soon the United States might be compelled, "not by our own purpose or desire," to embark on "a more active assertion of our rights" and a "more immediate association with the great struggle itself." Americans could be "provincials no longer," the president insisted. Their "fortunes as a nation" had become caught up in the European war, and there was "no turning back." On March 9, Spring Rice reported that in Washington circles it was now "generally considered that the country will drift into war, mainly because Germany wishes it." Berlin still had the ability to avert the clash, if it chose, because the vast majority of Americans still desired peace and "would do a great deal" to secure it.[33] But the general view was that the Germans were no longer interested in preventing war with the United States.

Any doubts were put to rest on March 18 when news came that three American ships had been sunk without warning by U-boats.[34] These were the "overt acts" that Wilson had spoken of. The next day three senators called for war. Wilson called a cabinet meeting for two days later to make a final decision.

Meanwhile, yet another stunning development was unfolding in this crowded hour. On March 15, the tsar was deposed by Russians who promised to establish a new constitutional democracy. Banner headlines in the United States reported news of the revolution. The implications were far-reaching, obviously for the belligerents, but also for Americans.

Russia's participation in the war had long been a problem. The tsarist government was extremely unpopular in the United States. To American Jews, tsarist Russia was the most hated regime in the world, and American strategic thinkers and policymakers had long regarded Russian expansionism as one of the great menaces.[35] The revolution came as a great relief, therefore. The United States, if it did join the war, would no longer have to fight alongside what the *New Republic* called "the most corrupt government, the most detestable despotism," but instead would be joining a broad international democratic alliance that now included the Russian people.[36]

For many American liberals, in fact, the Russian revolution so transformed the war as to "make one forget the original objects." Now the Allies were fighting not only to defend themselves but also to preserve the liberties of the Russian people.[37] The American tendency to view the world in terms of ideological struggle suddenly seemed apposite. The war was "only superficially a war among nations," liberals now believed. It was actually a global struggle "between the masses and their oppressors."[38] This belief, which would lead to much disillusionment in the years to come, only strengthened many Americans' willingness to go to war in 1917.

For Wilson, the Russian revolution made for one less argument against intervention, and possibly one more argument in favor, but it was hardly decisive. Although he spoke of "the glorious act of the Russians," he did not believe it right to ask the American people to go to war to save Russian democracy.[39] Although Lansing made a vigorous case for declaring that the United States enter the war to "advance the cause of Democracy," that the European war was in fact "a war between Democracy and Absolutism," and that the only hope of a lasting peace was the "establishment of democratic institutions throughout the world," Wilson did not agree. The justification "would have to rest on the conduct of Germany, the clear need of protecting our rights, of getting ready, and of safeguarding civilization against the domination of Prussian militarism."

As to the basic question of whether to intervene or not, there were no longer any dissenters in his cabinet. At the meeting on March 20, days after the ships were sunk, the more hawkish members predictably argued that war had become necessary. "We are at war now!" Lansing insisted. But so did those who until then had been adamantly opposed to American intervention. Labor Secretary William B. Wilson reached this decision only "with very great reluctance," but he now believed Germany had "made war upon this country" and that "Prussian rule" had become a menace to "human liberty and peace all over the world." Postmaster General Albert Burleson regretted having to support war but believed there was "no other way." When the president turned to Josephus Daniels, the navy secretary, who had always been closer to Bryan than to Wilson in his pacifism, said with a trembling voice and tear-filled eyes that he agreed there was no other choice.[40]

The next day Wilson announced that he would call Congress into special session on April 2 "to receive a communication concerning grave matters of national policy." "The die has been cast," Spring Rice reported with relief to London. The Americans had "drifted into war," and, he hastened to add, not because they "wanted it" but because their hand had "been forced by Germany."[41]

Wilson was miserable about the decision he felt compelled to make. A friend and supporter recalled the president saying he could see no alternative. He had "tried every way he knew to avoid war," had "considered every loophole of escape," but everything he tried the Germans had "deliberately blocked . . . with some new outrage." Was there anything else he could do? His visitor, Frank Cobb, editor of the New York *World* and a longtime supporter, said there wasn't. The president's "hand had been forced by Germany" and now "we couldn't keep out." "Yes," Wilson said, "but do you know what that means?" The president then proceeded to list all the ways America's entry into the war would be a disaster, both for the world and for Americans. The majority of Americans would go "war-mad, quit thinking and devote their energies to destruction." They would "forget there was such a thing as tolerance. To fight you must be brutal and ruthless, and the spirit of ruthless brutality will enter into the very fibre of our national life, infecting Congress, the courts, the policeman on the beat, the man in the street." The president feared the Constitution would not survive, that "free speech and the right of assembly would go. He said a nation couldn't put its strength into a war and keep its head level; it had never been done." He feared that his domestic reform program would be the first victim. "War means autocracy." The government would be dependent upon the steel, oil, and financial magnates, and so they would "run the nation."[42] America, he feared, "couldn't fight Germany and maintain the ideals of Government that all thinking men shared. He said we would try it but it would be too much for us."[43] What Wilson saw dying was the vision that American internationalists had long cherished, the idea of America not as a normal great power but as the disinterested arbiter of peace, a great power "in the finer sense," as Lodge had put it. At the end of the conversation he exclaimed again, "If there is any alternative, for God's sake, let's take it." Cobb recalled, "Well I couldn't see any, and I told him so."[44]

With his decision made, Wilson set these thoughts aside and began preparing the nation for war. He asked his advisers to ready the necessary legislation. He instructed Navy Secretary Daniels to establish a confidential liaison with the British Admiralty to work out means of protecting ships against submarine attack. He ordered American diplomats and relief workers out of Belgium. A few days later the secretary of war submitted a new army bill that federalized the National Guard, increased the strength of the regular army, and authorized the drafting of a "first unit" of 500,000 soldiers. The newspapers reported on plans being formulated to deploy the U.S. Navy to help the Royal Navy protect the transatlantic trade and take on the submarines.[45]

As Wilson set about these preparations, public support for intervention swelled. Patriotic rallies were held across the country, including in the Midwest and Far West. Twelve thousand people at Madison Square Garden cheered for war. Thousands marched in Philadelphia, Boston, Chicago, and Denver. Prominent Democrats, Republicans, and even progressives joined in the call. On April 2, 1917, the anticipated war announcement prompted even greater celebrations. More than a hundred thousand people, along with half a dozen bands and hundreds of veterans in uniform, assembled on Boston Common and sang patriotic songs while crowds surged through the city streets. Those old enough to remember said there had been nothing like it since the outbreak of the war with Spain. In Chicago, students turned from their lessons to sing patriotic songs and listen to speakers. In Kansas City, 60,000 schoolchildren pledged allegiance to the nation and saluted the flag. In Philadelphia, one thousand students from the University of Pennsylvania held a patriotic rally and pledged their loyalty to the government. In Ann Arbor, Michigan, Henry Stimson spoke before what was described as "the greatest patriotic meeting of students and townspeople ever gathered" since the firing on Fort Sumter.[46]

Leading Republicans supported war openly now, and for many of them it was a matter not only of interest but of morality and of honor. Root insisted the choice was either war or "submission to oppression." If the world determined that Americans were a "weak, flabby, divided, and indefinite people" who could be "insulted and assaulted and abused with impunity," then the tide of history would flow "over us and we are gone. Our country is gone. Our union is gone. Our liberty is gone."[47]

Antiwar dissent continued, especially out west. The Republican senator from North Dakota reported receiving a "vast number of antiwar telegrams, resolutions, and petitions." The Republican senator from Utah wrote in his diary that the impending war was "a very unpopular one."[48] In the days leading up to the president's address, peace groups and German American organizations engaged in intensive efforts to lobby against war. The Emergency Peace Foundation designated twelve

"Apostles of Peace" to travel the country speaking out.[49] When April 2 arrived, socialists gathered at Carnegie Hall "hissed and hooted" Wilson's anticipated request, shouting "No! No! Never!" and calling for revolution. Great numbers of antiwar protesters descended on the nation's capital to express their opposition and, if possible, to block the proceedings. One group entered a Senate office building and got into a fistfight with Henry Cabot Lodge, who got in his own licks and emerged happy, a momentary hero of the prowar patriots. The authorities had to scramble to regain control of the situation. "Two troops of the Second Cavalry guarded the approaches" to the Capitol building. Secret Service officers, postal inspectors, and police swarmed the area to "see that no harm from the lovers of peace befell the President of the United States in his discharge of a constitutional duty." The audience admitted to the Capitol building was "carefully sifted."[50]

The protesters represented a minority, however, and a beleaguered one. Across the country, and especially in the East, newspapers denounced them as pro-German traitors. Princeton's president refused to let former Stanford president David Starr Jordan speak on the campus, and when he did speak at a nearby church, he was booed by the assembled students.[51] Those western Republican senators who noted the apparent unpopularity of the war in their states nevertheless came out in support of war. By the time Wilson went to Congress to seek support, the nation had for the most part come around to a "single way of thinking."

With the protesters kept at bay, inside the Capitol building on April 2 official Washington was assembled as never before in recent memory. All the justices of the Supreme Court sat in the front row, along with the cabinet. The foreign diplomatic corps, which did not often attend such events, was out in force. At one dramatic moment the doors to the House chamber opened and in marched the senators, led by the vice president, "each man carrying or wearing a small American flag." (La Follette and one or two other senators were conspicuously without flags in their lapels.) When the president was finally announced, the Supreme Court justices stood up and led what became a raucous ovation, with members of Congress not merely cheering but screaming. It was two minutes before Wilson could begin.[52]

Wilson uncharacteristically delivered his speech with little emotion, reading from his typed manuscript, and only occasionally looking up from the pages. As with his previous speeches on the subject, the case he made was for the most part narrow and specific, even legalistic. The justification for war was based almost entirely on the issue of Germany's submarine warfare. "On the 3d of February last," he began, "I officially laid before you the extraordinary announcement of the Imperial German Government that on and after the 1st day of February it was its purpose to put aside all restraints of law or of humanity and use its submarines to sink every vessel that sought to approach either the ports of Great Britain and Ireland or the western coasts of Europe or any of the ports controlled by the enemies of Germany within the Mediterranean." He reminded Congress that after the Sussex Pledge on April 1916, the German government "had somewhat restrained the commanders of its undersea craft." Now those restraints had been lifted. "Vessels of every kind, whatever their flag, their character, their cargo, their destination, their errand, have been ruthlessly sent to the bottom without warning and without thought of help or mercy for those on board, the vessels of friendly neutrals along with those of belligerents."

Wilson admitted that he had been "for a little while unable to believe that such things would in fact be done by any government that had hitherto subscribed to the humane practices of civilized nations." Nations had long worked to establish a set of laws, albeit imperfect, that could govern the seas, "where no nation had right of dominion and where lay the free highways of the world." Germany had now "swept aside" those laws. Wilson emphasized that he was not talking about the loss of property so much as of the "wanton and wholesale destruction of the lives of noncombatants, men, women, and children." Property could be paid for and replaced. People's lives could not be. "The present German submarine warfare against commerce," the president continued, was really "warfare against mankind."

Americans now had to choose how to respond. Although American ships had been sunk and American lives had been lost, Wilson wanted the United States to act with "a moderation of counsel and temperateness of judgment," and with no desire for revenge. But there was "one choice we cannot make," he declared. "We will not choose the path of submission and suffer the most sacred rights of our nation and our people to be ignored or violated."[53]

No one heard him finish the sentence. At the word "submission," the *New York Times* reported, the chief justice of the Supreme Court, Edward White, rose up "with an expression of joy and thankfulness on his face." He raised his hands high in the air and "brought them together with a heartfelt bang." The members of the House and Senate, and all those in the galleries of the House chamber, "followed him with a roar like a storm. It was a cheer so deep and so intense and so much from the heart that it sounded like a shouted prayer."[54] Many years later the British ambassador said he would "never forget the cheer I heard at those words."[55] Cheers erupted again when Wilson asked Congress to accept on behalf of the nation "the status of belligerent which has been thrust upon it." Cheers again when he called for "the utmost practical cooperation" with the Allies, and again when he called for "the extension to those governments of the most liberal financial credits." And cheers again when he called for establishing a "first unit" of 500,000 soldiers to be selected by a universal draft.[56]

As far as his audience was concerned, Wilson could have stopped there. He had made the case for war, and Congress was ready to approve. He had not yet said a word about democracy, nor about America's future role in establishing peace, nor about a league of nations. He had talked only of German submarine warfare and its effect on American rights and commerce, on the rights and commerce of other neutrals, and on "the free highways of the world." It was to defend those rights that Wilson asked Congress to "accept" the state of belligerency into which Germany had driven the United States.

It was only in the second half of his speech that Wilson went beyond the reason for American intervention and explained what the war meant for the United States and what he hoped the war would accomplish. The days of American neutrality were over, he said. It was neither "feasible" nor "desirable" when the peace of the entire world was at stake and when the democracies were threatened by "autocratic governments backed by organized force." The United States could never trust such a government or treat it as a friend. Indeed, so long as an autocratic Germany remained powerful, "always lying in wait to accomplish we know not what purpose," there could be "no assured security for the democratic governments of the world." The world had to be "made safe for democracy."[57]

The revolution in Russia offered new hope. The Russian people had "shaken off" their autocracy and joined the forces "fighting for freedom in the world, for justice, and for peace." At some point, the German people would join them. The present war was a fight to protect those who desired democracy, "the German peoples included." A "steadfast concert of peace" could be maintained only by a partnership of democratic nations." No autocratic government "could be trusted to keep faith within it or observe its covenants." Only "free peoples" could "hold their purpose and their honour steady to a common end and prefer the interests of mankind to any narrow interest of their own."

To call for war, Wilson concluded, was "a distressing and oppressive duty." There were "many months of fiery trial and sacrifice ahead of us." Nevertheless, he declared, "the right is more precious than peace." Americans would "fight for the things which we have always carried nearest our hearts—for democracy, for the right of those who submit to authority to have a voice in their own governments, for the rights and liberties of small nations, for a universal dominion of right by such a concert of free peoples as shall bring peace and safety to all nations and make the world itself at last free." America was "privileged to spend her blood and her might for the principles that gave her birth and happiness and the peace which she has treasured. God helping her, she can do no other."

Wilson's address was widely applauded both at the Capitol and across the country. Even Lodge and Roosevelt offered congratulations. Lippmann was ecstatic. The president had put "the whole thing exactly where it needed to be put." Others had "led nations to war to increase their glory, their wealth, their prestige," but no other statesman had "ever so clearly identified the glory of his country with the peace and liberty of the world."[58] In the debate that followed over the coming days most members of Congress agreed that while the proximate cause of America's entry into the war was Germany's sinking of American ships, more was at stake than legal rights. The "knell of autocracy" had been sounded, Republican congressman August P. Gardner declared. The "democracies of the world" were "struggling to their feet," and Americans could no longer let the Allies "bear our burden in this war for liberty." Lodge proclaimed that the United States had to unite with those "fighting the common foe in order to preserve human freedom, democracy, and modern civilization," all of which were "in grievous peril."[59] On April 6, the Senate voted 82–6 and the House 373–50 to approve the resolution declaring America in a state of belligerency.

The lopsided votes somewhat overstated the breadth and depth of enthusiasm. Some members felt under pressure to vote for war "when away deep down in our hearts we are just as opposed to it as our people back home."[60] An Arkansas senator railed against a war fever brought on by "the Eastern papers yonder."[61] The fifty-six members in both houses who voted against the resolution, though outnumbered, certainly made their voices heard. Some progressive Republicans like La Follette and Nebraska senator George Norris charged that the United States was "going into war upon the command of gold."[62] The Democratic Senate Foreign Relations Committee chairman, William Stone, came out against the resolution, as did the Democratic House majority leader, Claude Kitchin, who declared that with "half the civilized world . . .

now a slaughterhouse for human beings," the United States was "the last hope of peace" and the "only remaining star of Christendom."[63] German American organizations and church groups once again sent cards and telegrams to congressional offices pleading for peace. Irish Americans railed against the hypocrisy of joining with Britain to secure the rights of humanity while Irish rights were being trampled under the British boot.[64]

Although the opponents had a chance to air their views, however, they paid a stiff price. Norris was shouted down by his Senate colleagues with cries of "Treason! Treason!"[65] Democrats called on Kitchin and Stone to resign, accusing them of taking the kaiser's side and playing to their "large populations of German constituents."[66] The *New York Times* listed on its front page the names of all fifty House members (including the sole woman in Congress) who had voted no. La Follette and other prominent opponents of intervention were burned in effigy. Others, like Bryan, quickly accepted the inevitability of war.[67] Prominent German American leaders professed their community's undivided loyalty; even the German-funded *Vaterland* declared, "We are American, and . . . our common duty demands that we stand behind our Government."[68]

Support for the war was far from unanimous, therefore, but by historical standards, it was substantial.[69] Nor was it the product of irrational whimsy, jingoism, or blind passion. When Americans finally entered the war, they did so enthusiastically, but they had not rushed into war.

The president, the Congress, and the public had resisted taking any part in the European conflict for the better part of three years, and for twenty-three months after the sinking of the *Lusitania*. Before February or March 1917, most Americans opposed intervention. Most had believed they were largely immune from what happened in Europe. Even those who did not think the United States was immune tended to support only aid and money for the Allies. Meanwhile, whatever pro-Allied exuberance there was had been balanced and often checked by the influential German American and Irish American populations, as well as by anti-Russian Jewish and Scandinavian Americans.

If a majority of Americans ultimately changed their minds about entering the European conflict, it was largely in response to German actions. American historians naturally tend to focus on American decision-making in the lead-up to war, but it is important to understand that it was Germany's decisions, not Wilson's, that played the decisive role in bringing the two countries to blows. By January 1917 German officials knew Wilson was desperate to avoid war and would seize almost any excuse to stay out. As Churchill later observed, however, the Germans left him "no loophole of escape."[70] As the American diplomat Henry White put it at the time, "Sad it is to think how different events might have been with a little more wisdom on the part of a nation which seems capable of everything except that clear perception of the sentiment of other peoples which is so indispensable to success in international affairs."[71]

In fact, it had taken a lot to drive Americans to war. Churchill later lamented that if only the United States had joined the war in May 1915, after the sinking of the *Lusitania,* "what abridgment of the slaughter; what sparing of the agony; what ruin, what catastrophes would have been prevented; in how many million homes would an empty chair be occupied today; how different would be the shattered world in which victors and vanquished alike are condemned to live!"[72]

This was true, and yet Churchill also understood why it had taken so long for Americans to arrive at their decision: "Time and distance interposed their minimizing perspectives." Americans in their entire history had never sent a soldier to fight in Europe, and Churchill admitted it was a "frightful responsibility" for a "vast, unarmed, remote community" like the United States to launch itself into Europe's bloody conflict. The "real wonder" was that America entered the war at all.[73]

Whether the country had always been ready to follow Wilson to war whenever he decided to lead it, as some critics then and later claimed, was hard to know. Lansing, who had been miserable at the president's refusal to act after the sinking of the *Lusitania,* admitted in his memoirs that it "would have been a serious mistake" even to suggest going to war at any time prior to March 1917.[74] The British ambassador, who had closely followed the ebbs and flows of public sentiment, thought at the time that Wilson had taken the nation to war "at the earliest possible moment" and that it was "extremely doubtful whether the country would have followed him" if he had tried any earlier. Wilson prided himself on gauging the public mood, and he generally had a better grasp than other politicians, including even those as successful as Theodore Roosevelt.[75] His "political method," Spring Rice observed, had always been "to ascertain from various sources of information" what was the "predominant sense of the country." He had always tried "to follow very exactly the dictates of popular opinion" and had "never taken any action in which he was not moderately sure of at least the acquiescence of the majority." Spring Rice made this observation not to praise Wilson—as a Briton, he had suffered terribly from what he regarded as Wilson's failure to lead rather than follow the public—but simply to record a fact. Wilson himself asserted that although his chief aim was always to avoid war, his secondary aim, if war could not be avoided, was to do his best to ensure that the country went forward in "a single way of thinking."[76]

What produced this broad popular support for Wilson's decision to go to war? It was not fear for America's immediate security. No plausible case was ever made, or could have been made, that the United States was vulnerable to invasion by any of the belligerent powers. Even the staunchest advocates of preparedness acknowledged that a German attack on the United States could come only after the conquest of Britain and the destruction of the Royal Navy. That seemed unlikely when, less than two weeks into the war, the German High Seas Fleet retreated to its home ports and the Royal Navy retook control of the Atlantic. Even in the extremely improbable event that Germany did eventually conquer Britain, that would have taken some time, and then it would have taken still more time for the Germans to mount a transatlantic invasion. There is of course no evidence that the Germans ever seriously considered such a massive undertaking, but even if they had, the United States would have had plenty of time to prepare—as Wilson and others argued at the time.

Economics were a much bigger factor shaping American policies than security concerns. Wilson did not focus much on economic questions in his public statements. For one thing, he had a strong aversion to admitting that the United States, or he himself, ever acted out of "selfish" interests. Moreover, with peace progressives like La Follette and other critics constantly charging that the administration's policies were driven by Wall Street bankers and munitions makers, Wilson and others were loath to admit the obvious: that the pro-British tilt of the administration's policies did serve American commercial interests. Nevertheless, economic considerations were at the forefront throughout. Lansing and others repeatedly warned that a substantial reduction in trade with the Allies would produce a severe economic downturn, with consequent unemployment and unrest.[77] When trade was temporarily cut off at the beginning of the war, both Congress and the White House leapt into action to ameliorate the worst effects. When Bryan's initial embargo against loans to the Allies threatened a sharp reduction of Allied purchases, the decision was immediately reversed. When Britain and France desperately needed a new mammoth loan in the summer of 1915, the administration approved it lest Allied purchases of American goods cease. Even Wilson's cutoff of short-term loans to the Allies at the end of 1916 lasted less than three months, until the American ambassador in London warned that Britain was running out of gold to purchase American goods.[78] No one in a position of responsibility ever suggested a total embargo on trade with all the belligerents. This was not because such a thing was impossible. Two decades later, the authors of the Neutrality Acts, remembering the role that economic interests had played, insisted on banning all commerce with the belligerents—as Charles Beard would put it, "no trade no war." But in 1917 not even Bryan was prepared to crash the American economy, and Beard himself supported going to war.

Considerations of national honor also played a critical role. This was not a major issue initially. Americans did not feel at the beginning of the war that honor required them to go to war for Belgium or for the Allied cause. The British blockade did raise questions of honor, harking back to the confrontation in 1812, but for most Americans, as for Wilson, the matter of honor was outweighed by the financial and commercial benefits of trading with the British. The question of honor only arose in a serious way when Germany declared its submarine blockade. The German decree in February 1915 put Wilson and the United States in a difficult position, for it not only required Wilson to abandon what he considered America's rights as a neutral but to do so humiliatingly under the threat of German attack.[79] Following the sinking of the *Lusitania,* Wilson would speak constantly of honor, as did Roosevelt, Lodge, and many other politicians from both parties.

The question of honor was closely tied to American perceptions of their own power. It was one thing for a weak nation to let its civilians be killed on the oceans or be driven off the seas by a stronger force. A weak nation faced a choice only between submission and destruction. But a powerful nation had other choices. It did not have to submit, and if it did, it risked dishonoring itself, in the eyes of other nations and, most importantly, in the eyes of its own people. Considerations of honor had long played a role in American foreign policy, as it has for all great powers throughout history. American leaders openly proclaimed that their war against Britain in 1812 was very much a matter of honor, and it was to honor that McKinley appealed when he declared it America's responsibility to alleviate Cuban suffering "ninety miles from our shores." Wilson learned his lesson the hard way. He was harshly criticized when he carelessly suggested that America was "too proud to fight" in May 1915; he received a thunderous ovation two years later when he declared that Americans "would not choose the path of submission."

What was remarkable, and to critics like Roosevelt appallingly shameful, was not that Americans ultimately went to war partly for reasons of honor, but how long and hard they tried not to let questions of honor drive them to war. For two years after the initial German decree, and for twenty months following the sinking of the *Lusitania,* Wilson had gradually pared down his demands to the bare minimum—from requiring a complete cessation of submarine warfare to asking that German submarine commanders not target passenger ships, to asking that they at least abide by the rules of cruiser warfare, to, in the end, asking only that American ships be spared. Much to his own advisers' dismay, he was reluctant to act even when Germany crossed successive lines that he had drawn. But when Germany after February 1, 1917, refused even to spare American vessels, Wilson believed he could back down no further. He had all along warned Americans that although he would do his best to preserve both peace and the nation's honor, as they wanted him to do, if forced to choose he would choose honor. By the time he made that choice, in March 1917, he had most of the country with him. If Americans were to "retain our self-respect" and not be regarded by the world as "a nation of degenerates and cowards," one congressman insisted, then there was "nothing else to do but acknowledge that Germany has made war on us and accept it."[80] Even Ambassador Bernstorff acknowledged that Wilson could not have taken any other course.

The Germans bore significant responsibility for painting Wilson into this corner, therefore, and this was only one of Germany's many tragic errors. By their actions both before and during the war, they created the context in which it was possible for many in the Western democracies to view Germany not only as a menace to their economy or to their security but to their very "civilization." It was not that the British and French didn't also use poison gas or aerial bombardment as weapons in the war, or that the Allies never committed atrocities. Yet there was no getting around the fact that Germany not only used these weapons first and committed the earliest and most systematic atrocities, but that they made it clear that they considered these violations of norms and conventions, just as they considered the violation of Belgian neutrality, as at worst the regrettable necessities of war. It was the Germans who called their submarine warfare "ruthless." It was the Germans who defended the use of terror or *Schrechlichkeit* as a tool of warfare against civilian populations. It could be said that the Germans were simply less hypocritical than their enemies—and the Germans did take pride in their unflinching "realism." But as the historian Paul Kennedy has argued, the Germans were at the very least imprudent in appealing "so often to the code of naked *Machtpolitik,* to revel in their superior 'realism' and to deprecate the hypocritical Liberal concern about means and ends."[81]

A few Germans understood the problem. Bethmann had always feared that a return to "ruthless" submarine warfare would result in "the condemnation of the entire world," would isolate Germany and make it appear "the mad dog among nations." But most Germans were oblivious to the costs of their behavior. As Kennedy notes, other nations, and especially the liberal powers of the West, "were influenced by questions of right or wrong" even if many Germans thought these distinctions were meaningless in time of war. Because German leaders never understood this or took the moral questions seriously, "Germany actually crippled itself in power-political terms." Even so hard-headed an American as Roosevelt, who well understood the concept of *raison d'état,* believed there was such a thing as "'right' and 'wrong' in international matters," and that Germany's behavior, with its "cynical brutality and bad faith," was simply "wrong." Nations had to be guided by an "international social consciousness," he insisted, by a morality that considered their own interests "as well as the interests of others." They could not act "without regard to the essentials of genuine morality."[82]

The extensive German program of spying and sabotage in the United States was, from this perspective, ill-advised. The officials who authorized these activities may have regarded American outrage as naïve or even hypocritical, but even so were the advantages gained by German spying and sabotage not outweighed by the damage done to Germany's image among the public of the world's most important neutral power? Over time a growing number of Americans came to see Germany not as just another European power making war against other European powers but as a nation that did not share American beliefs about humanity and that was even a threat to civilized existence.

Wilson is often singled out by historians and international relations theorists for viewing the war as a struggle between democracy and autocracy. But he was far from alone. Charles Evans Hughes, the Republican candidate for president in 1916, denounced Germany's "onslaught on liberty and on civilization itself."[83] According to Henry Stimson, the United States was not going to war with Germany merely because it had suffered "an incidental injury, gross and unbearable as that injury may be." It was because Americans realized that what was at stake "upon the battlefields of Europe" was "the future of the free institutions of the world."[84]

The war and German actions produced the first serious discussions of world order and the role the United States should play in upholding it. Instead of thinking only about security of the homeland or whether trade routes were at a given moment open or closed to American commerce, some came to think in a broader way about the kind of international order or system that best safeguarded those interests over the long term.

Walter Lippmann spelled out these broader interests in the *New Republic* in the weeks following Germany's January 30 announcement. He argued that the United States had an interest not in legalisms about neutral rights but in the preservation of an "Atlantic Community" made up of the Western and mostly democratic nations on both sides of the ocean. It had an interest in seeing to it that "the world's highway" should not be closed either to Americans or to the Western Allies. It had an interest in defending "the civilization of which we are a part" against the "anarchy" that would result from a German victory. Germany was fighting for "a victory subversive of the world system in which America lives."[85]

As Lippmann explained, the task of defending "civilization" had until recently been shouldered by the British. Britain had served as the guardian of an "international order" that produced immense benefits for the United States. British domination of the oceans, "the world's highway," had made the United States and the other nations of the Western Hemisphere safe from attack and kept open the trade routes that had allowed American commerce to flourish. More than that, British maritime supremacy had created an entire "Atlantic world" in which Americans had become "inextricably bound." The British Isles, France, Italy, Spain, Belgium, Holland, the nations of Scandinavia, and the Americas had all become "one community" with a "web of interest" that united the two shores of the Atlantic.

Britain was no longer capable of playing this role, however. The rise of a powerful Germany in Europe and a powerful Japan in Asia had signaled the end of British control of the seas. The outbreak of war in 1914 and Germany's rapidly achieved dominance across Europe and into Eurasia signaled that the old balance could never be restored by the Europeans themselves. Germany had grown too powerful to be balanced even by the combined forces of Britain, France, and Russia. British power had not prevented the war, and even with all its resources thrown into the European struggle Britain had been unable to achieve more than a stalemate against German power. The days when Britain could hover outside the continent, bringing its naval power to bear as necessary to restore or maintain the balance, were over. That role, Lippmann argued, had now passed to America. In the new configuration of global power, only the United States could "guarantee the equilibrium" in Europe and thus "maintain at least a temporary security in the world."[86] Americans had been placed in this predicament less by any actions of their own than as a result of the seismic shifts that had occurred in the international configuration of power in the decades leading up to the war. But now only the United States had the capacity to defend "the world system in which America lives," and, therefore, it had come to be in America's interest to take on that role.

To play such a role the United States would have to institutionalize and make permanent the role of balancer that it had now taken on by entering the conflict. It had to assume responsibilities, permanent responsibilities, that it had hitherto shunned. And it had to be willing to employ power. Before the war the preferred international role had been that of disinterested neutral mediator, not the wielder of great power—the arbiter of peace, not the makeweight in the international system. The new role would require that Americans both have power and be willing to use it, and not to protect narrow and immediate interests but to preserve an order in which American interests could be protected. What exactly that would mean and, perhaps more importantly, whether Americans were actually prepared to take on such a role, were questions yet to be answered.

CHAPTER NINE

America and the "War to End All Wars"

"Nous voilà, Lafayette!"

—American soldiers, arriving in Paris, July 4, 1917

THOSE QUESTIONS for the moment took a back seat to the practical problems that Americans faced in the spring of 1917. All that mattered now was winning the war, and Wilson gratefully turned to that task with all his energies. After two years of wrestling over whether or not to intervene, he was relieved to be able to focus exclusively on the "concrete and definite" task of defeating Germany.[1]

No one in the United States knew quite what that would entail. Most assumed the American contribution would be chiefly financial—more loans, more sales of food, weapons, and munitions—and that the navy would help protect shipping routes. Few contemplated sending an American army to Europe, at least in part because, as Lodge observed, there was "no army to send."[2] Americans also had not realized what desperate shape the Allies were in. The Allies had kept the bad news mostly to themselves, lest they discourage Americans from entering the war on what could appear to be the losing side. But now that the Americans were in, the desperate requests poured in. Britain's foreign secretary, Arthur Balfour, cabled House that Britain was "on the edge of a financial disaster."[3] Admiral John Jellicoe informed Wilson's naval envoy that the German submarine campaign had sunk so much tonnage since February—900,000 tons in April alone—that Britain would not hold out much longer.[4] The French pleaded for American forces to fill their depleted front ranks. Trained or untrained, equipped or not, it didn't matter, General Joseph Joffre insisted: "We want men, men, men."[5]

The United States could move quickly on two fronts. One was naval. The first six American destroyers arrived off the coast of Ireland at the beginning of May. By June German submarine attacks had declined. And by July it was clear that the British would not be brought to their knees, as the German naval command had promised six months earlier. Americans would eventually supply over seventy destroyers to protect convoy shipments across the Atlantic. Those German officials who had warned that unrestricted submarine warfare would bring the United States into the war and actually increase American trade with Britain were proved right.[6]

The Germans also miscalculated on the financial side. Their assumption that the United States could not possibly provide more money as a belligerent than it was already providing as a neutral proved a serious miscalculation. As a neutral, Americans could only provide private loans, which were substantial but limited by investors' willingness to take risks. Official belligerency, on the other hand, opened the doors to the federal treasury. While private loans to the Allies had totaled a little over $2 billion during almost three years of American neutrality, with the declaration of belligerency in April 1917, Congress immediately approved a $3 billion loan for the Allies.[7] Over the coming eighteen months it would provide $7–8 billion more. Many members of Congress were more than happy to provide the loans, moreover, because they hoped that American cash alone might win the war "before we send our boys to the trenches." They didn't even worry about whether the Europeans would ever pay the loans back. As the chairman of the House Appropriations Committee put it, "If by giving them money we can save the sacrifice of American lives, I do not care about the repayment."[8] It was only thanks to the rapid and massive infusion of financing that the British were able to continue fighting.

It was easy to send ships and make loans. Sending troops was a different story. Once it became clear that the Allies would eventually lose without an infusion of American troops, military planners estimated that at least two million soldiers would be needed to turn the tide in the war. But first they would have to be trained, equipped, and then somehow transported across the Atlantic. Neither American industry, nor the military establishment, nor the civilian administration was ready for this mammoth undertaking—which was one reason the Germans had always discounted the risk of bringing the Americans into the war. Wilson had to establish new agencies to oversee production of weapons and munitions. He instituted price controls on food and other goods to prevent producers from profiting excessively from the soaring demand. He nationalized the railroads to prevent paralyzing transportation bottlenecks. For this he was accused by Republicans of instituting "state socialism," but even these efforts fell short. Mobilization still depended on the voluntary efforts of major industries, and those industries failed to produce. In the nineteen months of America's involvement in the war, U.S. soldiers never had their own field artillery, their own tanks, their own planes, or their own transport ships. Britain and France provided everything except the rifles they carried into battle.[9] Meanwhile, the government administration, both civilian and military, had more than its share of failures. New recruits were trained at hastily constructed camps, sometimes armed with broomsticks instead of rifles. When the winter of 1917–1918 came— one of the coldest in memory—many suffered in subzero temperatures without blankets and overcoats. Hospitals were without heat; there were numerous reported deaths from pneumonia and meningitis; trainees' morale plummeted.

In its first year in the war, the American contribution on the battlefield was practically nil. At the end of June 1917, 14,000 troops arrived in France and immediately went into training camps well behind the lines. The next group of Americans did not arrive until September. In their first contact with German forces, the green American troops were outfought and humiliated. (Pershing wept when he received the report.)[10] When in November the British and French commanders meeting in Paris determined that the United States had to send twenty-four divisions to France by spring, Wilson had to ask his secretary of war, "Is such a program possible?"[11] It wasn't. Not until February 1918, almost a full year after the United States entered the war, did significant numbers of American troops begin taking part in the fighting alongside the Allies. And it wasn't until June 1918 that enough troops began arriving to make a substantial difference on the battlefield, though even then it was not as many as the Allies wanted. On many occasions throughout the first year of American intervention in the war, the Allies seemed on the verge of collapse, begging for American troops that did not arrive.

Wilson and his administration took a beating at home for these failures. Members of Congress in both parties demanded the secretary of war's resignation and wanted to create a congressionally appointed "war cabinet" to take the war out of Wilson's hands. It was only because the

Democrats controlled both houses that the proposal never came to a vote. Despite much talk about politics being "adjourned" now that the country was at war, this was a myth. Politics in America is never adjourned. Lodge declared there was enough damning information about the Wilson team's corruption and incompetence "to defeat a dozen administrations." Roosevelt swept into Washington looking like a man ready to take charge and set himself up for the presidency in 1920.[12]

Could another administration have gotten substantial numbers of American troops to the front much faster, or improved the speed and quality of weapons production? It was hard to know. Wilson had done far too little to prepare for the possibility of war during the period of neutrality. When war came, he appointed too many cronies who were not up to the task. Neutral observers agreed that mobilization proceeded at "an incredibly leisurely pace, amid a welter of graft, confusion, waste, and extravagance."[13]

But the fault was not all Wilson's. The nation as a whole had not been ready to raise a large army, train it, arm it, and ship it across three thousand miles of ocean—and this was deliberate. Both the executive branch and the Congress were responsible for inadequacies that long predated the Wilson administration. There were only 220,000 soldiers on active duty when war was declared, and that was double the number when Roosevelt was in office. Those forces had been trained chiefly in the art of suppressing Indian tribes, fighting Filipino guerrillas, or unsuccessfully chasing Pancho Villa around northern Mexico. Even under Roosevelt little thought had been given to preparing for modern warfare against a great-power opponent. Opposition to the very idea of a "standing army" led Congress to resist reforms that might have increased the size of the professional army, created a trained reserve force, and improved efficiency in weapons procurement.[14] Institutionally, the government was, in the words of the *New York Times,* "muddling along with old forms, methods, and procedure" that were "obsolete."[15] Much of the weapons procurement problems stemmed from indecision and poor judgment by the military leadership.[16] Roosevelt and other preparedness advocates railed at Wilson, and with some justice. But even if he had done everything they demanded in 1915, it would not have made more than a marginal difference by April 1917. The fact was, most Americans had not seen the need to prepare for war, and neither Wilson, his predecessors, nor successive Congresses had worked very hard to persuade them.

Opposition persisted even after war was declared. When officials testified in April about the possible need for American troops in Europe, the committee chairman exclaimed, "Good Lord! You're not going to send soldiers over there, are you?"[17] A majority of Americans supported the draft—and draft day in early June went off better than expected, with ten million men between the ages of twenty-one and thirty reporting to their local boards—but there were large pockets of resistance, especially beyond the Appalachians. The Democratic Speaker of the House, Champ Clark, remarked that "in the estimation of Missourians" there was "precious little difference between a conscript and a convict." Political warfare took a toll as well. Passage of the draft law was delayed by several weeks because Roosevelt, the now sixty-year-old hero of San Juan Hill, insisted on once again raising his own force of volunteers and leading it into battle in Europe. Military professionals found the idea absurd, and Wilson was not about to hand the war over to a bitter political enemy and aspiring presidential candidate. But Republicans supported Roosevelt, and his friend Lodge successfully pushed an amendment authorizing the plan through the Senate. Opposition in the House killed the measure, but the wrangling over making Roosevelt commander of American armed forces in Europe delayed the start of conscription and, until late May, the naming of Pershing as the commander of the American Expeditionary Force.[18]

Financing the war was also a political minefield. Wilson and McAdoo wanted to fund the war mostly through increased taxes. Populists and progressives wanted the rich and the corporations to pay the entire bill. The Democratic majority leader pushed through a $1.8 million revenue measure that sharply increased the new federal income tax, which fell almost entirely on the well-to-do, imposed "war profits" taxes on munitions makers, and largely exempted the cotton and grain growers of the South and Midwest. Republicans and business leaders denounced this "monstrosity," and it took six months to get the revenue bill through Congress.[19] Meanwhile, the costs of the war escalated far beyond McAdoo's initial expectations. Federal spending went from $800 million to over $15 billion in the first year.[20] The administration had no choice but to rely on borrowing as well as increased taxes. The government raised more than $15 billion by selling war bonds, known as Liberty Loans.[21] Lodge did not oppose the loans but scored political points by noting that the American people were "mortgaging . . . the future of coming generations."[22]

The two parties delighted in charging one another with disloyalty and even treason. Because the country entered the war after two years of official neutrality, votes cast prior to the declaration of war now took on a different and damaging aspect. Support for an arms embargo and opposition to preparedness in 1915 and 1916 were portrayed at the time as efforts to keep America at peace. Now they were labeled "pro-German." Wilson took the lead in this retroactive blame-casting, compiling a list of past votes that he claimed served as an "acid test" that revealed "true loyalty and genuine Americanism."[23] In Wisconsin he campaigned against La Follette due to the senator's "questionable support for the dignity and rights of the country on some test occasions."[24] Wilson's vice president declared that the entire Republican Party of Wisconsin, indeed the whole state, was "under suspicion."[25] The "acid test" was a problem for Democrats, too. The largely Republican National Security League rated every member of Congress on six "acid test" votes, and Democrats generally fared worse than Republicans.[26] The Democratic Party leadership intervened in the Massachusetts primaries to block the candidacy of John F. "Honey Fitz" Fitzgerald because his strong Boston Irish ties left him open to charges of pro-German pacifism.[27] Party leaders begged Wilson to count only votes cast after April 2, 1917, but instead the president campaigned against a number of Democratic senators in the South, defeating two of the most persistent opponents of the war, James K. Vardaman of Mississippi and Georgia's Thomas Hardwick ("Herr Hardwick, the Kaiser's friend," Republicans called him). In doing so, he put his own party's control of the Senate at risk.[28]

Those who continued to oppose the war after April 1917 risked more than political attack. The Espionage and Sedition Acts of 1917 and 1918 made it a crime to obstruct the war effort, and that included public statements about the government, the Constitution, or the flag that could be deemed "disloyal, profane, scurrilous, or abusive." Congress and the nation's newspapers forced the administration to drop its demand for official censorship of war-related news—the papers chose self-censorship instead—but Elihu Root expressed the general sentiment: "We must have no criticism now."[29] Among the chief victims of the new legislation were socialists. Wisconsin congressman Victor Berger and three other socialists were indicted by a grand jury for "obstructing recruiting, encouraging disloyalty, and interfering with the prosecution of the war."[30] Socialist Party leader Eugene V. Debs was sentenced to ten years in prison for giving antiwar speeches. Meanwhile, Wilson's postmaster general stripped second-class mailing privileges from publications that "impugn[ed] the motives of the government" or suggested that the government was "controlled by Wall Street or munitions manufacturers."[31] Wilson's attorney general warned that opponents of the war should expect no mercy "from an outraged people and an avenging government."[32]

German Americans were also victims. The prominent role played by German American organizations during the period of neutrality, their outspoken opposition to Wilson's policies, and the links they were presumed to have, and in some cases did have, with the German government—all made them vulnerable to attack from both official and unofficial quarters. Before April 1917 it had been acceptable to blame all sides, to argue that Germany was as much a victim as France, to deny claims of German atrocities in Belgium. After April 1917 official propaganda and public opinion decided that Germany alone was guilty. Prominent historians, including Charles A. Beard and Carl L. Becker, wrote essays under government auspices that documented Germany's responsibility for the war. The Committee on Public Information, created as an independent government agency and headed by the progressive George Creel, organized thousands of "four-minute men" to speak to audiences in local movie theaters, criticizing Germany and arousing patriotic support for the war effort. Government-issued cards and posters portrayed the "Hun" as blood-thirsty killers, with captions that read "HUNS KILL WOMEN AND CHILDREN!"[33] States banned the teaching of German in schools, on the grounds that it was a language "that disseminates the ideals of autocracy, brutality and hatred."[34]

Hostility to all things German was further inflamed by the widespread fear of spies and saboteurs. Sensational stories recounting German efforts to blow up munitions plants, poison waters, or engage in propaganda broke into the news every month, and sometimes every week. Over the course of two days in January 1918 the *New York Times* reported the arrest of a man presumed to be a spy (he spoke "broken English") hanging around the Navy Yard; the dispatch of two hundred soldiers to a New Jersey submarine plant in response to a rumored bombing plot; and the transfer of thirty-six convicted German "spies, agents, propagandists, and other enemy trouble makers" from Ellis Island to a Georgia prison camp, all of them reportedly singing *Deutschland über Alles* as their ferry passed the Statue of Liberty.[35] In this atmosphere of high anxiety and suspicion many German Americans were frightened for their lives, and with reason. A mob in a town outside St. Louis murdered a German-born American citizen on suspicions of disloyalty stemming from an overheard conversation. Defense attorneys for the arrested perpetrators called it a "patriotic murder"; and the jury acquitted the killers in twenty-five minutes. The *Washington Post* editorialized that although murder was excessive, the events revealed "a healthful and wholesome awakening in the interior of the country."[36]

Wilson had warned that Americans would "forget there ever was such a thing as tolerance" once they entered the war, and he played no small part in fueling that intolerance.[37] But he was also its victim. As Republicans enjoyed pointing out, his own past statements could not pass the "acid test." Had he not declared the nation "too proud to fight" after the sinking of the *Lusitania*? Had he not suggested many times that there was nothing to choose between the two sides in the European struggle? Had he not argued, as late as January 1917, that the best result would be a "peace without victory" that left Germany undefeated? Had he not opposed preparedness, and might not his failure to prepare the nation adequately before the war, and to mobilize effectively after war was declared, be signs that he was not committed to an all-out victory even now? Wilson constantly had to parry charges that he was not really committed to the complete annihilation of Germany. This would pose problems for Wilson politically, and it would also limit his diplomatic maneuvering room at the end of the war and during the peace talks that followed.

Meanwhile, as Americans squabbled and failed to ship troops to Europe in a timely manner, the Allies' situation grew steadily more dire. The quick infusion of American finance in April 1917 had helped stave off immediate collapse, but the months that followed were the darkest and most perilous of the entire war.

The biggest crisis came on the eastern front. Hopes that the February Revolution would bring new energy and resolve to the Russian people's struggle against Germany proved misplaced. Discipline at the front broke down when the Petrograd Soviet of Workers' and Soldiers' Deputies, set up as an alternative to the Russian Provisional Government, issued an order that soldiers need not obey their officers. After the German government smuggled the Bolshevik leader Vladimir Lenin into Russia, he rose to prominence chiefly by calling for an immediate end to the war, which others had been reluctant to do while the Germans were invading the motherland. By the summer of 1917, the Russian army began to weaken as hundreds of thousands deserted and the rest refused to carry out further offensives. When a new leader of the Provisional Government, Alexander Kerensky, ordered an ill-advised offensive in July that the Germans crushed, the Russian war effort all but collapsed and Lenin soon took power.

Russia was not the only Allied nation suffering morale problems. A disastrous Allied offensive on the western front in April and May 1917 produced almost 200,000 French and British casualties and led to a mutiny among French forces. The battered and demoralized troops refused to go "over the top" in further bloody offensives and for most of the remainder of the war would do no more than hold the line.[38] To take the pressure off the paralyzed French army, British generals launched new offensives in Belgium at the end of July. The Germans were pushed back several hundred yards, then held the line in the muddy slaughter of Passchendaele.[39] British casualties were massive, morale was badly shaken, and criticism mounted against the generals' sacrifice of tens of thousands of lives in these futile assaults.[40] Still more devastating for the Allies was the defeat of the entire Italian Second Army by Austrian and German troops at Caporetto in October. Finally, in the biggest blow of all, the Bolsheviks seized power in November and effectively took Russia out of the war. In November 1917, Colonel House reported from a meeting of the Allied military chiefs in Paris that unless there was a rapid "change for the better," the Allies could not win.[41]

The Central Powers also suffered in 1917. The Germans had just come through the 1916–1917 "Turnip Winter" in which tens of thousands starved, and severe malnutrition continued into the summer. Strikes plagued Berlin and other cities in April, with as many as 300,000 workers, the majority from munitions factories and related war industries, walking off the job. As in Russia, the workers in Leipzig followed the revolutionary Spartacists calling for "Peace! Freedom! Bread!"[42] In January 1918 massive strikes across Germany again saw workers demanding peace and political reform. The Austrian government was looking for a peace settlement, and feeling out the various Allied governments, because they were not confident they could fight much longer—"our weeks and months are numbered," the Austrian foreign minister told Bethmann.[43]

Pressures for a peaceful settlement came from all sides. In July 1917 in Germany an alliance of the moderate Catholic Zentrum party with progressives and socialists—together controlling nearly two-thirds of the seats in the Reichstag—passed a "Peace Resolution" calling for a "peace of understanding and the permanent reconciliation of the peoples" and a rejection of "forced acquisitions of territory" and "financial oppression."[44] In November in Britain a distinguished former statesman, the conservative Lord Lansdowne, rattled the government with a public plea for a negotiated peace, warning that continuing the war much longer would "spell ruin for the civilised world."[45] Morale on the home front was not just a political problem. It was also a war-fighting problem. To fill depleted military ranks, governments needed to conscript more men, young and old. To produce weapons and materiel, workers had to put in longer hours. After almost three years of horrific military stalemate, populations in all the warring states were demanding to know how long the war was going to last and, perhaps just as important, what exactly they were suffering, slaving, fighting, and dying for.

For the Allies that question became more complicated when the Russian Bolsheviks seized the tsarist government's diplomatic archives and revealed the extensive secret agreements that the Allies had made with Russia and each other for the postwar division of German, Austrian, and Ottoman territories. The French were to get Alsace and Lorraine, taken by Germany in 1871, as well as control of the mineral-rich Saar basin, which lay in German territory. In the Sykes-Picot agreement of 1916, Britain, France, and Russia agreed to divide up the remainder of the Ottoman Empire, with Britain getting Mesopotamia, parts of Persia, Palestine, the Transjordan, and Arabia; France getting Syria; and Russia getting Armenia and Kurdistan. Russia also demanded control of Constantinople and the Turkish straits. Other agreements were essentially bribes to bring other countries into the war on the Allied side. Italy demanded pieces of the Austro-Hungarian Empire, including the German-speaking Tyrol and the Slavic regions on the Dalmatian coast, parts of Albania, and some islands in the Adriatic. Japan demanded retention of territories in China's Tsingtao region, seized by Germany in the international suppression of the so-called Boxer Rebellion.

For the British and French, these treaties were different from war aims. Neither the British nor the French were fighting the war in order to expand their empires—though Italy and Japan arguably were fighting for that reason. The people of France were defending themselves from invasion; the British had entered the war to defend France, liberate Belgium and the Low Countries, and prevent German hegemony on the continent. They were also fighting to defend their democracies against what they regarded as a threat to "civilization." The trading of territories at the end of wars was a centuries-old European tradition, and it was not unusual for allies to decide beforehand who would get what, partly to strengthen allied solidarity. But these were ancillary to the main purposes of the war.

Revelation of the secret treaties was nevertheless highly embarrassing to the Allied governments. To those who had already concluded that the war was futile, and therefore immoral, the idea that millions should continue suffering and dying so that greedy empires might expand their territorial holdings, trading whole peoples back and forth as if they were chattel, was appalling. It was hardly in keeping with the professed goals of liberation and defense of "the people" against militarist autocracy. The Bolsheviks and like-minded revolutionaries across Europe insisted that the bloody war continued only to serve capitalists and imperialists. Lenin and Trotsky denounced the "secret diplomacy" of the "governing classes" and called for a "peace without annexations or indemnities" based on the "self-determination of peoples." They also called on the "proletarians of all countries" to unite and overthrow their governments.[46] And many liberals and socialists across Europe and in the United States harkened to the call. The Russian Revolution still seemed to many a triumph of progressivism and democracy, the empowering of workers and peasants against the tyranny of the tsar and the brutality of unfettered capitalism. "Self-determination" became the rallying cry for all those who sought a rapid and "just" end to the war. In late December 1917, the British Labour Party echoed the Bolsheviks in denouncing secret diplomacy and the "war of conquest," and called for a peace based on "self-determination" and the formation of a League of Nations.

With the liberals and the Left in Britain and the United States up in arms, and with the broader public's morale sinking, the embarrassed and embattled Allied governments felt compelled to respond lest support for the war, and for them, collapse. In early January, Prime Minister Lloyd George gave a speech to trade union leaders declaring that any territorial settlement must be based on the "right of self-determination." He also insisted that the Allies sought no indemnities beyond the cost of reparations, that their only goal was a just and durable peace and the creation of "some international organization" after the war to preserve it.[47]

It was not Lloyd George to whom European liberals and socialists looked for leadership, however, but to the American president. Wilson was the hero of liberals on both sides of the Atlantic. They recalled Wilson's "peace without victory" speech from January 1917, in which he had denounced the handing of "peoples about from sovereignty to sovereignty as if they were property" and boldly proposed a "League for Peace." Members of the British Labour Party regarded the United States and Russia as the only powers seeking a "democratic and international peace." The Left on both sides of the Atlantic wanted Wilson to force the Allies to renounce their territorial ambitions and accept a liberal settlement of the war, one that was generous to the German people.[48] Many argued, as well, that if Russia was to stay in the war, Wilson needed to make clear to its people that they were not fighting and dying in "a capitalist war for colonies, markets, and concessions."[49] Wilson's advisers agreed that he should launch a "liberal diplomatic offensive" that would at once "placate the moderate Left" in Britain and France, keep Russia in the fight, support liberal forces in Germany, and, not incidentally, make Wilson the leader of the democratic alliance. Ever since his January 1917 speech he had become the "spokesman for the liberals of the world," House and Lippmann argued. Now those liberals again needed to be shown the way forward.[50]

Wilson was ready to do his part to bolster liberal support for the war, but he did not entirely share the views of his left-leaning supporters. For instance, although he shared their hopes for a democratic revolution in Russia and sympathized with the plight of Russian workers and peasants, unlike many on the Left, he took a dim view of Lenin and the Bolsheviks, who were unremittingly hostile to the Western democracies, were not democrats themselves, and, most alarmingly, seemed determined to take Russia out of the war. Like Allied leaders, he feared the "Bolsheviki," and one of his principal goals was to diminish their appeal both inside and outside Russia.

More significantly, he was no longer interested in a "peace without victory," nor was he especially concerned about providing the most liberal settlement possible to the Germans. He was skeptical of the German liberals and socialists who, despite their "peace resolution," had done nothing to slow the German war machine. Wilson also knew that the American people favored total victory and that Roosevelt and Lodge would denounce anything short of that. But he also believed that a total victory over Germany was essential.[51] Speaking to the American Federation of Labor in November 1917, he affirmed that he wanted peace. What he opposed, he said, was "not the feeling of the pacifists, but their stupidity. . . . I want peace, but I know how to get it, and they do not." The only way to get it was to defeat Germany and remove its "military masters."[52] If some on the Anglo-American Left, like Britain's Ramsay MacDonald, were dismayed by Wilson's "complete reversal" of his "old views regarding the war and its settlement," this only further demonstrated how, on these matters at least, Wilson was not a man of the Left.[53]

The speech he gave on January 8, 1918 would become famous for its Fourteen Points. It was widely misunderstood at the time by supporters and critics alike, as well as by later historians. They thought it was but a continuation and fleshing out of the ideas he had broached a year earlier in his "peace without victory" speech. Liberals focused on his vague assurances that the United States and the Allies had no "jealousy of German greatness," that so long as the German people would accept "a place of equality" and not "a place of mastery" and join in "covenants of justice and law and fair dealing," they could attain any "achievement or distinction of learning or pacific enterprise." They ignored the terms that he put forth as the basis for any "stable and enduring peace." Peace could not be made with a Germany that ruled from "Hamburg to Bagdad," Wilson insisted. Under his Fourteen Points, Germany would not only have to be driven from Belgium and return Alsace and Lorraine to France. It would have to give up all the territory and influence it had acquired in eastern and central Europe, in Asia Minor and in the Middle East. The peace settlement had to rescue "the peoples of Austria-Hungary, the peoples of the Balkans, and the peoples of Turkey . . . from the impudent and alien dominion of the Prussian military and commercial autocracy." Any peace that permitted German hegemony in the east would only re-create the conditions that had led to this "iniquitous war."[54]

Since only a thoroughly defeated Germany would ever accept such terms, this was the furthest thing from a "peace without victory." Liberals might imagine that the Fourteen Points were an attempt to accommodate Berlin, but the Germans were under no such illusion. Kaiser Wilhelm called the Fourteen Points a "death knell" for Germany.[55] Wilson did not even want to negotiate with the present German government, which he believed had proven itself "without conscience or honor or capacity for covenanted peace." The Prussian autocracy had to be "crushed." Only when Germany was led by the people's "properly accredited representatives," ready to accept a just settlement and pay reparation for the "wrongs" the previous rulers had done—only then could the war be considered "won." On this fundamental point, Wilson and the Allies were in accord, and would be for the remainder of the war and during the peace negotiations that followed—much to the dismay of many American and British liberals. Wilson's Fourteen Points were not an attempt to save Germany from British and French vengeance but, on the contrary, were part of a pro-Allied diplomatic offensive.

If there was a gap between Wilson and the Allies, it was not on the question of Germany or Russia but on the future division of spoils. In his Fourteen Points, Wilson put the world on notice that the United States was not fighting to further the imperial ambitions of its partners. American soldiers were not fighting for *la gloire de la France* or to satisfy French (utopian?) desires for absolute and permanent security. Nor were they fighting to support Italian claims on the Dalmatian coast or to expand British imperial influence in Mesopotamia. Points Five and Twelve made clear that he would not endorse in advance all British, French, and Russian claims to parts of the Ottoman Empire or their division of the German colonies, nor would he endorse oppressive imperial domination of their existing colonies. Point Nine indicated that Wilson would not support all of Italy's expansionist demands. In an address to Congress a month before, he had stated bluntly that the future peace should not serve the "selfish claims" of the victors. This was the kind of statement that would later be treated as lacking in realism, typically "Wilsonian." Yet it was consistent with American interests. The United States, after all, made no claims on anything, anywhere. It did not seek territory either inside or outside Europe in return for its contribution to the war. By speaking out against the "selfish claims" of the victors Wilson was only insisting that Allies not aggrandize themselves at America's expense. Wilson understood that the Allies did not have "the same views with regard to peace that we have," and that this would become apparent once the war ended.[56] He would do nothing until then, but his Fourteen Points hinted at future disagreements.

Although both Lloyd George and Clemenceau publicly welcomed the speech, therefore—the latter declared that the Fourteen Points gave France "satisfaction in all the vital questions which concern her"[57]— privately they grumbled. The British prime minister took exception to Wilson's call for "freedom of the seas," which aimed to limit Britain's ability to use blockades against its enemies, and the French prime minister rejected any notion of tolerating German "greatness." But if the Allies, and especially the French, took a skeptical view of the Fourteen Points, it was not because they found Wilson's principles vague and otherworldly but because, on the contrary, they understood all too well the considerations of American interest that lay behind them. Both men recognized that even in this generally pro-Allied speech, which gave nothing away to the Germans, Wilson was staking out a strong independent position and that in an eventual peace settlement his views and American interests would have to be taken into account. They would not be organizing postwar Europe themselves but would have to bend to the desires of this figure who was at the moment arguably the most powerful man in the world.

No more than Wilson did they want to have a public fight over these issues, however. Victory was a long way off. In the early months of 1918,

German advances on the battlefield were a far more pressing concern. Indeed, if there was a problem with Wilson's Fourteen Points, it was that they bore no relation to what was actually happening on the battlefield in the winter of 1918. Although the Germans would later reach for the Fourteen Points as a lifeline, at the time of the speech they rejected them in their entirety.

CHAPTER TEN

The Great War Ends

I hope we may say that thus, this fateful morning, came to an end all wars.
—David Lloyd George

GERMAN LEADERS had some reasons for optimism in early 1918. Although their ranks were depleted and their people restive, they had successfully taken Russia out of the war. In mid-February negotiations with the Bolsheviks at Brest-Litovsk broke down, and the Germans launched a new offensive with fifty-two divisions advancing eastward. On March 2 they entered Kiev in the south and moved on Petrograd in the north. Lenin, fearing that the revolution was about to be obliterated under German boots, declared "we must sign at once. . . . This beast springs quickly."[1] The terms of the agreement signed on March 3 were a triumph for General Ludendorff and the high command and for German conservatives' most expansive territorial ambitions. The Russians were forced to give up all the Baltic provinces, Poland, Byelorussia, Finland, Bessarabia, Ukraine, and the Caucasus. These territories comprised one-third of Russia's population before the war, one-third of its arable land, and nine-tenths of its coal production.[2] With much of its border pushed back behind the Urals, Russia was effectively eliminated as a European great power.[3] Germany was now dominant across central and eastern Europe.

The harsh terms of Brest-Litovsk shocked and appalled Allied publics and their political leaders. Wilson called it a "moment of utter disillusionment" that ruled out any prospect of negotiating "a fair and just and honest peace" with Germany.[4] At the beginning of April 1918 he told Americans that it was no time for diplomacy but only for unrelenting war: "Force, Force to the utmost, Force without stint or limit, the righteous and triumphant Force which shall make Right the law of the world and cast every selfish dominion down in the dust!"[5]

The immediate effects of Brest-Litovsk were disastrous for the Allies. The collapse of the eastern front allowed Ludendorff to shift forty-two divisions totaling more than half a million men to the western front. This gave Germany a more favorable balance of forces in the west than at any previous time in the war. (The imbalance would have been even greater had the Germans not chosen to take and occupy so much Russian territory.) In the third week of March, Ludendorff threw everything he had into what he hoped would be the decisive offensive. With strength in numbers, air superiority, and two million shells filled with poison gas, the German attack drove the British, still understrength after the heavy losses at Passchendaele, back toward the Channel, splitting them off from the French further south and opening a path for an advance on Paris. By June 1, German forces had pushed their way to within forty miles of the French capital. The French government prepared to evacuate. General Pershing wrote to House: "The Allies are done for."[6]

The Allies pleaded for American forces to be rushed into the battle. Lloyd George warned Wilson that the war's outcome now rested entirely on the United States.[7] Wilson was eager to comply, but Pershing believed it would be a strategic mistake to throw American forces, still far below their eventual strength, into the lines in what he assumed would be a futile effort to stop the German advance.[8] Rather than "fritter away our resources," he wanted to hold his forces in reserve, build up the size of the army to three million, and then launch a triumphant counteroffensive in the following year. America's task would be to "win the war in 1919," Pershing believed, and largely on its own.[9] When France's General Ferdinand Foch asked if Pershing was "willing to risk our being driven back to the Loire?" the American general replied that he was. The time might come, he said, when the American army would have to "stand the brunt of this war," and it made no sense for it to be chewed up along with the Allies. Lloyd George was furious. It was "maddening" that with almost a million Americans in France (most in training camps behind the lines), the Allies faced defeat "because of the short-sightedness of one General and the failure of his Government to order him to carry out their undertakings."[10] In the end, and under some pressure from Washington, Pershing relented and agreed to allow about a third of the American forces then assembled in Europe—a little over 200,000—to operate in small formations under Foch's command. As he prepared to send troops of the First Division off to battle, he told them, "You are going to meet a savage enemy, flush with victory. Meet them like Americans. When you hit, hit hard and don't stop hitting. You don't know the meaning of the word defeat."[11]

Even in those smaller numbers, and despite what Lloyd George disdained as "a largely amateur United States Army," the involvement of American forces proved critical.[12] Although the Allies reeled under the German offensive in April and May, Ludendorff overestimated German advantages and underestimated the American contribution.[13] The Allies defended their positions more tenaciously than anyone could have reasonably expected given the condition of their forces, and the German advance, though deeper and more rapid than any since the beginning of the war, stalled for the same reasons as all previous offensives: the Germans simply lacked the manpower and equipment to sustain the drive. Although they came close to taking Paris, there was no decisive breakthrough. The British and French forces put up a staunch resistance, aided by the infusion of fresh American troops. In their first major encounter with the Germans at the Saint-Mihiel salient in April, American forces performed poorly, but at the end of May a brigade of four thousand American soldiers won a victory at Cantigny. Then in other major engagements at Château-Thierry and Belleau Wood in May and June, the Americans played critical roles in resisting the German onslaught and holding the line thirty miles from Paris.

By the summer, the war began to turn against Germany. The American intervention was decisive. The promise of a seemingly endless supply of fresh American troops provided the Allies a vital morale boost. As French soldiers watched U.S. marines hurl themselves at German positions at Belleau Wood—where Sergeant Dan Daly famously called out to his comrades, "Come on, you sons of bitches, do you want to live forever?!"—one remarked, "You Americans are our hope, our strength, our life."[14] The American presence, even in smaller numbers, acted as a "transfusion of blood" for the Allies at the front lines.[15] By July, Americans were arriving in France at a rate of 300,000 per month. Pershing formed the American First Army, which anchored the right flank of the French at Briey and Metz. Soon a Second and Third Army were formed.[16] At the pivotal Second Battle of the Marne, American forces helped hold off the German assault launched on July 15; it proved to be the turning point in the war. (The Third Infantry Division would thereafter be known as "the Rock of the Marne.") As the German chancellor at the time later recalled, when the Germans launched their major offensive in mid-July, they had expected they would soon be in Paris discussing terms

of peace. "That was on the 15th," but by the 18th "even the most optimistic of us knew that all was lost. The history of the world was played
out in three days."[17]

On July 18 Foch launched the counteroffensive that would eventually
drive the Germans back and produce the Allied victory. The fighting was
led by the French, still battling after four years of death and destruction.
But as one French general observed, the counteroffensive would have
been "an utter impossibility" without the Americans.[18] It was a matter
of sheer numbers. Throughout the war Allied forces had occasionally
been able to drive the Germans back, only to see their advances stall for
lack of troops to exploit openings and hold the newly gained territory.
The infusion of hundreds of thousands of American troops changed the
equation, allowing Allied armies to hold and then advance.[19] As German
analysts grimly noted at the time, "If only Hindenburg and Ludendorff
had behind them that inexhaustible strength in men and material which
Foch has, then the German soldiers would long ago have been sitting in
Paris and all over the world as victors."[20]

The effect on German morale was as devastating as the effect on the
battlefield. In mid-August Crown Prince Rupprecht of Bavaria, one of the
top army commanders, wrote from Flanders that the military situation
had deteriorated so rapidly that he did not believe the forces could hold
out through the coming winter; it was possible that a "catastrophe" could
come even earlier. His biggest worry was the Americans, who were "mul-
tiplying in a way we never dreamed of."[21] The American performance in
the battle of the Saint-Mihiel salient in mid-September, the first and only
American-led offensive in the war—with 550,000 American troops under
Pershing's command—left the German generals despondent. An officer
who visited Ludendorff on September 12 found him "so overcome by the
events of the day as to be unable to carry on a clear and comprehensive
discussion."[22] Hindenburg and Ludendorff then turned in desperation
to the navy, insisting that only submarines could win the war or prevent
total capitulation.[23] But that was now hopeless, too. The introduction of
some seventy U.S. destroyers over the previous year made possible the
new transatlantic convoy system that had proved vital to the war effort.[24]

By the end of September 1918, German forces were in full retreat.
Although the highly trained and disciplined troops pulled back in orderly
fashion, and continued to inflict heavy casualties on the advancing Allied
force, the army overall was in danger of collapse. Soldiers increasingly
sought to avoid contact with the enemy by surrendering, disappearing,
or feigning injury.[25] It was now possible to imagine not only defeat but

the war moving onto German soil, and once Allied forces occupied Germany, it would be at their mercy. The nation that had only been unified for forty-seven years might well be broken up again, as many in France were insisting. *Finis Germaniae,* the term Bethmann had used back in early 1917, was suddenly a real possibility. The situation was one of "utter hopelessness," Ludendorff concluded. "We cannot fight against the whole world," by which he meant Britain, France, *and* the United States.[26]

At the end of September Ludendorff and Hindenburg suddenly and frantically called on the kaiser and the civilian leaders to seek an immediate armistice. The civilians were stunned and disbelieving at first, for until that moment the military leaders had given little hint that things were going so badly. But by the beginning of October, they agreed. The chancellor sent a note to Washington requesting that "the President of the United States of America take the initiative in bringing about peace." The note further stated that the German government accepted Wilson's Fourteen Points "as the basis for peace negotiations."

The call for an armistice did not mean that Ludendorff had given up the struggle. He sought a pause in the war to halt the Allies' advance and allow the German military time to survive, regroup, replenish, and prepare for another day. Any peace settlement would be temporary. Nor did the acceptance of the Fourteen Points as the "basis" for negotiations mean the Germans were prepared to accept Wilson's terms. They had no intention of returning all of Alsace and Lorraine to France, for instance, nor would they concede any of the territory conquered in the east.[27] The Germans approached Wilson not because they genuinely saw the Fourteen Points as their salvation or believed that he still sought a "peace without victory," but because they assumed the American president would be a more accommodating negotiator than the French and British. It was not an unreasonable assumption. The Americans, who had suffered the least and had no territorial interests in the final settlement, were sure to be more flexible than the French, who had suffered by far the worst damage at the hands of German forces and who would demand not only compensation but a measure of revenge.[28]

Ludendorff and others knew that to entice Wilson they would have to accede to his repeated demand for a change of government. Ludendorff therefore orchestrated a "revolution from above." The chancellor resigned and was replaced by the more liberal-minded Prince Max von Baden, who enjoyed broader support in the Reichstag. The Reichstag itself was given some new powers. Leading members of the Reichstag majority, including two prominent Social Democrats, were brought into the cabinet. For Ludendorff, the "revolution from above" had the added advantage of ensuring that any armistice would be signed by civilians and liberals, not by the military.[29]

The Germans overestimated Wilson's willingness to act independently of the Allies, however, and they underestimated his determination to see Germany completely and irreversibly defeated. Although he did seek a peace that would be "as moderate and reasonable as possible" and worried that the terms imposed by a victorious France might be too harsh—and therefore unstable—his idea of a "moderate" peace bore no relation to what the Germans were hoping for.[30] He was also under great pressure at home. Public anger at the Germans had reached such a fever pitch by this point in the war—Lansing regarded Americans as "almost savage in their vindictiveness"—that Wilson was taken aback at "how war-mad" the once-pacific public had become.[31] The mere fact that he responded to the German note without first consulting with the Allies led to accusations from Republicans that he was about to accept a "German peace." Lansing urged Wilson to "keep in mind the coming elections" as he formulated his response to Germany.[32] Wilson resented the suggestion that he was being snookered by the Germans or had any intention of saving Germany from decisive military defeat, remarking that "it would relieve a great many people of anxiety if they did not start with the assumption that I am a damn fool."[33] To make this unmistakably clear, after conferring with the Allies, he sent two further notes insisting there could be no discussion of an armistice until German forces effectively made themselves defenseless and incapable of renewing hostilities. It was to be an "armistice" in name only. As House pointed out, it more closely resembled unconditional surrender.

Faced with Wilson's unexpectedly tough response, Ludendorff and Hindenburg argued for cutting off the negotiations, calling up another half-million conscripts, and resuming the fighting. The Germans' situation had deteriorated too far, however, and not only on the military front. Having begun the process of reform, "from above," the kaiser and the military were fast losing control of the process they had unleashed. The Berlin government continued making reforms to the constitution, hoping to satisfy Wilson and the public, but they were never enough for an increasingly radicalized German populace.[34] Revolution was in the air. Calls for the kaiser's abdication grew louder. On October 28 sailors from the High Seas Fleet at Kiel mutinied. Industrial workers then joined in rebellion against the authorities. By the first week of November revolts had spread to several major German cities. The revolutionary Left was on the rise. Soldiers' and workers' councils sprouted up across the country, modeled on the Russian soviets. The revolutionary Spartacist movement led by Karl Liebknecht seemed on the verge of establishing a parallel government, just as the Bolsheviks had in Russia. By November 2 prominent socialists warned that the question was no longer whether the kaiser would abdicate and make way for a German republic but "whether we shall have Bolshevism or not."[35] In Washington and London, top officials became concerned that the Spartacists were indeed following the Bolshevik model. Lansing feared "another Russian revolution" in Germany with all the "horrors" that entailed.[36]

To forestall a socialist revolution, and reflecting popular demands, Prince Max resigned as chancellor on November 9 and handed power over to the head of the Social Democratic Party, Friedrich Ebert. The kaiser, after being informed that the army would no longer follow his orders, abdicated the throne. Thus came to an end the five-hundred-year-old Hohenzollern dynasty, less than a year after the overthrow of the Romanov dynasty in Russia.[37] Ludendorff fled the country. Germany was now a republic, led, however shakily, by its liberals.

The new German government was prepared to accept practically any terms to end the fighting. The question for the Allies and the United States was whether to press ahead and invade German territory or impose an immediate armistice on terms that amounted to Germany's unconditional surrender. Wilson and his advisers favored an immediate armistice "moderate and reasonable" enough to help the new liberal German government survive.[38] Roosevelt and Lodge opposed an armistice and insisted on an invasion of Germany and a dictated peace. This was also General Pershing's view. He wanted Allied troops to enter Germany and continue advancing until German forces surrendered. An armistice, he feared, "would revivify the low spirits of the German army and enable it to reorganize and resist later on."[39] Pershing also envisioned American troops under his command leading the invasion and accomplishing the final conquest of Germany. In an act that bordered on insubordination, he sent his recommendation directly to the Allied commanders without first showing it to the president.[40]

In the end it was not Wilson who overruled Pershing, however, but the Allied military commanders. They had no desire to continue the fight one day longer than necessary. "I am not waging war for the sake of waging war," Foch told House. If the Allies could obtain the terms they wanted from Germany, then they had no right to "shed one more drop of blood." Both Clemenceau and Lloyd George dismissed Pershing's recommendation for continuing the war as "theatrical" and likely motivated by politics.[41] A top official in the Imperial War Cabinet, the South African general Jan Smuts, worried, like Wilson, that "the grim spectre of Bolshevist anarchy" was "stalking the front." The British also worried that the longer the war continued, the more powerful the United States would become and the more influence Wilson would have at the coming peace conference.[42] But above all they feared that the price of prolonging the war would be unacceptably high. The Allied armies were exhausted. Not fully aware of the dire condition of the German army, they believed the Germans would fight tenaciously to defend their homeland.[43] As House later recalled, the feeling among Allied commanders was that if Germany did hang on and the public later learned that the Allies had turned down an opportunity for peace in November 1918, "there would have been a revolution in every Allied country save the United States."[44]

On November 8, Allied military leaders and a German delegation met in a train car in the forest outside Compiègne, sixty miles north of Paris. The German side was led by Matthias Erzberger, the moderate leader of the Catholic Centre Party who had been brought into the government in early October. There were no high-ranking military officials with him. Ludendorff had fled and Hindenburg deliberately stayed away. The German civilian government hoped to negotiate better terms in this final negotiation but Foch stood firm. Erzberger contemplated holding out but was instructed to accept the Allies' terms by the new chancellor, the Social Democrat Ebert. The chancellor himself was following the advice of Hindenburg, who insisted that Germany had to agree immediately to whatever terms the Allies wanted, no matter how harsh.

The armistice agreement was signed on November 11. When the terms became known in Germany, Erzberger and the other civilians in the government were denounced for their shameful betrayal of the nation, including by military leaders who would soon claim that the German army had never been defeated by the enemy but had been "stabbed in the back" by the civilians. After the signing, General Pershing expressed his misgivings. "What I dread," he commented, was "that Germany doesn't know that she was licked. Had they given us another week, we'd have taught them."[45] Whether another week would have been enough was doubtful, but Pershing's concern was warranted. A great many Germans were surprised and embittered by the sudden surrender. They had witnessed no fighting on their soil and German military defeats had not been publicized, so most Germans did not understand what had happened. When Chancellor Ebert later welcomed the returning German troops marching in Berlin, he declared, "No enemy has conquered you!"[46] Many therefore regarded those who had signed the armistice as traitors to the fatherland. In 1921 Erzberger would be assassinated.

Whether or not Germans fully accepted their defeat, the Great War had finally been brought to an end. The Allies had triumphed. But the cost had been unimaginably high. Tens of millions had been killed, by war and the consequences of war, as well as by a global influenza pandemic that struck in 1918. With such unfathomable levels of death and destruction, it was natural that people soon began asking what had been the point of it all. Many hoped some way would be found to prevent such horrors from ever happening again. It was Lloyd George who put this universal sentiment into words, expressing his hope on the day of the armistice that on that "fateful morning, came to an end all wars." (Hence, the immortal phrase, the "war to end all wars," which would forever be mistakenly attributed to Wilson.)[47] In time many on both sides of the Atlantic would look back on the war as an act of collective madness.

It has become common, over a century later, to view the war in much that way, as a disaster into which the various participants stumbled or "sleepwalked." The perception that the war was meaningless and the victory hollow would play a major part in shaping American attitudes in the two decades that followed.

It is worth asking, therefore, what might have happened had the United States not intervened in April 1917. At that point in the war, the Allies had no prospect of defeating Germany and Austria-Hungary by themselves. In the most optimistic scenario, the war would have remained a stalemate. Eventually Britain and France would have been forced to sue for peace under terms that left Germany the dominant economic and military power on the European continent. Even as late as the summer of 1918 the German government was not prepared to give up most of its substantial conquests. Even if Germany agreed to withdraw its forces from France and Belgium, though not from Alsace and Lorraine, it would have retained control of a vast region stretching from the Rhine in the west to Ukraine in the east, with control, through the Austro-

Hungarian and Ottoman empires, of the Balkans, Constantinople, and the Straits, and with predominant influence in Asia Minor and the Near East. It would have controlled the great bulk of resources on the European continent, from the coal and iron ore of the Rhineland and the Saar Valley, to the wheat fields of Ukraine, and the oil of the Near East and Persian Gulf. If the peace settlement proved more favorable to Germany and more closely reflected the war aims outlined by Bethmann soon after the start of the conflict, German domination of Europe would have been even more comprehensive. Among the aims listed by Bethmann, the moderate civilian in the German hierarchy, was a Russia pushed back behind the Urals—which had already been accomplished at Brest-Litovsk. France was to be "so weakened as to make her revival as a great power impossible for all time." The French were to be forced to give up the iron ore fields of Briey, which were "necessary" to supply German industry. Belgium, if allowed "to continue to exist," would be "reduced to a vassal state," its military posts and North Sea coast placed at Germany's "disposal." Luxembourg would be incorporated into Germany. The Netherlands would be "left independent in externals, but be made internally dependent" on Germany. Poland, though nominally independent, would also be under German control, as would the "independent" states of Ukraine, Byelorussia, and the Baltics. Austria-Hungary was to be "a very junior partner." Finally, Germany would be the dominant economic power in "a central European economic association through common customs treaties to include France, Belgium, Holland, Denmark, Austro-Hungary, Poland, and perhaps Italy, Sweden, and Norway. . . . All its members would be formally equal but in practice would be under German leadership," thus cementing Germany's "economic dominance over *Mitteleuropa.*"[48]

German plans for a European customs union have led at least one historian to suggest that a German victory on these terms would have produced a moderate peace from which many Europeans would have benefited.[49] But Germany's treatment of conquered territory and peoples during the war suggests a less benign outcome. In Belgium, raw materials and semi-finished products, including copper pipes and iron roofs, were seized and shipped off to Germany. Belgian factories were systematically dismantled, partly "to eliminate Belgian competition in the future."[50] Of the 260,000 firms operating at the beginning of the war, only 300 survived at the end, and Belgian production of coke, iron, steel, lead, and zinc fell below 20 percent of prewar levels.[51] Meanwhile, beginning in the fall of 1916 over a hundred thousand Belgian men were rounded up and shipped to work in Germany or in labor battalions behind the front lines.[52] The original idea for a customs union, set out by the liberal Friedrich Naumann in 1915, had become "militarised" and was barely distinguishable from annexation and exploitation.[53]

Bethmann's memorandum stated explicitly that eastern Europe was to become a source of minerals for German industry and a region for colonization by Germany's expanding population. The peace settlement with Romania provided Germany a ninety-year lease on the conquered nation's oil wells. The treaty of Brest-Litovsk brought 90 percent of Russia's coal mines, 50 percent of its industry, and 30 percent of its population under German control.[54] In Poland the German army set out to establish a "sanitized ethnic barrier between Germany and the Slavic peoples to the east." A strip along the border was to be purged of Jews and Poles and resettled with Germans.[55]

Such were the ideas put forth by a German moderate. When Ludendorff, who was no moderate, effectively became military dictator in 1916, the "subjugation of economic life in the occupied areas . . . became ruthless." Factories in Belgium and parts of France were kept working to the point of exhaustion and then turned into scrap for shipment to Germany.[56] In the Baltic states, the native populations were taken off farms and dragooned into forced labor battalions. Without farmers to till the fields, a famine struck in the winter of 1916–1917. What food there was, however, fed the occupying army or was shipped to Germany.

These were actions taken in wartime and driven by wartime needs. Whether a victorious Germany, led by a victorious Ludendorff, would have pursued more moderate policies cannot be known. Germans' sense of their racial and civilizational superiority, already a key element of the "spirit of 1914," would have likely been enhanced by victory over Slavs, Anglo-Saxons, and the West generally. In terms of sheer economic, political, and military power, Germany's position in the world would have been immeasurably strengthened. A German *Mitteleuropa* reaching from Belgium to the Balkans, all dependent on and responsible to the rulers in Berlin, including a triumphant Hohenzollern dynasty, would have presented quite a geopolitical and geo-economic challenge to Britain, France, Russia, and even the United States. Even Germans of only moderate ambition during the war envisioned a vast colonial empire—a "German India"—perhaps in Africa that could "yield us all the raw material we need."[57] As one historian notes, it would have provided the foundation "on which Germany could compete for power on a worldwide scale."[58]

This was Britain's fear at the time. In June of 1918, Lloyd George's chief strategist painted a dire scenario: a "German-Austro-Turko-Bulgar bloc" that would be "master of all Europe and Northern and Central Asia up to the point where Japan steps in to bar the way." The Central Powers "under the hegemony of Germany" would then control "not only Europe and most of Asia, but the whole world."[59] One of the highest-ranking German generals during the war, Wilhelm Groener, reflected afterwards that Germany was defeated because it had striven for "world domination" without sufficiently preparing the German people for the struggle: "If one wants to fight over world hegemony one has to prepare ruthlessly with long term foresight."[60] This lesson would not be lost on influential Germans in the postwar period, including the Nazi political theorist Carl Schmitt and Adolf Hitler.

Had Wilhelmine Germany triumphed, it might well have acquired by 1919 what Nazi Germany acquired in 1941. This was what was at stake in the Great War. And this was what American intervention on the side of the Allies prevented. As Wilson put it in the summer of 1917, "the object of the war" was to deliver the world "from the menace and the actual power of a vast military establishment controlled by an irresponsible government."[61] As Roosevelt put it, Americans fought Germany in order to defeat an "arch foe of international right and of ordered freedom throughout the world."[62] The war had accomplished that.

To many, in retrospect, it all seemed for naught. Within twenty years the United States and its Allies would again be fighting a desperate struggle against an invigorated and well-armed Germany. That the costly successes of 1918 would be squandered completely over the next twenty years is one of the most astounding turns of events in modern history. But it should not diminish the importance and significance of the Great War for those who waged it, on both sides.

CHAPTER ELEVEN

America and the European Peace

*The more we can get the United States to realise her great responsi-
bilities for the peace and welfare of the world the better it will be for
us and for all mankind.*

—Canadian Prime Minister Sir Robert Laird Borden[1]

HOW WAS the European peace squandered? And how much responsibility did the United States bear for the breakdown? For decades historians
have generally answered: not much, except indirectly. Most tend to attri-
bute the breakdown of peace to the effects of the Great Depression, for
which the United States bears significant blame, but the modern consensus is that American policies in the 1920s were otherwise sensible and well
intended, even creative. Some suggest that the Republican presidents of
those years did their best to create a new liberal world order using only
peaceful diplomacy and America's enormous economic leverage. Their
tactics and strategy may have proved unequal to the challenge, especially
when the Depression struck, but the causes of the European breakdown
were to be found primarily in Europe, not in Washington.

This long-standing consensus, however, underestimates the central role
the United States played in the actions and calculations of all the European players. American power was so great in these years that both its
actions and its inactions had an outsized effect on everyone else. Americans were not isolationists in these years. They used their wealth and diplomatic muscle to pursue their economic interests. They established arms
control regimes; they tried to stabilize Europe through loans and financial maneuvers; they negotiated a treaty to "outlaw" war. Yet whatever
their intent may have been, their policies exacerbated existing problems
in Europe and created new ones.

Indeed, it is the contention of this book that the United States had it within its power to preserve the peace in Europe after 1919, and at a manageable cost. But for reasons having little to do with capacity, Washington policymakers would not take the steps necessary. And while it is customary to focus on the collapse of world order in the 1930s, it was in the 1920s that the peace was truly lost. By the time Franklin Roosevelt took office in March 1933, Hitler was already in power in Germany, and the self-described "have-not" powers, which included Italy and Japan along with Germany, had already embarked on their determined attempt to undo the fragile order that Americans were half-heartedly attempting to establish.

It is easy to miss the importance of that first postwar decade. The 1920s were a time of hope and optimism, in Europe as well as in the United States, when democracy seemed to be flourishing, when Weimar Germany was cooperating with erstwhile enemies in France and Britain to establish a stable peace, when the global economy seemed to be picking up steam. Yet it was in these halcyon years that the weak foundations undergirding the peace began to crumble.

The most important of those foundations was the new role of the United States. Prior to America's intervention after April 1917, the European conflict had reached its own internal equilibrium in the form of a military stalemate that left Germany the hegemon in Europe. That outcome reflected the existing power relationships in Europe, where even the combined power of Britain, France, and Russia could not defeat Germany but only check its further expansion—and perhaps over time not even that. The power of Germany had simply grown too great for the rest of Europe to handle. The intervention of the United States fundamentally changed the equation. Germany was not nearly strong enough to take on Britain and France plus the United States. The end of the war thus reflected the new balance of power in Europe and in the world.

That balance was even more lopsided in favor of the United States than before the war. Europe was in shambles. The end of the war revealed the full extent of the chaos and dysfunction into which Europe had driven itself. Almost all of the ancient dynasties collapsed or were overthrown—the Habsburgs, Hohenzollern, Romanovs, and the Ottoman sultanate—and their imperial lands were broken up into their component nationalities and ethnicities, few of which had any modern experience of sovereignty, let alone of self-government. Although the armistice was signed in November 1918, some countries were still at war over boundaries and other disputes well over a year into the "peace." The Poles invaded Soviet Russia, only to be driven back to a desperate if ultimately successful defense of Warsaw. Turkey was fighting Greece. Governments everywhere were unstable as the continuing shortages of food, millions of displaced peoples, and a deadly worldwide flu epidemic created a general sense of hopelessness. Riding these waves of discontent and despair, Mussolini launched his Fascist Party in 1919, denouncing the postwar Anglo-Saxon order as "a solemn 'swindle' of the rich against the proletarian nations."[2] On March 21, 1919, the Hungarian Communist leader, Béla Kun, overthrew Hungary's government and established the Hungarian Soviet Republic. The next month a Soviet republic was also established in Ukraine. In Germany, although moderate Social Democrats led the government, Communists rose up in January 1919 and again in March, with substantial support from Moscow. Battles raged in the streets of Berlin between government forces and 30,000 well-armed Spartacists.[3] On April 4, Communists overthrew the government of Bavaria and established a Soviet republic, which was then toppled by the German army on May 1. Lloyd George may have exaggerated the threat, but he was far from alone in fearing that "all Eastern Europe" might be "swept into the orbit of the Bolshevik revolution," producing a "vast red army under German instructors and German generals equipped with German cannon and German machine guns and prepared for a renewal of the attack on Western Europe."[4]

Even the victorious European great powers were badly and, in some cases, permanently damaged both by the conflict itself and by the overall shift in power globally. France lost 1.3 million soldiers in the war, a quarter of all men between the ages of eighteen and twenty-seven, with another 4 million wounded—a demographic catastrophe with long-term economic and strategic ramifications. The French industrial heartland was destroyed, damaging an economy already falling behind the other great powers. As the historian Adam Tooze observes, the war "confirmed the end of France's claim to be a power of the first rank."[5]

The British came out less crippled, but they had lost 700,000 killed and another 1.5 million wounded. Britain's postwar economy labored under a crushing debt and a depleted workforce. Its global empire was intact but vulnerable to both internal and external pressures.

The Europeon powers brought these weaknesses to the peace talks, desperate for some remedy. But they were divided. During the war the threat of Germany had bound them together. With that threat disposed of, at least for the time being, they resumed their long-standing impe-rial rivalry, scrambling for the remains of the Ottoman and German empires.⁶ Each accused the other of greed and sharp dealing. The British sniped that the French were "bitten with the mania for colonial expan-sion."⁷ Clemenceau called Lloyd George "a cheat" and denounced Brit-ain's "unbridled avarice."⁸ The French leader at one point accused his British colleague of acting like an "enemy of France," to which Lloyd George replied with a smile, "Was it not always our traditional policy?"⁹

Their most significant disagreement came over how to handle a defeated Germany. France's goal was to ensure that Germany would never again have the physical capacity to invade France, as it had twice in forty-three years. Germany had to be disarmed, occupied, impoverished, and dismembered. The French wanted Germany broken up into its pre-1871 component parts, with an independent Bavaria, an independent and reduced Prussia, and the Rhineland severed and transferred to France. At a minimum they wanted to see the Rhineland established as an inde-pendent buffer state under French economic, political, and military con-trol. Clemenceau made this demand explicit: "The Western frontier of Germany ought to be fixed at the Rhine."¹⁰ Along with the return of Alsace and Lorraine, and in addition, the Saar Valley and perhaps even Luxembourg, this would provide France the defense in depth that it had lacked in 1914. It would also deprive Germany of substantial raw materi-als and the industrial capacity that had allowed Germany to extend its economic hegemony on the continent.

The French also wanted to set up new allies on Germany's eastern flank to replace Russia, now in the throes of revolution and civil war. They sought the largest possible territory for a newly independent Poland, partly carved out of territories that had been German, and a new state of Czechoslovakia carved out of the ruins of the Austro-Hungarian Empire. German demography had been a French preoccupation before the war, made even more acute now that France's population of young and middle-aged men had been cut by a quarter in four years of fighting. The transfer of millions of German-speakers to the new non-German states, together with the separation of the Rhineland, would greatly reduce Germany's overall population. The French wanted Germany's economy crippled, too. The transfer of territories would deprive Ger-many of significant resources, particularly coal and iron, some of which would go to France. The French demanded sizable reparations, partly to pay back the Americans, partly to repair the damage the Germans had done to French industry, but partly to keep Germany down.

Clemenceau liked to say that he put his faith in that "old system" called "the Balance of Power,"[11] but what he and other French leaders wanted was not to restore the old European balance of power but to create a new *imbalance* of power to ensure that Germany could never rise again. To American and British observers, the French seemed bent on vengeance and self-aggrandizement at Germany's expense, and Clemenceau and Foch did exult at "the revenge at last obtained" for the humiliating losses of 1871.[12] The return of Alsace and Lorraine, the occupation of the Rhineland, the aspiration to add the Saarland and Luxembourg to France's domain—all were part of "a reassertion of national greatness," a return to France's "natural frontiers" as they had stood at the height of Napoleon's power, a reaffirmation of France as *la Grande Nation.*[13]

The British naturally did not share those goals—Lloyd George "had no intention of substituting France for Germany as the hegemonic power in Europe"[14]—but, most importantly, they did not share France's fears. As Clemenceau observed to Lloyd George, there was "a difference of psychology between your people and ours; you are on your island, behind the rampart of the sea; we are on the Continent, with a bad frontier."[15] Clemenceau was right. As an island power, Britain's greatest concern before the war had been the growth of the German navy. Now that navy was gone. With the German war machine defeated and disarmed, the danger of a German hegemony on the continent had been quashed, at least for some time. Britain's other main concern was for the empire, which prior to the war faced challenges from every direction. Now, although serious internal problems remained, and notwithstanding the tussles with France, the postwar empire faced fewer external challenges. The result was that the two nations had different perceptions of postwar reality. As Lloyd George told Wilson, "For France, the great danger is the German danger; I believe it is averted for a century."[16]

To the British, the greatest danger was no longer German militarism but German collapse and the threat of Bolshevik revolution. British and American officials both feared that French polices were "bolshevising" the German people and driving them into Russia's arms.[17] Far from sharing Clemenceau's goal of permanently weakening Germany, British officials tended to see Germany's return as a European power as a necessary bulwark against Soviet Russia—"I fear the Slavs much more" than the Germans, Lloyd George told Wilson.[18] It was also a bulwark against an overly ambitious France.

For economic reasons, the British had no interest in the destruction of the German economy or the breaking up of Germany into its pre-

Bismarckian state of disunity and weakness. The Germans were important trading and financial partners before the war, and only a healthy
German economy would be able to pay reparations. British demands for
reparations were at least as high as France's, but they were willing to be
flexible with Germany. As Lloyd George put it, "We cannot both cripple
her and expect her to pay."[19]

The British people's greatest concern was to ensure that they would
never again have to send their sons, brothers, and fathers to die in muddy
fields to save some other nation's skin.[20] If the French got their way, putting millions of Germans under alien rule, separating the Rhineland
from the rest of Germany, and establishing permanent occupations of
German lands, another war seemed certain. Lloyd George wanted no
"reverse Alsace-Lorraines," and the British people did not want to be
"France's underwriter" on what seemed a very risky insurance policy.[21]
What the British wanted was a Germany that was "chastened" but not
debilitated, and a "self-regulating mechanism" to keep the peace in
Europe that would not require British intervention. Britain would retain
influence, but "at the lowest cost possible," thus freeing it to defend its
imperial interests and keep up with its new economic and naval competitor, the United States.[22]

Unlike the French, the British really did want to establish some kind
of balance of power on the continent. Traditional British policy for over
a century had relied on such an equilibrium, which allowed Britain to
hover just outside the continent, weighing in as necessary to maintain the
balance. The British yearned to return to that nineteenth-century policy
that had preserved peace on the continent while allowing the British to
extend their empire by tens of millions of square miles, just as Americans
yearned to return to their summer sea. The British were aware, however,
that they no longer possessed the ability to preserve a stable balance in
Europe. For that they needed the help of the United States.

Indeed, one of the few things that the British and French agreed about
was the critical role of the Americans in the new global configuration of
power. American dominance of the postwar world was an inescapable
fact of life. This was most notable in the economic realm. Not only was
the American economy larger than those of all the other great powers
combined, but the United States held most of the world's gold reserves.
London's long-held position as the world's banking and financial hub
had passed to New York.[23] Britain and France alone owed the United
States almost $8 billion in war debts ($135 billion in 2019 dollars), and
the fate of Europe's postwar economy hinged on the continued availabil-

ity of American financing, the openness of the huge American market, and American consumers' willingness to purchase European goods.

British officials had long since determined that their primary postwar interest lay in forging a close, cooperative relationship with the United States.[24] Not only did they depend on American financing, they also needed American help preserving security in East Asia, and, of course, in Europe. As the British official Robert Cecil put it, the "greatest guarantee" of a "settled peace" in Europe lay in a "good understanding with the United States."[25] More than narrow interests were at stake. As Cecil wrote Balfour in the summer of 1917, it would be "of incalculable benefit to the human race" if America's growing power were wielded "in accordance with our ideas of right and justice." It would mean the dominance of the Anglo-Saxon vision "in all international affairs."[26] The world was increasingly going to "turn on the Great Republic as on a pivot," Balfour argued, and so, as Canada's prime minister, Sir Robert Borden, put it, "the more we can get the United States to realise her great responsibilities for the peace and welfare of the world the better it will be for us and for all mankind."[27] Although skeptics reminded their colleagues that "our friend America lives a long way off" and that, in the words of one senior Foreign Office official, the Americans were "so wedded to the almighty dollar that they cannot be judged even by the low standard of other nations in regard to matters of national honor," nevertheless, the general view was that Britain had little choice but to try to lock the Americans in.[28]

French views were much the same. The lesson not only of the recent war but of the war with Prussia four decades earlier was that France must never again be left to face the Germans alone. Had it not been for the intervention of both the Anglo-Saxon powers, Clemenceau believed, "France would perhaps no longer exist."[29] The French, like the British, were going to need American financing and access to the American market, as well as American leniency concerning the repayment of France's $3 billion wartime debt. Clemenceau's primary goal at Paris was to hold the three powers together. "To this unity," he told colleagues, he would "make every sacrifice."[30]

Even the Germans looked to the United States for their salvation. They had seized on the Fourteen Points not because they liked their substance but because they believed the United States, led by Wilson, could and would stand up to France's vengeful demands and insist on reasonable reparations, or none at all. Like other Europeans, the Germans assumed that Americans had two overriding concerns: to make money and to prevent Communist revolution. The liberal parties that made up the Weimar coalition had their own reasons for seeking close ties with the Americans. It was Wilson, after all, who had called the new democratic government in Germany into existence, and so it was reasonable to expect the Americans to want to support their own creation. The new German government counted on American investment and financing to hasten postwar recovery and hoped that American bankers and businesses, once invested in the German market, would further compel Washington to champion Germany's cause. From the moment the Weimar Republic came into being in early 1919, coaxing the United States back into greater involvement in European questions became the Weimar Republic's foreign policy priority, second only to throwing off the chains of Versailles.[31] They thought the Americans would help with that, too.

For all America's failings, therefore, and despite Europeans' concerns about American hegemony, nevertheless they wanted as deep an American involvement in Europe as the Americans themselves were willing to make. As one historian observed of a later period in transatlantic relations, if this was empire, it was empire by invitation.[32]

Whether Americans were up to this grand task, on the other hand, was questionable. Just three years earlier, the great majority of Americans had hoped to play no role at all in Europe, and even Wilson had pronounced the United States indifferent to the outcome of the war. There was good reason to suspect that the Americans would return to this view of Europe now that the war was over. That certainly seemed to be Henry Cabot Lodge's view. He suggested that the United States need only endorse whatever the British and French wanted in the way of peace terms, with the clear implication that the United States had no interests of its own in the way the European conflict was settled. Despite the two million soldiers sent "over there," Americans remained a parochial people, their perspective still shaped by geographical and psychological distance. Even Wilson's decision to attend the Paris talks raised a scandal. In the republic's one hundred and thirty years, no president had ever crossed the ocean.[33]

The perception of Americans' parochialism and unreliability was compounded by their unwieldy political and constitutional system. Britain and France were also democracies, and Lloyd George and Clemenceau had to be responsive to public opinion up to a point. But in both countries foreign policy was more insulated from politics. Neither Lloyd George nor Clemenceau had to worry much about treaty ratification.[34] Nor did they have to present themselves to the voters until they determined the moment was propitious. National elections in both countries were suspended between 1914 and 1918. Just one month after the armistice, Lloyd George called a snap election, which he and his coalition won in a landslide.[35]

An American president had no such control. The Constitution determined the dates of elections, and it was Wilson's misfortune that the 1918 midterm congressional elections fell on November 5, six days before Germany surrendered. With the war unsettled, Roosevelt and Lodge did their best to paint Wilson as pro-German at a time when the great majority of Americans were demanding complete destruction of "the Hun." They accused Wilson of seeking a "compromise peace" that would leave the German autocracy and its armies intact. The Fourteen Points, Roosevelt warned, days before the election, represented the "conditional surrender of the United States."[36] These charges evolved into a broader theme: that the real struggle was between patriotic "Americanism" and Wilson's suspicious and un-American "internationalism."[37] Roosevelt warned voters not to "trust the internationalists" because they were "the enemies of nationalism and Americanism."[38] Republican papers equated internationalism with Bolshevism, even hinting that some of Wilson's advisers were secretly Communists.[39] Whether these charges had any effect on the vote was hard to know, but Democrats believed they did.[40]

Partisanship on these foreign questions was especially intense because everyone knew that eventual ratification of any treaty was going to have weighty political consequences—all the more so if the treaty included Wilson's League. As the former Republican senator Albert Beveridge warned, if Wilson managed to accomplish "the greatest constructive world reform in history," Republican prospects would be "seriously, perhaps fatally, injured."[41] The "future of the party" was therefore in the hands of Lodge, soon to become both Senate majority leader and chairman of the powerful Senate Foreign Relations Committee.[42] Lodge had no doubt that his primary political task was to defeat Wilson's League of Nations. He and Roosevelt, notwithstanding their own earlier support for the League idea, now proclaimed their opposition—even before Wilson himself had decided what form it should take. Roosevelt declared that the League of Nations was the scheme of "professional internationalists" playing "the game of brutal German autocracy."[43]

Republicans may have started the fight, but Wilson was also a fighter and capable of intense partisanship. As many suspected, Wilson did entertain thoughts of running for a third term, and passage of the League and the treaty would give a significant boost to his own prospects or to whom-

ever the Democrats chose as their 1920 nominee. His concerns were sufficiently obvious that an astute British politician like Lloyd George could
see that, "politically," ratification of the League and the treaty were for
Wilson "a matter of life and death."[44]

With a justifiable confidence in his ability to sway Americans—his
speaking tour in 1916 had played an important part in securing passage
of his preparedness legislation—Wilson made the questionable decision to seek a mandate in the midterm elections. He asked Americans
to vote the Democratic ticket and not send him off to Paris with a vote
of no-confidence.[45] This strategy backfired when Republicans predictably
picked up enough seats in the House and Senate to give them control of
both houses.[46] Wilson thus arrived in Paris with Lodge and Roosevelt
proclaiming to allies and enemies alike that he no longer had authority
to speak for the country.[47] In a November 26 editorial Roosevelt insisted
that in any other democratic country Wilson would no longer even be in
office; he would "simply be a private citizen like the rest of us."[48]

This boded ill for any treaty Wilson brought home from Paris, and
everyone knew it. The requirement of a two-thirds vote in the Senate
had always been a significant hurdle to getting any treaty ratified, much
less one as momentous and controversial as this one. Treaties especially
ran aground when the opposition party controlled the Senate.[49] From the
beginning it was an open question whether a Republican Senate under
Lodge's leadership would ratify the president's treaty or "substitute for it
a program formulated by the senior Senator from Massachusetts."[50]

That was Lodge's plan. He and Roosevelt initially hoped that the
"whole thing" would "break down" at the peace conference and that
the Allies would kill the League idea before it could even come before
Congress.[51] With that in mind, Lodge visited the French and British
embassies to urge their governments not to follow Wilson's lead. Having
assumed leadership of the Senate, Lodge regarded himself as co-equal
with the president in the conduct of foreign policy and thought nothing
of communicating his own views directly with the Allied governments.
The quid pro quo he offered was clear: Lodge publicly declared that the
United States had no interest in the boundaries of Europe and would
support whatever arrangement the Allies decided upon.[52] But he warned
that if a league of nations was linked to the treaty, Senate passage would
be "extremely doubtful."[53] Roosevelt sent letters and private messages
to Lloyd George, Balfour, and Clemenceau encouraging them to oppose
Wilson and promising complete support from the Republican-controlled
Congress if they did. All these efforts took a toll on Wilson's ability to

negotiate effectively. When Wilson stepped onto the European continent at the end of January 1919, he was the most powerful leader in the world, but everyone could see that he was not necessarily the most powerful figure in his own country. As one member of the British delegation, Harold Nicolson, recalled, fear that the Americans might not honor any pledge Wilson made in Paris was "the ghost at all our feasts."[54]

The difficulties Wilson had in Washington at first seemed slight compared with the difficulties he and his colleagues faced in Paris. Things in Europe looked more manageable from distant Washington than they did in the maelstrom of the European capital inundated by delegations from every corner of war-torn Europe. Most Americans assumed that Britain and France were still their old great-power selves and were capable of reconstructing Europe as suited their interests—hence Lodge's belief that the United States need only ratify whatever the Allies decided on. The Americans, on the other hand, were notably out of their element. While British and French diplomats had been dividing and trading conquered territories and imperial holdings for a millennium, Americans had never given the smallest thought to the boundaries of Europe, the transfer of populations and economic resources, or the disposition of collapsing empires.[55] The collection of "experts" that House put together to advise President Wilson—known as "The Inquiry"—lacked relevant expertise and experience.[56] The senior Republican on the American delegation, Henry White, wrote to Lodge soon after he arrived in Paris: "We are now on a volcano which may explode at any time." Unless something was done, "the danger of war's breaking out somewhere, soon after the adjournment of this Conference," would only grow.[57]

What was the right answer? Wilson, at British urging, had latched on to the vague idea of a League of Nations to preserve the peace. To someone like White, sixty-eight years old, friend of Lodge and John Hay, and Roosevelt's ambassador to Italy and France, the League idea had not at first seemed very appealing. It seemed too extreme for the circumstances. Yet "contact with the terrible realities of Europe" changed his and other delegates' minds.[58] White came to believe that the League idea, however unusual and flawed it might be, was nevertheless "an eminently practical scheme which would minimize the danger of any great international conflict."[59]

The idea of the League of Nations as an "eminently practical scheme" runs counter to the mythologies that have grown up around Wilson and the League over the past century. Yet a good number of Americans in Wilson's day had latched on to the idea of a league as the best solution to a complex problem: how to bring American power to bear for the preservation of peace in the present without making ironclad commitments to go to war in the future. Long before Wilson came to embrace the idea, it was the Republican statesmen—Taft, Lodge, and Roosevelt—who were the League's first and most enthusiastic spokesmen.

Way back in the fall of 1914, beginning a month after the outbreak of the war, Roosevelt wrote a series of articles calling for establishment of a "League for the Peace of Righteousness." The recent war had proved the "worthlessness" of treaties, peace conferences, and arbitration agreements, he believed. The problem, of course, was that the international system lacked what a government possessed: the ability to enforce the law. As Roosevelt saw it, the international system was like the old American West, where men came together voluntarily to form a posse comitatus to administer a rough justice and protect themselves and others from outlaws. The international system needed its own posse comitatus, Roosevelt believed, some way of "putting the collective and efficient strength of all the great powers of civilization" behind a just peace.[60] Roosevelt envisioned an international tribunal, with representatives of all the nations serving as judges to adjudicate disputes, and a league made up of the strongest military powers to enforce the tribunal's decisions. For the system to work, the great powers had to commit to act when called upon. They had to be "solemnly covenanted" (yes, Roosevelt used that word before Wilson did) to use "their entire military force" against any aggressor and any nation that defied the tribunal.[61] Roosevelt knew that some would call his plan "utopian," and he had no illusions about the difficulty of implementing it. But the horror of the European conflict, which had drawn in the whole world from Asia to the Americas, was "too great to permit us to rest supine." It was "our duty" to devise "some efficient plan for securing the peace of righteousness throughout the world." The United States had to become "one of the joint guarantors of world peace," to play its part as "a member of the international *posse comitatus* to enforce the peace of righteousness." If that could be done, "then we would have come nearer to the day of world peace."[62]

For Americans, the great virtue of the League was that it was not an alliance. Alliances had been anathema to Americans for a century and they were in particularly bad odor after the outbreak of the Great War. Most Americans believed, as did many Europeans, that the European alliance system itself had been a major cause of the war. That system had produced not peace but a continent full of nervous nations, jealous and fearful of their neighbors, armed to the teeth and ready to strike at a moment's notice. The forty years of peace that preceded the war, it now appeared to many, had not been a real peace at all but "only a feverish truce" during which "national rivalries and racial hatreds" had burned ever hotter until the inevitable "day of reckoning."[63] The "bitter and vindictive" animosities of Europe, Roosevelt believed, could not be cured by a return to "shifty and uncertain" alliances.[64] Lodge, too, opposed "permanent alliances of any kind."[65] Peace would have to be established on "a new basis," Root believed, one that would be "free from the old virus."[66] Even the most committed American internationalists, who believed, as Taft put it, that the United States had no choice but to "depart from the traditional policy" of isolation, nevertheless balked at anything suggesting "a defensive alliance with European nations" that would "bind us to take part" in a future European war.[67] Wilson insisted that a league was the opposite of an "entangling alliance."[68]

The idea of a league was attractive to Americans for another reason as well. Americans still preferred not to take sides. Although genuine neutrality in any future war had become impossible—just as it had proved impossible to stay neutral in the recent war—when it came to *preventing* the next war, Americans believed their disinterested neutrality was an essential asset. It was interesting that Roosevelt himself believed, at least in the early months of the war, that Germany should be included in any future league. Back in 1914, he had criticized "extremists in England, France, and Russia" who yearned for "the utter dismemberment of Germany and her reduction to impotence." Such an outcome would be a "frightful calamity for mankind," no less than if Britain or France were crushed by Germany. What the world needed was "a stable, united and powerful Germany, too strong to fear aggression and too just to be a source of fear to its neighbors."

To accomplish this required active involvement by the United States in a postwar peace settlement, but not on one side or the other. The idea that the United States would ally with France in perpetuity against Germany after the war was unthinkable. No more than the British did Americans wish to keep the new, democratic Germany prostrate under the French boot. Prussian militarism had been destroyed and replaced by a liberal, pro-American, pro-capitalist government. Was the United States going to make a permanent security alliance with France and promise to go to war against this struggling new liberal Germany whenever France deemed itself provoked? Even at the start of the war, Roosevelt had argued that the "greatest service that could be rendered to peace would be to convince Germany" that the United States was just as committed to defending it as it was to defending the Allies.[69] Hence the need for a league in which all would be committed to the security of all. For some American internationalists, "collective security" was not merely an ideal. It was the only practical means by which the United States could participate in an international mechanism to preserve the peace, the only way it could be what Lodge had called a world power "in the finer sense," one whose "active participation and beneficent influence" would be "recognized and desired by other nations in those great questions which concerned the welfare and happiness of all mankind."[70]

Prior to 1917, the League had been chiefly a Republican idea. Following Roosevelt's lead, Taft and others had formed the League to Enforce Peace, and while many internationalists insisted that keeping the peace by threatening war was a contradiction, Taft and his colleagues generally favored a league capable of both imposing economic sanctions and going to war against would-be aggressors, if necessary. These Americans did not regard the League as a utopian scheme but rather as the most practical means of preserving international peace.

For many American internationalists, in fact, these League proposals were all too practical. They smacked of the old power politics. Most American internationalists opposed the idea of imposing sanctions, much less using force, to compel desirable international behavior. They looked to the evolution of international law, to new mechanisms of arbitration, to the establishment of a world court, to building on the modest achievements of the Hague conferences of 1899 and 1907. Or they looked to public opinion, to the gradual enlightenment of all civilized men and women. Nicholas Murray Butler, president of Columbia University, wrote of the emergence of an "international mind" that would increasingly govern the behavior of nations.[71] Others envisioned various forms of world government, a "Congress of Nations," or a "Parliament of the World."[72] Even Root before the war had argued that what was needed was not an "international policeman" but "a permanent court composed of judges" capable of deciding "upon rights in accordance with the facts and law."[73] As one leading American internationalist put it, "Peace is the outcome of justice, justice of law, law of world organization."[74] Roosevelt's posse comitatus, Taft's League to Enforce Peace, and, eventually, Wilson's League of Nations—all looked too much like the old concerts of great powers.

Some internationalists had changed their minds after witnessing the horrors of the Great War. Global public opinion had proved impotent. International tribunals seemed weak and far from realization. Changes in international law were slow and uncertain. The recent war had proven, after all, that powerful nations ignored laws and treaties and rejected arbitration. No "international mind" had stopped them. After 1914, even a legalist like Root believed that laws had to have "sanctions behind them," although he continued to worry about binding the American people to future actions.[75] The world seemed to require more than a slow evolution and more treaties. Any peace would have to do more than test theories of international relations. Any league had to have muscle behind it. When the war broke out in Europe, those urging support for a league included General Nelson A. Miles, who had served in every American war from the Civil War through the war with Spain. He told the *New York Times* that the conflict offered an opportunity, once the Europeans "open[ed] their eyes to their folly," to create a new organization, a "peace congress" with "full power" to order the armies and navies of its members to drive any "wayward nation into submission."[76]

Historians have generally erred in viewing the League as Wilson's personal dream, that he wished to fulfill Kant's vision of a league of peace, or that he had a long-standing Presbyterian fascination with covenants. In fact, Wilson was a latecomer to the idea, and his enthusiasm was not always unbounded. When the suggestion of American membership in a postwar league was first broached to House by Edward Grey in 1915, Wilson demurred. He changed his mind when it seemed that agreeing to a postwar league was the only way to bring a rapid end to the war and thus avoid American intervention. At that point, he supported the league chiefly as a quid pro quo, the price of admission for allowing him to mediate an end to the European war. Once that effort failed and the United States was compelled to intervene, Wilson for a time lost interest in the league as he concentrated on winning the war. Although he made reference to it in general terms in his Fourteen Points address, he gave little thought to the details until after the November 1918 armistice. On the voyage to Paris in December he was still discussing with his advisers the general principles that might guide such a league and the nature of the commitment that would be required by the United States.

In his mind, that commitment was far from ironclad. On board the *George Washington,* he spoke of an organization of powers that *might* impose an economic embargo on a nation threatening to go to war, but only if the members agreed. In general, each member state "would be free to decide for itself" what additional steps "if any" should be taken.[77]

Wilson was under no illusion that many Americans would automatically embrace membership in a league. William Borah had already accused him of "moral treason" for allegedly proposing to grant other powers that much authority over American actions.[78] He knew the Senate would "never ratify any treaty" that put the "force of the United States" at the disposal of an international body. Even Lodge, having fully reversed his earlier sentiments, had come out against the League as too likely to entangle the United States in "the field of European politics," where it had "no national or legal concern."[79] And of course Roosevelt, in the last months of his life, with his hatred for Wilson burning hot along with his desire for another shot at the White House, turned against the League, which he now insisted was a product of Wilson's dangerously un-American "internationalism."

Wilson knew he had to be careful with the League idea, therefore, but he and his fellow delegates quickly discovered at Paris that what seemed too much of a commitment to their fellow Americans was not enough of a commitment to satisfy the nervous French. Although French desires to dismantle and impoverish Germany at first struck White and his colleagues as evidence of ambition, they soon realized it derived mostly from fear.[80] Regardless of whether French anxieties were justified, they had to be addressed if there was to be any kind of stable peace settlement.[81] A League seemed the best answer.

That a stable peace was in America's interests few doubted at the time. Wilson himself was not in the business of providing charity to other countries, much less involving himself in matters of no concern to Americans. At Paris, he was a dogged defender of American interests. When the French sought forgiveness of their war debts and the continuation of wartime economic cooperation, he refused.[82] When it came to the terms of the peace settlement, Wilson was also determined to protect American interests. These were not very different from those of Britain. Americans sought a moderate peace, in which Germany was punished but also restored so that it would be capable of paying reparations and serving as a market for American goods. Above all, Americans shared Britain's desire for a settlement that would require as little future American involvement as possible. As House explained, it was "almost as important to us to have the settlement laid upon the right foundations as it is to the nations of Europe." If the war did not put an end to European "militarism," then the future would be "full of trouble for us."[83]

Those who accompanied Wilson to Paris could not believe that opponents of the League back home understood the risks they were taking.
Henry White continually chastised Lodge for his "marked ignorance of
the actualities of Europe." Lodge's repeated insistence that the United
States simply agree to whatever the British and French wanted in the
settlement struck White as both absurd and dangerous. For one thing, the
British and French did not agree. For another, French demands looked to
both British and American officials as certain to create chronic instability
in the center of Europe. At the end of May 1919, French-backed Rhenish
separatists made a failed bid for the Rhineland's independence, offering a
glimpse at future instability in the occupied territory.[84]

Under these dire circumstances, White and others in the delegation
found it maddening that Lodge and other Republicans were trying to
defeat the League. American membership was the League's "mainstay,"
David Hunter Miller wrote to Root. If the French felt that "we are likely
to retire during the first few years," there would be "no guarantee of protection left," and they would return to seeking the dismemberment of
Germany, with all the dangers that would bring.[85] The American delegation members in Paris understood that much American opposition to
the League was driven by the "desire to prevent our getting involved in
European affairs."[86] But the time to have thought of that, White wrote
Lodge, was back in 1917, not now. By entering the war, the United States
had completely reshaped the political, financial, and security structures
of Europe. To suggest that "we can divest ourselves of all responsibility for the condition which we have been chiefly instrumental in creating
seems to me an untenable proposition."[87]

This was certainly the view of the British and the French. Lodge and
Roosevelt had hoped that the British and French would oppose the
League, but this was just another example of their ignorance of the situation in Europe. The British delegation at Paris had no great objections
to the League idea. It had, after all, been a British idea first, and Britain's
delegation at Paris included two of the League's leading advocates, Robert Cecil and Jan Smuts.[88] Lloyd George was never very enthusiastic, but
he was prepared to support a league if that was what was required to win
an American commitment to European peace.[89] British strategy was "to
work with Wilson, not against him." Indeed, some British officials were
put off by Lodge, the onetime internationalist who now seemed willing to
put the Anglo-American relationship at risk for scarcely concealed parti-

san purposes. When Lodge came out against the League Covenant, Cecil remarked, "One more illusion gone. I thought Lodge was an able man."[90]

Clemenceau had even more disdain than Lloyd George for the League idea, and for Wilson personally, but even more than the British he believed France needed the United States.[91] He was not about to fight Wilson on the thing that mattered most to the American president and which seemed the only way of permanently engaging the United States on France's side in Europe's affairs.[92] Clemenceau's chief hope was to turn the League into a military alliance for the defense of France. The Allied leaders' very first action at Paris, therefore, was to ignore Lodge's warnings and join Wilson in making a League of Nations an integral part of the peace treaty.

This did not bridge the gap between American and French desires, however. The problem was not just the League. The French were suspicious from the beginning about *any* American promise to come to their defense. "America is distant," Clemenceau repeatedly remarked during the first days of the conference. American forces had taken "a long time to get here" even after the decision to enter the war, and during that time the French people had suffered terribly.[93] "Guarantees, Guarantees, Guarantees," blared the headlines in the French press, expressing the common view of what was needed to secure the peace.[94] Clemenceau insisted he could rely only on a "system of alliances."[95] If Wilson was insisting on a league, then the league itself would have to operate like an alliance. There had to be an international force of sufficient strength with contingents provided by the various members. There had to be a permanent "general staff" headed by a chief chosen for a three-year term. In case of war, this international army would be led by a "commander-in-chief" designated by the member states. The force would have to be "ready to act" with little or no advance warning.[96] Otherwise, the French complained, any league would be nothing "but a dangerous façade."[97] The French view, which spanned the political spectrum, was that a league which had "no army" and did not bind its members to act was "no League at all."[98]

The American and British delegations naturally balked at such ideas— Miller called Clemenceau's proposal a plan for "international control of our Army and Navy *in war and in peace.*" Wilson politely explained to the French that this was "impossible."[99] No nation in the world would agree to it, and the United States "because of our Constitution" certainly could not.[100] After several weeks of bargaining, the final language of what would become Article 10 of the League Covenant remained a carefully hedged commitment. It guaranteed the independence and territorial integrity of all member states, but stipulated only that, "in case of any aggression," an executive council of great powers would "advise the plan and the means by which this obligation shall be fulfilled."[101] Wilson went out of his way to note that the commitment could be fulfilled in many cases "without the necessity of war."[102]

The problem for the French was that Article 10 did not bind the United States to anything. The Americans could oppose action in the Executive Council, and if they were out-voted they could ignore any decision the Executive Council made.[103] As Miller, the delegation's international legal expert, put it, Article 10 entailed a "very limited obligation, much more limited legally than generally supposed or stated," which was why it was "certain to be regarded by the French as not enough."[104]

That was indeed how the French regarded it.[105] Wilson pleaded with Clemenceau to have "confidence in the good faith of the nations who belong to the League." Although he could not offer more than he had proposed in the way of guarantees, he assured the French leader that "when danger comes, we too will come, and we will help you, but you must trust us."[106] Cecil took the French delegates aside to warn that Wilson's offer of a league was "practically a present to France" and they had better not turn it down. It was the "only means" of getting the assistance of America and England, and if they rejected it, "they would be left without an ally in the world."[107]

The struggle between Wilson and Clemenceau has often been characterized as one between the hard-headed European's "realism" and the American president's "idealism." That was how Clemenceau and his allies portrayed it—Wilson, the "prophet," putting his faith in the "new diplomacy," while the French prime minister relied on the old diplomacy, alliances, and the "balance of power." That was also how Wilson's most ardent defenders described it, and often even Wilson himself—the virtuous American seeking a new and better world while the European imperialists remained mired in their power politics.[108]

But beneath the apparent clash of philosophies was a more fundamental clash of national interests, perspectives, and preferences. What the French called Wilson's "idealism" was really just America's reluctance, shared by the British, to be tied down by a security pact. The French wanted the Americans and the British to treat France's security as if it were their own vital interest too—or as one French senator put it, "The problem of the defense of civilization is the problem of the defense of France."[109] But while the Americans and British believed they had an interest in providing reassurance to France and deterring future German aggression, they also had an interest in protecting the right to make their own choices, and in protecting Germany from France.

Clemenceau would not budge, however. As the spring came, and with it the revolutions and chaos across Europe, Wilson's desperation to reach a settlement grew. France was not Wilson's only problem at Paris. The Japanese insisted on keeping the Chinese province of Shantung, which they had taken from the Germans at the start of the war. The Italians demanded the port city of Fiume on the Dalmatian coast, which was intended for the new South Slav state. Lloyd George demanded a halt to the U.S. naval program that threatened to outstrip the Royal Navy. Both the British and the French wanted a higher German reparations bill than the Americans thought wise or fair. All were emboldened to use the leverage provided by the growing opposition Wilson faced back home, where Lodge was busily assembling his forces to oppose the League. Wilson was growing exhausted and his health deteriorated alarmingly, probably the result of the flu. And still Clemenceau was holding out for stronger guarantees.

These dire circumstances led Wilson to make a rather desperate move.[110] In early March he agreed to Lloyd George's extraordinary suggestion that Britain and the United States offer France a formal security treaty against "unprovoked aggression" by Germany. In Wilson's mind the agreement was only a stopgap until the French learned to trust the League.[111] But his advisers were appalled when they learned of it.[112] They noted that if France could not rely on Article 10 and required a separate commitment to feel safe, then no one else would accept Article 10 as a sufficient guarantee either. The whole League would be discredited before it was born. In addition, there was the problem that a straightforward security pact with France, which was tantamount to a military alliance, would never be ratified by the U.S. Senate.[113] Lloyd George had already built this assumption into his proposal. He inserted a clause in the final text stating that Britain's obligation would be null and void if the United States failed to ratify.

It is unclear how seriously Clemenceau took the Anglo-American offer of a guarantee treaty. Foch immediately pointed out the difficulty, if not impossibility, of winning Senate approval.[114] Nor did the language of the guarantee treaty spell out what would constitute "unprovoked aggression" against France, what would trigger an Anglo-American response, or what that response would be. Wilson himself played down its significance—it "really amounted to very little more than Article 10 of the Covenant," he told Cecil.[115]

Clemenceau ultimately decided he had no choice but to accept, and he made a great show of declaring the tripartite agreement the "keystone of European peace," but it did not slow his efforts to get more solid guarantees.[116] He continued to press for an indefinite joint Allied occupation of the left bank of the Rhine as well as joint Allied control of the bridgeheads and a fifty-kilometer zone along the right bank. According to his plan, Germany would not be permitted to maintain military forces or fortifications in the Rhineland, could not recruit troops, and could not manufacture war materials. There would be a permanent Anglo-American-French Commission of Inspection to ensure German observance. Any German movement or attempted movement into the occupied zone would be regarded as an act of aggression.

Lloyd George and Wilson rejected these terms, and the bitter wrangling continued until Wilson, exhausted, ill, and angry, finally summoned the *George Washington* and threatened to return home. At that point, Clemenceau began to retreat. If the choice was between accepting a vague security guarantee from the two most powerful nations in the world or leaving France standing "alone on the left bank of the Rhine" against Germany, with only Poland, Czechoslovakia, and Yugoslavia as allies, he would take what he could get.[117] After three more weeks of painful bargaining, the leaders forged a compromise. The occupation of the Rhineland would only be temporary, as Lloyd George and Wilson insisted, but if at the end of fifteen years the security treaties had not been ratified, the occupation could continue.[118] In addition, the Rhineland would remain permanently demilitarized. The German military would be limited to 100,000 troops, with no tanks, no heavy guns, no air force, no submarines, and only a tiny navy that amounted to a coast guard. Any move by Germany to violate the terms of the agreement would be grounds for the forceful reoccupation of German territory by France and the Allies. Clemenceau put great stock in the joint Allied occupation of the Rhineland, which would last for at least fifteen years. He hoped that the presence of American and British troops would suffice to deter German revanchism, at least for as long as the occupation lasted.[119]

On the other major issues, Clemenceau backed down. There would be no independent Rhenish state, no permanent separation of the Rhineland, no buffer states of any kind, no shifting of France's strategic frontier to the Rhine. There would be no permanent international force ready to come to France's defense at the first sign of renewed German aggression. France would have to depend for its protection on the promises from the United States and Britain and on the workings of the new League.

House, seeking to reassure the French, observed that "if after establishing the League, we are so stupid as to let Germany train and arm a large army and again become a menace to the world, we would deserve the fate which such folly would bring upon us."[120]

The French were not impressed. Back in Paris the League Covenant was greeted with "universal scorn" and produced an outpouring of anti-American sentiment.[121] The political, military, and diplomatic establishments were almost unanimous in calling the treaty a "surrender" and a "German peace." They were not impressed by the side treaties, and Clemenceau remained under pressure to address France's security concerns by physical means rather than with the vague assurances from the unreliable Americans.[122] For the United States and Britain, one diplomat complained, the peace settlement was nothing more than "a piece of paper."[123] White reported that Marshal Foch was still demanding "an independent state in the Rhine Province" along with an "inter-allied army permanently stationed there for all time to come, to which we should contribute a contingent of about 100,000 men."[124]

A beleaguered Clemenceau defended the treaty as imperfect but workable, flawed like all human creations. The real problem, he said, was not the treaty but French birth rates—"if France does not have large families, it will be in vain . . . that you take away all the German guns. . . . France will be lost because there will be no more French." Within months Clemenceau's political career was over.[125]

The signing of the final treaty on June 28, 1919, brought little celebration in any quarter. The Japanese acquisition of Shantung sparked a popular nationalist and anti-imperialist uprising in China, which won much sympathy on both sides of the Atlantic. The Italians were angry that they did not get Fiume, and everyone else was angry about how much of the *irridenta* Italy did get. The transfer of substantial German-speaking populations to Italian, Polish, and Czech rule, and Japan's retention of Shantung, clearly violated any notion of self-determination, which many had assumed was the guiding principle of the peacemakers. The disposition of former German colonies and parts of the former Ottoman Empire was a barely concealed ratification of British and French imperial gains in the war. In Britain, the Independent Labour Party denounced the treaty as "a capitalist, imperialist and militarist imposition" that aggravated "every evil which existed before 1914" and assured "the certainty of other and more calamitous wars."[126]

Although the French called it a "German peace," many transatlantic liberals agreed with John Maynard Keynes that it was, on the contrary, a "Carthaginian peace," a merciless victors' settlement foisted on a naïve American president by the French with the intention of crushing Germany. The fact that the Germans were presented the treaty to sign with practically no opportunity to negotiate; that the treaty included the so-called "war guilt" clause, assigning full blame to Germany for starting the war; that German territories, colonies, and German-speaking populations had been parceled out to the victorious powers and their satellites; that Germans were likely going to have to pay a crushing reparations bill to the victors—all this struck British and American liberals as the very opposite of the kind of peace they had been led to expect. What had happened to Wilson's generous terms, to "peace without victory," and to the Fourteen Points, on which the treaty was supposed to have been based? Many believed the agreement was no model of the "new diplomacy" but reeked of the old, vengeful great-power politics that Wilson had sought to banish. In vain did the statesmen and diplomats who negotiated the treaty argue that the unhappiness on all sides signaled their success in balancing competing interests—"Our disappointment is an excellent symptom," Lord Cecil commented. "Let us perpetuate it."[127]

Many American progressives who had devoted themselves to what they had taken to be Wilson's vision were especially disillusioned. "We had such high hopes of this adventure," one commented. "We believed God called us, and now at the end we are put to doing hell's dirtiest work, starving people, grabbing territory—or helping to grab it for our friends; standing by while the grand gesture of revenge and humiliation links this war up with the interminable chain of wars that runs back to Cain!"[128] Some who went to Paris to provide advice felt ignored. Walter Lippmann and William Bullitt were especially embittered and, like Keynes, would soon take their anger out on Wilson.[129]

Wilson was aware of the treaty's shortcomings. He had, after all, tried to resist or modify most of the provisions the critics complained about.[130] Lippmann would later argue that Wilson underestimated his own strength and gave away more than he had to. This was probably true. In his desperation to get the League approved, and with his eye intently on the American public back home and the coming battle in Congress, Wilson may well have underestimated his ability to bully the British and French leaders. The toughest nut to crack was Clemenceau—the only leader truly fighting for the survival of his nation—and yet when Wilson threatened to quit the talks, Clemenceau quickly gave in.

The charge that Wilson was weak, however, presumes that Wilson agreed that the product of his efforts was a failure. He did not. The treaty was the product of a compromise among friendly powers, none of whom got everything it wanted. Some of the flaws could be fixed by the League, Wilson insisted. Mistakes could be brought "one by one" for "readjustment."[131] In the meantime, he believed, it was essential to focus on the "main objective," which was to establish the League as the necessary instrument of establishing a stable peace.[132] Wilson would tolerate a flawed settlement of the last war if he could put in place the means of preventing the next one.[133]

Wilson did not agree that the Versailles settlement had treated the Germans too harshly. The treaty was "undoubtedly very severe indeed," he said, ". . . but invariably my thought goes back to the very great offense against civilization which the German state committed and the necessity of making it evident once and for all that such things can lead only to the most severe punishment."[134] Wilson's attitude toward Germany, and toward Germans, had only hardened after the brutally harsh Brest-Litovsk treaty was endorsed by all the German political parties. If the Paris agreement two years later was also harsh, Wilson believed, the Germans had "earned that."[135] Even in 1919, with Germany defeated and a new democratic government precariously in place, Wilson did not feel confident that the Germans had learned their lesson. The foreign minister's angry protest at Versailles that "Germany was not alone at fault" had appalled him and left him wondering if the Germans even understood the wrongs they had committed.[136] The world, he thought, "had a moral right not only to disarm Germany but to subject her to a generation of thoughtfulness."[137]

Wilson knew, moreover, just how much he had protected the Germans from a truly Carthaginian peace. The French would have broken Germany into pieces and destroyed its economy for all time. The Germany that emerged from the peace agreement was not only largely intact but arguably in better shape than France. The war had not been fought on German soil, and although the German people had suffered hunger and deprivation, they had not experienced invasion and subjugation. Unlike those of the French and the Belgians, their industries and their economy had been left mostly intact. Even after losing the war, Germany remained Europe's "industrial powerhouse."[138] The fall of tsarist Russia and its replacement by a new revolutionary government mired in civil war removed Germany's chief geopolitical rival and opened up central and eastern Europe and the Balkans for eventual German economic and political penetration. The new, weak states on Germany's eastern and southern borders offered little barrier to a return of German influence, and many Germans continued to harbor dreams of *Mitteleuropa.*[139] Germany still retained the largest population in Europe after Russia, despite the 6 to 7 million Germans living under Polish, Czech, and Italian rule. Lippmann and other liberals were appalled that Germany had lost control of the Saar, that German-speaking populations had been transferred to Poland and Czechoslovakia, and that Austria and Germany were forbidden from uniting. Yet had the treaty allowed all German-speakers to remain united, and had Germany been allowed to unite with Austria, postwar Germany would have been larger in both population and territory than prewar Germany.[140]

The alleged mistreatment of Germany was therefore far from Wilson's primary concern as he headed back to the United States. He was much more worried about the need to reassure a "terror-stricken France." Yet at home he faced the biggest challenge of all: convincing the American people to do their part in stabilizing "a turbulent and too swiftly changing world."[141]

CHAPTER TWELVE

Wilson and the League Fight

*If you want to quiet the world, you have got to reassure the world, and
the only way in which you can reassure it is to let it know that all the
great fighting powers of the world are going to maintain that quiet.*

—Woodrow Wilson[1]

WHEN WILSON returned to the United States in early July after 127 days
overseas, the League fight had already been going on for over six months.
Both pro- and anti-League factions had been hard at work making their
case, and the ninety-six senators in the new Congress had already split
into groups of committed supporters, committed opponents, and those
in between looking for compromise. Lodge, from his new perch as Senate
majority leader, had already set in motion his plans for defeating Wilson's
league. The price that Wilson paid for making himself the negotiator of
the treaty and spending months abroad was that he was now arriving
late to the party. He knew he was "out of touch with the situation inside
America."[2]

By all indications, however, he was still in a strong position. The treaty
was broadly popular. The harsh treatment of Germany that so troubled
British and American liberals did not trouble the great majority of
Americans—most agreed that "the punishment fit the crime."[3] As for the
League, Wilson's success in revising the Covenant to meet some of the
Senate's objections—on preserving the Monroe Doctrine, for instance—
seemed to improve its chances of passage. While Lodge insisted the revisions had done nothing to fix the problems, Senator Charles L. McNary,
a pro-League Republican from Oregon, said Wilson had met "all the
legitimate objections."[4]

Lodge knew he faced a difficult challenge. Not only did the nation's elite support the League, he observed—the clergy, university professors, and newspaper editors—but so did the "great mass of the people," the "man in the street . . . the farmers, the shop keepers, the men in small businesses, clerks and the like, in short the people generally."[5] The Republican Party itself was "split this way and that way," according to its national party chairman, Will Hays.[6] Republicans from northern and midwestern states worried about being punished by pro-League constituents. Beveridge sneered at the "higgling, piddling side-stepping and shifting" of his Republican colleagues, but Hays insisted there was "no way to commit the party" against the treaty.[7] Republicans could not stand for "mere negation."[8] At the end of June, Hays himself came out for the League, with modifications. Even stalwart League opponents couldn't see how they were going to defeat it when "eighty percent of the people" seemed to be for it.[9] They were "in danger of being overwhelmed" by the popular demand for some kind of league, Root later recalled.[10] According to Lansing, when Wilson arrived back in the United States, "it was not even suggested that the Treaty would fail of ratification."[11]

It's important to recall that there was a time when almost everyone on both sides of the debate believed the treaty and the League would pass. Given what later transpired, it would be easy to assume that the American public would never have been prepared to join a league of nations and enforce the peace treaty. But like so many things that happen in human affairs, this was not foreordained. Politics, not fate or larger forces, decided Americans' response to Wilson's proposals. It took every bit of Henry Cabot Lodge's considerable skills as a politician and legislator to defeat the League and the treaty.

Lodge had a few advantages, bestowed by the American Constitution and the workings of the American government. As the new Senate majority leader, he controlled the timing and manner of the treaty's consideration. He also controlled committee assignments. In May he made himself chairman of the Foreign Relations Committee and stacked it with "irreconcilables"—as the staunchest opponents of the League and the treaty were known. He excluded even moderately pro-League Republicans from the all-important committee.[12] He then slowed things down as much as he could. The committee held several weeks of hearings from the end of July through mid-September, mostly devoted to testimony from treaty opponents and representatives of foreign nations unhappy with some aspect of the settlement. A number of days were devoted to the issue of Shantung, with American witnesses condemning that grave injustice done to China. Italian Americans like Congressman Fiorello H. La Guardia spoke on behalf of Italy's claim to Fiume. Irish Americans attacked Wilson's refusal to advance Irish independence.[13] The committee also heard sensational testimony from William Bullitt, the disgruntled former member of the American delegation who, along with Lippmann, leaked damaging insider information to Borah, including the fact that Lansing in Paris had privately opposed major provisions of both the treaty and the League.[14] According to Bullitt, Lansing had said the League was "entirely useless," that the European powers had "simply gone ahead and arranged the world to suit themselves," and that if the Senate and the American people only understood the treaty, "it would unquestionably be defeated." Lansing, though privately denouncing "the little traitor" for his "garbled" account of their conversations, refused to rebut Bullitt's testimony in public.[15]

Outside the hearings Lodge and other League opponents worked to shift public opinion. To mobilize disgruntled ethnic groups, Lodge publicly supported Italy's claim to Fiume and stirred up Irish Americans' hostility to the "British" League. German Americans needed little prodding to oppose the treaty.[16] To appeal to white Protestants, League opponents warned that the League would be controlled by Catholic nations subservient to the pope. Or they warned that it would be a "colored league" that would impose racial equality in the United States. "Chew on that quid in your reflective moments, you men of the South!" cried the renegade Missouri Democrat James Reed.[17]

A central plank of Lodge's anti-League campaign consisted of playing to traditional anti-European sentiments. He denounced the League as a new "Holy Alliance" that threatened American independence and security just as the monarchies of Russia, Austria, and Prussia had in the days of Monroe.[18] California's progressive Republican senator, Hiram Johnson, spoke of a "sordid, cunning, secret, and crafty" design of "European and Asiatic governments" to control "the economic destinies of peoples."[19] Beveridge had a simple message: "Get out of Europe and stay out." He warned that shady international financiers were "weaving a net that would entangle the American nation in a European-Asiatic balance of power."[20] The strident anti-European invective of Lodge and other League opponents was a marked shift from just a few months earlier, when Lodge and other Republicans were accusing Wilson of abandoning the Allies. But Lodge's political needs had changed.[21]

Lodge and other League opponents focused most of their fire on Article 10. Despite Wilson's repeated insistence that it did not bind the United States to act and did not take away Congress's constitutional right to declare war, Lodge and others warned that it would allow other nations to force America into foreign conflicts in which Americans had no interest. Lodge asked whether Americans were "willing to have the youth of America ordered to war by other nations without regard to what they or their representatives desire," to defend "the territorial integrity of the far-flung British Empire, including her self-governing dominions and colonies, of the Balkan states, of China or Japan, or of the French, Italian, and Portuguese colonies of Africa."[22] These were effective arguments even if inaccurate. As David Miller recalled, "The false and fantastic vision of American (or Canadian or Brazilian) mothers praying for their sons in the Balkans was as real to many uninformed minds as a movie."[23]

The debate took place against a backdrop that didn't inspire Americans to optimism or enthusiasm about grand enterprises. The months following the end of the war were a difficult time of adjustment. Wilson and his administration had made little preparation for inevitable economic dislocations, and the economy went through rapid cycles of boom and bust as producers adjusted to the sudden drop in orders from Europe. Wartime controls were lifted, which contributed to a rise in prices, but sharply declining foreign demand meant layoffs and stagnant or lowered wages. The nation was suddenly plagued with strikes. In 1919 harbor workers, dressmakers, shipbuilders, cigar makers, firemen, engineers, coal miners, and transportation workers went on strike in Chicago, New York, and other major cities. A great steel strike began in September and did not end until January 1920. Federal troops were called in and people were killed. That same September the Boston police went on strike. There were also "buyers' strikes," with consumers refusing to pay high prices for clothing and other items.[24]

Closely related to the economic disruptions was a growing fear of Bolshevism. Federal, state, and local governments and law enforcement agencies spread a wide net to prevent the revolution that a remarkable number of Americans believed could come any day. Police rounded up members of the Industrial Workers of the World, or "Wobblies," as they were popularly known, accusing them of seeking to overthrow capitalism. The Senate created a committee to investigate Bolshevik activities in the United States. A federal jury convicted a leading socialist and member of Congress, Victor L. Berger of Milwaukee, of sedition and disloyalty. The government arrested the leader of the American Socialist Party, Eugene V. Debs, in part for preaching that Lenin and Trotsky were the "foremost statesmen of the age."[25] Lippmann observed that people were "shivering in their boots over Bolshevism" and were "far more afraid of Lenin than they ever were of the Kaiser." Americans, he noted, were a "most frightened lot of victors."[26]

Some genuinely frightening events added to the general panic. A mysterious wave of bombings at the homes of judges, cabinet members, and other public officials raised alarms about secret plots of anarchists or communists. Sixteen packages containing explosives were discovered at the New York post office. Explosive-filled packages were sent to Justice Oliver Wendell Holmes, Postmaster General Albert Burleson, the governor of Pennsylvania, the mayor of New York, the secretary of labor, and Attorney General Mitchell Palmer. On a single day, June 2, bombs exploded at Palmer's home and at the homes of the mayor of Cleveland and judges in New York and Massachusetts.[27] There followed nationwide raids—the so-called Palmer Raids—in which the federal government arrested hundreds of suspected "Reds." Constant rumors spread of imminent "Red uprisings." The spring and summer of 1919 also saw the eruption of race riots across the country, including in New York, Chicago, and Washington, D.C. Hundreds died, mostly Black Americans. These were not times when Americans thought of expanding their involvement around the world. They were more inclined to insulate themselves from the world as much as possible.

These were also the months when American soldiers began returning from Europe, some percentage of them wounded, along with coffins filled with the corpses of dead husbands, fathers, and sons. Even many of the healthy soldiers returned with sour feelings about their experience. They had headed off to Europe in the spring or summer of 1918, spent months in training, and barely got into the fight when the armistice came, then spent months waiting to get home.[28] Many wondered what the point of it all had been. As one contemporary noted, the Germans at the end of the war "did not have the emotion of being beaten" and the Americans "did not have the emotion of winning."[29] Internationalism and idealism were in short supply, therefore, as Wilson tried to sell his League and treaty.

Lodge, meanwhile, had devised a clever strategy. The League could not be beaten on a straight up-or-down vote, he believed. If the only choice was the League or nothing, a good number of Republicans were likely to defect to Wilson rather than take a stance of "mere negation." Lodge needed an "indirect method." The way to beat Wilson was by attaching amendments to the League Covenant, ostensibly to repair its shortcomings and to protect American rights and interests, but actually to load it with so many caveats as to negate its purpose. Lodge had used this strategy with great success in defeating Taft's arbitration treaties with Britain and France back in 1911. He had larded those treaties with so many damaging amendments that Taft had ultimately refused to go forward with his own treaty. Lodge hoped Wilson could be forced to make the same decision.

One virtue of the strategy was that it also could heal the rift in the Republican Party. It allowed pro-League and anti-League Republicans to vote together to approve the amendments (which only required a majority vote). Then, once the amendments were attached, they could go their separate ways again on the vote for final ratification (which required a two-thirds vote). Pro-League Republicans could vote for the League as modified by the reservations, and anti-League Republicans could vote against it. This would provide the political cover that many Republicans representing pro-League constituencies needed. If the treaty failed because Wilson and the Democrats refused to support an improved, "Americanized" version, Republicans could hardly be blamed. As Lodge explained to Root, Wilson would have to bear responsibility for killing the treaty, and when he ran for re-election, he would be "the worst beaten man that ever lived."[30]

Keen observers at the time had no doubt that Lodge's overriding aim was to defeat Wilson's League by whatever means necessary. Lodge throughout the negotiations repeatedly assured the irreconcilables that he would support only the kind of amendments that "you and I believe in," namely, those that would fundamentally "change the treaty."[31] On September 10, his Foreign Relations Committee reported the treaty out with fifty amendments attached to it, most written by the irreconcilables. These were boiled down to fourteen so-called Lodge reservations. Some were designed to be unacceptable to both Wilson and the Allies. One disavowed the Shantung agreement, although it was inconceivable that Japan could be compelled to return it to China; another rejected the granting of votes in the assembly to the British "dominions," which included Australia, Canada, New Zealand, India, and South Africa. Lodge knew the British would find it very hard if not impossible to swallow either of these provisions.[32] To drive the stake deeper, he added a requirement that at least three of the four Allied powers had to give formal assent to the reservations before the Senate could ratify.

On the critical question of Article 10, Lodge's "reservation" simply rejected any hint of obligation. It stated that

> the United States *declines* to assume, under the provisions of Article X, or under any other article, any obligation to preserve the territorial integrity, or political independence of any other nation . . . or to employ the military or naval forces of the United States . . . ; or to adopt economic measures for the protection of any other country, whether a member of the League or not, against external aggression or for the purpose of coercing any other country, or for the purpose of intervention in the internal conflicts or other controversies which may arise in any other country, and no mandate shall be accepted by the United States under Article XXII, Part I, of the treaty of peace with Germany except by action of the Congress of the United States.[33]

Pro-League Republicans protested that this positive disavowal of all obligations was worse than removing Article 10 altogether and saw it as further proof that Lodge aimed to "kill the whole treaty."[34] Lodge admitted that his reservations were designed to "take the United States out of the treaty entirely on all points where we wish to refuse obligation."[35] Observers in both parties believed that Lodge's mind was "bent not on amendments which would render the present scheme acceptable but upon objections which would render it or any substitute impossible."[36] Stimson believed that if Wilson had presented Lodge and his colleagues "with the Kingdom of Heaven," they still would have rejected it as "immoral and un-American."[37] Elihu Root complained to Lodge that "extreme opponents of the Treaty" were driving the party toward "complete rejection."[38]

If Root believed that, it was not surprising that Wilson did, too. He insisted that what Lodge was proposing were not "reservations" but rather "nullification" of the treaty. The question was what to do about it. Since Wilson believed that his Republican opponents' main goal was "to discredit and overthrow him," he doubted they would accept any concessions, even if he were willing to make them.[39]

He wasn't. Partly it was a matter of pride, partly it was the innate stubbornness of the man, partly it was his intense hatred for Lodge. All these factors, as well as poor health, played a part in Wilson's unwillingness to engage in the political gamesmanship that might conceivably have extracted the requisite number of votes to pass the treaty and the League in some form.

But Wilson was also mindful of serious practical considerations that made him reluctant to compromise. He had just spent six months pleading with the French to have faith in the League and to trust that the United States would make good on its commitment under Article 10. He had offered these assurances in exchange for Clemenceau dropping demands for dismembering Germany and creating an independent Rhineland under French control, for establishing a permanent Allied occupation along the Rhine, for equipping the League with a permanent international army. To remove Article 10 now, or worse, to modify it with a "reservation" disavowing its obligations, would be a betrayal, perhaps with dangerous consequences.

The bilateral security treaty that Wilson had offered Clemenceau as further inducement was predictably going nowhere. Lodge made a great show of demanding that Wilson submit it and repeatedly suggested that he would be willing to bring up the French security treaty as a "distinct and separate thing which we could well afford to do." But he would do so only *after* the Senate voted on the League.[40] That turned out to be a lie. When Wilson finally did submit the treaty at the end of July, Lodge did not bring it to a vote but referred it to the Foreign Relations Committee, where it was buried, forever.[41] Even after the League was defeated and Republicans had taken control of both the White House and the Congress, Lodge never brought the French treaty back up for consideration.[42]

There was disingenuousness on both sides. Wilson, on the one hand, refused to acknowledge that Article 10 could ever lead the United States into war, insisting that "when this Treaty is accepted men in khaki will never have to cross the seas again."[43] Yet at the same time he tried to explain to Americans that to have peace the United States had to declare its willingness to go to war. "If you want to quiet the world, you have got to reassure the world, and the only way in which you can reassure it is to let it know that all the great fighting powers of the world are going to maintain that quiet."[44] The world had to know that "behind the moral judgment of the United States" stood the "overwhelming force of the United States."[45] The message was confusing, and it is likely that Americans were confused. His arguments certainly did not help his cause.

As the final votes on the League approached in November, the Republicans seemed all but locked down in support of the Lodge reservations.

As it became clear that the treaty would fail unless the reservations were included, some Democrats began to argue that it was better to have a treaty with reservations than no treaty at all. Wilson was bedridden from the end of September until well into 1920 and in the critical weeks leading up to the November vote, he made no public comment on the treaty. From his sickbed, however, he told League supporters to vote against the Lodge reservations, the sole purpose of which, he insisted, was "the nullification of the treaty."[46] The Democrats reluctantly complied, and on November 20 the treaty with Lodge's reservations was defeated 39–55, with Democrats joining the irreconcilables in opposition. Then the Senate voted on the treaty without reservations, which also failed, 38–53.

Wilson refused to believe that the Senate's action represented the true wishes of the people. Once again, he staked all on the next election. The approaching 1920 presidential and congressional elections, he insisted, would be "a great and solemn referendum" on the "part that the United States is to play in completing the settlements of the war and in the prevention in the future of such outrages as Germany attempted to perpetrate."

Whether the public would respond as Wilson hoped remained to be seen. The treaty failed for a final time in March 1920. Some Democrats broke ranks and voted for the treaty with Lodge's reservations, bringing the vote to 49–35 in favor of the treaty as amended. That was still seven votes short of the necessary two-thirds. For the remainder of Wilson's term at least, the treaty was dead.

There followed much finger-pointing, and many fingers pointed at Wilson, just as Lodge had hoped. Pro-League Republicans, the so-called "mild reservationists," were angered by his inflexibility and insulted when he claimed to see no "difference between a nullifier and a mild nullifier."[47] Democrats blamed him for not releasing them to negotiate with pro-League Republicans who had voted for the reservations. Many asked at the time, and many would ask later, whether Wilson erred in refusing to accept Lodge's reservations if that was the only way the United States could enter the League. "A few ill-chosen words, one way or another, were not going to make or break this great treaty," one historian later argued. Another insisted that all that mattered was turning the country's attention to Europe's political problems. Joining the League "with or without reservations might have done just that."[48]

Among those who made this case at the time was Edward Grey, the former British foreign secretary, who had first broached the idea of American participation in a league to preserve peace in Europe after the war. Horrified at the possibility that the United States might not join, and believing that without the United States the League would have neither the "overwhelming physical force" nor the "moral force" that it needed to succeed, Grey suggested that it would be better to have America enter the League "as a willing partner with limited obligations" than as "a reluctant partner who felt that her hand had been forced."[49]

Even a century later it is hard to know who was right. It is theoretically possible that had the League and treaty been approved with Lodge's reservations, the United States could have gone on to play the role in Europe that Grey wanted. What Europe needed, after all, was not philosophy but action. The French were not so reassured by Article 10 that its absence or even negation would have made that much difference to them. The real question was whether the United States was prepared to undertake any of the responsibilities and commitments that the Versailles Treaty called for. The two most important were American participation on the Reparation Commission to determine the amount Germany would have to pay, and the presence of American troops as one of the occupying forces in the Rhineland. Because these roles were part of enforcing the treaty, they did not require an Article 10 commitment or even League membership. As Herbert Hoover, a League supporter at the time, later observed, the "major functions" of the League would still have been in place even had the United States not joined.[50] Even David Hunter Miller later believed that Lodge's reservations left the league's "structure intact" and would not have "interfered with its workings."[51]

This was the theory, but the reality might have been different. League supporters on both sides of the Atlantic underestimated the importance of the political shift that had taken place in the United States in the course of the League fight. The fight had transformed the Republican Party, and to some extent American public opinion more generally, in ways that would have far-reaching consequences for American foreign policy. The triumph of the forces in the Republican Party that had opposed Wilson's League raised doubts about whether the United States would in fact have fulfilled its commitments under the treaty or played any role at all in the League, even if Wilson had swallowed Lodge's objections.

Parties and politicians have been known to shift their positions for partisan purposes, but no shift was more dramatic than the Republicans' turn on foreign policy in these months. Until the 1918 election, Republicans had been the internationalist party, the party of global responsibility, the party that had favored entering the war to defeat militarism and defend "civilization," the party bubbling with ideas for a World League for the Peace of Righteousness, for a League to Enforce Peace, for a United Nations. It was the party of the Theodore Roosevelt who had asked Americans to "take a risk for internationalism." But in the process of opposing Wilson and the League, Lodge and his colleagues had radically shifted. The Republican Party became the party it would be for the next quarter century, the party that equated internationalism with Bolshevism, the party of "Americanism" and insular nationalism, the party of rigid abstention from world politics, the party of William Borah. Republicans treated the League as if it were a European plot for world domination. They depicted France and Great Britain not as loyal allies who deserved American support but as greedy imperialists trying to bully and ensnare the United States in their wily scheme.[52]

Although some historians have described Lodge and Roosevelt as conservative "realists," as opposed to Wilson's supposed utopian idealism, it was Lodge and his colleagues who after 1918 employed the rhetoric of utopianism and American exceptionalism. In time-honored American fashion they contrasted the "New World's" purity and moral superiority with the debased and corrupt "Old World" of Europe. The League, they warned, would suck America into "the rapacious power of the imperial system of Europe." Instead of "Americanizing Europe," it would "Europeanize America."[53]

Some Republicans tried to stop the party's turn away from international responsibility. Root, in particular, spent the months leading up to the 1920 election trying to salvage some U.S. commitment to European peace. Privately, he warned that "abandoning" the Versailles Treaty "would bring chaos," the "entire loss" of the results of the war, and a "general disaster, involving [the] United States."[54] Publicly, he helped engineer a letter signed by more than two dozen Republicans arguing that "conditions in Europe" required "the stabilizing effect of the treaty."[55] Speaking to a Republican state convention in February 1920, he proposed that the next Republican president should immediately call a "Congress of all nations" to work on reforming the League Covenant.[56]

Root was stymied, however, by Lodge, who would not let Root write even a moderate endorsement of the League, with the Lodge reservations, into the party's platform. Root angrily suggested that if Lodge continued to back the irreconcilables, all his efforts to add reservations to the treaty over the past year would appear as "a mere subterfuge for the purpose of defeating by indirection a Treaty which the Senate did not dare defeat directly."[57]

In fact, Lodge faced enormous pressure from the irreconcilables to oppose a league in any form, with or without reservations.[58] Borah opposed "any political alliance, co-partnership, or league with Europe or the old world."[59] When Lodge at one point looked a bit too willing to discuss alternative means of supporting a league, Borah and other irreconcilables summoned him to a full-scale dressing down. They threatened to disrupt the convention and bolt the party if he permitted any endorsement of any kind of league. When Lodge offered to resign his post as majority leader, Borah responded, "You won't have a chance to resign! On Monday, I'll move for the election of a new majority leader and give the reasons for my action."[60] Lodge backed down and thereafter blocked all attempts by Root and others to insert an endorsement of a league, or indeed any kind of commitment to Europe, in the party platform.[61] In the end, Lodge would not even permit a Republican platform endorsement of *his own* reservations.[62]

Root and other Republican internationalists next turned to the newly minted Republican presidential candidate, Warren G. Harding. The senator from Ohio had not been their choice, since Harding had worked with Lodge to defeat the treaty.[63] But as Harding was widely assumed to have no strong convictions about anything, Root and others hoped to bring him around. Insisting that his apparent "irreconcilable opposition to any league" was being "misinterpreted," Root, Taft, Stimson, Hughes, and twenty-seven other Republicans published a letter asserting that a vote for Harding would not be a vote against the League but in fact would reaffirm America's commitment to do its "full part in association with other nations to prevent war."[64] Unfortunately and embarrassingly, Harding himself immediately repudiated Root's letter and took a straight, irreconcilable line. His goal was not to "clarify" America's obligations, he insisted, but to "turn my back on them." He sought not "interpretation" but "rejection." What America needed was "not nostrums but normalcy . . . not submergence in internationality but sustainment in triumphant nationality."[65] Republican newspapers commented that the irreconcilables had placed "a pistol to the head of the Republican candidate with so little secrecy that it might as well have been done on the front porch at Marion."[66] Thomas W. Lamont, the longtime Republican who had served on the American delegation in Paris, told friends that the Republican Party was "no longer our old party." It had "turned its coat" and was now "bowing down completely" to Senators Borah and Johnson.[67]

Harding won the 1920 election in the largest landslide in American history. The popular vote was 60.3 to 34.2. The Democrats won no states outside their historic southern stronghold. Republicans picked up 63 seats in the House, which they now held by the massive margin of 303–131. They picked up 10 seats in the Senate, increasing their margin there to 59–37.

The vote was about many things, of which foreign policy was but one. Most observers agreed that the lopsided vote was not a tribute to Harding, whom Senator Frank B. Brandegee called "the best of the second raters."[68] Nor was it about James M. Cox, the Democrat, who ran a respectable race. Insofar as the vote was about one thing more than any other, it was about Wilson. The president by the time of the election was "as unpopular as he once was popular."[69]

There could be no denying, moreover, that much of Wilson's unpopularity was a consequence of the League fight. German Americans disliked him for the peace imposed on Germany. Italian Americans disliked him because of Fiume. Irish Americans disliked him for opposing Irish independence. "Nearly every racial group of alien-born voters (except the Poles) had some such reason for disliking Wilson," one contemporary observed. "Something Wilson had done at the Peace Conference, some shifting of a national boundary in Europe, some denial of racial aspirations."[70] Nor was it just the ethnic groups. Wilson had become "the symbol both of the war we had begun to think of with disillusion, and of the peace we had come to think of with cynicism."[71] Insofar as the election was any kind of "solemn referendum" on the League, it had not come out as Wilson expected.[72]

In the months following the election, Harding, Lodge, and the leading Republicans in Congress made clear that any idea of American participation in any kind of league was dead. Lodge, Borah, Knox, and Brandegee opposed Root for secretary of state, though the party's senior statesman was an obvious choice, because they feared he might sway the president and the party toward internationalism and a league.[73] Soon Lodge, too, would be gone. By 1924 Borah would become chairman of the Senate Foreign Relations Committee. On matters of foreign policy, the Republican Party had indeed become Borah's party.[74]

So what would have happened had Wilson agreed to the treaty with Lodge's reservations? To focus only on "a few ill-chosen words" is to miss the significance of this dramatic shift in the Republican Party's stance on foreign policy. By 1920 Borah and the irreconcilables had become the dominant faction. They wrote the party's platform; they chose the party's presidential candidate; and they held a veto over his choice of secretary of state. Had they wanted, they could have unseated Lodge from the party's leadership—and they might well have done so if, contrary to Lodge's assurances to them, Wilson had accepted his reservations and thus brought the United States into the League. And it was more than just the League. As one contemporary noted, there had "developed in the United States a reaction against all things European," and even if the United States had entered the League in a technical sense, "the political situation in America would have prevented, for a few years at least, the exercise by the United States of any considerable influence in European affairs."[75]

Another question then is whether the outcome of the 1920 elections would have been different had the League passed with Lodge's reservations. It is impossible to know, but there is reason to doubt that passage of the League alone would have produced a Democratic victory. The 1920 election simply restored the Republican Party to the dominant position it had enjoyed for a dozen years prior to the freak election of 1912.[76] The return of Republican ascendancy was aided by a generally conservative shift in the electorate on a number of big issues, including immigration, race, and culture, all of which helped solidify Republican political advantages, especially as the party began courting white voters in the South. It would take the Great Depression and Franklin Roosevelt to change the electoral landscape again.

If the treaty had been approved, therefore, it would have been implemented not by a friendly Wilson or a Democratic successor but by a Republican president and Republican Congress heavily influenced, if not completely controlled, by Borah and his allies. The irreconcilables' battle against the League would have continued, and America's nominal membership in the League might not have provided the physical and moral force that Grey sought.[77] If the League's leading powers ever decided that a deployment of force or an economic embargo was necessary to prevent some act of aggression in Europe, Republicans could have pointed to Lodge's reservations and insisted that the League's decisions had no bearing on American policy, that the president as a legal matter could not even begin to cooperate with other League members without congressional authorization. Lodge's reservations actually gave Congress more control over League matters than over the normal conduct of foreign policy, including control over the appointment of American representatives to the League's various commissions, conferences, and agencies. Borah and his allies could have refused to send anyone to these posts, or they could have insisted on sending people who shared their hostility to the League. As it was, Borah and his allies spent the early 1920s blocking every conceivable American involvement with the new League. They refused to appoint representatives to commissions and prevented American diplomats from meeting with League officials. They even opposed American participation in the new World Court, which during the League debate they had claimed to support.[78]

When Wilson refused to accept Lodge's reservations, therefore, he may have been stubborn, prideful, spiteful, and perhaps even mentally impaired. But he also may have glimpsed this future more clearly than Grey and others did. Whatever mistakes Wilson made in creating the League and seeking Senate approval, and he made many, he may not have been wrong to believe that accepting the Lodge reservations was tantamount to defeating American participation in the League—just as Lodge intended.

What about the American public? Did Americans turn against the League only because of Lodge's maneuverings? Or was American participation doomed from the start because it was simply more of an international commitment than most Americans were willing to make in 1919? Again, there is no sure way of knowing. Lodge and his allies could not have successfully played on fears about being dragged into future wars by foreign governments had those fears not been there. They could not have made Americans feel anxious about "internationalism" were Americans not prepared to feel anxious. And they could not have convinced Americans that they were safe behind their oceans and need not worry about what happened in Europe if the American people were not ready to be convinced.

Given America's history and physical circumstances, such responses were predictable. Even the British, separated from Europe by only twenty miles and having already been involved in several wars on the continent, somehow could believe they had the option of turning away from it. Americans, who lived three thousand miles away and had never taken part in European politics, much less a European war, could not be expected to embrace a new commitment with enthusiasm. Lodge and others insisted that Germany no longer posed a threat, that the Allies could take care of themselves, and that the United States could continue relying on the Monroe Doctrine and Washington's great rule to preserve its security. Most Americans were inclined to believe it.

And yet, the most remarkable thing about the League fight was that for all of Wilson's failures and Lodge's maneuverings, Americans and their representatives in Congress had initially been prepared to approve the Versailles Treaty and join a league in some form. Lodge went to extraordinary lengths to defeat them, and it required transforming his party's views on foreign policy. Had Lodge been either less skillful or less committed to the treaty's defeat, the treaty and the League might have passed. Moreover, had Lodge been willing to see the league approved, it would have been approved, probably with a few mild reservations that Wilson would have accepted. The Republican Party would have remained the party of internationalism and global responsibility as it had been for decades, and not become the party of insular nationalism and narrow self-interest.[79] The United States would have ratified the Versailles Treaty and entered a league in some capacity. Whether that would have made a difference in the direction events took over the next two decades can never be known, but there is good reason to believe it would have.

Much ink has been spilled on the failure of the Versailles Treaty. Generations of critics have argued that its terms were both too harsh and too lenient. The Germans felt aggrieved by the take-it-or-leave-it terms of the Versailles "diktat," and by the "war guilt" clause, but the terms were not so oppressive as to prevent the Germans from trying to overturn it. The emphasis on national and ethnic self-determination was both hypocritical—since in fact many peoples were placed under regimes they did not choose—and too sincere—in that the fulfillment of multiple national aspirations led to a breakdown of stability. Some believe that Wilson betrayed his own principles; others, like Henry Kissinger, believe that the treaty adhered to those principles all too closely.[80]

By far the biggest problem with the treaty, however, had nothing to do with its terms but with America's unwillingness to implement and defend the agreement against inevitable challenges. The treaty was never intended to be implemented without the United States, and it could not be.[81] The agreement reflected the balance of power as it existed on November 11, 1918, in which American power was central. The Germans would not have accepted the peace had the United States not brought its weight to bear. In all likelihood they would not even have lost the war. So the peace reflected the fact that the United States had indeed become part of the equation. When the United States failed to ratify, the peace no longer reflected the distribution of power in Europe. The potential strength of Germany remained enormous. France was weaker than it had been before the war. Russia was out of the picture. Without continued American involvement, it was only a matter of time before Germany regained its hegemonic position on the continent, with all that meant for European stability. With American involvement, the crisis in Europe could possibly have been managed. Without the United States, there was almost no chance.[82] As the historian Margaret MacMillan observes, when war came again in 1939, it was "a result of twenty years of decisions taken or not taken, not of arrangements made in 1919."[83] What MacMillan does not note is that the most critical of those decisions were made by the United States.

CHAPTER THIRTEEN

A Return to "Normalcy"?

The difficulties which beset Europe have their causes within Europe and not in any act or policy of ours.

—Secretary of State Charles Evans Hughes[1]

WHY DID the United States withdraw from the European settlement? The 1920s may be one of the most misunderstood decades in the history of American foreign policy. For some years after World War II, the policies of the three Republican administrations—Harding, Coolidge, and Hoover—were generally condemned for inaction in the face of the European crisis. In recent decades their reputations have been rehabilitated. They are credited with clever use of American economic tools, such as the 1924 Dawes Plan, which provided American loans to Germany in an effort to calm tensions that had led to French invasion in 1923, as well as for engineering agreements aimed ostensibly at a new peaceful order, the Washington naval treaties of 1921–1922 and the Kellogg-Briand Pact "outlawing" war in 1928.

As is often the case with historical revisionism, the original account was closer to the truth.[2] The core principle that guided all three administrations was abstention, and especially in Europe. The conferences they hosted and the treaties they signed were chiefly defensive efforts to limit American commitments and avoid any association with the new League. To understand American policy in these years, it is not enough to look at what policymakers did and said. It is also necessary to place these actions and statements in their political and diplomatic contexts. Although historians these days credit Charles Evans Hughes and others with a "doctrine," American policies were more a haphazard response to domestic pressures and foreign crises. Most of what Republican administrations did was aimed at mollifying public opinion at home. Republican foreign policies were shaped most by what Americans did *not* want to do. This reflected a national mood that was pessimistic about any good that might be done abroad by the United States.

This shift in mood may have been the single most important factor in shaping American policy in the 1920s. Before their entry into the war in 1917, Americans had generally viewed the world as a source of opportunity, not danger. They shared a general belief in the inevitability of peace, progress, and civilization, and saw the United States leading the way, lending its hand in the establishment of international institutions and providing its good offices to mediate disputes. The presidents they elected encouraged this expansive view of America's place in the world. For two dozen years, from McKinley and Roosevelt through Taft and Wilson, Americans were led by the most internationalist-minded administrations in the nation's history up to that point. All believed that a newly powerful America had acquired some responsibilities in the world, that honor and decency required Americans to think not just about their own narrow interests but to recognize that they had broader interests in the overall state of the world. The "selfish avoidance of duty to others" was a "wretched thing," Roosevelt wrote in 1914, and every president since McKinley, each in his own way, said the same.[3]

After the war, the League fight, and the 1920 election, however, Americans became suspicious, anxious, and pessimistic about the world. Instead of offering opportunities, overseas involvement seemed to bring only dangers and unwanted burdens.

This shift in the national mood was not a response to economic problems. Although postwar dislocations threw the country into a deep recession in 1920–1921, by 1922 the U.S. economy came roaring back, and for the remainder of the decade Americans enjoyed the greatest period of prosperity in their history. Real GNP rose by 39 percent between 1919 and 1929. Wages rose by 22 percent to the highest levels ever, and working hours declined thanks to an explosion in productivity. The United States in these years produced as much wealth annually as Britain, France, Germany, Japan, and a dozen other nations combined. Many Americans remained poor, and the gap between rich and poor also reached unprecedented heights, but the general prosperity left the vast majority of Americans contented. The conservative tenor of the times and the dwindling ranks of reformers, labor activists, and socialists attested to this—as La Guardia put it, "it's damned discouraging to be a reformer in the wealthiest land in the world."[4]

Nor was Americans' desire to pull back due to national weakness or incapacity. Never in its history had the United States been stronger relative to the rest of the world, and probably no nation ever enjoyed the combination of wealth, power, and global influence that Americans wielded in the years following the Great War. Germany was defeated and no longer an enemy. The American navy was on its way to surpassing the Royal Navy. The British economy was reeling from the war; it had lost substantial markets in Latin America and elsewhere to the United States; and it owed the United States $4 billion. The empire's very survival depended on American money and power.

The possession of such overwhelming power might have tempted Americans to expand their holdings or their position in the world. That certainly had been the reaction of the British during their nineteenth-century hegemony—they expanded their empire by hundreds of millions of square miles. But Americans had a different aspiration after the war: to be left alone. America's unprecedented power would protect the United States. There was no need to venture out in the world to achieve security. If Americans feared anything after the Great War, it was that they would be dragged into war again. And it was not just other powers that they feared would lure them into war. They also feared themselves, or rather, those amongst themselves—the bankers, the weapons manufacturers, the idealistic internationalists, the eastern elite establishment—who seemed not to have learned the lessons of the Great War.

American disillusionment with the war and the peace that followed was not just a response to the loss of life and treasure. There was a widespread conviction that the war had served no purpose and that the United States had erred in entering it. The disillusionment was greatest among those liberals and progressives who had overcome pacifist inclinations to support a war to end all wars. They now regretted their enthusiasm. Appalled at the "victor's peace" imposed on Germany, they exaggerated its failings. It was "the most iniquitous peace document ever drawn," a "Covenant of Death," "purple with revenge."[5] Some liberals undoubtedly suffered from guilty consciences.[6] Some admitted that they had been carried away, that, as Lincoln Steffens put it, their progressive "theories didn't stand up under the crisis of the war."[7] Others preferred to lay the blame elsewhere, conjuring various conspiracies that had allegedly fooled Americans into intervening. Upton Sinclair believed he had been "trapped into supporting" the war. The historian Harry Elmer Barnes, who had produced patriotic pro-war propaganda during the war, afterwards complained of "how totally and terribly we were 'taken in'" by the "salesmen of this most holy and idealistic world conflict."[8] Some blamed Wilson, their "prophet of righteousness," for failing to see through the Europeans' "diplomatic perfidy."[9]

The release of new documents about the war and the new interpretations of the war's origins offered by "revisionist" historians over the course of the 1920s only deepened the impression that Americans had been the victims of a "fraud" and a "hoax."[10] The source of much of the revisionism was Germany itself. Proving that Germany was "not alone at fault" was a primary foreign policy objective for Berlin after the war, and not just as a matter of fairness but as a lever to "force open the Treaty of Versailles."[11] The leading lights of the formidable German historical profession joined in the task, producing and organizing a "veritable avalanche" of German diplomatic documents for release to the world. The curated collections revealed, among other things, that the kaiser had not been quite the madman salivating for war that Americans had imagined but rather a sometimes indecisive, hesitant decision-maker who at the last minute made some minor, meaningless gestures for peace.[12] None of this proved that the Germans were not responsible for the war. Even Charles Beard warned against attempts "to white-wash" Germany's role.[13] But for many the contrast between what the documents showed and what Americans had believed during the war was enough to force a painful re-examination.

Many who had fervently supported the war now just as fervently condemned it. As Niebuhr wrote in his diary in 1923, gradually "the whole horrible truth about the war" was being revealed. "Every new book destroys some further illusion." Instead of a moral war between good and evil, the conflict now seemed to have been "simply a tremendous contest for power between two great alliances of states in which the caprice of statesmen combined with basic economic conflicts to dictate the peculiar form of the alliances." The "moral pretension of the heroes" had turned out to be "bogus," and "the iniquity of the villains" now seemed "not as malicious as it once appeared. . . . How can we ever again believe anything?"[14]

Many chose not to. Barnes warned that Americans must be "on our guard" the next time someone proposed going to war to "'crush militarism,' 'make the world safe for democracy,' 'put an end to all further wars,' etc."[15] Most Americans decided to blame the Europeans for the failure of the peace to live up to their hopes. Lippmann, who had justified intervention in 1917 on the grounds that America's "own existence" depended on the survival of the "Atlantic community," now argued for leaving Europe to its fate and finding "our own security in this hemi-sphere."[16] It was necessary to sever ties, steer clear of them, and, as Beard suggested, to regard all of Europe's quarrels "with cold blood."[17]

Americans did not become "isolationists" after the war; that term never fit them in any era. Their immigrant character, their natural inclination to trade, their universalist ideology, and their general openness as a people precluded any genuine walling off from the rest of the world. In the 1920s American businesses continued to seek greater access to foreign markets. They opened plants and offices in Europe and around the world. Bankers and financiers looked to invest abroad. Artists, writers, and intellectuals poured into postwar Europe, as did hundreds of thousands of tourists. Americans who did not travel abroad became more aware of the world with the expansion of newspaper and radio coverage, which brought more and more of the world into Americans' daily lives. *Time* magazine began publishing in 1923, and in just its first twelve months sported pic-tures of Mussolini, Atatürk, Churchill, Poincaré, Asquith, Hugo Stinnes, and Egypt's Fuād I on its covers.

The postwar disillusionment had not altogether extinguished interna-tionalist sentiments. Although midwestern farmers and most small and medium-sized domestic manufacturers tended to support traditional Republican high-tariff policies and the nationalist foreign policies that went with them, multinational corporations like General Electric and the Radio Corporation of America and big financial houses like J. P. Morgan and Company favored a more open and cooperative relationship with the rest of the world, and especially with Europe.[18] They believed American foreign policy had to keep pace with a changing global economy, with the growing "interdependence of all civilized nations in matters of commerce and industry," and also with America's expanding role within this chang-ing world.[19] Between 1919 and 1929, U.S. overseas investment climbed from just under seven billion to over seventeen billion dollars.[20] As GE chairman Owen D. Young put it, the United States might stay out of the League of Nations, but it could not stay out of "the great economic movements throughout the world." It was already "inescapably there."[21] The business-minded Herbert Hoover believed—in the early 1920s—that solving America's "domestic problems" required a degree of "stability abroad," which meant reducing armaments, establishing mechanisms for the peaceful settlement of disputes, and destroying the "economic barri-ers" that prevented "the free entry of our commerce over the world."[22]

A number of Americans had not stopped thinking of the United States as a moral beacon to the world. As the former suffragist turned peace advocate Carrie Chapman Catt put it, there had to be more to American foreign policy than "trade and dollars."[23] No one spoke anymore of making the world safe for democracy, but on the great question of international peace, many still felt that the United States had to "fulfill its real destiny and contribute to the real peace and security of the world." It had to "lead . . . in the war on war."[24] During and after the war American peace organizations proliferated. As the historian Robert H. Ferrell summed up the decade: "Peace echoed through so many sermons, speeches, and state papers that it drove itself into the consciousness of everyone. Never in world history was peace so great a desideratum, so much talked about, looked toward, and planned for, as in the decade after the 1918 Armistice."[25]

The American peace movement lacked unity and a consistent message—or even a coherent theory of what was wrong and how to fix it. The movement included genuine pacifists with a "deep-seated opposition to sanction-based collective security," as well as onetime League supporters who still believed that, on the contrary, no peace could be built without international enforcement mechanisms.[26] Very few internationalists still believed peace should be preserved by American power, however. Legalists looked to a third Hague Conference or membership in a World Court, believing, with Elihu Root, that the only "true remedy" to international chaos and aggression was "the most perfect establishment and enforcement of law."[27] "Community internationalists" looked to the evolution of a shared, "organic social consciousness" across national boundaries.[28] Some saw the answer in disarmament, others in arbitration and non-aggression pacts, and others still in the "outlawing" of war. Some believed that "only a spiritual and economic revolution" could "save mankind and make possible a genuine association of free peoples."[29]

Some League supporters still hoped the United States would one day join or at least cooperate with the League and the European powers. Perhaps "we can put a new label on it," Taft hoped, "as soon as Wilson is forgotten."[30] Some believed that joining the Permanent Court of International Justice, or World Court, a League creation, might be a first step.[31] But whether the United States was inside the League or outside it, many American internationalists and even some pacifists believed the United States had to be involved with other nations in establishing a durable international peace. They doubted that Europeans could cure their ills without American assistance. They were too dependent on the United States, "financially, morally and spiritually."[32] "How can there be security," former secretary of war Newton Baker asked, "with us standing aloof and playing a lone hand?"[33] But these voices were distinctly in the minority. Most peace advocates, like most Americans, opposed the League and any involvement with Europe.

"Normalcy," it turned out, was closely tied to xenophobia and racism. Mistrust of all things foreign was rampant in the postwar years. Many in white Protestant America were consumed with fear that, as the eugenicist Madison Grant put it, "the old stock" of Americans was being "crowded" out and overwhelmed by "these foreigners."[34] The remarkable rise and popularity of the "second" Ku Klux Klan in the 1920s testified to widespread concerns that, as Imperial Wizard Hiram Wesley Evans put it, "aliens" were trying to "force us to change our civilization" and "wrest from us control of our own country."[35] In the Harding administration's first months, Congress passed the Emergency Quota Act, the most restrictive immigration measure in American history. Rushed through to address expected massive inflows from war-torn Europe, it cut back especially on the number of immigrants permitted from southern and eastern Europe. The Immigration Act of 1924 sharply curtailed immigration from all except northern European nations.

The same allergy to foreigners spurred support for the Fordney-McCumber Tariff Act of 1922, which raised rates on dutiable imports by a massive 38.5 percent. The *Wall Street Journal* called it "one of the most selfish, short-sighted and extravagant laws of the kind ever enacted" because its chief effect was to leave hungry Europeans with no money to buy food from distressed American farmers.[36] But the high tariff offered satisfaction to those who believed the average American was being "robbed" by foreigners.[37]

Such concerns naturally affected foreign policy, shaping attitudes toward the League, toward Europe, and toward American involvement in world affairs more generally. Klan followers and millions of others feared being made "a tool or cat's-paw" in "the hatreds and quarrels of the Old World" and saw a clear link between external and internal threats, between "radicalism, cosmopolitanism, and alienism of all kinds."[38] These fears bolstered William Borah and the other "irreconcilables" in their ongoing battle against the League and "internationalism."

That battle did not end with Wilson's defeat. Borah and his colleagues spent the next decade fighting every form of international commitment, no matter how minor, on the suspicion that it was a way of sneaking America into the League through the "back door."[39] They had defeated Root's candidacy for secretary of state, but they viewed Charles Evans Hughes and Commerce Secretary Herbert Hoover with suspicion, too.[40]

Borah, who succeeded Lodge as chairman of the Senate Foreign Relations Committee in 1924 and would remain in that powerful position until 1933, kept a tight leash on Hughes and other policymakers. They, in turn, did everything they could to avoid reviving what Hughes called the "old controversy."[41]

Avoiding that "old controversy" required going to unusual lengths. In the early years of the Harding and Coolidge administrations, Congress prohibited American representatives from attending the League's meetings in an official capacity. When the administration occasionally sent "unofficial observers" to Geneva and other League conferences, Borah cried foul.[42] Harding's new ambassador to Great Britain, the staunchly anti-League journalist George Harvey, announced that the United States would have no dealings with the League or with any "commission or committee appointed by or responsible to it, directly or indirectly, openly or furtively."[43] So fearful was the State Department of congressional ire that for a time it would not even open mail from the League.[44]

For Borah and a significant portion of Congress and the public, it was not just a matter of staying out of the League. It was also about staying out of Europe. From their first days in office, Harding and Hughes had to bend over backwards to prove to both Americans and Europeans that the United States really was out. The "difficulties which beset Europe," Hughes repeatedly declared, "have their causes within Europe and not in any act or policy of ours."[45] American diplomats serving in Europe were instructed to steer clear of all "political questions of purely European concern."[46] When they did attend international conferences, they had to travel incognito or pretend they were vacationing. When Hughes himself attended an international conference in London, he arrived not in his role as secretary of state but as president of the American Bar Association.[47] Even in their day-to-day diplomacy, American diplomats in Europe were constrained by a State Department policy of "enforced inactivity."[48]

Americans would have had an easier time disentangling themselves from Europe had they not insisted on full repayment of the war debts, with interest. Most leading economists, bankers, and businessmen argued that demanding repayment was short-sighted. The postwar economy of Europe was in dire need of stimulus that only American money could provide.[49] As the influential financier Paul Warburg put it, there was "infinitely greater value" for the United States in reconstructing "a world in which we can trade in peace and security" than in having "on our books obligations of our comrades at arms which they cannot pay."[50] Secretary of State Hughes privately admitted to the British that "it was altogether against the interests of the United States that the debt owed by Great Britain and the other Allies should be repaid."[51]

Public attitudes in the United States made it hard for Congress to show any flexibility, however. The main lines of U.S. policy on the debt were laid down during the brief but deep postwar recession. Unemployment had temporarily reached roughly 12 percent while GDP dropped by almost a quarter.[52] Farmers sought federal subsidies to compensate for falling prices. The unemployed sought financial support. Returning war veterans and their families sought bonuses. Everyone wanted relief from the high war-time taxes. And all these demands came as the federal budget deficit had ballooned from $1 billion in 1915 to more than $20 billion in 1920.[53] Under the circumstances, forgiving Europe's debt was not the road to re-election. What was more, the federal deficit was directly tied to the European loans, inasmuch as the loans were funded in part by selling "Liberty Bonds" to the public. The bondholders would eventually have to be paid back with interest. To make those payments, the Treasury was counting on the Europeans making good on their debts.[54] If the Europeans did not pay, the government would either have to run a bigger deficit or raise taxes.[55] When the Harding administration asked Congress for some latitude in negotiating easier terms with European debtors, therefore, Senate Democrats and Republican irreconcilables joined together to reject the idea.[56] Instead, Congress set up a War Debt Commission with strict instructions on what terms could be negotiated. Harding even bragged that in the debt settlement negotiated with Britain in 1923, the U.S. negotiators had driven a "hard bargain" and came away with a "substantial profit."[57]

Europeans were furious—a British official later recalled that the whole affair made "the average Englishman think of the Americans as dirty swine," while French newspapers took to calling the U.S. "Uncle Shylock."[58] From the European perspective, the loans had been America's contribution to the overall struggle to save civilization—Europeans had paid in blood; the Americans had paid in dollars.[59] Now the Americans were treating the loans as if they had simply been business transactions. Calvin Coolidge may or may not have remarked, "They hired the money, didn't they?" but this reflected the common view.[60] Economic nationalism was the order of the day. Harding had promised to put "our own house in order," to "prosper America first," not to help Europe.[61]

Far from helping Europe, American policies exacerbated the European crisis. Hughes and other American officials could claim all they wanted that Europe's difficulties had their "causes within Europe and not in any act or policy of ours," but this was not true.[62] Practically every action taken by the Europeans in this period was influenced by American policies. On questions concerning the League, French security, disarmament, reparations, and overall European peace and stability, American power and American preferences could not be ignored, even if Americans pretended that they had no interests at stake one way or the other.

What most worried American diplomats on the ground in Europe was the possible resumption of war between France and Germany. From the moment the Senate failed to ratify the Versailles Treaty for the second and final time in March 1920, it was clear to them that Europe faced an "impending cataclysm."[63] There were two ways to prevent it. Either the United States could provide meaningful reassurance to the French that they would not be left to fend for themselves against a reinvigorated Germany, or they could ease the pressures on both Germany and France by forgiving some of France's debt and keeping the German reparations bill low enough for the German economy to recover. The United States did neither.

French fears of German recovery remained the core of the crisis. The French had legitimate doubts as to whether they could remain a viable power in the European system if Germany was not compelled to abide strictly by the terms of the Versailles agreement.[64] Indeed, with the Americans out of the League and the treaty, the French had reason to wonder whether even the terms of Versailles would be enough to protect them. As Churchill observed at the time, Clemenceau at Paris had given up immediate security in exchange for American and British promises. "Well, America did not make good," and so the French, having been "abandoned by the United States," were "terrified."[65]

Under the terms of Versailles, the French had one big lever. The treaty stipulated that if Germany was not living up to its obligations, the Allies could occupy cities and regions on the right bank of the Rhine to compel compliance. Following the U.S. Senate's final rejection of the treaty and the League in 1920, the French thus embarked on an aggressive strategy in the Rhineland not only to force Germany to live up to the terms of the treaty but to acquire the "physical guarantees" and the strategic frontier on the Rhine that Clemenceau had been denied at Paris.[66] In April 1920 French forces occupied Frankfurt and Darmstadt, technically in response to an unauthorized German dispatch of troops to put down a Communist revolt. A few months later, when the Germans failed to make deliveries of coal as part of their in-kind reparation payments, the French sent troops to occupy Düsseldorf, Duisburg, and Ruhrort. When Raymond

Poincaré took over as premier in January 1922, he began threatening to send French forces into the Ruhr, Germany's industrial heartland, to seize control of German mines and factories and thereby ensure German payments that had not been forthcoming—to obtain what the French government called "productive guarantees." As the commander of U.S. occupation forces in the Rhineland, General Henry T. Allen, noted, they had decided "to take every possible measure" to weaken Germany, to cripple its economy and wrest control of the Rhineland while they still had the power, and the nominal right, to do so.[67]

In addition to wanting to weaken Germany, the French also had their own economic problems to address. They owed the Americans over $3 billion, and the French public was understandably unenthusiastic about paying it back, with interest, over the next half century or more. The French insisted they would pay no more to the Americans than they received from Germany in reparations. It was precisely this linkage that the Americans vigorously denied, but that had no effect on French thinking. Perhaps if the United States had taken its seat as chairman of the Reparation Commission established by the treaty, as the other powers still favored even after the Senate's failure to ratify, it might have been able to blunt the more extreme French actions. But Borah and other irreconcilables forbade the Harding administration from sending an official representative. Instead, the French took the chair and used it both to demand the maximum from Germany and to authorize the use of force to collect.

The French were not wrong to be concerned, both about the Germans' long-term capabilities and about their short-term intentions. The Germans did not want to fulfill the terms of the Versailles Treaty, and particularly the payment of steep reparations. Even in the best of circumstances, convincing the German public to transfer hundreds of millions of dollars to the treasuries of other countries—and to do so every year for decades—would have been difficult. Adolf Hitler was not the only German who believed that the Versailles "diktat" had turned Germany into the "wage slave of international capital" and that German workers had been turned into "international slave workers" for foreign bankers.[68]

As a purely financial matter, the Germans were theoretically capable of paying the reparations demanded by the Allies.[69] They could do it by raising taxes, cutting expenditures on welfare and other social programs, and achieving a favorable balance of payments by exporting more and importing less. Yet in the real world, and in a nascent democracy, it was doubtful that any German politician could survive in office after proposing such painful measures to a beleaguered German public.[70] From the beginning, therefore, successive Weimar governments did their best to evade the reparations burden. They failed to make payments on time or at all. They inflated their currency to depreciate the value of whatever they did pay. They complained constantly to the British and the Americans that the reparation demands would destroy the German economy. They particularly looked to the Americans, who had, after all, refused to ratify the Versailles Treaty. If the richest and most powerful of the victor nations was not going to enforce the treaty, Germans did not see why they, as the weakest and poorest, had to abide by it.[71]

The Weimar Republic entered the world burdened with life-threatening handicaps. It had been born in defeat. Its civilian leaders were discredited from the beginning for signing the shameful Versailles "diktat." The revered Hindenburg and other German military leaders had dishonestly accused the Weimar leaders of stabbing the German army in the back, which provided rich propaganda material for nationalist groups. So did the fact that some of the more prominent members of the democratic political coalition that took power in the November 1918 revolution—the "November criminals," as right-wing critics called them—were Jews.[72]

In addition to bearing "the heavy historic burden of a lost war," the newborn republic also bore the burden of paying for it.[73] The kaiser's government had not financed the war by raising taxes but instead had piled up debt in the expectation that, after victory, the defeated powers, that is, France and Russia, would pay reparations to Berlin. But instead, it was Germany that was defeated, and it was Germany that had to pay. The debt crisis fell squarely into the laps of Weimar's new democratic leaders. In addition to paying off the wartime obligations, plus the reparations, the new government also had to pay the costs of rebuilding Germany: war victims had to be given some assistance; ethnic Germans evicted from territories lost in the Versailles agreement had to be resettled back in Germany; civil servants' salaries had to be paid, as did welfare benefits to the needy, along with all the other expenses of facilitating Germany's recovery from the war.[74] Instead of cutting spending and raising taxes, the early Weimar governments took the politically safer route: they just printed more money.[75] The resulting inflation managed to preserve social peace, barely, but it soon spiraled out of control.

Germany in these years was highly unstable, prone to radicalism and violence. Discharged soldiers from the vast army made the difficult

adjustment to civilian life at a time of economic hardship and uncertainty. Some portion of them joined paramilitary groups, which played
an outsized role in postwar German society. The German army was
reduced by the treaty to 100,000, which meant that the Weimar government often relied on the paramilitary organizations to help keep order.
In 1919 the government turned to the right-wing *Freikorps* to put down
a Communist uprising, which resulted in the deaths of two prominent
Communist leaders, Rosa Luxemburg and Karl Liebknecht. The Communist Party had its own private army, as did the numerous right-wing
organizations, including the National Socialist German Workers' Party
(or Nazis, as they were known in Britain and America), as did the Social
Democrats and other more moderate political parties. These private
armies battled in the streets and used violence and intimidation as political tools. There were repeated uprisings by both Left and Right, but the
government responded more harshly to Communist challenges than to
right-wing violence. In March 1920, a rightist putsch led by Wolfgang
Kapp succeeded in capturing Berlin and forced government leaders to
flee first to Dresden and then to Stuttgart while the German military
stood by and did nothing. When widespread protests and strikes against
the Kapp Putsch led to another Spartacist uprising in the Ruhr in 1920,
the government sent in the army, which in turn led to the intervention of
the French.

Early Weimar was plagued by political assassinations. In 1919, Kurt
Eisner, the socialist premier of Bavaria and a Jew, was assassinated by
a German nationalist. In 1921, Matthias Erzberger, the leader of the
Catholic Centre Party and one of the signers of the armistice in November 1918, was assassinated by an ultra-nationalist paramilitary group. In
1922, the foreign minister, Walter Rathenau, another Jew and a moderate
who tried to negotiate a reparations compromise with France, was assassinated by the same group.

Many Germans, especially in the upper reaches of society, were simply
not committed to democracy, a form of government that had been essentially imposed on them by Wilson as a condition of peace. German aristocrats, senior military officers, and some corporate leaders would have
preferred a return to the monarchy or some other hierarchical system of
rule. German big business was not happy with the new social compact of
Weimar democracy, which provided unprecedented protections for labor
and, in the business owners' view, increased wages without increasing
productivity. They saw Bolshevism lurking everywhere, especially among
the workforce, and so hedged their bets by funneling money to right-wing

organizations with paramilitary arms, including the National Socialists led by the dynamic young Hitler. Leading figures like Hindenburg, who enjoyed immense prestige and popularity despite the loss of the war, also had no affection for democracy, and even less for the Social Democrats who predominated in Weimar. Even an up-and-coming political leader like Gustav Stresemann began as a monarchist and converted to democracy chiefly out of necessity and political ambition.

Postwar Germany would have been unstable had it faced no external pressures, therefore, but French actions to compel reparations payments aggravated Weimar's difficulties. The Weimar governing coalition could not win: If they paid reparations, they were selling out the fatherland and robbing the German people of their hard-earned wages; if they refused to pay, they could not defend the German people against French retaliation. Many Germans started looking to the Communists or to the right-wing nationalist groups that promised liberation from foreign oppression and humiliation. These pressures also produced splintering within Germany's federal system, as strong states like Bavaria toyed with the idea of seceding from the democratic republic and establishing their own monarchy. The French were not sorry to see this splintering. It encouraged them to press harder. Preparations for an invasion of the Ruhr quickened.

Both British and American officials took a dim view of French policies, but they did little to address the burgeoning crisis. The British were far more willing to be flexible than the Americans, however, especially on the debt and reparations question. As a nation that was both a debtor and creditor from the war, the British would have been happy to cancel the debts they were owed, by France and others, in exchange for the United States canceling the debts that Britain owed. This would have relieved pressure on Germany to pay reparations. Foreign Secretary Arthur Balfour suggested this in a public note in August 1922. Expressing concern about the "weight of international indebtedness, with all its unhappy effects upon credit and exchange, upon national production and international trade," he bluntly observed that only the United States, which insisted on looking at all these debts as commercial transactions, stood in the way of solving the great international problem. Balfour's note did not go over well in the United States, where even sympathetic internationalists like Bernard Baruch responded angrily to the suggestion that America was being "ungenerous." As one newspaper put it, "Lord

Balfour seems to think he can call us sheep thieves in language so eloquent that we shall not understand it."[76]

The British also looked for ways to provide France some reassurance on the security front. The French, for instance, demanded greater clarity on how the League of Nations would designate an aggressor, when and how the League would impose sanctions, and whether the British were committed to implementing League decisions. The British responded with the Draft Treaty of Mutual Assistance, which aimed at defining aggression and strengthening the League's mechanisms to respond. A year later, League diplomats produced the Geneva Protocol, which also looked to establish the means for designating an aggressor and triggering League action.

The British were wary of making such commitments without American approval, however. Not only did they not want to be left alone defending France, but they feared clashes with the United States. If Germany or some other power committed an act of aggression, and the League agreed to impose sanctions, would the United States take part or ignore them? If the United States refused to participate, the aggressor would enjoy unlimited access to the vast American financial and material resources. The League's sanctions would be meaningless. If Britain and other League powers tried to block American trade with the aggressor, it could lead to an unthinkable war with the United States.[77]

The Harding administration, meanwhile, worked to kill the League diplomats' handiwork. Secretary of State Hughes expressed concern lest the Draft Treaty of Mutual Assistance "impose specific commitments on the United States, infringe upon the nation's freedom of action, undermine traditional neutrality policy, or link the United States to the League of Nations."[78] He condemned the Geneva Protocol as a "new Holy Alliance," warning rather absurdly that it would permit the European powers to intervene in the Western Hemisphere.[79] Most importantly, he made it clear to the British that the United States did not approve of these League measures. Britain withdrew its support, and the effort collapsed. French diplomats complained that the British always had "their eyes on Washington" and that it was "a fundamental principle of English policy in any international crisis to humor the opinion of the United States."[80]

Washington's push for disarmament also created problems in Europe, especially with the French. The Washington Naval Treaty of 1921–1922 was widely celebrated in the United States for putting a cap on the multisided naval arms race which Wilson had helped kick off with his wartime naval program. With only minimal consultation with the other powers, Hughes declared a moratorium on naval construction and the scrapping of enough existing vessels to establish a new fixed naval hierarchy, with the United States and Britain on top, the Japanese next, and the French lumped in with the Italians at the bottom (the ratios were set at 5:5:3:1.5:1.5). The French were outraged in part because they were not consulted, in part because they were insulted to be given such a lowly position, but mostly because, for France, all questions of disarmament, on land or on sea, were inseparable from its security needs vis-à-vis Germany. The Americans had not even taken this into consideration in formulating their proposal. In the years that followed, the French would refuse to disarm, or even to attend further conferences, without some guarantee that the League would come to France's assistance in the event of German aggression. Without American help, there was little the British could do to satisfy French concerns. As one prominent British general noted, British power after the war was "spread all over the world, strong nowhere, weak everywhere, and with no reserve."[81]

As the American General Allen observed in the spring of 1921, England had gone as far as it could attempting to restrain the French without "increasing the friction" between the two erstwhile allies. The French were "intent on the occupation of the Ruhr" and could be "restrained only by the attitude of the United States."[82] Instead, Americans' policy of aloofness and "enforced inactivity" only worsened the situation. As the French moved closer to the threatened intervention in the Ruhr, British officials repeatedly beseeched the American government to do something: to lean on the French, to limit their power in the Reparation Commission, to propose a moratorium on German reparations payments, to show flexibility on the war debts, or even just to show up at an international conference to discuss these matters.[83] The Germans, too, begged the United States to get involved. In April 1921, the Weimar government formally asked Washington to serve as mediator or arbiter on the reparations question, promising to abide by whatever plan the Americans proposed.[84] Even French officials hinted that American mediation would be welcome, especially if accompanied by concessions on the war debts.[85]

It was not only foreign governments that pressed Harding and Hughes. American diplomats in Europe bombarded the White House and State Department with requests for some kind of action. The U.S. ambassador in Berlin, Alanson B. Houghton, a Republican business tycoon highly regarded by both Harding and Hughes, repeatedly warned that the Weimar government, if pressed too hard, could fall to radical forces on either the Right or the Left. Houghton reported that as Germany's young parliamentary system faltered, armed groups were "working toward dictatorship." He singled out Hitler, who had 30,000 followers in his National Socialist German Workers' Party and who on the strength of his "vehemence and fanaticism" was "rapidly becoming leader of a whole movement . . . following the pattern of the Fascisti in Italy."[86] State Department officials in Washington warned that a French military occupation of the Ruhl would inspire "the undying hatred of the German people—a hatred which must eventually result in war."[87]

American diplomats in Europe believed that the mere hint of U.S. flexibility on the question of war debts could keep the French from drastic action. It would "turn [the] scale," advised the American ambassador in Paris, another Republican political ally of Harding.[88] General Allen, too, believed that "measured action now would prevent serious discomforts for us later."[89] Houghton sent an impassioned cable to Hughes analyzing the European problem and proposing the American remedy. "Each of these nations is caught in the gin of its own historic continuity," Houghton wrote. "It is in a sort of groove. It cannot escape. If relief is to come, it must come from without. And the only people who possess the power to give the necessary impulse are the people of the United States." Houghton argued for a policy of generosity rooted in enlightened self-interest. "God has been good to us in America. He has made it possible for us to create and pile up huge wealth. . . . He has given our people also the vision, once the essential facts are laid before them, to use any necessary part of this wealth to bring about a real and, it may be, a lasting peace, among the four great nations involved."[90] Either course was open, Houghton wrote in another cable. "We can make the conditions under which millions of human beings in Europe must live almost infinitely better, or we can make them infinitely worse. It is for us alone to decide."[91] The issue was not just a humanitarian one. Houghton warned that "the German people were desperate, that Western civilization was collapsing, and that social upheaval was imminent. . . . American interests would be damaged."[92]

Hughes and his colleagues in the Harding administration did not disagree with the analysis. "We do not wish to see a prostrate Germany," Hughes made clear. He believed, as well, that there could "be no economic recuperation in Europe unless Germany recuperates."[93] But as "anxious" as he was to avoid "a German collapse," he feared that even discussing the debt question with Europeans would produce "violent opposition" in Congress.[94] At that very moment, the War Debt Commission created

by Congress was publicly calling on France to begin repayments immediately.[95] According to the British ambassador in Washington, Harding
and Hughes were "frightened of their own political shadows."[96] General
Allen, too, could see that "public opinion" in the United States and the
"approaching elections" prevented "President Harding doing what seems
to be of the greatest benefit to the world just now."[97]

Hughes therefore rejected the requests for American action. He
rebuffed German calls for American mediation, British calls to attend a
conference, and his ambassadors' calls for almost any action to prevent
the coming crisis. "The key of the settlement" of the Europeans' problem, he insisted, was "in their hands not ours."[98] Harding complained
that "the nations of the Old World" wanted to "put upon our shoulders
the main burden of finding a way out from the present deplorable state
of affairs."[99]

The Americans had other tools they could have used besides war debt
cancellation. Their troops in the Rhineland also gave them considerable
leverage over all the parties, if they chose to use it. Since the end of 1919,
the number of American forces had dropped considerably from the initial
200,000, but there were still 15,000 left, led by the formidable General
Allen. Although Allen received no instructions from Washington at any
time, in his three years in command at Coblenz, he had played a critical
role unofficially and discreetly mediating disputes between the French
occupation authorities and the German population. As Under Secretary
of State William Phillips explained in a memorandum in the late spring
of 1921, every one of the European powers wanted American troops to
stay in place. The Germans saw American troops as their only protection
from the French; the British looked to the United States to discipline
the French in ways they could not; and the French continued to value
America's continuing presence as a deterrent to Germany.[100] General
Allen repeatedly made the case to visiting American politicians and businessmen that the small U.S. occupation force was well worth the price,
for it served to stabilize the European economy for American exports.
One Republican senator declared that if keeping "American soldiers on
the Rhine will tend to restore the equilibrium in Europe and bring back
a market for the excess products of the United States, it seems to me to
be a good business investment."[101] Harding on the campaign stump in
1920 had promised that the "boys over in Germany" hadn't "any business there" and would be brought home "just as soon as we have formal
peace," but by the fall of 1921 he had changed his mind.[102] In October the

secretary of war reported that 5,600 American soldiers would remain in Germany indefinitely.[103]

But pressure began to grow in the United States to pull the troops out. Borah and other irreconcilables worried that the continuing occupation would drag the United States back into Europe's conflicts. "We are drifting into the League," Brandegee warned, and Hiram Johnson insisted that "whether England wishes it, or France wishes it, whether the Entente desires it, or whether Germany now asks for it, I want them brought home."[104] The axe fell in January 1922 when the question of paying for the occupation force came up and the Allies notified Washington that it would not receive the $230 million for the cost of the occupation out of the first tranche of German reparations payments. Congress and the Harding administration exploded at what the president called European "ingratitude," and within a month General Allen received orders to bring the entire force home by July 1.[105]

The European powers pleaded with the United States not to pull out. The British warned that the departure of American forces would be a "great calamity for Europe." The Germans sent word that the proposed withdrawal was "causing great anxiety to the population of the Rhineland and the German Government" and urged the United States to continue to exercise its "impartial and moderating influence." Even the French, though moving closer to intervention in the Ruhr, worked to reverse Harding's decision. The American ambassador in Paris sent a cable urging the retention of both the troops and General Allen.[106] Harding's mind was made up, however. Although he had earlier praised the "mollifying and harmonizing influence" of Allen and his troops, he now warned that their continued presence "might involve us" in European difficulties.[107] On January 6, 1923, the Senate passed a resolution calling for their removal. The measure had strong bipartisan support, including, by this point, Lodge, who now said he had "favored for a long time the withdrawal of troops." The irreconcilables argued that Americans should get out precisely because Europe was in a "highly inflammable state." Better to "keep our hands out of this hell pot they are brewing over there." They hoped to have seen "the last American boy cross the seas to fight the wars of Europe or Asia."[108]

As the last American troops in Europe prepared to move out, the French moved in. In January 1923 the Reparation Commission, now chaired by France, with the American seat empty, and with the British representative casting a lonely dissent, officially declared Germany to be in default on its payments. Spearheaded by the French 32nd Division, French and Belgian engineers and troops moved into the Ruhr to take control of German mines, factories, and railroads to ensure delivery of coal and steel to France. Hughes, finally roused to action, tried to use the impending withdrawal of American forces as leverage to forestall the invasion, warning Poincaré that it would lead to the withdrawal of all American troops from Europe.[109] The French had made their decision, however, knowing that the Americans had already made theirs. As the invasion commenced, Hughes announced there was nothing America could do but "maintain a dignified position" in "accord with the traditional policies of nonintervention."[110]

CHAPTER FOURTEEN

The Collapse of Europe and the Rise of Hitler

All of us are suffering to a greater or lesser extent from the situation in which we find ourselves as regards the United States.

—Raymond Poincaré to Gustav Stresemann[1]

THE FRENCH invasion of the Ruhr, and the more than two years of military occupation that followed, had much the effect on German politics and the economy that American and British officials had feared. The Weimar government at the time was led by Chancellor Wilhelm Cuno, a moderate businessman whom Houghton knew well and regarded as not at all "warlike."[2] Cuno feared that to acquiesce to this latest French use of force, however, would spell the end not only of him but of Weimar.[3] Facing a "wave of national fury that crossed all social and political divides," Cuno ordered a policy of "passive resistance" to the French.[4] German workers in the occupied regions were encouraged not to cooperate as the French tried to extract resources and manufactures from German mines and factories. There were widespread strikes, and in the confrontations between French occupying forces and local workers, some Germans were killed. The rest suffered severe deprivations, even with the government providing financial support. Reinhold Niebuhr, visiting the homeland of his parents, found such misery among the Germans in the occupied territories that he thought it "the closest thing to hell I have ever seen." He was also struck by the bitter hatred the average German felt for the French occupiers.[5]

The suffering and anger extended well beyond the occupied territories.

To sustain the resistance, the Weimar government had to pay the striking Ruhr workers their wages. But there was not enough money in the treasury to cover this unexpected cost. So the government printed more money, sending the currency into hyperinflation. By the summer of 1923 the mark had fallen to 3.3 million to the dollar. Germans were buying groceries with wheelbarrows of cash in the "single greatest destruction of monetary value in human history."[6]

The material and psychological trauma for average Germans as they watched their life savings vanish dealt a deadly blow to the Weimar democracy. Some of the effects were not immediately obvious and would take a few years to play out. But the French intervention did give an immediate boost to the republic's enemies on both left and right.[7] Communist and other Far Left uprisings spread across Germany, as well as in the Ruhr itself. The Communists and Socialists formed coalition governments in Saxony and Thuringia.[8] To put down these challenges, and also to prepare whatever defense might be necessary against further French attacks, the Cuno government and what remained of the post-Versailles German military turned to right-wing paramilitary groups. Hitler agreed to place his party's storm troopers, the SA, under the army's command if necessary.[9]

Thus began Hitler's legitimation by elements of the German business and military establishment. At the outset of the crisis Hitler was a well-known figure chiefly in Bavaria, but the Ruhr occupation helped give him a national reputation and made him something of a cult figure. Nazi party membership more than doubled over the ten months of the French occupation, from 20,000 to 55,000.[10] Hitler did not use his new popularity to attack the French, however. Instead, he went after Germany's "domestic political enemies," the "November criminals," the national government leaders in Berlin who had failed to resist the French invasion. Sensing that his moment had come, he led a putsch in November 1923, and although it was easily put down and resulted in his imprisonment, his eloquent statements at trial only further cemented his reputation as a force on the nationalist right.[11]

Cuno had hoped that the policy of passive resistance and national suffering would convince the Americans and British to step in and pressure France to withdraw.[12] But both powers held back, waiting for the French to realize on their own that the intervention was only damaging French economic interests and isolating France diplomatically. And the invasion did turn out to be a disaster for France. Economically, the French may have extracted significant income from the occupation. But diplomatically, the French had badly alienated both the Americans and the British. Nor had the French relieved their dependence on American financing.

Germany meanwhile was coming apart. By September 1923 the Cuno government had run out of answers. It fell. It was eventually replaced by a new government led by the conservative Gustav Stresemann, who called for an end to passive resistance. This ended the worst of the economic crisis, although the whole experience left Germans humiliated and bitter.

To many observers, including American diplomats on the scene, the damage was incalculable. Houghton predicted that as a result of the economic destruction and the hatred spawned by the French occupation among the Germans, "we may look forward confidently . . . to a time not far off when another war will lay prostrate what is left of European civilization."[13] For the rest of his life he would believe that "the Ruhr crisis had sown the seeds of a second world war."[14] Dean Acheson, looking back from the perspective of 1936, called the Ruhr invasion "the most disastrous single step taken in Europe during this century," for it "brought on the German inflation, made the Nazi movement inevitable and revived in Europe the conviction that the only basis of international politics was force."[15]

With Germany's surrender and French willingness to declare victory and go home, the Americans finally stepped in to offer help arranging a settlement of the reparations question. The decision was more a response to political pressures at home however, than to any newfound desire to involve the United States in Europe's problems. The French intervention shifted public sentiment in the United States: The once-beloved French were now the greedy aggressors; the once-hated Germans were now the helpless victims. Perhaps just as significant was that the collapse of the German and French economies during the Ruhr crisis rippled through global markets and cut into American exports. Agricultural interests suffered as wheat prices declined due to Germans' inability to buy.[16] Even Borah now clamored for American involvement, calling for an international financial conference to find solutions to Europe's economic crises. "We want the European markets open for our farm products. Millions are hungering and dying in Europe for products which are rotting on our farms. We are directly, immediately, and vitally concerned."[17] The war debt question also lingered. Germany was not paying reparations; France was not negotiating a debt settlement. Something had to be done.

The Ruhr crisis fell into the lap of Calvin Coolidge, who became president in the summer of 1923 after the sudden, unexpected death of

Harding. Coolidge, in the estimation of Elihu Root, "did not have an internationalist hair in his head" and was at least as wary of Congress as Harding had been.[18] In the face of growing pressure, however, he approved an idea that had earlier been floated by Hughes. The plan was to form an international committee of non-government financial "experts" to determine the proper level of German payments and to ensure they were made. The negotiations would be carried out by private individuals acting on their own. Private bankers would handle the arrangements. "I do not propose to implicate ourselves in Europe," Coolidge declared. "We have interests there that I want to look after for our own sake, but we cannot attempt to shield them from the results of their own actions."[19]

American willingness to support an international discussion of reparations, even if indirectly and unofficially, was greeted with relief by Europeans on all sides. The Germans looked to an easing of reparations, protection against further French incursions, and to American financing to stabilize their economy and ease the suffering of the population. The French were just as desperate. With the franc collapsing almost as fast as the German mark, the government had long sought a $100 million credit from the Morgan bank, only to have it repeatedly blocked by a State Department unhappy with French policies. After the Ruhr debacle, French officials feared that "failure to procure the grand loan" would be "the death blow to the franc."[20] Although they had resisted Hughes's suggestion of an "experts" committee before, therefore, they now grasped it as a lifeline.[21] The British were naturally delighted to see the Americans finally addressing the whole crisis, relieving them of the burden.

The plan that emerged from weeks of negotiations and a conference in London—known as the Dawes Plan, after the commission's American chairman, banker and politician Charles G. Dawes—offered what on the surface was a strictly financial solution to the crisis. The plan called for a reduction in Germany's annual payments for the first five years, with future payments rising as Germany's economy recovered. Meanwhile, foreign banks—meaning American banks—would provide Germany a loan of $200 million both to help stabilize the economy and to allow the Germans to resume reparations payments to France and Great Britain. The plan did not reduce Germany's overall reparations bill, because the French refused to agree to a reduction unless the Americans also reduced the war debt. But it did leave room for future adjustments depending on how quickly the German economy recovered. The key to the whole plan was the large private loan for Germany. By getting money flowing again, from U.S. private banks to Germany, from Germany to France and Great

Britain, and from them to the United States, credit would be eased, confidence restored, European economies given a chance at recovery, and the Europeans' debt to the United States paid.

For the Coolidge administration, the plan was ideal, for it allowed the United States to continue collecting European debts while retaining high tariffs, reducing the budget deficit, and cutting taxes. American taxpayers would not have to shoulder any part of the burden. No money would come from the Treasury. In addition, the European situation could be stabilized without any new security commitment by the United States. Announcement of the plan brought cheers for the administration, which, it seemed, had deftly defused the European crisis and without direct U.S. involvement. Dawes won the Nobel Peace Prize and became Coolidge's running mate for the 1924 presidential campaign, which the Republicans again won handily.

The Dawes Plan was never meant to be more than a temporary fix, however, and some critics, like John Maynard Keynes, worried that it was a shell game. Germans would not be working more or consuming less. "Nothing real" was happening. The Dawes Plan had produced "a great circular flow of paper," but for Keynes the question was "How long can the game go on?"[22]

The Dawes Plan certainly showed how much influence the United States could wield when it chose to. Neither the French nor the Germans liked the plan, but they so desperately needed American financing that they had no choice but to accept. At the London conference of experts, the bankers and the British publicly took the lead in pressing the French to make concessions, but it was senior American officials (pretending to be in town visiting Savile Row tailors) who privately brought the full weight of the United States to bear. This was not a negotiation. Hughes bluntly told Poincaré, "Here is the American policy. If you turn this down, America is through."[23] In Berlin, Houghton similarly told German industrialists and nationalist leaders that if they did not accept the plan, "it might be a hundred years" before America again "extended her hand to Germany."[24] As the American ambassador in Paris wrote Coolidge, "The fact that America is the creditor nation and is trusted in all Europe, even where she is despised . . . gives us a potential power to straighten out affairs over here."[25]

The question, however, was straighten out which affairs? Hughes and his colleagues may indeed have hoped to use American private capital for diplomatic purposes, to calm the Franco-German crisis and get Europe back on its feet. But they were not the ones making the deal and setting the terms. Those decisions were in the hands of the private bankers whose willingness to lend their money was the key to everything. If they weren't happy, there could be no deal of any kind. The private bankers were not in it for the diplomacy, nor did they wish to be told what to do by the diplomats. As J. P. Morgan, Jr., whose bank would take the lead in floating the German loan, wrote to Hughes, "If politicians, feeling themselves incompetent, request intervention of private parties," then those private parties had to be given "complete freedom to arrive at their conclusions."[26] Morgan was quite intent on ensuring that his bankers, in helping the Coolidge administration "straighten out the tangled affairs of Europe," not be led "away from the [banking] fundamentals."[27]

Fidelity to banking fundamentals, however, had strategic and political ramifications. At the heart of the Dawes Plan was the loan to Germany of $200 million. To float a private loan of that size J. P. Morgan and Company needed to be able to convince potential subscribers that the investment was relatively secure. This was not easy to do under the circumstances. In 1924, following the Ruhr debacle, Germany still suffered from the effects of hyperinflation; it had suspended reparations payments; and French troops still occupied the German industrial heartland, much to the bitter and sometimes violent resentment of the German population. Germany under these conditions hardly seemed like a safe investment. Significant steps had to be taken to provide some reasonable assurance that the loan could and would be repaid.

The bankers insisted, for instance, that the German government carry out "responsible" economic policies. Inflation needed to be tamed. The budget needed to be balanced, taxes raised, and expenditures, including for social welfare, kept under control. Since German governments had already proven themselves "irresponsible" and too easily swayed by voters on these matters, the American bankers demanded direct control over core elements of the German economy. The Dawes Plan thus placed Germany's central bank in the hands of an international board. It put the German national railway system under international control, as well, both as a source of revenue and as collateral for the loan. To ensure that Germany made its reparations payments on time, an "agent-general"—the former U.S. Treasury official S. Parker Gilbert—was put in charge of making the payments. The Germans, in short, had to forfeit a substantial degree of economic sovereignty. Not surprisingly, this aroused intense opposition in Germany. Right-wing nationalists and Communists alike denounced the Dawes Plan for turning Germany into the "slave" of international capitalists.

The other problem with the plan, for Germans, was that it did not lower their overall reparations burden. Although in theory the "experts" were supposed to be acting independently of their governments and calculating reparations based on Germany's "capacity to pay," the American experts knew that the Coolidge administration remained rigid on Allied war debts and that France would not accept less in reparations from Germany than it owed the United States. That meant that Germany's overall obligation could not be lowered. For Germans this was not only an economic problem but a psychological blow, for it seemed they would never be free of the burden of reparations.

There was some good news for Germany. If the bankers were to convince anyone to lend money to Germans, they would have to provide some guarantee against further pressures from the French. There could be no more threats to punish Germany for non-payment of reparations or any other treaty violation; no more incursions into German cities on the right bank of the Rhine. As one Morgan partner put it, France's desire to weaken Germany and punish it for non-compliance was understandable, but it was "not very alluring to the American who is asked to put money into a German bond."[28] The Dawes Plan thus took several steps to deprive France of the leverage that had been bequeathed by the Versailles Treaty: The agreement stripped the French-chaired Reparation Commission of its power to declare Germany in default and compelled France to renounce its right to impose sanctions on Germany unilaterally; it required France to withdraw all its forces from the Ruhr within a year and anticipated a general withdrawal from the Rhineland as soon as possible.[29] Henceforth, the issues that had preoccupied France and other European powers—security against Germany, the Rhine frontier, the continental balance of power, Anglo-American guarantees—would be subordinated to the requirements of the international financial community.[30] Investors wanted to see a "new order" in Europe—"a tranquillized and hard-working Germany, Allies working in harmony, no more Ruhr invasions, no more sanctions, Germany paying reparations at last upon a scale steady and fairly adequate."[31]

The strategic implications were clear. For France, the Dawes arrangement marked the end of security based on legitimately applied force within the Versailles framework. The French had been able to wield power against Germany only so long as it had the permission, if not the backing, of the United States and Britain. Once that permission was withdrawn, France's natural weakness was starkly revealed. As General Allen observed, France after the war had occupied a status in Europe that it could never have achieved on its own and could never sustain on its own. Without the backing of the United States and Britain, the "inexorable laws of force" must eventually reduce France to the status "to which her own potentiality and merit entitle her."[32] The Dawes Plan left the French little choice but to reverse course. Having tried and failed to weaken Germany, it would now have to accommodate it. This was in keeping with American desires. As one administration official put it, the "only way for France to obtain real security is by taking Germany into camp."[33]

But did Germany want to come into camp? For Gustav Stresemann, the Dawes Plan was the beginning of Germany's deliverance from the prison of Versailles. With the treaty's enforcement mechanisms dismantled, Germany could press forward on all aspects of treaty revision: the end of the Rhineland occupation, adjustment of the German boundaries in the east, especially with Poland, and a final end to reparations. The key to everything was to end the foreign occupation of German territory. Thus, while German nationalists, Communists, and financiers called for rejecting the harsh economic terms of the Dawes Plan, Stresemann insisted, "We must accept. . . . We must get the French out of the Ruhr. We must free the Rhineland."[34]

Stresemann moved quickly to exploit the opening created by the Dawes Plan. Within months of the London Conference, he advanced a plan for a final settlement of Germany's western boundary. All French and Allied occupation forces would withdraw from the Rhineland. Germany and its western neighbors would sign non-aggression pacts. His appeal was for a lasting peace and an end to the confrontation between France and Germany.

The French had little choice but to accept. With the Dawes Plan already severely limiting French options and the Anglo-Saxon powers unwilling to guarantee French security in any meaningful way, the only hope was to put their faith in German good intentions. Stresemann was, in the eyes of many, a "good European," who sought only the peaceful reintegration of Germany into the European economy and society. He appealed to the French for a relationship of "cooperation and understanding" between equals, agreement by mutual consent. The best defense for France, he argued, was to win German friendship.[35]

The French remained doubtful, but American financial pressure pushed them along. The Coolidge administration placed an informal embargo on private loans to France through most of 1925, and Houghton, now ambassador in London, gave a speech warning that new loans to Europe depended on a peaceful environment. Coolidge more bluntly told the British ambassador that any additional American private loans would be forthcoming only if there was a new security pact.[36] As one French official put it, the United States "had the money bag at its disposal," and given France's dire financial situation at the time, it was impossible to say no.[37]

In the Swiss town of Locarno in October 1925, Stresemann and his French counterpart, Aristide Briand, along with representatives from Great Britain, Belgium, Italy, Poland, and Czechoslovakia, signed five agreements, including non-aggression and demilitarization pacts for the Rhine powers, arbitration conventions for all, including the eastern powers, and a treaty of mutual guarantee among Germany, France, Belgium, Britain, and Italy, in which the first three promised not to attack each other, and the latter two would act as guarantors and come to the assistance of any power or powers threatened by aggression. The treaty of mutual guarantee and the non-aggression pacts notably did not apply to Germany's eastern borders, including the one with Poland, which the Germans made clear they would seek to revise.

A hopeful world celebrated the agreements, which seemed to have finally put an end to the European war. The *New York Times* headline read "France and Germany Bar War Forever." Stresemann and Briand shared the Nobel Peace Prize in 1926. That year Germany was admitted to the League of Nations, a symbol of its return as a member in good standing of the European family. The agreements were welcomed by the two Anglo-Saxon powers. As Foreign Secretary Austen Chamberlain put it, the British wanted to "close the war chapter and start Europe afresh as a society in which Germany would take her place as an equal with the great nations."[38] The Americans were pleased because, as Coolidge told Congress, the French and Germans were working out "their own political problems without involving this country."[39]

Few French officials believed that the "spirit of Locarno" actually solved France's problems. A non-aggression pact with Germany was good only for as long as Germany wished to abide by it. France had been stripped of the means, institutions, and legal right to deter an attack. The mutual guarantee treaty made Britain the guarantor of *both* Germany and France against aggression from the other, but in theory only. In practice it was the guarantor of neither. In the age of modern warfare, joint defense required extensive advance planning and pre-positioning, and in secret. The British military could hardly engage in such planning with both France and Germany, so it would engage with neither. Without Anglo-French military planning, Britain would not be able to respond quickly to a future German attack. That was fine with the British. British officials could not envision a scenario in which they would actually have to come to France's defense under the terms of the new agreement. Neither the public nor the government had any interest in doing so.[40] Winston Churchill, then serving as chancellor of the Exchequer, refused to "accept it as an axiom that [Britain's] fate was involved in that of France."[41] Both the Dawes Plan and the Locarno agreements gave the British an excuse to stop worrying about French insecurity.

In addition to weakening the already tenuous security ties between France and Britain, the Locarno agreements also severed the strategic ties that France had attempted to forge with Poland and Czechoslovakia on Germany's eastern flank. According to the agreements, France could no longer attack Germany in the west in response to a German attack on Poland or Czechoslovakia in the east—that would violate the non-aggression pact. But the accords explicitly opened the door for Germany to seek territorial revisions in the east—and not necessarily by peaceful means.[42] As one Polish official sarcastically put it, Germany had been "officially asked to attack the east, in return for peace in the west."[43] Ambassador Houghton commented, with some prescience, that the real accomplishment of Locarno was to determine "the point where the next great war will begin, i.e., the German-Polish frontier."[44]

Not surprisingly, it was around this time that the French military drastically revised its defensive strategy. With the option of launching offensives against Germany from the Rhineland ruled out, the French abandoned forward strategies for deterring Germany. Instead, military planners proposed an elaborate network of fortifications on French soil to slow and halt another German attack like the one launched in 1914. Construction on what became known as the Maginot Line began in 1928.

With the Versailles Treaty all but dismantled and the physical barriers to Germany being removed, everything would now depend on Germany's intentions. The British and Americans put a great deal of faith in Germany's evolution from the expansionist, militarist power it had been to the modern, liberal, integrationist power that they hoped it was becoming under the moderate guidance of Stresemann.[45]

The focus on Stresemann as the indispensable German was understandable, but it failed to acknowledge both the continuities of German foreign policy aims and the breadth of public support for those aims. Whether or not Stresemann was a "good European," he was without question "a great German nationalist dedicated to restoration of the Reich's power."[46] Like almost all Germans his primary objective was to overthrow the Versailles system, remove foreign troops from German soil, regain the Saar and the German-speaking territories lost to Poland and Czechoslovakia, establish union (*Anschluss*) with Austria, undo the one-sided disarmament provisions that left Germany naked to its potential enemies, and end reparations. That he hoped to accomplish these objectives peacefully and through "understanding and cooperation" may have distinguished him from some Germans who favored a more aggressive and even violent route. As foreign minister he repeatedly insisted that "the new Germany and its recovery" could "only be based on peace."[47] But how much of this was a matter of principle and how much simply a response to circumstances was hard to measure. During the years when Stresemann was calling the shots in Germany, American military intelligence reported considerable German efforts to evade the Versailles agreement's limitations on armaments, regain territory lost to Poland, unite with Austria, hasten the evacuation of foreign troops from the Rhineland, and in general return to a position of predominance in central Europe. Germany, the intelligence officials reported, was "like a young giant in chains, whose growing . . . powers cause him to expand in one direction as rapidly as constrictions are applied in another."[48]

So long as French and British forces sat in German territory and occupied the bridgeheads across the Rhine, however, the chains would remain. The vulnerability of Germany's industrial heartland induced moderation in any German leader. The Rhineland occupation was the "rope of the strangler who has us by the neck," as Stresemann put it. Together with the disarmament provisions of the Versailles Treaty, it left Germany in a state of "complete military helplessness."[49] But what would Germany do if that rope were ever removed?

Stresemann was not the only German voice that mattered, moreover. Weimar Germany *was* a democracy, and that meant Stresemann's policies faced vigorous opposition at every stage, regardless of the gains he achieved. Right-wing nationalists and Communists alike opposed the Locarno agreements just as they had opposed the Dawes Plan. Locarno, they insisted, was a sellout because it left Alsace, Lorraine, and the Saar in French hands, and German-speaking lands in the east remained under Polish and Czech rule. Austen Chamberlain rightly wondered about "the value of any pact" that aroused so much opposition in Germany. Even Stresemann's great partner in peace, Aristide Briand, had to admit that sometimes Stresemann's fiery speeches "stood my hair on end."[50] French and British officials alike wondered whether Germans could ever be successfully appeased.[51]

The French by this point had all but given up trying to contain Germany. Their concerns were now almost exclusively economic and focused on the debt to the United States. In 1926, in the wake of Locarno, the French and Americans finally negotiated a debt settlement agreement, the Mellon-Bérenger accord. By its terms, France still owed the United States almost $7 billion—the roughly $4 billion of the original loan plus interest—to be paid annually for sixty-two years. From the American point of view, it was a generous settlement, better than the one the British got, but the French public was outraged. With the final payment to be made in 1988, their great-grandchildren would still be paying off a debt to the Americans for a war they fought together seventy years before. The French parliament refused to ratify the agreement without a guarantee that France would not pay one cent more to the United States than it received from Germany every year until the debt was paid off. The French wanted a reparations settlement that provided what they called "absolute financial security." With such an agreement in hand, the parliament could ratify the Mellon-Bérenger agreement and the war debt issue with the Americans would be settled.[52] In return for Germany's agreement to such a plan, even Raymond Poincaré, the old hawk and author of the Ruhr invasion of 1923, was prepared to withdraw French troops from the Rhineland substantially ahead of the schedule laid out in the Versailles Treaty.

As it happened, the authors and implementers of the Dawes Plan were also looking to wrap up a final reparation settlement. The 1924 arrangement was always meant to be temporary, and although it solved the crisis of the moment, American financial experts had always worried about its fundamental soundness. Germany had become too dependent on foreign loans, and American creditors were too exposed. American banks had lent nearly $3 billion to German borrowers, mostly in short-term loans. (In constant dollars this was more than twice what Germany would receive from the Marshall Plan two decades later.) By 1928 American financial institutions held about 50 percent of the $2 billion worth of short-term credits in Germany.[53] Much of this lending the financial experts viewed as irresponsible. With no U.S. government oversight, the private lenders tripped over each other hoping to make a profit in Germany and did not care very much how their loans were used.[54] In Germany the recipients of American lending were not only private businesses but city governments, regional authorities, public utilities, and public credit institutions. The unending flow of dollars financed substantial government spending on programs that Germany otherwise could not have afforded.[55]

Gilbert, along with other private bankers and some Germans, worried that German prosperity in the late 1920s was thus built on a house of cards. Public spending and imports were high. Exports were low. The German government was running large deficits, which it financed with the endless succession of short-term loans. The constant flow had allowed both voters and their representatives to avoid the hard choices necessary to make the economy self-sustaining over the long run, capable both of growing without artificial outside stimulus and also of paying reparations without constant recourse to foreign lending. For Gilbert, the bottom line was this: The Weimar government's failure "to exercise proper restraint in its expenditures" raised doubts about Germany's commitment to its "reparations obligations."[56] And that, after all, was Gilbert's sole responsibility as agent-general.[57]

The solution, in the view of Gilbert and others, was to cut off foreign lending to Germany and thereby force the government to take the necessary steps to put its economic house in order.[58] Budget austerity would compel Germans to reduce imports, improve their balance of trade, and thus earn sufficient foreign exchange to pay reparations without American loans.[59] In the fall of 1927 Gilbert convinced the State Department to begin expressing official disapproval of new private American lending to Germany. At the same time he released a public memorandum highly critical of the German government's "constantly enlarging programs of expenditure and borrowing, with but little regard to the financial consequences of their actions."[60] In Berlin he teamed up with the president of the central bank, Hjalmar Schacht, to block a major new foreign loan sought by Germany's finance minister and to discourage further borrowing at all levels of the German government.[61] By the fall of 1928 the flow of new American loans to Germany was slowing.

Then came some unexpected events on far-off Wall Street that shook the German economy to its foundation. It was not the market crash of October 1929, however, but the Great Bull Market of 1928 that started the unraveling of the German economy. Wall Street's speculative boom saw average stock prices climb by 50 percent over eighteen months. The world's investors, eager to get a piece of the action, moved their money into American stocks. The short-term loans that had been floating the German economy suddenly became much harder to come by.[62] With the foreign credit spigot all but closed, the German economy slipped into recession beginning in early 1929. Industrial production stagnated, and unemployment began to rise.[63] German federal, state, and local governments were forced to undertake a "vigorous fiscal retrenchment."[64]

Then came October 24, 1929, Wall Street's "Black Thursday," when the American speculative bubble burst, stock prices crashed, and stockholders began scrambling to meet their obligations. American banks started calling in the short-term loans they had made to German public and private institutions. As the American economy began to sink into depression, American demand for German goods declined and German exports to the United States collapsed.[65] With the German government no longer able to use foreign loans to provide economic stimulus, industrial production plummeted further; unemployment soared; domestic demand for all goods, including food, fell; farmers went into foreclosure as banks called in their loans; agricultural workers joined the unemployment rolls; and Germany, too, slid into depression.

As all this was occurring, another experts group came together, headed by the American financier and businessman Owen D. Young, to come up with the final reparation settlement that Gilbert, the French, and the Germans all wanted. Germans naturally looked to the Young Commission to reduce if not suspend or even end reparations payments as a partial solution to the German economic crisis. Germany's "capacity to pay," which Americans claimed was the proper means of calculating reparations, would certainly call for a substantial reduction in annual payments, especially if Gilbert and other American financial experts wanted Germany to stop relying on foreign loans.

Young, his colleagues, and Parker Gilbert had other problems to deal with, however. One was the continuing tangle of war debts and reparations. The newly elected Herbert Hoover had already rejected any forgiveness of the war debts as "both inequitable and impolitic."[66] The French (and the British) still refused to accept less in German reparations payments than they owed the Americans. Since it made no sense to devise a plan that the Americans, British, and French would not accept, Young and his colleagues once again left the greatest financial burden on the Germans. The Young Plan reduced Germany's overall reparations bill only marginally, and annual reparations payments were based not on any technical evaluation of Germany's "capacity to pay" but on what Britain and France owed the United States. German annuities were reduced slightly from the Dawes levels for ten years, but the average annuity over the life of the plan actually increased. And the life of the plan stretched out over decades—Germans would be making payments until 1988, which, not coincidentally, was the last year of the Allies' scheduled payments to the United States.[67]

The Young Plan was a crushing blow to German hopes for a financial reprieve and sparked widespread hostility to the Americans. The Nazi ideologist Gregor Strasser may have exaggerated when he claimed that an "anti-capitalist yearning" took hold of "95 percent of our people," but Germans at all levels of society now did see themselves as victims of an Anglo-Saxon-dominated international financial order, which they also identified with Jewish bankers. Schacht, the German central bank president, denounced the planned payments as "absolutely impossible"[68] and began a flirtation with the Nazis that eventually would culminate in his joining Hitler's government. Keynes predicted the Young Plan would "not prove practicable for even a short period" and prophesied "some sort of crisis in 1930."[69] As Poincaré put it to Stresemann, "All of us are suffering to a greater or lesser extent from the situation in which we find ourselves as regards the United States."[70]

The silver lining for Stresemann was that, in exchange for German acceptance of the deal, Poincaré was willing to begin withdrawing all forces from the Rhineland almost immediately and to have them all out by the end of June 1930, five years ahead of the Versailles schedule. This was the goal Stresemann had been aiming for since he joined the government in 1923. He would not live to see it fulfilled, however. The great statesman, who had overthrown the Versailles regime and brought his nation back to a state of near equality with the other European powers, died in October 1929.

When Briand heard of Stresemann's death, he remarked that they should order two coffins—one for the German and one for himself. Briand personally and the French in general had put great stock in Stresemann's good intentions and had always wondered what course Germany might take without him. Now they would find out, and just as the French were agreeing to an early departure from the Rhineland. The British wondered, too. As Austen Chamberlain put it to Mussolini, "Only the future would show whether Germany would really accept her present position, or whether she would once again resort to arms and stake everything on the hazards of a new war." British policy remained to "take away all provocation and all excuse for a new war," an approach that became known as "appeasement." But Chamberlain worried that "Germany was still restless, still prone to suggest that her good behavior must constantly be bought by fresh concessions."[71] The Rhineland occupation had kept the Germans in a "chastened mood" and encouraged them to "walk warily." The end of the occupation would therefore "produce a remarkable effect" in Germany, one British official commented, but "not, I am afraid, quite the effect which we all desire and hope for."[72]

—

The German economic downturn, the cutoff of American lending, and the end of foreign control of the Rhineland as well as the German economy had a combustible effect on German politics. The new financial arrangements put immense pressure on the fragile Weimar coalition. With no relief on reparations and no more access to foreign loans, the only option left was austerity. Taxes would have to be raised and/or public spending cut, while national income was falling and unemployment rising. This inevitably put significant strain on the coalition of Social Democrats and business-backed parties of the center and center right that had run Germany since the end of the war. For three years the steady flow of foreign loans had greased the gears of the political system, allowing the parties to strike compromises, buy off constituencies, and maintain a tenuous social peace. When the financing dried up beginning in 1928, the weaknesses of the young political system were exposed. In the new scarcity, choices had to be made, but the squabbling parties couldn't make them. Their futile haggling tended to discredit a system that had not enjoyed much public confidence to begin with. In the months before his death Stresemann warned that the parliamentary system was becoming a "caricature" and that a turn to dictatorship was not inconceivable.

Rumors of an impending coup were indeed rife. As the economy sank, industrial leaders who had never been enthusiastic about the new democracy held it responsible for the meltdown. Some industrialists thus withdrew their political and financial support from the parties of the middle.[73] At the same time, the army, which had also never fully accepted the Weimar constitution, began agitating for a return to the authoritarianism of the imperial era.[74] Conservatives and army leaders around President Hindenburg began urging that the great war hero himself take charge.

Until the Young Plan, German dependence on Western, and particularly, American lending had acted as a powerful check on such antidemocratic impulses. With Germany reliant on a constant supply of loans from the United States, with international control of the central bank and railroad, and an American "agent-general" ensconced in Berlin directing the payment of German obligations, conservative industrialists dared not challenge the parliamentary government that still enjoyed the favor of the United States and Britain. Powerful industrialists like Hugo Stinnes floated trial balloons with American officials about possible coups and the establishment of a business-friendly dictatorship but received little encouragement. America's preference for parliamentary government and

German dependence on American loans "precluded overt constitutional experiments." Throughout the 1920s, influential Germans also knew that the "formation of a right-wing dictatorship would have led to the loss of the Rhineland."[75] The "anti-republican Right found itself obliged to work out some form of accommodation with existing parliamentary institutions."[76]

That obligation ended after 1929. The effect of the Young Plan and the Rhineland evacuation was the opposite of what the French, British, and Americans had hoped. They were intended to appease the Germans, but instead they "burst the bonds of pent-up German nationalism."[77] The submission of the Young Plan to the Reichstag in March 1930 blew up the Grand Coalition and led to the formation of a conservative government and the exclusion of the Social Democrats, the party most dedicated to the Weimar constitution. Hindenburg appointed as chancellor Heinrich Brüning, a staunch nationalist, avowed monarchist, and an "authoritarian at heart."[78] Brüning was indeed no democrat. His ultimate goal was the dismantling of Weimar and restoration of some form of constitutional monarchy. American embassy officials reported from Berlin that the September 1930 elections had dealt a "body blow to the republican form of government" and reflected a "dangerous mentality" on the part of a "large portion of the population."[79] Although the republic might not fall immediately, the fact was that "some thirteen odd million Germans have by their votes declared their hostility to the present republican form of government."[80]

Communists and right-wing parties benefited from this anger, but none more than Hitler and the Nazis. After facing near extinction in the 1928 elections, the National Socialists had made some headway in the faltering economy of 1929 and 1930. Everyone expected the Nazis to do well in the September 1930 elections, but not even Hitler anticipated the magnitude of Nazi gains. The National Socialists won 18.3 percent of the vote, up from the 2.6 percent they had managed in 1928. The Nazis' total vote went from 810,000 to over 6 million. The 107 seats they picked up in the Reichstag made them the second-largest party by a significant margin, behind only the Social Democrats. The Communists also increased their percentage, picking up 77 seats in the Reichstag.[81] As the British ambassador in Berlin observed, the "first electoral campaign which has taken place in Germany *without the shadow of the Rhineland occupation* has brought out into the open, through one party or another, all that Germany hopes for and intends to strive for in the field of external affairs."[82] As Hitler put it, "Germany will either be a world power or nothing, but to be a world power one needs the necessary size."[83] In fact, every one of Germany's twenty-four political parties greeted the Rhineland evacuation with demands for the restoration of the German-speaking territories that had been given to Poland, Belgium, France, and Italy in the 1919 settlement. The conservative chancellor Brüning, now fighting for his political life against Hitler and other Far Right forces, declared that the precondition for a "just and lasting European order" was that Germany be granted "sufficient natural living space."[84]

All this occurred in first year of Herbert Hoover's term as president. Hoover was at heart no isolationist, or at least he hadn't been throughout his long and impressive career in government service. He had run humanitarian food operations in Belgium after the Great War and then in the Soviet Union during the Russian famine. As commerce secretary under Harding, he had pushed for lower tariffs to enhance American trade overseas. He had initially supported the Versailles Treaty as essential to the peace of Europe. By the time he became president, however, he had molded his views to accord with the predominant sentiments of the Republican Party.[85] With the party's foreign policy still dominated by Borah and his old irreconcilable allies, Hoover could not have won the nomination otherwise. In addition, he was almost immediately preoccupied with the American economic crisis. The market crash occurred just eight months into his presidency. It was no surprise that he had no interest in an active foreign policy.

By the time he entered the White House, Hoover had convinced himself that the problems that ailed the American economy had nothing to do with the well-being of the global economy. The American economy was "remarkably self-contained," he argued, and could "make a very large degree of recovery independently of what happened elsewhere."[86] Republican congressional leaders agreed. Utah's Republican senator Reed Smoot argued that "the most striking feature of America's rise to the position of foremost industrial nation in the world" had been the "creation of our immense domestic market."[87] The solution, therefore, was to protect that market further against foreign competition. In the summer of 1930, Congress passed the Smoot-Hawley Tariff, dramatically raising rates on imports and further shutting the American market to European, and German, goods. Nor was Hoover at all interested in forgiving any of the European debt.

Germany's slide toward authoritarianism prompted no course change or new policies. Indeed, far from wanting to get involved in keeping the German economy, and German politics, from going off the rails, the general view in Washington was that the United States was already too enmeshed in European affairs. With the German economy in free fall, one official complained, European bankers wanted "to burden us with the responsibility of maintaining German credit. We cannot assume this responsibility."[88] Even Hoover's secretary of state, Henry Stimson, though a consistent internationalist, would not cross Borah when it came to involvement in Europe.[89] "We can properly take no leading part" in addressing Europe's problems, he insisted. It was up to the "parties to the controversies"—Britain, France, and Germany—to "work out their problems with such friendly help as we can give."[90]

To the extent the Hoover administration was concerned about Germany, its concerns were, as always, strictly financial. The radicalization of the German electorate was a problem because it threatened the payment of reparations, which in turn would give France and Britain the excuse not to make their war debt payments.[91] The Hoover administration supported the anti-democratic Brüning as the best hope of seeing responsible German economic policies.[92]

In fact, American officials and private bankers were far more worried about threats from the Left than from the Right. A political analysis by the investment banking firm Harris, Forbes, and Company saw some good news in the September 1930 election results. The "decided swing to the Nationalist parties" had offset the gains of the "large parties of the Left."[93] Stimson, like many in both the United States and Britain, believed Communism remained the "real menace to the peace of Europe."[94] Even as embassy officials observed the growing tendency of German conservatives to accept the Nazis as a plausible partner and to include them in plans for restructuring the government, American policy did not reflect concern.[95] The American ambassador continued to worry more about the "deep and dangerous extent of American banking involvement in what could become a financial catastrophe" if Brüning was overthrown. He was frustrated that the Hoover administration made only "minimal" efforts to help Brüning and keep Hitler out of power.[96]

It was only when the European problems began to hit American financial interests directly that Hoover and his advisers took notice. The Nazis' success in the September 1930 elections drove Brüning to more desperate measures. In an effort to get out ahead of the right-wing nationalists, he proposed creation of a German-Austrian customs union in March 1931.[97] The move was correctly perceived internationally as a preliminary step toward *Anschluss* with Austria—long desired by many Germans, demanded by right-wing nationalists, but forbidden by the Versailles Treaty. It was no coincidence that Brüning made his proposal soon after the withdrawal of French forces from the Rhineland.

The effect in international financial circles was disastrous. Within weeks of the announcement, banks in Vienna began to fail, whether out of general nervousness or because French lenders deliberately set out to punish Brüning. On May 11, 1931, the Creditanstalt, Austria's largest provider of credit, revealed it had lost almost all of its capital, setting off a cascade of bank failures, first in Germany and then spreading throughout Europe. It would not be long before the contagion spread to America.

As Hoover later wrote in his memoirs, Americans suddenly learned "about the economic interdependence of nations through a poignant experience which knocked at every cottage door."[98] Facing this dire threat to the already shaky American banking system, Hoover finally took the step that he and his Republican predecessors had refused to take for a decade: He turned to the question of the war debts. Stimson and others favored cancelling the debts entirely, but that remained politically unthinkable. Hoover instead proposed a one-year moratorium on both war debt and reparations payments. The measure was necessary, he explained, because under the current conditions of global depression, "the whole fabric of intergovernmental debt" was coming apart.[99] Americans were "now faced with the problem, not of saving Germany or Britain, but of saving ourselves."[100]

The "Hoover Moratorium," however, proved to be too little and too late to prevent collapse. Despite the moratorium, the worldwide depression worsened, as did the depression in the United States. The whole issue of war debts became moot, moreover, for in the summer of 1932, the Europeans meeting at Lausanne agreed to a 90 percent write-off of the reparations, provided the United States did the same. The Americans refused, but the Europeans suspended war debt payments anyway. The Lausanne decision stood as a "final resolution of the war debt-reparation question."[101]

The Hoover Moratorium also did nothing to improve the situation in Germany. By early 1932, unemployment hit 40 percent of the workforce. The government was bankrupt, so unemployment benefits were cut back and eventually ended. Millions of Germans began to go hungry.[102] The moratorium was supposed to help Brüning in his struggles with Hitler, but it didn't. Germans weren't interested in temporary reprieves. They wanted an end to reparations altogether. Whatever leverage American financing might once have provided, it no longer made a difference in the politics of 1932 Germany.[103] In May Hindenburg dismissed Brüning and named Franz von Papen chancellor. But Papen had no support in the Reichstag, and so it was dissolved and new elections were called. In July 1932 the Nazis scored their biggest electoral victory yet, doubling their votes from 6.4 million to 13.1 million, winning 37 percent of the electorate, and gaining 230 seats in the Reichstag, a hundred more than the next-largest party. The election confirmed the Nazis as a "catch-all party of social protest," a "rainbow coalition of the discontented," now with "a greatly increased appeal to the middle class."[104] Less than six months later President Hindenburg reluctantly named Hitler as the new German chancellor. After another round of elections in March 1933 added to the Nazi vote, the American ambassador in Berlin reported that German democracy had "received a blow from which it may never recover." Germany had been "submerged under a huge Nazi wave." The Third Reich had "become a reality," although what form it would take was "not yet clear in these critical days of political confusion and uncertainty."[105]

Hoover throughout his life would believe that the United States bore no responsibility for what happened in Germany, and in Europe more generally, and that view was shared by the American public. A people so intent on staying out of Europe could not see how any actions of theirs could have affected the course of European politics. There was certainly no shortage of explanations for the failure of German democracy—the repeated devastation of the middle class, first by inflation, then by depression; the lack of deep-rooted support for the Weimar Constitution; the widespread perception by Germans that they were not in control of their own fates. Many Americans and Britons assumed that it was the unjustness of the Versailles Treaty that had sparked such German bitterness and led to the triumph of the man most committed to overthrowing the treaty's terms. And if any outside power deserved blame, it was France, which had so aggressively and unreasonably bullied and oppressed a German nation that posed no threat to anyone after the war.

Some American officials at the time had a different view, however. They saw the enormous strain placed on all the European governments by the American insistence on having its war debts paid in full and how that had driven French policy toward Germany. This was compounded by America's unwillingness to play any role in providing security for both France and Germany. The United States had failed to reassure the French sufficiently to blunt their aggressive policies, and it had failed to protect Germany from the disaster of the Ruhr invasion and occupation. Americans on the scene—career diplomats, military officers, and political appointees alike—warned throughout the 1920s that the danger of another war was high, that American economic interests were threatened, and that absent a more active American diplomacy a "catastrophe" loomed.

What frustrated Americans serving in Europe in these years was how little effort it would have required to preserve relative peace and stability on the continent, especially where it was most needed, on the border between France and Germany. The "unofficial" representative to the Reparation Commission, Roland W. Boyden, lamented that the United States had "failed to act with the definiteness which might have changed the whole course of events."[106] A timely reduction of the war debts, a more active and steady involvement in the reparations settlement, the maintenance of a few thousand American troops in the Rhineland— fewer than were then deployed in the Philippines—these moderate measures, American diplomats and observers on the scene in Europe believed, could have made all the difference. Other critics pointed to the risks of leaving German and European economic recovery in the hands of private American lenders. They argued that the task of bringing "order out of world chaos" was "too vital to our security and prosperity" to be left to such "haphazard treatment."[107] Early on Briand told General Allen that American "prestige" was so great, along with its financial and potential military power, that in many cases "a word would have sufficed." In the 1920s the United States did not have to go to war again to keep the peace, nor did anyone suggest that it should. The United States did not have to embroil itself deeply in order to have influence.[108] It only had to embroil itself enough. Allen himself found that "our mild participation" often had a "wholesome effect" on European policies.[109]

Why was this "mild participation" opposed in Washington? American officials were capable of taking action elsewhere.[110] Outside of Europe, the United States was no more "isolationist" in the 1920s than it had been during the presidency of Theodore Roosevelt. Officials continued to govern and troops continued to be deployed in the Philippines, Haiti, the Dominican Republic, and Nicaragua. In 1927 the Coolidge administration dispatched three thousand troops to put down an insurgency in Nicaragua, demonstrating, among other things, that the U.S government was not entirely averse either to risk or to combat. In 1921 Charles Evans Hughes negotiated agreements regarding East Asia and the Pacific that, while innocuous and non-binding, far exceeded what he was willing to negotiate in Europe. As one historian has noted, commitments that were tolerable elsewhere were "not acceptable in Europe."[111]

The disparity between American involvement in these other parts of the world and its involvement in Europe could not be explained by their relative importance to American interests.

American officials insisted there were no "vital" interests at stake in Europe. But it was hard to argue, in the 1920s, that Europe mattered less to the United States than Haiti or Nicaragua or the Philippines.[112] The fact that Americans had undertaken the greatest mobilization of power and resources since the Civil War had been some indication of Europe's importance in the eyes of most, including Republicans, in 1917 and 1918. Those interests had not suddenly disappeared after 1919. The postwar American economy was even more entangled with the economies of Britain, France, and Germany than it had been before the war, as Hoover eventually had to acknowledge. Many of those in senior policymaking positions throughout the 1920s had not doubted American interests in European peace and stability prior to 1920.[113]

That successive administrations rejected even "mild participation" in Europe's affairs, except on matters pertaining to war debts, could not be explained as some recalculation of costs and benefits. The truth was, Americans steered clear of Europe not because they perceived no vital interests there but precisely because many feared that their economic interests, which were tied more broadly to European peace and stability, would drag them back into a European entanglement and possibly war.

In abstaining, however, the United States played a central part in making that war more likely. A key turning point was the French and British departure from the Rhineland in 1930, five years ahead of schedule. Europeans knew that, as one British general put it, the only "real security" for the continent lay "in the occupation of the Rhineland and the Rhine bridgeheads."[114] Had the French remained in the Rhineland until 1935, as stipulated in the Versailles Treaty, or even for an additional two or three years beyond 1930, events in Germany might have unfolded differently. Would Hindenburg and the conservative forces around him, as well as the industrialists, have moved toward the "veiled dictatorship" of Brüning with French forces still occupying parts of Germany, or would they, as in the past, have been nervous about the French and British and possibly even the American reaction to the overthrow of the Weimar Republic? Would they have made Hitler chancellor in 1932? Even if they had, how differently might events have unfolded if French forces had remained in the Rhineland as the Nazis took power? What might Hitler have done had he been confronted by the continued presence of French troops throughout his first two years in power?

As the historian Adam Tooze has noted, there was nothing "predetermined" about Hitler's appointment to the chancellorship on January 30, 1933. Had Hitler been kept out of the government for a few months longer, Tooze argues, "the world might have been spared the nightmare of a National Socialist dictatorship."[115] Hindenburg made the decision, but timing was driven largely by American policies. The Hoover administration's insistence on a $400 million war debt payment in August 1929 pushed Poincaré to seek a rapid, final settlement of the debt and reparations question that year, for which he was willing to trade a significantly accelerated timetable of withdrawal from the Rhineland. The timing was also dictated by the American reparations agent in Berlin, who since 1927 had sought to wean Germany off the steady stream of American loans that followed implementation of the American-brokered Dawes Plan. More broadly, the fact that the French were even considering withdrawing sooner than the treaty required was the result of several years of American and British pressure.

It was coincidence that the American stock market boom and crash helped drive Germany into a deep depression, thus radicalizing German politics and fueling Nazi electoral triumphs, just at the moment the French were giving up the only means left to control German behavior. But it was a coincidence made more likely by American policies. The Americans had done little to prevent the disastrous French invasion of the Ruhr. They had helped create German dependency on foreign loans and then abruptly cut them off. They had forced the French to abandon the Versailles framework and pull its forces from the Rhineland. They had stood by as Germany descended to authoritarianism under Hindenburg and Brüning; and, indeed, even as Hitler climbed to power, senior American officials still worried more about the Communists. Both by the actions the United States took, and by the actions it did not take, American policy decisively influenced decisions made in France, Britain, and Germany at critical moments that together shaped the new European order, or perhaps more accurately, the disorder, of the 1930s.

CHAPTER FIFTEEN

Toward a New Order in Asia

Everywhere in the world the so-called Americanism is advanced, and conditions have definitely altered from the days of the old diplomacy.

—Japanese delegate to the Paris Peace Conference, 1919[1]

IT IS a recurring fact of history that the seeds of future turmoil and destruction are often sown in placid and prosperous times. The 1920s, and especially the latter half of the decade, were a time of renewed optimism about the prospects for peace. The "spirit of Locarno" produced hopefulness even among such hard-headed realists as Winston Churchill. Writing in 1928, Churchill proclaimed that the 1925 European agreement, together with the Washington Treaties of 1921–1922, were "twin pyramids of peace rising solid and unshakable on either side of the Atlantic." There were still risks of conflict, but hope now rested on a "surer foundation." The horror of war had produced a "blessed interval" during which the world's great nations could "take their forward steps to world organization."[2]

Yet the new order, such as it was, was already collapsing. It had never been much more than a mirage. The common thread running through all these agreements was the American unwillingness to support or uphold any of them, which, given the realities of power, meant they couldn't be enforced. The Washington Treaties deliberately lacked any mechanisms of enforcement. The Locarno agreements, which did not even mention the United States, also had no genuine enforcement (other than the hollow promise that Britain would come to the aid of either side in the event of aggression).

The quintessential expression of the American approach in the 1920s was the Kellogg-Briand Pact to "outlaw" war, known officially as the

General Treaty for Renunciation of War as an Instrument of National Policy. Although the formal proposal came from France's Aristide Briand, the idea had been born in the United States, the brainchild of a Chicago corporate lawyer, Salmon O. Levinson. Levinson believed the great obstacle to world peace was that nations and peoples had always regarded war as a lawful and legitimate act. If the nations of the world could agree to make war illegal, it would have the same deterrent effect as domestic law. Once international conflicts were posed as lawsuits, he argued, "these large questions would then be fought out by experienced statesmen in the council chamber rather than by boys on the field of battle."[3] John Dewey, who became a great supporter of "outlawry," believed that war could only be eliminated "if the world stopped thinking in terms of war."[4] When asked how nations that did not stop thinking of war would be deterred and punished, Levinson and his allies pointed to the power of international public opinion. They rejected any enforcement mechanisms, in part because this would require the United States to take part with other nations.[5] The great virtue of "outlawry" was that it had nothing to do with the League, nothing to do with Europe. It was a unilateral declaration, a "purely" American peace plan.[6] It was immediately embraced, not surprisingly, by Senator Borah, who saw it as a weapon against all "pro-European peace plans."[7] Borah argued that "those who cry: Peace, Peace" but who urged the United States "to become politically a part of Europe" were actually "destroying the last great hope of peace." Agreeing that the United States had a "tremendous service to perform," Borah insisted that "we must perform it independently."[8] As one leading activist put it, "If the foreign nations do not want peace, we shall pursue the paths of peace alone."[9]

The Republican administrations of the 1920s had little use for any of the proposals, whether from League supporters or outlawrists. Charles Evans Hughes complained about the constant carping from internationalists pressing the "barren controversy" of League membership or some other form of "association" with Europe, and Coolidge's secretary of state, Frank Kellogg, was known to curse the outlawrists as "pacifists."[10]

Pressure from internationalists grew after Locarno, however. Internationalists believed the European agreement had opened the way "to a new era of international cooperation and friendship" in which nations agreed to settle their differences "by right reason and the rule of law rather than by appeal to force."[11] But where was the United States? Even if it was not going to join the League, the United States needed to place itself "on the side of organized peace."[12] It had to be willing to back up the arbitration treaties among the powers by refusing to conduct business as usual with those deemed aggressors.[13] Otherwise, it would become "the greatest single obstacle on the road to world peace."[14] The world needed to know, argued the prominent British journalist Wickham Steed, that when nations banded together to restrain an aggressor, they would "never find the United States ranged against them."[15] The United States needed to revise its conception of neutrality and offer a "negative guarantee" that even if it refused to join the League in actively punishing an aggressor, it would not make it impossible for the League to do so.[16]

To generate pressure on the Coolidge administration, one prominent internationalist, Columbia professor James T. Shotwell, turned to the French foreign minister, Aristide Briand. It was not an obvious choice given the poor relations between the United States and France at the time. But the hero of Locarno and winner of the Nobel Peace Prize was eager to repair relations, remove the Americans as an obstacle to better Anglo-French security ties, and perhaps persuade Washington to provide the "negative guarantee" that the French felt they needed. At Shotwell's suggestion, and in a statement to the American people that Shotwell helped draft, Briand declared that France was willing to join the United States in "any mutual engagement tending 'to outlaw war.'" More specifically, Briand proposed that the two nations in dealing with one another renounce war "as an instrument of national policy." Although he thereby hoped to play on the popularity of the phrase "outlaw war," his aim was the opposite of the outlawrists. He aimed to "tie the United States into the collective responsibility system being established in Geneva."[17]

Coolidge and his advisers were not happy. The president believed the "outlawry" concept was unconstitutional. The State Department saw that Briand's real aim was to get the United States to agree to a "negative military alliance."[18] Kellogg commented that while there was a "tremendous demand" in the United States and abroad "for the so-called outlawry of war . . . no one knows just what that means."[19]

But the administration was cornered by the combination of growing domestic demands and now an appeal from Briand that could not simply be ignored, especially as the 1928 election season approached. In the *New York Times* Shotwell's colleague, Columbia University president Nicholas Murray Butler, challenged the administration to respond. France "has called out to us across the ocean. What answer is he to hear?"[20]

Borah was no happier than the administration with Shotwell's maneuver. As the champion of peace and outlawry, and as an aspiring presidential candidate himself, Borah could not oppose Briand's proposal, even though he saw it for what it was. His solution was simple and ingenious: Instead of a bilateral treaty with France, Borah proposed turning it into a multilateral agreement to be signed by all the nations of the world. And rather than commit the United States not to violate international sanctions against a designated aggressor, he would limit the treaty to a statement declaring war illegal, without any explanations or enforcement mechanisms. As one of Borah's colleagues put it, "That was the best way to get rid of the damn thing."[21]

Briand resisted. A pact in which the United States and dozens of other nations agreed to renounce war did nothing for France. It was not the "negative guarantee" he sought. The treaty had become meaningless, which was Borah's intent.[22] In some ways the treaty was worse than meaningless, for it treated France and Germany as equals. If France went to war with Germany in response to a German attack on Poland or Czechoslovakia, as it was bound to do under the League Covenant and other agreements, France might itself become a target of American sanctions. By the time the Kellogg-Briand Pact was signed by the United States, France, and Germany, eventually to be joined by sixty other nations, the French had lost interest.

None of the parties involved fully embraced the pact, but all made use of it for their own purposes. Republicans, though never genuinely enthusiastic, ran on the treaty as the Coolidge administration's greatest, and perhaps only, foreign policy success. Hoover, the party's nominee, called it a "magnificent step toward world peace." Coolidge, in his last annual message, spoke mostly about national defense but hailed the treaty as promising "more for the peace of the world than any other agreement ever negotiated among the nations."[23] Most Americans regarded the pact as a great achievement of American diplomacy. Kellogg won the Nobel Peace Prize, the crowning achievement of a record that most regarded as otherwise lackluster. It was quite an accomplishment for someone who had opposed the outlawry idea, who had been bullied into engaging with it, and who then had successfully turned a genuine effort to involve the United States in preserving the peace into a guarantee that it would not have to.

In Europe, many engaged in wishful thinking, misreading the pact as "the beginning of a regular and responsible participation of America in European affairs."[24] But American internationalists knew it was not that. Kellogg made clear that the treaty in no way involved the United States in European affairs.[25] Henry Stimson, the onetime League supporter and Root disciple, hoped that the pact could become "the basis of a system of organic law into the development of which the United States could throw its whole weight and strength."[26] But others were dubious. Britain's Austen Chamberlain mused that the pact could mean "very much for the peace of the world" or it could mean "very little." It all depended on what the United States wanted to do in the world. That was "a riddle to which no one—not even themselves—can give an answer in advance. But perhaps this is only saying that the United States has no foreign policy. The ship drifts at the mercy of every gust of public opinion."[27]

The test of the new "peace machinery" came not in Europe but, quite unexpectedly, in Asia. Neither Americans nor Europeans paid much attention to Asia during the 1920s. The rise of Japan to near-great-power status over the previous three decades had been noticed, and sometimes feared—both Americans and Europeans spoke of the "yellow peril." But despite Japan's success, most in the West still regarded Asians as backward and therefore weak. Anti-Asian prejudice was rampant in the United States, as well as in Australia and other parts of the British Empire. The rejection of a "racial equality" clause in the League Covenant was a symbol of the Western powers' lack of regard for both Asia and Japan. As for the Kellogg-Briand Pact and other elements of the peace machinery, Hoover's secretary of state, Henry Stimson, expressed the general sentiment when he commented that the "peace treaties of modern Europe" no more fit the three Asian races (by which he meant Russia, as well as China and Japan) than a "stovepipe hat" fit an "African savage."[28]

Notwithstanding this Western contempt, however, Japan's rise had fundamentally altered the strategic equation in East Asia and the western Pacific. For almost a century before 1914, the dominant powers in Asia had not been Asian. Britain controlled most of the key regions in central China, with Hong Kong under a ninety-nine-year lease, special treaty rights in Shanghai and other Chinese port cities, and effective control of the Yangtze River valley. It also controlled the strategic port of Singapore. France controlled Indochina. The Dutch controlled what is now Indonesia. Late in the century Russia drove across Siberia and into Manchuria and Korea. The Germans seized Shantung in 1898. The United States that same year took the Philippines.

Japan had emerged as a player in this imperial competition only in the last decade of the nineteenth century. To avoid the fate of China and other victims of European colonialism, the Japanese had begun a revolutionary process of political and economic reform beginning in the late

1860s—a period marked by the restoration of the Meiji emperor—to meet and resist Western power, in part by copying Western ways. Without giving up core traditions, the Japanese adopted many "Western" governmental forms, economics, and technologies. It soon became clear that in order to compete, and perhaps even to survive in the multi-sided Asian geopolitical struggle, Japan would also need to replicate Western imperialism. Many Japanese leaders believed their nation had to expand in order to survive. With its growing population and long but narrow, mountainous strip of islands, Japan needed access to resources and territory for settlement. With the European powers increasingly staking claim to northeast Asia, the most natural arena for Japanese expansion, Japanese leaders decided they either had to join the Western powers as a "guest at the table" or, like China, become "part of the feast."[29]

Prior to the world war, the imperial competition in Asia operated according to a brutal but relatively stable set of rules that had been set by the European powers. Staking a claim to territory or a sphere of influence required gunboats, battleships, and armies, and the proven willingness to use them. But the competing powers also tried to keep the competition in Asia from escalating into wars that could spill back into Europe. An informal "diplomacy of imperialism" allowed the powers to operate within their various spheres of influence without constant warfare. Every now and then one power tried to muscle its way into another power's sphere, and there were occasional new entrants to the competition, such as Russia and Germany, who had to be accommodated. Tensions might rise and conflicts might erupt, but great-power bargaining usually restored peace and a new equilibrium. The imperial powers generally agreed that all should share in the fruits of the imperial project.[30]

The Japanese adapted to and played by these rules—they had little choice. Their successful war against China over control of the Korean Peninsula in 1894–1895 won them territory in northeast China, including the important naval base at Port Arthur—only to have to give it up under threat by the combined forces of Russia, France, and Germany, who promptly took the spoils for themselves. The so-called Triple Intervention was a humiliation the Japanese never forgot, but it also taught lessons: first, that it was a rough world in which only power mattered, and second, that it was dangerous to make a move without the support of at least one European power capable of checking the others. The Japanese wisely chose the British for their ally. The world's greatest naval power was looking for help in Asia against Russia as German power threatened close to home. The Anglo-Japanese alliance formed in 1902 became a cornerstone of Japanese foreign policy. Symbolically, it marked Japan's arrival as a great power and its acceptance as a peer by the West. Strategically, it provided vital backing when in 1904 the Japanese waged another successful war, this time against Russia. The peace that followed, brokered by a sympathetic Theodore Roosevelt, gave Tokyo substantial control over Manchuria and established Japan once and for all as a major player, and the only local great power, in the imperial competition on the Asian mainland.

The British alliance served as a shield for Japanese expansion, but also, in the first decade, as a check against excessive ambition. Japanese statesmen were wary of overreaching and losing British support. "The high tree encounters strong wind," warned Ito Hirobumi, among the most respected of the old Meiji oligarchs.[31] So while the Japanese fought their way to a seat at the main table with bold military action, they also operated within the constraints of imperial diplomacy and the region's rough balance of power.

The Great War upset that balance. The Europeans' power and influence in Asia fell sharply as they bled each other on their own distant continent. With Russia racked by revolution, Japan was the only power in Asia untouched by the war. Indeed, it was, like the United States, a net beneficiary of the war. The British gladly ceded policing of the region to the Japanese navy, and, together with the French, looked to Japan to distract or destroy German naval assets in the region.[32] To entice the Japanese into a war that otherwise did not concern them, the Allies secretly promised Tokyo it could keep territory seized from Germany—the Chinese province of Shantung and the string of German-controlled islands in the Pacific straddling the passage between Hawaii and the Philippines.

After 1914, the Japanese suddenly found themselves in a strong position and with few obstacles to further expansion. They were divided about how to respond. The older generation of Meiji leaders characteristically advised "showing solidarity with the Powers," but a younger generation was less patient and less inclined to subservience. They believed Japan needed to act quickly, before the Europeans recovered their strength. The war was the "chance of a millennium," a "divine aid . . . for the achievement of Japan's destiny."[33] In addition to driving the Germans out of Shantung and seizing German-held islands in the Pacific, the Japanese saw a chance to take substantial control of China. In 1915 they confronted the Chinese government with a set of proposals that became known as the Twenty-One Demands. These included the permanent stationing of Japanese troops in Shantung, the extension of Japanese leases in Manchuria to ninety-nine years, and the installation of Japanese political, military, and economic advisers to oversee Chinese industry, railroads, and ports. China would become a virtual protectorate. In the end, international opposition convinced the Japanese to back away from their most extreme demands, but the powers acknowledged Japan's special interests on the mainland. Japan's stature as a power to be reckoned with in Asia was secure.

The end of the war in Europe, however, seemed to bring another shift in the Asian power balance. Not only did the British return, but there was a new major player on the scene: the United States. Although U.S. forces had not played any part in the Asian theater against Germany, the end of the war left the United States in a potentially dominant position. As formidable as Japan's had become over the previous two decades, America's actual power was greater and its potential power was almost unlimited. The postwar American economy was twelve times the size of Japan's. The Japanese depended on the United States for practically everything an industrializing society needed—oil, steel, machine tools, loans, and access to the vast American market. The United States had a powerful navy and was still in the midst of a wartime buildup that, if completed as planned, would give it by 1924 a "monster battle force" of over fifty first-line battleships. According to the Japanese navy minister, this would create "such a great disparity in the balance of naval power as to reduce the Pacific Ocean to an American lake."[34] The Japanese navy had plans for building a modern fleet of eight new battleships and eight new heavy cruisers, but the government was already spending half the national budget on defense, and the navy minister warned that Japan would bankrupt itself trying to keep pace with a nation that possessed "unlimited wealth and resources."[35] Some leaders worried that Japan had overreached during the war and could find itself isolated in an American-dominated world.

Japanese leaders decided at war's end that the nation needed to adapt to the new Anglo-American world, which meant adapting to the new rules and principles of international behavior articulated by the American president at Paris. It had to cooperate with others, and "especially the United States," if it was to "restore the world's confidence" and "emerge as a great power in the new era of peace."[36] The "old diplomacy" had to be abandoned. "Duplicity," "intrigues," and "coercion" had to give way to "fair play, justice, and humanitarianism."[37] Armed competition had "become obsolete" and was being replaced by economic competition in a world that was becoming "one, large, open economic organization."[38]

At first even the military supported this view, agreeing that it was time for consolidation rather than expansion.[39] For the Imperial Navy, "the essence of national defence" boiled down to a single strategic imperative: "avoidance of war with America."[40]

Just as Japan during the Meiji era had transformed its political system and economy to respond to the challenges of late-nineteenth-century imperial competition, in the new Taisho era it transformed itself again.[41] The appointment in 1918 of Hara Takashi as prime minister, the first party politician ever to lead a Japanese government, was itself a response to what many regarded as the "inevitable trend in human affairs" toward American-style democracy.[42] After the victory of the democracies in the Great War, Japanese liberal intellectuals argued that Japan had to "move with the currents in the world."[43] Japanese life had to become more "cosmopolitan," Japanese commerce, industry, and agriculture had to become "internationalized,"[44] if Japan was going to compete in "a liberal, capitalist, internationalist world order rather than a world of power politics."[45]

The era of "Taisho democracy" was, in fact, one of remarkable individual freedom by traditional Japanese standards, akin in many ways to the Weimar period in Germany and the American "Jazz Age" of the same period.[46] Sexual mores were relaxed and Western cultural influences pervaded society. The franchise was expanded. Universal manhood suffrage was introduced in 1925, with the voting population rising from under 3 million voters to over 12 million by 1928. Laws banning labor unions were abrogated.[47] Japanese civilian leaders wielded unprecedented influence. The military's share of the national budget fell from nearly 50 percent in 1921 to 30 percent in 1923, forcing the Imperial Army to cut four divisions.[48]

This social, economic, and political revolution caused resentments, of course. Many Japanese believed their country was becoming a slave to Western culture and Western power. Nationalists and conservatives inside and outside the military, like the young aristocrat and future prime minister Prince Fumimaro Konoe, believed Japanese leaders were selling the nation out. They regarded Wilson's "new diplomacy" as hypocrisy. After colonizing the world for three centuries, the Western powers now declared it immoral and unacceptable just as "late developing countries" like Germany and Japan started to do the same. The British and French grabbed up pieces of the Ottoman Empire and Germany's former colonies in Africa, but it was Japan's retention of Shantung they complained about.[49] For the moment, this was but a subcurrent in Japanese thinking, albeit a powerful one. Most Japanese leaders in the early postwar years believed Japan had no choice but to adjust to the new fact of American dominance. If Japan did not conform to the new rules, they feared, it would "suffer the miserable fate of being excluded from the community of world powers."[50]

Anticipating an American-dominated world was not unreasonable in the first couple of years following the war. Nor was concern that American power might be directed at Japan. Both Wilson and Harding had supported the naval buildup in part as a check against growing Japanese power. American naval strategists warned that with the weakening of Britain and France, the collapse of Russia, and the defeat of Germany, there was "no power in the Pacific" to check Japanese sea power, and only American "naval preponderance" could "contain Japanese expansionism" and curb Japan's "dangerously aggressive temper."[51] Henry Cabot Lodge had begged Harding to resist calls for cutting back the naval program "in view of the way Japan is behaving."[52] John Van Antwerp Mac-Murray, the American minister to Tokyo and the State Department's top Asia expert, agreed it was essential to restore "the equilibrium in the Far East" by increasing American naval power in the western Pacific.[53] Some Americans also still retained a romantic, paternalistic protectiveness toward China, which was also a potential source of tension with Japan. The U.S. minister to China, Paul Reinsch, warned that if Japan were not contained, it would become "the greatest engine of military oppression and dominance" that the world had ever seen and that a "huge armed conflict" would be "absolutely inevitable."[54]

But despite the concerns of officials and a few interested Americans, Congress and the broader public had no more interest in Asia than in Europe. Any possibility that the United States was going to restore the "equilibrium" of East Asia through "naval preponderance" ended at the Washington Conference nine months into Harding's term. The decision to suspend Wilson's naval buildup and scrap existing and planned battleship construction, together with the agreement not to fortify American or British bases within three thousand miles of Japan, gave the Japanese, according to British naval estimates, "an effective guarantee of security."[55] And that, in turn, gave Japan "the power to do what she liked in China." As a gesture toward helping China, constraining Japan, and preserving peace and stability in Asia, Hughes and company had therefore produced two further agreements: a Four-Power Treaty between the United

States, Britain, Japan, and France replaced the Anglo-Japanese Alliance, which Americans believed had emboldened Japanese aggressiveness; and in a Nine-Power Treaty, the signatories promised to respect the "sovereignty, the independence, and the territorial and administrative integrity of China" and to abstain from establishing new spheres of influence or interfering with the commercial rights of the other powers—effectively codifying America's "open door" principles.[56] The treaties deliberately contained no mechanisms for monitoring and enforcement—as it was, Borah denounced the new arrangement as tantamount to another League. The agreements were to be preserved only by "good faith," "pacific intentions," "mutual self-restraint," and a "forbearing spirit."[57] The Harding administration hailed the agreements as a "Magna Carta" for China and "the beginning of a new and better epoch in human affairs," and prepared to engage as little as possible in the region.[58]

This seemed like a workable strategy given the liberal-minded Japanese government that emerged from the war. Even MacMurray, who had viewed the Japanese with such extreme suspicion before the conference, afterward decided that the Japanese were actually a "friendly people," willing to "put aside mutual distrust and rivalry and to cooperate loyally with us in our traditional Far Eastern policies."[59] The relative strengthening of Japan's military position would not matter if Japanese foreign policy sought only peaceful cooperation in China. As Franklin Roosevelt, who had served as Wilson's assistant secretary of the navy, put it, even if the United States had "seriously crippled" its strategic position in the western Pacific, it had done so with "eyes open." Conflict between the two nations would be "ridiculous and futile" and was therefore most unlikely.[60]

The new Japanese government was indeed committed to peaceful cooperation. There was grumbling in certain quarters about the Washington Treaties, which most Japanese observers regarded as "at least a partial failure."[61] The end of the Anglo-Japanese alliance left a "great sense of loneliness" and betrayal.[62] Nor did the Japanese fail to see that the Nine-Power Treaty was directed at them. As the British ambassador in Tokyo reported, the feeling among Japanese was that they had "yielded everything and gained nothing."[63]

The new leaders of Japan nevertheless determined to use the agreements to strengthen cooperation with the United States and Britain. Embracing the "new and better epoch in human affairs," they were willing to trade tangible strategic assets for "intangible promises of cooperation."[64] The lead negotiator at the Washington Conference, Kijuro

Shidehara, who would serve as foreign minister for most of the remainder of the decade, declared that Japanese policy in China would henceforth be conducted "within the framework of the Washington Treaties."[65] And Japan made good on this promise for the next few years, as American officials acknowledged.

Indeed, as soon became clear, the Japanese sought and expected more active cooperation than Washington was prepared to offer. The Japanese may have believed that the Washington Conference had established a new "system" for managing the problems of China and other regional issues, but American officials at the highest levels did not see it that way.[66]

The difference in expectations soon became evident as China gradually slipped into crisis. Even as the powers were meeting in Washington, long-simmering nationalist passions were erupting in China, accompanied by a breakdown of authority and descent into political turmoil. The sources of Chinese discontent were of long standing. Since the mid-nineteenth century, Britain and the other imperial powers had demanded and enforced special rights and privileges in the parts of China where they did business, especially in such "treaty ports" as Shanghai, Nanking, and Canton. These agreements, which the Chinese and those who sympathized with them called the "unequal treaties," had also allowed those foreign governments effectively to control Chinese taxes and tariffs. Foreign nationals living in China enjoyed immunity from Chinese laws and judicial institutions; foreign police forces operating in Shanghai and elsewhere in the country acted autonomously to defend foreign nationals and their property; and they were backed in times of unrest by the Royal Navy or other foreign forces. Combined with the economic controls exercised by foreign powers and the long-term leases on territory and facilities, the "unequal treaties" had deprived the Chinese government of anything resembling sovereign control over its people and national territory.

A series of events over the course of the previous decade had brought much of the Chinese population to the boiling point. The overthrow of the Manchu dynasty and establishment of a nominal republic in 1912 gave the people a greater say in their fate and led to growing demands for an end to the foreign impositions. It also destroyed the central authority that had usually acted as intermediary between such popular demands and the foreign powers. In the decade between the end of the imperial dynasty and the Washington Conference, China had descended into warlordism, with more than a dozen local military chiefs and cliques controlling provinces and cities across the country and rival governments in the north and south vying unsuccessfully to unite the country under their rule.

The effects of the European war in Asia had fanned these flames. On the one hand, the Chinese were forced to swallow most of Japan's Twenty-One Demands, but, on the other hand, the defeat of Germany and Austria-Hungary put an end to the unequal treaties with those two powers. The Chinese delegation at the Paris peace talks tried to get the other powers to renounce their own special rights as well, and also to get Japan to return Shantung. With all the talk of "self-determination" and Wilson's professed anti-imperialism, they expected progress. When the powers instead decided to allow Japan to keep Shantung, therefore, it set off an explosion of demonstrations across China, chiefly led by students and intellectuals, the so-called May Fourth Movement. When the West, including the United States, still refused to help, the Chinese nationalist leader Sun Yat-sen turned to the Soviet Union, which was only too happy to support an anti-imperialist revolution against the Western powers. In 1921 the Chinese Communist Party was founded, and Sun's Nationalist Party (the Kuomintang or KMT) soon allied with it. Indeed, at the very moment when the great powers were negotiating the Washington Treaties, representatives of the Communist Party and Sun Yat-sen's KMT were in Moscow for a meeting of the Comintern.

The Washington Treaties did almost nothing to address Chinese demands. The Nine-Power Treaty, which Hughes called China's "Magna Carta," was chiefly an agreement among the powers and barely mentioned Chinese interests. American officials rejected the Chinese delegation's request that all existing "special rights, privileges, immunities or commitments . . . be deemed null and void." [67] Although the powers were to "provide the fullest and most unembarrassed opportunity to China to develop and maintain for herself an effective and stable government," the agreement said nothing about the unequal treaties that were the greatest obstacles to achieving that goal. The Americans agreed to hold a future conference to discuss revisions of tariff policies, with an eye toward making more revenue available to a Chinese government, should one ever form, and to appoint a commission to look into the question of "extraterritoriality." But the treaty did not even establish a roadmap to these gains, much less to actual Chinese independence. [68]

Americans were not indifferent to Chinese desires—on the contrary, they thought of themselves as the only well-meaning foreign power when it came to Chinese interests. But no more than in the past were they prepared to sacrifice much to help. American businesses and citizens also benefited from the "unequal treaties," after all, and Hughes worried that the burgeoning Chinese nationalist movement endangered "the whole system of treaty rights under which foreign trade with China is carried on."[69] During the negotiations MacMurray frankly warned the Chinese delegation not to imagine that the United States was operating out of "altruistic motives."[70] The general consensus of the powers, shared by MacMurray, was that the Chinese had to get their own house in order before concessions could even be considered.[71] MacMurray was unimpressed by the "juvenile nationalistic influences" in China. He saw little difference between Sun Yat-sen and the warlords. "They all look alike to us," he wrote to Washington, advising that until some leader was able to "lick his rivals completely enough" to form a durable government, the United States would do well to "keep out of the mess."[72]

That would not be easy, however. Within a year of the ratification of the Washington Treaties, a Chinese nationalist movement erupted with a depth, breadth, and force not seen since the anti-foreign uprisings of 1899–1901. The manifesto of the First National Congress of the revitalized, militarized, and now Soviet-backed Kuomintang in January 1924 condemned the unequal treaties, and Sun Yat-sen, on his deathbed in 1925, called for abolishing the treaties in the "shortest possible time."[73]

Growing nationalist demands were accompanied by mounting violence against foreign interests. In the spring of 1925, labor disputes in Japanese-owned textile mills led to skirmishes and the killing of a Japanese employer. When police fired on the striking workers, killing one, crowds of students and laborers entered the International Settlement in Shanghai to protest. A British officer ordered his forces to fire into the crowd, killing twelve and wounding seventeen, which in turn set off anti-British and anti-Japanese strikes, boycotts, and demonstrations nationwide, including in the British colony of Hong Kong and the treaty port of Canton. The strikes and protests continued for months. In January 1926, the Second National Congress of the KMT issued an anti-imperialist manifesto calling for the abolition of the unequal treaties and all foreign privileges in China.[74] That spring, Chiang Kai-shek, replacing Sun as head of the Kuomintang, launched the Northern Expedition to defeat the northern warlords and unify the country. Fighting under the banner of nationalism, anti-imperialism, and treaty annulment, and with the continued support of the Soviets, Chiang's northward offensive put at risk the peace and stability the Washington Treaties were designed to preserve. The turmoil in China also raised questions in American foreign policy circles about whether the United States could remain passive in the face of the mounting crisis.

MacMurray, who had just arrived as minister in Beijing, insisted it could not. Together with his Japanese and British colleagues, he proposed a united show of force by the three powers under the rubric of the Nine-Power Treaty. The Chinese public, aroused to the point of "fanaticism," he argued, was trying to deprive the treaty powers of their rights through violence and intimidation. In MacMurray's view, the Chinese were thus themselves in violation of the Nine-Power Treaty. Like most Americans, he favored treaty revision, but he insisted it had to be negotiated with a "stable and effective" Chinese government capable of protecting foreign interests and citizens.[75] MacMurray recommended that the three powers threaten a naval blockade or some other "feasible forceful measure" to make the Chinese back down. If the Chinese "realized that the Powers were in earnest," he believed, "no drastic action would in fact be necessary." Then the powers could offer the Chinese real concessions. The powers had an obligation to "adopt a firm policy" in order to save "the Chinese from their own folly."[76] He was particularly concerned that the three powers work together, because he feared that if they went their own ways, conflict was inevitable.[77]

The historian Akira Iriye has speculated that "the subsequent course of Chinese history might well have been different if these proposals had been accepted."[78] The United States was, in fact, prepared to make concessions to the Chinese, on tariff autonomy and the "gradual relinquishment of extraterritorial rights," and so were the other powers.[79] In response to the strikes and boycotts, the British Foreign Office had begun to review China policy and in December 1926 issued a statement recognizing "the essential justice of the Chinese claim for treaty revision."[80] Foreign Minister Shidehara of Japan still preferred to befriend the Chinese rather than to coerce them, despite the attacks on Japanese citizens and companies, in part because the boycotts were wreaking havoc on Japanese exports to China.[81] MacMurray and his Japanese and British counterparts in Beijing therefore worked to put together a coordinated policy, including a show of force if necessary.[82]

The diplomats' suggestion met a consistent wall of opposition in Washington, however. Not only was American opinion "very strongly opposed to military action in China," Kellogg sharply reminded Mac-Murray, but the idea of any kind of joint action with the other powers was also objectionable.[83] Senator Borah denounced the idea of using

American forces to defend British imperialism.[84] In February 1927, the House overwhelmingly passed a resolution calling on the Coolidge administration to support Chinese demands and free the United States from "entangling relations with other powers" whose interests were not the same as America's.[85] Kellogg told MacMurray that the United States had to "do its own thinking."[86]

Far from cooperating with the other treaty powers, in fact, the Coolidge administration sought to satisfy public opinion by repeated declarations of support for the Chinese and their demands. President Coolidge promised to "assist and encourage every legitimate [Chinese] aspiration for freedom, for unity, for the cultivation of a national spirit and the realization of a republican form of government."[87] Such statements reflected genuine American sentiments, but they left the British and Japanese hanging out on their own. Neither London nor Tokyo was ready to make the same concessions, which left them alone to face Chinese anger while the Americans engaged in "popularity-courting."[88] As one Japanese liberal complained to MacMurray, the Americans could afford to "indulge" in "idealistic" gestures, because they had so little at stake, but Japan's "economic and political existence" was on the line.[89] American policies left the Foreign Ministry "shocked and embittered."[90]

Nor would the United States support the other powers when they asked for help. When foreign citizens, including Britons and Americans, were attacked in Canton, the British sent naval forces to defuse the crisis and asked if the United States would "associate itself" with the action. Kellogg declined.[91] When a year later Chinese forces in Nanking went on a rampage of killing and looting against foreigners, attacking the American, British, and Japanese consulates, as well as the American-run University of Nanking, killing six and wounding several others, MacMurray and his British and Japanese counterparts once again worked to fashion a joint response.[92] But editorial opinion in the United States was almost unanimous against taking forceful action or cooperating with the other powers. It was not America's job to uphold "a one-sided treaty system forced upon China by the European Powers," the New York *World* commented. The United States should be pulling "nobody's chestnuts from the fire."[93]

The Americans' determination to go it alone convinced the British that they, too, should go their own way. Indeed, without American support, without the Japanese as allies, and with problems in Europe looming, the British sought as much as feasible to wash their hands of the China problem.[94]

That left the Japanese essentially alone to manage the crisis in China. No nation had more at stake. With 250,000 nationals living and working on the mainland, Japanese citizens made up 75 percent of the foreign population, far more than the British or any of the other treaty powers. Japanese business investments in China accounted for over 80 percent of all Japan's overseas assets.[95] The biggest investment of all was in Manchuria. With a territory as large as France and Germany combined, and four times the size of Japan, Manchuria had over the past two decades become a critical source of lumber, coal, iron, grain, and soybeans.[96] Hundreds of Japanese companies did business there, employing more than 100,000 Japanese citizens. The South Manchurian Railway alone was a mammoth Japanese enterprise. The company that owned it was the largest corporation in Japan, and in the 1920s it was responsible for more than a quarter of the nation's tax revenues. Japan's Manchurian interests were protected by a permanent garrison force of roughly 10,000 troops, the Kwantung Army, which wielded significant influence within Japanese military circles and enjoyed considerable independence.

No Japanese government could ignore the burgeoning threat posed by the Chinese nationalist movement as Chiang led his armies northward toward Shantung and Manchuria. Shidehara had done what he could to address the problem without force and coercion.[97] He made repeated overtures to the United States. He proposed international support for moderate nationalist factions in China.[98] He called for a conference of the treaty powers to address Chinese demands under the rubric of the Nine-Power Treaty. But to no avail.

One result was that by the late 1920s, Shidehara's policy of peaceful cooperation came to be regarded by many Japanese as too "soft." Both the Japanese military and the broader public grew increasingly angry as the strikes against Japanese companies, the involvement of the Soviets, the killing of Japanese nationals, and Chiang's Northern Expedition threatened what all regarded as Japan's vital interests on the mainland. Even diplomats in the Foreign Ministry believed more "positive" action was needed.[99] The result was a gradual turn in Japanese policy toward the unilateral use of force to preserve Japanese interests.

In April 1927, a month after the Nanking incident, Shidehara's government fell and was replaced by a cabinet led by the politician-general Tanaka Giichi. The new prime minister sent 2,000 troops from Manchuria down to Tsingtao, prompting complaints from the Chinese and the other powers about an "invasion." Two months later an additional 2,000 troops were sent to Shantung province. The following spring, Tanaka sent 20,000 troops from Japan to confront Chiang's nationalist forces at Tsinan, temporarily halting Chiang's drive northward toward Beijing. Tanaka's aim was to prevent by force what international diplomacy was failing to prevent. The Chinese government vainly appealed to the League of Nations.[100] Chinese nationalist anger at Japan continued to grow.

Some American officials saw the writing on the wall. As early as November 1927 the U.S. consul general in Mukden predicted that Japan's new direction under Tanaka would eventually lead to the "political absorption" of Manchuria, unless the United States took steps to prevent it.[101] In June 1928, junior officers of the Japanese Kwantung Army assassinated the Manchurian warlord Chang Tso-lin, whom they suspected of working with Chiang Kai-shek against Japanese interests. The move was not approved by Tanaka, but it nevertheless served warning to the Chinese and everyone else that further assaults on Japanese interests would be met by force.[102]

Tanaka continued trying to work with the other powers. In the fall of 1928, he sent a prominent Japanese emissary, Count Uchida, to Washington and London to formulate "common policies" toward China. Secretary Kellogg wasn't interested, and neither were the British.[103] Uchida would soon become a leading voice for taking Manchuria by force.[104] This became such a dominant trend in Japanese thinking that even Shidehara's return as foreign minister in 1929 could not reverse it.

CHAPTER SIXTEEN

The Manchurian Crisis

We had better quit writing notes . . .

—Will Rogers[1]

WASHINGTON WAS largely oblivious to the shifting currents in Japan.[2] The assistant secretary of state for Asia at the time assumed the "friendliest feelings between us and the Japanese" and saw no reason why they shouldn't "continue more or less indefinitely."[3] In fact, anti-American sentiments had roiled beneath the surface throughout the period of Taisho democracy, and by the latter half of the 1920s they were bubbling over. Much of this was due to economic factors. Over the course of the 1920s the Japanese economy was buffeted by global forces and natural calamities. There were bank panics in 1922, an earthquake in 1923 that destroyed much of Tokyo and necessitated heavy foreign borrowing for reconstruction, and then a full-blown financial crisis in 1927 that led to the formation of the Tanaka government. American bankers did the bulk of the lending, making Japan even more dependent on the United States. Meanwhile, American protectionist trade policies had hurt Japanese pocketbooks. The Fordney-McCumber Tariff of 1922 raised duties on some of Japan's leading exports, including silk goods produced by small farmers in rural Japan.[4] When the U.S. stock market crashed in 1929 and depression struck the American economy, Japanese exports to the United States fell by over 40 percent in a year, and the collapse in the demand for silk drove Japanese small farmers into bankruptcy and starvation.[5]

By the end of the decade, Japan's economic difficulties added to the growing conviction among leading Japanese officials and politicians that peaceful and accommodating policies were not paying off. The much-vaunted cooperation with the United States and the West had proven to be a mirage, and now Japan's economic dependence on the Anglo-American global economy had produced decline and widespread suffering. The Anglo-American liberal world order, moreover, had proved far less liberal than advertised. In the supposedly liberal West, and especially in the United States, xenophobia rather than cosmopolitanism was the order of the day. In 1924 Congress passed the Asian Exclusion Act, shutting the door to Japanese immigration entirely. The following year, elections in Australia reaffirmed the "White Australia" policy. On the economic front, neo-mercantilism and high tariffs had triumphed over free trade. The Smoot-Hawley Tariff Act in 1930 raised import duties on Japanese goods by an additional 23 percent.[6] The British by 1931 had begun enacting their own protectionist imperial preference system. The world was heading toward the creation of "large economic blocs," Japanese officials observed, and many believed Japan would have to follow this global trend.[7] The idea of an Asian "co-prosperity" sphere led by Japan had long been discussed in some nationalist circles. By 1930 it took on a new salience. "Co-prosperity," meaning, above all, "an exclusive and unequal economic partnership between China and Japan," became the "slogan of the decade."[8]

These trends strengthened the hands of conservatives who had argued from the beginning for a more aggressive and independent foreign policy. While liberals like Shidehara had sought to pursue Japan's interests in China peacefully through "economic diplomacy" and cooperation, and regarded a clash with the United States as both dangerous and avoidable, many conservatives inside and outside Japan's military had come to believe that conflict with the United States was inevitable and that Japan had to prepare itself.[9]

If conflict was inevitable, then Japan's economic dependence on the United States was a fatal weakness. The lesson of the Great War, some influential army officers believed, was that only nations with self-sufficient and self-reliant economies, with significant domestic industrial capacity and unhindered access to raw materials, had a chance of surviving in the new age of modern "total" war. An American trade embargo could bring Japan to its knees, just as it had done to Germany. Japan could only escape this perilous dependence through expansion on the Asian mainland and beyond. Influential Japanese military leaders believed the constraints imposed at the Washington Conference had been designed to keep Japan down.[10] With its "limitless economic resources," its "policies of economic aggression," and its "provocation of anti-Japanese activities" in China, the United States already threatened Japan's position on the Asian mainland, "for which our nation has risked its destiny."[11] If Japan did not overthrow the "Anglo-American-Centered Peace," it would remain "a backward country . . . forever subordinate to the advanced nations."[12] The United States and Britain would never allow Japan "equal access to the markets and natural resources of the colonial areas," therefore the Japanese people had no choice but to "destroy the status quo for the sake of self-preservation."[13]

Such thinking harkened back to an earlier, more martial phase of Japanese foreign policy. After all, Japan had become one of the world's great powers not through a subservient accommodation but through imperial conquest and the triumphs of its military. Most Japanese, both in the elite and among the masses, still took pride in those victories and thought that perhaps the time had come to repeat them.[14]

The new thinking also harkened back to a less liberal Japan. The turn to liberalism after the Great War, the era of Taisho democracy, had not come without opposition and resistance. As in other countries experiencing liberal politics and economics for the first time, Japanese society was divided between those who welcomed the new system and those who lamented what was being lost: the culture and traditions, the familial and societal relationships, Japan's special place in the world—all the things that made up a distinctive Japanese nationalism.

These divisions were exacerbated by Japan's increasing dependence on and vulnerability to the global economy. Until the 1850s, Japan's only trading relationship with the outside world was a small artificial island off Nagasaki where Dutch traders were allowed to sell their wares. The Japanese people had been poorer but also more self-sufficient, and more equal. The heavy reliance on foreign markets, foreign goods, and foreign financing had disrupted this centuries-old societal order. The new class of pro-Western, cosmopolitan Japanese businessmen developed strong relationships with foreign, increasingly American, capitalists and financiers. Even in prosperous times, less privileged Japanese outside the big cities tended to resent this cozy capitalist relationship.[15]

In Japan as elsewhere, anti-capitalist sentiments only intensified as economic hard times hit. While many were suffering, a few grew immensely wealthy, and often because of their access to Western financiers and industries. Wealth thus became associated with foreign influence. The man who assassinated a leading Japanese capitalist in 1921 declared it was necessary to punish "the traitorous millionaires."[16] In the eyes of the "total war" school in the military, liberal civilian leaders' determination to preserve good relations with the West at the expense of military power, economic self-sufficiency, and territorial expansion was indeed treason.[17] The democratic capitalist system was an obstacle to the "completion of national defense."[18] Civilian rule itself was "an anachronism."[19]

The answer, they believed, was to return to the more traditional "imperial way." Military officials and their conservative supporters had long believed that the emperor's "right of supreme command," as specified in the Meiji Constitution, meant that matters of national defense, including the size of the military budget and questions of disarmament but also the broad direction of Japanese foreign and military policy, were to be decided by the emperor advised by his military chiefs, not by democratically elected civilian cabinets. As Prince Konoe declared, "The country demands national reform, and the government . . . must listen to its call. The impetus of the great [Meiji] Restoration has carried us thus far with honor and success; but now it is for the young men to take up the task and carry the country forward into a new age."[20] And this was the direction Japan took. In a world where democracy was under assault everywhere, Japanese liberals put up little struggle. As one historian put it, "Taisho democracy and Taisho internationalism" proved to be "fragile plants, for no one cared as much about their preservation as some cared about their destruction."[21]

The first blow struck for the new Japan was in Manchuria. The "total war" faction was well placed in the large Kwantung Army that protected Japanese interests in that vast, nominally Chinese province. In the late 1920s, top officials began looking for a provocation that would allow them to invade and seize all of Manchuria. The 1928 assassination of the leading Chinese warlord in Manchuria was made to look like the work of a Chinese rival. Then, in September 1931, Kwantung Army soldiers exploded a bomb under a stretch of the South China Railroad, again blaming Chinese saboteurs for the act. This time the Japanese "responded" by attacking Chinese positions in Mukden. Although launched technically without the direct approval of commanders either in Manchuria or in Tokyo, it was no act of insubordination but had been approved in principle.[22] The project of making Manchuria a formal part of the Japanese empire had begun.

The Hoover administration responded hesitantly. Although Washington officials had been warned that Japan might take such an action, they were reluctant to believe the government could have approved it. Most believed that "liberalism was too firmly seated in Japan."[23] Some thought the Chinese must indeed have done something to provoke the Japanese. Secretary of State Stimson, assuming that the Kwantung Army acted without orders and that Foreign Minister Shidehara would soon bring them to heel, and fearing that any foreign denunciation could whip up nationalism and strengthen hardliners, opposed invoking the Nine-Power Treaty or the Kellogg-Briand Pact or having the matter raised by the League of Nations. It was enough to "let the Japanese know that we are watching them." He held to that posture for almost three months, as the Japanese expanded their military operations throughout Manchuria.[24]

The Hoover administration's reluctance to see the Japanese action as a deliberate act of aggression was understandable. In the decade since the Washington Conference, the United States had been able to pose as a defender of China without taking any action or incurring any risks. But that policy had sufficed only because Japan had pursued a peaceful and accommodating policy. If the world was now dealing with a different, more aggressive Japan, the United States was going to have to choose between being a friend to the Chinese and risking war or abandoning the Chinese to Japanese mercies.

The Japanese military action in Manchuria, in fact, did not produce quite the usual outpouring of support for the Chinese in the United States. On the contrary, there was a good deal of caution and some sympathetic understanding for Japan's behavior.[25] Self-described "realists" at the State Department and among strategic thinkers and writers argued that even if Manchuria was legally part of China and becoming "more Chinese every day," it nevertheless was in Japan's natural sphere of influence.[26] As the journalist Herbert Bayard Swope, winner of the first Pulitzer Prize, put it, "Sixty-three million people living on rocky islands . . . have the right to exist. If existence demands expansion . . . then why forbid Japanese expansion to follow natural lines?"[27] The financial and business community, led by the Morgan bank, also sided with Japan. Many influential Americans continued to believe for some time that the Chinese had actually provoked the Japanese. Elihu Root, Stimson's mentor, questioned whether Japan was "doing anything more than defending herself" from Chinese aggression, while the State Department's William Castle, Jr., complained of China's "bloody and endless provocations."[28] Such statements were so patently at odds with what was happening in Manchuria that they could best be explained by the strong American desire to avoid hard questions about U.S. policy.

Those questions became impossible to avoid, however, as Japanese military actions expanded across Manchuria and into other parts of China. The bombing of Chinchow in October was the first unmistakable evidence that Japan was not merely responding to a "provocation" but was engaged in what Stimson called "a widely extended movement of aggression." Chinchow was some two hundred miles from the South China Railroad and Mukden. To Stimson it was now clear that Shidehara and the civilian government had lost control. Japan, he believed, was in "the hands of virtually mad dogs."[29] In December the government in which Shidehara served was indeed replaced by a more militant cabinet, depriving Stimson of his last hope for a reversal of Japanese policy.[30]

At the end of January 1932, the Japanese government escalated dramatically. Using another "provocation" as pretext—the killing of a Japanese Buddhist monk by Chinese rioters—the Tokyo government launched a combined naval and ground attack on Shanghai. As the foreign community in the International Settlement watched in shock and horror, the Japanese deployed over 100,000 troops and some 80 naval vessels, including an aircraft carrier and 300 aircraft, in an attack that killed between 10,000 and 20,000 civilians. In a historic first, the Japanese launched bombing sorties from their carrier against the Shanghai civilian population. Civilians faced a "dilemma of terror," American journalists reported: whether to burn to death in their homes or be shot in the streets. Chiang's armies put up unexpectedly stiff resistance, but they were outgunned. Five thousand Chinese and over 3,000 Japanese soldiers were killed in the fighting. In March, the Chinese surrendered the city. The "ceasefire" agreement required the Chinese to remove all troops from Shanghai and the surrounding region. The Japanese kept a small force in the city, taking another large step toward control of northern China.

The Shanghai "incident," as the Japanese called it, had a dramatic effect on American attitudes toward Japan. Daily descriptions of the horrors flooded the papers. Analogies to Germany's actions in the Great War abounded. Some compared the attacks to the "rape of Belgium," others to the sinking of the *Lusitania*.[31] Stimson later recalled feeling that he did not want to be another Wilson, "who did nothing to show the shame that we felt in regard to Belgium."[32]

Even before Shanghai, the Sino-Japanese crisis had begun to take on a different aspect for Stimson and others. As the first major act of territorial aggression since the Great War, it had ceased to be only about China. The "whole world" was watching to see whether the various international peace treaties were "good for anything or not," Stimson believed, and if the United States and others allowed another set of treaties to be treated like "scraps of paper," then all the institutions of peace "laboriously constructed since the great war" would be "irreparably damaged, if not completely overthrown."[33]

The difficulty, of course, was finding some way to defend the treaties that did not risk conflict, new commitments in Asia, or deeper entanglement with Europe and the League of Nations. Even the horror of the Shanghai attacks did not alter the overwhelming postwar determination to avoid at all costs being dragged into another foreign war. Edward R. Murrow, then a twenty-four-year-old director of the National Student Federation, reminded the membership that millions had been "needlessly sacrificed in the great war," and Charles A. Beard asked what the United States had to gain by defeating Japan if it came at the price of "two or three million American doughboys."[34] Whatever public sympathy may have existed for the Chinese, Will Rogers probably spoke for most Americans when he suggested that "America could hunt all over the world and not find a better fight to keep out of."[35]

If war was to be avoided at all costs, that left few viable policy options. Many peace activists favored sanctions, but others pointed out that sanctions could easily lead to war. Jane Addams opposed "ruthless" sanctions that might punish innocent Japanese workers.[36] Some favored a private boycott, against Japanese silk products, for instance. The peace activist Dorothy Detzer stopped buying silk stockings.[37] But still others questioned whether a private boycott would have much effect and, if it did, whether it, too, might prompt a violent Japanese response. The idea of an arms embargo or an embargo on loans, either against both belligerents or only against Japan, raised similar questions. Would the pacifists' demand for sanctions drive the United States into a war? The *Chicago Tribune* editorialized jocularly about "Pacifists Running Amock."[38]

Many peace activists wanted it both ways. They believed it essential to the cause of peace that the Kellogg-Briand Pact and Nine-Power Treaty be upheld, but they opposed any means of enforcing them. Dewey spoke for many when he insisted that the "enforcement of peace" was a contradiction.[39] And the peace activists were not alone in their indecision. Walter Lippmann changed his mind almost weekly, calling for sanctions one moment and in the next sneering at the "belligerent pacifists at Geneva" who wanted "another war to end war and another war to make Asia safe for democracy."[40]

The Hoover administration was also torn. The State Department drew up a proposal for sanctions, estimating that Japan could not withstand a boycott for "more than a very few days, or weeks," but President Hoover steadfastly opposed any measure that might provoke Tokyo. He had no interest in "sticking pins in tigers."[41] The State Department's Stanley Hornbeck, exasperated by the activists' constant demands for firmer action, warned Detzer that she did not seem to understand: "This situation is so serious that it literally may mean war for us—not this year, or next year, but sometime in the near future."[42]

It was Lippmann who first recommended the approach that Stimson and Hoover would pursue: non-recognition.[43] The idea was that if the United States and the member states of the League of Nations refused to recognize the new state of Manchukuo or Japan's control of Manchuria, Japan's grasp would become so tenuous that eventually it would have to withdraw. Lippmann's non-recognition strategy essentially depended on the functioning of the global economy to squeeze Japan. The world's "money markets" would be closed to Japan until a "recognized legal order" was established, and eventually this would force the Japanese to withdraw.[44]

Hoover and Stimson were both easily sold on the idea, and in early January 1932, Stimson sent notes to both Japan and China stating that the United States would not "admit the legality" of any changes of border resulting from aggression in violation of the Kellogg-Briand Pact and would not "recognize any treaty or agreement" between China and Japan that impaired the rights of the United States or the territorial and administrative integrity of the Republic of China.[45]

In the United States, the non-recognition policy won almost unanimous approval—indeed, as one historian observes, "few actions in the entire interwar period received such enthusiastic support." The promise of "painless but effective action" leading to Japan's "inevitable downfall" was naturally appealing. Internationalists and peace activists saw non-recognition as a means of putting some teeth in the Kellogg-Briand pact.[46]

The problem was getting the other great powers to go along, especially the British, without whom non-recognition would be futile. Unfortunately for Stimson, the record of American unilateralism over the previous decade proved to be a serious obstacle to winning London's cooperation in this moment of crisis.

Stimson himself had from the beginning been wary of involving the United States in international deliberations on the Manchurian crisis, since those deliberations were conducted almost entirely at the League Council in Geneva. He worried that the French and British would use the Asian crisis to draw the United States into League discussions more generally, including on European matters.[47] And he was right to worry. When he finally agreed to let an American representative sit with the League Council, the event was treated in Europe as an historic occasion. The council hall "was filled to overflowing with a hushed expectant crowd," all eager to welcome "the prodigal propounders of the League returned after years of absence."[48] Borah and the old irreconcilables were outraged, and Stimson had to withdraw the representative from further interactions with the overeager Europeans.[49]

Stimson also worried that on the specific question of Manchuria, the European powers wanted to push the United States out front. He was right about that, too. The other powers believed that Japan would only respond to the League's demands if the United States was clearly in the lead.[50] The League was continually trying to "pass the buck to us," Stimson complained, and he made clear that American "leadership" was out of the question. President Hoover was upset that Stimson had already gone too far.[51]

When it came to winning British support for non-recognition, therefore, Stimson found London reluctant. British officials regarded the non-recognition idea as absurd. They believed Japan could "only [be] checked by force." Britain lacked sufficient power in the region to act alone, and they did not trust the Americans to act with them.[52] The Americans had been "erratic and inconsiderate in the past," British diplomats complained, and were "quite capable of backing out after we had agreed to give our support, leaving us to clear up the resultant mess."[53] Stimson would later complain that the British "let us down" and railed at the "yellow-bellied responses" from Britain and the other powers. But the fact was, as Hornbeck noted, that in this moment of crisis there was not a single power in the world that the United States could "count on . . . as a firm 'ally' or associate."[54]

Meanwhile, the repeated U.S. remonstrances, warnings, and verbal threats were having no effect whatever on Japanese military activities. Will Rogers quipped that every time the Japanese received a note, they took another town. "We had better quit writing notes," he suggested, or Japan would have "all China."[55]

Stimson knew that he was likely to get nowhere without the threat of force to back up his diplomatic efforts. The problem he faced, however, was twofold: The United States had too little force in Asia to threaten Japan, and Hoover wasn't interested in making the threat. Charles Evans Hughes and Henry Cabot Lodge had proven right about the mood of

Congress. Over the course of the 1920s Japan had been able to catch and surpass the United States in important categories of vessels because year after year Congress would not vote the funds necessary to build the navy even up to treaty limits. In the ten years following the Washington Conference, Japan built 196 ships of all varieties while the United States built 40.[56] By the time of the Manchurian crisis the Imperial Navy enjoyed an absolute superiority in both numbers of vessels and tonnage.[57] Since the non-fortification agreement of 1922 had prevented the United States and Great Britain from building defensible bases within three thousand miles of Japan, Tokyo's strategic position had become "impregnable."[58] This fact had shaped the calculations of key figures in the Japanese military before launching the attacks in Manchuria, and it continued to shape Japanese calculations as the U.S. escalated its warnings and threats.[59]

It also placed a limit on how far the United States could go in attempting to intimidate the Japanese into backing down. At various moments Stimson proposed deploying naval forces in order to signal American resolve, only to find the navy reluctant.[60] After a decade of neglect, the Asiatic Fleet was "undermanned, inadequately trained," and too old to be a match for Japan's newly built warships.[61] Budget cuts threatened to reduce naval personnel further, close shipyards, and put one-third of the fleet out of service. Six out of the eleven destroyers were to be delayed or abandoned. No new keels were scheduled to be laid in the following year.[62] Stimson became "much alarmed about the present situation of the Navy" when he discovered that it was "more unequal" than he had thought "to meeting Japan."[63]

Stimson tried to get by with bluff. Regardless of the navy's actual existing strength, he hoped and believed that the Japanese had to fear America's "great size" and potential strength.[64] When Japan attacked Shanghai, he persuaded Hoover to dispatch a cruiser and six destroyers, along with 1,400 soldiers and marines, as a show of strength. When a fleet of nine U.S. battleships, thirty destroyers, six submarines, and two aircraft carriers just happened to be conducting long-planned exercises off Hawaii, Stimson hoped this would remind the Japanese of America's "ultimate military strength."[65] He also tried to unnerve the Japanese by hinting in a public letter to Borah in February 1932 that if Japan abrogated the Nine-Power Treaty, the United States might resume construction of battleships and fortify the bases at Guam and the Philippines.

Stimson's bluffs, however, were consistently undermined by the realities of the naval balance. When the single American cruiser and six destroyers arrived in the waters off Shanghai in January 1932, they found the Japanese Imperial Navy already there with seven cruisers, twenty-one destroyers, and one aircraft carrier.[66] The American presence was so weak that the admiral in command regarded himself as nothing more than an "innocent bystander."[67] As for the battle fleet's maneuvers off Hawaii, which Stimson hoped would have a "steadying effect" on the Japanese, one of the exercises included defense against a mock attack on Pearl Harbor. At dawn on a Sunday morning, the "enemy" planes launched from "enemy" carriers took the U.S. defenders completely by surprise, "sinking" every battleship in the harbor and "destroying" every airplane on the ground.[68]

President Hoover, meanwhile, refused to engage in bluff. While Stimson wanted to keep the Japanese guessing and not "disclaim publicly our willingness to fight," Hoover did exactly that. He declared publicly that the United States would never "fight for Asia."[69] Two weeks after the Japanese intervention, the president announced a cut in naval construction for the coming year and the elimination of all building for the year after that.[70] Stimson complained that Hoover refused to let him wield American power effectively, and Hoover complained that Stimson "would have had us in a war with Japan before this if he had had his way."[71]

It is not possible to know how Japan might have reacted had the United States and the other powers responded with greater unity and vigor. According to reports at the time, in the twenty-four hours following the seizure of Mukden, officials in Tokyo waited "with some anxiety" to see what the foreign reaction would be.[72] Thereafter they closely followed the League's deliberations and did their best to disrupt or delay unified council action.[73] These were not "mad dogs," whatever Stimson may have thought. They believed the United States, Great Britain, and the League would do little beyond declarations of disapproval. Even Shidehara believed "the United States would never fight for the sake of China."[74] This assessment played a key role in Japanese planning and decision-making. The historian and diplomat Sadako N. Ogata has argued that "the absence of international opposition with teeth" was "the overall factor that helped the Japanese military feel free to advance into Manchuria." Stimson's early passivity in response to the initial Japanese actions, which he hoped would strengthen the hands of Shidehara and other moderates, actually had the opposite effect.[75] By taking the pressure off, Stimson's reticence made the civilian government "less resolute than it might otherwise have been in resisting the rapid expansionist flow." Shidehara might have been better served by a loud, immediate, and unified international condemnation.[76] So long as "international opposition contained elements of indecisiveness, ambiguity, or sympathy," Ogata argues, "Japan found herself possessed of a safe margin within which to consolidate and expand her control."[77]

In the end, of course, the Japanese faced neither the threat of military force, nor economic sanctions, nor even a unified international diplomatic condemnation. Only after Japan had all but completed its occupation and absorption of Manchuria did the League and the United States come together, albeit without recommending any action. In October 1932, the League of Nations released the report of the Lytton Commission, which had been charged with investigating the conflict. The commission's findings, though carefully balanced, made clear that Japan's invasion had been an act of unprovoked aggression, that Manchuria should be returned to China, and that the Japanese-backed government of Manchukuo should not be recognized. In early 1933 the League, with America's tacit support, approved the Lytton Report. This prompted the Japanese delegation to walk out and announce Japan's official withdrawal from the League. It was a proud and defiant moment for Japan. Yosuke Matsuoka, the diplomat who led the Japanese delegation out of the hall at Geneva, was greeted as a hero upon his return to Tokyo. The American ambassador, Joseph Grew, reported that "his fellow countrymen looked upon him as a modern Horatius defending his people against the onslaughts of the world."[78] Matsuoka would later become the leading advocate of closer ties with Nazi Germany.

Looking back on these events from the perspective of 1935, MacMurray wondered whether it might have been possible to manage the growing conflict between Chinese nationalism and Japanese interests had the Washington Treaty powers been truer to the spirit of cooperation and consultation established by the Washington Conference.[79] As one historian suggests, it was not impossible that Japan, under the right leadership and aided by the cooperation of the United States and Britain, might have redefined its goals in Manchuria "in such a way as to permit acceptance of real Chinese sovereignty." Throughout the 1920s liberalism was strong enough in Japan that a more friendly and accommodating international environment might have made it possible to move gradually in this direction.[80]

As in Europe, however, Americans feared that any involvement risked total involvement, including ultimately the use of force and possibly war. This fear was more reasonable in Asia than in Europe. Japan was not, like

Germany, prostrate and under the thumb of foreign powers. Its military strength was growing, as was the combination of ambition and insecurity common to rising powers. While a light touch in Europe might have solved many problems, in Asia it would have taken a deeper American commitment. Dealing with the Chinese revolution and adjusting the interests of the powers required cooperation with the British and Japanese, a willingness to threaten and possibly use force against the Chinese to protect foreign interests, and taking a leadership role in treaty revision. For Americans in the 1920s, such a role was all but inconceivable.

Instead, however, Americans chose to promote principles without any intention of enforcing them. American policymakers somehow expected the Japanese to sacrifice what they regarded as vital interests and abide by American principles, even while giving Japan neither incentive to do so nor disincentive not to. The combination of a lack of cooperation, accommodation, and adroit diplomacy, on the one hand, and inadequate military deterrence, on the other, was almost a perfect formula for producing the Japanese decisions and actions of 1931. Perhaps Japan would have ended up in the same place no matter what the United States did, but American policies did nothing to steer Japan in a different direction.

CHAPTER SEVENTEEN

The Fascist Challenge

Quite frankly, the wind everywhere blows against us.
—Franklin D. Roosevelt, 1936[1]

WHEN THE fighting in China finally stopped in 1933, most Americans quickly put the episode behind them.[2] Hoover and Stimson put the best face on what they had accomplished. Hoover was proud to have "avoided precipitate action and allowed time to work out proper solutions." He was proudest of the non-recognition doctrine. "I have projected a new doctrine into international affairs," he declared, and it had "been accepted by all nations of the world."[3] It was a genuine source of pride for Stimson and other internationalists. After a decade of U.S. refusal to cooperate with the League, and despite the continuing complexity of that relationship, the United States and the League had come together to denounce an act of aggression. Stimson thought this was an important and hopeful step, even if it had not succeeded in this first test.[4] If the "people of the world" were willing to make their voices heard, he believed, the "sanctions" of international public opinion would be "irresistible."[5] The League had functioned. It had ordered a high-level international investigation. It had received and voted to approve the report, which was a politely worded condemnation of Japan's actions. Perhaps the system was starting to work. Many American opinion leaders were more optimistic about prospects for international cooperation at the end of the Manchurian affair than they had been at the beginning.[6]

As for Japan's unfortunate actions, American policymakers and political leaders were convinced that Tokyo had overreached and would be forced to retreat. China was too big and too populous to be conquered. Japan would bankrupt itself in the attempt. The *Wall Street Journal* observed in early 1933 that Japan's situation was becoming "more palpably hopeless every day."[7] American leaders were also not prepared to write Japan off as irrevocably committed to militarism and aggression. When the intervention in Manchuria and northern China inevitably failed, they believed, the Japanese militarists would be discredited, and the liberal forces that had opposed the Manchurian affair would return to power.

Looking back on the entire period in his memoirs, Stimson recalled "no sense of general frustration" and no "foreboding of inevitable war." Over the next three years, as a private citizen, he even felt a "cautious optimism." He did not believe that Germany and Japan were "wholly lost to liberalism." The passage of time and the "continuing pressure of world opinion" would force both nations back onto the liberal democratic path. This was a widespread view that carried Americans through the 1920s and well into the 1930s, what Lionel Trilling would later call "the simple humanitarian optimism" that the world system was progressing despite the occasional setback.[8]

As part of their Enlightenment inheritance, liberals by nature tended to see the world in evolutionary terms. They anticipated a gradual, steady movement toward ever greater peace, freedom, and prosperity, driven by expanding global commerce and advances in communications and transportation, as well as by the growing power of international public opinion. When nations or movements emerged to oppose that vision, liberals regarded them as aberrations, fleeting and ephemeral, bumps on the long road of human progress. And the cure for these unfortunate renegade anti-liberal forces was more liberalism, deeper economic ties, more successful capitalist economies, more open political systems. Once satisfied, the people of these nations would see the great benefits of joining the order. Until they did, they would suffer the misfortunes and disadvantages of refusing to take part in the system.

Liberals were confident that this upstart Hitler could not survive unless he adapted to "reality." Japan's aggression against China could not succeed. Mussolini's dictatorship was a necessary step in the inevitable evolution toward liberalism. Such assumptions underlay the optimism that prevailed after the signing of the Kellogg-Briand Pact and which lingered six years later.

This powerful, almost religious conviction, however, tended to blind Americans to the underlying realities of power that had produced the world they considered the triumph of liberal principles. They did not realize that if the world seemed to be moving in a liberal direction, it was because liberal powers had held a near monopoly of power since the end of the war, and this state of affairs was coming to an end.

For the first dozen years after the war, the three powerful democracies—the United States, Britain, and France—were in substantial control of world affairs, economically, politically, and militarily. They established the terms of the peace settlement, redrew the borders of Europe, summoned new nations into being, distributed pieces of defunct empires, erected security arrangements, determined who owed what to whom and how and when debts should be paid. They called together the conferences that determined the levels of armaments the major nations could possess.

All this was possible because they had won the war; because the United States and Britain controlled the banks and the seas; because France wielded predominant military power on the European continent. With this power, the three Western democracies sought to establish and consolidate a world system favorable to their interests and preferences. They argued over how best to do this, whether through coercion or inducement of Germany, for instance, and they became increasingly estranged from each other in these years. But they all wanted a stable, prosperous, and peaceful Europe. They all sought to preserve their global empires, or, in America's case, its hemispheric hegemony. They all sought to defend the liberal capitalist economic system that enriched and protected them and in which they believed. None doubted the rightness of their vision of international order or much questioned the justice of imposing it.

And there had been successes, certainly from their point of view. By the second half of the 1920s, the world had grown less violent and marginally less miserable. In Europe especially, economies were recovering, living standards were rising, general violence was down from the immediate postwar years, and the dangers of war and aggression seemed as low as they had been in decades. Internationally, trade had risen by more than 20 percent, despite growing protectionism, driven largely by the American economic boom. Nations spent more time discussing measures for peace than preparing for war. The League of Nations had come into its own. Germany seemed to be on a moderate, democratic course. In general, the threat of a return to autocracy and militarism seemed low. Democracy seemed to be in the ascendant.[9]

While the democracies were more or less content with the world they were trying to create, however, the postwar settlement had left other major powers with significant grievances. This was true not only of the war's big losers—Germany, Austria, Hungary, and the Ottoman Empire—but also some of those nominally on the winning side. Japan and Italy had hoped to gain much more from the war and were unhappy with what they were granted at Paris by the Big Three. Japan had been forced to give up some of its wartime gains. Italians were bitter at what nationalists called their "mutilated victory" (*vittoria mutilata*). The Soviet Union was also a "loser" in the war, shorn of territories lost in the Brest-Litovsk agreement, under siege both from within and from without, the Bolsheviks' hope of world revolution largely set aside for the time being.

In the first decade after the war these self-described "have-not" nations had adapted as best they could to the new realities of international power. To the degree they sought revisions of the postwar settlement, they sought them by means acceptable to the dominant democratic powers. Some, like Stresemann's Germany and Shidehara's Japan, sought to conform themselves to the liberal order, to integrate and gain acceptance in the new system. But even those who openly defied the new order had to move cautiously—the Bolsheviks, with their mission of overturning capitalism, and Mussolini, who rode to power on the resentment over the *vittoria mutilata*. The Soviets promoted their revolution abroad but not so aggressively as to challenge the dominant powers, and they wound up settling for "Socialism in one country." Mussolini, ruling an Italy surrounded in the Mediterranean by British and French naval power and dependent on the United States for financial support, thought it best to play the responsible European statesman. The 1920s were his "decade of good behavior."[10]

Adolf Hitler, too, proceeded with caution as he ascended to power in the early '30s. Impressed by the United States as "a giant state with unimaginable productive capacities" and by Anglo-American domination of the global economy, and well aware of the role it had played in selecting Germany's past governments, he worked at first to soften Washington's opposition to his rise.[11] He reached out to the American ambassador, gave numerous interviews to prominent American journalists, including William Randolph Hearst, in the hope of making "the personality of Adolf Hitler more accessible to the American people."[12] He promised to pay Germany's "private debts" to American bankers and went out of his way to assure the English-speaking world that his national socialist movement would gain power only in a "purely legal way" in accordance with the "present constitution." After taking power, he told the press and his own officials to play down the campaigns of anti-Semitism that began immediately. He sought to keep German rearmament under wraps in what he called the "perilous interval" during which the "whole world" was "against us." Until the economy recovered and German rearmament was further along, he feared that the national socialist revolution could be crushed at any time by the superior power of the democracies.[13]

The victory of the democracies in 1918 had also produced an unprecedented spread of democratic governments. By 1920, there were twenty-four elected governments in Europe, compared with just nine in 1914. Some of this was due to the war, which had empowered citizens in a way they had not been before, as governments relied on workers at home to keep armies in the field and on the general population to bear wartime sacrifices. But there were not many cases where democratic government sprouted indigenously in response to popular demand. The democratic wave was largely a response to the democracies' military victory and subsequent economic, political, and military hegemony. In Germany and Austria, democracy was essentially imposed by Wilson as a condition of peace. In other nations the external pressures to democratize were more subtle but still potent. Old nations and empires that had seen their dynastic rulers toppled in the war could not restore the old dynasties without running afoul of the victorious powers that still controlled their economic and political fates. The leader of Hungary's first government had hoped that establishing a democracy would "soften the Allies' hostility."[14] Some nations, like Japan, chose to join what seemed to be the prevailing currents. The newly formed eastern and central European nations that depended on the West for their security mimicked western political systems. Nations with no history or tradition of legitimate government chose democracy to win international acceptance. But if democracy was now regarded as the only legitimate form of government, it was in large part because the dominant powers of the postwar world were democracies.[15] Few outside the United States would have claimed before the war that democracy was the only legitimate form of government. In most countries such views were a ticket to prison. Now democracy was the approved form of government for everyone.

It was remarkable how quickly the winds then shifted. An American journalist, looking back from the end of that decade, identified the moment when history pivoted. "In the first five years after the World War," he wrote, "the nations of Europe, on their backs and seeking American aid, took all pains to avoid offending us and therefore appeared to give careful and weighty consideration to our altruistic advice. The succeeding five years have changed that."[16]

One indicator of the shifting trends was the declining fortunes of democracy throughout Europe. It was inevitable that some of the new democracies, implanted in lands that had never known such a form of government, would not survive. The rise of dictatorship in various forms in Hungary (1920), Italy (1925), Lithuania, Poland, and Portugal (1926), Yugoslavia (1929), Romania (1930), Germany and Austria (1933), Bulgaria and Latvia (1934), and Greece (1935) had many internal and external causes, including the global depression that began after 1930. But the overall decline of European democracy from the second half of the 1920s onward, and the turn away from democracy in Japan, also reflected the declining influence and appeal of the great-power democracies and their order.

Liberal democracy was not just losing ground. It faced a potent challenge from a vibrant and revolutionary anti-liberal doctrine that attracted followers and imitators throughout Europe and beyond. Americans, British, and French during the war and for decades afterward assumed that Bolshevism posed the greatest threat to liberal democracy. But Bolshevism proved less easily exported than both its proponents and its opponents believed. When Jozef Pilsudski's Polish army defeated the Red Army outside Warsaw, Bolshevik hopes for rapid world revolution were dashed. Ostracized by the rest of Europe, the Soviet Union turned inward to wrestle with the transformation of its society. When democracies fell in the 1920s and '30s, they fell to the Right, not the Left.

Mussolini and his fascist movement, which seized control of Italian politics in the early 1920s and which in various forms spread across the continent, had many roots. Some of the fascist worldview was unique to the Italian experience, but some of it transcended national boundaries. Above all, fascism represented a rejection of liberalism and the postwar Anglo-American political and economic order that had been imposed on the peoples of the "have-not" nations. It was an answer to those who felt oppressed by "Demo-Liberal rule," as Mussolini called it.[17] It was a response to growing cosmopolitanism, to the blurring of national distinctions, to the growth of a common commercial culture dominated by the Americans. Fascism promised to restore national and ethnic identity and culture even while modernizing the nation to compete in an industrializing world. It glorified the people not as individuals but as a collective, with the nation serving as the vehicle for their common destiny. Individual rights and legal processes had to be subordinated to the popular will, a will that could only be understood, articulated, and executed by a single, charismatic national leader, *Il Duce* or *Der Führer,* in whom the people could place their trust. By 1925 Mussolini introduced the idea of the "totalitarian" society, in which the state oversaw every aspect of life, or as he put it, "everything within the state, nothing outside the state."[18]

This desire to remold society combined with an ambition to revise or overturn an international system that had deprived these nations of their opportunity for greatness. As the historian Robert Paxton has noted, it was no accident that "fascist success" followed closely "the map of defeat in World War I."[19] Fascism was a reaction to the humiliation and insecurity brought on by defeat, or, in the case of Italy and Japan, by the imposition of an unjust settlement that had deprived them of their expected fruits of victory.

Fascism was not an ideology of peace. To revise or overthrow this unjust order would require military power and the will to use it. The fascist ideologist Giovanni Gentile wrote of the "centrality of war to human existence," and the means by which superior nations and races subdued the weak and inferior and fulfilled their destiny. "Words are beautiful things," Mussolini said, "but rifles, machine guns, ships, aircraft, and cannon are still more beautiful."[20] Society had to be purged of flabby liberalism, quarreling political parties, and alien elements, and forged into one unified collective fit for war. The people needed to be prepared for war by rigid control of politics, economics, and society, and the elimination of all institutions that could stand in the way of the leader's total power, from the church to the aristocracy to the remnants of monarchy.[21] Hitler's entire program was aimed at creating a new Germany that would not fail as Imperial Germany had in 1918. Democracy was "the most disastrous thing there is," he told his top generals on the eve of taking power. "Only one person can and should give orders." The German population had to learn to "think nationalistically and thus be welded together," and this could only be accomplished by force.[22]

This fervent nationalism had transnational appeal. "Whoever says that fascism is not an exportable commodity is mistaken," Mussolini declared.[23] He hoped and expected that it would become to the twentieth century what liberalism had been to the nineteenth.[24] He even tried to promote fascism in the United States.[25] He saw himself as "the Pope of anti-democracy" leading an "anti-democratic crusade throughout the entire world."[26] In the 1920s and '30s "almost every nation on earth, and certainly all those with mass politics, generated some intellectual current or activist movement akin to fascism."[27] It made less headway in Britain and the United States, where democracy was more firmly rooted, but it thrived in countries where liberal democratic institutions were new and fragile, including in France. Where fascism did not succeed in taking power, as in Romania and Hungary, it was usually because the government was already sufficiently right-wing and nationalist that fascists could not find an opening. Even in far-off China, Chiang and his advisers in the 1920s marveled at how Mussolini had become "the greatest and most picturesque statesman in Europe" and thought that fascist Italy offered a model for how China could restore its national strength "through the revitalization of a past great civilization."[28]

Mussolini always had international ambitions, even if in the 1920s he lacked the means of pursuing them. While "pretending respect for the postwar order," he awaited the opportunity to break the iron "chain" by which Italy was imprisoned in the Mediterranean, and to embark on a career of imperial conquest befitting the inheritor of Rome's glory.[29] He longed to find an ally to establish a "new order" in Europe of which he would be the "supreme Pontiff."[30] He lent support to those across Europe who for their own reasons wished to undermine the political and territorial arrangements of Versailles: nationalist movements in Hungary, nationalist terrorist groups in Croatia and Bulgaria, and the nationalist right in Germany. Any disruption in the existing international system was good for Italy, regardless of where or why it occurred.[31] He was encouraged by the Japanese aggression in Manchuria and the weak and faltering response of the League and the United States.[32] When Japan announced its withdrawal from the League in 1933, it was a sign that the other "have-not" nations might be willing and able to mount a rebellion against the Anglo-American system. But ultimately, it was to Germany that Mussolini looked for salvation. As far back as 1923 he had believed that the "axis of European history passes through Berlin." He saw in Hitler's rise to power the historic opportunity for which he had been waiting.[33]

No one was more committed to overthrowing the postwar order than the man who took power in Germany in 1933. Many of Hitler's aims were not different from those of Stresemann and other German leaders: to regain sovereignty over German territory, including the Rhineland; to revise the borders in the east to bring more, if not all, Germans back under German rule; and to rebuild Germany's military, economic, and political strength and restore the nation to something approaching its prewar status as a great power and *primus inter pares* in Europe.[34] Stresemann and other Germans had sought to accomplish these goals within the existing postwar liberal order—"a peaceful Germany at the center of a peaceful Europe" was Stresemann's stated ambition[35]—and had done so with some success. Hitler, however, aimed to overturn the order by force. He opposed Germany's continued participation in the Anglo-

American global economy, which made Germans dependent on trade and access to the markets of the United States and other democracies. He did not want Germany to rely on exports, because it meant "competing with the world" in a system designed to favor others. Germans must create for themselves "a new market through the expansion of our living space." With the vast continental domestic market of the United States as his model, Hitler saw the conquest of eastern lands, from Poland and Ukraine to the Balkans, as vital for Germany's future.[36]

To accomplish this goal, there could be no cooperation with the reigning powers, except to buy time, no participation in multilateral institutions like the League of Nations, no international agreements to reduce arms. These were the means by which the liberal powers kept Germany down. Only German power and German unity mattered. Germany's position in the world, Hitler believed, would be "decisively conditioned upon the position of the German armed forces."[37] War was his objective, and all his policies—military, diplomatic, and economic—aimed at preparing Germany for war. That included his extreme racialism and his determination to "purify" Germany of alien and destructive elements, particularly the Jews but also Roma, homosexuals, and people with mental and physical handicaps, as well as his aim to create, like Mussolini, a "totalitarian" state that guided every aspect of German life.

Although cautious about challenging the democracies prematurely, Hitler could also be bold and opportunistic. He looked for weaknesses to exploit and early on perceived that the Western powers lacked the determination and coherence to defend their order. Like Mussolini, he gleaned this in part from the weak international response to Japan's actions in Manchuria and China. Just one month after Hitler took office, the League finally voted to declare Japan an aggressor, but there was no punishment or sanction. When, in the following month, the Japanese delegation walked out of Geneva and announced its decision to pull out of the League, it suffered no repercussions. Japan's successful defiance of the democracies, despite its relative weakness, helped convince Hitler that Germany, too, could defy them with minimal risk.[38] Within months of taking power, he publicly announced his plan to rearm Germany and withdrew from disarmament talks at Geneva and then, like the Japanese, from the League of Nations. Less than two years later he publicly repudiated the disarmament clauses of Versailles, unveiled a new German air force, reintroduced military conscription, and announced plans to build an army of thirty-six divisions and half a million men.

The rise of Hitler's Germany changed the dynamics of the international system. Before 1933, Italy and Japan were isolated in their resistance to the dominant powers. The mere arrival on the scene of a defiant Germany, with its inherent capacity to overturn the European settlement, opened a whole new vista of possibilities. The three defiant powers had few interests in common—indeed, Italian and German interests clashed in Austria and the South Tyrol, Germany and Japan were at odds over China, and race was a barrier—but they shared a common enemy in the postwar liberal order.[39] Whether they cooperated or not, their individual pursuit of their interests challenged and pressured the Western powers and opened opportunities. Fear of Hitler's Germany made Britain and France reluctant to alienate Mussolini. Concerns about Mussolini distracted attention from Germany. Both Hitler and Mussolini saw an increasingly aggressive Japan as a valuable strategic asset forcing Britain and the United States to attend to the rising challenge to their interests in Asia. "Every Japanese advance frees Germany," observed one Nazi publicist.[40] And the same was true for Japan. The Manchurian incident had left Japan isolated against a united Europe and United States. The arrival of Hitler fractured Europe and turned its attention inward. As the American ambassador in Tokyo, Joseph Grew, observed, "the increased tension in Europe" made Japan "safer from foreign interference than at any time since the termination of the Anglo-Japanese alliance."[41]

Although lacking specific common interests, their shared hostility to democratic liberal capitalism and Anglo-American hegemony drew them together in a common worldview. For Hitler, both were victims of "Jewish controlled international finance capitalism."[42] Japan's leaders were drawn to the German view that the world was dividing into regional blocs, and that each nation would rise and fall based on its ability "to acquire more resources, mobilize its people, and drive out other nations' economic and political influences from the region under its control."[43]

Many in Japan wanted to emulate Germany's political trajectory. Yosuke Matsuoka, the diplomat who had triumphantly led the Japanese delegation out of the League of Nations, became a leading advocate of closer ties with Nazi Germany. He argued in 1933 that the "Western style of party government" did not "conform to the conditions of our country nor the character of our people."[44] While the United States and the other Western democracies were mired in the Great Depression, the Soviet and Nazi governments appeared to "radiate dynamism."[45] By the mid-1930s a Japanese version of fascism had emerged. There was no führer or duce because the emperor still enjoyed ultimate legitimacy among conservatives and traditionalists. And there was no mass movement or single party. In traditional Japanese style, the system was transformed from the top by a collective of military and civilian leaders. As in Europe, violence and assassinations were rampant, as was the encouragement and, when necessary, the enforcement of a conformity of views. In Japan, as in Germany, a people who had briefly experimented with forms of democracy but had never developed any deep commitment to it bade it farewell without obvious regret.

Hitler saw the fascist seizure of power in Italy as "a harbinger of his own success" and had such admiration for Mussolini that when they met for the first time in the summer of 1934, he had tears in his eyes.[46] Mussolini believed a "community of destiny" united the fascist powers.[47] The "alliance between the two nations," his foreign minister declared, was based above all on the "identity between their political regimes."[48] By the mid-1930s, the Japanese had joined the anti-liberal club. As Matsuoka argued, each of the have-not nations was fighting for "recognition and its place in the eyes of the world."[49]

The entry of Japan into what Hitler would call the "triangle" of challengers to the Anglo-American system was the final step in a geopolitical revolution. As one Japanese author noted in 1934, the world now contained "two tinderboxes," one in the western Pacific and one in Europe, and the two were "interlocked." A crisis in one "can easily extend to the other and assume a global character."[50] Hitler believed that if the British were confronted not only by Germany and Italy in Europe but also by "a common organized force in the Far East," they would have no choice but to accept Germany's rise and even seek "common ground with this new political system."[51]

He was not wrong. By the mid-1930s the Royal Navy faced challenges from three directions: from the Germans in the North Sea, the Italians in the Mediterranean, and the Japanese in the western Pacific. British grand strategy for more than a century had depended on maintaining naval supremacy in all three theaters. The new, combined challenge seemed to defy solution. The British public would not support building a navy sufficient to meet all the possible threats at once. The only other hope was to get the Americans to shoulder some of the burden, to reverse the course of abstention they had taken since 1919.

CHAPTER EIGHTEEN

Franklin D. Roosevelt: Isolationist

These are not normal times; people are jumpy and very ready to run after strange gods.

—Franklin D. Roosevelt[1]

THE ELECTION of Franklin D. Roosevelt initially offered reason for hope. Everyone on both sides of the Atlantic knew that the new American president's instincts were internationalist. He not only served under Wilson but had been a fervent Wilsonian.[2] He had been a leading proponent of the League of Nations[3] and as late as 1928 was still arguing that the United States should cooperate with it "as the first great agency for the maintenance of peace." He had criticized the Republican administrations for continuing to demand full repayment of Europe's wartime debts while continually raising tariffs on European products.[4] British diplomats in Washington reported that the new president was "strongly opposed" to the dictatorships and wished to "support united action by League members to preserve peace or penalise aggression."[5] Leaders in France and Britain welcomed his election, hoping and believing that he would set a new course in American foreign policy, with greater involvement in international efforts to preserve peace and greater cooperation to address the global economic crisis.

At first, Roosevelt seemed to live up to their expectations. Within weeks of taking office, he addressed a message to fifty-four heads of state calling for "peace by disarmament" and "the end of economic chaos," signaling American interest in the two big conferences dominating the international scene at the time: the World Disarmament Conference in Geneva, which had been meeting for more than a year with little progress, and the World Economic Conference, which was to open that summer in London. The Hoover administration had treated the Geneva talks as "a European peace conference with European political questions to be settled." Roosevelt looked to be more forthcoming. Privately, he told the British prime minister, Ramsay MacDonald, and the French prime minister, Edouard Herriot, that in the event of war in Europe the United States would "refrain from any action that would tend to defeat the collective effort against an aggressor." The French had longed to hear these words from an American president. As for the coming economic conference, Roosevelt publicly expressed his hope that it would "establish order in place of the present chaos by a stabilization of currencies, by freeing the flow of world trade, and by international action to raise price levels."[6] The promise of American engagement on these issues immediately catapulted Roosevelt into a position of world leadership in the eyes of many.

It quickly became clear, however, that, notwithstanding the internationalist rhetoric, Roosevelt's actual policies would be almost indistinguishable from those of the previous administration. His course was one of strict economic nationalism and abstention from European affairs. Like his predecessors, he rejected British and French pleas for debt reduction, complaining about the "debtor countries" that had left American investors with "worthless and depreciated bonds." He supported legislation punishing debtor states, like France, that defaulted on their payments. His early trade policies had the effect of increasing tariffs, in response to foreigners "dumping" their products in American markets.[7] Then, in the summer of 1933, he effectively blew up the international economic conference in London by rejecting currency stabilization. Determined to push up domestic commodity prices by letting the dollar fall, he insisted that the United States would not allow other nations to control its domestic prices based on the "old fetishes of so-called international bankers."[8]

As for the disarmament talks in Geneva, despite his private assurances to MacDonald and Herriot, he offered nothing to indicate that the United States would cooperate in sanctions against an aggressor. On the contrary, and much like Hoover, he declared that the United States was not interested "in the political element or any purely European aspect of the picture." He suggested that all the world's nations sign a non-aggression pact, urged Europeans to "get down to brass tacks," and suggested a meeting between MacDonald, the French premier, Édouard Daladier, Mussolini, and Hitler.[9] The new German chancellor quickly capitalized on Roosevelt's proposal by giving a speech expressing his sincere desire to live with other nations "in peace and friendship."[10]

The disappointment in democratic Europe was palpable. In London Roosevelt's rejection of currency stabilization was denounced as a "manifesto of anarchy."[11] Ramsay MacDonald said he found "the whole thing . . . depressing."[12] To foreign observers it seemed clear that whatever might be Roosevelt's natural internationalist inclinations, he was "extremely sensitive to public opinion," heavily influenced by "the exigencies of domestic politics," and worried about "the isolationist element" in both parties. This explained what the British and French soon came to regard as the "fundamental inconsistency" of his behavior.[13]

In fact, Roosevelt had been trimming his internationalist sails since before he was elected. By the late 1920s, no politician in either party could rise as a proponent of the League or any other foreign commitment. As governor of New York with presidential ambitions, Roosevelt had carefully avoided talking about foreign policy. When he threw his hat into the national ring he ostentatiously renounced his earlier views, appearing "in sackcloth and ashes" before William Randolph Hearst, the publisher and Democratic party kingmaker, whose newspapers had been attacking Roosevelt's "internationalism."[14] Roosevelt gave no major foreign policy address during the campaign, but his few comments reflected the prevailing "nationalistic mood."[15] In his inaugural address he promised to put "first things first": the "emergency at home" took priority over international cooperation.[16] Given the state of the economy he inherited, it was hardly surprising that foreign policy took a back seat.

The effects of the Depression did not begin to hit most Americans until the beginning of 1931, but within a year the unemployment rate soared to 25 percent and GDP plunged by 13 percent. A sense of helplessness pervaded society from top to bottom as the economy declined with no end in sight. As former president Coolidge put it a few days before his death in January 1933, in other periods of economic depression it had "always been possible to see some things which were solid and upon which you could base hope." But now he saw "nothing to give ground for hope."[17] From 1930 onward, the Hoover and Roosevelt administrations flailed and experimented without any sure formula for success. Roosevelt's skill as a politician lay in inspiring hope among the general public, something Hoover had failed at, but Roosevelt made no secret of the fact that in pushing forward his New Deal policies he was feeling his way without a roadmap. From the beginning, powerful critics emerged on both the right and the left, with one side warning about the New Deal's creeping socialism and the other warning of capitalist fascism. Across the political spectrum serious people doubted not only whether their democratic leaders were up to the task but whether democracy and liberalism themselves were viable. As the historian Will Durant noted, on both sides of the Atlantic democracy's reputation had fallen sharply "from the high prestige it had at the Armistice."[18]

The loss of faith and confidence in democracy and liberalism in turn affected how people viewed the rising dictatorships in Europe and Asia. While most Americans opposed fascism and communism at home, the fascist and communist governments abroad seemed to be handling things better than their own chaotic and flailing democracy. The weaknesses of liberalism in the global struggle suddenly seemed glaringly apparent. Reinhold Niebuhr noted in 1935 that fascists had a feeling for "the organic character of society" that liberals lacked. Although they might seem "ridiculous" and practiced "particularly atrocious forms of injustice and tyranny," they gave expression to "impulses and forces in society" which a "rationalistic and mechanistic" liberalism had suppressed or ignored.[19]

It was not just in the spiritual and emotional realm that fascism seemed superior to liberalism. The leaders in Rome, Moscow, and Berlin, with their four-year and five-year plans and their government-directed support of heavy industry, including armaments, seemed to have found a formula for success that eluded the liberal democracies. Mussolini had been well regarded even before the Depression set in, especially among American conservatives and the business community.[20] *Fortune* magazine in 1934 devoted an entire issue to Mussolini's "Corporate State," observing that in a worldwide depression "marked by government wandering and uncertainty," Mussolini showed the "virtue of force and centralized government acting without conflict for the whole nation at once."[21] Americans of all political and ideological perspectives thought Mussolini was exactly what the backward Italian people needed, someone to get the country shaped up and modernized.[22] The humorist Will Rogers, after interviewing the Italian leader, commented that "Dictator form of government is the greatest form of government there is; that is, if you have the right Dictator. Well, these folks have certainly got him."[23]

Americans were less susceptible to Adolf Hitler's charms than some British statesmen, like Lloyd George, who expressed a certain admiration for the Führer's "magnetic, dynamic personality." In New York ten thousand marched to protest Nazi anti-Semitism just five months after Hitler took office, and the following year the *New York Times* condemned the Nazi regime's "ruthlessness in the suppression of liberalism and in racial persecution," behavior which "harked back to medieval days."[24] But some Americans also saw Hitler as a legitimate voice of the German

people. Whatever his failings, his rise to power was the inevitable consequence of the unjust Versailles Treaty and the greed and selfishness of
the European democracies in the decade after the war. In Hitler, Walter
Lippmann argued, one could hear "the authentic voice of a genuinely
civilized people." As for the Nazis' treatment of the Jews, Lippmann,
himself a Jew, urged his readers to keep an open mind. It was necessary
to understand the "dual nature of man. . . . To deny today that Germany
can speak as a civilized power because uncivilized things are being done
in Germany is in itself a deep form of intolerance."[25] American businessmen and other conservatives were impressed by Nazi efforts to revive the
German economy.[26] In the first two years of Hitler's rule, the number
of unemployed Germans fell by half, from over 5 million to under 2.5
million.[27]

Many Americans believed, moreover, that whatever the sins of the
Nazis and the *Fascisti,* they paled next to the sins of Communism. Moscow and the Bolsheviks were the real enemy, and Nazi Germany was a
potential ally against them. As Charles Lindbergh put it, Germany could
"either dam the Asiatic hordes or form the spearhead of their penetration into Europe."[28] The Ohio Republican Robert A. Taft, like many
American conservatives, believed that "the victory of communism in the
world would be far more dangerous to the United States than the victory
of fascism."[29]

There was no separating American attitudes toward these foreign
dictators from the political, economic, and ideological battles raging in
the United States in these years. As always in American politics, debates
about foreign policy were also debates about the meaning and purpose
of the United States at home. Conservatives regarded Roosevelt's New
Deal as but a step away from socialist tyranny, an assault on property and
individual liberty, on religion and nationalism. Their constant warnings
about international communism were also aimed at Roosevelt and the
New Deal. Many Americans sympathized with the fascist regimes abroad
that seemed to share their pro-capitalist, pro-Christian, pro-nationalist
principles. *The Saturday Evening Post,* one of the leading opponents of
Roosevelt and the New Deal, provided its 3 million readers with sympathetic views of Nazi efforts to liberate Germany as well as sometimes
favorable portraits of Mussolini.[30]

The Catholic Church under Pope Pius XI was pro-Mussolini, accommodating to Hitler, and pro-Franco, partly because the fascists were
fighting communism, partly because they were fighting the often violently anti-clerical Spanish Republican government, and partly because

many Catholics sympathized with the fascist resistance to modern liberalism.[31] American cardinals and bishops, priests and monks, and the Jesuits produced "the most impressive and astounding anthology of Fascist glorification made in any country outside Italy." Prominent Catholic intellectuals, like the poets T. S. Eliot and Ezra Pound, "dismissed liberalism as a nineteenth-century illusion . . . rejected[ed] the idea of democracy . . . and opted for a Christian culture based on some form of distributive justice, integral humanism, and authoritarian order."[32]

While conservative Americans tended to take a benign view of the fascist leaders, ignoring or explaining away the harsher aspects of their regimes, many liberals and progressives took a similarly sympathetic view of Stalin's Soviet Union. They were untroubled by the growing repression or by reports of the devastating manmade famine that killed up to 3 million people in Ukraine and other Soviet republics. The *New York Times*'s Walter Duranty, who dismissed reports of atrocities as "mostly bunk," described Stalin as "a quiet, unobtrusive man" whose mission was to "train and discipline and give self-respect to a nation of liberated slaves."[33] The progressive muckraking journalist Lincoln Steffens, who famously commented after a visit to the Soviet Union in 1921, "I have seen the future and it works," did not change his mind after a decade of Stalin's rule. In 1935 he reported that "Russia just now is a sort of heaven, where humans have got rid of the great primitive problems of food, clothing and a roof."[34]

By the early 1930s American intellectuals had fallen into a "profoundly anti-liberal mood," what John Diggins has called an "intellectual malaise."[35] There was a general loss of confidence in democratic government, in capitalism, in liberalism, in the very idea of progress. As the British historian Arnold Toynbee put it in 1931, "The members of this great and ancient and hitherto triumphant society were asking themselves whether the secular process of Western life and growth might conceivably be coming to an end in their day."[36]

Some, like Walter Lippmann, moved right. In these bitter years, Lippmann became a "cynic and antidemocrat," or, as he put it, a "realist." He opposed the New Deal and in 1936 voted against Roosevelt.[37] Others moved left. Niebuhr flirted with Marxism as the only practical response to the "new ruthlessness of the twentieth-century situation." Convinced of "the futility of liberalism," with its "gray spirit of compromise," and fearing "the inevitability of fascism," he and others admired the toughness, the militancy, the self-confidence, and the sheer "realism" of the communists.[38] "We need something less circumspect than liberalism to save the world," Niebuhr argued. The inadequacy of the New Deal they attributed to Roosevelt's compromises with the capitalists.[39] Those who still clung to liberalism's tenets criticized Niebuhr for his "cynicism," his "unrelieved pessimism," and even his "defeatism," but he was hardly alone.[40] Many liberals and progressives looked to Marxism as the only answer to fascism, and to the Soviet Union as the leader of the anti-fascist camp, especially in the early and mid-1930s.[41] As the *New Republic* put it in June 1935, there was "no longer a feasible middle course."[42]

With such views prevalent among American thought leaders, it was not surprising that enthusiasm for defending liberalism and democracy abroad was tepid. The one thing liberals, progressives, and conservatives agreed upon was that an active foreign policy would only exacerbate America's domestic ills. For Charles Beard, an internationalist foreign policy stood in the way of the needed transformation of the American economy into a "collectivist democracy" and a "workers' republic"; Americans had to concentrate "on tilling our own garden."[43] For John Dewey, the real threats to American democracy were not Hitler, Mussolini, or Imperial Japan but the fascism that lurked "within our own personal attitudes and within our own institutions."[44] If the United States took part in another war, the result would be a "semi-military, semi-financial autocracy."[45]

Conservatives agreed that it was no time for Americans to be involved in "foreign battles," albeit for different reasons. Robert A. Taft warned that there was "a good deal more danger of the infiltration of totalitarian ideas from the New Deal circle in Washington than there will ever be from any activities of the communists or the Nazi bund."[46] If the nation did go to war, he warned, it would lead to "a Socialist dictatorship."[47] The American public broadly agreed that no good could come from involvement in the world's crises.

Depression-era Americans were more receptive than ever to the argument that the nation had been duped and driven into war by a conspiratorial alliance of internationalists, bankers, and arms manufacturers and that this same group could push the United States into a European war again. A best-selling book, *Merchants of Death,* argued that the American arms industry had pushed the United States into war in 1917. Following the book's publication in 1934, a special Senate committee under the chairmanship of Republican senator Gerald P. Nye of North Dakota began a two-year investigation of the munitions industry and other war "profiteers."[48] The investigation, driven by a progressive Republican, was "as antibusiness as it was antiwar."[49] The hearings confirmed for many that the greedy corporate desire for profit had been the chief motivation for war, just as that same greed had produced the economic calamity from which average Americans were suffering.

Those who did not entertain conspiracy theories about "plutocrats" blamed trade in general. As Senator Arthur Vandenberg put it, the benefits of wartime trade with Great Britain and France had been so great that Americans were "sucked into that war irresistibly."[50] Restricting trade with belligerents would keep the United States from being sucked into the next war. To ensure that Americans would have no financial interest in the outcome of a future conflict, to curb businessmen's appetite for profits and the government's appetite for revenue, Congress had to legislate "positive restraints" on American trade during wartime.[51]

The breakdown in European security after Hitler's rise to power, far from provoking Americans to greater activism, strengthened the hands of Borah and other isolationists. As the danger of another European war increased in the 1930s, the antiwar mood intensified. In 1935, another national bestseller, Walter Millis's *Road to War: America, 1914–1917,* bluntly warned against being pulled into a European war again.[52] The *Nation*'s Oswald Garrison Villard hoped Americans would not once again "be moved by the argument that wrong may triumph."[53] Peace movements again sprouted across the country. In 1935, on the eighteenth anniversary of America's intervention in the Great War, 50,000 veterans came to Washington to march for peace; 175,000 college students conducted sit-in strikes against war, demanding the abolition of Reserve Officers' Training Corps on campuses, and the building of "schools, not battleships."[54] Across university campuses, students fearing a future draft voted for resolutions declaring they would not fight for their country no matter what the cause.

The result of this national anti-interventionist consensus was a succession of Neutrality Acts, the first of which Congress passed in 1935. Despite the name, the aim of the legislation was actually to prevent the United States from asserting and defending the traditional rights of neutrals in wartime. Guided by the experience of the last war, the authors of the new neutrality acts sought first to prohibit the sale of "arms, ammunition, and implements of war" to all belligerents. Then, over the next two years, they gradually tightened the prohibitions to ban public and private loans to belligerents (another suspected cause of America's entry into the Great War), as well as the provision of assistance to belligerents in a civil conflict (to block support for either side after the outbreak of the Spanish Civil War). The neutrality legislation, designed to tie the hands of the president and even to tie Congress's own hands, was the final victory of the policies that William Jennings Bryan had futilely sought before America's entry into the European war two decades before.

While Roosevelt and others argued that this was no time to make it harder to use sanctions against an aggressor, Senator Nye argued that the legislation was necessary *because* Germany was rearming and *because* aggression was mounting around the world, including the pending Italian war against Ethiopia.[55] The authors of the legislation sought to make sure that the United States would play no role whatever in any conflict, directly or indirectly. It would not participate in an embargo against an aggressor. It would not provide assistance, even in accord with legitimate neutral rights, to the victims of aggression. Indeed, Congress refused to give the president leeway even to designate an aggressor.[56] Senator Hiram Johnson celebrated the passage of the first Neutrality Act as a "triumph of the so-called isolationists" and "the downfall . . . of the internationalist."[57] The aim, he explained, was to prevent "those internationalists who love every country but their own" from formulating "neutrality policies and treaties for the introduction of lop-sided embargoes and nebulous definitions of 'aggressor.'"[58]

Roosevelt got the message. At a time when he was trying to build public confidence in the nation's economic prospects, in his New Deal policies, and in himself, he did not want to jar the public with foreign involvements. Many Americans on both ends of the political and ideological spectrum were all too ready to believe that any international cooperation, especially with Britain, was part of some international bankers' conspiracy to undermine American sovereignty. Even on relatively innocuous matters like membership in the World Court, populists with wide followings like Huey Long and Father Charles Coughlin warned that America was about to be made "the hunting ground of international plutocrats."[59] Another problem was that a good number of the senators Roosevelt relied on to pass his New Deal legislation were western progressive Republicans like William Borah and Hiram Johnson, the old irreconcilables who continued to man the barricades against the League and anything that resembled international commitments.[60] Roosevelt also believed he would need to pick up at least some midwestern Republican progressive voters if he was going to win re-election in 1936, something that was by no means assured given the state of the economy and a decade of Republican electoral dominance.[61] Roosevelt was an internationalist by background and disposition, and his calls for international political and economic cooperation were sincere. He wanted to keep hope alive both at home and abroad. But he was not about to weaken himself or imperil his policies for marginal gains on the international scene. Even if Roosevelt had been willing to buck public opinion and take on Borah and his allies, it was not obvious what the United States could do—unless it was prepared to throw itself much more actively into the mounting European crisis. It would have taken more than a few successful international conferences to reverse the global trends.

As the situation in Europe began to turn ominous after 1933, therefore, Roosevelt felt his hands were tied. When Hitler announced Germany's withdrawal from both the Geneva disarmament conference and from the League of Nations in October 1933, Secretary of State Cordell Hull observed that although there was "widespread resentment against the Hitler Government" in the United States, Americans remained "unanimous" in opposing any further involvement in Europe. He predicted the administration would adopt "a distinctly passive role for some time to come." Roosevelt continued to make idealistic pronouncements, insisting that "we could get a world accord on world peace immediately if the people of the world could speak for themselves," but he made sure to stipulate that the United States "would not sign any accord obliging it to use its armed force for the settlement of any dispute whatever."[62]

His one nod in the direction of internationalism failed miserably. With a 58–37 Democratic majority in the Senate, he hoped to win support for the United States to join the World Court, an institution created by the League but separate and independent from it. Even Republican presidents had tried to join the court in the 1920s. But with the Hearst papers, Will Rogers, and Father Coughlin condemning the court as a tool of international "plutocrats," and with Johnson, Borah, Norris, and Nye leading the opposition in the Senate, the treaty fell seven votes short.[63] An angry and dejected Roosevelt commented that "we shall go through a period of non-cooperation in everything . . . for the next year or two."[64]

Roosevelt was therefore loath to take a strong stand on the neutrality legislation. Ideally, he wanted some flexibility to impose an embargo against aggressors when and as he thought appropriate. This was what he had promised MacDonald and Herriot. But his efforts to persuade Congress failed. As the columnist Arthur Krock put it, Senators Johnson and Borah could "tell a hawk from a handsaw" and were not about to leave loopholes for Roosevelt to slip through.[65]

Roosevelt was also stymied by ethnic politics. When Italy invaded Ethiopia in October 1935, and Roosevelt, unable to block vital oil shipments to Italy by fiat, tried to impose a "moral embargo," Italian Americans, who saw Mussolini as "the savior of Italy," were furious. This important constituency also lined up against him on revision of the Neutrality Act.[66] Hopes of revising the legislation during the Spanish Civil War similarly ran into a wall of opposition from Catholics.

It was not that Roosevelt himself cared so much about the fates of either Ethiopia or the Spanish republic.[67] What most concerned him was the growing likelihood of another European war and what he regarded as the American public's unreadiness for that challenge. In his 1935 State of the Union address he warned of dangerous trends in Europe, where "old jealousies" had been "resurrected," "old passions aroused," and where "new strivings for armament and power" were rearing "their ugly heads."[68] The following year he appealed to Americans to "take cognizance of growing ill will, of marked trends toward aggression, of increasing armaments, of shortening tempers—a situation which has in it many of the elements that lead to the tragedy of general war."[69] But he deliberately did not recommend any action on the part of the United States. Nor did he suggest who was responsible for the resurrection of "old jealousies." In private correspondence with friends and advisers, he expressed concern that there was a "very large and perhaps increasing school of thought" in the United States that believed that "we can and should withdraw wholly within ourselves and cut off all but the most perfunctory relationships with other nations." If the "civilization of Europe" was bent on destroying itself, this segment of the public believed, then "it might just as well go ahead and do it" while the United States stood "idly by."[70] But Roosevelt did not see that there was much to be done about it. The problem was "a large misinformed public opinion," compounded by the economic crisis. In normal times, he told Henry Stimson, the extravagant claims of Father Coughlin, Huey Long, and the more extreme Hearst papers would not be so effective. "However, these are not normal times; people are jumpy and very ready to run after strange gods." He hoped things would change eventually, but for the moment, he told Root, "quite frankly, the wind everywhere blows against us."[71]

Roosevelt's policies reflected this fatalism. He did almost nothing to hinder Italy's conquest of Ethiopia, and even less to help the Spanish government.[72] His administration had nothing to say about Hitler's announced plan to rearm and build an army of a half-million soldiers and was silent when Hitler sent German troops into the Rhineland in 1936. When the Japanese announced the Amau doctrine in 1934, shutting the door to Western support of China in any form, the administration went out of its way to say nothing provocative.[73] Nor did it complain when Japan signed the Anti-Comintern Pact with Nazi Germany in 1936. Instead, Ambassador Grew in Tokyo launched a charm offensive designed to smooth relations between the two powers, insisting to the Japanese public that "it should not be at all difficult for our two nations to live in peace and harmony and to cooperate."[74] Here, too, Roosevelt and his advisers hoped the American people would eventually come around to see the dangers. "Enlightenment with regard to this matter comes slowly," the State Department's Stanley Hornbeck mused. "Some people learn by observation, reasoning, and the use of the imagination. Others learn only by experience."[75]

The one moderately controversial move Roosevelt made in his first term was to launch a significant naval buildup to try to make up for the neglect of the previous decade. It was chiefly directed at the growing threat of Japan. The American people might consider war with Japan "unthinkable," Ambassador Grew noted, but it would be "criminally shortsighted" not to prepare for one. The Japanese military and its nationalist supporters understood only power, and therefore strengthening the navy was "peacetime insurance both to cover and to reduce the risk of war."[76] Hornbeck agreed that the best hope of preventing conflict was to convince those in "ultimate authority" in Tokyo that Japan had "no chance of success and would be doomed to decisive defeat" in a war with the United States.[77] Within three months of taking office, Roosevelt allocated over $200 million from his inaugural New Deal program for the construction of thirty-two warships, including twenty destroyers and two aircraft carriers. The next year he supported the Vinson-Trammell Bill, which authorized, though it did not pay for, the construction of sixty-five destroyers, thirty submarines, and another aircraft carrier, as well as over a thousand naval airplanes. Construction was to begin over the coming three years and be completed by 1942.[78] The proposed buildup was not as controversial as it might have been because the isolationists were divided. Some, like Hearst, believed that the best means of keeping the United States out of war was to maintain a large enough navy to deter any possible challenge. For Roosevelt, the naval buildup was also a jobs program, part of his effort to use government spending to put people back to work and stimulate the economy.

Even so, he faced strong opposition. Many in Congress remained resistant to naval expenditures. Senators Gerald Nye and Hiram Johnson denounced the "crazy, insane" naval race and argued that parity with Japan would ensure peace.[79] Oswald Garrison Villard, editor of the *Nation,* accused Americans of "rapidly sinking to the level of Hitler and Mussolini in our bowing down before the God of war." How could Washington spend over a billion dollars on the military when more than twenty million Americans were on the dole?[80] The White House received more than two hundred letters a day opposing the buildup as wasteful and contrary to peaceful aims. When the U.S. Navy conducted maneuvers in the northern Pacific, pacifist societies "bombarded the government with thousands of protest letters." Roosevelt had to reassure critics that the money for the naval buildup had only been allocated, not yet appropriated.[81]

Americans' allergy to overseas involvement extended even to the Western Hemisphere. Since 1900 administrations of both parties had pursued essentially the same approach to the region. Theodore Roosevelt's concern that "bad behavior" by the little states of the Caribbean Basin, which included non-payment of debts, would lead to European intervention remained a chief guide to policy. But after the smashing of Germany and the overall shift of power from Britain to the United States, the risk of European encroachments in the hemisphere was practically nil from 1919 until at least 1935. Therefore, the strategic rationale for deep U.S. involvement all but disappeared. All that was left was the habit of hegemony, reinforced by the Monroe Doctrine, as well as by the impulse to help the Caribbean and Central American republics achieve some semblance of peace and prosperity so that the United States might finally end its interventions. The Republican administrations looked to end the ongoing occupations in the Dominican Republic and Haiti, both legacies of Wilson, as well as in Nicaragua, which was a legacy of the Taft administration.

The shift in American intellectual currents played a big part in undermining support for continuing American military involvement in the hemisphere. By the early 1930s the quasi-Marxist-Leninist interpretation of foreign policy, including American foreign policy, had become dominant in the American academy and filtered its way into the arguments of congressional leaders like Nye. This produced a great deal of retroactive revisionism. Policies that had once enjoyed support across the ideological spectrum—the American "liberation" of Cuba, for instance—were now reinterpreted as having been driven by financial interests and by "imperialists" like Theodore Roosevelt and Henry Cabot Lodge.[82] All American diplomacy in the region was assumed to be "dollar diplomacy," that is, conducted for the purpose of aiding American bankers or businessmen.[83] In 1928, Nye introduced a resolution declaring that "it shall never be the policy of the United States to guarantee nor protect by force the investments and properties of its citizens in foreign countries."[84] From the Harding administration onward, there was a "definite trend toward a policy of less interference in the internal political affairs of the Central American and West Indian republics."[85]

As past U.S. officials had discovered, however, getting out was not as easy as it sounded. Pulling U.S. troops out of places like Haiti, the Dominican Republic, and Nicaragua led almost invariably to instability and revolution, as political forces once held in check by American power were unleashed to fight it out for the levers of power and wealth. The effort to pull out of Nicaragua had especially disastrous consequences when a minor revolt led by Augusto Sandino led to the deployment of several thousand marines in an unsuccessful counterinsurgency operation. Coolidge all but confirmed the critics' charges when he insisted that America's "proprietary rights" to a Nicaraguan canal route and American investments in Nicaragua put the United States in a position of "peculiar responsibility."[86] Sandino became a symbol of Latin American anti-imperialism and enjoyed support in some U.S. circles. Nor did the irreconcilables and progressives in Congress fail to note that the Coolidge administration, by "carrying on an unauthorized and indefensible war against Nicaragua," was establishing a precedent that Congress needed to stop.[87]

By the time Roosevelt came into office, the United States was ready to liquidate its occupations and interventions and embrace what first Hoover and then Roosevelt endorsed as the Good Neighbor Policy. The unintended though not unpredictable result was the establishment of what would become long-lasting dictatorships throughout the region: Anastasio Somoza in Nicaragua, Rafael Trujillo in the Dominican Republic, and eventually Fulgencio Batista in Cuba. As one official put it, the State Department generally preferred to establish democracies, which they believed were more stable than dictatorships. But the only way to prevent dictators from taking and holding power was through heavy-handed interference, and the United States was, for the moment, done with that.[88] As the threat from Europe and Japan rose, Roosevelt was increasingly inclined to keep the dictators close in the interest of hemispheric solidarity.

By the end of 1935, it was no secret that Roosevelt's foreign policy actions, or lack thereof, were aimed at bolstering his chances of re-election. As the British ambassador observed, Roosevelt would have to be "more than ever cautious in the conduct of his foreign policy not to offend the electorate" and play into the hands of the Republicans.[89] The Republican Party was, in fact, divided between western progressive "isolationists" like Borah and an eastern "internationalist" wing epitomized by Henry Stimson, but Borah and his colleagues were still in control. The Republican presidential candidate, Alf Landon, was a moderate internationalist from Kansas, but it was Borah who wrote the 1936 Republican platform.[90]

Roosevelt did not merely try to avoid offending the electorate; he made an active play for progressive Republican support and conducted his campaign to appeal to pacifists and isolationists.[91] His only major foreign policy speech of the campaign was an August address at Chautauqua, New York.[92] Proclaiming "I hate war!" Roosevelt promised to choose "peace over profits," to resist the "greed" of the financiers and munitions makers, and to "isolate" Americans from any future conflict.[93] Feeding the conspiratorial mindset that pervaded Nye's investigations, he warned that "if war should break out in another continent, let us not blink the fact that we would find in this country thousands of Americans who, seeking immediate riches—fool's gold—would attempt to break down or evade our neutrality. . . . It would be hard to resist the clamor of that greed." Americans could "keep out of war," he insisted, "if those who watch and decide . . . possess the courage to say 'no' to those who selfishly or unwisely would let us go to war."[94]

Roosevelt likely believed that his re-election was more important than any particular policy he might have pursued at that moment or any statement he might have made. He believed that the very survival of democracy was at stake in 1936. He said as much publicly, and privately he commented that the election had "in a sense, a German parallel. . . . Democracy is verily on trial."[95]

Presidents often feel that the fate of the nation and the world rests on their re-election, but in this case, Roosevelt was not alone. Despite the disappointments of his first term, Europeans continued to believe Roosevelt at his heart was an internationalist, and they knew where Republicans stood. *The Times* of London opined that Roosevelt's victory was "a matter of supreme importance at the moment when English-speaking nations are becoming more isolated as the champions of democracy in a world 'blown about by all the winds of doctrine.' "[96] After his election, when Roosevelt traveled to South America, people in the streets chanted "Democracy! Democracy!"[97] French newspapers hailed him as "the statesman on whom every hope is to be pinned if the great liberal and democratic civilization of the west is one day threatened, either by Bol-shevism or by autocracy."[98] William Bullitt, then ambassador to Paris, reported that on the day of Roosevelt's election, Prime Minister Léon Blum rushed into the embassy, bounded up the stairs, and kissed him ("violently!").

In Europe many still believed that Roosevelt alone was the man who could keep the world from plunging into war. "You are," Bullitt told him, "beginning to occupy the miracle man position."[99] For Europeans the hope for a miracle reflected desperation more than a sober assessment of American politics. As Europe slid toward another disastrous conflict, Roosevelt inspired hope primarily because he was the leader of the one nation that had the capacity, if it chose, to make a difference. Even in the midst of the long Depression, the United States remained the world's strongest nation in terms of raw potential power. Its economy was three times the size of the British and German economies and five times the size of the French and Japanese. American industry produced one-fifth of the world's total economic output, and its industrial capacity far out-stripped that of the other powers.[100] If the United States ever chose to turn its energies to weapons production, it could significantly outbuild all other powers. If it ever exercised the full extent of its capacities, with universal conscription and full economic and industrial mobilization, the effect would be decisive, just as it had been in 1918. As Arnold Toyn-bee noted, the United States was "lazily playing with a fraction of her immeasurable strength."[101] What the world wanted to know was whether the United States would bring more of that strength to bear on the grow-ing crises.

CHAPTER NINETEEN

The United States and Appeasement

What the British need today is a good stiff grog, inducing not only the desire to save civilization but the continued belief that they can do it.

> —Letter from Franklin D. Roosevelt to
> Roger B. Merriman, February 15, 1939[1]

You will get nothing out of the Americans but words. Big words, but only words.

> —British prime minister Stanley Baldwin[2]

ROOSEVELT HOPED that in a second term he would have more flexibility to exercise American power in some measured but still useful way. His landslide victory in 1936 (he won the popular vote 61 to 31 percent and the electoral college by 523 to 8) put him in a stronger position to do so. Democrats extended their overwhelming dominance of Congress, gaining a 76–16 margin in the Senate and 333–89 in the House. With such lopsided majorities Roosevelt and his advisers hoped for better luck with the neutrality legislation, at least. He had less need to cater to western progressive Republicans like Borah, who were a vanishing species anyway (the Idaho senator turned seventy-two in 1937). Borah's old ally, Senator Hiram Johnson of California, himself past seventy, worried that "the views of men like myself" would henceforth "receive scant attention" and that Roosevelt would become another "Wilson," seeing himself as "the arbiter of the world."[3]

Yet Roosevelt still faced significant obstacles, not the least of which were his own political caution and policy priorities. Roosevelt had not sought a foreign policy mandate in his re-election campaign. On the contrary, he had promised, like Wilson in 1916, to keep America out of foreign conflicts. His landslide victory, therefore, did not signal any greater public desire for overseas involvement. A poll taken in 1937 confirmed that Americans still believed the country's entry into the European war in 1917 had been a terrible mistake, not to be repeated.

For all his genuine concern about the international situation, moreover, Roosevelt's first priority remained the U.S. economy. He used his electoral mandate to fight the domestic and constitutional battles over his Second New Deal policies, and those battles were fierce. In an effort to change the complexion of the Supreme Court, which had struck down key parts of his economic policies, he proposed legislation allowing him to appoint additional justices. This "court-packing scheme" aroused intense opposition in both parties, with some accusing Roosevelt of a tyrannical power grab, and Roosevelt suffered a series of defeats. It did not help that the economy fell into a deep recession beginning in the late spring of 1937, with unemployment jumping to 19 percent and manufacturing falling back to 1934 levels. Having taken credit for the recovery, the president was now saddled with responsibility for what critics called the "Roosevelt Recession." Within months after his landslide re-election victory, Roosevelt suddenly found himself weaker than at any time in his presidency.

This inevitably affected his approach to foreign policy. On the most important issue he faced, revision of the neutrality legislation, he decided not to press the matter in 1937. The middle of the "court-packing" fight was not an opportune moment to seek greater presidential authority in matters of war and peace. The "permanent" Neutrality Act, which he signed into law in May, marginally increased his flexibility, but it did not permit him to designate and level sanctions at an aggressor—which was what mattered to the Europeans.[4] Roosevelt swallowed his defeat quietly.

He was just as timid on the other major foreign policy issue at the time: the civil war in Spain, which by the start of his second term had become a full-blown international conflict. The capture of Italian soldiers by Spanish government forces in March 1937 removed any doubt that the "civil war" had become "a foreign war of the Fascist Powers against the Government of Spain," as Roosevelt's ambassador in Madrid put it. That reality was driven home the following month with the bombing of Guernica by the German Condor Legion.[5] Nevertheless, neutrality legislation passed in January 1937 retained the embargo on both sides, thus starving the Loyalists of support, except from Moscow. General Franco and the

Nationalists, meanwhile, had both the support and the active intervention of Germany and Italy.

Roosevelt approached the Spanish crisis with caution. The issue was politically fraught in the United States, deeply dividing those who paid attention. American liberals, progressives, and Socialist and Communist Party members supported the Loyalists fighting to defend the left-wing Popular Front government that won a narrow electoral victory in February 1936. The *Nation* called it the most "encouraging" advance of democracy in Europe in years, and it was a rare bright moment in an otherwise dark time for European democracy. It was also an unaccustomed triumph for the Left. Spain under Republican rule became a series of local and national experiments in socialist, communist, and even anarchist government, with workers controlling much of the Spanish Republic's economy and anarchists controlling much of Catalonia's.[6] That their opponents included Franco's Nationalist forces, the fascist Falangists, assorted monarchists, the Catholic Church, and the pope, as well as Hitler and Mussolini, made it easy for the American Left to choose sides. Roughly three thousand American volunteers joined the Abraham Lincoln Brigade and other international groups to fight with the Loyalists.[7] Three-quarters of them were members of the Communist Party or its youth league. Half were Jewish. "For us it wasn't Franco," one volunteer recalled, "it was always Hitler."[8]

The politics of the Spanish war even caused a bit of a split in American anti-interventionist ranks. Left-leaning anti-interventionists like Charles Beard wanted the United States to help the Loyalists in their battle against Franco. Senator Gerald Nye, the driving force behind strict neutrality legislation, wanted the embargo against arms sales to the Spanish Republic lifted. Norman Thomas, the Socialist Party leader and a committed pacifist, visited Roosevelt to argue that American neutrality was objectively aiding the fascist powers in Europe in what was likely a preview of the next war. The president's wife, Eleanor, was "dismayed and disgusted" by Roosevelt's failure to do anything to help the Loyalists by lifting the embargo and providing them the aid they desperately needed.[9]

Although Roosevelt sympathized with the Loyalist cause, however, he steered clear of any deeper involvement. As passionate as the American Left was about aiding the Spanish Republic, American conservatives, and, more importantly, American Catholics were just as passionately opposed. The Spanish Civil War had been extremely violent, and at times barbaric, with atrocities committed by both sides. Franco's forces executed entire villages, including women and children, and imprisoned tens of thousands more in brutal conditions. But the Loyalists and their supporters were hardly more humane. Among their primary targets was the Catholic Church, which had aligned itself on the side of Franco and the Nationalists against the "godless" communists and socialists. Loyalist crowds and workers' militias burned churches and allegedly murdered as many as seven thousand priests. They even "executed" a famous statue of Christ.[10] The Catholic Church in Rome, which had already accommodated Mussolini, joined Italy and Germany in recognizing Franco as the legitimate ruler of Spain in the summer of 1937, even though the conflict was still raging.

American Catholics were outraged at the treatment of fellow Catholics in Spain, and equally by the lack of outrage this sparked in the United States, especially among the dominant eastern urban press and opinion makers. Father Coughlin, whose weekly radio show was heard by an estimated 30 million Americans, called Franco a hero, "a rebel for Christ, a rebel for humanity's sake," and he mourned the murdered priests buried "beneath the crimson cross of Communism upon which the brothers of Christ had been crucified."[11]

Roosevelt's New Deal coalition depended on the Catholic vote—more than 70 percent of Catholics had voted for him in 1936.[12] A journalist who met with Roosevelt to try to persuade him to aid the Loyalist cause was perplexed when, at the end of his brief presentation, the president said, "I can't hear you." Roosevelt explained: "I can hear the Roman Catholic Church and all their allies very well. They speak very loudly. Could you and your friends speak a little louder, please?"[13] The whole issue was political dynamite. As one senior State Department official observed, "The bitterness inspired by this Spanish strife among the Left Wingers on the one hand and the Catholic conservative elements on the other surpasses anything I have seen for years."[14]

Roosevelt had an easy excuse for doing nothing. The British and French governments, trying to avoid confrontation and a wider European conflict with Hitler and Mussolini, had pursued an official policy of "non-intervention" and imposed a strict embargo on arms sales to both sides. Roosevelt argued that he was only cooperating with the democracies by doing the same. To do more would be to involve the United States "directly in that European strife from which our people desire so deeply to remain aloof."[15]

Although American policy remained unchanged, the debate over the Spanish Civil War nevertheless revealed a subtle shift of attitude in some quarters. While the broader American public remained indifferent, liberals, progressives, and the American Left, on one side, and Catholics and conservatives, on the other, saw the conflict as a proxy for a larger global ideological battle, in which both sides believed the United States had a stake.[16] Liberals in particular seemed to be shedding their disillusioned cynicism and renewing their enthusiasm for the cause of liberalism abroad. How far they were prepared to go down this path, which many had sworn they would not go down again, was unclear, even to them. It would depend on events.

But the events continued to tumble out, and not only in Europe. In July 1937, a new round of conflict erupted in Asia. Seizing on a minor incident southeast of Beijing, Japanese forces invaded an area of China "roughly equivalent to the United States east of the Mississippi River."[17] Within the first three days, the forces of the Japanese Kwantung Army occupied Beijing and Tientsin. Then the army headed south into central China, aiming toward Wuhan and Nanking, the capital of Chiang Kai-shek's Nationalist government. In the middle of August Chiang's air force bombed the Japanese naval installation at Shanghai in an effort to divert Japanese forces and drag the Western powers, whose interests in Shanghai were substantial, into the fray. The new Japanese premier, Prince Konoe, declared that Japan's objective was to crush the Chinese will to resist and then to erect "a permanent structure of peace in the Orient in collaboration with all the constructive forces in China which will be liberated by our present action."[18] In short, Chiang had to be overthrown. On September 19, Japanese air forces began bombing the city of Nanking, with dreadful consequences for civilians.

For the first few months of the invasion, the Roosevelt administration took the same approach as in Spain: It did nothing and said little. Rather than pursue "the righteous indignation theme" in the manner of Stimson, Ambassador Grew in Tokyo argued that American interests were best served "by a policy of dignified silence." The "fundamental objectives" in this latest crisis were to "avoid involvement," protect the lives and property of American citizens, and maintain "our traditional friendship with both combatants."[19] Secretary Hull agreed. He had no intention of making "uncalled for and likely to be futile protests or gestures of interference."[20]

Roosevelt also agreed. When the commander of the U.S. fleet asked for four cruisers to aid in the evacuation of American citizens from China, Roosevelt refused, fearing it would provoke the military leaders in Tokyo.[21] He declared that Americans who remained in China did so "at their own risk," much to the chagrin of the missionary community.[22] As for the Chinese themselves, even Stanley Hornbeck, the leading anti-Japanese hardliner at the State Department, informed them that the United States did not have "much to lose" from further Japanese aggression. American principles and ideals "with regard to world peace" might be "further scratched and dented." American trade might be "somewhat further impaired." But "from the point of view of material interests," there was nothing in China that Americans considered "vital."[23]

Although few advocated deeper American involvement in East Asia, however, many were outraged and concerned about Japan's renewed aggression. With Germany and Italy fully involved in Spain, the latest Japanese assault on China was no longer an isolated case of the Japanese having their way on the mainland. To the State Department, Japan's attack appeared to be part of a coordinated strategy with Germany and Italy. But whether this was true or not, and whether or not officials saw American vital interests at stake in China, the combined actions of the three aggressive states seemed to threaten the general peace and well-being of the world.[24] As Walter Lippmann put it, there was "no use pretending to deny that the three fascist powers" had gained "the initiative in world affairs," and "that with great skill and daring" they were "pressing home the advantage." Although "potentially weaker than the rest of us," the fascist powers were "in fact stronger," because they had "the will to fight for what they want and we do not have it."

This was an increasingly common view. But so was Lippmann's insistence that he did not mean to suggest, "even indirectly and by implication," that there should be any particular American response. He certainly was not proposing "a military alliance to oppose this world-wide aggression" and he did not see how anyone could "responsibly favor so desperately dangerous a remedy." Lippmann admitted he did not know what to do. He knew only that there was "accumulating evidence to show that, as the liberal powers retreat, the aggression becomes more intense and that there is increasing reason to fear that if the liberal powers do not stand together they will fall separately."[25]

Roosevelt and most of his advisers also saw the Japanese actions less in terms of their specific impact in China and more as part of a broader international trend of aggression and brutality. Secretary Hull worried about the effect of Japanese aggression on "the courses pursued by other countries."[26] As one senior State Department official put it, American policies in the Far East had to be "determined with respect to analogous situations elsewhere."[27] There was a growing conviction that ignoring aggression in one corner of the world only encouraged aggression elsewhere.

Roosevelt was both concerned and annoyed at his inability to take any useful action. Everyone was looking to him "to *do* something," he complained. Everyone was looking "for somebody . . . to come forward with a hat and a rabbit in it. Well," he said, "I haven't got a hat and I haven't got a rabbit in it."[28] He searched for purely diplomatic gestures that he might make—a peace plan, a conference, a statement—anything that might address the growing crisis without requiring "a definite response or action on the part of anybody."[29] He invited the new British prime minister, Neville Chamberlain, to meet him in Washington (apparently the idea of Roosevelt himself crossing the Atlantic was inconceivable), vaguely suggesting that "Anglo-American cooperation" might somehow improve the global situation.[30] He wrote to Mussolini ("My Dear Duce"), seeking a meeting to discuss their supposedly common concern that the international situation was "ominous to peace."[31] He looked to improve relations with the Soviet Union and instructed his new ambassador "to win the confidence of Stalin."[32] He discussed various broader plans with his advisers: Perhaps he could send a letter to all the nations of the world, except Germany, Italy, and Japan, suggesting that in the case of future aggression, the "peace-loving nations would isolate" the aggressor nation, "cut off all trade" and "deny it raw materials." This would not apply to the current crises in China and Spain, of course—"what has happened in those countries has happened." It would be a "policy for the future" and "a warning to the nations that are today running amuck."[33] Perhaps he could offer his good offices to help other nations resolve their disputes peacefully. Sumner Welles, a close adviser at the State Department, suggested a conference where the world's neutral powers could work out "fundamental norms" and "standards of international conduct," with the aim of establishing an "international economy based upon reduced armaments, a greater common use of world resources and the improvement and simplification of economic relationships between all peoples."[34]

Little came of these ideas. Chamberlain was not interested in a meeting, and the approaches to Mussolini and Stalin came to little. As for the Welles plan and similar ideas, Secretary Hull rejected them as "illogical and impossible" and likely to lead to embarrassment for the president at a time when he could ill afford it.[35]

Hull and others recommended instead that Roosevelt give a speech "on international cooperation" in order to begin "to edge our own people gradually" out of the "slough of isolation into which so many had sunk."[36] Roosevelt himself had been thinking for some time about giving a major address that would not be "simply another speech" but "a dramatic statement." Hull recommended giving it "in a large city where isolation was entrenched." Roosevelt chose Chicago.[37]

The speech, delivered to a large audience on October 5, 1937, was indeed dramatic, and also strikingly at odds with the policies that Roosevelt had been pursuing for the previous four-plus years. Without naming names, he excoriated the "three bandit nations" that were carrying out a "reign of terror" around the world.[38] Civilians, "including vast numbers of women and children," were being "ruthlessly murdered with bombs from the air." Great powers were "fomenting and taking sides in civil warfare in nations that have never done them any harm." Innocent people were "being cruelly sacrificed to a greed for power and supremacy" that was "devoid of all sense of justice and humane considerations." Hopes for peace, the "high aspirations expressed in the Briand-Kellogg Peace Pact," had given way "to a haunting fear of calamity" that threatened "the very foundations of civilization."[39]

If these dangerous trends continued, he warned, "let no one imagine that America will escape, that America may expect mercy, that this Western Hemisphere will not be attacked." War was a "contagion." It could "engulf states and peoples remote from the original scene of hostilities." The Congress and administration had adopted measures to "minimize our risk of involvement," but it was foolish for Americans to hope for "complete protection in a world of disorder in which confidence and security have broken down." With the world heading rapidly toward "international anarchy," it was necessary to stop this "epidemic of world lawlessness." To do that, the "peace-loving nations" of the world had to make a "concerted effort" against those bent on destroying civilization. "When an epidemic of physical disease starts to spread the community approves and joins in a quarantine of the patients in order to protect the health of the community against the spread of the disease." Without elaborating further on this intriguing metaphor, Roosevelt concluded by declaring that "America hates war. America hopes for peace. Therefore, America actively engages in the search for peace."

Despite the alarmist nature of the address, it was well received even in Chicago. The initial reaction in the national press was also favorable—a State Department official observed a general sense of "jubilation that somebody should have expressed in clear terms what everybody has been feeling." But Roosevelt was nervous, and rightly so.[40] Within a few days the tone of commentary changed. Opponents charged that the speech reflected Roosevelt's "overwhelming propensity" to involve the United States "in the quarrels of Europe and the Orient, with all the fateful potentialities for war."[41] The ranking Republican on the House Foreign Relations Committee, Hamilton Fish, threatened to impeach Roosevelt for violating the Neutrality Act. And while Republican critics assailed him for abandoning "Americanism" for "internationalism" and wanting to fight "other people's battles all over the world," not a single Democratic leader in Congress spoke out to support Roosevelt's position.[42] To one adviser he privately commented that it was "a terrible thing to look over your shoulder when you are trying to lead—and to find no one there."[43]

Roosevelt quickly backed away from his tough rhetoric. When pressed to explain what he had meant by "quarantine"—did it mean sanctions? collective security? an international conference?—he angrily denied that it meant any of those things. "Sanctions" was "a terrible word to use," he told the press. "They are out the window." Even a conference was also "out the window."[44] When the editors of *The Times* of London suggested that Roosevelt had offered only "an attitude and not a program," albeit an attitude they approved of, Roosevelt agreed. "It is an attitude and it does not outline a program. . . . But it says we are looking for a program."[45]

Roosevelt's quarantine speech and his rapid backtracking afterwards showed how torn he was between his fears about the rising dangers in the world and his concern that the public was not ready to support any action to meet them. He was searching for a way to awaken Americans to the dangers without frightening them deeper into their "slough of isolation." It was a difficult balancing act, and the early indications were that he was not succeeding.

Roosevelt had also hoped his speech would have some effect on the behavior of other nations by at least raising the possibility of eventual American involvement. Like Stimson in 1932, he hoped that the vague and uncertain prospect of bringing America's vast potential power to bear might be enough both to deter the aggressor states and to put some backbone into the other democracies to stand up to them. The speech was a bluff as far as American policy was concerned, but he hoped it would have an effect on the decisions of the other powers.

It didn't, at least not in the ways he hoped. The speech had no effect on the aggressive policies of the "bandit" nations. The Japanese advanced deeper into China. At the beginning of December, Prime Minister Konoe authorized Japanese forces to take Nanking, hoping that Chiang's government would collapse once his capital fell.[46] Chiang retreated from Nanking, Japanese forces entered, and for the next several months, the city became the scene of mass atrocities. Estimates of the number killed in Nanking ranged from 40,000 to 300,000. In one case, a hundred men were tied up, had gasoline poured on them, and were set on fire. Women of all ages were raped, in many cases repeatedly.[47] An American missionary recorded the morning when "a stream of weary wild-eyed women" arrived after a night of "horror" during which "again and again their homes had been visited by soldiers."[48]

A *New York Times* journalist, Tillman Durdin, who reported from inside Nanking throughout the attacks, believed that the Japanese soldiers were not simply out-of-control young men engaging in random acts of cruelty. They were executing a deliberate strategy to terrify the population in order to "impress on the Chinese the terrible results of resisting Japan."[49] The U.S. ambassador in China also speculated that Japanese brutality was "partly motivated by a desire to convince the Chinese that they must not depend on white intervention." In Berlin, Ambassador William E. Dodd heard his Japanese counterpart boast that while the Imperial Army had killed 500,000 Chinese, the government in Tokyo knew that the West would do nothing about it.[50]

The Japanese were so little deterred by Roosevelt's speech that they even targeted Americans. As Japanese forces began their occupation of Nanking in mid-December 1937, naval aircraft bombed the USS *Panay,* a river gunboat on the Yangtze that was evacuating Americans from the city. The U.S. naval vessel displayed two large American flags, stretched across the deck so as to be visible from the air, but the Japanese fighters—who flew close enough that their faces could be seen by Americans on board— not only sank the gunboat, they strafed the smaller boats attempting to take the wounded to shore. In the end, one American aboard the *Panay* was killed and forty-five were injured. Roosevelt bruited about various actions he could take to punish Japan short of war, and Secretary of the Treasury Henry Morgenthau, Jr., insisted the United States could not let the Japanese "put their sword into our insides and sit there and take it and like it, and not do anything about it."[51]

Yet even though Americans were outraged by the *Panay* incident, there was no popular demand for retaliatory measures, not even sanctions. Instead, peace groups and anti-interventionists demanded the withdrawal of all American civilians and military personnel from China. In

Congress the Ludlow Amendment, a long-standing anti-interventionist effort to amend the Constitution so that declarations of war could be made only by national popular referendum, not by Congress, came as close as it ever had to being brought to a vote. "This nation wants peace," Roosevelt privately observed, and when the Japanese government quickly apologized for the *Panay* incident, he let the matter rest.[52]

Hitler's reaction to the quarantine speech was no more encouraging. Although he had long regarded the United States as a power to be reckoned with, and perhaps *the* power that Germany would ultimately have to grapple with, his estimate of the Americans had declined substantially in recent years.[53] The unwillingness of successive U.S. administrations to act in Europe, or to spend more than a small fraction of American wealth on military power, compounded by the nation's economic collapse after 1930, and then the passage and repeated reaffirmation of the Neutrality Act, all contributed to his "negative assessment of America's power potential." It was all further proof, he told his generals, that the United States was "not dangerous to us." Not only would the Americans refuse to fight, but in the event of war he had reason to hope they would not even provide assistance to the British or French.[54]

When Hitler took the dangerous gamble of moving troops into the Rhineland in the spring of 1936, he had counted not only on British and French passivity but also on American indifference. His propaganda minister, Joseph Goebbels, recounted the Führer's satisfaction at how well he had predicted the world's reaction: "The Führer beams. England remains passive. France won't act alone. Italy is disappointed and America uninterested."[55] Now, a year later, Roosevelt had given a tough-sounding speech, but with little behind the words. Hitler's ambassador in Washington interpreted Roosevelt's speech as nothing more than a maneuver by a "tremendously shrewd politician" to distract attention from the worsening economy. The threat of a quarantine was not "truly serious."[56] As Hitler planned his next moves at the beginning of 1938, he again assured his nervous generals that the Americans were "incapable of waging war and would not dare go beyond empty gestures in international affairs."[57]

Roosevelt's quarantine speech did convince Hitler that the American president was an implacable enemy, however. He had not assumed that to be the case before. American interests, he believed, were unaffected by what happened in Europe. That, after all, was the clear message sent by successive administrations since 1920, including FDR's. Nor was Hitler quite prepared for the moral indignation in the United States. He had long considered Americans as predominantly northern Europeans who shared his belief in the superiority of the white race, as their immigration policies indicated. But now here was Roosevelt comparing Germany to a disease, an epidemic—metaphors that Hitler himself used to describe the Jews. Indeed, the best explanation of Roosevelt's behavior was that he was under the influence of his Jewish advisers and Jewish bankers. For perhaps the first time, Hitler began to regard the United States less as a nation competing with Germany for leadership of the Aryan world than as a nation corrupted by its mongrel population and especially by Jews. It had become a leader of the international Jewish conspiracy to destroy Germany. This did not change his plans in the near term, for he was just as sure that, during the next few critical years, the United States would do nothing to stand in his way. But it contributed to his belief, which grew over time, that eventually, perhaps not during his lifetime, the Third Reich and the United States must inevitably clash.

Hitler, Mussolini, and the Japanese were therefore undeterred by Roosevelt's strong words. Just as troubling was the fact that neither Britain nor France was very impressed by Roosevelt's vague assurances either. Not that London and Paris didn't yearn for any sign of renewed American interest in world affairs. The foreign secretary, Anthony Eden, regarded American power as "the one unexploited reserve which must make itself felt if the world was to be saved," and the permanent under secretary, Robert Vansittart, believed that close Anglo-American cooperation alone offered "one of the faint hopes for the democratic world."[58] Eden certainly wanted to believe that Roosevelt's quarantine speech was evidence that "the most powerful republic in the world" was finally coming out of its "psychological withdrawal."[59]

But as the British and French probed to learn what Roosevelt meant in practical terms, they quickly discovered he hadn't meant anything. With Japanese forces still brutalizing the Chinese and driving for control of the entire country, British officials asked whether Roosevelt's talk of "quarantine" meant that he would support a joint boycott on Japanese imports.[60] The French asked for an assurance of U.S. assistance in the event that Japan invaded French Indochina, and they also suggested that Roosevelt call a meeting of the democratic nations so that they might stand together against the dictatorships.[61] The League of Nations queried whether Washington would support an arms embargo. Even the Soviets offered to join in a common effort against Japan, so long as Moscow could be assured it "would not be left with the bag to hold."[62]

Roosevelt's response to all these anxious queries was annoyance. He was annoyed at the British for trying to "pin the United States down to a specific statement as to how far it would go and precisely what the President meant by his Chicago speech," and he asked his diplomats to remind London that there was "such a thing as public opinion in the United States."[63] He was annoyed at the French for asking a "hypothetical question" about a Japanese attack in Indochina, which was "such a remote contingency" that it "should not even be discussed."[64] As for the League, Roosevelt instructed his diplomats that the United States would not be "pushed out in front as the leader in, or suggestor of, future action."[65] As one American official put it, rather than offer actual policy proposals, Roosevelt preferred to "embroider on the theme of the eternal question mark of American foreign policy."[66]

Roosevelt was certainly not looking to take the lead. He hoped that his rhetorical flourishes would put some spine in the democracies' backs. To a French diplomat he complained that "some of the great powers with territorial interests in the Far East were behaving 'like scared rabbits.'" To which the French premier, when told of Roosevelt's comment, responded that while this might be true, "the rabbit which was behaving in the most scared manner since there was no gun pointed toward it was the United States."[67]

Roosevelt's tough speech, in the end, did nothing to shake the dominant view in British and French foreign policy circles that the United States remained "incurably isolationist."[68] If anything, it highlighted the degree to which Roosevelt was isolated in his own country. Whatever the president's personal views, the French concluded, he was blocked by "the Babbitts" who wished only to sit behind their "impregnable fortress."[69] Even pro-American British officials like Eden, Churchill, Vansittart, and the ambassador in Washington had come to regard the Americans as "pusillanimous," lacking in "political virility," and all in all just a "dreadful people to deal with." Most agreed with Prime Minister Stanley Baldwin that "you will get nothing out of the Americans but words. Big words, but only words."[70]

This was the view in Moscow, as well. Like Britain and France, the Soviet Union by the mid-1930s was desperately looking for allies. With a hostile Nazi Germany in the west and a hostile Japan in the east, Stalin faced the prospect of a two-front war. It made sense to look to the United States for help, especially against Japan—after all, the United States had engineered the Nine-Power Pact back in 1922 supposedly aimed at constraining Japanese expansionism.[71] Hopes for a rapprochement with the Republican administrations in the 1920s had foundered on the rocks of American anti-communism, fueled by the extravagant rhetoric of world revolution pouring out of the Comintern, but prospects seemed to improve with the arrival of Roosevelt. When William Bullitt arrived as the first U.S. ambassador to Moscow in 1933, Stalin broke protocol by greeting him personally.[72]

The Soviets did not ask for much: a non-aggression pact, a token visit to Vladivostok by an American warship, some expression of solidarity. As Soviet foreign minister Maxim Litvinov told Bullitt, Moscow would welcome any gesture that could "make the Japanese believe that the United States was ready to cooperate with Russia," even if there was "no basis for the belief."[73] But Bullitt made clear that even symbolic shows of support were impossible, and Litvinov reluctantly concluded that "there was not much point in fussing over the United States." As he told Bullitt, if Washington persisted in remaining "aloof from all active interest in international affairs," then good relations between the two countries were "of small importance to the Soviet Union."[74] By the time of the Czech crisis in 1938, the American ambassador in Moscow reported, presciently, that the Soviets were "rapidly being driven into a complete isolation" to the point where they might seek agreement with Germany "in the not distant future."[75]

Despite Roosevelt's hopes, in short, his "quarantine" speech, and the public reaction to it, only added to doubts about America's willingness to play any role in the burgeoning international crises. The perception of America's unreliability at a time of mounting threats played a critical role in convincing Neville Chamberlain, who became Britain's prime minister in the second half of 1937, to pursue a policy of appeasement toward Hitler and Mussolini.

British appeasement did not begin with Chamberlain, of course. Both the British elite and the general public had long been prepared to allow substantial revision of the Versailles agreement. Britain and France had been trying to wean Mussolini away from Hitler for two years, and they had tried to reach agreement with Hitler, too. The British public's blasé response to Hitler's reoccupation of the Rhineland was a sign of how little they wished to stand in Germany's way. Nor was the unreliability of the United States the only factor pushing Chamberlain toward this approach. The sorry state of the British economy also contributed, along with public opposition to significant spending on defense, the widespread view that Britain should not again come to France's defense on the continent, and the long-standing British inclination to focus on protecting the empire.

But by 1937 appeasement had taken on a different aspect. It was one thing to try to be generous to a weak and defeated Germany. But by 1937 the balance was shifting quickly. The primary motive for appeasement had become fear. Successive British governments were increasingly worried about the German military buildup and whether Britain could keep up. The likelihood that the British might be left to fight Hitler, Mussolini, and the Japanese alone, without the aid of the United States and with only a weakened France by their side, was alarming. An influential secret report by British military planners in 1937 emphasized how vitally important it was to reduce the number of Britain's "potential enemies and to gain the support of potential allies."[76]

The only potential ally that mattered was the United States.[77] But Roosevelt's behavior had convinced Chamberlain, along with many of his colleagues, that the Americans could not be "depended upon for help if we should get into trouble."[78] As one close adviser recalled, it was Chamberlain's conviction that the Americans could not be relied upon, "more than any other reason," that forced his "mind in the only direction that seemed likely to avert war, the negotiation of specific, and probably limited, agreements, first with Mussolini, and secondly with Hitler."[79]

Chamberlain therefore devoted his energies not to improving Anglo-American relations, but to pursuing, independently of the United States, a "general settlement" in Europe by which "reasonable grievances may be removed . . . suspicions may be laid aside, and . . . confidence may again be restored." To accomplish this required a "real understanding and effort to meet others' needs."[80] Of course, it was Germany's needs above all that had to be met if war was to be avoided. When Chamberlain took office in mid-1937, he believed there was no time to waste. With Hitler preparing his next moves, Mussolini actively engaged in both Spain and North Africa, and the Japanese on the march in the Far East, the British prime minister believed it would be "dangerous in the extreme" to delay seeking a European settlement in the hope that America would eventually come around and join in "salvaging the ruins."[81]

He was right to think that time was running out. Indeed, it was probably already too late. Hitler was already convinced that the circumstances were ripe for making his boldest moves. The remilitarization of the Rhineland, the intervention in Spain, the ongoing German military buildup, and the evident unwillingness of the democracies to bring their substantial power to bear either against him or against Italy or Japan had given Hitler supreme confidence in his ability to lead Germany to the ultimate triumph. Meeting with his top military and diplomatic advisers in November 1937, he declared that "German foreign policy no longer had to lead from weakness or rely on bluff." He also believed Germany had to move quickly before the democracies woke up to what was happening and prepared themselves for the war that was coming.[82]

First, he intended to deal with the Austrian and Czech "problems."[83] The Versailles Treaty had forbidden any union between Austria and Germany, but Hitler, like many Germans, passionately believed that "one blood demands one Reich." "German-Austria" had to "return to the great German mother country."[84] As for Czechoslovakia, in which some 3 million German-speakers of the Sudetenland had been left unhappily under Czech rule, Hitler insisted on uniting these Germans to the fatherland, as well. The acquisition of Czechoslavakia was itself only a step toward Hitler's grand plan to conquer vast territories in the east, including parts of Poland and Ukraine, as well as the Balkans, to provide the growing German population both lebensraum and vital economic resources—to create what Hitler called a *Grossdeutschland.*

It was to forestall all this, and the Europe-wide war that would inevitably result, that Chamberlain embarked on his effort to satisfy Hitler's demands peacefully. But he had barely begun when Hitler opportunistically made his first move. When the Austrian leader, Kurt Schuschnigg, in a desperate attempt to prevent a German takeover, called for a referendum in which Austrians could choose whether they wanted to join Germany or remain independent, Hitler angrily pounced. He demanded that the referendum be cancelled, that the Austrian Nazi Party be legalized, and that the Austrian Nazi leader, Arthur Seyss-Inquart, be made minister of the interior with control of Austria's security forces. In a meeting at Godesberg, Hitler bullied Schuschnigg into agreeing to his terms rather than face a full-scale military occupation. But afterwards, Hitler decided to send troops in anyway. On March 12, 1938, German forces marched triumphantly into Austria, after a fruitless appeal by Schuschnigg to London. The *Anschluss* was a fait accompli.

Chamberlain and his colleagues, as well as the French, were not especially troubled by this latest move by Hitler. It seemed inevitable, and the fact that, despite polls suggesting Austrians wished to remain independent, there were thousands lining the streets to cheer the arrival of German troops suggested that union with Germany was not entirely unwelcome. If anything, Britain and France were glad to have the troublesome issue behind them—as one British official put it, "Thank goodness Austria's out of the way."[85]

Their main focus was Czechoslovakia, where the French had far more at stake. Czechoslovakia had long been the linchpin of French strategy for containing Germany on its eastern borders, the most powerful of the Little Entente with whom France had forged security relationships after the Great War. Chamberlain understood that if Germany attacked Czechoslovakia and France came to the Czechs' aid, the British might find themselves unavoidably drawn in. Chamberlain was therefore prepared to make significant concessions on the Sudetenland question.[86] Believing that Hitler did not seek all of Czechoslovakia but only the parts that were predominantly German-speaking, he was prepared to support autonomy for the Sudetenland, so long as it was accomplished by "peaceful means."[87]

Hitler's latest triumph in Austria, however, and the weak response to it by Britain and France, convinced him that they had no stomach for confrontation. The *Anschluss* had also strengthened Germany considerably. The economic benefits of swallowing Austria were substantial and compensated somewhat for the crisis in production that was hampering Hitler's rearmament program. The addition of Austrian troops added 100,000 regular soldiers to the Wehrmacht. *Anschluss* also meant that Czechoslovakia was now surrounded by German-controlled territory on three sides, leaving it highly vulnerable to attack. Less tangible, but just as significant, was the political boost the bloodless triumph gave to Hitler's standing in Germany. Germans had believed for more than a decade that no such gains could be made without risking a devastating war with the better-armed democracies. Hitler had proved that the democracies were unwilling to take Germany on even when it blatantly violated the postwar settlement.[88]

This confidence made Hitler much less susceptible to Chamberlain's efforts at appeasement. The fact was, Hitler did not want to take Czechoslovakia peacefully. He intended to eliminate the Czech state entirely, and by force. As he explained to his military staff in May 1938, the elimination of Czechoslovakia would "clear the rear for advancing against the West, England and France." His plan was to "smash Czechoslovakia by military action in the near future," and the only question was how soon he could "bring about the suitable moment from a political and military point of view."[89] Two days later he signed a directive for military action

to begin at the beginning of October at the latest. He also greatly accelerated German rearmament, with the goal of being ready for a war against
both Britain and France by April 1939.[90]

Hitler's new mood of confidence was one problem for Chamberlain.
Another was Mussolini. The Duce had opposed Hitler's earlier attempts
to take Austria, fearing the presence of German troops along Italy's
northern border. But after the invasion of Ethiopia and its denunciation
by Britain and the League, Mussolini had fully embraced Hitler and by
the end of 1936 was referring publicly to the Rome-Berlin "Axis." In September 1938 the Italian foreign minister told the British ambassador that
although bound by "no treaty, alliance, or military agreement," Italy's
"interests, honor, and pledged word required she should actively and
fully side with Germany."[91] When Mussolini signaled his acquiescence to
the *Anschluss,* a grateful Hitler relayed word that "I will never forget him
for it, never, never, never, come what may."[92]

A third problem concerned Britain's readiness for war. When Chamberlain asked the military chiefs for an assessment, based on the assumption that the United States would refuse "any significant help," they not
surprisingly concluded that under those circumstances, war over Czechoslovakia would be disastrous. Britain would have to fight Germany, and
possibly Italy and Japan as well, with only France and Czechoslovakia on
its side.[93] Significantly overestimating German capabilities, they judged
that Hitler could field nearly ninety divisions against the fifty that Britain,
France, and the Czechs together could field. Nothing that Britain and her
"possible allies" could bring to bear could prevent Germany from inflicting on the Czechs a "decisive defeat." Britain would then be fighting to
liberate Czechoslovakia, and this could only be accomplished by defeating Germany and only after "a prolonged struggle." During that struggle,
the Luftwaffe would dominate the air; Germany's bombers would destroy
British cities; and if Italy and Japan should "seize the opportunity to further their own ends," it would no longer be a European war but a "World
War." With only France able and willing to lend support, it was almost
impossible for British forces "to safeguard our territory, trade and vital
interests against Germany, Italy, and Japan simultaneously."[94]

To avoid such a catastrophe Chamberlain was prepared to go to great
lengths to give Hitler what he wanted. That meant forcing the Czechs
to accept at least the autonomy and probably the independence of the
Sudetenland—in short, the dismemberment of their young state.

It was not only the Czechs who would need substantial persuading
to make such painful and possibly fatal concessions. The weakening or

destruction of Czechoslovakia directly affected French security. The alliance system designed to contain Germany on its eastern borders was now about to be destroyed, with British acquiescence and with the Americans nowhere to be seen. French officials shared none of Chamberlain's optimism about the prospects for satisfying Hitler. They believed Hitler sought the destruction of the Czech state and would not stop until he had achieved it.

French options were also limited, however. Chamberlain and his advisers warned that Britain would not come to France's aid in the event of a war with Germany over Czechoslovakia. French military leaders insisted that France could take no action if it meant being left "alone before Germany and Italy without any assurance of British assistance." When the Socialist leader Leon Blum's government fell in April 1938, it was replaced by a cabinet led by Édouard Daladier, who quickly fell into line with the British appeasement strategy.[95] Together the French and the British set about convincing Czech president Edvard Beneš to make maximum concessions.[96] Bullitt reported to Hull that the French under Daladier had come to believe that "the ultimate dissolution of Czechoslovakia is inevitable."[97] Here again was the cascading effect of American decisions: America's unreliability left Chamberlain with few options other than appeasement; British unreliability, in turn, left the French feeling they had no choice but to go along.

Back in Washington, Roosevelt and his advisers seemed not to know how to respond to the Munich settlement. "I want you to know that I am not a bit upset over the final result," the president told one State Department official. Welles publicly echoed Chamberlain's claim to "peace in our time," declaring that there were now real prospects for building "a new world order based upon justice and upon law." The *New York Times,* representative of respectable eastern opinion, suggested that no one should say "that too high a price" had been paid for peace unless they were "willing to risk" the lives of their loved ones in war.[98]

Yet Roosevelt also expressed disdain for Chamberlain's appeasement strategy, as well as concern for its effect on American security. He believed that Britain, France, and the Czechs together had the military strength to defeat Germany if it came to a war. He saw Chamberlain as lacking in courage—what the British needed, he later remarked, was "a good stiff grog."[99] At each stage of the 1938 crisis, from the *Anschluss* to the growing threat of German aggression against Czechoslovakia, he privately urged both London and Paris to stand firm. At one point he bluntly told Chamberlain that "if a Chief of Police makes a deal with the leading gangsters, and . . . the gangsters do not live up to their word the Chief of Police will go to jail."[100] To the French he privately argued that Hitler understood "only force" and that France had no choice but to "risk war" with a nation led by such a man.[101] In a continuing attempt to put some steel in their spines, he made cryptic statements suggesting American toughness in the manner of the quarantine speech. He declared, for instance, that America would not "stand idly by" if "any other Empire" threatened "Canadian soil."[102] Secretary Hull warned the Axis powers not to "count us out in pursuing their plans for conquest."[103]

But every tough-sounding statement was accompanied by a reaffirmation that the United States had "no political involvements in Europe" and would "assume no obligations in the conduct of the present negotiations."[104] More importantly, Roosevelt continued to refuse to provide any assurances that if Britain and France did stand up to Hitler, the United States would support them even with material assistance. In 1938, again, he made no serious effort to revise the Neutrality Act, assessing that the mood in Congress and among the general public remained hostile. In May, as tensions over Czechoslovakia were peaking, Ambassador Bullitt told the French air minister that France "could not count on receiving a single American plane after a declaration of war."[105] Given French fears of German air superiority and their belief that "French cities would be laid in ruins" by the Luftwaffe in the event of war, the American posture was one more reason to avoid conflict. French panic was fanned by Charles Lindbergh, who reported (inaccurately) that German air superiority was "overwhelming."[106] In mid-September Sumner Welles told French leaders that 80 percent of the American public opposed any intervention in Europe. The French would later justify deserting Czechoslovakia on the ground that France could expect no aid from the United States.[107]

The American government was, in fact, sharply divided in these months. While Hull and Morgenthau opposed seeking a settlement with Hitler, Welles and others believed, like Chamberlain, that Hitler's goals were limited and could be satisfied short of war, that he was more moderate than some of his entourage, and that tough statements by the West would only strengthen the "war party." They regarded the *Anschluss* as "probably necessary" and in any case "not alarming."[108] While officials in Washington denounced appeasement, Ambassador Bullitt and the U.S. ambassador in London, Joseph Kennedy, were among the leading advocates of appeasement in Europe.[109]

In the end Britain and France together forced the Czechs to relinquish control of the Sudetenland and allow German troops to occupy significant parts of Czech territory. The final settlement was agreed at Munich, with Hitler, Chamberlain, Daladier, and Mussolini, but not the Czechs, present. Hitler was actually angry that he had been forced to take peacefully what he had wanted to take by force, and he was determined never to let that happen again. Chamberlain returned to London proclaiming "peace for our time."

Roosevelt cabled to Chamberlain, "Good man," and publicly celebrated the preservation of peace.[110] Privately, he remarked that the British and French would have to "wash the blood" from their "Judas Iscariot hands." He believed the surrender of Czechoslovakia would only lead to new demands from Hitler: "Denmark, the [Polish] Corridor or most likely of all a dangerous and forcible economic or physical penetration through Roumania."[111] Walter Lippmann called the Munich agreement "the equivalent of a major military disaster."[112] Roosevelt feared it was a step on the road to an all-out European war.

Indeed, the Czech crisis may have been the last chance to prevent a general European war. Hitler had, in fact, pursued a bold and even reckless course that could have proved his undoing. Contrary to the inflated assessments of the British and French, Germany was neither economically nor militarily prepared for a major war. As the historian Williamson Murray has observed, the Third Reich in 1938 "presented the world with an imposing façade of military and political power," but behind the façade there were glaring weaknesses, of which the Germans themselves were acutely aware. Rearmament was stalled by shortages of key materials, including steel, which the German economy could neither produce nor purchase in sufficient quantity. The formidable German military machine of 1940 did not yet exist. Had Britain and France gone to war with Germany in defense of Czechoslovakia, which itself was remarkably well prepared for war, Murray concludes, the conflict might have been costly, but "the results would have been inevitable and would have led to the eventual collapse of the Nazi regime at considerably less cost than the war that broke out the following September."[113]

Had Hitler led Germany into a losing war in 1938, he might well have lost power. In the weeks and months before the final crisis, he faced intense opposition from his top generals and diplomats, who were convinced that the British and French would come to the aid of Czechoslovakia, and probably backed by the inexhaustible resources of the United

States, just as in the last war.[114] The British might or might not be ready for war, the German finance minister warned, but they possessed "two great trump cards." One was the "soon-expected active participation of the United States," and the other was Germany's own "financial and economic weaknesses." Taking on this potent "world coalition," the German foreign minister warned, would eventually lead to Germany's "exhaustion and defeat."[115] Hitler was furious—"What sort of generals are these, whom I, the head of state, have to force into making war?"[116]—but they stuck to their assessment. Some of the generals were so concerned that they plotted to overthrow Hitler if he took them to war and they were defeated.[117] Popular support might also have dissolved. Hitler was upset prior to the Munich settlement that "the German people had remained apathetic and in some cases hostile to the idea of war with Czechoslovakia." Imagine how they would have felt if Hitler took them to war and lost.[118]

But that was not what happened. Instead, the democracies compromised and the United States was absent. The bloodless conquest of Czechoslovakia proved that Hitler had been right. His critics were discredited. Any thoughts of overthrow fizzled. Hitler would never face serious domestic opposition again until the end of the war, not from the German people and not from his own generals. He had been right, moreover, not because he read the military balance correctly but because he read his opponents correctly. He had insisted that Britain and France would not go to war for Czechoslovakia; that Poland and Hungary were just waiting to "pluck the carcass"; that the Red Army, because of Stalin's purges, was in no condition to fight; and that the United States would do nothing.[119] As one respected senior general noted, Hitler took dangerous risks, but he "always judged the political situation correctly."[120] Whether this would always be true, it certainly seemed so at the time.

If anything, Hitler felt that he had underestimated Chamberlain's desperate desire to avoid war. "I myself" would never have thought it possible, he commented soon afterwards, that "Czechoslovakia would be served up to me, so to speak, by her friends. . . . I did not believe that England and France would go to war, but I was convinced that Czechoslovakia would have to be destroyed by a war. The way in which everything happened is historically unique."[121]

The consequences were far-reaching. The Munich settlement left the rest of Czechoslovakia at the mercy of Germany, both economically and militarily. Under the terms of the agreement Chamberlain struck with Hitler, the Czechs lost 27 percent of their heavy industry, 32 percent of their lumber industry, and 30 percent of their chemical manufactures. The loss of Sudetenland coal left Czechoslovakia dependent on German-controlled electricity. Within three weeks of the agreement, Hitler ordered preparations for taking the rest of Czechoslovakia, violating the promise he had just made and on which Chamberlain based his hopes for peace. In February 1939, German troops entered and occupied Prague. Czechoslovakia effectively ceased to exist, just as Hitler had all along intended. The seizure of the rest of Czechoslovakia gained Germany substantial new resources and industrial capabilities that would allow Hitler to overcome shortages and redouble rearmament efforts in preparation for the next war.[122]

With Czechoslovakia in his grasp, Hitler also established German hegemony in eastern and central Europe. The powers to the east and southeast were now effectively defenseless against German arms. Most governments moved quickly to strengthen political and economic ties with Berlin.[123] Britain's ambassador in Paris observed that France now found "herself in a position where her efforts of twenty years to assure her peace and security are in ruins. The League of Nations and her continental alliances have collapsed. Her one remaining standby is her entente with Great Britain."[124] As Winston Churchill put it in a speech to the Commons, "The whole equilibrium of Europe has been deranged" and this was "only the beginning of the reckoning."

The responsibility for the Munich settlement is usually laid at the feet of Chamberlain, and there are good reasons for that. He badly misread Hitler, genuinely believing that the Nazi leader had limited aims and that if he achieved what he wanted in Czechoslovakia, he would then be willing to accept a general European peace. Chamberlain stubbornly persisted in this view despite abundant evidence that it was mistaken.[125] Even to the end, Chamberlain remained convinced that "Herr Hitler . . . would not deliberately deceive a man whom he respected and with whom he had been in negotiation, and he was sure that Herr Hitler now felt some respect for him."[126]

Roosevelt and other Americans believed Chamberlain had acted in a cowardly and shameful fashion. And so of course did many Britons. But the Americans had somewhat less right to sit in judgment, for they shared responsibility. If Chamberlain clung to unreasonable hopes that Hitler could be appeased, it was partly because the alternative was a war that he feared Britain would have to fight alone, without assurance of American material assistance. Chamberlain might have made a different calculation had he felt able to count on the Americans. The same was true of the

French, and possibly even the Soviets. Roosevelt wanted them all to fight the Germans, but they had no idea whether the United States would help them if they did.

Roosevelt complained throughout the crisis that no one was listening to him, that neither Hitler, nor Mussolini, nor Chamberlain, nor the French seemed to give "a continental damn about what the United States thinks or does."[127] That was mostly wrong. It was true that Hitler, who had once thought a great deal of the United States, had stopped worrying about Washington's views. Roosevelt's own actions had done much to encourage that. But Britain and France cared intensely about the United States. It was only when they became convinced that the United States would do nothing in the event of a European confrontation that they went their own way and made their fateful choices.

As one historian has noted, "Europe's leadership in the 1930s was not capable of mustering the continent's strength" to deter or defeat Hitler. This could be viewed as a failing on their part. Or it could be viewed as the new reality, the inevitable product of the shifts in the international distribution of power that had begun early in the century. Whether their weaknesses were psychological or material, or both, the Europeans had proven that they could not preserve the peace without the added weight of the United States. Europe's leadership had not been capable of preventing war in 1914. It had not been capable of prevailing in that war until the United States entered the struggle. It was not surprising that, as Hitler threatened to engulf the continent in a new war, the Europeans felt helpless to meet the challenge alone. The peace settlement established after the war had depended on American power to provide reassurance to victors and victims alike, and when the United States withdrew, the settlement had collapsed, gradually and then suddenly.

CHAPTER TWENTY

Kristallnacht *and Its Effect on American Policy*

The Jews should for once get to feel the anger of the people.

—Adolf Hitler

MANY ON both sides of the Atlantic could see that the Munich settlement made a general European war almost inevitable. It was also clear that the American public remained uninterested in any deeper American involvement. Yet much as the *Lusitania* sinking had no immediate effect on U.S. policies but changed the lens through which many Americans viewed Imperial Germany, Hitler's actions in the fall of 1938 provided a new perspective on world events. Many again saw the "civilized" world engaged in a struggle against evil. A new phase of persecution of German Jews, culminating in the brutal attacks on the night of November 9–10, 1938—the infamous *Kristallnacht,* named for the shards of glass from Jewish stores that covered city sidewalks—fundamentally changed the contours of the American debate.

Hitler's rise to power had from the beginning carried ominous implications for Germany's Jews. In his first three years, widespread attacks on Jews were accompanied by the enactment of legal restrictions stripping them of their rights as Germans, including the right to own property, and forbidding their employment in certain professions. In 1935 the Reichstag passed the Nuremberg Laws, which defined a Jew by birth and stripped all Jews of their German citizenship.

During the early years of his rule, Hitler focused less on his mission to remove all Jews from Germany than on restoring German power, territory, and autonomy. Persecution of Jews increased but "without frequent or coherent central direction." Hitler kept his distance from anti-Semitic actions, lest he be discredited as a world leader or, worse, provoke the democracies to strangle Nazism in the cradle. On this as on other issues, he moved cautiously. In 1936, when Germany hosted the Olympic games in Berlin, the government actively suppressed anti-Semitic acts to avoid criticism from the thousands of foreign visitors—for instance, signs designating places where Jews were forbidden were removed in all areas where foreigners could see them.[1]

As Hitler grew more confident and secure, however, and as the democracies proved unwilling to challenge him even as he defied treaty commitments, he pursued his dream of a *judenrein* Germany with greater rigor and determination. If Britain, France, and the United States could allow him to send German troops back into the Rhineland, to intervene militarily in Spain, to resume universal conscription and build an air force and a navy in violation of treaties and promises—all barely with murmurs of complaint—they were unlikely to come to the defense of Germany's Jewish population. As Lewis Mumford observed just a few months after *Kristallnacht,* "the very ruthlessness of fascism has been in proportion to the lack of opposition it has encountered."[2]

When Hitler moved against Austria and Czechoslovakia in 1938, life for German and Austrian Jews became a series of mounting horrors. The arrival of German troops in Austria in March brought an extension of the Nuremberg Laws and an explosion of anti-Semitic violence, with beatings and killings in the streets of Vienna where most Austrian Jews lived. In Germany that May, a thousand-person gang roamed Berlin smashing Jewish shop windows, and the police responded by taking Jewish owners into "protective custody."[3] Nazi Party activists across the country vandalized synagogues and Jewish cemeteries. The main synagogue in Munich was destroyed in June, and two months later, the main synagogue of Nuremberg was demolished by the authorities, as tens of thousands watched. In August all Jews were required to add the names "Israel" or "Sarah" to their identification papers. In October, all Jewish passports were declared invalid and had to be replaced by passports with a red letter "J" stamped in them. As Goebbels explained: "We're now proceeding more radically."[4]

The democracies reacted with a combination of outrage and inaction. In the summer of 1938, between the *Anschluss* and Munich, Britain, the United States, and more than two dozen other nations met in Evian, France, to address the growing crisis of Jewish refugees. It was Roosevelt's initiative, but even he was not prepared to do much. Immigration restrictions in all countries, including the United States, left little room for German and Austrian Jewish refugees to escape the new wave of persecution. The conference ended with all but one nation, the Dominican Republic, refusing to raise their quotas, the United States among them. Hitler taunted the world for its hypocrisy. If the international community had "such deep sympathy for these criminals," he quipped, Germany was more than ready to hand them over.[5]

The democracies' refusal to open their doors turned German and Austrian Jews into hostages as well as victims. In July, Hitler told Goebbels that the Jews had to be "removed" from Germany within ten years, but until then they were to be held as "surety" for "whatever world Jewry undertakes against Germany."[6] In the meantime, they would be stripped of all their wealth and expelled from the German economy. Throughout 1937 and 1938, more and more Jews were driven from their professions as doctors, lawyers, university professors, and civil servants. Non-Jewish colleagues took their jobs.

The persecution culminated in November 1938 in the worst anti-Jewish pogrom in modern European history. On November 7, a seventeen-year-old Polish Jew named Herschel Grynszpan, driven to fury after his family's deportation, entered the German embassy in Paris and shot and killed a German diplomat. There followed an explosion of anti-Semitic hatred and violence in German cities. During what Nazi officials called *Reichskristallnacht,* large gangs smashed and looted over 7,000 Jewish-owned stores, burned some 1,400 synagogues across Germany, and invaded and looted hundreds of Jewish homes. Jews on the streets, including women and children, were beaten. Ninety-one Jews were reported killed. Others committed suicide. Although average non-Jewish Germans took part in the persecution, most of the looting and destruction was not spontaneous but orchestrated and carried out by Nazi Party activists with the government's approval. "The Jews should for once get to feel the anger of the people," Hitler said. His lieutenants made sure of it.

The persecution also filled the Nazi government's depleted coffers with money and property seized from Jewish merchants, professionals, and bankers. Police were ordered to arrest as many male Jews as the prisons could hold, and to focus on the wealthy. Some 30,000 were sent to prison camps at Dachau, Buchenwald, and Sachsenhausen. The Jewish community was then ordered to pay an "atonement fine" of a billion marks (equivalent to $400 million in 1938 and $7 billion in today's dollars) for the damages done to German property.[7]

The violent persecution of Jews was also intended to rouse the German public to meet the enemy at home and abroad. After Chamberlain's appeasement had deprived him of the chance to launch a war against Czechoslovakia, Hitler worried that the German people would think all goals could be accomplished peacefully. Unleashing anti-Semitic fury was partly designed to get the blood flowing, literally and figuratively. Hitler and other Nazi leaders portrayed the international struggle as a fight between Germany and international Jewry, rather than against Britain and France. Either Germany and Italy would be "annihilated," the SS leader, Heinrich Himmler, declared, or the Jews would be.[8]

As an American diplomat in Berlin put it, the Germans were "in a mood of triumph and victory over their success in Czechoslovakia" and believed their "course forward" was "positively irresistible." They had "embarked on a program of annihilation of the Jews," and there was little for the West to do but "save the remnants if we choose."[9]

In the United States, the events surrounding *Kristallnacht,* thoroughly covered in the American press, sparked widespread outrage.[10] The German ambassador in Washington reported a "storm of anti-German feeling," and not just in the "Jewish press" but also in "respectable circles." Even "the most bitter anti-Semites," he noted, were "anxious to disassociate themselves from methods of this kind."[11] Roosevelt spoke for most Americans in remarking that he "could scarcely believe that such things could occur in a twentieth century civilization."[12] Even before *Kristallnacht,* German officials had noted in the United States a "shift in emphasis toward an ideological interpretation of world developments which involved a contest between democracy and totalitarianism, freedom and despotism, Christianity and paganism."[13] But after *Kristallnacht,* Americans' "rage against Germany" reached heights not seen even during the last war.[14]

This shift in public opinion came well before most Americans regarded Germany as a direct threat to American security. The neutrality laws remained in effect, and there was little increased support for deeper involvement in Europe. Yet it was not long before moral outrage began to have an effect on the way many regarded the nature of the German threat.

The shift was, not surprisingly, most notable among American liberals. Reinhold Niebuhr, whose postwar disillusionment had led him to become first a pacifist, then a Marxist, and who believed even in early 1938 that the United States should remain out of any international conflict, began to shift again after *Kristallnacht.* For him as for a growing number of

Americans,[15] Germany was no longer a "have-not" power unjustly vic-
timized by the victors at Versailles, but a "fascist" regime with dangerous
and unlimited aspirations.

As always, American views on foreign questions were closely related
to domestic political battles. Liberals did not just worry about fascism
abroad. Some feared that the United States was becoming increasingly
susceptible to fascism. By the winter of 1938 the once-powerful engine
of New Deal reforms had ground to a halt, and the events in Europe
coincided with a period of conservative reaction in the United States.
The "Roosevelt recession" of 1937 produced a sharp drop in GDP and a
new wave of mass unemployment. Many Americans were on the brink of
starvation—in cities like Chicago, families searched for food in garbage
cans.[16] Meanwhile, conservative, anti–New Deal forces, which had been
routed by the Roosevelt juggernaut for four years, were making a come-
back. The unpopularity of Roosevelt's court-packing efforts contributed
to a general weakening of his mandate for reform. The 1938 midterm
congressional elections, which took place one day before *Kristallnacht,*
delivered a significant defeat to Democrats and to liberals and progressives in both parties. Democrats lost eight seats in the Senate and eighty
in the House. Although they retained substantial majorities in both, the
ideological complexion within the party shifted as conservative southern
Democrats gained at the expense of midwestern and western progressives.[17] Liberals, like the journalist Max Lerner, worried that a "new tidal
wave of reaction" had descended upon America and that "corporate capitalism" would soon take over.[18]

Still, while many liberals now saw international politics as a global
struggle between fascism and "civilization," they continued to oppose
American military intervention. Nor, at first, were they even interested
in providing aid to Britain and France, since the "exploiting classes" in
those countries had already made themselves "subservient clients of fascism."[19] A letter to Roosevelt from ninety-five prominent liberals just one
day after *Kristallnacht* called on the president to "make it clear to the
democratic powers of Europe that the American people" would not take
kindly to "further concessions to the totalitarian States at the expense
of the democratic peoples and ideals." But their only specific recommendation was to normalize commercial relations with Republican Spain,
which by that point was close to defeat.[20] Liberals also split over attitudes toward the Soviet Union. Some insisted that both the Soviets and
the Nazis were equally "totalitarian."[21] Others still believed that only the
Soviets stood in the way of a fascist victory in Europe.

Many Americans took nearly the opposite view. Taft believed that "the victory of communism in the world would be far more dangerous to the United States than the victory of fascism,"[22] and polls showed the majority of Americans agreed. Roosevelt, one Republican elder states-man complained, had "gone over hook, line and sinker to the Com-munists and Socialists by whom he is surrounded." Hearst assailed the "imported, autocratic, Asiatic Socialist party of Karl Marx and Franklin Delano Roosevelt."[23]

There was also widespread concern about an international Jewish conspiracy to undermine Christian America.[24] Some spoke of the "Jew Deal." Jews were attacked both as communists and as leaders of global capitalism. They also controlled Hollywood, which many blamed for undermining the nation's Christian morality.[25] Polls in 1938 showed that between 30 and 40 percent of Americans believed that Jews had "too much power." A majority also believed that the Jews were either partly or entirely responsible for their own persecution.[26]

Hitler's rise in Germany led to a significant increase in anti-Semitism in the United States.[27] William Dudley Pelley founded his Silver Legion in 1933 in direct response to Hitler's accession to the chancellorship, just one of a hundred new anti-Semitic organizations that were established in the United States between 1933 and 1941.[28] Many resented the sym-pathetic treatment the Jews received in the major American newspapers after *Kristallnacht.* The most powerful spokesman for this resentment was Father Charles E. Coughlin, the "Radio Priest" who at his peak in the mid-1930s reached as many as one-third of all Americans.[29] The uproar over the Nazi persecution was itself a sign of Jewish dominance, he told his millions of listeners.[30] Coughlin noted that while the Nazi seizure of $400 million from German Jews was receiving a "super-abundance of publicity," the $40 billion worth of "Christian property" that had been appropriated by the "atheistic Jews and Gentiles" who led the Bolshevik revolution and the Soviet government had received barely a mention.[31] As proof of the Jews' responsibility for Communism, Coughlin read from a list, compiled by Nazi propagandists, which alleged that fifty-six out of fifty-nine members of the Soviet Communist Party's central commit-tee were Jews, and the other three were "non-Jews married to Jewesses." Nazism, he argued, was a "defense mechanism against Communism."[32] In what quickly became a common trope for many anti-interventionists, Coughlin warned that if American Christians had to send their sons to die in Europe again, it would be because of the Jews.

The idea that Jews were pushing the United States into a war to save their co-religionists in Germany and Europe gained increasing currency as the European crisis deepened and as Roosevelt pressed for measures to aid Hitler's opponents. As one Catholic newspaper in Cincinnati summed up the general view, American Jewry, a "highly organized minority" possessed of "great wealth and extraordinary influence," had become "the war party in our country."[33] This belief sprang naturally from the revisionist accounts of World War I and the findings of the Nye committee. If bankers, financiers, and munitions makers had led the United States into war in 1917, many Americans assumed this meant Jews. In 1920, Henry Ford, through his personal newspaper, the Dearborn *Independent,* began publication of four volumes addressing the Jewish "question," the first of which was entitled *The International Jew: The World's Foremost Problem.*[34] Alleged Jewish responsibility for America's entry into the First World War was a major theme.[35] Senator Nye himself charged that Hollywood studios, swarming with "refugees" and run by men "born abroad and animated by the persecutions and hatreds of the Old World," had begun to operate as "war propaganda machines almost as if they were being directed from a single central bureau."[36]

Coughlin spread this message to millions of Americans, and especially to American Catholics.[37] In response to his call for a "crusade against the anti-Christian forces of the Red Revolution," a group of predominantly Irish Catholic Americans, including the Catholic bishop of Brooklyn, founded the Christian Front, which organized boycotts of Jewish stores, confronted and attacked Jews on the streets, and held rallies where speakers praised Franco and Hitler and denounced Jewish warmongers and President "Rosenvelt."[38]

Catholics were not alone. Many Protestants and Evangelicals saw Hitler as God's "rod of correction" for "Jewish sin and unbelief."[39] Gerald Winrod, a Christian evangelical pastor from Kansas, founded the Defenders of the Christian Faith in 1925 in response to the Scopes "Monkey Trial," but in the mid-1930s he shifted his focus to exposing the threat posed to America by the Jews. His newspaper, *The Defender,* had a monthly circulation of 100,000.[40] When Winrod ran for the U.S. Senate from Kansas in 1938, he submerged his anti-Semitism but warned against the "greasy," "unassimilated," "foreign population" that violated "the Christian Sabbath," didn't "speak our language" or "breathe our air."[41]

Among the most visible and colorful of the anti-Semitic organizations was the German American Bund, a pro-Nazi organization founded and led by Fritz Julius Kuhn, a Munich-born naturalized American citizen. Although the Bund probably never numbered more than 25,000 national members, the group garnered significant publicity, especially in the months following Munich and *Kristallnacht.* Typical Bund rallies featured Nazi and American flags, the singing of the German National Socialist anthem, the "Horst Wessel" song, fascist salutes and shouts of "Heil Hitler, Heil America!" Kuhn led his audience in chants of "Free America!" and the Bund's professed aim was "to combat the Moscow-directed madness of the red world menace and its Jewish bacillus-carriers."[42]

The Bund's actions did inspire counter-protests. On October 1, 1938, the day Germany annexed the Sudetenland, thousands of protesters showed up at a Bund rally in Union City, New Jersey, where a group of veterans from the Andrew Jackson Veterans Democratic Club sent Kuhn running for his life.[43]

The biggest clash occurred at Madison Square Garden in February 1939. With the great Manhattan sports palace festooned with swastikas, American flags, a thirty-three-foot painting of George Washington (the "first fascist"), and huge banners that read "Stop Jewish Domination of Christian Americans" and "Smash Jewish Communism," Kuhn and other speakers, guarded by men in Nazi-inspired uniforms, exhorted the cheering crowd to fight against "International Jewry." When journalist Dorothy Thompson, rather boldly seated in the audience, began to laugh in response to one of the speeches, she was forcibly removed. Meanwhile, outside the Garden, tens of thousands of protesters, more or less organized by the Socialist Workers Party, heckled and shouted at the Nazis, while some 1,700 members of the New York Police Department— enough to "stop a revolution," the police commissioner boasted—turned the Garden into "a fortress impregnable to anti-Nazis."[44]

These fascist and overtly anti-Semitic organizations represented no more than a tiny portion of the American population. But the views they expressed were widely shared in less extreme form by more mainstream groups. While few members of Congress were openly anti-Semitic, in private they were more expressive. California senator Hiram Johnson, writing to his son, feared that Roosevelt was pandering to the Jews, who were "willing to fight to the last American."[45] Charles Lindbergh raised a ruckus in 1941 when he accused the Jews of pushing the United States into war "for reasons which are not American."[46] Nor were Republicans averse to helping and working with some of these fringe characters, whatever their own view of Jews might be.[47]

The paradoxical result of *Kristallnacht,* therefore, was that while it did change the views of many Americans about the threat posed by Germany and Nazism, it also mobilized the anti-interventionists to try to stop what they feared might become a Jewish-inspired rush to war. The rising pitch of anti-Semitism in the country also posed a conundrum for Roosevelt and others who hoped to see the United States take a more active role in the European crisis. They feared that if Washington appeared to be responding to the plight of the Jews, this would help neither the Jews nor the internationalist cause.

Roosevelt almost never mentioned the Jews himself. In his annual message to Congress in early January 1939, he spoke of the Nazis' threat to "religion" and to freedom of worship. Dorothy Thompson pleaded with American Jews not to make this about Jews alone but about all those persecuted for their beliefs, because she did not want to alienate an "overwhelmingly middle-class," "native born, northern European," "Christian and Protestant" America.[48] The main Jewish organizations in America also feared making the issue about Jews, lest they provoke an explosion of anti-Semitism. When the question arose of changing the immigration quota system to make room for Jews fleeing Germany and Austria, even many Jewish leaders were opposed because they feared a rise in anti-Semitism.

Munich and *Kristallnacht* nevertheless set off the first significant national discussion of foreign policy since the League fight two decades earlier. The arguments in the 1920s over the World Court and the "outlawry" of war had been confined to comparatively small groups fighting for symbolic and theoretical victories in a time of relative peace and security. Nor had there been any real challenge to the reigning postwar orthodoxies. Democrats no less than Republicans disavowed the League in the party platforms. The events of the fall of 1938, however, produced the first serious challenge to the postwar consensus. Internationalists now rose up to sound the alarm. They were encouraged, no doubt, by the fact that, for the first time since 1920, the man in the White House shared their views.

Roosevelt, too, was emboldened by events and the general public's reaction to them. The always politically attuned president had every reason to shift his focus from domestic to foreign policy.[49] The 1938 congressional elections dealt a blow to the old New Deal political coalition and made further reforms difficult. But they also strengthened support for a more internationalist foreign policy. The defeat of western progressives, as well as the advanced age of such old warhorses as Borah and Johnson, had weakened the anti-interventionist forces in Congress. A new alliance among the urban northeast liberals who dominated the press and academia, the Wall Street bankers who dominated the financial world, and the conservative southern Democrats "provided the rockbed political base for the president's increasingly internationalist foreign policies."[50] For the next two years, as Roosevelt sought to increase defense expenditures and provide weapons and assistance to Britain and France, he could generally count on the kind of bipartisan coalition that could no longer be mustered for further New Deal reforms.[51] In January 1939, Roosevelt told Congress that "events abroad made it increasingly clear to the American people that dangers within are less to be feared than dangers from without."[52]

Roosevelt's message in 1939 was more alarmist than any of his previous discussions of the global situation. "World events of thunderous import" had moved with "lightning speed," he noted, and Americans who once "clung to the hope that the innate decency of mankind" and "two vast oceans" offered protection against aggression needed to understand now that this was an illusion. "All about us rage undeclared wars. . . . All about us grow more deadly armaments. . . . All about us are threats of new aggression." The world had "grown so small and weapons of attack so swift" that attacks could now be launched from "distant points."[53] The United States had to do more to meet this challenge, Roosevelt insisted. He promised to employ methods "short of war," but they had to be "stronger and more effective than mere words." In a confidential meeting with members of Congress at the end of January, he said that he didn't want "to frighten the American people" but he was "very much exercised over the future of the world," as well as of American security.[54]

Events quickly confirmed these fears. In March 1939 Hitler forcefully occupied the rest of Czechoslovakia, including the large non-German populations of Bohemia and Moravia, fulfilling the goal that had eluded him at Munich. Five days later, he delivered an ultimatum to Lithuania, demanding that the territory of Memel, detached from German control by the Versailles agreement, be ceded back and threatening invasion if the Lithuanian government refused. All of this prompted even Senator Borah to exclaim, "Gad, what a chance Hitler has! If he only moderates his religious and racial intolerance, he would take his place beside Charlemagne. He has taken Europe without firing a shot."[55] In April Franco's forces defeated the Republicans in Spain, prompting Roosevelt to lament that the embargo on arms to the Spanish Loyalists had been "a grave mistake."[56] That month, too, Mussolini invaded Albania, unseated its ruler, King Zog I, and made it a protectorate of the Italian Empire. The Japanese meanwhile occupied the Spratly and Paracel Islands in the South China Sea.

Roosevelt and his advisers were genuinely alarmed, as, of course, was all of Europe. After the German seizure of Memel, Ambassador William Bullitt wrote from Paris that "unless some nation in Europe stands up to Germany quickly, France and England may face defeat." The French and British fleets might end up in the hands of the Axis powers, and "we should then have the Japs in the Pacific and an overwhelming fleet against us in the Atlantic."[57] Bullitt also relayed reports that Hitler intended to take control of central and eastern Europe in the summer, and that in 1940 he planned to invade and conquer France. In 1942, allegedly, Hitler planned a joint attack with Japan on North and South America.[58] Even Joseph Kennedy now worried that France and Britain might well fall, with dire implications for the world and for American security.[59] Many suspected that Hitler's next move would come against Poland. In March, he began demanding the return of Danzig to Germany and the construction of a road across the "Polish corridor" that separated East Prussia from the rest of Germany. The French foreign minister warned Bullitt that time was running out: "It was five minutes before twelve."[60]

In candid conversations in early 1939, Roosevelt insisted that while he did not propose to take the United States to war—"about the last thing that this country should do is ever to send an army to Europe again"[61]—he did plan to provide what Britain and France needed to help them "rearm against the threat of dictators in this world." It was no longer possible to "draw a line of defense around this country and live completely and solely to ourselves," he argued. America's "first line of defense" was the "continued independent existence of a very large group of nations," which included not only Britain and France but the Baltic states, Scandinavia, Poland, Hungary, Czechoslovakia, the Balkans, Turkey, and Persia. If these lines were breached, Germany's "sphere of action" would be "unlimited" and might extend even to the Americas. Japan would dominate "the entire Pacific Ocean," up to and including the Pacific coast of South America. The result would be America's "gradual encirclement."[62]

In a speech on April 14, Roosevelt declared that Americans had "a stake in world affairs," a set of interests "wider than that of the mere defense of our sea-ringed continent."[63] The next day he sent public messages to Hitler and Mussolini asking them to "give assurance" that they would not attack or invade a list of thirty-one nations for a period of ten years. He also sent Congress a request for substantial increases in aircraft production, believing, as many observers did, that air power would be decisive in the next war and that Germany already enjoyed a dangerous advantage.

Finally, he resumed his quest for revision of neutrality legislation. There were reports that the German foreign minister, Joachim von Ribbentrop, was urging Hitler to move quickly against Poland while American neutrality legislation still prohibited the provision of arms and supplies to Britain and France.[64] British and French leaders believed that a quick revision might give Hitler pause and prevent the coming war.[65] Roosevelt sought outright repeal of the Neutrality Act but was prepared to settle for expanded discretionary authority to impose embargoes against aggressors only. As things stood, he complained, "If Germany invades a country and declares war, we'll be on the side of Hitler by invoking the act." At least if Congress did away with the mandatory arms embargo, "it wouldn't be so bad."[66] This time Roosevelt felt more confident of success. Polls in March 1939 showed 66 percent of the public favored selling war materials to Britain and France if they were attacked by Germany and Italy—up from just 34 percent before Munich and *Kristallnacht*.[67]

The first skirmish of this new American struggle over foreign policy showed the anti-interventionists still in charge, however. They played down the severity of the international situation. Accusing Roosevelt of politically motivated alarmism, they denied that a crisis was imminent. "We are not going to have a war," Borah insisted in July 1939. "Germany isn't ready for it."[68] Hamilton Fish, the ranking Republican on the House Foreign Affairs Committee, also insisted there would be no war in Europe unless "the hate and war-crazy administration in Washington goad[ed] the British and French into it."[69] Republicans were far from ready to abandon the foreign policy they had been running on, mostly successfully, for a quarter century. In June, the House defeated legislation to repeal the arms embargo, with Republicans voting 150–7 against.[70] They were joined by 61 Democrats (out of 226), who shared Charles Beard's fear that Roosevelt was "blundering into war" in part to distract attention from the economy.[71] The following month the Senate Foreign Relations Committee voted 12–11 to put off further action on the matter until 1940, with five out of the sixteen Democrats on the committee joining all seven Republicans.[72] Hull told legislators that they were "making the mistake of their lives" if they thought this was "another goddam piddling dispute over a boundary line" when, in fact, it was going to be a global struggle against "a philosophy of barbarism."[73] Senator Nye told reporters that Congress's actions served "notice to France and Great Britain that we are not going to fight any more of their wars."[74] Roosevelt remarked bitterly that there would be "great rejoicing in the Italian and German camps."[75]

CHAPTER TWENTY-ONE

Blitzkrieg and America's "Great Debate"

And if, which I do not for a moment believe, this island or a large part of it were subjugated and starving, then our Empire beyond the seas, armed and guarded by the British fleet, would carry on the struggle, until, in God's own time, the New World, with all its power and might, steps forth to the rescue and liberation of the old.

—Winston Churchill speech, June 4, 1940

THE FOLLOWING month, the world awoke to the surprising news that Hitler and Stalin, until then bitter enemies, had signed a non-aggression pact. Keen observers knew this was a prelude to the invasion and dismemberment of Poland.[1] Roosevelt's close adviser Adolf Berle, who just a year before had regarded fears of Hitler's intentions as overblown, wrote in his diary, "I have a horrible feeling of seeing . . . a civilization dying even before its actual death. . . . How delicate a fabric this thing we call modern civilization really is."[2] On September 1, 1939, the months of anticipation ended and German troops invaded Poland. When Bullitt called to inform Roosevelt that Germany had launched its attack, the president said, "It's come at last. God help us."[3]

Poland fell quickly. Against a poorly prepared and outgunned Polish force, the Germans threw 60 divisions—a million and a half soldiers—as well as 2,750 tanks and over 2,000 aircraft in a combined armor and air attack that awestruck observers called "blitzkrieg." In five weeks, Poland was defeated and its territory was divided between Germany and the Soviet Union. Stalin also took the opportunity to annex the three Baltic states of Estonia, Latvia, and Lithuania, and then, in November, he invaded Finland. Great Britain and France declared war on Germany, in keeping with their recent guarantee, but they could do nothing to come to Poland's defense. There followed several months of relative quiet—anti-interventionists in the United States sneered at the "phony war"—during which the Western powers hoped Hitler might be satisfied digesting his eastern conquests.

On the day of Hitler's invasion of Poland, reporters posed the inevitable question to Roosevelt: "Can we stay out?" Roosevelt responded that he sincerely hoped so and that his government would make an effort to keep Americans at peace.[4] But in a fireside chat two days later, he harkened back to a similar moment twenty-five years before, saying that while the United States would remain neutral in the new European war, he would not ask Americans to "remain neutral in thought as well." Even a neutral had to "take account of facts"; even a neutral could not "close his mind or his conscience." And where Wilson had expressed hope in August 1914 that the European war would not touch Americans, Roosevelt insisted that, on the contrary, "every ship that sails the sea, every battle that is fought, does affect the American future."[5]

Roosevelt now believed that the "recrudescence of German power" had "completely reoriented" America's security situation.[6] Should France and Britain fall, which he considered a reasonable possibility, the United States would be left alone to confront a single dominant power across the Atlantic, hostile to democracy, hostile to America, and possessing all the resources and manpower of the entire European continent. He feared the Luftwaffe had 1,500 aircraft capable of crossing the Atlantic to Brazil, from where they would be able to strike New Orleans. Americans would quickly find themselves "surrounded by hostile states in this hemisphere."[7] To those who claimed that the Axis powers would "never have any desire to attack the Western Hemisphere," Roosevelt insisted that this was "the same dangerous form of wishful thinking" that had already "destroyed the powers of resistance of so many conquered peoples."[8]

Even if the United States faced no immediate threat of military attack, Roosevelt warned in his January 1940 State of the Union address, the world would be a "shabby and dangerous place to live in—yes, even for Americans to live in" if it were ruled "by force in the hands of a few."[9] Such a world would threaten "the institutions of democracy."[10] To live as a "lone island" in a world dominated by the "philosophy of force" would be a "helpless nightmare of a people without freedom . . . a people lodged in prison, handcuffed, hungry, and fed through the bars from day to day by the contemptuous, unpitying masters of other continents."[11]

A week after the invasion of Poland, he declared "a limited national emergency," signing executive orders to increase further the size of the army and navy and adding an additional 150 agents to the FBI. He also called the Congress into special session to revise the neutrality legislation. This time, revision passed: 63–30 in the Senate and 243–181 in the House. The new legislation repealed the requirement for a mandatory arms embargo on both sides of a conflict and reinstated the "cash-and-carry" provision that allowed other nations to purchase American products, including weapons and ammunition, if they transported them in their own ships—a provision that largely benefited the British, who still controlled the Atlantic trade routes.

Roosevelt continued to insist that he wanted to keep the United States at peace. To prove it, he sent Sumner Welles on a mission to Europe in February 1940. But Welles returned convinced that there was only one thing in the world that could make Hitler and his acolytes pause to reflect: the certitude that if they did decide to plunge Europe into a war of devastation, the United States would go to the aid of the democracies.[12]

Less than three weeks after Welles returned, on April 9, 1940, German troops invaded Denmark and Norway. A month later German armies invaded Belgium and the Netherlands. British and French forces attempting to block the advance were routed. On May 12, German forces crossed into France. Over the next two weeks, Allied forces were driven back to the sea, and the entire British army had to be evacuated under fire at Dunkirk. On May 27, Belgium surrendered. On June 14, German troops marched into Paris. On June 22, France surrendered. In less than two months Germany had conquered almost all of western and central Europe. In Britain, Neville Chamberlain's government fell and Winston Churchill became prime minister of a new unity government.

Across the Atlantic, Americans were stunned. Before Munich, and even after the German invasion of Poland, most assumed that France was strong enough to fend off a German invasion. With the famed Maginot Line in place, they expected at worst another bloody stalemate like the First World War. To see French defenses collapse in just a few weeks was shocking. Americans suddenly confronted a situation most had not thought possible: a European continent dominated by Nazi Germany, with Great Britain possibly the next to fall. The German blitzkrieg brought a new age of warfare as mechanized armies, supported from the air, moved with lightning speed over great distances, through, around, and over previously impenetrable defenses.

Hitler's advances in the spring of 1940 jolted the American political system. On May 16, as the Germans drove British and French forces back toward the English Channel, Roosevelt addressed a joint session of Congress. As he walked into the House chamber, members of both parties "sprang to their feet and began applauding wildly in . . . a demonstration of national unity in a time of international crisis." The American people needed to "recast their thinking about national protection," the president declared. The last weeks had shown the "brutal force of modern warfare," with its "motorized armies," "lightning attacks," "parachute troops," and, above all, the threat of attack from the air. So-called "impregnable fortifications" no longer existed. Attacks could be launched in hours rather than days or weeks—from Greenland, Bermuda, the Azores, and the Caribbean—and not only against American coastal cities, he pointedly noted, but against the cities of the Midwest as well. "No attack" was so "unlikely or impossible" that its possibility could be ignored. The United States needed to produce, quickly, the weapons necessary "to make this country's defenses impregnable to modern lightning warfare," and he called for a ramping up of American industrial capacities to produce 50,000 aircraft annually—a number almost equal to all belligerent air forces combined. This call for an "aerial armada second to none" was greeted with the "wildest cheering and applause."[13]

The public response was also overwhelming—polls showed 93 percent of Democrats and 83 percent of Republicans in support of greater defense spending—and the massive increases sailed through Congress. Over the next two months Congress also approved the Two-Ocean Navy Act, the largest naval procurement bill in American history, which expanded naval combat forces by 70 percent, adding some 250 ships, including 18 aircraft carriers, 7 battleships, 27 cruisers, 115 destroyers, 43 submarines, and 15,000 naval aircraft. The appropriation, amounting to $8.55 billion ($158 billion in 2020 dollars), passed the House 316–0 after less than an hour of debate. Then, in September 1940, Congress passed the Selective Service and Training Act, the first peacetime draft in American history. All males between the ages of twenty-one and forty-five were required to register, and, if drafted, to serve a minimum of a year, chiefly for training.

Although Roosevelt's plans aimed at augmenting American power, most of the new measures would not begin to have an effect until 1942 and later. Roosevelt's chief near-term concern was to provide Britain all it needed to resist Hitler. The situation was "extremely serious," he told members of Congress in May, even before the fall of France. The "complete domination of Europe by the Nazi forces" was now likely, and the

Germans seemed determined to destroy the power of Britain, as well. That did not necessarily mean "they will be coming over here." But who could be sure? "A victor of that kind may think at the beginning that he is not going to conquer the whole world but, when the time comes and he has conquered Europe and Africa and got Asia all settled up with Japan and has some kind of practical agreement with Russia, it may be human nature for victors of that kind to say, 'I have taken two-thirds of the world and I am all armed and ready to go, why shouldn't I go whole hog and control, in a military way, the last third of the world, the Americas?'"[14]

Roosevelt and his advisers also worried Hitler might move next in South America. Those nations were virtually defenseless, and some of them, like Brazil, had large German populations that, Americans feared, would support Hitler's aims. If Britain were defeated, Roosevelt warned Americans in December 1940, the Axis powers would "control the continents of Europe, Asia, Africa, Australasia, and the high seas" and be "in a position to bring enormous military and naval resources against this hemisphere." Americans would be living "at the point of a gun—a gun loaded with explosive bullets, economic as well as military." Thus he called upon Americans to make the United States the "arsenal of democracy" and press ahead with the building of "more ships, more guns, more planes—more of everything" that could be shipped to the people of Great Britain and the British Empire, who were serving as "the spearhead of resistance to world conquest."[15]

The British indeed faced their most perilous moment in the summer of 1940. The evacuation of British forces from Dunkirk was completed on June 4. German forces marched into Paris ten days later. The "Battle of Britain" commenced in the second week of July, as the German Luftwaffe began attacking British shipping in the Channel, as well as industrial plants and other military targets in the British Isles, eventually escalating to the terror-bombing of British civilian areas, including London. Hitler's goal was to force the British to accept a negotiated peace on his terms, and many influential Britons, including the foreign secretary, Lord Halifax, favored talks lest Britain be defeated. Hitler simultaneously ordered preparations for an amphibious invasion of Britain, Operation Sea Lion, to be launched once the Luftwaffe had destroyed enough of the Royal Air Force to achieve air superiority. Churchill and a majority of the new cabinet overruled Halifax, and Churchill brought his considerable talents to bear in bucking up the morale of a fearful British public. On June 4 he gave the historic speech that galvanized British resolve, declaring in words that produced tears among Parliament ministers that "we shall defend our island, whatever the cost may be. We shall fight on the beaches, we shall fight on the landing grounds, we shall fight in the fields and in the streets, we shall fight in the hills; we shall never surrender . . ."

The speech ended, however, with a poignant hope and a scarcely concealed plea: "And if, which I do not for a moment believe, this island or a large part of it were subjugated and starving, then our Empire beyond the seas, armed and guarded by the British fleet, would carry on the struggle, until, in God's own time, the New World, with all its power and might, steps forth to the rescue and liberation of the old."

The note of reproach was no doubt intentional and certainly understandable. Churchill did not believe the war could be won without the Americans, even if the British people survived the Blitz. But at that moment, the Roosevelt administration, Congress, and the American public were reluctant to provide Britain even the weapons it needed to survive. Roosevelt and his military advisers feared that, after the fall of France, the odds were "about one in three" that Britain would fall, too, and perhaps by the end of the summer.[16] On June 18 Churchill appealed to Roosevelt again. With Germany's conquest of the coastline from Norway to the Channel, the addition of Italian submarines, and the sinking of almost half of Britain's fleet of destroyers, the British were in desperate need of immediate American assistance. The United States had hundreds of World War I destroyers, which the U.S. Navy had begun to deploy in Atlantic patrols. Britain's acquisition of a good number of these could prove critical—"a matter of life or death."[17]

But American military planners were reluctant to provide these and other weapons and supplies to the British. If Britain then surrendered, it would be a double loss. Not only would the United States not have those weapons for its own defense, but they would fall into the hands of the Germans. Roosevelt also believed Congress was "in no mood" for such a transaction. On June 24, Roosevelt approved his military advisers' recommendation that war materiel be sold to the British "only if the situation should indicate that Great Britain displayed an ability to withstand German assault, and that the release of such equipment as we could . . . spare would exercise an important effect in enabling Great Britain to resist until the first of the year."[18]

It was only when the bleak picture of June 1940 began to brighten somewhat at the end of July that Roosevelt reconsidered. Churchill, who was well aware of the reasons for American hesitation, cabled the president on July 31: "I am beginning to feel very hopeful about this war."

Britain could survive the next three or four months, but only if it could acquire some 50 to 60 of the old destroyers. "The whole fate of the war may be decided by this minor and easily remediable factor," he told Roosevelt, adding that "with great respect I must tell you that in the long history of the world, this is the thing to do now."[19]

Roosevelt was persuaded. To sell the idea to Congress and the American public, Roosevelt proposed trading the destroyers for ninety-nine-year leases on British naval and air bases in the Western Hemisphere. Normally such a deal would be unthinkable to a British leader, and Churchill tried to suggest that the United States provide the destroyers simply "in recognition of" what the British had done "for the security of the United States." This was obviously not going to work for Roosevelt, so Churchill gave in.

As it was, Roosevelt faced substantial opposition in Congress. Many regarded the deal as a blatant violation of the Neutrality Act—the former ambassador to London, Joseph Kennedy, called it an "unneutral" act likely to lead to war.[20] Roosevelt feared the decision could cost him the next election. He had decided to run for an unprecedented third term, which by itself was causing critics, and even supporters, to wonder about the president's "dictatorial" tendencies. Now critics pounced on this unprecedented executive order, which looked, among other things, like a barely concealed military alliance with Britain, as proof that Roosevelt was an aspiring tyrant. In late October, with his lead over the Republican candidate, Wendell Willkie, diminishing in the polls, Roosevelt attacked the "fantastic" charge by Republicans that he had "secretly entered into agreements with foreign nations" and gave his "solemn assurance" that he made no agreement, secret or otherwise, to "involve this nation in any war."[21] On October 30, with the latest Gallup poll showing Willkie pulling to within four points, Roosevelt declared, "I have said this before, but I shall say it again and again and again: Your boys are not going to be sent into any foreign wars."[22]

Roosevelt's re-election in November 1940, by a larger margin than the polls had predicted, allowed him to press forward with the assistance to Britain. By the end of 1940 it was clear not only that the British lacked the weaponry necessary to fend off the Germans indefinitely, but they also lacked the money to pay for weapons. "Well boys," the British ambassador told American reporters at the end of November, "Britain's broke."[23] In response to more pleading from Churchill, Roosevelt himself came up with the idea of "Lend-Lease." The United States would not ask for payment, in either cash or loans, for the ships and other war materiel. When "the show was over," the British would repay the United States "in kind." In selling this novel idea to the American public, he resorted to a "homely analogy": if a neighbor's house is on fire, he said, "I don't say to him before the operation, 'Neighbor, my garden hose cost me $15; you have to pay me $15 for it.' . . . I don't want $15—I want my garden hose back after the fire is over." In January 1941 Democrats introduced H.R. 1776, "An Act to Further Promote the Defense of the United States," which gave the president latitude "to sell, transfer title to, exchange, lease, lend, or otherwise dispose of . . . any defense article" to "any country whose defense the President deems vital to the defense of the United States" and also to determine whether repayment should be "in kind or property, or any other direct or indirect benefit."[24]

The congressional battle over Lend-Lease sparked an intense nation-wide argument, what Roosevelt would later call a "great debate." The fact that there was debate at all signaled a shift from the broad anti-interventionist consensus that had dominated American politics for almost two decades. In the months following the fall of France, the American public mood, which had already begun to shift in response to Munich and *Kristallnacht,* shifted further. In May 1940, before the Germans entered Paris, two-thirds of Americans polled believed it was more important for the United States to stay out of the war than to aid Britain if it increased the risk that the United States could be pulled in. By October 1940, after the fall of France, a majority of Americans believed it was more important to aid Britain than to stay out of the war. Only on the question of whether the United States should itself declare war were majorities consistently opposed.

Much of Americans' views on the European crisis depended, as always, on ethnicity, geography, and party. By late 1940, the new "internationalist" coalition included American Jews, a majority of Americans of Anglo-Saxon backgrounds, and the eastern establishment of bankers, lawyers, educators, and newspaper editors. Roosevelt's supporters were mostly Democrats, with a smattering of Republicans like Stimson, who for the second time in two decades found themselves in league with a Democratic president.

Not all who supported Roosevelt's policies could be called "internationalists," however. Many Democrats simply followed their president's lead, and the troubling events in Europe made it easier for them to explain the switch. Roosevelt's most reliable supporters were in the South. In the critical vote on Lend-Lease in March 1941, southerners in the Senate voted 29–1 to approve, and southerners in the House voted 120–5.[25] This made the South "the least isolationist section of the nation," but it was not because southerners were necessarily more internationalist than their midwestern neighbors.[26] Rather it was because the South was overwhelmingly Democratic; the influential cotton growers depended on the British market; and the predominantly white Anglo-Saxon Protestant South lacked what other parts of the country had in abundance—ethnic Germans, Irish, Italians, and Catholics.

A good number of Americans had genuinely changed their minds, however. The polls made that clear. The most visible shift was among liberals. The editors of the *New Republic*, who just three years earlier had vigorously opposed any involvement in the European crisis, now argued that Hitler was "a menace to this country" and, therefore, "England's battle is our own."[27] Walter Millis, author of the revisionist bestseller *Road to War*, became an outspoken supporter of helping Britain. Robert Sherwood, author of the 1935 Pulitzer Prize–winning antiwar play *Idiots Delight*, was now writing Roosevelt's speeches and ad copy for pro-Allied lobby groups.[28] Reinhold Niebuhr, whose postwar disillusionment led him to become first a pacifist, then a Marxist, then a "realist," and who believed even in early 1938 that the United States should remain out of any international conflict, shifted again after *Kristallnacht*. Having seen the "racial fanaticism inherent in the Nazi creed," he worried that the world was approaching "the final destruction of every concept of universal values upon which Western civilization has been built."[29]

Among liberals there was much rethinking of old judgments about the Great War and the peace that followed. With all that had happened since, the much-reviled Versailles Treaty did not look so terrible, and the passionate opposition to the treaty by liberals and progressives did not look so noble. The historian and social critic Lewis Mumford marveled at the "pert young men" of 1919 who had believed that after "a war of unparalleled brutality," a "perfectly just and generous treaty could be composed" in "less than six months."[30] Nor did the economic explanation of events, the blaming of the war on bankers and munitions makers, seem applicable to the present situation. "If the United States does become a belligerent," Walter Millis argued, it would "not be for business reasons."[31]

In retrospect, abstention from Europe's affairs did not seem to have been such a wise strategy. "In 1919 we had a golden opportunity," Henry Luce argued. "We bungled it in the 1920s and in the confusion of the 1930s we killed it."[32] As Lippmann put it, "Having disarmed ourselves and divided the old Allies from each other, we adopted the pious resolutions of the Kellogg Pact, and refused even to participate in the organization of a world court. Then, having obstructed the reconstruction of the world, and having seen the ensuing anarchy produce the revolutionary imperialist dictatorships of Russia, Italy, and Germany, we tried to protect the failure of isolation by the policy of insulation—by the neutrality acts which were to keep us safe by renouncing our rights."[33] "Errors of commission and omission," Max Lerner argued, had brought the world to "the threshold of an ice age, in which we shall have to fight and endure."[34]

Among internationalists there was much talk, again, of "responsibility." It was time for the United States to accept "our responsibility as a world power," Senator Harry Truman declared in early 1938.[35] Niebuhr set out the maxims of the new era: "balance of power politics" were not "sufficient to guarantee the world's peace"; Europe was no longer at the world's "strategic center" and could no longer maintain order in a "total world"; Britain no longer had "sufficient power to manipulate a balance of power alone"—in short, that there was no alternative to the consistent exercise of American global power and influence.[36]

These had been Woodrow Wilson's maxims, too. Wilson's reputation enjoyed a revival. As Sumner Welles asked, "Who saw straight and who thought straight twenty years ago?"[37] The "men of Wilson's generation," Lippmann wrote, were not "the deluded, starry-eyed, hysterical fools that our cynical historians have taught us to think they were." It had been easy "to sneer at Woodrow Wilson's demand that the world must be made safe for democracy," but now that a Nazi victory loomed, it was again obvious, as it had been to Wilson, that such a victory would leave America "morally and politically isolated" and in mortal danger.[38]

A number of national organizations formed to support Roosevelt's policies, most notably the Committee to Defend America by Aiding the Allies, founded in the wake of Germany's advances in May 1940 and chaired by the Kansas newspaper editor and lifelong Republican William Allen White. The committee declared in its founding statement that the war in Europe was a "life and death struggle for every principle we cherish in America: and it was time for the United States to "throw its economic and moral weight on the side of the nations of western Europe, great and small, that are struggling in battle for a civilized way of life."[39] Its bipartisan membership included Niebuhr, Stimson, Sherwood, the cotton-trading magnate Will Clayton, and the *Nation*'s editor, Freda Kirchwey. Anti-interventionists attacked the organization as a front for British interests and the Morgan bank, but the committee played an important role in the debates over Roosevelt's destroyers-for-bases deal, Lend-Lease, and, later, on the question of allowing U.S. naval vessels to convoy merchant ships across the Atlantic.[40]

The anti-interventionist coalition included most Republicans, naturally opposing the other party's president and sticking rigidly to long-held foreign policy principles. There was a handful of renegade Democrats, whom Roosevelt, like Wilson, had tried and failed to defeat. There were peace progressives and outright pacifists, midwestern farmers and voters in far-western mining states. A critical core came from regions with heavily Irish American, Italian American, and German American populations.[41] Each of these groups had its own reasons for opposing Roosevelt's trajectory, and not all were directly related to foreign policy. For many Catholics it was a fight against liberalism and communism at home as well as abroad. For many Republicans and conservatives, opposition to Roosevelt's foreign policies was an extension of their opposition to his domestic policies.[42] In May 1940, while the British army was facing annihilation at Dunkirk, Robert Taft declared that it was "no time for the people to be wholly absorbed in foreign battles." It was "the New Deal which may leave us weak and unprepared for attack."[43] Nor was it surprising that opponents of the "Jew Deal" opposed Roosevelt's interventionist approach to a conflict in which Jews were the most prominent victims, or that German, Irish, and Italian Americans opposed a pro-British, anti-German and anti-Italian foreign policy.[44] For almost two years after the August 1939 Nazi-Soviet Pact, the anti-interventionist coalition also included American Communists and pro-Soviet socialists following the Moscow line. They would flip back into the internationalist camp after Hitler invaded the Soviet Union in June 1941.

Among those who opposed intervention in Europe in these years were self-described "realists." They decried the "giddy" moralism and emotionalism that, in Beard's words, prevented Americans from dealing "with the world as it is."[45] Hugh Wilson, a senior member of the "realist" camp at the State Department in the 1930s, observed of Americans in general that "our most certain reaction to the stimulus of a piece of news from a foreign land is to judge it 'good' or 'bad,' 'righteous' or 'unjust.' . . . We instantly assess it by a moral evaluation based on our own standards." This moralistic approach had "poison[ed] our relations with Japan" ever since the Manchurian incident, and it poisoned America's relations with the Nazis as well.[46] As Vandenberg noted, Americans had "openly embraced" a "belligerent" stance toward Germany when Congress repealed the arms embargo in the fall of 1939, and indeed, America's hostile stance to both Germany and Japan had been clear at least as far back as 1937, when Roosevelt denounced the "bandit nations" in his quarantine speech.[47] C. Hartley Grattan, a leading revisionist, complained that such "powerful currents of emotion and opinion" had led Americans to "throw cold reason out of the window."[48]

This new breed of professional foreign policy and military experts, priding themselves on "realistic thinking," the "banishment of altruism and sentiment" from their analysis, and "single-minded attention to the national interests," insisted that contrary to Roosevelt's fear-mongering, the United States was safe from the threat of foreign invasion.[49] The United States did not have a "vital" interest in Hitler's defeat, or in Japan's.[50] Nicholas Spykman, a professor at Yale and one of the founders of the school of "classical realism," argued that with "the European neighbors of the United States . . . three thousand miles away" and the Atlantic Ocean still "reassuringly" in between, America's "frontiers" were secure. So long as the United States maintained a strong navy capable of protecting its shores and so long as "the cruising radius of bombing squadrons" remained less than four thousand miles, the Atlantic and Pacific would remain "the chief elements in the defense of the United States."[51] Hanson Baldwin, the military editor of the *New York Times,* explained in detail what an attack on the United States would require, in order to show that it was inconceivable.[52] Based on these kinds of calculations, Senator Taft argued that no other power "would be stupid enough" to try to land "troops in the United States from across thousands of miles of ocean."[53] The fall of France did not affect these assessments.[54]

Anti-interventionists also rejected Roosevelt's claim that American democracy would be at risk after a German victory.[55] They did not believe that even American trade would be affected by German and Japanese victories. The historian Howard K. Beale argued that nations did not trade with one another because they like each other's governments. If Hitler controlled Europe, Americans would still want European goods, and Europeans would still want American goods.[56] Joseph Kennedy suggested that increasing trade with Germany would actually "enmesh the Nazi government in a mutually profitable relationship that would moderate its behavior in the future."[57]

In any case, the realists ridiculed the idea that the United States could do anything to help the situation in Europe, even if that were the right thing to do. The war was the product of "national and racial animosities" that had existed for centuries and would continue to exist "for centuries to come." "European quarrels" were "everlasting" due to the "welter of races," which made even the drawing of boundaries impossible "without leaving minorities" that were a "perpetual source of friction." American involvement in the last war not only "failed to solve Europe's problems" but "helped bring about the present situation." It had been "childish" to try to impose democracy on Germany, where the "conditions" for "self-government" did not exist. Europe had to "work out its own salvation." Americans lacked the power and the wisdom, even if they had the will, to be Europe's "savior." History showed that "we can make war in Europe, but we cannot make enduring peace," Herbert Hoover argued. The "ideals of America" were "not fitted to solve these problems of Europe."[58]

American entry into the war could only bring disaster, Lindbergh and other anti-interventionists argued. The U.S. military would face the "superhuman task of crossing an ocean and forcing a landing on a fortified continent against armies stronger than our own and hardened by years of war," an operation that would mean "wholesale death" on both sides.[59] Beale suggested that before "interventionists rush our country into war they need to enlighten us on some of the practical problems involved."[60]

Accepting the world "as it is" meant adjusting rationally to the shifts in power that had already taken place in Europe.[61] George F. Kennan, then serving in the American embassy in Prague, applauded the Munich settlement and praised the Czechs for eschewing the "romantic" course of resistance in favor of the "humiliating but truly heroic one of realism."[62] Hitler, these analysts believed, was likely to win the war and probably would defeat Great Britain, too. Ever since the summer of 1939 Ambassador Joseph Kennedy had been predicting from London that the British were finished. ("I am also a bear on democracy," he commented to Lippmann. "It's gone already.")[63] Lindbergh a year later predicted that Britain's defeat would "come fast."[64] His wife, the bestselling author Anne Morrow Lindbergh, suggested that perhaps it was not "courage" but "stupidity" that made the British fight on.[65] German weaponry had shifted the balance of power in Europe irrevocably. Charles Lindbergh believed American policy should respect "the right of an able and virile nation to expand."[66] If dissatisfied "have-not" powers like Germany were bent on changing the existing system, E. H. Carr argued, the satisfied powers ought to make the necessary concessions. Indeed, "the responsibility for seeing that these changes take place . . . in an orderly way" rested as much on the defenders of the existing order as on its challengers.[67]

Americans would do better to concentrate on their own democracy, anti-interventionists argued. After the fall of France, the former editor of the *Nation,* Oswald Garrison Villard, argued that the United States could best protect itself not by "guns and warships . . . but only by greater economic and industrial wisdom, by social justice, by making our democracy work."[68] Americans, Beard argued, should "leave disputes over territory, over the ambitions of warriors, over the intrigues of hierarchies, over forms of government, over passing myths known as ideologies—all to the nations and peoples immediately and directly affected."[69]

The alternative, the anti-interventionists warned, would be a career of imperialism "wholly foreign to our ideals of democracy and freedom."[70] "We will be involved in war for the rest of our lives," Taft insisted.[71] American forces "would have to police Europe"; American garrisons "would be manning the islands of the South Seas" as well as the "ports of Latin America."[72] Vermont Republican George Aiken accused Roosevelt and his supporters of yearning to see "their flag waving in glory over the oil fields of Asia Minor and the plantations of the East Indies."[73] The pacifist A. J. Muste worried that "we shall be the next nation to seek world-domination—in other words, to do what we condemn Hitler for trying to do."[74] Taft acknowledged that a German victory might well "mean a world in which force had triumphed and international good faith had vanished." But better that than the "death and wounding of our boys, the terrible destruction of life and property, the practical establishment of a dictatorship in this country through arbitrary powers granted to the President, and financial and economic collapse." It was not "selfish," Taft insisted, to put the interests of the American people "ahead of any prejudices or sympathies with other peoples."[75] The historian William Henry Chamberlain warned that "a nation which embarks on a *crusading war* is far more likely to endanger its own liberty than to plant it elsewhere."[76] The world was "big enough to contain all kinds of different ways of life," Taft argued. The United States could not be ranging "over the world like a knight errant," protecting "democracy and ideals of good faith" and tilting, "like Don Quixote, against the windmills of fascism."[77]

To turn the public around and block Roosevelt's increasingly interventionist policies, anti-interventionists formed the America First Committee in September 1940. Although often depicted as a movement of middle American populism, the organization was founded and led by members of the American elite. Established originally by a group of Yale students, the committee soon boasted an impressive list of wealthy and influential supporters that included the textile magnate Henry Regnery; the chairman of the board of Sears Roebuck, General Robert E. Wood;

Chester Bowles, an advertising executive; H. Smith Richardson of the Vick Chemical Company; and the president of the Hormel meatpacking company. It had the support of several prominent generals from World War I, as well as such potent public figures as former ambassador Joseph Kennedy and the famed aviator Charles Lindbergh. The list of younger America First supporters included two future presidents of the United States, John F. Kennedy and Gerald Ford; a future Supreme Court justice, Potter Stewart; a future president of Yale, Kingman Brewster; and the novelist Gore Vidal. By December 1941 the America First Committee counted 800,000 members in over 400 chapters in cities and towns across the country.[78] In its first and biggest fight, against the Lend-Lease Act in early 1941, the committee distributed hundreds of thousands of pieces of literature and coordinated its membership to flood congressional offices in Washington with mail, phone calls, and telegrams.[79] What effect all this had was less clear. Public support for Lend-Lease actually grew during this impressive publicity campaign, even in areas of the country where the committee boasted the largest following.[80]

America First came late to the fight, however. By the time of the "great debate" of 1940–1941, U.S. policy was already well down the road to intervention. The repeal of the arms embargo and the implementation of "cash-and-carry" in 1939, the launch of the enormous arms buildup in 1940, which the majority of anti-interventionists supported, and the "destroyers-for bases" deal in September 1940 had all but locked American policy into a pro-British and anti-German course. As the historian Harry Elmer Barnes tartly observed, it was hard to imagine that the United States could have done much more to help the British than it had already done. Had "Germany wished to declare war on us," Roosevelt had already "offered her many opportunities to do so on the best legal grounds."[81] The anti-interventionists made their stand against Lend-Lease, but they were trying to shut the barn door long after the horses had departed. The only hope of keeping the United States out of the war was for Britain to be defeated—which many anti-interventionists quietly expected and hoped for. They never won a policy battle after July 1939.

Roosevelt was a formidable adversary. In the "great debate" over the League, twenty years before, Henry Cabot Lodge could count on Wilson's self-righteous stubbornness and a commitment to principle that limited his ability to outmaneuver his opponents. But Roosevelt was a far more slippery and savvy politician. He generally told the American people what he knew they wanted to hear and no more than what he thought they needed to hear. Although the anti-interventionists incessantly charged that Roosevelt's real aim was to get the United States into the war, or, at the very least, that he was willing to provoke Hitler until *he* fired the first shot, Roosevelt simply accused them of lying.[82] The nastiest exchange occurred in early 1941, when Senator Burton K. Wheeler, a leading anti-interventionist Democrat from Montana, called Lend-Lease "the New Deal's triple 'A' foreign policy—it will plow under every fourth American boy." Roosevelt called it "the most untruthful" and "most dastardly, unpatriotic thing that has ever been said."[83] He promised categorically—too categorically, Stimson and other advisers thought—that "your boys are not going to be sent into any foreign wars!"[84] The anti-interventionists called him a liar, but the public either believed him or didn't hold his dissembling against him.

Of course, it is possible that Roosevelt would not admit to himself that his policies might lead to full-scale American intervention. There is no evidence that, prior to Pearl Harbor, Roosevelt ever seriously considering sending American forces to Europe. He was counting on the navy and strategic bombing as the key to winning the war.[85] Among his top advisers, only General George C. Marshall believed in 1941 that a massive ground assault on Europe would be necessary. Only in late September of 1941 did the army and navy come up with a plan for defeating Hitler, and the army's planners estimated it would take a force of at least 5 million troops, and eventually as many as 8.8 million. Roosevelt put the plan on hold, firmly of the belief that the American people would never tolerate sending such a massive force to Europe.[86] He continued to suggest, and perhaps to believe, that a sizable deployment of American forces would not be necessary. Meanwhile, he only sought public approval for measures well short of that, thereby offering the anti-interventionists no opening to exploit public opposition to full-scale American intervention.

Roosevelt enjoyed one enormous advantage. When Henry Cabot Lodge waged his fight against Wilson, the Republicans controlled the Senate and employed all the powers of Congress to block Wilson's program: lengthy congressional hearings, delayed votes, and a steady stream of complicating amendments and reservations. In 1940 and 1941, by contrast, the anti-interventionist Republicans did not control Congress, its key committees, or the legislative agenda. Despite picking up seats in the 1938 elections, the party remained badly outnumbered—68–25 in the Senate, 252–172 in the House. This was a serious impediment to battling any president, let alone one as crafty as Roosevelt. The president and his allies in Congress brought measures to the floor only when sure of victory; they squelched legislative measures designed by Roosevelt's opponents to embarrass or corner the administration. Anti-interventionist resolutions, such as one opposing the convoying of ships across the Atlantic by the U.S. Navy, were bottled up and defeated in committee.[87] A straightforward declaration of war, which the anti-interventionists demanded be put to a vote, never made it to the floor.[88] Instead, Roosevelt had the luxury of picking his battles, seeking authorization only for those steps "short of war" that he knew the public would support.[89]

Finally, the Republican Party itself suffered from internal weakness and division, and the anti-interventionists were far from dominant. The Republican convention in the summer of 1940 was a free-for-all. France was falling just as the convention opened in June in Philadelphia. Four days before the convention, Roosevelt named two Republicans to his administration, Henry Stimson as secretary of war and Frank Knox as secretary of the navy. At the convention, the leading anti-interventionist candidates—Taft and Vandenberg—were defeated by the popular dark horse, Wendell Willkie, who ran an unorthodox, renegade campaign outside the control of the party bosses. One reason for Taft's loss, in addition to his limitations as a politician, was that eastern delegates, representing the more internationalist wing of the party, voted overwhelmingly against him, partly because of his stance toward the European war.[90] In 1920, Borah and the irreconcilables were in full control, able to block internationalist candidates and force the chosen nominee, Harding, to toe the anti-League line. Twenty years later, the anti-interventionists could not even prevent an internationalist from winning the Republican presidential nomination.

Willkie was a former Democrat, a past supporter of the League of Nations, and fundamentally in agreement with Roosevelt's foreign policies. Once nominated, he refused to read off the anti-interventionist script until near the end of the campaign. Republican Party operatives naturally wanted to cast Roosevelt as the man who would drag Americans into war. In one Republican radio ad the announcer darkly warned, "When your boy is dying on some battlefield in Europe and he's crying out 'Mother! Mother!'—don't blame Franklin D. Roosevelt because he sent your boy to war—blame yourself, because you sent Franklin D. Roosevelt back to the White House."[91] But Willkie for much of the campaign refused to play this card.[92]

Roosevelt also benefited from Americans' somewhat contradictory views of the international situation. On the one hand, Americans overwhelmingly opposed going to war. But polls also showed that 80 percent of Americans believed the United States would end up at war anyway. If so, a large majority believed Roosevelt would do a better job leading the nation than his untested challenger. Indeed, Willkie's campaign manager later concluded that Roosevelt was "invincible" in 1940 precisely because the American people thought he would be the "best able to prosecute a war."[93]

Roosevelt feared the election would be close, if only because of opposition to an unprecedented third term. It was not. Roosevelt won by a landslide: 54.7 percent to 44.8 in the popular vote; 449–82 in the Electoral College. He swept both coasts, the South, and the Northeast, leaving Willkie only the plains states and part of the Midwest. This thrashing may not have been a direct repudiation of the anti-interventionists, since Willkie was not their candidate, but no one doubted that their preferred candidates would have fared just as badly. More importantly, the election results freed Roosevelt to move more quickly and boldly and left the anti-interventionists little if any hope of stopping him.

CHAPTER TWENTY-TWO

Accelerating Toward War

When you see a rattlesnake poised to strike, you do not wait until he has struck before you crush him.

—Franklin D. Roosevelt, September 11, 1941[1]

If I am told to fight regardless of the consequences, I shall run wild for the first six months or a year, but I have utterly no confidence for the second or third years.

—Admiral Isoroku Yamamoto[2]

What is America but millionaires, beauty queens, stupid records and Hollywood?

—Adolf Hitler[3]

FOLLOWING THE fall of France and his re-election, Roosevelt substantially increased American involvement in what had become the critical "Battle of the Atlantic." The conquest of France gave the Germans new bases on the Atlantic coast from which to operate against British shipping and their naval convoys. This greatly extended the reach of the German U-boat fleet, which had grown and become more sophisticated in its tactics. Now attacking in the waters around Greenland and the western Atlantic, the Germans by early 1941 were sinking British merchant ships at a rate more than five times Britain's capacity to replace them. Roosevelt's alarmed advisers, led by Stimson, army chief of staff George Marshall, and the chief of naval operations, Admiral Harold Stark, argued for direct American military involvement to protect Britain's transatlantic lifeline. They also recommended shifting the bulk of the Pacific fleet to the Atlantic. Roosevelt, who feared that the public was not yet ready, was reluctant to take such a big "step forward"—to which Stimson replied, "Well, I hope you will keep on walking, Mr. President. Keep on walking."[4] Once Lend-Lease became law in March, however, and it became clear that it would serve no purpose if all the new outpouring of American supplies ended up at the bottom of the ocean, Roosevelt started taking steps. He began allowing British ships to be repaired in American ports. He transferred coast guard cutters to the Royal Navy. He gained the Danish government's permission to place Greenland under American control and authorized the establishment of bases there to help defend transatlantic shipping. In April he authorized the navy to begin working with the British on plans for escorting convoys. And although he continued to shy away from announcing such a policy openly—an April poll suggested the public was still opposed, 50–41—he ordered U.S. naval patrols to help the British spot German subs.[5]

A string of Nazi victories in the spring of 1941 made the situation more dire. German forces invaded and occupied Greece, after the Italians had failed to accomplish that task. Yugoslavia fell in eleven days. With General Erwin Rommel leading his Afrika Korps, the Germans were punishing British and Australian forces in North Africa. Churchill, who feared that the next move would be an attack on the British stronghold of Gibraltar, giving the Axis powers control of the mouth of the Mediterranean, begged Roosevelt to step up American assistance and even to enter the war officially. Unless the United States took "more advanced positions now, or very soon," he warned, ". . . vast balances may be tilted heavily to our disadvantage."[6]

Roosevelt agreed that the situation was grave and pushed ahead as far as he thought the American public would allow. "Unless the advance of Hitlerism is checked now," he warned in a speech at the end of May, "the Western Hemisphere will be within range of the Nazi weapons of destruction." Referring to Cape Verde and the Azores as the "island outposts of the New World" (although they were between 2,100 and 3,000 miles from the closest North American coast), he warned that if they fell, along with the "Atlantic fortress of Dakar" on the westernmost tip of Africa, then Hitler would be poised to threaten "the ultimate safety of the continental United States itself."[7] He issued a proclamation that "an unlimited national emergency exists" and called for "strengthening of our defense to the extreme limit of our national power and authority."[8] In June he ordered 4,000 U.S. Marines to take positions in Iceland, to relieve British forces and allow them to operate elsewhere.

The symbolic climax of this growing American involvement in the war came in August when Roosevelt and Churchill met on a warship off the coast of Newfoundland. There they produced a document outlining their joint vision of a postwar peace, or as Roosevelt put it, a list of "certain principles relating to the civilization of the world." What became known as the Atlantic Charter signaled a degree of Anglo-American cooperation that was tantamount to a military alliance in all but name. Churchill came away from the meeting with the impression that Roosevelt "was obviously determined that they should come in." He was "skating on pretty thin ice in his relations with Congress," however, and although he did not regard the Congress "as truly representative of the country," nevertheless, if he sought a declaration of war, there would be three months of debate with a most uncertain outcome. Instead, Roosevelt planned to "wage war, but not declare it." American policy would become "more and more provocative" in the hope of forcing an "incident" that would justify "opening hostilities."[9]

Churchill probably exaggerated Roosevelt's determination to "force" an incident. The president continued to regard the public as wary of a declaration of war, even while supportive of helping Britain survive the Nazi onslaught. As Lord Halifax observed, Roosevelt's "perpetual problem was to steer a course between . . . (1) the wish of 70 percent of Americans to keep out of war; (2) the wish of 70 percent of Americans to do everything to break Hitler, even if it means war." As far as Roosevelt was concerned, Halifax quipped, "declarations of war were out of fashion."[10] Even Churchill had to admit, moreover, that Hitler's cautious policies toward the United States offered little prospect of an "incident" that could justify a declaration of war. To one adviser Roosevelt commented that while it was easy for an individual to swing quickly from one extreme position to another, "governments, such as ours, cannot swing so far so quickly. They can only move in keeping with the thought and will of the great majority of our people."[11]

Roosevelt was certainly willing to make use of an incident to expand America's undeclared participation in the Atlantic war, however. Three weeks after the Roosevelt-Churchill meeting, on September 4, a German submarine fired torpedoes at an American destroyer, the USS *Greer,* which in turn dropped depth charges. Even American officials believed the U-boat commander did not know he was firing at an American warship, but Roosevelt made the most of the incident. "This was no mere episode in a struggle between two nations," he declared in a radio talk. It was part of a determined effort by Germany to create "a permanent world system based on force, on terror and on murder." American security, he insisted, was now directly threatened. "For if the world outside of the Americas falls under Axis domination, the shipbuilding facilities which the Axis powers would then possess in all of Europe, in the British Isles, and in the Far East would be much greater than all the shipbuilding facilities and potentialities of all of the Americas—not only greater, but two or three times greater—enough to win."[12] Roosevelt warned again that it was "time for all Americans . . . to stop being deluded by the romantic notion that the Americas can go on living happily and peacefully in a Nazi-dominated world." He then announced his new policy. "We have sought no shooting war with Hitler," he told Americans, and "we do not seek it now." But "when you see a rattlesnake poised to strike, you do not wait until he has struck before you crush him." The "Nazi submarines" were "the rattlesnakes of the Atlantic," he declared. Therefore, "our patrolling vessels and planes will protect all merchant ships— not only American ships but ships of any flag—engaged in commerce in our defensive waters. . . . Let this warning be clear. From now on, if German or Italian vessels of war enter the waters, the protection of which is necessary for American defense, they do so at their own peril." Roosevelt would later be accused of misleading Americans about the risks he was taking. In this case, however, he said he had "no illusions about the gravity of this step. I have not taken it hurriedly or lightly. It is the result of months and months of constant thought and anxiety and prayer. In the protection of your Nation and mine it cannot be avoided."[13]

As he no doubt hoped and expected, the majority of Americans were with him on this latest escalation. Sixty-two percent of those polled approved of a policy of "shoot on sight."[14]

As he also may have feared, however, Congress was less supportive. In an effort to bring the neutrality legislation in line with his new policies, Roosevelt first asked Congress to revise the legislation to allow American-flagged merchant ships to arm themselves for the transatlantic crossing. This passed on October 16, the day after a German submarine attacked the U.S. destroyer *Kearny.* Then he asked Congress for a further revision allowing American vessels to deliver Lend-Lease goods directly to British ports, a repeal of cash-and-carry. This passed the Senate, but only by 50–37, the smallest majority of any foreign policy vote taken since the outbreak of the war. Given that Democrats enjoyed a 66–28 majority, it was no wonder that Senator Hiram Johnson celebrated the "nearness" of the tally. In the House, revision passed by only 18 votes, 212–194, despite the

Democrats' 268–162 majority.[15] It was clear to Roosevelt that it would take more time and more severe "incidents" to bring the country around.

If Roosevelt was waiting for Hitler to fire the first shot, however, he would have to wait a long time. Hitler's attitude toward the United States had gone through a rapid evolution after the invasion of Poland. From giving almost no thought to the United States as a factor in the war, he had since come to regard the Roosevelt-led Americans as a serious obstacle. By late 1940, all his strategic plans revolved around keeping the United States out of the war until he was ready to take it on.

Hitler certainly knew the role the United States was capable of playing in Europe. In 1922, asked by a friend, "Why did we lose?" he responded, "Because America came in."[16] In *Mein Kampf* and in his unpublished second book, completed in 1928, Hitler had regarded the United States as a "new force" that threatened to "upset the existing balance of power among nations."[17] The Americans had everything Hitler wanted for Germany: a vast continent, unlimited resources, and a large, predominantly northern European population. He had admired the restrictive immigration law of 1924 that seemed to ensure America's place as the supreme "Aryan" nation in the world.

Two decades of determined American passivity and abstention from European politics, however, and the onset of the Great Depression had made him almost forget that the United States mattered.[18] Like that of most German leaders, Hitler's strategic vision did not extend far beyond the European continent anyway—his "land-mindedness" was a "barrier to any realistic comprehension by the Führer of America's role."[19] He had also developed a deep disdain for American society. To someone like Hitler, American behavior since the war had been both baffling and contemptible. As one German official put it, "Here was a country which had decided the last war, without seizing advantage at the peace conference, had proposed the League of Nations and let it fail, and now was making grandiose gestures while keeping its hands tied with neutrality legislation." Hitler and others concluded that Americans were decadent and incapable of overcoming the internal contradictions of their society.[20] "What is America but millionaires, beauty queens, stupid records and Hollywood?" he later remarked. It was a "decayed country, with problems of race and social inequality, of no ideas," "half Judaized half negrified with everything built on the dollar." The Americans, he said, "live like sows, though in a most luxurious stye," controlled by "Jewish robbers and moneybags." Especially after the hostile American reaction to *Kristallnacht,* Hitler regarded the nation as "a Jewish rubbish heap."[21]

When Congress refused to amend the neutrality legislation in the summer of 1939, Hitler was even more convinced that the United States was hopelessly weak and incapable of getting in his way.[22] Berlin officials saw Congress's failure to act as "a severe defeat for warmonger Roosevelt" and further proof that, notwithstanding Roosevelt's anti-German prejudices, the American public was more intent than ever on "neutrality and isolation."[23] Even if Congress eventually changed its mind, American arms industries were only just beginning to move to large-scale production. In two years the United States would be producing more weapons and materiel than any other power, but it would be too late to make a difference. As Hitler and his military advisers looked ahead to the anticipated attack on Poland, and the likely reaction of Britain, France, Russia, and other powers, they didn't even discuss the United States.[24]

This long period of indifference ended with the invasion of Poland and the first in a series of misjudgments by Hitler. After his successes in Austria and Czechoslovakia, Hitler assumed the British would not fight over Poland either. He therefore expected the war to remain localized and limited.[25] When Britain and France shocked and infuriated him by making good on their pledges and declaring war after the invasion of Poland, America's role suddenly began to loom larger. For one thing, some German officials, including the former ambassador to Washington, Hans Heinrich Dieckhoff, believed that the hope of eventual American support had toughened the British and French response to the invasion of Poland. In any case, the war would now be neither short nor limited, which meant that both America's own rearmament and its ability to aid the allies with arms, materiel, and money were now critical factors. On September 12, Foreign Minister Ernst von Weizsäcker told Ribbentrop that Germany had "a great interest in preventing the United States from throwing her weight into the scales on the side of our foes."[26]

Hitler, who was capable of rapid shifts both in his analysis and his policies when circumstances changed, now acknowledged that time was "working against Germany." He worried that, in a prolonged conflict, "certain states" would be "drawn into the enemy camp."[27] He continued to hope that the American public and Congress would resist Roosevelt and the Jews—the German press still emphasized American "isolationism," running the photographs and statements of Borah, Lindbergh, Father Coughlin, and others under the heading, "The Commonsense

Front."[28] But in December German intelligence noted that interventionist sentiment seemed to be growing, thanks largely to Roosevelt. The president's mastery of American politics made him a formidable enemy. As one German official put it, "It would be a mistake to compare Roosevelt with Wilson, a lethargic politician." Roosevelt's "sole aim" was to "gain time in order to muster all his propaganda machinery" against Germany.[29] Ambassador Dieckhoff warned in a memorandum in January 1940 that if the Americans were drawn into the conflict, they would "step up their production of arms and munitions to the maximum with the result that material aid to England will also be considerably increased." The "compromise peace" that Hitler hoped to force on the British would be "out of the question once America entered the war, since there would then be doubts about Germany's final victory."[30]

Roosevelt's re-election to a third term in November 1940 made America's eventual involvement almost a certainty. Hitler and his advisers knew that in 1941 U.S. aircraft production would exceed that of the Reich and that by the end of 1941 the U.S. would possess a modern, well-equipped army with 1,500,000 troops. Hitler told General Alfred Jodl in December 1940 that Germany needed to solve all continental problems in 1941 "because in 1942 the United States will be ready to intervene."[31]

The dilemma Hitler faced was the same one faced by the German General Staff after 1914. To force Britain out of the war required cutting off its American lifeline, which could only be accomplished, if at all, by a full-scale U-boat campaign. Yet such a campaign was almost certain to bring the United States into the war. In the first war Germany had suspended attacks for as long as possible in order to keep the Americans from intervening. Hitler tried to do the same. When a German submarine on September 3, 1939, sank the passenger ship SS *Athenia,* bound from Liverpool to Montreal, killing all 117 passengers and crew, including 28 Americans, Hitler immediately issued an order forbidding attacks on passenger ships. He forbade use of the term "unconditional submarine warfare." Unlike German military leaders in 1917, he was not about to let a U-boat captain bring the United States into the war before he was ready.[32] In February 1940 he vetoed the navy's suggestion of sending submarines to patrol near Halifax, Canada, because he worried about "the psychological effect on America." After the fall of France, when military advisers told him that American intervention on Britain's side was inevitable, Hitler still resisted actions that might provoke Roosevelt. Even when American forces occupied Greenland and Iceland in July 1941, and his naval advisers urged Hitler to declare war, he held back. Three months later, he rejected the navy's request to shell the Dutch island of Aruba in the Caribbean, because the oil facilities there belonged to Standard Oil.[33]

The need to gain his objectives before the Americans entered the war led Hitler to two momentous and related decisions. The first was to try to convince the Japanese to step up their aggression in the Far East against British holdings in the hope of drawing the United States into the East Asian imbroglio. The second was to speed up the timetable for his planned attack on the Soviet Union, in the hope of completing his conquest of the continent before the Americans could bring their power fully to bear.

German officials had long regarded Japan as a critical asset when it came to the United States. They recalled how concerned Wilson and other Americans had been about Japan during the first war—Wilson had repeatedly justified his reluctance to enter the war against Germany on the grounds that it would free Japan to pursue its ambitions in the Far East—and that was when Japan was still nominally an ally.[34] Now Japan had joined the Axis. The Germans assumed that the United States would do anything to avoid a two-front war—always the Germans' own nightmare—and that fear of Japan would force Roosevelt to keep the bulk of the American fleet in the Pacific rather than the Atlantic.[35] In September 1940, Hitler told Mussolini that "a close cooperation with Japan" was the "best way either to keep America entirely out of the picture or to render her entry into the war ineffective."[36]

Whether the Japanese could be induced to play this role, however, was uncertain and would be a continuing source of anxiety for Hitler for the next two years. Unlike Hitler, Japanese leaders had never lost sight of the importance of the United States to all their calculations. The threat posed by the United States had been the subject of unending debate and discussion since the First World War, when the Japanese had been forced to back down in the face of Wilson's opposition to their attempt to control China and Manchuria. Then in the immediate postwar years the Japanese had adjusted themselves to a new American-dominated liberal world order. Except for the most extreme factions in the military and various civilian imperialist and patriotic societies, most of the leading politicians and military officials believed that war with the United States should be avoided if at all possible.

By the 1930s, however, the Japanese had shifted course. A critical turning point had been the conquest of Manchuria, which had badly damaged relations between Japan and the United States. The attack itself both revealed and strengthened some new trends in Japanese society, particularly the growing influence of the military, and within the military, the growing influence of younger, more aggressive army officers. This was part of a broader shift in Japanese society, an increasingly widespread rejection of the Anglo-American liberal capitalist world order, and, indeed, of liberalism itself.

Many factors contributed to shaping this course. One was the Great Depression, which many regarded as a failure of Anglo-American democratic capitalism. For decades the United States had been "the model for Japanese businesses." Japanese elites had partnered with American businessmen and financiers, sent their sons to American universities, and generally thought of themselves as part of the global liberal economic order. In Roosevelt's first term, business interests on both sides even tried to repair the damage to economic relations caused by Japan's military actions in Manchuria. The Japanese sent business missions to the United States, and the United States sent Charlie Chaplin and Babe Ruth to Japan as goodwill ambassadors to promote cultural exchange. But the persistence of the Depression in the United States led to questions about the viability of the American system, and Japanese observers came to regard the United States as suffering from terminal economic decline. It didn't help that the Roosevelt administration, which had not moved past the Manchurian affair, imposed limits on American private lending to Japan.[37]

The American turn to more protectionist trade policies, along with the British imposition of imperial trade preferences, also had a significant impact on Japanese attitudes. The Anglo-American world itself was no longer devoted to free trade, and Japan was among the primary victims. Japanese businessmen who had advocated cooperation with the Anglo-American economic order could see that the world was moving away from free trade and toward the formation of competing economic blocs. As the director general of Mitsubishi Bank lamented, "Every country is today more nationalistic in its commercial policy than ever before." He feared that "economic nationalism" would not only prevent global economic recovery but also "engender international ill will and . . . threaten international political stability."[38] Those of a less liberal disposition believed that Japan had no choice but to form its own economic bloc. In the present struggle of great powers, each would rise and fall based on its ability "to acquire more resources, mobilize its people, and drive out other nations' economic and political influences from the region under its control."[39]

These changes in the external environment coincided with the ongoing cultural, social, and political struggles that had roiled Japan since its drive to adopt "modern" Western practices in the Meiji era. Economic, political, and social "modernization" naturally clashed with powerful ancient Japanese traditions. When times were good and Japan prospered, some of these divisions were submerged, but they never disappeared. The global depression, though it did not hit Japan as hard as it hit the United States and Britain, brought these divisions back to the surface. American protectionism and Britain's imperial preference system, combined with the Depression-era collapse in the demand for Japanese silk and other products, fell particularly hard on Japanese farmers, who formed a key constituency of the anti-liberal and anti-modern forces. Japanese nationalists and conservatives, long dissatisfied with what appeared to them as Japanese subservience to the West, demanded a rejection of "inauthentic modernism," "individualism," and the licentious "sensuality" of urban life, all of which they blamed on Japan's attempt to integrate itself into the Anglo-American liberal capitalist world system. This included such foreign imports as democracy.[40] As in Weimar Germany, democracy looked to many Japanese as divisive and dysfunctional—the endless squabbling of the political parties pursuing the selfish interests of their constituencies. As in Germany, liberal "individualism" was increasingly seen as antithetical to Japanese traditions and its vital interests.[41] Conservatives and nationalists demanded a return to the "imperial way," which could once again unite the Japanese people in an organic, traditional polity under the divine authority of the emperor.

The "resulting discontent" introduced a "note of stridency into Japanese politics," including violence.[42] Successive prime ministers, high-ranking civilian officials, and private business leaders were assassinated by young army and navy officers and others belonging to or influenced by the more radical patriotic societies—"government by assassination."[43] After 1932, the party cabinets that had led governments during the era of Taisho democracy died out. With few exceptions, Japanese prime ministers would henceforth be chosen from the senior ranks of the army and navy. By the end of the decade the political parties had simply disappeared. The demand for uniformity of thought and action increasingly silenced opposition and dissent. The Justice and Home Ministries "strengthened their programs of thought control." In 1934 the Army Ministry published a pamphlet denouncing the "ideas of liberalism, individualism, and internationalism which neglect the nation." It called for "the education of the people in order to organize and control the great potential spiritual and physical energy of the imperial nation for the sake of national defense and to administer it in a unified manner."[44]

As in Germany, much of the drive for unity and national organization aimed at preparing the people for the great struggle ahead. If saving the Japanese soul, spirit, and nation meant throwing off the dominating influences of the Anglo-American order, that could hardly be done while Japan remained dependent on, and therefore vulnerable to, American economic power. Military and civilian leaders insisted, as some of them had been doing for decades, that Japan's survival required further expansion to acquire the resources necessary to relieve the dangerous dependence.

Liberals like Foreign Minister Shidehara had argued that Japan could get what it needed through peaceful cooperation with both the West and the Chinese. But this view was largely discredited over the course of the 1920s, both by the violent resistance of the Chinese and by Washington and London's refusal to work with Japan to defend their common interests.[45] Many Japanese officials had come to regard the "existing international order with disdain, distrust, and hostility." What they sought was a "new order" in Asia, an "autarkic economic bloc under Japanese leadership." Japanese thinkers and officials envisioned a sphere of "co-prosperity" among Asian peoples.[46] This "pan-Asian" ideal had animated Japanese foreign policy at least as far back as the Great War, and Japan's desire at the Paris Peace Conference, thwarted by Wilson, had been to gain the world's recognition of Japan as the leader of the Asian peoples. In the 1920s this pan-Asian outlook took a back seat to cooperation and integration with the West. Now the priorities were reversed: "coexistence with the West, which had been primary, became secondary; relationships with Asians, which had been secondary, became primary."[47]

Some advocates of the "new order" in Asia believed it could be achieved without collision with the United States. Others feared that the United States would never tolerate Japanese expansion and control of China and would eventually seek to thwart it, just as it had in Paris in 1919 and at the Washington Conference of 1922.[48] Therefore, Japan had to move quickly to acquire the resources and power necessary to prevail in the inevitable conflict. In the new international circumstances, with the rise of competing economic blocs, survival depended on a nation's ability "to acquire more resources, mobilize its people, and drive out other nations' economic and political influences from the region under its control."[49]

In practical terms, this meant extending Japan's control of China. But it also meant striking out in new directions to end Japan's dependence on the United States, particularly for that most vital of military resources: oil. The Imperial Navy, which had been left out of the recent military actions, argued for an expansion of naval power into the South Pacific to gain access to natural resources—and, above all, oil—in advance of any possible conflict with either the United States or the Soviet Union. Only with secure access to the oil reserves of the Dutch East Indies could Japan safeguard what it had already gained on the mainland and prepare for future contingencies. In 1936 the Japanese leadership decided to pursue this southward advance.[50]

Events in Europe and the shifting power balance within the West encouraged this more aggressive course. Before 1933 the Anglo-American liberal world order had been the only game in town—the United States itself was the only power, other than Japan, left standing after the Great War—and the Japanese had accommodated themselves to this reality. But by the mid-1930s, with Germany and Italy challenging the Anglo-American hegemony in Europe with increasing success, the Japanese saw a more open field in Asia. As in 1914, war in Europe opened new opportunities for Japan on the other side of the planet.

A decisive turning point came in the spring of 1937. A new government came into office, headed by Prince Konoe, the man who two decades earlier had denounced the "Anglo-Saxon peace" and the relegation of Japan to the status of "have-not" nation. As prime minister, Konoe declared that peace could no longer be the sole object of Japanese foreign policy. It was time for Japan to "work out new principles of international peace from our own perspective."[51] The July 1937 "incident" on the Marco Polo Bridge provided the occasion, and the full-scale invasion of China launched that month brought into the open the fundamental clash between Japan and the West that had been simmering below the surface since the Manchurian incident six years before. After Japanese forces seized Shanghai, Nanking, Hangchow, Canton, and Hankow, Konoe proclaimed the "New Order" on November 3, 1938, which was the birthday of the Meiji emperor. It was also, perhaps not coincidentally, just a month after the British and French retreat at Munich.

The war boldly defied the West and accelerated the evolution of Japanese politics toward authoritarianism and militarism. To meet the war's demands, and in keeping with the conservative, anti-democratic trend, Konoe's ministry launched the nation into a full-scale war economy. A National Mobilization Law gave the government broad powers as Japan poured more than a million troops into China over the first year of the war. When the Konoe government resigned at the end of 1939, amidst popular frustration with the high cost and indeterminate results of the war, a new government led by a leading right-wing politician and founder of one of the nationalist anti-democratic societies further deepened the role of the state and the organization of society around the war effort. To Western observers, Japan had moved "a long way on the road to totalitarian statehood."[52]

It had also moved a long way toward an alliance with Nazi Germany. In November 1936, Japan had signed the Anti-Comintern Pact in Berlin, but that was only a first step.[53] The strategic benefits of an alliance with Germany seemed obvious. The Soviet Union would be restrained in the east by fear of a German attack in the west. Britain, France, and the Dutch would have to think twice before challenging Japan's expansion southward against their colonial holdings. The Chinese would see that all their potential supporters in Europe were unwilling to challenge the Japanese position on the Asian mainland and thus would be more likely to accept Tokyo's terms.[54] The Imperial Army, which was carrying the burden of the war with China, was particularly eager to strengthen military ties with Germany.

Japanese leaders were still divided, however. The war in China was not going well. By early 1939, the army seemed hopelessly bogged down, unable to strike a fatal blow against Chiang Kai-shek, but consuming massive quantities of oil, machine tools, steel, and other critical resources, which only increased Japan's dependence on the United States.[55] Another problem was the growing strength of the Soviet Union in the Far East. In the spring of 1939, Japan's Kwantung Army in Manchuria engaged in border skirmishes with Soviet and Mongolian forces that quickly escalated into full-scale war. The result was a humiliating and costly defeat of the Japanese Sixth Army by a superior Soviet force led by the legendary general Georgy Zhukov (later to be the architect of the defense of Leningrad, Moscow, and Stalingrad). The Japanese sued for peace and reached a truce in September; the two powers would not fight again until the Soviets joined the Pacific war in August 1945.[56]

The biggest blow to those advocating closer ties with Germany, however, was the surprise announcement of the Nazi-Soviet Pact in August 1939. Occurring almost exactly as the Japanese were being defeated by the Soviets, Hitler's diplomatic reversal, with no advance warning to Tokyo, left the Japanese suddenly isolated. The pro-German approach now looked like a disaster. News of the pact led to the resignation of the government and the naming of a new cabinet under General Nobuyuki Abe, with instructions from the emperor to "cooperate with England and the United States."[57]

By 1939, however, there was little interest in either London or Washington for rapprochement with Tokyo. The predominant view for some time had been that Japan was bent on achieving "absolute economic domination" in East Asia and beyond. This view only hardened with the Japanese invasion of China in the summer of 1937 and Konoe's announcement a year later of the "New Order" in Asia.[58] The Japanese desire for rapprochement in 1939 was therefore greeted with suspicion and cynicism. As one Asia hand in the British Foreign Office put it, Japan's "new friendliness" was simply due to fear of the Soviets. Once the Japanese got past the crisis, there was no guarantee that the Anglo-Americans would not be "next on the menu."[59]

Joseph Grew, the long-serving U.S. ambassador in Tokyo, disagreed. With the new Abe government in place, he thought there was hope for another swing of the pendulum and a revival of "Shidehara Diplomacy." "We are here dealing not with a unified Japan," he cabled Hull, "but with a Japanese Government which is endeavoring courageously, even with only gradual success, to fight against a recalcitrant Japanese Army, a battle which happens to be our own battle." Grew believed the United States had a choice: either "direct American-Japanese relations into a progressively healthy channel," or "accelerate their movement straight down hill."[60]

Stanley Hornbeck, another longtime State Department Asia hand who had worked closely with Henry Stimson during the Manchurian crisis, thought it was a mistake to imagine that the "civilian" element in Japan would ever regain control of the "military" element. Changing military and economic factors would determine the course of "the Japanese military machine." American diplomacy could only "slightly accelerate or slightly retard the movements of that machine." "Practically the whole of the Japanese population" enthusiastically supported "expansion and aggrandizement of the Japanese empire," Hornbeck argued. Unless and until the Japanese military met with "reverses," this course would not change. There might be "slightly perceptible" changes in "strategy and tactics," but not of "attitude nor of heart."[61]

For Roosevelt, and for many others, however, Japanese behavior could not be viewed in isolation from other disturbing trends around the world. After the German takeover of Austria in March 1938 and the Munich agreement in September, followed a few months later by Hitler's takeover of all of Czechoslovakia, Japan's aggression in China and its internal evolution toward authoritarianism came to be viewed as part of the overall assault on the democracies. Whether or not American interests were directly affected—and even Hornbeck did not believe the United States had interests in China worth fighting for—Japan's war in China and its ambitions in Southeast Asia were, as one American diplomat put it, part of a much larger "world problem."[62] Even Grew sometimes worried that the day might be approaching "when we shall have to fight in self-defense . . . against the danger of *world* fascism."[63]

From 1939 onward it was this global perspective, rather than a narrower view of U.S. interests in Asia, that shaped American policies. Roosevelt had no interest in improving relations with Tokyo if it meant in any way accommodating, or even appearing to accommodate, Japanese demands for control of mainland China. Such "appeasement" had been discredited by events in Europe, and from the global perspective, appeasement of "the bandit nations" anywhere only strengthened the forces of aggressive fascism everywhere. In Grew's discussions with the Abe government in 1939, therefore, the United States would not budge from its demand that Japan pull its forces out of China and return to the principles of the Nine-Power Treaty.[64]

The same global perspective that made Roosevelt unwilling to accommodate Japan also made him reluctant to antagonize Japan to the point of provoking a war. If Hitler's aim was to embroil the United States in a conflict with Japan in order to distract it from Europe, Roosevelt's aim was not to be distracted. The primacy of the European crisis and of the need to stop Hitler had guided Roosevelt's policies ever since the Japanese invaded China in 1937. Throughout 1938, the State Department studied options for economic sanctions, which would require abrogating the 1911 Treaty of Commerce and Navigation with Japan, but Roosevelt had not been ready to take that step. In 1939, as public and congressional pressures increased, Roosevelt imposed what he called "moral embargoes" on aircraft and air munitions, intended to discourage American companies from selling such items. But that restriction proved limited. American companies were still allowed to export steel, aluminum, technology, and aviation gasoline.[65] Only when Senator Vandenberg introduced a bill to abrogate the trade treaty, which seemed likely to pass with bipartisan support, did Roosevelt preempt congressional action by announcing his intention to withdraw from the treaty.

In early 1940, the United States notified Tokyo of the decision to abrogate the 1911 trade agreement. This was a potentially "severe blow," since

Japan depended on the U.S. for about 80 percent of its strategic goods and materials.[66] But that was as far as he was willing to go. The decision had no immediate effect. Trade continued as usual. When a congressional commission recommended the fortification of the naval base at Guam, now that the Washington Naval Treaty prohibiting it had expired, Roosevelt declined that suggestion, too.[67] He hoped the mere warning of future sanctions would have a "sobering effect" on the Japanese.[68]

It didn't. Although there were many in Japanese leadership circles who believed the war in China had become a disastrous drain on the nation's resources and had only increased dependence on the United States, no one dared suggest withdrawal on American terms. Instead, the Abe government sought to change the subject by offering to negotiate a new trade agreement. When the Americans showed no interest, the talks collapsed. And so did the Abe government.[69] In January 1940 army leaders forced Abe's resignation and the appointment of Admiral Mitsumasa Yonai as prime minister. At the end of March, Japan recognized a new puppet government in China as an alternative to the Chiang government, further infuriating the Americans. Tokyo also took steps to expand Japan's reach southward in the hope of acquiring more resources to meet the war effort and relieve the dependence on the United States. In February 1940, Tokyo presented the Dutch East Indies authorities with a demand for an end of restrictions on Japanese commercial activity and an end to export restrictions.[70] Secretary Hull condemned the ultimatum, and the administration authorized a new loan to Chiang Kai-shek in response.

Grew warned that the two nations had entered a vicious cycle. Japan was acting aggressively in Asia in large part because it wanted to reduce its dependence on the United States and gain a greater degree of economic self-sufficiency. American sanctions only increased Japanese fears of dependence and vulnerability, thus spurring them to more rapid efforts to expand control of resources. Grew also believed that Japanese "moderates" were having second thoughts about the direction Japan had taken and that the U.S. should encourage this by not imposing sanctions, which he believed only strengthened the hardliners. Hornbeck believed quite the opposite. The Japanese were an "Iron and Blood" nation like Germany and would not respond to diplomacy and moderation, only to pressure. Roosevelt and Hull generally agreed with Hornbeck's view of Japanese intentions, but in the interests of avoiding war they were both inclined to the caution and moderation advocated by Grew.[71]

The result was an American policy that neither accommodated nor deterred the Japanese. By abrogating the trade treaty and refusing to discuss a new agreement until the Japanese withdrew from China, Roosevelt put the Japanese on notice that the resources they relied on, especially oil and steel, could be cut off whenever the United States chose. As Harold Ickes put it, dependence on American resources was a "noose" around the Japanese neck. Roosevelt was "unwilling to draw the noose tight" lest he force Tokyo's hand, but he was willing to "give it a jerk now and then" to remind the Japanese of the possibility of strangulation.[72]

At the same time, it was clear from the president's other actions that he was not looking for a conflict.[73] For one thing, the United States was in no condition to go to war. After years of not building naval forces even to the levels permitted in the Washington Naval Treaty, Roosevelt had launched his naval construction program in 1939. But its effects would not be felt before 1942 at the earliest. In the meantime, Japan enjoyed a substantial naval advantage in East Asia and the western Pacific. American holdings in the region, including the Philippines and Guam, were essentially indefensible in the event of a conflict.

Roosevelt's ambivalent approach created a dilemma for the Japanese. As Foreign Minister Yosuke Matsuoka put it at a critical meeting of senior officials in the fall of 1940, Japan could seek a return to cooperative relations with the United States and Great Britain. But it could only do so on the Anglo-Saxons' terms. Any settlement would require giving up many of the gains made over the previous two decades. Japan might retain Manchuria, but it would have to give up its ambition for hegemony in China and might even have to live with the defiant government of Chiang and the Nationalists. It would certainly have to give up the dream of a "New Order" for Asia led by Japan. In short, it could go back to being "little Japan," as General Hideki Tojo, the minister of war and future prime minister, called it.[74] Alternatively, the Japanese could proceed in their difficult, expensive, and so far unsuccessful efforts to establish hegemony in China and get used to living with the American noose around their necks. Or they could try to remove the noose by acquiring the territory and resources that would relieve their dependence on the United States. This was what the Imperial Navy proposed to do with its plan for a southward advance into Indochina and toward the oil supply of the Dutch East Indies. That meant risking war with the United States.

At no time were the Japanese convinced they could win such a war. More than Hitler, they were acutely aware of their own vulnerability to America's superior economic and industrial strength, its seemingly limitless resources, and its large population. War games consistently showed that Japan could score short-term victories owing to their initial military superiority over Anglo-American forces in the region and also to the inadequacy of American bases in the western Pacific. But within two or three years the United States would develop sufficient military power to roll back Japanese victories and eventually threaten Japan itself. As the brilliant naval commander and tactician Admiral Isoroku Yamamoto put it, "If I am told to fight regardless of the consequences, I shall run wild for the first six months or a year, but I have utterly no confidence for the second or third years."[75] The Imperial Navy was naturally more conscious of this medium-term weakness than the Imperial Army, which tended to be more concerned about the dangers posed by Soviet Russia's land forces in Siberia. Still, when Emperor Hirohito periodically asked at cabinet meetings, "Will we win? Can you say we will definitely win?," none of his military advisers could answer affirmatively.[76] When the Imperial Navy's chief of staff briefed him on the latest war planning, the emperor asked if he could expect "a big victory such as our victory in the Sea of Japan [during the Russo-Japanese war]?" The admiral replied that he was "uncertain as to any victory, let alone the kind of huge victory won in the Sea of Japan." To which the emperor exclaimed, "What a reckless war that would be!"[77]

Japan's best hope was that the Americans would choose not to fight. Ambassador Grew had long worried that Japanese planners might make such a judgment, overly influenced by the "apparent strength of the pacifist element in the United States."[78] Some Japanese officials did believe that Americans lacked the stomach to fight their way back across the Pacific after they had been driven out—certainly the United States had done little to suggest otherwise since 1919. The Japanese had an impressive history of defeating stronger powers. As Tojo pointed out, "We did not go to war with Russia thinking that we would win, but we did win."[79] Much of this success they attributed to the superiority of Japanese courage and mettle—the "Yamato spirit," they called it.[80] Still, there was no escaping the fact of America's superior power, once mobilized, and fear of the consequences of a war with the United States hung over all discussions of Japan's foreign policy, right up until the end.

In this state of uncertainty and indecision, the Japanese policy debate was heavily influenced both by internal struggles between the army and navy and by external events that affected their assessment of the risks of one strategy or another.

The policy battle between the army and navy was partly a fight over the allocation of increasingly scarce resources such as steel and oil and partly a disagreement over the best means of securing Japan's continued access to those resources. The army still favored a northern advance against the Soviets, a strategy that had little if any role for the navy and would require giving the army the lion's share of available resources. The navy preferred the southward advance into French Indochina, hoping that it would provoke no response from the United States. Senior navy officials therefore pushed for the southern strategy but accompanied by diplomatic efforts to win American acquiescence.

The two services also had different views of a German alliance. The army preferred closer relations with Germany. The navy feared that the closer Japan got to Germany, the harder it would be to work with the United States.[81] Many of those who favored a German alliance believed that the prospect of a two-ocean war would deter the United States and make it more accommodating to Japanese aims. Opponents worried that an alliance with the Nazi government would have the opposite effect.

There were also domestic political and economic matters at stake. The navy's approach required no great transformation of Japanese politics and society. Indeed, it would encourage Japanese businesses to continue pursuing cooperative relationships with their American counterparts. The army's approach, which anticipated an eventual war with the United States, required preparing the Japanese people for struggle, which meant greater regimentation and discipline in Japanese society and greater government control of the economy. Japanese society would be more closely modeled on the apparently successful example of the "totalitarian" nations: Nazi Germany, Fascist Italy, and the Soviet Union.

The nature of the Japanese regime made it difficult to come down cleanly on one side or the other. The only person with the authority to make a final decision was the emperor, but he preferred that the services work out their disagreements and arrive at a common plan for his approval. This encouraged cooperation and compromise but also stalemate. It also meant that no decisions were ever really final. The Nazi-Soviet Pact of August 1939, for instance, coming on the heels of the army's defeat by Soviet forces, temporarily discredited both the army and the advocates of a military alliance with Germany. This gave the navy the upper hand, for a while, and led to a decision both to proceed with the southward advance into Indochina and to seek rapprochement with Washington.[82]

Given the unsettled nature of the Japanese policy debate, it wasn't surprising that Hitler's astounding victories in Europe in the late spring of 1940 had a decisive effect on the course chosen. Those who had warned of the dangers of alienating Britain and the United States now appeared both timid and foolish. The British ambassador in Tokyo reported widespread popular "indignation" at the "governing classes" who had "completely misjudged the development of the world situation," while strengthening the hand of those who had "consistently favored the Rome-Berlin Axis." Many Japanese of all political and ideological persuasions believed that events in Europe had created "the opportunity of a century for the advancement of Japan's destinies," one that "must not be missed."[83]

The fall of both France and the Netherlands, and the anticipated defeat of Britain, certainly seemed to open a wide path for further Japanese expansion as well as for breaking the long and costly stalemate in China. With French Indochina now under the control of the Vichy government, the Japanese looked to close off French supply routes to Chiang and British support along the Burmese Road.[84] The Dutch East Indies, and its supplies of oil, also seemed to be in reach. With the Netherlands government in exile, the local leaders of the Dutch colonies were left to their own devices in dealing with the Japanese. Nor could the British, fighting for their very existence, prevent a Japanese drive on Hong Kong and Singapore. As Grew reported in early July, the Japanese were "well aware that Great Britain" was now "impotent in the Far East."[85]

Japanese military officials held conferences in June and July to draft plans to take quick advantage of these dramatic "Changes in the World Situation." According to the plan, the army would move as rapidly as possible into northern Indochina and Thailand, and take over air, land, and sea bases, ideally with the acquiescence of Vichy. From these bases Japanese forces would be in position to strike at the Dutch East Indies if and when that became necessary.[86] By September 1940, the Vichy government had given in to Tokyo's demands and granted Japan military rights in Indochina. The Japanese established bases at Haiphong and Saigon, the latter within striking range of Singapore.

Germany's victories strengthened the case for closer relations between the two powers. Older members of the emperor's inner circle, as well as top naval officials and even some senior army officials, continued to argue against an alliance with Germany.[87] The president of the emperor's Privy Council predicted that Washington would react by imposing draconian economic sanctions.[88] But after the fall of France, these arguments carried less weight. The army pushed out the more moderate government and brought Prince Konoe back as prime minister.[89] Three months later, on September 27, 1940, Konoe announced the Tripartite Pact, which turned the Anti-Comintern Pact of 1936 into a full-fledged military alliance. Konoe hoped that the Americans, as well as the British, Dutch, and Chinese, would be sufficiently intimidated by Japan's alliance with such a formidable power that they would accommodate Japan's southern advance.[90] Japanese officials were not shy about declaring that the Axis pact was "a military alliance aimed at the United States."[91] Within days after its signing, Konoe publicly warned that if the United States continued its "provocative acts," Japan would have no other option "but to go to war."[92]

As always, Japan's foreign policy and its internal politics were intimately connected. The British ambassador in Tokyo reported that the German successes in June 1940 "did more than anything else to fasten totalitarianism on the Japanese back."[93] The charismatic Konoe was a strong proponent of the more hawkish army officers' call for further transformation of the economy and society.[94] His "New Order Movement" and its organizing institution, the Imperial Rule Assistance Association, looked to dissolve all independent civic and political entities and to create one national unity organization with local branches in every neighborhood.

To outside observers, this looked very much like an attempt to copy Hitler's Germany and Mussolini's Italy. But Japanese traditions and the constitutional system established in the Meiji period were incompatible with European-style fascism. The role of the emperor as the son of God and living symbol of the Japanese nation and people left no room for an alternative leadership by a Hitler or a Mussolini. As Grew explained in a long cable in June 1940, the key issue remained the role of the military. As the political parties disappeared, the army had increasingly "usurped their place as the driving force behind Japanese politics." This was more a "reversion to old forms and traditions" than a replication of the populist demagogic dictatorships of Europe.[95]

To Grew and other Americans, however, it was a distinction without a difference. The goal in Japan seemed the same as in Hitler's Germany and Mussolini's Italy: to expunge liberalism and democracy, and with the aim, as Konoe himself put it, of uniting "the total energies of the State and the People" to enable the "powerful pursuance of any policy when the necessity arises." As Grew explained, in establishing an ever more authoritarian government, exercising total control of all political organizations down to the local level, demanding the subordination of "the individual to the larger interest of the state," and taking "rigid control over the economic life of the nation," Japan was, for all intents and purposes, following the example of the new European dictatorships, combining, as always, "their genius for imitation and their sure sense of tradition."[96]

Grew was in despair. Ever the optimist when it came to the possible return of Japanese liberalism at home and abroad, he had to admit that the German victories had "radically altered" Japanese politics and policy. And whereas in recent years Grew had consistently urged patience and conciliation, and warned of the "hazards involved in a strong policy," he now emphasized the hazards of a "laissez-faire policy." American interests in the Pacific were "definitely threatened" by Japan's new policy of southward expansion, which he identified as "a thrust at the British Empire in the East." Believing that the survival of the British Empire was an element in America's own security, Grew thought it was no longer enough simply to register disapproval. Only "a show of force, together with a determination to employ it if need be," could change Japan's trajectory.[97] In December 1940 he lamented, "This, indeed, is not the Japan that we have known and loved."[98] For Cordell Hull, the only question was "how long we maneuver the situation until the military matter in Europe is brought to a conclusion."[99] To "maneuver" the situation meant, on the one hand, to do what was possible to blunt or at least slow Japanese expansion, while, on the other hand, not provoking a war before the United States was ready.

CHAPTER TWENTY-THREE

The United States Enters the War

*Occasionally, one must conjure up enough courage, close one's eyes,
and jump off the platform of the Kiyomizu.*

—Hideki Tojo

*Now at this very moment I knew the United States was in the war, up
to the neck and in to the death. So we had won after all! . . . Hitler's
fate was sealed. Mussolini's fate was sealed. As for the Japanese, they
would be ground to powder. . . . I went to bed and slept the sleep of the
saved and thankful.*

—Winston Churchill[1]

ALTHOUGH ROOSEVELT still hoped to avoid war with Japan, the new
circumstances were making that harder. With Japan now formally allied
to Germany, Americans assumed much greater coordination between
the two powers. Administration officials feared, for instance, that Japan
might choose to strike Singapore just as Germany attacked Gibraltar,
thus dealing a fatal blow to the British Empire at two critical nodes.[2] At
their meeting in mid-August, Churchill had asked Roosevelt to consider a
warning and ultimatum to Japan. The most "unthinkable" possibility, he
warned, was a Japanese attack on British interests with the United States
standing aside. If Japan succeeded in cutting Britain off from the dominions, "the blow to the British Government might be almost decisive."[3]

In the summer of 1941 Roosevelt also had another factor to consider.
On June 22 Hitler invaded the Soviet Union. From the Anglo-American
perspective, this was good news, so long as Soviet forces could hold out.
Roosevelt hoped that if the attack was more than just a "diversion," it
would swallow immense amounts of German troops and resources and

allow "the liberation of Europe from Nazi domination." Determined to provide as much assistance as possible as quickly as possible, he agreed to Stalin's request for $1.8 billion worth of supplies to keep the Soviet Union in the fight. Roosevelt hoped that if Soviet forces could hold out until October, the Russian winter would bog Hitler's forces down until the following spring. He also hoped that if the Soviets stayed in the war, he would not have to send troops to fight in Europe. Although he faced opposition at home to aiding the Communist government, especially from Catholics, his top military advisers believed the United States had a vital interest in supplying Stalin what he needed, even if it meant drawing down American stocks.[4]

Roosevelt remained eager to avoid war with Japan, but these developments reinforced his determination to make no concessions to Japan that might impair either the British or, now, the Soviet war effort. He hoped to prevent the Japanese from moving either southward against British interests and the Dutch East Indies or northward against the Soviets in Siberia. He knew that the Japanese were "having a real drag-down and knock-out fight among themselves . . . trying to decide which way they are going to jump—attack Russia, attack the South Seas (thus throwing in their lot definitely with Germany), or whether they will sit on the fence and be more friendly with us." Regardless of which path they chose, he hoped to slow the Japanese without diverting resources from the Atlantic. As he told Ickes on July 1, it was "terribly important for the control of the Atlantic for us to help keep the peace in the Pacific. I simply have not got enough Navy to go round—every little episode in the Pacific means fewer ships in the Atlantic."[5] For the first six months of 1941, therefore, Roosevelt combined carefully calibrated but increasing economic pressure on Japan with support for China and others threatened by Japanese expansion, while at the same time negotiating with Japan to try to delay war.

On the economic side, the administration had already put in place an expanded export licensing program, partly to ensure that raw materials and manufactured products needed for American rearmament were not sold either to allies or to potential adversaries. Using this licensing procedure, in July 1940 Roosevelt placed an effective embargo on the sale to Japan of high-octane aviation fuel (but not low-octane fuel) and high-grade scrap metal (but not all scrap metal). When Japan entered northern Indochina in September 1940, and in the same month signed the new Tripartite Pact with Germany and Italy, Roosevelt cut off all types of scrap iron and further reduced the level of octane. By early 1941 the

United States had put a number of such de facto embargoes in place, and although most could be justified as necessary for American arms production, they had a significant impact on the Japanese war economy.[6] From the American point of view, these steps were calibrated to make the Japanese pause their expansion without provoking them to war, tugging on the noose but not too hard. In Congress and among the public, pressure grew for tougher measures, including a full embargo on oil, but Roosevelt and Hull both continued to resist a measure they were confident would drive the Japanese to attack either north or south.[7] Roosevelt continued to keep his biggest weapon holstered.

At the same time, Roosevelt supported a new round of talks with Japan. In January 1941, two American priests traveled to Japan hoping to find some basis for a peaceful settlement of the two nations' differences and returned with an unofficial proposal from Prince Konoe. Talks began in April between Secretary Hull and the Japanese ambassador, Admiral Nomura, who, representing the navy's preferences, eagerly sought some kind of agreement.

Grew had long argued that a more accommodating American approach would help the Japanese moderates, while tougher measures would only strengthen the "militarists" in the Japanese government. In fact, while some Japanese officials seized on the chance to work things out with the United States and avoid war, the more hawkish officials saw Roosevelt's moderate response and apparent eagerness for negotiations as a sign that the Americans were indeed cowed by the Tripartite Pact. It was obvious that as Roosevelt took the United States deeper into the war in the Atlantic, he was eager to avoid a simultaneous crisis with Japan. This perception was strengthened when Nomura sent a copy of a draft understanding, written largely by the two American priests, suggesting American willingness to permit Japan to keep its troops in China even after an end to the war, as well as other concessions. Japanese officials did not learn until later that the Roosevelt administration had never approved the terms. So while navy officials, along with an increasingly worried Konoe, looked hopefully to negotiations, the army pushed for more aggressive actions on the assumption that Roosevelt would not respond with harsh measures. With Germany "winning the war now," the army chief of staff argued, the Americans were not "going to war with us over French Indochina." The perception of American reluctance was such that even the navy could not oppose more aggressive steps, especially since doing so would only undermine their case for more resources.[8]

On July 2, 1941, therefore, an Imperial Conference met and ratified the army's policies in both north and south. Preparations for possible war with the Soviets would continue, including the reinforcement of troops in Manchuria. But the main thrust would be southward. The army would move into and occupy the south of Indochina and prepare for a possible attack on the Dutch East Indies. The hope was to accomplish this peacefully, but if the result was a war with the United States and Britain, the final document stated, "The Empire shall not flinch."[9] Since Japanese naval planners had become increasingly convinced that an attack on the East Indies would bring the United States into the war, senior naval officials were stunned by the decision. "What if a war really broke out?" the commander of the Second Fleet exclaimed. "We won't win!"[10] The decision had been taken, however, mostly in the hope that it would not come to war with the United States, partly in the hope that even if it did, the Japanese might once again astonish everyone and prevail. Two weeks later, Tokyo presented Vichy with another ultimatum: for the occupation of all of Indochina, including an additional eight air bases and two naval bases in the south.[11] On July 28 Japanese forces began the occupation of southern Indochina unopposed.

Roosevelt learned about the decisions taken at the Imperial Conference a week later thanks to American intelligence, which was by then intercepting and decoding Japanese communications. The decision of the Imperial Conference followed by the ultimatum to Vichy convinced American officials that Japan would carry out its southern advance no matter what the United States did. Roosevelt still remained unwilling to pull the trigger on an oil embargo, but he agreed to Welles's suggestion to freeze all Japanese assets in the United States, which, as it turned out, amounted almost to the same thing. At a July 18 cabinet meeting, Roosevelt agreed to a complete ban on all high-octane gasoline and to limit oil shipments to prewar levels, which were dramatically lower than what Japan needed for continued prosecution of the war in China and any further aggressive actions. The person in charge of approving licenses, the State Department's Dean Acheson, effectively ensured that Japan received no oil at all.[12] The British, Dutch, and Canadians soon followed suit.

Whether or not Roosevelt knew and approved of this stringent enforcement of the asset freeze, he had ample reason to believe the time had finally come to shut off the oil flow.[13] More importantly, the Roosevelt administration had concluded that the Japanese were determined to launch an attack whether the United States imposed an embargo or not. Roosevelt had held back for fear of provoking the Japanese to attack the

Dutch East Indies, but with the Japanese move into southern Indochina, American officials believed Japan was already preparing to do just that. Intercepts of Japanese army communications suggested that the move was only a precursor to a broader attack that would include Singapore and the Dutch East Indies.[14] So now the question was no longer whether an embargo would provoke the Japanese to attack, but whether American oil was literally going to fuel Japan's further aggression.[15] Although there remained some doubt whether the Japanese intended to launch their major attack southward against British and Dutch colonies or northward against the Soviets, for Roosevelt both options were bad. If anything, he worried more about the Japanese going north against the Soviet Union. Roosevelt wanted to ensure that Soviet forces continued to wage war on Germany's eastern front, where they were tying down a huge portion of Hitler's armies. He hoped limiting Japanese oil supplies would "increase Japan's hesitation." He certainly didn't want to be providing the Japanese army with the fuel it needed to wage a war against the beleaguered Soviets.[16]

While imposing these economic costs, however, Roosevelt also hoped to continue pursuing diplomacy, ideally to prevent a Pacific war altogether but short of that at least to delay it. At the Atlantic Conference in August, Roosevelt told Churchill that he would seize opportunities for negotiations, slim as they were, if only to give both the British and Americans more time to strengthen Pacific defenses. Upon his return to Washington, Roosevelt met with Ambassador Nomura. He told him that if Japan was ready "to suspend its expansionist activities," the United States would consider "resumption of the informal exploratory discussions."[17]

Roosevelt was not willing to concede much in order to reach agreement, however. He and Hull were prepared to accept Japan's control of Manchuria, but beyond that Roosevelt did not want to make any concession that either the Chinese or the British could regard as a betrayal. If the United States wavered and appeared willing to strike a deal at the expense of the other powers, Roosevelt feared that the "ABCD" [American, British, Chinese, Dutch] coalition he was trying to establish would collapse. As it was, even with the talks going nowhere, the Chinese and the British frequently worried that Roosevelt was about to cut a deal with Japan at China's expense.[18] Roosevelt wanted to make it abundantly clear that he would do nothing of the kind.

Roosevelt and Hull approached talks with the Japanese with significant skepticism. As long as the military controlled Japan, they believed—and they saw no real prospect of that changing—there would be no fundamental change in foreign policy. They had serious doubts, justified, as it turned out, about whether Nomura, or the Japanese foreign ministry, or even Prime Minister Konoe himself actually spoke for Japan. In one meeting, Roosevelt jokingly but pointedly asked Nomura "whether [an] invasion of Thailand can be expected during these conversations just as an invasion of French Indochina occurred during Secretary Hull's conversations with your Excellency."[19] Hull repeatedly asked the Japanese to repudiate the pact with the Axis powers, insisting that he could hardly convince Americans that Japan was interested in peace while it remained "tied in an alliance with the most flagrant aggressor who has appeared on this planet in the last 2,000 years."[20]

In fact, although there were deep divisions among Japanese officials—deeper than the Americans even knew—the Japanese military was calling the shots. The American freeze on Japanese assets left roughly four months of oil reserves. Despite the fact that a number of Japanese officials had predicted the United States would take precisely such action if Japan moved into southern Indochina, Army officials had convinced themselves that the United States would take no drastic action until Japan moved against the Dutch East Indies. The embargo's effect on Japanese thinking was, therefore, the opposite of what Roosevelt and Hull intended. Instead of making the Japanese hesitate, the decision convinced most Japanese officials that they had to move quickly, before the embargo made any action impossible and before the American naval buildup tilted the scales against them.[21]

Japan's civilian leaders were in a panic. With a war with the United States looming on the horizon, even Prince Konoe, who had been responsible for so many of the key decisions that had led Japan to this point, was filled with regret. He told a colleague he had made "a big mistake on Japan's relations with China," since the war had weakened rather than strengthened Japan's position. The occupation of Indochina had also been a mistake, and now threatened to "inflict serious damage."[22] All he could do was "pray for a miracle and divine intervention."[23]

He did more than pray. He began pressing for direct negotiations between himself and Roosevelt, in the hopes that he could strike a deal with the Americans and compel the military to accept it as a fait accompli. It was clear that the current Japanese negotiating position was unacceptable to Roosevelt—among other things, it did not promise to withdraw Japanese troops from either China or Indochina, even if the Sino-Japanese conflict was settled peacefully.[24] At a high-level conference in early September, with senior officials agreeing that "Japanese-

American differences were irreconcilable," military officials agreed to let Konoe and Nomura pursue a settlement with the United States. But they demanded a deadline. If no agreement was reached by mid-October, Japan would move against British, Dutch, and American interests. In the meantime, as negotiations proceeded, Japanese forces would make the necessary preparations for such a war.

Receipt of the latest Japanese proposal did not surprise Roosevelt and Hull, nor did they consider trying to accommodate Tokyo. Polls showed a large majority of Americans opposed any "appeasement"—67 percent of those asked said they were ready to risk war with Japan if necessary to keep it from expanding its power through aggression—and Roosevelt's advisers warned him not to do to China what Chamberlain did to Czechoslovakia.[25] Roosevelt also knew through intercepts and observation that, even as the talks continued, Japan was mobilizing and repositioning its forces for attacks in the south, and possibly in the north. Hull complained to Nomura, and Prince Konoe himself later complained that "while my government was negotiating with all its energy, the military were pursuing war preparations. . . . Washington got to know that our ships were being switched about and became very skeptical."[26] In fairness to the military, that was the agreed Japanese policy.

The Americans were not the only ones trying to gauge and influence Japanese actions. Hitler and his advisers were frustrated and worried that the Japanese feared taking on the United States. Tokyo's evident eagerness to continue talks held out the possibility of a settlement that would leave Roosevelt free to focus entirely on the Atlantic war. The former German ambassador to Washington had no doubt about what Roosevelt was up to. His diplomatic proposals, Ambassador Dieckhoff observed in May, aimed only to "gain time." Roosevelt wanted to "lull Japan to sleep until such time as he can intervene in the fight for England with a war industry operating at full capacity and with a full mobilization, especially with a larger navy." If the Japanese were to "play his game," Roosevelt would soon be able to "turn all his forces against the Axis powers, since he would be free to the rear."[27] Indeed, Ribbentrop feared that Roosevelt's more aggressive actions, such as his decision in June to send American marines to Iceland, could only have come about because of some secret agreement with Tokyo.[28]

By the summer of 1941 Hitler had grown increasingly desperate to keep the United States out of Europe, and therefore all the more desperate for aggressive Japanese actions to tie the Americans down in the Far East. His answer was to speed up the timetable for the attack on the

Soviet Union. An invasion of the Soviet Union had always been central to Hitler's overall plan—that, after all, was where he looked for the "living space" that would make Germany powerful and self-sufficient. But he had always hoped to knock France and Britain out of the war first, so that he would have a free hand in the east—hence the Nazi-Soviet Pact, which was intended only to buy time. But Britain's stout resistance, made possible by American assistance, had foiled these plans. Now keeping the Americans out of the war became essential, and the best tool, perhaps the only tool, for that was Japan. Germany had yet to acquire the naval power to take on the Americans—that was years away. In the critical months ahead, he looked to the Japanese navy to do the job for him.[29]

The timing of his invasion of the Soviet Union was thus determined almost entirely by the need to keep the Americans out of the war in Europe and to embroil them in a war with the Japanese in the Far East. If the Japanese did not have to worry about the Soviet Union, they could take more aggressive action against American and British interests. The United States, he told his advisers, would have "less inclination to enter the war due to the threat from Japan."[30] As one of his top naval advisers put it, "The Führer . . . [was] most anxious to postpone the United States entry into the war for another one or two months." A "victorious campaign on the Eastern Front" would have a "tremendous effect on the whole situation and probably also on the attitude of the U.S.A."[31]

The need for speed may have led Hitler to a fateful mistake. As one historian notes, "In order to destroy the Soviet armies before the United States intervened in the conflict, Hitler was bound to opt for a Blitzkrieg strategy which, on the vast Russian plains lacking up-to-date communications network, was to invite failure."[32] But from Hitler's perspective, the victory had to be swift to give the Japanese the confidence they needed to take on the Americans. Hitler's nightmare was Roosevelt leading the United States into the war in Europe while peace reigned in the Far East. "The main aim of German policy" was to "make sure that the Japanese entered the war in time."[33] The rapid "smashing of Russia," Hitler believed, would accomplish that objective.[34]

But would the Japanese go along? German doubts about Japan's intentions continued throughout the summer and into the fall of 1941. Frustrated German officials had long spoken of the "childlike" views that the Japanese had of America and how their dependence on American trade made them fearful of doing anything to provoke war. From the German point of view, they overestimated American power and American will, and they underestimated the effect on Americans of the alliance with

Germany.[35] The Japanese had been shocked by Roosevelt's reaction to their occupation of Indochina, for instance, but Ribbentrop complained that they failed to realize how timid that response actually was. The fact that the United States had responded "only with economic sanctions" and that the Roosevelt-Churchill meeting had "produced only words" were "clear signs of weakness" and proof that the Americans would "not risk any serious military action against Japan." The American military was not yet ready for war; the U.S. Navy was inferior to the Imperial Navy in the western Pacific; and the "real attitude" of the American people was opposed to war. Japan was therefore still in a position "to impose whatever decisions she chooses. But the longer she waits, the more the balance of forces will change to her disadvantage."[36]

Throughout 1941 German diplomats repeatedly urged the Japanese to take action, against Singapore, in particular. Ribbentrop told the Japanese ambassador in Berlin that the "occupation of Singapore" would be both "a critical blow at the heart of the British Empire" and would likely "keep America out of the war." The Americans were still rearming and were "very reluctant" to expose their navy "to danger West of Hawaii." If, moreover, the Japanese refrained from attacking the Philippines, this would make an American declaration of war even less likely. America could "scarcely afford to declare war and then have to watch impotently while the Japanese took the Philippines, without being able to do a thing about it."[37]

A good number of Japanese officials were not convinced, however. For one thing, it was clear that the Germans wanted war in the Pacific solely to keep the Americans out of the war in Europe, just as the Japanese hoped that the Americans would enter the war in Europe and leave Japan alone in East Asia. Nor could the Japanese be sure that, if they did find themselves at war with the United States, Hitler could be relied upon to join in. As one Foreign Ministry official told the German ambassador in Tokyo, Hitler himself was still doing everything he could to avoid war with the United States, despite Roosevelt's provocations in the Atlantic. It seemed "tactically correct" for Japan to do the same. Even hardline Japanese officials no longer hoped that the alliance with Germany would deter Roosevelt. His actions since July certainly did not indicate fear of a two-front war. Japan's situation had only become steadily more dire since the Tripartite Pact was signed.[38] Hitler thus felt compelled to promise the Japanese repeatedly that he would declare war on the United States immediately if war erupted between the United States and Japan.[39]

What impact these promises and urgings from Germany had on Japanese decision-making is hard to know. Hitler's invasion of the Soviet Union did tempt the army to return to its preferred strategy and take on the Soviets in Siberia. It breathed new life into the northern advance, at least until the surprising resistance of the Soviets suggested that the project might be no easier to accomplish than before. For the most part, the Japanese proceeded less on the basis of German promises and more in response to their own difficult predicament.

Negotiations with the Americans were still going nowhere. At a meeting on October 2 in Washington, Hull and Nomura could agree on nothing. Konoe continued to press for a summit meeting in a last desperate effort to bypass the military, but Roosevelt was persuaded by Hull and others that without some prior agreement on basic issues, such a meeting would be useless or worse. The Americans did not believe that Konoe spoke for the military, which was true, and they did not believe that any agreement reached with him could be sold to the military, which was probably also true.[40] Since any summit with Konoe was also likely to stir fears of appeasement among the Chinese and the British, and the American public, it was easy to reject. As Ambassador Nomura put it, the problem from the beginning was that the two sides had "fundamental differences in policy" and a "long list of divergences dating from the Manchurian Incident."[41] By the end of November Hull was telling Stimson that he washed his hands of the diplomatic effort, and now matters were "in the hands of you and Knox—the army and the navy."[42]

With diplomacy failing, and economic sanctions not yet biting, Roosevelt scrambled for other means of delaying and deterring further Japanese aggression. There was not much left in his toolbox. In its current state, the Pacific fleet was no match for Japanese superiority in the western Pacific. The Imperial Navy outnumbered the combined Anglo-American-Dutch forces in the Pacific theater, with eleven battleships and ten aircraft carriers against nine battleships and three carriers, and the latter force was spread out across the six thousand miles between Pearl Harbor and Singapore.[43] With the confrontation in the Atlantic growing, available warships could not be spared for the Pacific. Over the course of the next two years, 178 additional destroyers would be completed, and some 17 battleships and a dozen attack carriers were either in the last stages of completion, under construction, or on order by the end of 1941.[44] But even when these additional warships came into service, Roosevelt assumed they also would be needed in the Atlantic. The Pacific fleet would remain understrength for some time.

To compensate, Roosevelt, like Stimson before him, tried to bluff. He ordered the Pacific fleet stationed at Hawaii instead of California, hoping its mere presence in the middle of the Pacific would make the Japanese hesitate. When the fleet's commander, who insisted the fleet was dangerously exposed and would be safer on the West Coast, asked why it remained at Hawaii, the chief of naval operations, Admiral Harold Stark, replied, "You are there because of the deterrent effect which it is thought your presence may have on the Japs going into the East Indies." Then, anticipating the next question, Stark said, "Suppose the Japs do go into the East Indies? My answer to that is, I don't know, and I think there is nobody on God's green earth who can tell you." The only thing to hope was that "the Japs don't know what we are going to do, and so long as they don't know, they may hesitate or be deterred."[45]

As another somewhat desperate measure of deterrence, the Roosevelt administration undertook to make the Philippines defensible against a Japanese attack. In the summer of 1941 General Douglas MacArthur was sent to the Philippines to raise an indigenous army. Roosevelt also ordered the deployment of some three dozen B-17 bombers, which would presumably be capable of hitting Japanese ships and bases.[46] Secretary of War Stimson thought they were a "big stick" that would end America's impotence in the region, and even George Marshall hoped they would "restrain" Japan from advancing south into Malaysia or north into eastern Siberia.[47] Even if the planes could serve such a purpose, however, it would be months before they could be used. Runways had to be extended, supplies and personnel had to be shipped over, and the long-neglected bases still had to be fortified.

As the possibility of war increased, Marshall and Stark urged caution. In early November they noted that not until the middle of December could American "air and submarine strength in the Philippines" pose any threat to "Japanese operations south of Formosa." Not until February or March 1942 could American air strength possibly deter Japanese actions south and west of the Philippines. In any case, an "unlimited offensive war" against Japan would "greatly weaken the combined effort in the Atlantic against Germany, the most dangerous enemy." Roosevelt told an impatient Churchill that "in Japan's present mood" any further warnings or ultimatums from the United States would have the opposite of the intended effect.[48]

Time was running out for the Japanese, too. Because their military advantage would diminish and eventually disappear, just as Marshall and Stark claimed, with the oil embargo threatening to grind Japanese military operations to a halt, a last chance to strike was fast approaching.[49]

As the Japanese contemplated their next move, nothing Roosevelt had done to try to deter Japan in the near term had any effect. The B-17 bombers in which the Americans put such stock were no deterrent whatever, inasmuch as the Japanese planned to overrun American bases in the Philippines within days of the initial attack. The fleet that Roosevelt had based at Hawaii in the hope of giving the Japanese pause had the opposite effect. It made the fleet a target.

Ironically, Pearl Harbor became a target thanks to the genius of a senior Japanese naval official who not only opposed war with the United States but had declared on many occasions that Japan would certainly lose. That official was Admiral Isoroku Yamamoto, who would serve as commander of Japan's Combined Fleet throughout the war.

Yamamoto and other Japanese military planners had long argued that the likely outcome of the "southern strategy" was going to be war with the United States. Whether or not the Americans would tolerate the occupation of Indochina, they were unlikely to tolerate an attack on the Dutch East Indies and seizure of the oil fields. Yamamoto and others believed it was folly not to assume American entry into the war, and if that was the case, Japan ought to fight the United States on the most advantageous terms possible. That meant striking preemptively. In the last months of 1940, Yamamoto had successfully made the case that rather than attacking the Dutch East Indies, seizing the oil, and then waiting for the Americans and British to counterattack, Japanese forces should launch a preemptive attack on the Philippines to seize Manila and either sink the American fleet or drive it back to Hawaii and the American Pacific coast. With no bases in the western Pacific, the American fleet would have to reassemble at Hawaii and then steam back across to launch a counterattack. This would take weeks, during which time the Japanese could consolidate their position, access the new resources, and prepare to fight the coming battle from a stronger position. Such had been the finding of recent war games, which demonstrated that Japan could score significant victories in the early stages of a war with the United States, perhaps for a year or more, even though in the long run it would probably lose.[50]

Beginning in February 1941 Yamamoto took this logic further. If war with the United States was inevitable, he argued, why not employ the more "radical tactic" of attempting to destroy the American fleet before it could even begin the long trip to the western Pacific? That would give Japanese forces even more time to consolidate the empire before the United States could muster its response. Perhaps the Americans would be so demoralized that they would seek a negotiated settlement.[51] He and his planners immediately began working out the tactical and logistical details of a surprise attack on the U.S. Pacific Fleet that was now based at Pearl Harbor. Thus, even as Yamamoto and other top naval officials continued to argue against war with the United States, the brilliant tactician was devising the strategy most certain to bring the United States into war with a vengeance.

The consensus among the top naval officers was still that it was "folly to start a war with the United States." They even agreed "in principle" that Japanese forces might begin withdrawing from China as a way of satisfying American demands. But they knew the army would be outraged at such a suggestion, and they were unwilling to fight that battle.[52] Senior officials in the army also had trepidations. A high-ranking general expressed his concern that with "one misstep" a war could end up "destroying the state." He had supported the war against China in 1937 but now, like Prince Konoe, he believed that had been a mistake.[53]

Despite such doubts, however, the army pressed to implement the plans that had been approved by the emperor and his imperial council. Army officials recorded their disgust with the navy's hesitations. "What are they talking about at this stage? The navy is selfishly trying to nullify the sacrosanct decision made at the imperial conference. Unspeakable! How irresponsible the navy is! How untrustworthy! The navy is actually destroying our nation!"[54] The bottom line, as the army chief of staff put it, was that "[we] cannot afford to waste time. If the decision doesn't get made soon and we waste more time, we'll end up not being able to launch a war at all, either in the south or the north."[55] The momentum built over recent years as a result of critical Japanese decisions, starting with war against China, was too powerful to stop. The decisions of the Americans had now increased the pressure to act swiftly. There was, in the minds of senior Japanese officials, no turning back.

In the end, the Japanese leadership was willing to take a leap of faith. As Tojo put it to Konoe, "Occasionally, one must conjure up enough courage, close one's eyes, and jump off the platform of the Kiyomizu"— which was another way of saying "take the plunge and hope for the best."[56] Konoe responded that this might be an acceptable choice for an individual, "but if I think of the national polity that has lasted twenty-six hundred years and of the hundred million Japanese belonging to this nation, I, as a person in the position of great responsibility, cannot do such a thing."[57] Tojo suggested that if he felt that way, he should resign as prime minister. On October 16, Konoe did resign and was replaced by

Tojo. That same month the Imperial Navy adopted Yamamoto's Pearl Harbor strategy.

That decision was momentous. As the prospect of war grew, Roosevelt's biggest worry was that the Japanese might strike only at British and Dutch holdings, and he would be left with the job of explaining to the American people why the United States should go to war to protect British and Dutch colonies. Anti-interventionists in Congress were already making this point. On December 3 Senator Burton Wheeler observed to reporters that Japan "had not threatened us." The "only time the Administration had intimated that we should go to war with Japan" was when the British Empire was threatened. The America First Committee warned that if war with Japan came, its sole purpose would be to "save the British and the Dutch empires in Asia."[58] Roosevelt later admitted to Stalin and Churchill that he would have had a difficult time making the case for war if the Japanese had limited their attack to British or Dutch possessions.[59] And indeed, in the final weeks before the attack on Pearl Harbor, Konoe had asked Tojo if it were possible to attack only the British and Dutch and leave the Americans alone, but Tojo insisted that the navy's plans allowed "for no division."[60] Roosevelt might have been unsure about his ability to persuade the American public to go to war for a British colony, but Japanese planners believed they had to assume he could.

Right up until the end, the president and his advisers had expected an attack in Southeast Asia, quite possibly including American bases in the Philippines. What Roosevelt did not anticipate was the surprise attack on Pearl Harbor on December 7, 1941. The attack was also more devastating than Roosevelt and his advisers had imagined, and also more far-reaching. In a few hours, Japanese aircraft, launched from aircraft carriers that had managed to sneak within range without being detected, sank eight battleships and ten other naval vessels, destroyed or disabled some three hundred aircraft, and killed over two thousand soldiers—including over a thousand trapped in the battleship *Arizona* when it sank. Pearl Harbor was only one part of a multi-pronged attack that day. An hour before Japanese planes appeared over Pearl Harbor, the Imperial Army and Navy launched a coordinated attack on British bases in Malaysia; and several hours after the Pearl Harbor attack began, Japanese bombers attacked Clark Field and Cavite Naval Base in the Philippines. The three dozen B-17 bombers, in which Roosevelt had placed so much confidence, were destroyed in minutes on the ground along with two hundred other aircraft. It was one of the most brilliantly coordinated attacks in military history, and one of America's most disastrous defeats.[61]

Roosevelt was pained by the scale of the damage and outraged at what he regarded as Japanese treachery. But he was also relieved. The attack took the question of war or peace "entirely out of his hands, because the Japanese had made the decision for him." Eleanor Roosevelt recalled that "in spite of his anxiety" that day, "Franklin was in a way more serene than he had appeared in a long time."[62]

Winston Churchill was more than serene; he was jubilant. "To have the United States at our side was to me the greatest joy," he later wrote. "Now at this very moment I knew the United States was in the war, up to the neck and in to the death. So we had won after all! . . . Hitler's fate was sealed. Mussolini's fate was sealed. As for the Japanese, they would be ground to powder . . . I went to bed and slept the sleep of the saved and thankful."[63]

Churchill was more sanguine about the prospects for American entry into the European war than Roosevelt. The president still would not declare war on Germany and Italy. Formal and informal samplings of public opinion before December 7 showed little evidence that the American people were ready to send troops to Europe. In the Midwest especially, there was "tremendous fear" of another American Expeditionary Force. Polls showed Americans evenly split on the question, with much lower support than Roosevelt had enjoyed for his other measures. After the Japanese attack, Roosevelt told Lord Halifax, he remained "conscious of a still lingering distinction in some quarters of the public between war with Japan and war with Germany."[64]

But Roosevelt's adversaries solved that problem, too. On December 8, Japanese ambassador Oshima met with Ribbentrop to nail the Germans down on a formal declaration of war against America. Ribbentrop stalled for time; he knew that Germany was under no obligation to do so under the terms of the Tripartite Pact, which promised help if Japan was attacked, but not if Japan was the aggressor. Ribbentrop, who had for so long dismissed the American threat, now worried that America's entry into the war would overwhelm the German war effort.

Hitler did not hesitate, however. He had watched nervously for months as the Japanese and Americans played at negotiating their differences, and he was immensely relieved when the Japanese attacked Pearl Harbor. Although the specific nature of the attack was as much a surprise to him as to the Americans, he wasted no time in fulfilling his part of the bargain and declaring war on the United States. In addition to making good on his promise to the Japanese, he was convinced that if he did not declare war, Roosevelt soon would. The U.S. Navy was already attacking German U-boats and working closely with the British in convoying, and Roosevelt had extended the American "security zone" almost to the European shores of the Atlantic. Hitler also believed that Japan was much stronger than it was, and that the United States was weaker, or more corrupt, or simply more cowardly. Once Japan had defeated the United States, he hoped, it would turn and help Germany defeat Russia. So at 3:30 p.m. (Berlin time) on December 11, the chargé d'affaires in Washington handed Hull a copy of Germany's declaration of war.

That day, Hitler addressed the Reichstag to defend the declaration. The failure of the New Deal, he argued, was the real cause of the war, as President Roosevelt, supported by plutocrats and Jews, attempted to cover up for the collapse of his economic agenda. "First he incites war, then falsifies the causes, then odiously wraps himself in a cloak of Christian hypocrisy and slowly but surely leads mankind to war," Hitler declared. The assembled Reichstag delegates leapt to their feet in thunderous applause.

Conclusion

AMERICA'S INTERVENTION was at first disastrous. As Yamamoto predicted, the Japanese did "run wild" for the better part of a year. Ten hours after the attack on Pearl Harbor, Japanese forces attacked American bases in the Philippines. They destroyed half of the U.S. Far East air force on the ground along with its installations. American and Filipino army forces were driven back to Bataan, where they fought tenaciously before succumbing to hunger and disease. General MacArthur was evacuated from the Philippines on March 11, 1942, and the remaining American and Filipino fighters surrendered on April 9. Overall, tens of thousands were captured. Thousands died in the infamous Bataan death march, and those who survived spent the remaining years of the war in POW camps. Guam fell quickly, as it was almost entirely undefended, just as it had been for more than four decades. Americans suffered more casualties in a shorter span of time than in any conflict in their history other than the Civil War.

Meanwhile the British were suffering the "greatest disaster" in their entire history. They surrendered Hong Kong in a matter of weeks. Malaya fell in two months, as British and Indian forces were chewed up, British warships sunk, and tens of thousands taken prisoner.[1] By the end of February, the Japanese Imperial Navy had met and destroyed the combined naval forces of the United States, the Dutch, and the British. Rangoon and Burma fell on March 8.[2] In less than six months, Japan had conquered a new empire of some 350 million people, three-fourths the size of the British Empire. All told, Japan conquered more territory in a shorter period of time than any nation in history.[3] To win the war would require the United States, practically by itself, to fight its way back across the Pacific and roll back these massive strategic gains one island at a time.

At the same time, the United States began operations against German forces on the other side of the world. Taking the lead from the British,

American forces drove the Germans out of North Africa and then began the attack through Italy. It would be two more years of brutal fighting, especially on the eastern front, before the United States led the Allied invasion of Germany that ultimately ended the war in Europe.

The Americans started slowly, just as they had during the First World War, but once the American economy shifted fully into war production and as the large and healthy population geared itself up for war-fighting, the tide turned, just as it had in 1918. The U.S. Army, which had numbered 188,000 in 1939, swelled to 1.5 million by December 1941, and rose to 5.4 million by the end of 1942. At the end of the war 12 million Americans were under arms, second in number only to the Soviet Union.[4] American weapons production eclipsed all previous efforts. Shipyards produced almost 9,000 "major naval vessels" between 1941 and 1945, ten times the number produced by Britain in the same period and sixteen times the number produced by Japan. In 1943 alone the United States built fourteen new aircraft carriers, which more than replaced their early losses. The Japanese, who lost just as many in the early fighting, built none.[5] American industry produced over 300,000 military aircraft during the war, more than Britain, Germany, and Japan combined. The United States also produced 90 percent of the Allies' aviation fuel and, through Lend-Lease, supplied a quarter of all British munitions and over half of all military vehicles used by the Red Army. The Soviets acknowledged then and later that they never could have held out against the German onslaught without American financial and material assistance. "I drink to the American auto industry and the American oil industry," Stalin remarked with conscious irony in 1943.[6]

Meanwhile, the American economy soared. While every other great power's economy collapsed under the strain of total war, U.S. GNP more than doubled. Eleven million Americans joined the armed forces, but six million more joined the ranks of the civilian workforce. This expansion allowed the American economy to increase military production without greatly limiting production of many non-war-related goods.[7]

The phenomenon of a single power fighting two full-scale wars on land and sea, financing and producing enough military equipment for itself and its allies, while at the same time also raising its people's standard of living, was so unprecedented that Hitler could be forgiven for not having anticipated it. He admitted to the Japanese ambassador, soon after declaring war, that he did "not know yet" how "one defeats the USA." He soon came to regard the war with America as "a tragedy, illogical, devoid of fundamental reality."[8]

In light of his belated realization that going to war with the United States was a mistake, might Hitler have been more effectively deterred by different American policies? Hitler's disastrous misjudgment about the United States was not his only error, but it was the one that ultimately brought him down. Why had he so discounted the effect of the United States entering the war, just as a previous generation of Germans had?

The America trap

PART OF the answer lay in the fact that Hitler, like everyone else, including Americans, had not fully realized how much the world had changed and how much America's overwhelming power, both existing and potential, could affect the fate of would-be hegemons in Europe and Asia. But his underestimation of American power was reinforced by Americans' behavior over the previous two decades.

Hitler fell into a trap unwittingly laid by American policymakers, Congress, and the public. In the critical years of his rise to power, the consolidation of his rule, and then his first moves against the Versailles order, the democratic powers were passive and accommodating—not least because the United States was unwilling to play any role in European security beyond providing private loans. In those critical early years, Hitler feared and expected the democracies would come after him during what he called that "perilous interval." When they did not, and he was allowed to pass undisturbed through his time of greatest vulnerability, he grew overconfident. As early as 1935, Hitler and his lieutenants were already "absolutely drunk with power," convinced that "the whole world" was afraid of them and would not move against them "no matter what" they did.[9] He was emboldened to re-occupy the Rhineland in 1936 and then to move on to fulfill his ambitions in central Europe. When Roosevelt took office, it was already too late to knock Hitler off his course merely with strong words or even sanctions. By the time Roosevelt actually began trying to convince Americans that they would have to become involved in the general international crisis—beginning with his quarantine speech in 1937—both Hitler and the Japanese were so far down the road that they could not be deterred by anything short of a genuine threat of war, and perhaps not even by that.

It mattered a great deal that the United States and the democracies did not successfully contain either Germany or Japan in the late '20s and early '30s. The simultaneous rise of two aggressive major powers in two core regions of the world was harder to manage than each would have been by itself. Even though the two powers were never truly allied and consistently mistrusted one another, every German success in Europe spurred further Japanese aggression in Asia, and every Japanese victory in Asia strengthened Hitler's resolve to press forward in Europe. Both assumed that the Allied powers, and especially the United States, would be distracted by the aggressive moves of the other and fearful of a two-front war. Strengthening this assumption was their common belief—in Japan's case it was more of a wish and prayer—that the Americans would not fight for anything outside the Western Hemisphere. Certainly American leaders, including Presidents Hoover and Roosevelt, had repeatedly said as much. How were the leaders of Japan and Germany to know that there would come a point at which Americans would completely change their minds and decide that the stakes were worth risking war? Here the America trap was sprung. By the time the United States finally decided to use its power, after almost two decades of deliberate inaction, it was too late for the Japanese to turn back without a catastrophic humiliation. For Hitler, any hope of deterrence ended after 1936, at the latest. As Churchill put it, "When the situation was manageable it was neglected, and now that it is thoroughly out of hand, we apply too late the remedies which then might have effected a cure."[10]

A "war of necessity"?

WHY DID Americans finally decide to bring their power to bear? For years, American leaders had insisted the United States had no vital interests at stake in Europe, or in Asia. Nor, despite Roosevelt's exaggerations, was there serious prospect of a full-scale attack on the United States. Even Pearl Harbor was not a prelude to an amphibious invasion of the West Coast, for which the Japanese lacked capacity. It was an act of pre-emptive defense. Although Hitler declared war against the United States, it was to keep his word to the Japanese and encourage their attacks on the United States. He had no intention of fighting the Americans directly while he was still at war with the Soviet Union. Until December 1941, he had even avoided sinking American commercial ships, deliberately denying Roosevelt the casus belli that Wilson had used to justify intervention against Germany in 1917.

Perhaps Germany and Japan might eventually have turned on the United States, once they had accomplished the subjugation of their respective regions. There were times when Hitler contemplated going to war against the United States. But consolidation of German gains in Europe was going to take time, even if the war with the Soviets went well, and so, at other times, Hitler thought that an attack on the United States, if it came at all, would not come during his lifetime. In any case, the anti-interventionists were not wrong to insist that an invasion was all but impossible in the near term, and that the United States would have a long interval in which to prepare if the danger increased in future years.[11]

Americans began significant efforts to support Britain against Germany, moreover, well before anyone believed Hitler could conquer Europe, much less attack the United States. Steps to aid Britain began before the invasion of Poland, when almost no one thought France, with its Maginot Line, could be overrun by German forces. The decision to go ahead with Lend-Lease, the destroyers deal, the revision of the Neutrality Act, and the other measures to help Britain and the Allies, "short of war," preceded any notable increase in the actual threat to American security.

As for Japan, it was clear that war could be avoided if the United States simply let the Japanese do what they wanted in East Asia. But avoiding war with Japan was never Roosevelt's primary objective. Instead, he chose a course of opposing Japanese expansion that he knew could lead to war. As the anti-interventionists insisted at the time, American actions cornered the Japanese and forced them to make a decision they would have preferred not to make. As Hoover put it, if the United States insisted on "putting pins in rattlesnakes," it should expect to get bitten.[12]

Why, then, did the United States put pins in rattlesnakes, aggressively deploying economic sanctions against Japan and expanding the American naval role in the Atlantic against Germany, if its security was not threatened? The answer had less to do with material national interests such as immediate physical security than with moral and ideological considerations that shaped perceptions of a longer-term threat. Most American liberals believed that Germany and Japan, because they were fascist and "totalitarian" states, might pause but would never cease their struggle against democracy and liberalism. Their "propulsive system of beliefs" would drive them onward until the world was "made over in the fascist image."[13] Even in 1937, long before most Americans could envision a war with Hitler, the American diplomat George Messersmith insisted that what was occurring was a "basic clash of ideologies" and that the dictators were embarked on "a long road" that must end in an attack on the United States. Much as Lincoln insisted the United States could not permanently endure "half slave and half free," so there was an assumption among liberal interventionists that the world must ultimately go in one direction or the other.

Although Roosevelt often spoke of the risk of an imminent German attack on the Western Hemisphere, his most arresting image of the world he feared did not even require an eventual war. Rather, he painted a picture of American democracy isolated in a world of totalitarian dictatorships, a "lone island" in a world dominated by the "philosophy of force," "a people lodged in prison, handcuffed, hungry, and fed through the bars from day to day by the contemptuous, unpitying masters of other continents."[14]

Setting aside Roosevelt's colorful rhetoric, the question of whether Americans could live relatively content in a world in which Europe was dominated by Nazi Germany and East Asia by Imperial Japan was at the heart of the "great debate." The anti-interventionists insisted that the United States could remain secure and content even in a world dominated outside the Western Hemisphere by Germany and Japan. How the Germans and Japanese treated their own people was none of Americans' concern, nor, from a strictly strategic perspective, did it matter how they treated those whose territory they conquered. The United States was not morally responsible for the well-being of people in distant lands, so long as American interests were not threatened. A world dominated by Germany and Japan might not be Americans' preference, but it could be tolerated, especially when the alternative was a devastating war.

But Roosevelt and an increasing number of Americans disagreed. To them such a world was a nightmare, and they were not willing to wait and find out whether it could be tolerated. They preferred the risk of war to accepting a fundamental shift in the global ideological balance of power. After Munich and *Kristallnacht,* Roosevelt and others concluded that "the Nazi regime was too insatiably aggressive and untrustworthy ever to be incorporated into a stable, norm-governed European order."[15] That judgment had more to do with world order than national security. It was about the kind of world Americans were willing to live in. They almost certainly could have lived in such a world. They could have built a navy sufficient to protect their coasts and taken other measures to keep the hostile powers at bay. The question was whether Americans could accept their fate as a lone democratic island.

It seems unlikely, and here it was the anti-interventionists who were being unrealistic. A world dominated by Hitler and Imperial Japan would have been odious to a great majority of Americans. Hitler's plans for ruling conquered peoples and territories were no secret. He had already begun to implement them. All Jews were to be killed wherever German forces established control. The Roma, homosexuals, and the handicapped would also be targeted for elimination. In Germany and elsewhere, those thought likely to give birth to defective babies were to be sterilized. Such programs had already begun.[16] There were also to be mass deportations of the populations of conquered territory, so that German families could be settled on the "empty" lands. The "General Plan for the East," prepared at the orders of Heinrich Himmler, "envisaged the deportation over the subsequent thirty years of 31 million persons, mainly Slavs, beyond the Urals and into western Siberia."[17] This "Germanization," or what the Nazis called the "New Order," was already being carried out in Poland by the time the United States entered the war, involving "massive expulsions, killings, resettlements, deportations, and other procedures." In time Hitler planned to eliminate the Polish clergy and intelligentsia and to lower the standard of living of the remaining Poles, many of whom would be forced into slave labor.[18] On the other side of the world, Japanese mistreatment of conquered peoples was already notorious following the "rape of Nanking" and other Japanese atrocities, and it would become even more so during the war.

Anti-interventionists insisted that Americans not let moral and humanitarian considerations get in the way of pursuing their "interests," but throughout American history there had always been a sizable number of Americans inclined to protest doing business as usual with regimes they regarded as unsavory. Such protests had disrupted and damaged relations with tsarist Russia, Imperial Germany, and Meiji Japan in the past. They could be counted on to produce tensions in any relationship with Nazi Germany and Imperial Japan. Nor would these tensions be ameliorated by the allegedly calming effect of trade. Even if Hitler had believed in international trade, which he did not, many Americans would have opposed trading with the destroyer of so many innocent people's lives. Nor would Americans have conducted normal trade relations with a Japanese regime that was not only expanding its empire by millions of square miles and hundreds of millions of subjects but committing numerous deliberate atrocities in the process.

There was also the strategic situation to consider. Even if the war between the Axis powers and Russia and Great Britain settled into a prolonged stalemate, the territorial and resource gains of both Germany and Japan would have made them formidable regional and, possibly, global powers. In Europe, a stalemate would have meant at least a continental victory for Germany, with the annexation of Denmark, Norway, Sweden,

Finland, Switzerland, Belgium, and parts of France all but certain. Spain and Portugal with their important Atlantic bases were to become German satellites. Poland, the Baltic states, and, depending on the status of Germany's invasion of the Soviet Union, Ukraine and other parts of the western Soviet Union were all to be absorbed into Germany, along with the Caucasus. This huge expanse of territory with its reserves of coal, oil, wheat, and other grains would have significantly increased Hitler's power and reach. Even if Hitler had no thought of attacking the United States, Americans would have felt compelled to arm themselves against the possibility that he would change his mind, as he often did.

The Japanese would also have held a commanding position in East Asia and the western Pacific. Even if they did not disturb the United States in the Philippines, the American position in the Pacific, including the strategic approaches to Hawaii and to the West Coast, would have been precarious. Nor was there any way of knowing how Japanese ambitions might be affected by their massive gains in East Asia. Even if an actual war in Asia never came, therefore, the United States would have had to be in a constant state of preparation for the possibility. The United States ultimately went to war because Roosevelt and many other Americans found such a prospect to be unacceptable. They were willing to do almost anything to prevent the fall of Britain, and later the Soviet Union, and even if it meant entering the war themselves.

If World War II was a "war of necessity" for the United States, then, it was in this broader sense. A majority of Americans decided that it was necessary to prevent the establishment of a new international power arrangement that favored the German and Japanese "totalitarian" dictatorships, and to do so long before that new arrangement could pose an immediate risk to the United States and the Western Hemisphere. That was why majorities of Americans favored Roosevelt's measures "short of war," but it was also why Roosevelt and a majority of Americans were willing to risk war with both Germany and Japan if it came to that. If the war was "necessary," it was not to protect the American homeland but to defend and restore the kind of liberal order in which Americans preferred to live and which provided the greatest degree of protection against possible future threats.

Power and hegemony

BEHIND THAT assessment lay great fear, but also a consciousness of great power. This "sense of power" was a critical factor in all American decisions from the late 1930s until Pearl Harbor.[19] Had Americans not felt capable of defeating the Axis powers, they would have acted differently. Americans in the 1820s reasonably feared that the Holy Alliance might intervene in the Western Hemisphere, but no one dared suggest that the weak, early-nineteenth-century republic take on the combined forces of Alexander I's Russia, Metternich's Austria, and Frederick William III's Prussia. A century later, the transatlantic power balance had shifted so dramatically that Roosevelt and his advisers, and most Americans, did not doubt that, if it came to war, the United States could defeat the combined military machines of Germany and Japan, and largely on its own, if necessary. It was remarkable, and to the Germans and Japanese almost incomprehensible, how little Roosevelt and his advisers feared the prospect of fighting two such powerful adversaries in two distant theaters simultaneously. Roosevelt's main worry, before and after Pearl Harbor, was that Hitler might not declare war on the United States.

This "sense of power" did not by itself lead Americans to risk intervention in the Second World War. For the anti-interventionists, after all, America's strength and relative invulnerability were the reasons the United States did not have to involve itself in Europe's crises. Still, for Roosevelt and a majority of Americans, the consciousness of great power blended with their moral and ideologically driven fear of Hitler and Japan to produce policies that made American involvement all but inevitable.

Americans saw all this in purely defensive terms, but it was also an exercise in global political, ideological, and military hegemony. It was the imposition of American preferences on a resistant world. Germany, Italy, and Japan, however unpleasant or "illegal" their methods, were attempting to break free of the restraints of an Anglo-American world order that they had no part in establishing, which did not serve their interests as they perceived them but which, on the contrary, was created specifically to constrain them. Americans satisfied themselves that they were in the right because the other powers were the aggressors, but in what other way, except by force, could the aggrieved nations change the world to suit their interests and preferences?

In accepting the new arrangements in 1919, Germany and the Central Powers had succumbed to power, not to superior claims of justice. And now, a little over two decades later, they, along with Japan and Italy, would succumb to power again, as Americans decided, for a second time in the century, that war was preferable to a shift in the global balance of power toward the dictatorships. For a second time Americans would defend what Lippmann called the "Atlantic community" in which friendly democracies held both shores of the vital ocean waterway. Americans naturally believed they were in the right, but viewed from a more objective, neutral perspective, Americans were only in the right if one believed liberalism itself was right and that the opponents of liberalism were wrong. Absent that moral judgment, the world order the Americans wanted to uphold, as well as the means they used to uphold it, was no more just than any other world order established and upheld by force. It was simply better for Americans and for those who shared their liberal faith.

Thanks to the Japanese attack—that act of "infamy"—Americans did not have to examine these questions, or the implications of their actions for the future. The Second World War was the "good war" mostly because Americans believed they had nothing to do with starting it. They were attacked and they responded. This perception absolved Americans of responsibility for going to war, as well as for the moral consequences of fighting the war. The legacy of the First World War was complicated by the fact that the United States technically declared war first. It had therefore seemed like a choice, which meant that the United States bore responsibility for all the consequences, including the supposedly unsatisfactory peace. But the second time around, the aggressors had struck first and declared war first. Whatever the United States did after that, including the firebombing of German and Japanese cities and the dropping of atomic weapons on civilian populations, could be excused because the United States had not sought the fight—or so most Americans believed then, and most still believe now.

American decisions in this period were not a "bid for world supremacy," nor were they driven by anxiety over America's status as the world's "Number One power."[20] Americans had not been jealous of British and French world leadership prior to World War I. On the contrary, they would have preferred to see that leadership resumed after the war rather than take on the responsibilities themselves. Americans simply could not conceive of themselves as would-be global hegemons. Their historic traditions told them that the exercise of power for any purpose other than self-defense was immoral, and so if they went to war it could only be for self-defense. When critics pointed out that their actions nevertheless had hegemonic consequences, that their policies served their economic and other selfish interests, individual Americans disavowed any such motives in themselves. They had only been responding to Japan's infamous and supposedly unprovoked attack.

Most Americans, therefore, did not heed the anti-interventionists' warnings during the great debate about where all this might lead. Since they did not acknowledge their hegemonic intentions, they did not consider what it would take to preserve the liberal order they were rescuing and restoring. Above all, they did not consider that to preserve the liberal peace after the war would require a tremendous and continuous exertion of power. The anti-interventionists warned that if Americans took on this task, it would mean policing the oceans and keeping troops deployed thousands of miles from home, perhaps forever. They warned of the large military budgets, the temptations to imperialism, and the loss of independence and freedom of action that would come from taking on such vast global responsibilities. Meanwhile, those who favored American intervention, including Roosevelt, rarely talked about the postwar future except in vague and visionary ways. Lippmann was among the few to acknowledge that the United States was embarking on a dramatically new course of global leadership that would require "giving the law" to the world.

Roosevelt never fully spelled out the role he expected the United States to play after the war. Perhaps he himself had an unrealistic sense of what it was going to take to preserve a liberal peace, but he certainly knew that Americans would balk at any suggestion that they were about to take on the role of global hegemon. He preferred to speak in homely metaphors that greatly understated the role he was asking Americans to undertake. Just as the Lend-Lease program meant a good deal more than lending a neighbor a garden hose, the world role the United States had taken on was not just a matter of going "out in the street" and using American "influence to curb the riot."[21] Many Americans, probably a majority, did not believe they were fighting to establish an American-led and -policed global order. They believed they were fighting so that they might return to that summer sea on which they had sailed so peacefully and happily before the First World War. They did not foresee that in this new global configuration of power, the sea would be kept calm only by a constant global American involvement that itself would often stir up the waters.

It may have been too much to ask Americans to see what they were doing and to understand why they were doing it, much less to acknowledge it to themselves and others. Power, geography, contingent historical events, and Americans' own political, ideological, and economic preferences had catapulted the United States into the center of world affairs. But Americans still clung to an old image of themselves, not isolationist perhaps but certainly insular. They still interpreted their interests as defense of the homeland, even though they had now twice intervened in major wars when the homeland was not under any immediate threat. They had no language, no theory, and no justification for the role they had actually come to play in the world. This would become a great and often debilitating source of the confusion, misunderstanding, and recrimination that characterized debates about American foreign policy in the decades to come. For Americans, the ideal solution was to create a liberal order with mechanisms for adjudicating differences among nations short of war, a self-regulating system that did not have to be constantly enforced and reinforced by American power. They had sought that unsuccessfully in the Western Hemisphere, and now they would discover that, in the new geopolitics, there could be no liberal peace without the consistent exercise of American power.

The road not taken

THE IRONIC tragedy was that Americans had had an opportunity to achieve something approximating this ideal of a self-regulating, largely democratic liberal world order—in 1919 and the years that followed. Although those years were full of turmoil and dislocation in both Europe and Asia, as nations and peoples tried to adjust to a new postwar world, the basic international conditions were remarkably conducive to a lasting peace based on liberal principles. The United States enjoyed overwhelming predominance, more even than it would after 1989. In 1919 liberalism was in the ascendant globally. Two of the three other most powerful nations—Great Britain and France—were friendly democracies, while the third, Japan, was in a democratic phase and prepared to accommodate itself to a U.S.-led liberal world order. Among the defeated powers, Germany was flat on its back but had also taken a democratic path, and its democratic government was also friendly to the United States and prepared to integrate Germany into an American-led international order. Challengers to the order were few and weak. Mussolini had yet to engineer his fascist revolution in Italy. Hitler was still a young rabble-rouser. Soviet Russia was in crisis at home and abroad.[22]

Crucially, the world was still multipolar after 1919, more than it would be at any time over the next century. Had the United States accepted its role then, it would not have been alone. Other great powers, especially Britain and France, would have shared a greater burden for managing the international peace. The lack of a power bloc of challengers meant that the United States would not have had to deploy large numbers of troops in distant theaters, as it would after World War II. There was no Soviet

Union in control of half of Europe, not even a united, if weak, Communist China virulently opposed to the liberal order.

In such circumstances, not only would the United States have needed to exercise less power, at least for some time. But in addition, international law and international institutions might have had a better chance of taking hold. Even more than after the Second World War, Americans in 1919 were happy to share as much global responsibility as possible. The United States would have been hegemonic, but it would have been a softer, less militarized hegemony.

Critics at the time and later questioned whether Americans would have been willing to go to war to enforce this liberal peace if they had chosen this path in 1919. But they might not have had to. With such great disparities of power between the proponents of a liberal order and their adversaries, the U.S. would have been able to manipulate the scales with minimal effort. It simply had to stay involved, maintain a few thousand troops in Europe—no more than it kept in the Philippines during this entire period—and use its economic influence not to ensure repayment of war debts but truly to stabilize Europe. The formula for that was the same as it would be after the Second World War: to encourage German economic recovery and make it compatible with French security. The tools for that were an active diplomacy with all the European powers, a small but continuing U.S. troop presence to reassure both the French and the Germans, a substantial reduction if not elimination of the war debts, and hence a reduction if not the elimination of German reparations.

Where was the danger of war in this scenario? It is not even clear who in Europe would have objected to such an American role, outside of the Bolsheviks, the Nazis, and the Fascisti, all of whom remained too weak to do anything about it. In fact, this was the American role that almost every major power in Europe hoped for throughout the 1920s, Germany no less than France and Britain, if only as the best means of accessing the American financing they all desperately needed. It was also what the very capable American diplomats and military officials on the ground in Europe begged for in cables to their superiors in Washington.

This was not the course the Americans took. Their determination in the 1920s and '30s never to be drawn into a war in Europe again had the effect of depriving them of the means and the mentality necessary to avoid precisely that fate. Instead, disillusioned Americans withdrew from the peace and thereby destroyed what they alone had the power to create.

Could the United States have gone in a different direction in 1919? Given that Americans did choose a different direction after 1945, the answer is surely yes. It would have required them to recognize that their interests had broadened as a result of their growing power, that their fate was ultimately bound up with the fates of other key parts of the world. Above all, it would have required self-understanding, a recognition early on that they would not tolerate a shift in the balance of power in favor of global dictatorships and therefore should work consistently to ensure that the risks of such a shift were kept to a minimum. Instead, Americans continued to imagine that what happened in the world was mostly a matter of indifference to them. When the United States abstained, events in Europe took their natural course, based on the realities of power. The result was that the United States would end up at war again, only under much worse circumstances.

In some respects, as Churchill later noted, there was nothing new in the story. It fell into that "long dismal catalogue of the fruitlessness of experience and the confirmed unteachability of mankind."[23] Americans added to these common human failings their own peculiarities as a people and a nation: their complex attitudes toward power and morality, their sense of distinctness and remoteness, their tumultuous and highly contested political system, which made consistent action difficult if not impossible, their tendency to see all world problems through the lens of their own domestic disputes. Perhaps above all, Americans brought to these issues the confusion and dissonance that came from being a hegemonic world power with a small, isolated nation's worldview and sensibility. Americans' difficulty squaring their traditional sensibilities with the new realities of their power was the source of much of the world's drama in the first half of the twentieth century. It would continue to roil the world in the decades that followed.

ACKNOWLEDGMENTS

This book would not have been possible without the support and friendship of many people. I am especially indebted to the Brookings Institution, to its president, John Allen, and to his predecessor, Strobe Talbot, for their exemplary leadership and support for scholarship, as well as to my wonderful colleagues, past and present: Martin Indyk, Bruce Jones, Suzanne Maloney, Mike O'Hanlon, Tom Wright, and many others. I have also been blessed with a succession of outstanding research and program assistants: Will Moreland, Tesia Schmidtke Mamassian, Laura Daniels, Chris Miller, Aroop Mukharji, Maame Boakye, Katherine Elgin, Brad Porter, and Rob Keane. No one put more time and effort into making this book a reality than Kristen Belle Isle. I must also thank the incomparable staff of the Brookings library, led by Laura Mooney.

Throughout the research and writing of this book I have benefited from the generous support of Brookings donors, and especially Stephen and Barbara Friedman and Phil Knight. (Activities supported by Brookings donors reflect a commitment to independence, and the analysis and recommendations are solely determined by the scholar.) The Smith Richardson Foundation also provided support. No one has been a more generous and consistent supporter than Roger Hertog, whom I have relied on not only as a benefactor but as a friend, mentor, and intellectual companion.

I also want to thank those who read and commented on early drafts: Mike O'Hanlon, Roger Hertog, Hal Brands, Frank Gavin, and Mel Leffler. And, of course, my late father, whose enthusiasm and love for the craft of history were a continuing source of inspiration. All helped immensely in making this a better book. They are not responsible for its flaws and inadequacies.

I owe everything to my wife and children. No one ever had a more wonderful, supportive family. My wife, Victoria Nuland, in addition to reading every word of this book, multiple times, and serving as an irreplaceable editor, has also been a loving and devoted partner to me and to our children. This book is dedicated to Leni and David. My best friends, my soulmates, they have given me endless joy.

NOTES

1. Harold Nicolson, *Peacemaking, 1919* (Houghton Mifflin Company, 1933), 108.

Introduction

1. James Bryce, *The American Commonwealth: The National Government*—The State Governments, vol. 1 (Macmillan, 1891), 303.
2. Mark Sullivan, *Our Times: The United States, 1900–1925,* vol. 1, *The Turn of the Century* (Charles Scribner's Sons, 1926), 33.
3. Between 1890 and 1907, British steel production rose from 3.6 to 6.5 million tons per year, while America's rose from 4.3 to 23.4 million tons. W. Arthur Lewis, "International Competition in Manufactures," *The American Economic Review* 47 no. 2 (1957), 580; Aaron L. Friedberg, *The Weary Titan: Britain and the Experience of Relative Decline, 1895–1905* (Princeton University Press, 2010), 25.
4. In 1900, the U.S. share of world trade was 10 percent. Britain's share was more than twice that, and even Germany's was higher. Paul M. Kennedy, *The Rise of the Anglo-German Antagonism, 1860–1914* (Allen & Unwin, 1980), 292.
5. Arthur S. Link, *Wilson,* vol. 3, *The Struggle for Neutrality, 1914–1915* (Princeton University Press, 1960), 26; Stephen Gwynn, ed., *The Letters and Friendships of Sir Cecil Spring Rice*, vol. 2 (Constable & Co., 1929), 320, 345.
6. Howard K. Beale, *Theodore Roosevelt and the Rise of America to World Power* (Collier, 1962), 342.
7. John A. S. Grenville and George Berkeley Young, *Politics, Strategy, and American Diplomacy: Studies in Foreign Policy, 1873–1917* (Yale University Press, 1966), 173.
8. Germany spent more than 3 percent and the United Kingdom spent almost 7 percent of GDP on defense.
9. Quoted in Robert L. Beisner, *From the Old Diplomacy to the New, 1865–1900* (Wiley-Blackwell, 1986), 13. Lodge's friend, the historian Henry Adams, observed that when it came to foreign policy, the American public didn't "want to think about it." And perhaps, he thought, they were "quite right." William C. Widenor, *Henry Cabot Lodge and the Search for an American Foreign Policy* (University of California Press, 1980), 122.
10. Widenor, *Henry Cabot Lodge,* 106. For the best argument that the United States had a more coherent and sophisticated foreign policy in this period, see Beisner, *From the Old Diplomacy to the New.*
11. Bryce, *American Commonwealth,* 1:302–3.

12. Richard H. Collin, *Theodore Roosevelt's Caribbean: The Panama Canal, the Monroe Doctrine, and the Latin American Context* (Louisiana State University Press, 1990), 70.

13. David F. Healy, *U.S. Expansionism: The Imperialist Urge in the 1890s* (University of Wisconsin Press, 1970), 216.

14. Robert Kagan, *Dangerous Nation: America's Foreign Policy from Its Earliest Days to the Dawn of the Twentieth Century* (Vintage Books, 2006), 357–58; Charles W. Calhoun, *Gilded Age Cato: The Life of Walter Q. Gresham* (University Press of Kentucky, 1988), 135, 155, 134–35.

15. Such concerns went back to the debates over the Constitution, when anti-Federalists like Patrick Henry warned that the "splendid government" that Madison, Hamilton, and Washington envisioned would produce "empire" and undermine "liberty." Henry worried that if the United States adopted the "strong, energetic government" that Hamilton and the other founders sought, it would be only a matter of time before Americans turned this "splendid government" into a "great and mighty empire," with an army and a navy and the other accoutrements of great power. "When the American spirit was in its youth," he declared, "the language of America was different: liberty, sir, was then the primary object." Patrick Henry, Speech Before Virginia Ratifying Convention, June 5, 1788. The Debates in the Several State Conventions on the Adoption of the Federal Constitution of the United States, 1787–88, ed. Jonathan Elliot (Brooklyn, NY, 1892). Gresham feared that even the comparatively modest naval buildup of the 1880s—the "splendid naval establishment," as he sarcastically called it—was not "consistent with the early policy" of the Republic. Calhoun, *Gilded Age Cato*, 135, 155, 134–35.

16. Kagan, *Dangerous Nation*, 357–59, 363–65; Calhoun, *Gilded Age Cato*, 6, 171.

17. John Adams to John Jay, December 6, 1785, in C. F. Adams, *Works of John Adams* (Little, Brown, 1856), 8:357.

18. Alexander Hamilton, "Camillus," in *The Works of Alexander Hamilton*, ed. Henry Cabot Lodge, 12 vols. (J. F. Trow, 1850–51), 5:206; Burton Kaufman, ed., *Washington's Farewell Address: The View from the 20th Century* (Quadrangle Books, 1969), 171; Kagan, *Dangerous Nation*, 127–28.

19. Russell F. Weigley, *A Great Civil War: A Military and Political History, 1861–1865* (Indiana University Press, 2000), xviii.

20. Bradford Perkins, *The Creation of a Republican Empire*, vol. 1 of *The Cambridge History of American Foreign Relations* (Cambridge University Press, 1993), 170–71.

21. Weigley, *A Great Civil War*, xv.

22. Benjamin Harrison, "Speech in Galveston, Texas," April 18, 1891, quoted in R. Hal Williams, *Years of Decision: American Politics in the 1890s* (John Wiley and Sons, 1978), 60–61.

23. Henry Cabot Lodge, "Outlook and Duty of the Republican Party," *Forum* 15 (April 1893), quoted in William C. Widenor, *Henry Cabot Lodge and the Search for an American Foreign Policy* (Berkeley: University of California Press, 1980), 53; Kagan, *Dangerous Nation*, 281–84.

24. In the last two decades of the nineteenth century, the White House changed hands in four consecutive elections—the Democrat, Cleveland, won in 1884, then lost to the Republican Benjamin Harrison in 1888, then won the White House back in 1892, and then the Democrats, led by William Jennings Bryan, lost to the Republican McKinley in 1896. Between 1875 and 1897 there were only two two-year periods when one party controlled the White House and both houses of Congress. The

rest of the time Congress was divided, with the Democrats usually holding the House and Republicans the Senate.

25. The term "internationalists" is a broad one, but efforts by historians to delineate clear ideological strands within the overall category—to distinguish "conservative" internationalists from "progressive" internationalists—are unsatisfying and generally say more about the prejudices of the historians than about the distinctions between the various actors. See, for instance, Thomas J. Knock, *To End All Wars: Woodrow Wilson and the Quest for a New World Order* (Oxford University Press, 1992), chap. 4.

26. Robert Endicott Osgood, *Ideals and Self-Interest in America's Foreign Relations* (University of Chicago Press, 1953), 87.

27. Sondra R. Herman, *Eleven Against War* (Hoover Institution Press, 1969), 11.

28. Williams, *Years of Decision,* 134–35.

29. See Sidney Ratner et al., *The Evolution of the American Economy: Growth, Welfare, and Decision Making* (Basic Books, 1980), 384: "[T]he United States was becoming relatively more important in the world economy at the same time that the world economy was becoming relatively less important to the United States."

30. W. T. Stead, *The Americanization of the World; or, The Trend of the Twentieth Century* (Horace Markley, 1901), 181, 349.

31. Lance E. Davis and Robert J. Cull, "International Capital Movements, Domestic Capital Markets, and American Economic Growth, 1820–1914," in *The Cambridge Economic History of the United States,* vol. 2, *The Long Nineteenth Century,* ed. Stanley Engerman and Robert E. Gallman (Cambridge University Press, 2000), 796.

32. Carl Russell Fish, *American Diplomacy* (Henry Holt and Co., 1938), 427.

33. Judy Crichton, *America 1900: The Turning Point* (Henry Holt and Co., 2000), 91.

34. Stead, *Americanization,* 357.

35. Crichton, *America 1900,* 91; Manfred Jonas, *The United States and Germany: A Diplomatic History* (Cornell University Press, 1984), chap. 2 passim, 49.

36. Stead, *Americanization,* 179, 170–71.

37. Widenor, *Lodge,* 107.

38. Charles Callan Tansill, *The Foreign Policy of Thomas F. Bayard, 1885–1897* (Fordham University Press, 1940), 29.

39. Widenor, *Lodge,* 105–6.

40. Ibid., 105–6. This was the extent of the "Large Policy" that the two men hoped to implement when war with Spain came in the spring of 1898. See Julius Pratt, "The 'Large Policy' of 1898," *The Mississippi Valley Historical Review* 19, no. 2 (1932), 230.

41. Kagan, *Dangerous Nation,* p. 352; Healy, *U.S. Expansionism,* 103; Oliver Wendell Holmes, Jr., "The Soldier's Faith" (speech, Harvard University, May 30, 1895), in *The Essential Holmes: Selections from the Letters, Speeches, Judicial Opinions, and Other Writings of Oliver Wendell Holmes, Jr.,* ed. Richard A. Posner (University of Chicago Press, 1992), 89–93.

42. Widenor, *Lodge,* 83.

43. Osgood, *Ideals and Self-Interest,* 63.

44. William McKinley, First Inaugural Address, March 4, 1897.

45. Williams, *Years of Decision,* 133–35.

46. Ibid., 48, 211.

47. Andrew Preston, *Sword of the Spirit, Shield of Faith: Religion in American War and Diplomacy* (Alfred A. Knopf, 2012), 203.

48. Ibid., 177.
49. Ibid., 185.
50. Peter Balakian, *The Burning Tigris: The Armenian Genocide and America's Response* (Harper, 2003), xix, 69; Preston, *Sword of the Spirit*, 196–97.
51. Preston, *Sword of the Spirit*, 196.
52. Widenor, *Lodge*, 95; Balakian, *Burning Tigris*, 131–32.
53. Fish, *American Diplomacy*, 428.

Chapter One: A Tale of Two Wars

1. Mark Twain, *Boston Herald* transcript of a speech,1900, quoted by the Library of Congress, "The World of 1898: The Spanish American War." https://www.loc.gov /rr/hispanic/1898/twain.html.
2. In Richard Harding Davis's best-selling novel of 1897, *Soldiers of Fortune,* the hero, asked about his past, replies, "My Father, Miss Hope, was a filibuster, and went out on the Virginius to help free Cuba, and was shot, against a stone wall." Richard Harding Davis, *Soldiers of Fortune* (Broadview Press, 2006), p. 164.
3. Louis A. Pérez, *Cuba Between Reform and Revolution* (Oxford University Press, 1988), 164–65.
4. Ibid., 167.
5. John L. Offner, *An Unwanted War: The Diplomacy of the United States and Spain over Cuba, 1895–1989* (University of North Carolina Press, 1992), 46–47, 80–81, 112. It is remarkable how often the extent and details of the humanitarian disaster are barely mentioned in standard surveys of American foreign policy.
6. Philip S. Foner, The *Spanish-Cuban-American War and the Birth of American Imperialism, 1895–1902* (Monthly Review Press, 1972), 1:185. The *Journal of the Knights of Labor* called the Cuban revolution "one of the most righteous ever declared in any country" and deserving the support of "every lover of liberty and free government in this country." Jules R. Benjamin, *The United States and the Origins of the Cuban Revolution: An Empire of Liberty in an Age of National Liberation* (Princeton University Press, 1990), 27.
7. Ann Marie Wilson, "In the Name of God, Civilization, and Humanity: The United States and the Armenian Massacres of the 1890s," *Le Mouvement Social* 2, no. 227 (2009), 43. According to the *New York Morning Journal,* the American people would "not tolerate in the Western Hemisphere the methods of the Turkish savages in Armenia, no matter what the cost of putting an end to them might be." David Nasaw, *The Chief: The Life of William Randolph Hearst* (Houghton Mifflin, 2000), 125–26.
8. "Weyler in Cuba,*" New York Times,* Feb. 12, 1896.
9. Talcott Williams, "Cuba and Armenia," *Century,* February 1899, 635.
10. As one historian has observed, even had there been no sensational journalism, the American public "would have learned about the terrible conditions in Cuba [and] would have wanted Spain to leave." Offner, *Unwanted War,* 229–30. Hearst's biographer, David Nasaw, concurs: "Even had William Randolph Hearst never gone into publishing, the United States would nonetheless have declared war on Spain." It was his "genius as a self-promoter" that he convinced the nation he had led the country to war. Nasaw also debunks another common myth: When Hearst told his reporter on the scene, "You furnish the pictures, and I'll furnish the war," he was referring to the one already being fought between the Cubans and Spain, not the one the United States would eventually fight. "There is no mention of or reference to American intervention in the telegrams." Nasaw, *The Chief,* 125, 127.

11. Preston, *Sword of the Spirit,* 214.

12. Merle Curti, *Peace or War: The American Struggle, 1636–1936* (Angell Press, 2007), 171. It seems unlikely that Stanton proposed "fighting for American manhood." See Kristin L. Hoganson, *Fighting for American Manhood: How Gender Politics Provoked the Spanish-American and Philippine-American Wars* (Yale University Press, 1998).

13. Preston, *Sword of the Spirit,* 213.

14. Roger Hollingsworth, *The Whirligig of Politics* (University of Chicago Press, 1963), 134. Bryan was just one of many. Populists like Nebraska's Senator William V. Allen were among the first and loudest in their support for Cuban independence, and he was joined by other Populist senators and by populist-style Silver Republicans like Colorado's Henry Teller and Utah's Frank Cannon. Paul S. Holbo, "The Convergence of Moods and the Cuban Bond 'Conspiracy' of 1898," *Journal of American History* 55, no. 1 (June 1968): 58. People in the West and South who "were disposed to see themselves as underdogs in their own country" also "viewed the Cubans as the oppressed victims of Spanish tyranny." Hollingsworth, *Whirligig of Politics,* 130–1.

15. Roosevelt and Lodge were exceptional in this regard, even though Republicans had been the party of greater foreign policy activism since the Civil War. Woodrow Wilson was even more of an anomaly in the generally "isolationist" Democratic Party elite represented by Cleveland and Olney.

16. Editorials in the business press expressed overwhelming opposition to Cuban independence or recognition of the rebels. Jules R. Benjamin, *The United States and the Origins of the Cuban Revolution: An Empire of Liberty in an Age of National Liberation* (Princeton University Press, 1990), p. 36. As one Massachusetts businessman wrote to Lodge, what the business community wanted was "peace and quiet," not war. John A. Garraty, *Henry Cabot Lodge: A Biography* (Alfred A. Knopf, 1953), 182.

17. The president of the Spanish-American Iron Company and the representative of Bethlehem Steel's Juragua Iron Company wrote the secretary of state warning that "our interests will be jeopardized if belligerency is recognized, as the protection of troops will be withdrawn, which means the immediate closing of our mines, and the probable destruction of our properties, particularly the railway and the dock and harbor improvements." Foner, *Spanish-Cuban-American War,* 1:183; "Despite their losses, early in the war U.S. investors saw no alternative to Spanish protection, however inadequate." Benjamin, *The United States and the Origins of the Cuban Revolution,* 35.

18. Foner, *Spanish-Cuban-American War,* 1:181fn.

19. The *Journal of the Knights of Labor* expressed little surprise that the Cleveland administration was doing nothing to help the Cuban revolution, "one of the most righteous ever declared in any country," but was instead serving "the interest of tyranny and oppression." Kagan, *Dangerous Nation,* 384.

20. Foner, *Spanish-Cuban-American War,* 1:203.

21. "Nothing [could] stop it," he told McKinley. Kagan, *Dangerous Nation,* 381, 395; Offner, *Unwanted War,* 41, 54–55.

22. Williams, *Years of Decision,* 136.

23. McKinley's campaign manager and friend, Mark Hanna, warned that any intervention in Cuba would be "a dangerous and costly venture into the unknown." Along with Hanna, this view was shared by the powerful group known simply as "The Four," Senators Nelson Aldrich of Rhode Island, William Allison of Iowa, John Spooner of Wisconsin, and Orville H. Platt of Connecticut. Horace Samuel

Merrill and Marion Galbraith Merrill, *The Republican Command, 1897–1913* (University Press of Kentucky, 1971), 49.

24. William McKinley, "First Inaugural Address," March 4, 1897 (University of Virginia, Miller Center, https://millercenter.org/the-presidency/presidential-speeches/march-4-1897-first-inaugural-address). The night before his inauguration he told Cleveland that if he could leave office at the end of his term knowing he had done everything possible to avoid the "terrible calamity" of a war with Spain, he would be the happiest man in the world. Sullivan, *Our Times,* 1:302. Cleveland came away "impressed by McKinley's desire to avoid war."

25. McKinley felt a "deep moral concern" for the "massive civilian suffering in Cuba." He was "genuinely moved by descriptions of starving and diseased women and children in Reconcentration camps." Offner, *Unwanted War,* 38.

26. The most that a majority of Cubans would accept was autonomy, and not a nominal autonomy but one akin to the autonomy that Canada enjoyed within the British Empire, which was virtual independence, and then only if guaranteed by the United States. As one prominent liberal Spanish politician reported from Cuba, most people there "who at one time had championed autonomy were now unwilling to take up the cause." American officials told the Spanish government that it was "visionary" to continue hoping that Cuba could ever return to its old relationship with Spain. "There was 'no prospect of immediate peace,' nor of a return to a level of economic prosperity that could provide stability on the island, unless the Spanish made concessions." Offner, *Unwanted War,* 79; Kagan, *Dangerous Nation,* 397. This had also been the conclusion of the London *Times* correspondent in Havana back in the summer of 1896, as reported in the *New York Times.* "Spain on the Defensive," *New York Times,* June 7, 1896.

27. Offner, *Unwanted War,* 43.

28. Robert L. Beisner, among other historians, has refuted the claim that the Spanish offered reasonable terms that McKinley, stampeded into war, rejected. As Beisner notes, McKinley never received the answer he sought from Spain, and that was partly because no Spanish government could do anything that amounted to granting Cuba independence. See Beisner, *From the Old Diplomacy to the New,* 113.

29. Offner, *Unwanted War,* 124.

30. McKinley later insisted that if only he had had more time he might have brought about a peaceful settlement. This seems fanciful, unless he was willing to back off his demands for a negotiated settlement between Madrid and the rebels. McKinley himself had set terms that the Spanish would not accept, and he held to them knowing that the likely outcome was war.

31. Lewis L. Gould, *The Spanish-American War and President McKinley* (University Press of Kansas, 1982), 48.

32. David M. Kennedy and Lizabeth Cohen, *The American Pageant: A History of the American People* (Cengage Learning, 2018), 611, 621; Robert H. Wiebe, *The Search for Order, 1877–1920* (Hill and Wang, 1967), 241.

33. Richard Hofstadter advanced the "psychic crisis" thesis in his essay "Cuba, the Philippines, and Manifest Destiny": "The primary significance of this war in the psychic economy of the 1890s was that it served as an outlet for expressing aggressive impulses while presenting itself, quite truthfully, as an idealistic and humanitarian crusade." In Richard Hofstadter, *The Paranoid Style in American Politics and Other Essays* (Harvard University Press, 1996), 161. The argument that Americans were responding to "status anxiety" can be found in Wiebe, *Search for Order, 1877–1920.* The argument that Americans were fighting to prove their manhood is in Hoganson, *Fighting for American Manhood.*

34. Offner, *Unwanted War,* 132–33.

35. The *Wall Street Journal* reported that Proctor's account "converted a great many people" who had until then believed that "the United States had no business to interfere in a revolution on Spanish soil." Offner, *Unwanted War,* 134. It produced "a raising of the blood and temper," one senator recalled, "as well as of shame that we, a civilized people, an enlightened nation, a great republic, born in a revolt against tyranny, should permit such a state of things within less than a hundred miles of our shore.'" Gould, *Spanish-American War,* 40.

36. Offner, *Unwanted War,* 134.

37. Hay to Roosevelt, July 27, 1898, in William Roscoe Thayer and John Hay, *The Life and Letters of John Hay* (Houghton Mifflin, 1915), 2:337.

38. In two years of fighting, well over 200,000 Cubans had died, and there was no reason to doubt that another year or two would produce deaths at roughly the same pace.

39. David F. Healy, *The United States in Cuba, 1898–1902: Generals, Politicians, and the Search for Policy* (University of Wisconsin Press, 1963), 63.

40. Ibid., 64.

41. Army Major William Crawford Gorgas, quoted in Sullivan, *Our Times,* 1:440.

42. Hubert Herring, *A History of Latin America* (Jonathan Cape, 1966), 408.

43. James Ford Rhodes, *The McKinley and Roosevelt Administrations* (Macmillan, 1922), 179.

44. The anti-imperialist politician Carl Schurz observed that the war had begun as an act of "liberation, of humanity, undertaken without any selfish motive." It was a "war of disinterested benevolence." Louis A. Pérez, Jr., "Incurring a Debt of Gratitude: 1898 and the Moral Sources of United States Hegemony in Cuba," *American Historical Review* 104 (April 1999): 358; Kagan, *Dangerous Nation,* 412.

45. Quoted in Hofstadter, *The Paranoid Style in American Politics,* 161.

46. Fred Harvey Harrington, "Literary Aspects of American Anti-Imperialism, 1898–1902," *New England Quarterly* 10, no. 4 (December 1937): 660. The intervention was a "righteous war," and "by the grace of that war we set Cuba free." Mark Twain, *Boston Herald* transcript of a speech, 1900, quoted by the Library of Congress, "The World of 1898: The Spanish American War." https://www.loc.gov/rr/hispanic/1898/twain.html.

47. Richard Drake, *The Education of an Anti-Imperialist: Robert La Follette and U.S. Expansion* (University of Wisconsin Press, 2013), 124.

48. No leading American in a position of influence had entertained ambitions for acquiring those Spanish-held islands in the South Pacific prior to April 1898—not McKinley or his advisers, not Roosevelt or Lodge, not Alfred Thayer Mahan.

49. It also gave the U.S. Asiatic Squadron something to do. See Philip Zelikow, "Why Did America Cross the Pacific? Reconstructing the U.S. Decision to Take the Philippines, 1898–99," *Texas National Security Review* 1, no. 1 (November 2017): 43–45. Once war began, planners knew, the squadron would no longer have a port from which to operate. Hong Kong was controlled by Britain, and according to laws of neutrality could not allow a belligerent vessel to use its ports. When war broke out, therefore, the Asiatic fleet would have to either return to California or attack and take Manila Bay. There was a brief moment when U.S. planners considered launching an attack on Spain's Canary Islands in the Atlantic, but that was rejected.

50. Ivan Musicant, *Empire by Default: The Spanish-American War and the Dawn of the American Century* (Henry Holt, 1998), 102.

51. Many historians over the decades erroneously claimed that Roosevelt effectively launched the war in the Pacific by himself. See Beale, *Theodore Roosevelt,* 63. Julius

W. Pratt, *Expansionists of 1898: The Acquisition of Hawaii and the Spanish Islands* (Quadrangle Books, 1964), 226. As an example of the later distortions regarding the actions and intentions of American officials, see George F. Kennan, *American Diplomacy, 1900–1950* (University of Chicago Press, 1985), 14, in which he writes that Roosevelt "had long felt that we ought to take the Philippines," that "he had some sort of a prior understanding with Dewey to the effect that Dewey would attack Manila, regardless of the circumstances of the origin or the purpose of the war," and that, therefore, the attack on the Spanish fleet at Manila Bay was "determined primarily on the basis of a very able and quiet intrigue by a few strategically placed persons in Washington." In 1967, Robert H. Wiebe, in his influential book *The Search for Order, 1877–1920,* wrote that the McKinley administration "agreed with an ambitious Assistant Secretary of the Navy, Theodore Roosevelt, that in the event of war a portion of the fleet should move against Spain's Philippine colonies . . ." However, neither Kennan nor Wiebe was correct. The attack on Manila was not Roosevelt's idea, though he certainly favored it, but was part of long-standing plans in the event of war with Spain set forth by naval planners. Wiebe, *Search for Order, 1877–1920,* 241. A good summary of the facts can be found in Zelikow, "Why Did America Cross the Pacific?": 43–44.

52. John M. Dobson, *Reticent Expansionism: The Foreign Policy of William McKinley* (Duquesne University Press, 1988), 79–82; William Reynolds Braisted, *The United States Navy in the Pacific, 1897–1909* (University of Texas Press, 1958), 21–22; Grenville and Young, *Politics, Strategy, and American Diplomacy,* 273–76; Richard H. Miller, ed., *American Imperialism in 1898* (John Wiley and Sons, 1970), 9–10.

53. H. Wayne Morgan, *William McKinley and His America* (Syracuse University Press, 1963), 294.

54. Ibid., 294.

55. Major General Nelson A. Miles to Russell A. Alger in *Correspondence Relating to the War with Spain Including the Insurrection in the Philippine Islands and the China Relief Expedition* (Department of the Army, 1902), 648–49; Zelikow, "Why Did America Cross the Pacific?," 43–45.

56. Ephraim K. Smith, "'A Question from Which We Could Not Escape': William McKinley and the Decision to Acquire the Philippine Islands," *Diplomatic History* 9, no. 4 (Fall 1985): 370–71. McKinley hoped that in addition to securing Manila for Dewey, the capture might shorten the war by convincing the Spanish that their situation was hopeless and getting worse.

57. At the time and later, both publicly and privately, he insisted that after Dewey's victory, he "did not know what to do with them." Stuart Creighton Miller, *Benevolent Assimilation: The American Conquest of the Philippines, 1899–1903* (Yale University Press, 1984), 14. No evidence has ever emerged to suggest otherwise.

58. It was notable that when the British inquired early on what terms the United States would accept for ending the war with Spain, the State Department listed as demands the cession of Cuba and Puerto Rico and a coaling station somewhere in either the Philippines or the Caroline Islands chain. But the State Department explicitly stated that the Philippines themselves would "remain with Spain." Zelikow, "Why Did America Cross the Pacific?," 47–48.

59. As Brian McAllister Linn has argued, "Efforts to prove that the president was guided by an imperial master plan have lacked documentation sufficient to raise them above speculation." Far better documented, he suggests, is the "argument that American involvement in the Philippines was accidental and incremental. Under this view, neither the president nor his key advisers sought an empire. Essentially pragmatic and opportunistic, they viewed Manila as a bargaining chip with Spain

for Cuba or for securing trade interests in Asia. As the consequences of their actions unfolded, they expanded their horizons from Manila to Luzon, and then the entire Archipelago, but each time they were following less a premeditated course than seeking to deal with an immediate crisis. Each decision, in turn, committed them further." Brian McAllister Linn, *The Philippine War, 1899–1902* (University Press of Kansas, 2000), 3–5.

60. Ephraim K. Smith, "'A Question from Which We Could Not Escape,'" 373. One prominent senator remarked that he would "as soon turn a redeemed soul over to the devil as give the Philippines back to Spain." Zelikow, "Why Did America Cross the Pacific?," 52.

61. Ibid., 55.

62. Ibid., 52.

63. Collin, *Theodore Roosevelt's Caribbean,* 70–71.

64. Jonas, *The United States and Germany,* 60. It did not help that when German warships arrived at Manila Bay, they engaged in maneuvers which Dewey found so unnerving that at one point he told a German officer that "if Germany wants war, all right, we are ready." Collin, *Theodore Roosevelt's Caribbean,* 71–72.

65. A telegram to the German ambassador in Washington stated that "His Majesty the Emperor deems it a principal object of German policy to leave unused no opportunity which may arise from the Spanish-American War to obtain maritime fulcra in East Asia." And if Germany did not get the Philippines, they wanted "an equivalent compensation." The Germans at first mistakenly convinced themselves that the Filipinos wanted to give a throne to a German prince. Lester Burrell Shippee, "Germany and the Spanish-American War," *American Historical Review* 30, no. 4 (July 1925): 767.

66. Zelikow, "Why Did America Cross the Pacific?," 50.

67. *Census of the Philippine Islands, Taken Under the Direction of the Philippine Commission in the Year 1903* (United States Bureau of the Census, 1905), vol. 2, 46; Golay, *Face of Empire,* 51; Zelikow, "Why Did America Cross the Pacific?," 50.

68. Jack C. Lane, *Armed Progressive: General Leonard Wood* (Bison Books, 2009), 103.

69. Zelikow, "Why Did America Cross the Pacific?," 50. *Census of the Philippine Islands, Taken Under the Direction of the Philippine Commission in the Year 1903* (United States Bureau of the Census, 1905), vol. 2, 46; Golay, *Face of Empire,* 51.

70. McKinley and his advisers were also acutely aware that the situation in East Asia had been tense ever since the German seizure of Kiaochow. British officials feared the weakening and possible disintegration of the Chinese Empire would lead to international conflict. Even in 1895, following China's defeat by the Japanese, the British worried about "an Armageddon between the European Powers struggling for the ruins of the Chinese Empire." Quoted in T. G. Otte, *The China Question: Great Power Rivalry and British Isolation, 1894–1905* (Oxford University Press, 2007), 1; see Zelikow, "Why Did America Cross the Pacific?," 51.

71. H. Wayne Morgan, *America's Road to Empire: The War with Spain and Overseas Expansion* (John Wiley & Sons, 1965), 88; George F. Kennan, looking back on the decision, argued that the "alternative to the establishment of American power in the Philippines . . . was not a nice, free, progressive Philippine Republic: it was Spanish, German, or Japanese domination." Quoted in Robert L. Beisner, *Twelve Against Empire: The Anti-Imperialists, 1898–1900* (McGraw-Hill, 1968), 231.

72. Miller, *Benevolent Assimilation,* 20; Ephraim K. Smith, "'A Question from Which We Could Not Escape,'" 369.

73. Sullivan, *Our Times,* 1:535.

74. Linn, *Philippine War,* 30.

75. Miller, *Benevolent Assimilation,* 134.

76. Ibid., 21.

77. Some tried to argue that the Philippine archipelago, along with Japan, Formosa, and Australia, were somehow "pickets of the Pacific, standing guard at the entrances to trade" with the rest of Asia. But even they had to acknowledge that the Philippines were not exactly in "the direct line of ocean traffic" to the Far East. See Frank A. Vanderlip, assistant secretary of the treasury, "Facts about the Philippines with a Discussion of Pending Problems," *The Century,* August 1898; Curti, *Peace or War,* 180; Garraty, *Lodge,* 198.

78. Sullivan, *Our Times,* 1:535.

79. Harley A. Notter, *The Origins of the Foreign Policy of Woodrow Wilson* (The Johns Hopkins Press, 1937), 118.

80. Garraty, *Lodge,* 200.

81. See Widenor, *Lodge,* 108–109, 98, 87.

82. Miller, *Benevolent Assimilation,* 146.

83. Ibid., 23.

84. Pratt, *Expansionists of 1898,* 324.

85. William Day, quoted in Zelikow, "Why Did America Cross the Pacific?," 55.

86. Alan Dawley, *Changing the World: American Progressives in War and Revolution* (Princeton University Press, 2003), 19.

87. Beisner, *Twelve Against Empire,* 48.

88. Dawley, *Changing the World,* 18.

89. Mark Twain, "To the Person Sitting in Darkness," *The North American Review* (Feb. 1901), quoted by the Library of Congress, "The World of 1898: The Spanish American War." https://www.loc.gov/rr/hispanic/1898/twain.html.

90. The editor of *The Nation,* E. L. Godkin, opposed annexation of Hawaii in part because it would admit "alien, inferior, and Mongrel races to our nationality." Former president Grover Cleveland quipped that "Cuba ought to be submerged for a while before it will make an American state or territory of which we will be particularly proud." Miller, *Benevolent Assimilation,* 120–24.

91. Miller, *Benevolent Assimilation,* 125–26.

92. Carl Schurz recommended giving the islands to Belgium or Holland. Fish, *American Diplomacy,* 420.

93. Beisner, *Twelve Against Empire,* 32.

94. The treaty acquiring the Philippines, for example, fared better than the Hay-Pauncefote treaty negotiated with Britain over a future canal in Central America.

95. Notter, *Origins of the Foreign Policy,* 130. Morgan, *America's Road to Empire,* 88–89.

96. As a legal matter, the Teller Amendment was "a sweeping and categorical commitment by the United States to forego either annexing Cuba or making a protectorate of it." Healy, *United States in Cuba,* 23, 27.

97. Ibid., 28.

98. If the U.S. commander, General Leonard Wood, had had his way, it would have been years before American troops left. Healy, *United States in Cuba,* 36.

99. The amendment was passed as part of the 1901 Army Appropriations Bill.

100. Perez, *Cuba Between Reform and Revolution,* 187–88.

101. Linn, *Philippine War,* 31.

102. Golay, *Face of Empire,* ix, 35.

103. Linn, *Philippine War,* 64.

104. Otis wanted to "revive local government," put an end to "disorder in the country-

side," and expand the army's campaign of building roads and schools and medical clinics to show that American rule was preferable to chaos and violence. Linn, *Philippine War,* 200.

105. Linn, *Philippine War,* 89.
106. Ibid., 201.
107. Ibid., 190.
108. Ibid., 211.
109. Miller, *Benevolent Assimilation,* 80.
110. Ibid., 81.
111. Ibid., 102.
112. Linn, *Philippine War,* 209.
113. The officer continued, "It would surprise you what a close watch these people keep on American politics—every disloyal sentiment uttered by a man of any prominence in the United States is repeatedly broadcast through the islands and greatly magnified." Miller, *Benevolent Assimilation,* 185. And it was quite true. As one insurgent general put it in the summer of 1900, "Let us for a little while longer put forth heroic deeds of arms," because as "McKinley falls by the way side, the people abandon him and incline to the party of Mr. Bryan whose fundamental teaching is the recognition of our independence." Linn, *Philippine War,* 187.
114. "We had begun the Spanish War as a fight against a major European power, for the purpose of freeing the oppressed Cubans," one observer recalled. "We now found ourselves fighting a weak people, and in a role similar to what had been Spain's. There was no pride or other satisfaction to be got out of it." Sullivan, *Our Times,* 1:536.
115. Sullivan, *Our Times,* 1:538.
116. Harry Thurston Peck, *Twenty Years of the Republic* (Dodd, Meade and Co., 1929), 647.
117. Miller, *Benevolent Assimilation,* 107.
118. Ibid., 141.
119. As one sergeant wrote home, "Every soldier in the Eighth Army Corps understands that the responsibility of the blood of our boys rests on the heads of [Senators] Hoar, Gorman & Co." Miller, *Benevolent Assimilation,* 178.
120. Peck, *Twenty Years of the Republic,* 646.
121. Widenor, *Lodge,* 120.
122. Miller, *Benevolent Assimilation,* 137.
123. Beisner, *Twelve Against Empire,* 129.
124. Notter, *Origins of the Foreign Policy,* 130; Beisner, *Twelve Against Empire,* 122.
125. Widenor, *Lodge,* 120.
126. Ephraim K. Smith, "'A Question from Which We Could Not Escape,'" 373.
127. Linn, *Philippine War,* 214. Miller, *Benevolent Assimilation,* 208; Linn, *Philippine War,* 94.
128. Linn, *Philippine War,* 214–15.
129. Miller, *Benevolent Assimilation,* 163.
130. Linn, *Philippine War,* 312.
131. Miller, *Benevolent Assimilation,* 228.
132. Linn, *Philippine War,* 195.
133. Miller, *Benevolent Assimilation,* 179.
134. Richard H. Collin, *Theodore Roosevelt, Culture, Diplomacy, and Expansion: A New View of American Imperialism* (Louisiana State University Press, 1985), 144–45.
135. Miller, *Benevolent Assimilation,* 251.

136. Ibid., 104–105.
137. Beisner, *Twelve Against Empire,* 49.
138. Notter, *Origins of the Foreign Policy,* 133.
139. Akira Iriye, *From Nationalism to Internationalism: US Foreign Policy to 1914* (Routledge and Kegan Paul, 1977), 158–59.
140. Henry F. Pringle, *The Life and Times of William Howard Taft* (Archon Books, 1964), 1:160.
141. Quoted in Rhodes, *McKinley and Roosevelt Administrations,* 183. "I know of no chapter in American history more satisfactory than that which will record the conduct of the military government of Cuba," Root observed. American soldiers had "governed Cuba wisely" and "with sincere kindness" had helped the Cuban people establish "their own constitutional government." Rhodes, 182.
142. Perez, *Cuba Between Reform and Revolution,* 195–98.
143. Although large producers benefited most and small producers tended to be wiped out, "the export-oriented economic growth did bring about a significant level of prosperity that trickled down through the social class structure," as the historian José Domínguez notes. José Domínguez, *Cuba: Order and Revolution* (Belknap Press of Harvard University Press, 1978), 23, 28.
144. By the mid-1920s, Cuban capital, mostly accumulated during the sugar boom, dominated some 1,000 factories and businesses across the island. Perez, *Cuba Between Reform and Revolution,* 231.
145. Domínguez, *Cuba: Order and Revolution* 26.
146. Lester D. Langley, *The United States and the Caribbean in the Twentieth Century* (University of Georgia Press, 1982), 43.
147. Figures from U.S. State Department, Office of the Historian: https://history.state .gov/milestones/1899-1913/foreword.
148. Widenor, *Lodge,* 151.
149. William N. Tilchin, *Theodore Roosevelt and the British Empire: A Study in Presidential Statecraft* (St. Martin's Press, 1997), 216.
150. Beisner, *Twelve Against Empire,* 28, 33–34.
151. Miller, *Benevolent Assimilation,* 262–63, and also 253: "When the dream soured, the American people neither reacted with very much indignation, nor did they seem to retreat to their cherished political principles." "Anti-imperialism had never been a popular issue, although it was impossible to convince the diehards of it."
152. By comparison, the French lost more than 138,000 in six months of fighting against Prussia in 1870; the Chinese army suffered 2,000 dead in one day of fighting against Japan at Pyongyang in 1894.
153. Miller, *Benevolent Assimilation,* 269.
154. The first elected national assembly in 1907 was dominated by the conservative wing of the independence-minded Partido Nacionalista.
155. Sullivan, *Our Times,* 1:534. As the scholar Robert Osgood once put it, "Having acquired an empire, the American people were quick to exercise their privilege of ignoring it." Osgood, *Ideals and Self-Interest,* 79.
156. Miller, *Benevolent Assimilation,* 264–65.
157. Sullivan, *Our Times,* 1:55.

Chapter Two: Empire Without "Imperialism"; Imperialism Without "Empire"

1. Lars Schoultz, *Beneath the United States: A History of U.S. Policy Toward Latin America* (Harvard University Press, 1998), 234.

2. Margaret Leech, *In the Days of McKinley* (Harper and Bros., 1959), 464.

3. Sullivan, *Our Times,* 1:5.

4. The phrase is from George C. Herring, *From Colony to Superpower: U.S. Foreign Relations Since 1776* (Oxford University Press, 2011), 335. Defining "imperialism" is famously problematic. The tendency of most historians of American foreign policy has been to employ a fairly loose and all-encompassing definition. William L. Langer described it as "the rule or control, political or economic, direct or indirect, of one state, nation or people over other similar groups, or perhaps one might better say the disposition, urge or striving to establish such rule or control." Langer, *The Diplomacy of Imperialism, 1890–1902* (Alfred A. Knopf, 1935), 67. Many American historians, led by William Appleman Williams, have insisted that political and commercial hegemonism constitutes a form of imperialism or at least "neo-imperialism." The problem with these definitions is that they can apply to any great or even not great power that exerts predominant influence, economically, politically, or both, over other nations. Although all definitions are disputable, and imprecise, I prefer a more traditional definition of imperialism as being the direct exercise of sovereign power over a subject people.

5. Ronald Hyam, *Britain's Imperial Century, 1815–1914: A Study of Empire and Expansion* (Palgrave Macmillan, 2016), xvii–xviii.

6. Since they were paid for entirely out of revenues raised in India, this allowed Britain to compete globally without sparking rebellion by the British taxpayer. D. K. Fieldhouse, *The Colonial Empires: A Comparative Survey from the Eighteenth Century* (Delacorte Press, 1967), 272; John Darwin, *Unfinished Empire: The Global Expansion of Britain* (Bloomsbury Press, 2012), 390; Hyam, *Britain's Imperial Century,* 37.

7. Margaret MacMillan, *Paris 1919: Six Months That Changed the World* (Random House, 2003), 44.

8. Lawrence James, *The Rise and Fall of the British Empire* (St. Martin's Press, 1996), 204.

9. Hyam, *Britain's Imperial Century,* 35.

10. Chamberlain observed that "the crowded population of these islands" could not survive "for a single day" if Britain "cut adrift" the "great dependencies" that were the "natural markets" for British trade. Bernard Semmel, *Imperialism and Social Reform: English Social-Imperial Thought, 1895–1914* (Cambridge University Press, 1960), 85.

11. Nor was this just an aristocratic elite feeling. The British people wanted "two things," remarked Austen Chamberlain, "imperialism and social reform," and the liberal imperialists of the day thought the two went hand-in-hand. Semmel, *Imperialism and Social Reform,* 95, 25.

12. Neither of these matched the expanse of the Spanish empire at its height in the seventeenth century, of course, of which Samuel Johnson had once asked: had "heaven reserved . . . no pathless waste, no undiscovered shore, no secret island in the boundless main, no peaceful desert yet unclaimed by Spain?" Simon Collier, "The Spanish Conquests, 1492–1580," in *The Cambridge Encyclopedia of Latin America and the Caribbean,* ed. Simon Collier, Thomas E. Skidmore, and Harold Blakemore (Cambridge University Press, 1992), 194.

13. Jean-Marie Mayeur and Madeleine Rebérioux, *The Third Republic from Its Origins to the Great War, 1871–1914,* trans. J. R. Foster (Cambridge University Press, 1984), 273; Frederick Quinn, *The French Overseas Empire* (Praeger, 2000), 185.

14. Quinn, *French Overseas Empire,* 183, 176.

15. Ibid., 186.

16. It proved less than they hoped, but even so, when the war finally came in 1914, 134,000 Africans were thrown into the front lines and 30,000 of those would die fighting for *La France*. Quinn, *The French Overseas Empire,* 186–87.

17. Ibid., 113.

18. Viscount Grey of Fallodon, *Twenty-Five Years, 1892–1916,* 2 vols. (Frederick A. Stokes, 1925), 2:88. There were some similarities. Americans had treated the acquisition of the Philippines as an act of responsibility and a civilizing mission, which was the way Britons and French often spoke of their empire, too. The difference was that the British and French had no plans to let their imperial holdings go, even when the civilizing mission was complete, because they needed them. As the historian Bernard Semmel notes, even at the turn of the century "there were few men in [British] public life who still insisted that the inevitable tendency of the colonies was independence." Semmel, *Imperialism and Social Reform,* 55. For Americans, eventually letting go was the whole point, at least in theory. As one historian of comparative empire notes, they insisted on treating their colonies "either as proto-states of the Union . . . or as sovereign states with whom [they were] allied and who would finally throw off [their] tutelage." Fieldhouse, *The Colonial Empires,* 343. As Fieldhouse notes, unlike the British and French, the Americans made no attempt "to construct principles or institutions suitable for permanent colonial dependencies." The "underlying liberalism" of the "four colonial constitutions [Hawaii, Alaska, Puerto Rico, Philippines] indicated that they would eventually become states of the Union or fully independent." Fieldhouse, *The Colonial Empires,* 345. The chief exception was Puerto Rico, which occupied a permanent no-man's-land between colony and state.

19. Aside from the constant conquest of Indian lands, the most notable example of American rule over a people against their will was Jefferson's constitutionally dubious purchase of the Louisiana Territory, with its large French population.

20. Widenor, *Lodge,* 152–55.

21. Osgood, *Ideals and Self-Interest,* 78–79.

22. James A. Field, Jr., "American Imperialism: The Worst Chapter in Almost Any Book," *The American Historical Review* 83, no. 3 (June, 1978): 648, 653fn27.

23. Kenneth J. Hagan, *This People's Navy: The Making of American Sea Power* (Free Press, 1991), 233, 241. All this was in keeping with Mahan's strategic advice, for the man often described as among the leading "imperialist" theorists focused almost exclusively on defending American security in the Western Hemisphere. For this he believed the United States needed a high-seas battleship fleet, but only to meet another fleet if it attempted to cross one of the oceans. Field, "Worst Chapter," 647.

24. As late as 1917, the U.S. Navy remained "primarily a regional force." Its operational plans were premised "on the expectation that a single surface fleet would be met as it approached the western hemisphere. The Navy did not look far beyond that horizon." George W. Baer, *One Hundred Years of Sea Power: The U.S. Navy, 1890–1990,* 62.

25. In 1900, the U.S. share of world trade was ten percent. Britain's share was more than twice that, and even Germany's was higher. Kennedy, *Rise of the Anglo-German Antagonism,* 292.

26. William H. Becker, *Dynamics of Business-Government Relations: Industry and Exports, 189–1921* (University of Chicago Press), 42.

27. Beisner, *From the Old Diplomacy to the New,* 19.

28. On the other hand, 80 percent of American exports went to Europe and Canada. Figures from Beisner, *From the Old Diplomacy to the New,* 24–25.

29. Becker, *Dynamics of Business-Government Relations,* 14. Businesses seeking greater access to these markets did not look to gunboats. They looked for reciprocal tariff reductions and an easing of antitrust restrictions at home so they could compete more effectively with foreign cartels. They didn't have much luck with either because politicians from both parties cared more about the thousands of businesses and their employees producing for the home market than about increasing exports for the handful of firms that stood to gain from overseas sales. Becker, *Dynamics of Business-Government Relations,* 69–71. The same Republican Party that supposedly promoted "open door" imperialism to conquer foreign markets also stood for the high tariffs that stifled exports.

30. Field, "Worst Chapter," 656–57.

31. Harold Sprout and Margaret Sprout, *The Rise of American Naved Power, 1776–1918* (Princeton University Press, 1939), 264–67.

32. Ibid., 311.

33. Hagan, *This People's Navy,* 233, 241.

34. A contemporary observer called Hay's efforts "one of the most creditable episodes in American diplomacy, an example of benevolent impulse accompanied by energy and shrewd skill in negotiation." Sullivan, *Our Times,* 1:509.

35. Thomas A. Kohut, *Wilhelm II and the Germans: A Study in Leadership* (Oxford University Press, 1991), 150–51.

36. Widenor, *Lodge,* 155.

37. The founders' injunction against foreign "entanglements," the tradition of "operating alone," and the inability of American democracy to make reliable commitments all had the result, as one historian notes, of decreasing "both the immediate effectiveness and the larger impact of American foreign policy." A. E. Campbell, *Great Britain and the United States, 1895–1903* (Longmans, 1960), 192.

38. Zara Steiner and Keith Nelson, *Britain and the Origins of the First World War: The Making of the Twentieth Century* (MacMillan Press, 2003 [1977]), 175–76.

39. Alexander Hamilton, quoted in Helene Johnson Looze, *Alexander Hamilton and the British Orientation of American Foreign Policy, 1783–1803* (Mouton, 1969), 35.

40. Widenor, *Lodge,* 106.

41. Russia faced a similar problem but had no similar solution.

42. W. R. Grace ran a steamship line from Peru to New York beginning in 1893, but it was under the British flag.

43. Thomas M. Leonard, "Central America: The Search for Economic Development," in Thomas M. Leonard, ed., *United States–Latin American Relations, 1850–1903* (University of Alabama Press, 1999), 96.

44. In 1906 two-way trade between the United States and Latin America and the Caribbean was $36 million. Two-way trade with Europe was $1.8 billion. Leonard, ed., *United States–Latin American Relations,* 94.

45. Historians trying to argue that American imperialism in Central America was driven by U.S. investors searching for markets for "surplus capital" note that investments in Central America climbed from $21 million in 1897 to $93 million on the eve of World War I. See Walter LaFeber, *Inevitable Revolutions: The U.S. in Central America* (W. W. Norton, 1983), 35–37. But American investment in Europe and Canada over that same span of time climbed from $341 million to $1.558 billion. The figures for U.S. foreign investment (combined direct and portfolio) in this period are as follows:

	1897	1914
Central America	21	93
Europe	151	691
Canada	190	867
Mexico	200	853
S. America	38	365
Cuba/West Indies	49	336
Asia	23	245

Source: Cleona Lewis and Karl T. Schlottelbeck, *America's Stake in International Investments,* (Brookings, 1938), 606.

As Langley has noted, contrary to "Marxian analysis," American interventions were not followed by increased private investment, except in Cuba. Lester D. Langley, *The United States and the Caribbean, 1900–1970* (University of Georgia Press, 1980), 91.

46. As Walter LaFeber has noted, "These new states were . . . so untutored in self-government, so small, and so lacking in apparent natural resources, that a responsible, self-sufficient system would have been a miracle." LaFeber, *Inevitable Revolutions,* 27.

47. The United States did this less frequently and generally with less violence than the European powers, and Americans living in the region often complained about Washington's indifference. Dana Gardner Munro, *Intervention and Dollar Diplomacy in the Caribbean, 1900–1921* (Princeton University Press, 2016), 14–15. American warships landed marines in Haiti eight times between 1867 and 1900, for instance, and made other landings in the Dominican Republic, Panama, and along the Atlantic coast of Nicaragua. Britain had long been in the practice of sending warships to Latin and Caribbean shores to collect unpaid debts or to provide protection to British citizens. When Haitian authorities sentenced the son of a German father (and Haitian mother) to a month in prison for assaulting a policeman in 1897, Germany sent two warships and threatened to shell public buildings in the Haitian capital. The United States was less aggressive and less consistent than other powers, with administrations more likely to take the view that American citizens did business abroad at their own risk. As the international legal scholar John Bassett Moore put it in 1905, although governments liked to insist that their citizens traveled and did business abroad at their own risk, "no respectable government acts on any such theory." Munro, *Intervention and Dollar Diplomacy in the Caribbean,* 12–14.

48. The governments in Bogotá relied on the U.S. Navy to help put down rebellions in the Colombian-owned Panamanian isthmus. American troops were landed in Panama thirteen times between 1856 and 1902. When Roosevelt "took" the Panama Canal in 1902, it was chiefly by not helping the government put down the latest Panamanian rebellion. Political leaders in the Dominican Republic regularly offered to sell or lease control of the island's harbors and bays in exchange for U.S. protection against their opponents. Central Americans repeatedly called on the United States (and Mexico) to fend off aggression by their neighbors or against internal revolts supported by their neighbors.

49. Roosevelt regarded Venezuela's president as an "unspeakably villainous little monkey." Pringle, *Theodore Roosevelt: A Biography* (Harcourt Brace, 1931), 282; Philip

C. Jessup, *Elihu Root,* vol. 1, *1845–1909* (Dodd, Mead, 1938), 493. In 1895 a publicist had made much of alleged gold deposits, but Americans had little interest in Venezuela's markets or resources in 1902.

50. That domestic politics explained much of Cleveland's response in 1895, for instance, is well demonstrated in Grenville and Young, *Politics, Strategy, and American Diplomacy,* 158–60.

51. Munro, *Intervention and Dollar Diplomacy,* 70–71; Pringle, *Theodore Roosevelt,* 282; Jessup, *Elihu Root,* 1:493.

52. Mahan had warned that as soon as the canal was built the Caribbean would go from being a "comparatively deserted nook of the ocean" to a potential arena of strategic competition among the great powers. Alfred Thayer Mahan, *The Interest of America in Sea Power, Present and Future* (Little, Brown and Co., 1897), 12.

53. Special Message on Cuban Reciprocity, June 13, 1902, James D. Richardson, A Supplement to a Compilation of the *Messages and Papers of the Presidents,* 1789–1902 (Bureau of National Literature and Art, 1903), 356.

54. As Roosevelt put it, "If we intend to say, 'Hands off' to the powers of Europe, then sooner or later we must keep order ourselves." Munro, *Intervention and Dollar Diplomacy,* 77.

55. David F. Healy, *Drive to Hegemony: The United States in the Caribbean, 1898–1917* (University of Wisconsin Press, 1988), 106.

56. Ibid., 117, 113.

57. Munro, *Intervention and Dollar Diplomacy,* 76.

58. Ibid., 91. Even in Cuba, where he felt compelled to send troops in 1906 in fulfillment of the Platt Amendment, Roosevelt knew the American public was not interested in a prolonged occupation. Langley, *United States and the Caribbean,* 44.

59. Munro, *Intervention and Dollar Diplomacy,* 113.

60. As an unmistakable sign of his concern and the priority he placed on improving relations with Latin America, Root as secretary of state actually went on a months-long tour of the region, speaking and being feted in each South American capital. See note 69 below.

61. Munro, *Intervention and Dollar Diplomacy,* 114.

62. Jessup, *Elihu Root,* 1:158–517; Emily Rosenberg has referred to an ideology of "liberal-developmentalism." Emily S. Rosenberg, *Spreading the American Dream: American Economic and Cultural Expansion, 1890–1945* (Hill and Wang, 1982), 7.

63. Healy, *Drive to Hegemony,* 113, 117: If it was "absolutely necessary to do something," he wanted to do "as little as possible." Munro, *Intervention and Dollar Diplomacy,* 91.

64. Kris James Mitchener and Marc Weidenmier, "Empire, Public Goods, and the Roosevelt Corollary," *Journal of Economic History* 65 no. 3 (September 2005): 659–60, 690.

65. Jessup, *Elihu Root,* 1:541–42.

66. Langley, *United States and the Caribbean,* 44.

67. The Costa Rican foreign minister declared that "the names of Roosevelt and Diaz" would "always be remembered with gratitude by the humble citizens" of Central America who would "profit the most by stable peace." James Brown Scott, "The Central American Peace Conference of 1907," *American Journal of International Law* 2, no. 1 (January 1908): 132–33.

68. Healy, *Drive to Hegemony,* 137.

69. The bright spot for Root was that the government of Costa Rica requested arbitration by the new Court of Justice, which ordered the belligerents to withdraw from Honduran soil. Less promising was that the court imposed no sanctions on the

aggressors and each of the judges defended their own nation rather than acting with the impartiality for which Root had hoped. Langley, *United States and the Caribbean,* 49.

70. As one State Department official put it, "I shall be ashamed to look Mr. Root in the face. This intervention is contrary to his policy and what he has been preaching in Latin America." Healy, *Drive to Hegemony,* 139.

71. Ibid., 176.

72. As the historian José Domínguez has noted, it "enabled opposition politics to operate effectively in Cuba," and during the era of the Platt Amendment, Cuba enjoyed a high degree of "economic and political openness." Domínguez, *Cuba: Order and Revolution,* 52.

73. As Langley observes, when out of power, "they learned how to exploit American sentiment and precipitate American action by condemning the party in power and openly championing American intervention." When in power, "they learned how to plant in impressionable [American] minds the fear of disorder and disruption. Langley, *United States and the Caribbean,* 91.

74. The idea, as one senior official explained, was to substitute "dollars for bullets." Healy, *Drive to Hegemony,* 146.

75. Ibid., 149.

76. Kendrick A. Clements, *William Jennings Bryan: Missionary Isolationist* (University of Tennessee Press, 1983), 77; Healy, *Drive to Hegemony,* 146. Bryan's charge had more to do with American domestic politics and social conflict than with American policy in Central America. As one contemporary observer explained, at a time of increasingly radical progressivism it was "only necessary to hang a Wall Street tag on any proposition to make most politicians wary of it." See A Veteran Observer, "Will the Democrats Reverse Our Foreign Policies?," *American Review of Reviews,* January–June 1913.

77. As Langley recounts, in the Dominican Republic, there was a humorous proverb: "Two revolutions ago my son took a gun and went into politics." Langley, *United States and the Caribbean,* 58, 80.

78. Ibid., 80–83.

79. Walter Vinton Scholes and Marie V. Scholes, *The Foreign Policies of the Taft Administration* (University of Missouri Press, 1970), 54.

80. Zelaya had appointed as his successor another leader from his Liberal Party. The Taft administration, seeing this as a ruse, withheld recognition and waited for the anti-Zelaya revolution to triumph, which it soon did, with some timely, indirect assistance from the U.S. Navy. The navy declared a key town on the Atlantic coast off-limits to fighting, thereby preventing the rebels' defeat.

81. Scholes and Scholes, *Foreign Policies of the Taft Administration,* 65.

82. Munro, *Intervention and Dollar Diplomacy,* 208–9.

83. Langley, *United States and the Caribbean,* 62.

84. Jessup, *Elihu Root,* 1:505.

85. Ibid., 1:469, 482.

86. Ibid., 1:474.

87. Ibid., 1:484.

88. This was a deliberate repudiation of Secretary Olney's declaration in 1896 that the United States was "sovereign" in the hemisphere. Jessup, *Elihu Root,* 1:481.

89. The rights and wrongs of the situation were not as clear as some have imagined. As one historian has observed, "backing Colombia over Panama was no more correct than choosing Panama" over Colombia. Collin, *Roosevelt's Caribbean,* 561. Most Latin leaders shared Roosevelt's contempt for the Colombian government, which

had flippantly rejected the treaty that its own foreign minister had earnestly negotiated with John Hay for a lease on the Panamanian land.

90. As even the staunchly Democratic *Atlanta Constitution* put it, the American people "want and mean to have that canal, and they will visit their wrath upon whatever man or party may defeat their treaty." Collin, *Theodore Roosevelt's Caribbean,* 296. Peck, *Twenty Years of the Republic,* 703–4.

91. After proffering a lengthy defense of his actions to his cabinet, he asked, "Well, have I answered the charges? Have I defended myself?" To which Root responded, with characteristic barbed wit, "You certainly have, Mr. President. You have shown that you were accused of seduction, and you have conclusively proved that you were guilty of rape." Jessup, *Elihu Root,* 1:404–5; Rhodes, *McKinley and Roosevelt Administrations,* 272.

92. Woodrow Wilson, Message to Democratic Rallies, November 2, 1912, *The Papers of Woodrow Wilson,* ed. Arthur S. Link et al., vol. 25, 502–3; Mark T. Gilderhus, *Pan American Visions: Woodrow Wilson in the Western Hemisphere, 1913–1921* (University of Arizona Press, 1986), 8.

93. Healy, *Drive to Hegemony,* 165.

94. Arthur S. Link, *Wilson,* vol. 2, *The New Freedom* (Princeton University Press, 1956), 335, 337.

95. Healy, *Drive to Hegemony,* 192; Clements, *William Jennings Bryan,* 90.

96. Haiti was also given a new constitution, allegedly drafted by the then assistant secretary of the navy, Franklin Delano Roosevelt.

97. Link, *Wilson: Struggle for Neutrality,* 495; see also Knock, *To End All Wars,* 84.

98. Schoultz, *In Their Own Best Interest: A History of the U.S. Effort to Improve Latin Americans* (Harvard University Press, 2018), 84; Link, *Wilson: New Freedom,* 375.

99. John Gallagher, "Nationalisms and *the Crisis of Empire, 1919–1922,"* *Modern Asian Studies* 15, no. 3 (1981): 355–68; Darwin, *Unfinished Empire,* 304.

100. Hyam, *Britain's Imperial Century,* 187.

101. Darwin, *Unfinished Empire,* 225.

102. Quinn, *French Overseas Empire,* 121; Darwin, *Unfinished Empire,* 396–97.

103. Hyam, *Britain's Imperial Century,* 185.

104. Enrique Krauze, *Mexico: Biography of Power* (Harper, 1997), 263.

105. "By the standards of Latin America," one British observer noted, "there was nothing very novel about the Mexican revolution of 1912–1913, and, by those standards, the problem for foreign governments was simple. They had to await the emergence, from the welter of competing revolutionaries, of a government stable enough to maintain law and order and fulfill its international obligations; and they had to recognize it, at least de facto, as soon as possible after it had emerged." Link, *Wilson: New Freedom,* 370.

106. Ibid., 349–350.

107. Gilderhus, *Pan American Vision,* 19, 33.

108. Link, *Wilson: New Freedom,* 367, 373.

109. Schoultz, *Beneath the United States,* 234.

110. House recorded in his diary at the end of October 1913 that "the President has in mind to declare war against Mexico." Link, *Wilson: New Freedom,* 379, 380–81.

111. Ibid., 396–98.

112. Ibid., 404.

113. Ibid., 399-402.

114. His adviser, Colonel House, did not see why Mexicans should "object to our helping adjust [their] unruly household," especially since "our motives were unselfish." Gilderhus, *Pan American Visions,* 33.

115. Or at least this is how one Mexican historian characterized his views. Krauze, *Mexico,* 346. Wilson and his advisers, in turn, marveled at the Constitutionalists' "admirable skill" in "preventing their friends from helping them." Link, *Wilson: New Freedom,* 400, 383, 384.

116. Knock, *To End All Wars,* 29; Link, *Wilson: New Freedom,* 394.

117. Karl M. Schmitt, *Mexico and the United States, 1821–1973: Conflict and Coexistence* (John Wiley & Sons, 1974), 136.

118. Link, *Wilson: Struggle for Neutrality,* 240.

119. Link, *Wilson: New Freedom,* 393–94.

120. Ibid.

121. Ibid., 393–34.

122. Knock, *To End All Wars,* 28–29; Link, *Wilson: New Freedom 393–94.*

123. In Mexico, there was an alliance between the Catholic Church and "the educated, privileged, and propertied class . . . owning and running everything, the reactionary class." This, Wilson insisted, was also "the wedge in our own domestic politics." Knock, *To End All Wars,* 28.

124. Wilson, "Address before the Southern Commercial Congress, Mobile, Ala., October 27, 1913" (The American Presidency Project, https://www.presidency.ucsb.edu/documents/address-before-the-southern-commercial-congress-mobile-alabama).

125. Jessup, *Elihu Root,* 2:260–61.

126. Widenor, *Lodge,* 178. Lodge argued that denying Huerta recognition would probably only "increase the anarchy now existing and leave the situation worse than before."

127. To Root, it was comic opera: "Mr. Villa seems to indicate the same disposition to eat Mr. Carranza up that Mr. Carranza exhibited as to eating Mr. Huerta up, following Mr. Huerta's example in eating Mr. Madero up because Mr. Madero had eaten Mr. Diaz up." Jessup, *Elihu Root,* 2:260–61.

128. In retrospect, even Wilson's admiring biographer wondered how he could have "seriously contemplated lending any support at all" to Villa, much less imagined him as the next leader of Mexico. Link, *Wilson: Struggle for Neutrality,* 238–39.

129. The journalist John Reed, whose writings helped turn Villa into a hero, frankly admitted that the man's "misdeeds" were greater than "those of any other celebrated person in the world." Krauze, *Mexico,* 307.

130. Ibid., 315.

131. Ibid., 318, 311. Whether despite or because of these exploits, Villa became a living legend in the United States. A Hollywood film company even made a movie of his exploits, *The Life of General Villa,* filmed on location. (The actor playing Villa recalled, "In the mornings we succeeded in postponing the executions from five to seven o'clock so that there would be good light.") It opened in New York in May 1914.

132. Link, *Wilson: Struggle for Neutrality,* 239.

133. Jessup, *Elihu Root,* 1:260–61.

134. In one instance, Villa's men stopped a train, removed eighteen American passengers, robbed them, stripped them, and executed all but one of them.

135. Arthur S. Link, *Wilson,* vol. 4, *Confusions and Crises, 1915–1916* (Princeton University Press, 1964), 204–14.

136. Ibid., 214.

137. "If the thing were reversed," one adviser noted, "we would not allow any foreign army to be sloshing around in our country 300 miles from the border, no matter who they were." Link, *Wilson: Confusions and Crises,* 214–15, 282.

138. Ibid., 305.

139. Ibid., 314.
140. Ibid., 307.
141. Merlo J. Pusey, *Charles Evans Hughes* (Columbia University Press, 1963), 1:354.
142. Link, *Wilson: Confusions and Crises,* 199–200.
143. Ibid., 313.
144. Ibid.
145. Link, *Wilson: New Freedom,* 328n30.
146. Link, *Wilson: Confusions and Crises,* 200.
147. Sullivan, *Our Times,* 1:55.
148. This was true in congressional elections, as well. The Republican Party, the more internationalist of the two parties, controlled both houses from 1896 to 1910, losing only when the internationalist Woodrow Wilson came into office.
149. Widenor, *Lodge,* 168.
150. Henry L. Stimson and McGeorge Bundy, *On Active Service in War & Peace* (Harper & Brothers, 1947), 82–83.

Chapter Three: Collapse of the Nineteenth-Century World Order

1. Woodrow Wilson, Address at Independence Hall: "The Meaning of Liberty," Philadelphia, July 4, 1914. (The American Presidency Project, https://www.presidency.ucsb.edu/documents/address-independence-hall-the-meaning-liberty).
2. Out of 130 peace groups in the world in 1914, over 60 were American. Kuehl, *Seeking World Order: United States and International Organization to 1921* (Vanderbilt University Press, 1969), 172.
3. On Roosevelt, see Kuehl, *Seeking World Order,* 72.
4. They were limited because they agreed to submit disputes to international tribunals, except in matters concerning "vital interests" and "national honor." Root believed it was utopian foolishness to ask nations to go further than this. Kuehl, *Seeking World Order,* 113.
5. Theodore S. Woolsey, Yale professor of international law, thought it an admirable idea to begin the quest for an international legal regime in the New World, to establish there a "concert of nations" to maintain stability and promote trade, employing "an American police power in the hands of all the stable, responsible and orderly states of this hemisphere." Kuehl, *Seeking World Order,* 114, 118.
6. Ibid., 114.
7. See, for instance, Evan Thomas, *The War Lovers: Roosevelt, Lodge, Hearst and the Rush to Empire, 1898* (Little, Brown and Co., 2010).
8. Theodore Roosevelt's first annual message to Congress, December 3, 1901 (University of Virginia, Miller Center https://millercenter.org/the-presidency/presidential-speeches/december-3-1901-first-annual-message); quoted in James R. Holmes, *Theodore Roosevelt and World Order: Police Power in International Relations* (Potomac Books, 2006), 69.
9. He spoke optimistically of a growing sentiment "among the civilized nations" to settle disputes by such "rational" means and thereby "do away with much of the provocation and excuse for war." Theodore Roosevelt, "Second Annual Message," December 2, 1902 (University of Virginia, Miller Center, https://millercenter.org/the-presidency/presidential-speeches/december-2-1902-second-annual-message); Theodore Roosevelt, "Third Annual Message," December 7, 1903 (University of Virginia, Miller Center, https://millercenter.org/the-presidency/presidential-speeches/december-7-1903-third-annual-message).
10. Curti, *Peace or War,* 190–91.

11. Kuehl, *Seeking World Order,* 124.
12. Ibid., 95.
13. Osgood, *Ideals and Self-Interest,* 87.
14. Theodore Roosevelt letter to Hugo Munsterberg, October 3, 1914, in A. Scott Berg ed., *World War I and America: Told By the Americans Who Lived It* (Library of America, 2017), 45.
15. When advocates of world government envisioned how it would be structured, they saw the American Constitution writ large, with an executive, a legislature, and a judicial branch. Kuehl, *Seeking World Order,* 87; David C. Hendrickson, *Union, Nation, or Empire: The American Debate over International Relations, 1789–1941* (University Press of Kansas, 2009), 294.
16. Iriye, *From Nationalism to Internationalism,* 183–84.
17. Raymond A. Esthus, *Theodore Roosevelt and the International Rivalries* (Regina Books, 1970), 1–2.
18. Widenor, *Lodge,* 134.
19. These included Jamaica, the Bahamas, Bermuda, the Virgin Islands, Grenada, British Honduras, and British Guyana.
20. Campbell, *Great Britain and the United States,* 4, 47.
21. Again, as Campbell puts it, "Britain had no interests conflicting with those of the United States because she chose to have none." Campbell, *Great Britain and the United States,* 79.
22. Charles S. Campbell, Jr., *Anglo-American Understanding, 1898–1903* (Johns Hopkins University Press, 1957), 47.
23. C. J. Lowe and M. L. Dockrill, *Mirage of Power: British Foreign Policy* (Routledge and Kegan Paul, 1972), 1:96–97.
24. Garraty, *Lodge,* 152.
25. By 1900, during the Boer War, Lodge had concluded that "the downfall of the British Empire" was something that "no rational American could regard as anything but a misfortune to the United States." Campbell, *Anglo-American Understanding,* 180.
26. Darwin, *Unfinished Empire,* 401.
27. Paul Kennedy, *The Rise and Fall of the Great Powers. Economic Change and Military Conflict From 1500 to 2000* (Random House, 1987), 155.
28. Esthus, *Theodore Roosevelt and International Rivalries,* 60. On British suspicions, see 39–40. At one point he advised his friend the British ambassador that Germany ought to be "counted as a great factor in favor of and not against England." Theodore Roosevelt to Cecil Spring Rice, Nov. 19, 1900, Elting E. Morison, ed., *The Letters of Theodore Roosevelt,* 2 vols. (Harvard University Press, 1951), 2:1422–23. An exasperated Prime Minister Lansdowne once commented that "Roosevelt terrifies me almost as much as the German Emperor." Esthus, *Theodore Roosevelt and International Rivalries,* 58.
29. Esthus, *Theodore Roosevelt and International Rivalries,* 57.
30. Ibid., 56.
31. Ibid., 83. Lodge responded that neither the Monroe Doctrine nor the "great rule" prohibited the United States from participating "in any European engagement of any kind whatever." Lodge, "The Monroe Doctrine and Morocco," *Harper's Weekly,* March 10, 1906.
32. After Hawaii was safely annexed to the United States. The McKinley administration and Republican supporters in Congress had feared that the Japanese, with a navy that "surpasses ours in strength," might get Hawaii first. They rushed to

annex the island kingdom in what the Senate Foreign Relations Committee called a "preliminary skirmish in the great coming struggle between the civilization and the awakening forces of the East and the civilization of the West." Akira Iriye, *Pacific Estrangement: Japanese and American Expansion, 1897–1911* (Harvard University Press, 1972), 51–52.

33. TR to Spring Rice, Nov. 19, 1900. *Roosevelt Letters,* vol. 2, 1422–23.

34. The great concern in those years was that an expansive Russia, moving with the power of a glacier across the Eurasian continent, was about to swallow up China, which, in the calculations of Alfred Thayer Mahan and other turn-of-the-century students of "geopolitics," would mean dominance of Eurasia and eventually the world—not to mention the closing of the Open Door to American trade. As Henry Adams had expressed the general concern, "the vast force of inertia known as China was to be united with the huge bulk of Russia in a single mass which no amount of new force could henceforward deflect." Henry Adams, *The Education of Henry Adams* (Houghton Mifflin, 1918), 415; Pringle, *Theodore Roosevelt,* 375; Tilchin, *Theodore Roosevelt and the British Empire,* 58.

35. Theodore Roosevelt, quoted in Frank Ninkovich, "Theodore Roosevelt: Civilization as Ideology," *Diplomatic History* 10, no. 3 (Summer 1986): 238.

36. Akira Iriye, *Across the Pacific: An Inner History of American–East Asian Relations* (Harcourt, Brace & World, 1967), 105–6; Iriye, *Pacific Estrangement,* 217, 164, 263 fn47.

37. Iriye, *Across the Pacific,* 106.

38. Charles E. Neu, *The Troubled Encounter: The United States and Japan* (Wiley, 1975), 47.

39. Iriye, *Across the Pacific,* 120.

40. Ibid., 107.

41. The United States should "not take any steps as regards Manchuria which will cause the Japanese to feel . . . that we are hostile to them, or a menace . . . to their interests." Kennan, *American Diplomacy,* 46; Iriye, *Across the Pacific,* 107–8.

42. Ibid., 107–8.

43. Iriye, *Pacific Estrangement,* 163.

44. Ibid., 163.

45. Beale, *Theodore Roosevelt,* 328 fnB. Admiral Zinovy Petrovitch Rozhdestvensky was the commander of Russian naval forces defeated by the Japanese in the Russo-Japanese War of 1904–1905.

46. Iriye, *Across the Pacific,* 112.

47. The Chinese agreed, for the most part, for although Americans had always demanded the same rights and privileges for themselves that China had been forced to grant the imperial powers, and had thus benefited from China's oppression, nevertheless leading Chinese officials and reformers from the late 1890s through the first two decades of the twentieth century did often look to the United States for support against the more aggressive empires. In 1908 Chinese officials even tried to convince the United States to enter into an alliance that would "seal the bonds of friendship" and, more importantly, "guarantee China against the ambitions of Japan." Michael H. Hunt, *The Making of a Special Relationship: The United States and China to 1914* (Columbia University Press, 1983), 189–93, 205.

48. Ibid., 210.

49. On the Open Door as "a myth," see Iriye, *Across the Pacific,* 80–81. As the historian Michael Hunt has observed, Hay's notes had been "a token nod to the future possibilities of the China market, but not much more." They had offered no protec-

tion for American investments in China. They had promised no effort by the U.S. government to promote trade. They had contained no measures to prevent other powers from closing the open door if they chose to do so.

50. Hay to TR, August 2, 1903. A. Whitney Griswold, *The Far Eastern Policy of the United States* (Harcourt Brace and Co., 1938), 86.

51. Theodore Roosevelt, quoted in Kenneth B. Pyle, *Japan Rising* (PublicAffairs, 2007), 188.

52. Philander Knox, quoted in Iriye, *Across the Pacific,* 123.

53. While acknowledging that they were a "cause of uneasiness in European diplomacy," Taft officials insisted the United States "was involved neither directly nor indirectly with the causes or questions incident to . . . these hostilities" and "maintained in regard to them an attitude of absolute neutrality and complete political disinterestedness." Sprout and Sprout, *The Rise of American Naval Power,* 282.

54. Link, *Wilson: Struggle for Neutrality,* 1.

55. Britain and France signed only after the outbreak of the war. Germany and Austria never signed.

56. Daniel T. Rodgers, *Atlantic Crossings: Social Politics in a Progressive Age* (Harvard University Press, 2000), 57, 273.

57. Ibid., 75.

58. Kuehl, *Seeking World Order,* 144; Notter, *Origins of the Foreign Policy,* 276.

59. Calvin DeArmond Davis, *The U.S. and the Second Hague Peace Conference* (Cornell University Press, 1962), 143.

60. Kuehl, *Seeking World Order,* 61.

61. Osgood, *Ideals and Self-Interest,* 136.

62. Roosevelt Nobel Lecture, May 5, 1910, Christiania (Oslo), Norway. The proposal was at least as much Carnegie's as Roosevelt's. The steel magnate, philanthropist, "anti-imperialist," and founder of the Carnegie Endowment for International Peace had been pushing the idea of a "League" in public speeches since 1905. During Roosevelt's post-presidential African safari (for which Carnegie was footing the bill), the peace philanthropist pressed the ex-president to raise the idea in Europe. Roosevelt, reassured by Elihu Root's enthusiasm for the idea, and perhaps feeling beholden to the man paying for his very expensive vacation, complied. Although Roosevelt read Kant (see Theodore Roosevelt, *Theodore Roosevelt, an Autobiography* (Scribner's and Sons, 1922), 334, there is no evidence he took his idea for the League from Kant. Joseph Frazier Wall, *Andrew Carnegie* (University of Pittsburgh Press, 1989), 919–36.

63. A. J. P. Taylor, *The Struggle for Mastery in Europe, 1848–1918* (Oxford University Press, 1954), 427.

64. Ibid.

65. Annika Mombauer, *The Origins of the First World War: Controversies and Consensus* (Longman, 2002), 150–51.

66. Isabel V. Hull, *Absolute Destruction: Military Culture and the Practices of War in Imperial Germany* (Cornell University Press, 2006), 165.

67. Ibid., 166–67.

68. Roger Chickering, *Imperial Germany and the Great War, 1914–1918* (Cambridge University Press, 2004), 8. Faced with these circumstances, an anxious German leadership was increasingly prepared to take risks, including "cutting the Gordian knot with the help of a liberating war against the Reich's external enemies." Volker R. Berghahn, *Imperial Germany, 1871–1918: Economy, Society, Culture and Politics* (Berghahn Books, 2005), 263.

69. Martin Gilbert, *The First World War: A Complete History* (Holt, 2004), 8–9.

70. Ibid., 13. In speaking of "preventive war," he was not talking about launching war on Russia before Russia could launch war on Germany. As the German historian Fritz Fischer explained, the idea of preventive war in 1914 was "to defeat the enemy powers before they became too strong" to resist a rising Germany's influence and ambitions, which Fischer summed up as "hegemony over Europe." Mombauer, *Origins*, 153.

71. Gilbert, *First World War*, 13.

72. Ibid., 18–19. As Moltke told his opposite number on the Austrian general staff, any delay in war "meant a lessening of our chances." Gilbert, *First World War*, 13.

73. Ibid., 19.

74. Ibid., 23.

75. Ibid., 24–25.

76. The whole country, reported the British ambassador, had "gone wild with joy at the prospect of war." Gilbert, *First World War*, 24.

77. "To try and avoid such a calamity as a European war, I beg you in the name of our old friendship to do what you can to stop our allies from going too far." Gilbert, *First World War*, 26.

78. Ibid., 26.

79. Mombauer, *Origins*, 23.

80. Ibid., 204.

81. Ibid., 23.

82. Ibid., 193.

83. Gilbert, *First World War*, 25.

84. Ibid., 33–34.

85. The British ambassador in Paris, at the height of the crisis, told a reporter that the British did not trust the Russians and were "not going to feel comfortable about entering a quarrel in which the Serbs and Russians are involved." Max Hastings, *Catastrophe 1914: Europe Goes to War* (Alfred A. Knopf, 2013), 35.

86. Gilbert, *First World War*, 23. Prime Minister Asquith himself told the king that while Europe was "within measurable distance of a real Armageddon. . . . [,] [h]appily there seems to be no reason why we should be anything more than spectators." Gilbert, 22.

87. Ibid., 26.

88. Hastings, *Catastrophe*, 90–91.

89. Ibid., 92–93.

Chapter Four: The European War and American Neutrality

1. Gwynn, *Letters and Friendships*, 2:320.

2. Link, *Wilson: Struggle for Neutrality*, 31.

3. Ibid., 7.

4. Gilbert, *First World War*, 72.

5. *Chicago Daily Tribune*, Aug. 4, 1914; *St. Louis Post-Dispatch*, Aug. 8, 1914; "No Favoritism to the Stranded," *New York Times*, Aug. 6, 1914.

6. Although Mahan had four years earlier warned about the dangers to the United States of a British defeat at German hands.

7. "President Advises Nation to Be Calm," *New York Times*, Aug. 3, 1914; Ray Stannard Baker, *Woodrow Wilson: Life and Letters*, vol. 5, *Neutrality, 1914–1915* (Doubleday, Doran & Co., 1938), 2–3.

8. On August 3 the German government released its "White Book," entitled "How Russia and her Ruler betrayed Germany's confidence and thereby caused the Euro-

pean War," a curated set of documents purporting to show that the tsar had mobilized his armies while pretending to negotiate for peace, while the German emperor tried to avoid war. "The German White Book: Germany's Reasons for War with Russia," *New York Times,* Aug. 15, 1914. The British put out a "Blue Book" with their own collection of documents purporting to show that it was the kaiser who had talked peace while preparing for war. It included the comment by the German chancellor that would become notorious among those Americans who held Germany responsible for the war—when he referred to the seventy-five-year-old Treaty of London guaranteeing Belgium's neutrality as a "scrap of paper." *Great Britain and the European Crisis,* (Taylor, Govnet, Evans and Coe, 1914). (The account was from the British ambassador's meeting with Bethmann Hollweg on Aug. 4, in which the German chancellor expressed outrage that the British had gone to war "just for a word—'neutrality,'" and "just for a scrap of paper." "Goschen's Story of German Break," *New York Times,* Aug. 28, 1914.)

9. The first quotation is from Col. House, the second from Root. Charles Seymour, *The Intimate Papers of Colonel House: Behind the Political Curtain, 1912–1917* (Houghton Mifflin, 1926–1928), 1:285; Philip C. Jessup, *Elihu Root* (Dodd, Mead and Co., 1938), 2:313.
10. Garraty, *Lodge,* 305.
11. Gwynn, *Letters and Friendships,* 2:218–19; Joseph Bucklin Bishop, *Theodore Roosevelt and His Time* (Charles Scribner's Sons, 1920), 2:370–71.
12. Jessup, *Elihu Root,* 2:315, 318–19.
13. John Milton Cooper, Jr., *The Vanity of Power: American Isolationism and the First World War, 1914–1917* (Greenwood, 1969), 87.
14. Even in the East only 40 percent had a clear preference for the Allies. Cooper, *Vanity of Power,* 20–21. These surveys of newspaper editors were the closest thing to a national poll in those days.
15. Nasaw, *The Chief,* 241. It is interesting to note, given Hearst's alleged role in bringing on the war with Spain in 1898, that he had no interest in getting the United States into war between 1914 and 1918. Either he no longer had an interest in selling newspapers, or he did not believe he had to support war in order to sell them.
16. Someone had to "keep cool," he said, "while our people grow hotter with discussing the war and all that it involves!" Link, *Wilson: Struggle for Neutrality,* 73. Spring Rice believed the reason Wilson did not cite the Hague Conventions in response to Germany's invasion of Belgium, as Roosevelt privately demanded, was because he genuinely feared "provoking civil commotion in the United States." Gwynn, *Letters and Friendships,* 2:346-47.
17. "Paraders Cheer Times War News," *New York Times,* Aug. 6, 1914.
18. Link, *Wilson: Struggle for Neutrality,* 66–67.
19. Woodrow Wilson, "Message on Neutrality," Aug. 19, 1914). (University of Virginia, Miller Center, https://millercenter.org/the-presidency/presidential-speeches/august-19-1914-message-neutrality).
20. "Schiff Sees Dangers in a Loan to Russia," *New York Times,* Nov. 26, 1915.
21. Schiff lobbied Wilson for an arms embargo that would have favored Germany. See Baker, *Woodrow Wilson: Life and Letters,* vol. 5, *Neutrality,* 188–89, and Link, *Wilson: Struggle for Neutrality,* 168. In a letter to the *Times,* the prominent millionaire and philanthropist August Heckscher, a German Jew who had emigrated from Hamburg in 1867, complained that "the great New York dailies have practically taken it for granted that in the present war Germany is at fault, and have wrung

the changes on that conclusion." August Heckscher, "The Case for Germany" *New York Times,* Aug. 8, 1914.

22. Campbell, *Anglo-American Understanding,* 3; Gwynn, *Letters and Friendships,* 2:309fn2.
23. Garraty, *Lodge,* 306.
24. The American people, he observed, did not want to be pushed into an anti-British posture by Irish American or German American pressures, but they also didn't want him "to favor England at the expense of Ireland or Germany." Widenor, *Lodge,* 149. Privately, he could be heard railing against "the hyphenated American, the German-American, the Irish-American." Alexander DeConde, *Ethnicity, Race, and American Foreign Policy: A History* (University Press of New England, 1992), 56. But, and much to the dismay of his British friends, Roosevelt favored Irish home rule, as did Wilson, who insisted that "there never could be a real comrade-ship between America and England" until the question of Ireland was "out of the way." Seth P. Tillman, *Anglo-American Relations at the Paris Peace Conference of 1919* (Princeton University Press, 1961), 197.
25. Francis M. Carroll, "America and the 1916 Rising," in *1916: The Long Revolution,* ed. Gabriel Doherty and Dermot Keogh (Mercier Press, 2008), 131.
26. Justus D. Doenecke, *Nothing Less Than War: A New History of America's Entry into World War I* (University Press of Kentucky, 2011), 17.
27. According to the 1910 census, more than eight million Americans had been either born in Germany or born in the United States to a German parent, and that did not include the many German Americans who had begun migrating to the United States since as far back as the 1840s. See Link, *Wilson: Struggle for Neutrality,* 20.
28. During the confrontation between Roosevelt and Germany over Venezuela in 1902, many had regarded the coverage of the matter in the American newspapers as slanted against Germany and suspected an English plot to subvert relations between Washington and Berlin.
29. Carl Wittke, "American Germans in Two World Wars." *The Wisconsin Magazine of History* 27, no. 1 (1943): 3, Link, *Wilson: Struggle for Neutrality,* 21; Clifton James Child, *The German-Americans in Politics, 1914–1917* (University of Wisconsin Press, 1939), 23.
30. Drake, *Education of an Anti-Imperialist,* 137.
31. Petra DeWitt, *Degrees of Allegiance: Harassment and Loyalty in Missouri's German-American Community During World War I* (Ohio University Press, 2012), 36; Child, *German-Americans in Politics,* 24.
32. Child, *German-Americans in Politics,* 27, 33–34.
33. Wilson might be an "Orangem[an] . . . by descent . . . and by education a Presbyterian," the British ambassador observed, but as the leader of the Democratic Party he would be "bound in every way" to take Irish American demands seriously. Gwynn, *Letters and Friendships,* 2:393.
34. Joseph P. Tumulty, *Woodrow Wilson As I Know Him* (HardPress Publishing, 2012), 145–46.
35. Bucklin Bishop, *Theodore Roosevelt and His Time,* vol. 2 (Charles Scribner's Sons, 1920), 398–99.
36. *New York Sun,* Aug. 23, 1914, quoted in Henry Cabot Lodge, *The Senate and the League of Nations* (Charles Scribner's Sons, 1925), 372–73. Lodge professed to believe that Wilson was among those college professors who supported Germany because of their "intellectual connection with German thought, German books and German writers." But he refused to condemn Germany's violation of Belgian

neutrality publicly, insisting that while he retained "the deepest sympathy" for Belgians' sufferings, his duty as a senator required "an attitude of exact neutrality." Garraty, *Lodge,* 305–6.

37. Theodore Roosevelt, "The World War: Its Tragedies and Its Lessons," *Outlook,* Sept. 23, 1914.

38. Theodore Roosevelt, "The International Posse Comitatus," *New York Times,* Nov. 8, 1914; Theodore Roosevelt, "The Foreign Policy of the United States," *Outlook,* Aug. 22, 1914; "Theodore Roosevelt on Ultimate Cause of War," *New York Times,* Oct. 11, 1914; "Col. Theodore Roosevelt Writes on What America Should Learn from the War," *New York Times,* Sept. 27, 1914; Roosevelt, "The World War." These were not off-the-cuff comments made in the hazy confusion of the early days of war. They were the product of thought and consideration, offered in print over several weeks during which Louvain was destroyed, Belgian civilians were executed en masse, the cathedral at Rheims was shelled, and the German army was racing toward Paris. Roosevelt took note of German actions but explained that "in matters of vital national moment" German leaders believed there were "no such things as abstract right and wrong." Whatever Americans might think of it, all great nations, including the United States, had often taken the same view. His writings prompted letters from English and French acquaintances "upbraiding" him for his "pro-German leaning," and even Edward Grey thought it necessary to explain to him what a disaster it would be for civilization if Germany won. Grey, *Twenty-Five Years,* 2:143–45.

39. Lodge admitted it was risky to say what he really believed in "a country where there are large foreign groups." Widenor, *Lodge,* 194. The war had broken out in an election year, and Roosevelt was trying to save his collapsing Progressive Party from oblivion while also testing the waters for another run at the presidency. He did not want to alienate German Americans, with whom he had always enjoyed a good relationship, and his political advisers begged him not to criticize Wilson's popular neutrality policies. Roosevelt admitted the situation put him "in a very difficult position." The German Americans knew that he always kept his eye on "the large German vote," as one German-language newspaper put it. See John M. Thompson, "Theodore Roosevelt and the Politics of the Roosevelt Corollary," *Diplomacy and Statecraft* 26, no. 4 (Dec. 2105): 576. Roosevelt promised to hold off until after the campaign, at which point he would "smite the administration with a heavy hand." Roosevelt letter to Lodge, Dec. 8, 1914, Theodore Roosevelt and Henry Cabot Lodge, *Selections from the Correspondence of Theodore Roosevelt and Henry Cabot Lodge, 1884–1918,* 2 vols. (Scribner's, 1925), 2:449. Only when the congressional elections were over, he told Grey, could he begin to air his views "much more openly." Grey, *Twenty-Five Years,* 2:146. Even Roosevelt's Republican friends, he recounted disgustedly, "fell over themselves" praising Wilson "for his noble and humanitarian peace policy" and argued "how splendid it was that Wilson . . . had preserved such absolute neutrality in the European war." He waited until five days after the election, a full three months into the war, before stating publicly that Germany's "invasion and subjugation of Belgium" represented a clear "breach of international morality." Theodore Roosevelt, "The International Posse Comitatus," *New York Times,* Nov. 8, 1914. Unshackled at last, he was thankful that he no longer had to "consider the effect of my actions on any party." Roosevelt to Lodge, February 18, 1915, *Selections from the Correspondence,* 2:456. When Roosevelt later republished his early essays on the war in book form, he changed some of the passages, cutting out those sentences where he refused to pass judgment on German actions, as well as his early insistence that the United States "should remain entirely neutral." Pringle, *Theodore Roosevelt,* 579–80.

40. Daniel M. Smith, "Authoritarianism and American Policy Makers in Two World Wars," *Pacific Historical Review* 43, no. 3 (Aug. 1974): 306.

41. Apparently Wilson's eyes grew moist when Spring Rice recited some lines from Wordsworth's sonnet "We Must Be Free or Die," composed during the war with Napoleon. Gwynn, *Letters and Friendships,* 2:223. Contrary to Lodge's charge that Wilson was pro-German because he had a soft spot for German intellectuals, Wilson had a decided affection for British writers and thinkers.

42. In particular, he had to avoid saying or doing anything that might cause a collision with one of the belligerents. See Ernest R. May, *The World War and American Isolation, 1914–1917* (Quadrangle Books, 1966), 44.

43. Tumulty, *Wilson As I Knew Him,* 226. According to Joseph Tumulty, his de facto chief of staff, had Wilson been free to say what he pleased, "he would have yielded to the impulse of championing a cause that in his heart of hearts he felt involved the civilization of the world." (Tumulty's memoirs are not regarded as entirely reliable in all their recollections. Published in 1920, the year after Wilson left office, they are clearly intended, among other things, as a defense of the president from the many attacks he suffered in his last two years in office. Therefore, I have tried to use Tumulty's recollections of Wilson's attitudes and feelings only in conjunction with other sources confirming the same impression.)

44. Link, *Wilson: Confusions and Crises,* 92. This contemporary account contradicts the assertion of many later historians that Wilson took advice from no one and charted his own course independently. It was true that he did not often listen to advisers or always take seriously the opinion of members of Congress. He did, however, generally obey faithfully public opinion as best he was able to discern it.

45. Even in private, Roosevelt or Lodge would not suggest that the United States should join the fight.

46. This point is made by Robert W. Tucker in *Woodrow Wilson and the Great War: Reconsidering America's Neutrality, 1914–1917* (University of Virginia Press, 2007), 64–65.

47. T. W. Gregory, "Wilson and the War: An Account of His Attitude as Seen by His Attorney General," *New York Times,* Jan. 29, 1925. In the second week of the war the Royal Navy, having driven the German fleet back into port, imposed a blockade to choke off neutral trade with the Central Powers. The navy patrolled the Atlantic passages and laid mines in the North Sea, effectively blockading the coasts not only of Germany but of Norway, Sweden, Denmark, and the Netherlands—all neutral nations. Some aspects of the British blockade—the seizure of contraband that could directly aid the enemy's war effort, for instance—were consistent with the traditional laws of war on the high seas. Other aspects skirted the edges of the law, as when the British delayed or seized shipments bound for neutral nations on the suspicion (sometimes justified) that their ultimate destination was the Central Powers. And some British actions were simply blatant violations of international law, in particular, the mining of the North Sea and the blockading of neutral coastlines. According to traditional law, a blockade could only be instituted along the enemy's coastline, not along the coastlines of neutral powers, even if they were suspected of acting as transshipment points to the enemy. Doenecke, *Nothing Less Than War,* 46–47.

48. There were no reliable unemployment statistics in those days. Link, *Wilson: New Freedom,* 445.

49. Doenecke, *Nothing Less Than War,* 41.

50. The great bulk of transatlantic trade was not carried on American vessels—the U.S. merchant fleet was remarkably small given the nation's size and the volume

of its oceangoing trade. The chief reason for this was that American producers were content to ship their goods in foreign vessels, investors saw more money to be made in other areas of the economy, and the U.S. government had not intervened to address the issue, even though many recognized it as a potential vulnerability in time of war.

51. "Big Drop in Exports," *New York Times,* Sept. 26, 1914.

52. McAdoo said he spent "more sleepless nights thinking about cotton" than anything else he had had to deal with. Link, *Wilson: Struggle for Neutrality,* 98. As early as August 7 a congressional committee was already investigating the crisis and promising there would be "ample transportation" to ship the crop across the Atlantic. "Big Drop in Exports," *New York Times,* Sept. 26, 1914; "Cotton Situation Promises Improvements, Says Congress Committee," *New York Times,* Aug. 7, 1914.

53. "Wheat Conference to Be Momentous," *New York Times,* Aug. 13, 1914.

54. Baker, *Woodrow Wilson: Life and Letters,* 5:98; Link, *Wilson: Struggle for Neutrality,* 102.

55. As the *Times* reported, any hope for "the continuance of foreign exchange and commercial intercourse with Europe" depended on "the course that England takes." With Britain in the war, "her fleet may be relied on to keep the Atlantic clear of German warships and thus maintain the ocean highway so that the English and French lines of steamers can be kept running between New York and English and French ports." "Look to England to Keep Sea Lanes Clear," *New York Times,* Aug. 4, 1914.

56. "May Handle Our Goods"*New York Times*, Aug. 6, 1914.

57. "Wheat Conference to Be Momentous," ibid., Aug. 13, 1914; "Shoe Factories Reopen," ibid., Sept. 1, 1914; "Warring Nations to Buy Our Steel," ibid., Sept. 27, 1914; "Business World," ibid., Oct. 3, 1914; "Britain Sending Trade Conferees," ibid., Oct. 11, 1914; "Business World," ibid., Oct. 25, 1914; "Allies Placing Big War Orders," ibid., Oct. 30, 1914; "Russia Can Import Cotton," ibid., Nov. 4, 1914; "Foreign Trade Shifts," ibid., Nov. 18, 1914; "Our Prosperous Foreign Trade," ibid., Nov. 18, 1914; "Thousands Back at Work," ibid., Nov. 24, 1914.

58. "The British Ambassador (Spring Rice) to the Secretary of State, January 19, 1915," "The Ambassador in Great Britain (Page) to the Secretary of State, January 21, 1915"; "The Secretary of State to the Ambassador in Great Britain (Page), January 23, 1915," *Foreign Relations of the United States Diplomatic Papers,* 1915, vol. 2, ed. Joseph V. Fuller et al. (Government Printing Office, 1938), Documents 949–951.

59. Link, *Wilson: Struggle for Neutrality,* 115, 131. Grey worried that if Britain "exasperated the cotton States by making cotton contraband," it would only add to the political pressures on Wilson to take a tougher line with Britain. Grey, *Twenty-Five Years,* 116.

60. "Britain Sending Trade Conferees," *New York Times,* Oct. 11, 1914; "England to Take Cotton for Debts," *New York Times,* Oct. 22, 1914.

61. Robert H. Zieger, *America's Great War: World War I and the American Experience* (Rowan and Littlefield, 2000), 21.

62. On this point, see Heribert von Feilitzsch, *The Secret War on the United States in 1915: A Tale of Sabotage, Labor Unrest, and Border Troubles* (Henselstone Verlag, 2015), xix.

63. Money was "the worst of contrabands," Bryan argued, because "it commands all other things." Link, *Wilson: Struggle for Neutrality,* 63–64. The *Times* surmised that Bryan's decision was at least partly aimed at proving to German Americans

that the administration was not hostile to the German cause. "Opposes Loans to Those at War," *New York Times,* Aug. 16, 1914.

64. May, *World War and American Isolation,* 45–47. As the German ambassador reported to Berlin, the Wilson administration realized that "big trade" with the belligerents would have to be paid for by American loans.

65. Doenecke, *Nothing Less Than War,* 44–45.

66. Link, *Wilson: Struggle for Neutrality,* 161–64; After receiving a catalogue of complaints from the famed psychologist Hugo Münsterberg, Wilson wrote Lansing that the German American case was "prima facie very plausible indeed." It took both Lansing and Bryan to reassure him that he was pursuing a course of neutrality that was both legal and defensible. Baker, *Woodrow Wilson: Life and Letters,* 5:225. He had to be reminded that, according to law and tradition, a neutral's policies did not have to benefit both sides equally. If the neutral acted consistently, but circumstances beyond its control produced unequal results, that was not the neutral's problem. See Tucker, *Woodrow Wilson and the Great War,* 59. As Lansing and international legal experts explained, it was not America's fault that Britain controlled the oceans and could receive American arms shipments while denying them to Germany. The United States was not required to compensate for Britain's advantage. Indeed, to the contrary, any effort to do so—for instance, by putting an embargo on trade to both sides—would itself be a violation of neutrality. In Lansing's words, "If one belligerent has by good fortune a superiority in the matter of geographical location or of military or naval power, the rules of neutral conduct cannot be varied so as to favor the less fortunate combatant. To change such rules because of the relative strength of the belligerents and in order to equalize their opportunities would be in itself an unneutral act, of which the stronger might justly complain." Baker, *Woodrow Wilson: Life and Letters,* 5:208n2. This applied to the weapons and munitions trade just as much as to wheat and tobacco. The German government was actually fully versed in the laws of neutrality. German companies had sold weapons to Spain in 1898 and to Russia during its war with Japan, though Germany was neutral in both conflicts. German officials, therefore, could not and did not claim that either private loans or arms sales to the Allies violated the neutrality laws. The Berlin government even sent a memorandum to the State Department in December formally acknowledging that "under the general principles of international law" Britain and the Allies were allowed to purchase arms and other "war material" from private companies in the United States. The fact that the government would send such a memo showed just how little senior German officials were thinking about the role American trade might play in the war, even four months in. "The Ambassador in Germany (Gerard) to the Secretary of State," Dec. 14, 1914, *Foreign Relations of the United States, 1914, Supplement,* The World War, Document 789, x–xi; Link, *Wilson: Struggle for Neutrality,* 169. "Every sympathizer with Germany pursued the President relentlessly," his chief of staff, JosephTumulty recalled, insisting that England be "brought to book for the unreasonable character of the blockade." Tumulty, *Wilson As I Know Him,* 146. Wilson during the campaign wrote Democrats and friendly editors in areas with large German American populations seeking their advice on "the best means of handling . . . the mistaken sentiment growing up among German-Americans" that his policies were unneutral. Baker, *Woodrow Wilson: Life and Letters,* 5:236.

67. Lansing reported that "thousands of former friends of the Administration" were becoming "bitter adversaries." Link, *Wilson: Struggle for Neutrality,* 163. As Spring Rice put it, the German American vote "has always been Republican and now it

is strongly anti-Democratic." Gwynn, *Letters and Friendships,* 2:248. The German ambassador reported happily to Berlin that the Democrats were "beaten in the last elections in all districts where the German and Irish votes were the decisive factors." Link, *Wilson: Struggle for Neutrality,* 161.

68. Tumulty, *Wilson As I Know Him,* 147.
69. Baker, *Woodrow Wilson: Life and Letters,* 5:168–70.
70. Even an arms embargo "would have resulted in an economic shock that American business was unprepared to withstand." Baker, *Woodrow Wilson: Life and Letters,* 5:181, 184–85. As House put it, "Our whole industrial and agricultural population would cry out against it." Kendrick A. Clements, "Woodrow Wilson and World War I," *Presidential Studies Quarterly* 34, no. 1 (March 2004): 70.
71. Tucker disagrees and believes Wilson did not press Britain as hard as he might have to alter the terms of its blockade. Wilson was "at liberty to follow any one of several quite different courses." Most modern historians disagree with Tucker's view, as Tucker also notes. See Tucker, *Woodrow Wilson and the Great War,* 74–79, 82.
72. Wilson's resistance to taking a more confrontational course with Britain was also a recognition of how hard Grey was working to minimize the hardships for the United States. He authorized measures to ease inspections of American cargoes and reduce delays. He offered to purchase contraband goods like copper and cotton. Most importantly, he let the South's cotton shipments go to Germany for six months. In both cases he overruled the Admiralty and placed himself at odds with the British public. Grey couldn't solve all the problems caused by the blockade, but he was obviously trying his best to be helpful. If Wilson tried to wring more concessions through confrontation, he feared it would only make Grey's job harder. May, *World War and American Isolation,* 31, 66. As May observed, thanks to Grey's efforts, Wilson was "rarely confronted with a serious threat to American trade." The "conciliatory policy of the British government" was a critical factor in preserving a strong Anglo-American relationship in this critical period. Tumulty recalls Wilson arguing it was better to give Grey "a chance to adjust these matters" rather than "force reparation" through threats of war. Tumulty, *Wilson As I Know Him,* 147.
73. Ross Gregory, *Walter Hines Page: Ambassador to the Court of St. James's* (University Press of Kentucky, 1961), 68.
74. Baker, *Woodrow Wilson: Life and Letters,* 5:207–8. See Gwynn, *Letters and Friendships,* 2:243, 246. Wilson "would do all that he could to maintain absolute neutrality," Spring Rice reported to Grey, but in the end the president believed that "a dispute between our two nations would be the crowning calamity." Tucker, *Woodrow Wilson and the Great War,* 88.
75. May, *World War and American Isolation,* 336.
76. Even the advocates of preparedness could not paint a plausible scenario for war with Germany that did not first require Germany's defeat of Britain and the Royal Navy, an outcome that in early 1915 seemed not only implausible but impossible. Roosevelt thought a victorious Germany more likely to challenge American hegemony in the Caribbean, but that was something he had been worrying about since the 1890s. William Henry Harbaugh, *Power and Responsibility: The Life and Times of Theodore Roosevelt* (Octagon Books, 1975), 475. The sober-minded Root at this point in the war "had no thought that the United States should or would become a belligerent. Osgood, *Ideals and Self-Interest,* 137. Jessup, *Elihu Root,* 2:314. It is a common error of later historians and political scientists to suggest that this was the choice Wilson faced in 1914 when he was establishing the terms of neutrality, when

in fact by the time it became clear that war with Germany was possible, American policy had already been set. At that point, it would have required Wilson to retreat from his initial policies in order to mollify Germany. That was a more difficult thing to do.

77. Woodrow Wilson, "Jackson Day" Address at Indianapolis, Indiana," Jan. 1915 (The American Presidency Project, https://www.presidency.ucsb.edu/documents/jackson -day-address-indianapolis-indiana); Link, *Wilson: The Struggle for Neutrality,* 56; Woodrow Wilson, "Message on Neutrality," Aug. 19, 1914 (The American Presidency Project, https://millercenter.org/the-presidency/presidential-speeches/august -19-1914-message-neutrality); Woodrow Wilson, "Address at the Associated Press Luncheon in New York City," Apr. 20, 1915 (The American Presidency Project, https:// www.presidency.ucsb.edu/documents/address-the-associated-press-luncheon -new-york-city.)

78. "Mediation Offers Futile, Says Lodge," *New York Times,* Sept. 24, 1914. In August Root had guessed that within a few months the war would be "fought out" and then it would be time for "reason" to prevail. At that point the United States as the world's great neutral power would be uniquely positioned to help bring peace between the powers. Jessup, *Elihu Root,* 2:313–14.

79. Grey, *Twenty-Five Years,* 2:147–48; Theodore Roosevelt, "The International Posse Comitatus," *New York Times,* Nov. 8, 1914.

80. Seymour, *Intimate Papers,* 1:368, 363.

81. There were plans on the shelf in case of a naval confrontation in the Caribbean, and had been for years, but the United States had not figured at all in the planning for the European war.

82. May, *World War and American Isolation,* 119.

83. Hull, *Absolute Destruction,* 215.

84. Only a few far-seeing naval strategists glimpsed the potential value of the small and stealthy but also quite vulnerable vessel. "The only prewar study of submarine requirements for a campaign against British merchant shipping was prepared by an obscure lieutenant named Ulrich-Eberhard Blum at the Submarine Inspectorate." Karl Lautenschlager, "The Submarine in Naval Warfare, 1901–2001," *International Security* 11, no. 3 (Winter 1986–1987): 110.

85. Occurring just as the High Seas Fleet was suffering its unexpected humiliation, these submarine attacks were the only bright spot in an otherwise dismal naval performance. Following the battle of the Marne, in fact, they were Germany's only military successes in the west. As Ernest May put it, "Submarines achieved surprise successes at a time when no other German forces were making news." May, *World War and American Isolation,* 113.

86. Ibid., 115; Link, *Wilson: Struggle for Neutrality,* 314–15.

87. Gordon A. Craig, *Germany, 1866–1945* (Oxford University Press, 1980), 369.

88. Link, *Wilson: Struggle for Neutrality,* 316–17.

89. Ibid., 318.

90. This Colonel House reported back to Wilson during a visit to Berlin. May, *World War and American Isolation,* 131.

91. Link, *Wilson: Struggle for Neutrality,* 351. At some point Germany would finish with its "open enemies," one editorial noted, but "behind them stand other enemies who pretend to be neutral" but who actually "assist them in their war against us." Ibid., 349, 353.

92. Those restrictions, imposed to avoid offending the Americans, had resulted in the deaths of German submarine crews and had limited the damage to British trade.

Two months of submarine warfare had only destroyed 132,000 tons of shipping, hardly enough to justify the effort and the risks. Link, *Wilson: Struggle for Neutrality,* 349, 355.

93. Critics would later argue that it was Wilson's neutrality policies that provoked Germany into launching submarine warfare against the U.S. trade with Britain. But even if Wilson had been tougher with the British and forced them to limit the blockade, this would not have changed German calculations. The main problem for Germany was not the British blockade; it was Britain's ability to purchase an endless supply of food, goods, and munitions from the United States. The Germans would have happily forgone trade with the United States in exchange for blocking all U.S. trade with Britain. Unless Wilson was prepared to stop selling American goods to the Allies, the Germans were going to pursue their own means of accomplishing that end.

94. Unlike surface vessels, submarines could not safely warn ships and then wait for passengers to be evacuated before firing their torpedoes—the traditional practice of commerce raiders. The mere act of surfacing subjected submarines to deadly risk; once visible they could be rammed by the larger vessels or fired upon by guns mounted even on merchant ships. To avoid destruction, submarines had to approach their targets by stealth, fire their torpedoes while submerged, and make a quick getaway. Loss of civilian life was therefore unavoidable.

95. Link, *Wilson: Struggle for Neutrality,* 358–60, 363–64; May, *World War and American Isolation,* 146–47.

96. It is possible the Germans did not know the freighter was American. The British were escorting the *Gulflight* because they wrongly suspected it of carrying fuel bound for Germany. In fact, it was bound for France. See Link, *Wilson: Struggle for Neutrality,* 365–67. As Link notes, there is no record of exactly why Wilson chose not to take action at this point, so this must be a matter of speculation. He may have considered these isolated instances, the result of errors by low-ranking German officers, and calculated that the occasional sinking of an Allied merchant ship with an American on board or even the occasional accidental attack on an American vessel was not sufficient grounds for a confrontation with possibly dire consequences.

97. By all but announcing their intention of "drowning the crews" of neutral vessels and committing "murder" on the high seas, Grey chortled, the Germans had made the British blockade look positively humane. Link, *Wilson: Struggle for Neutrality,* 335. Winston Churchill declared it of the "utmost importance to attract neutral shipping to our shores, in the hope especially of embroiling the U.S. with Germany." Martin Gilbert, *Churchill and America* (Free Press, 2005), 57.

98. House to Wilson, March 14, 1915, in Arthur S. Link et al, eds., *The Papers of Woodrow Wilson,* (Princeton University Press, 1981), 32 (1915): 372–82, 274.

99. As the *New Republic* put it, "When arguing with Germany and Great Britain we are comparable to a man who does not want and cannot afford to bet more than a hundred dollars, but who is participating in an unlimited game. If it comes to a serious difference . . . we are sure to lose, because we are not willing to back our opinion with the only chips that count." "Getting It Both Ways," *The New Republic,* Feb. 27, 1915, 87.

100. " 'We want to stay out of everything' is the single rule," Bernstorff reported. May, *World War and American Isolation,* 131. The Wilson administration was "continually attempting to squirm out of every problem without getting into severe difficulties." Link, *Wilson: Struggle for Neutrality,* 357.

101. May, *World War and American Isolation,* 131, 201.

102. Ibid., 131.
103. Ibid., 134.
104. Link, *Wilson: Struggle for Neutrality*, 370–72. There have been suggestions that Schwieger's log was doctored after the fact to add some words of compassion that he may or may not have felt for those passengers in the water. See Diana Preston, *A Higher Form of Killing: Six Weeks in World War I that Forever Changed the Nature of Warfare* (Bloomsbury Press, 2015), 283.

Chapter Five: *Schrechlichkeit* and the Submarine War

1. Preston, *Higher Form*, 169–70.
2. Mark Sullivan, *Our Times: The United States, 1900–1925*, vol. 5, *Over Here: 1914–1918* (Charles Scribner's Sons, 1930), 120.
3. Link, *Wilson: Struggle for Neutrality*, 373; Preston, *Higher Form*, 169.
4. Child, *German-Americans in Politics*, 67–68.
5. Link, *Wilson: Struggle for Neutrality*, 375.
6. Ibid., 374.
7. Osgood, *Ideals and Self-Interest*, 163.
8. Ibid., 164.
9. Ibid., 163.
10. Cooper, *Vanity of Power*, 35.
11. John Milton Cooper, Jr., *Woodrow Wilson: A Biography* (Alfred A. Knopf, 2009), 291.
12. Pringle, *William Howard Taft*, 2:874–75.
13. Ibid., 2:876–77.
14. Ibid., 2:878–79.
15. Link, *Wilson: Struggle for Neutrality*, 375.
16. Harbaugh, *Power and Responsibility*, 475.
17. Link, *Wilson: Struggle for Neutrality*, 439.
18. Link, *Wilson: Struggle for Neutrality*, 375.
19. Preston, *Higher Form*, 169–70.
20. He assumed that Democrats on Capitol Hill echoed "a great part of public opinion." Cooper, *Woodrow Wilson*, 291.
21. Tumulty, *Woodrow Wilson As I Know Him*, 148–49.
22. Lodge himself did not call for intervention but would say only that the United States had to be "prepared to take further steps" if Germany continued to sink passenger ships. He also privately ruled out sending ground forces: "[W]e could not, if Germany involved us in war, send great armies to France or Russia." Widenor, *Lodge*, 212–13. William Howard Taft believed that if Wilson had merely called Congress into session, it would have been difficult to prevent it from declaring war, whether Wilson sought it or not. See Tucker, *Woodrow Wilson and the Great War*, 109.
23. Link, *Wilson: Struggle for Neutrality*, 431.
24. Cooper, *Woodrow Wilson*, 286.
25. Cooper, *Vanity of Power*, 36.
26. He told a friend the next morning, "That was just one of the foolish things a man does. I have a bad habit of thinking out loud." Link, *Wilson: Struggle for Neutrality*, 382. Wilson may not even have been thinking about the *Lusitania* as he spoke (as usual without notes). He may have simply been responding clumsily to those calling for immediate intervention. Some speculate that Wilson's thinking was a blur because he had just proposed to Edith Gault and, as he wrote her the next

morning, "I do not know just what I said at Philadelphia (. . . I found myself a little confused as to whether I was in Philadelphia or New York!) because my heart was in such a whirl . . ." John A. Thompson, *Woodrow Wilson* (Longman, 2002), 110–11.

27. Tumulty, *Woodrow Wilson As I Know Him*, 151. In his remarks, to newly natural-ized citizens in Philadelphia, Wilson repeated sentiments he had expressed many times: that America's role was not to fight but to be the neutral arbiter of peace. Some weeks earlier he had said the same thing, only in different words, in a speech delivered at a banquet of the Associated Press in New York: "My interest in the neutrality of the United States is not a petty desire to keep out of trouble. I am interested in neutrality because there is something so much greater to do than fight. There is a distinction awaiting this nation that no nation has ever yet got. That is the distinction of absolute self-control and mastery." This was standard interna-tionalist rhetoric. Lodge and Root had both said the same—before the sinking. Three days after the sinking, however, the words did not seem to fit as well, espe-cially when Wilson embellished by talking about being "too proud to fight."

28. Link, *Wilson: Struggle for Neutrality*, 383–84.

29. Ibid., 396–97. As Henry Stimson observed, it was a pledge to use force if Germany persisted in attacking civilians on the high seas. Stimson and Bundy, *On Active Service in War & Peace*, 84–85.

30. Even the "possibility of war," Bryan told Wilson, was intolerable. May, *World War and American Isolation*, 148.

31. Ibid., 152–53.

32. Ibid., 151.

33. Link, *Wilson: The Struggle for Neutrality* 405.

34. Cooper, *Vanity of Power*, 87, 89. He charged that Wilson was following the "old system" that rested on military force and that it was precisely the policy of "firm-ness, supported by force" that had produced the Great War. Bryan called for a "new system," based on "universal brotherhood" and the "uplifting power of example." The United States must lead the world "out of the black night of war into that light of day" when the nations "will place their trust in love, the weapon for which there is no shield." "Mr. Bryan's New Position, *New York Times*, June 11, 1915.

35. Both nations were "contending for the same great object," i.e., "freedom of the seas."

36. Link, *Wilson: Struggle for Neutrality*, 446–49. Both the press in Germany and the German-language papers in the United States denounced Wilson for his unfair treatment of Germany.

37. Ibid., pp. 452–53.

38. Ibid., 406–9.

39. Wilson wrote House that the American people were still counting on him to keep the country out of war and that it would be a "calamity to the world at large if we should be drawn actively into the conflict and so deprived of all disinterested influence over the settlement." With something approaching desperation he asked House whether there was any chance of getting the British to rescind their Order in Council of March. House advised against turning to England without first settling the issue with Germany. Link, *Wilson: Struggle for Neutrality*, 567–68.

40. He sent the warning via a leak to the *New York Times*. Link, *Wilson: Struggle for Neutrality*, 569; May, *World War and American Isolation*, 162.

41. Link, *Wilson: The Struggle for Neutrality*, 571, 575n76.

42. Karl E. Birnbaum, *Peace Moves and U-Boat Warfare: A Study of Imperial Ger-many's Policy Towards the United States, April 1, 1916–January 9, 1917* (Archon

Books, 1970), 35. The Germans declared that the new orders were "so stringent that the recurrence of incidents similar to the *Arabic* case" was out of the question. May, *World War and American Isolation,* 163; Link, *Wilson: Struggle for Neutrality,* 581.

43. Birnbaum, *Peace Moves and U-Boat Warfare,* 35–36.
44. Link, *Wilson: Struggle for Neutrality,* 571–72.
45. Birnbaum, *Peace Moves and U-Boat Warfare,* 37–38.
46. James W. Gerard, *Face to Face with Kaiserism* (George H. Doran Co., 1918), 31.
47. For an account of the German reaction, see Willi Jasper, *Lusitania: Kulturgeschichte einer Katastrophe* (Bebra Verlag, 2015).
48. Hew Strachan, The *First World War* (Viking, 2003), 59.
49. John Horne and Alan Kramer, *German Atrocities 1914: A History of Denial* (Yale University Press, 2009), 285.
50. Speeches by Asquith at Edinburgh, Sept. 18, 1914; to the House of Commons, Aug. 6, 1914; and at Guildhall, Sept. 4, 1914; in *War Speeches by British Prime Ministers,1914–1916* (T. Fischer Unwin, 1917), 26, 8, 17, 34.
51. Fritz Fischer, *Germany's Aims in the First World War* (W. W. Norton, 1968), 156.
52. Heinrich August Winkler, *The Age of Catastrophe: A History of the West, 1914–1945* (Yale University Press, 2015), 10.
53. Wolfgang J. Mommsen, *Imperial Germany, 1867–1918: Politics, Culture, and Society in an Authoritarian State* (Arnold, 1995), 209.
54. Ibid., 212.
55. Ibid., 209–10.
56. Preston, *Higher Form,* 46, 190.
57. Hull, *Absolute Destruction,* 223.
58. Ibid., 104.
59. The Reichstag's control of the military's budget was mostly a matter of rubber-stamping what the government proposed. Hull, *Absolute Destruction,* 122–23.
60. Ibid., 129.
61. Memories of the *franc-tireurs,* the irregular forces of popular French resistance in the Franco-Prussian War of 1870, were fresh in the minds of German soldiers and their commanders. There was no such resistance in Belgium, but the myth quickly spread among German troops that civilians were taking up arms and engaging in surprise ambushes of German soldiers. See Horne and Kramer, *German Atrocities,* chapters 3 and 4.
62. Gilbert, *First World War,* 42.
63. Preston, *Higher Form,* 54–55.
64. Horne and Kramer, *German Atrocities,* 419.
65. Gilbert, *First World War,* 42; Preston, *Higher Form,* 68–69, 184–85; Doenecke, *Nothing Less Than War,* 22.
66. Preston, *Higher Form,* 86–87, 102.
67. Ibid., 173–74.
68. Ludwig Dehio, *Germany and World Politics in the Twentieth Century* (Chatto & Windus, 1959), 95–96.
69. Hastings, *Catastrophe,* 95. In 1913, when Belgium's King Albert visited Berlin, the kaiser and Moltke had no compunction about telling him that "small countries, such as Belgium, would be well-advised to rally to the side of the strong if they wished to retain their independence." Hastings, 89.
70. Horne and Kramer, *German Atrocities,* 155. Bernhardi's book, *Germany and the Next War,* was translated and published in Britain in 1912 and in the United States in 1914. As the historian Gerhard Ritter notes, Bernhardi's book by itself did much

"to confirm the impression abroad that the German mind was giving way more and more to innate instincts of pugnacity, that under Prussian influence the nation which had given birth to Goethe had ardently embraced the cult of militarism." Gerhard Ritter, *The Sword and the Scepter: The Problem of Militarism in Germany* (University of Miami Press, 1969), 2:116.

71. Richard F. Hamilton and Holger H. Herwig, *Decisions for War, 1914–1917* (Cambridge University Press, 2004), 90. On the widespread support for these "annexationist ambitions," including by liberal intellectuals like Max Weber and even some Social Democrats, see David Blackbourn, *History of Germany, 1780–1918: The Long Nineteenth Century* (Blackwell, 2002), 363.

72. As Frederick C. Howe put it, Germany offered an example of "the kind of democracy we might have if we but saw the state as an agency of service." Quoted in Rodgers, *Atlantic Crossings,* 68.

73. Ibid., 271–72.

74. Ibid., 273–74.

75. Horne and Kramer, *German Atrocities,* 280–81.

76. Rodgers, *Atlantic Crossings,* 275.

77. Ibid., 273.

78. Lewis Mumford, "The Aftermath of Utopianism," *Christianity and Crisis* 3, no. 24, (1941), 2–7, quoted in Stuart Rochester, *American Liberal Disillusionment in the Wake of World War I* (Penn State University Press, 1977), 1–2, 100.

79. Child, *German-Americans in Politics,* 70–71; DeWitt, *Degrees of Allegiance,* 39.

80. Sullivan, *Our Times,* 5:122–23.

81. Child, *German-Americans in Politics,* 112.

82. "The German Americans and the United States," *New York Times,* Sept. 26, 1915.

83. Ibid.

84. Ibid.

85. Richard Wightman Fox, *Reinhold Niebuhr* (Cornell University Press, 1996), 43–46.

86. Link, *Wilson: Struggle for Neutrality,* 545–55.

87. Birnbaum, *Peace Moves and U-Boat Warfare,* 43.

88. Feilitzsch, *Secret War,* 1–6.

89. Link, *Wilson: Struggle for Neutrality,* 561–62.

90. Ibid., 563.

91. Ibid., 555–56.

92. "Facing Facts," *New York Times,* Aug. 26, 1915.

93. "La Follette Assails Loan," *New York Times,* Sept. 20, 1915; Drake, *Education of an Anti-imperialist,* 150–51.

94. "Organized Efforts Against Big Loan Threatens Banks," *New York World,* Sept. 17, 1915; "Our Exports and the Loan," *New York Times,* Sept. 20, 1915.

95. Since the beginning of the war they had purchased hundreds of millions of dollars in goods, supplies, and materiel in the United States but had been able to pay for only half of it. Most of the money was owed to the Morgan bank, which served as the agent of the British treasury in the United States. The British trade deficit with the United States was on pace to reach over two billion pounds for the calendar year 1915. The pound was falling, and without the extension of further loans the Allies would be unable to make further purchases after the end of the year. Link, *Wilson: Struggle for Neutrality,* 617.

96. Ibid., 623, 621.

97. Child, *German-Americans in Politics,* 76–79.

98. Back in the fall of 1914 Grey had acceded to Wilson's request not to put cotton on

the list of absolute contraband, but as the war had dragged on there was pressure to reverse that decision. Britons were appalled that the United States had reacted so timidly to the sinking of the *Lusitania*. Now, the Americans wanted to sell cotton to the Germans. The British public and most of the government were having none of it. A new cotton ban looked likely. As Arthur Link put it, "No government that opened passage for American cotton to Germany could have survived for many days in London." Link, *Wilson: Struggle for Neutrality,* 605.

99. Ibid., 606. As Link notes, British cooperation on the cotton issue provided further proof that Grey and his government "meant to avoid as far as possible any substantial injury to American economic interests while prosecuting its maritime war." Link, *Wilson: Struggle for Neutrality,* 615.

100. Ibid., 610.

101. In mid-September the administration leaked word that it would have no objection to American bankers lending the Allies whatever they needed. Link, *Wilson: Struggle for Neutrality,* 624. To do it required embarrassingly reversing the policies Bryan had laid out at the beginning of the year opposing "the flotation of any general loan by a belligerent." But at this point, it was not a hard decision for Wilson. Neutrality laws had never required a ban on loans, as both McAdoo and Lansing pointed out, and the secretary of state asked whether it made sense "to let a declaration as to our conception of 'the true spirit of neutrality' made in the first days of the war stand in the way of our national interests which seem to be seriously threatened?" Link, *Wilson: Struggle for Neutrality,* 624.

102. As Link notes, the decision on the loan was "in certain measure a consequence of the overshadowing and ever-present threat of rupture with Germany." Link, *Wilson: Struggle for Neutrality,* 616. As the *New Republic*'s editors put it, the episode proved once again that Britain and the United States were "to a very exceptional extent interdependent countries" and had little choice but to cooperate, especially with the Allies engaged in a "desperate contest with a ruthless and terrifying enemy." David W. Levy, *Herbert Croly of the New Republic: The Life and Thought of an American Progressive* (Princeton University Press, 1985), 228–29.

Chapter Six: "He Kept Us Out of War"

1. "Roosevelt Attacks Wilson," *New York Times,* Nov. 4, 1916; Osgood, *Ideals and Self-Interest,* 150–51.

2. Robert D. Ward, "The Origin and Activities of the National Security League, 1914–1919," *Mississippi Valley Historical Review* 47, no. 1 (June 1960): 52–53.

3. Based on a book by Hudson Maxim, brother of the inventor of the famous Maxim gun, the film was screened at the National Press Club in Washington with Secretary of War Lindley M. Garrison, Admiral George Dewey, and a number of influential senators on hand. In the film, enemy battleships shelled Manhattan; enemy airships dropped bombs on civilians; foreign armies marched through the New York streets driving "panic-stricken crowds" before them. And lest anyone miss the point, the movie recounted how, prior to the invasion, the enemy employed American pacifists to ensure that the United States did not build up its defenses. Its producers expected it to be seen by fifty million Americans. See "*Big Invasion* Film," *New York Times,* Aug 11, 1915.

4. Stimson and, Bundy, *On Active Service in War & Peace,* 86.

5. "T. R. Talks at Plattsburg," *New York Times,* Aug. 26, 1915.

6. Cooper, *Woodrow Wilson,* 297.

7. Seymour, *Intimate Papers,* 2:19; Edward H. Buehrig, *Woodrow Wilson and the Balance of Power* (Indiana University Press, 1955), 115–16. Tucker, *Woodrow Wilson and the Great War,* 44.

8. Gerard, Diary, December 1915, in *Face to Face,* 60. Gerard to Lansing, Oct. 25, 1915, enclosure in Lansing to Wilson, November 12, 1915, in Link et al, *The Papers of Woodrow Wilson,* 35 (1915–1916): 193–94.

9. Wilson remarked to House, "Is not the last paragraph amazing?" Link, *Wilson: Struggle for Neutrality,* 309–10, 311n6.

10. House assumed there would be attempts to blow up waterworks and electric light and gas plants, as well as subways and bridges in cities like New York. He relayed that he had been told by the New York police commissioner of a building in which Germans were suspected of storing shipments of arms. Seymour, *Intimate Papers,* 2:33–34.

11. Child, *German-Americans in Politics,* 90.

12. Woodrow Wilson, "Third Annual Message," December 7, 1915 (The American Presidency Project, https://www.presidency.ucsb.edu/documents/third-annual-message-19).

13. It is worth noting that there were also German Americans troubled by the behavior of their ethnic brethren. Wittke, *German-Americans and the World War,* 42.

14. For defense spending in this period see http://www.usgovernmentspending.com/spending_chart_1904_1924USb_30t#view.

15. Baer, *One Hundred Years of Sea Power,* 61–63; Hagan, *This People's Navy,* 252.

16. As Link relates, the November 4 speech set off "a storm of opposition and marked the beginning of one of the fiercest legislative controversies of the decade." Link, *Wilson: Confusions and Crises,* 23.

17. Link, *Wilson: Struggle for Neutrality,* 592.

18. As one political scientist at the time put it, it was the Republicans who had long favored "an aggressive policy of interest, participation, and often interference in affairs beyond our borders and in every corner of the globe." It was the Democrats who had wanted to "hold aloof from Europe" and could be expected to seek conciliation with other nations. Cooper, *Vanity of Power,* 87.

19. In the House some thirty members from the party's more progressive and pacifist wing—over a fifth of the caucus—opposed Wilson's plan. See Cooper, *Vanity of Power,* 90.

20. Knock, *To End All Wars,* 49–50. Only a few progressives, like Roosevelt and House, saw no contradiction between opposing corporations and plutocrats in domestic politics while supporting a military buildup and the wielding of force in the international realm. Some, like the editors of the *New Republic,* thought the mobilization of the nation would force Americans to abandon their laissez-faire approach to government involvement in the economy and enact the progressive social program. It was to them all part of obtaining "mastery" and advancing the cause of liberal civilization. Levy, *Herbert Croly,* 226.

21. Democratic congressman Clyde Tavenner's attack on the "World Wide War Trust" was reprinted in labor journals and newspapers across the country. See, for instance, the *Loveland (Colo.) Daily Herald,* no. 261, June 9, 1915.

22. The unions were heavily involved, since union leaders feared with some justification that "a larger army would be a weapon in the hands of the employing class during strikes." Curti, *Peace or War,* 235.

23. "I have unlimited faith in President Wilson," Jane Addams had insisted before becoming disillusioned by his call for a historic military buildup. Knock, *To End All Wars,* 51–52, 55. Why they should have had such faith in Wilson is unclear. He

had never been a peace progressive. He had supported the intervention in Cuba and the taking of the Philippines. As president he had already used force more often in four years than Roosevelt had in seven.

24. Link, *Wilson: Confusions and Crises,* 28.
25. Knock, *To End All Wars,* 64.
26. Link, *Wilson: Confusions and Crises,* 32.
27. The president worried he would be in trouble without the support of "Mr. Bryan." Cooper, *Vanity of Power,* 91; Cooper, *Woodrow Wilson,* 142.
28. Defeat was a real possibility. Head counts in the House showed at least thirty Democrats and two dozen Republican progressives were "almost fanatical" in their determination to block the military buildup. Link, *Wilson: Confusions and Crises,* 28. Tumulty reported on Jan. 17 that there was "no enthusiasm on the 'hill' for preparedness." The American public also seemed indifferent and unable to "grasp the importance of this question." Ibid., 45.
29. Ibid., 45–47; the most recent such effort had been President Andrew Johnson's disastrous "Swing Around the Circle" in 1866. Harbaugh, *Power and Responsibility,* 482.
30. Excerpts from speeches given by Wilson in the course of his tour from Jan. 27 through Feb. 4, 1916. See speech excerpts, Jan. 27–Feb. 3, 1916, in Oliver Marble Gale, ed., *Americanism: Woodrow Wilson's Speeches on the War* (Chicago, 1918), 14; Link, *Wilson: Confusions and Crises,* 46–48; "A Review of the World: Effect of the President's Appeals to the People for National Defense," *Current Opinion* 60, no. 3 (March 1916), 199.
31. He said something similar to Lillian Wald, who was leading a delegation of the American Union Against Militarism. Wald argued that the buildup of the army and navy would "neutralize and annul the moral power which our nation ought, through you, to exercise when the day of peace negotiation has come." Wilson had used much the same argument himself when he opposed preparedness back in December 1914. Now he rejected it as naïve. "In the last analysis," he told Wald, "the peace of society is obtained by force. . . . [I]f you say we shall not have any war, you have got to have force to make that 'shall' bite." Knock, *To End All Wars,* 66; Cooper, *Woodrow Wilson,* 326.
32. Speech excerpts, Jan. 27–Feb. 3, 1916, in Gale, *Americanism,* 14.
33. Link, *Wilson: Confusions and Crises,* 48–50.
34. Cooper, *Vanity of Power,* 97.
35. Bishop, *Theodore Roosevelt and His Time,* 2:401.
36. In Chicago Wilson spoke for forty-five minutes and was interrupted by applause forty-seven times. "Roosevelt in his palmiest days never received from the American people a noisier demonstration of their regard," one editor commented. "A Review of the World: Effect of the President's Appeals to the People for National Defense," *Current Opinion* 60, no. 3, Edward J. Wheeler, ed. (March 1916), 148.
37. Link, *Wilson: Confusions and Crises,* 48–50. He also preserved the allegiance of the *New Republic,* which until his bold defense of preparedness had been casting about for a candidate to support in 1916.
38. Pacifists and non-interventionists opposed it, as did others who considered a large standing army contrary to American traditions. Southern members worried that the new army would be populated by blacks. Most of all, there was widespread concern that it would supplant the National Guard. The guard, controlled by state governors and filled with loyal constituents, wielded enormous influence, and its defenders lobbied to make it the reserve force. Army leaders and Secretary of War Garrison hated the idea, believing the guard could never be turned into a profes-

sional army. But Wilson bowed to congressional pressure, and Garrison promptly resigned.

39. Link, *Wilson: Confusions and Crises,* 332.

40. There was more largesse to be thrown around congressional districts eager for ship-building contracts. As for the effect of Jutland, that massive clash of the British and German fleets, though inconclusive, convinced many that the battleship was indeed a vital weapon and that the United States had better start building to catch up.

41. Link, *Wilson: Confusions and Crises,* 336–37.

42. In the middle of his speaking tour, Wilson received the German government's refusal to accept responsibility for the *Lusitania,* raising doubts about its future intentions. Link, *Wilson: Confusions and Crises,* 46.

43. In the summer of 1915 Falkenhayn had been worried about the desperate situation in the Balkans and in Turkey. Neutral Bulgaria and Greece were deciding whether to remain neutral; the Allied campaign to take the Gallipoli peninsula and control access to the Dardanelles and Constantinople threatened to split the Ottoman Empire in two, and he feared that if the United States joined the war, this would tilt Bulgaria against the Central Powers and, with Serbia's help, cut the supply line to Constantinople. But by the beginning of 1916, Bulgaria had joined the Central Powers, Serbia was practically defeated, the Allies' Gallipoli campaign had failed disastrously, the Dardanelles remained under Turkish control, and the route to Constantinople was secure. Largely because of this hopeful shift in Germany's military fortunes on the continent, he thought the United States "was no longer in a position to do us injury." May, *World War and American Isolation,* 230.

44. Birnbaum, *Peace Moves and U-Boat Warfare,* 52–53; Link, *Wilson: Confusions and Crises,* 87–88.

45. Birnbaum, *Peace Moves and U-Boat Warfare,* 64.

46. The secretary of state wrote Wilson that the administration could "no longer temporize . . . when Americans are being killed . . . by the illegal and inhuman conduct of the Germans." Link, *Wilson: Confusions and Crises,* 229–31.

47. Ibid., 234–35.

48. Ibid., 235.

49. May, *World War and American Isolation,* 193.

50. Link, *Wilson: Confusions and Crises,* 236–37.

51. Ibid., 249.

52. Woodrow Wilson, "Message Regarding German Actions," speech, Washington, D.C., April 19, 1916. University of Virginia, Miller Center https://millercenter.org /the-presidency/presidential-speeches/april-19-1916-message-regarding-german -actions).

53. Wittke, *German-Americans and the World War,* 80–81.

54. *Source Records of the Great War,* vol. 4, ed. Charles F. Horne (National Alumni, 1923).

55. Ibid. 100–101.

56. Ruhl J. Bartlett, *The League to Enforce Peace* (University of North Carolina Press, 1944), 60; Saladin Ambar, "The Campaign and Election of 1912," Miller Center, University of Virginia.

57. This included the infamous Chesapeake Affair of 1807, in which a British ship fired on the USS *Chesapeake* when the Americans refused to let British sailors board and search for alleged English deserters pretending to be Americans. The incident, which eventually led to the War of 1812, was regarded by many at the time and later as one of the great humiliations in American history. Arthur S. Link, *Wilson,*

vol. 5, *Campaigns for Progressivism and Peace, 1916–1917* (Princeton University Press, 1964), 43–44.

58. Sullivan, *Our Times,* 5:236.
59. Republicans might say that "all our present policy is wrong," Wilson declared, but if so then they had to be for war, for that was the only other option. Ibid., 5:238.
60. Ibid., 5:238.
61. Albeit only for federal government employees. Seymour, *Intimate Papers,* 2:343–44.
62. That there were political motives behind these various moves was clear. One Democratic senator urged him to adopt as much of the 1912 Progressive platform as possible "as a means of attaching to our party progressive Republicans who are in sympathy with us in so large a degree." Cooper, *Woodrow Wilson,* 335.
63. Ibid., 351.
64. Pusey, *Charles Evans Hughes,* 1:350.
65. As his onetime progressive ally Amos Pinchot later recalled, Roosevelt was no longer seized with the domestic reform agenda. The "most important thing in the world was for America to enter the war on the side of the Allies." Harbaugh, *Power and Responsibility,* 491.
66. The American people, he observed, would have to be in a "heroic mood" to embrace his cause, but clearly they were not. The "prevailing currents of American opinion" were flowing in the opposite direction. He was "out of sympathy" with the people. Bishop, *Theodore Roosevelt and His Time,* 2:399; Harbaugh, *Power and Responsibility,* 485.
67. Link, *Wilson: Campaigns for Progressivism and Peace,* 3.
68. Harbaugh, *Power and Responsibility,* 487.
69. As Roosevelt put it, "No human being knows how he stands on Preparedness . . . or whether he has real and effective convictions about International Affairs." Link, *Wilson: Campaigns for Progressivism and Peace,* 4.
70. Pusey, *Charles Evans Hughes,* 1:358. He generally avoided discussing foreign policy and stuck to "secondary issues." Pusey, 1:350; Ronald Steel, *Walter Lippmann and the American Century* (Little, Brown, 1980), 106; Link, *Wilson: Campaigns for Progressivism and Peace,* 136.
71. Harbaugh, *Power and Responsibility,* 481.
72. Ibid., 491.
73. Widenor, *Lodge,* 234; Henry Cabot Lodge, *War Addresses* (Houghton Mifflin, 1917), 134–35.
74. Betty Glad, *Charles Evans Hughes and the Illusions of Innocence: A Study in American Diplomacy* (University of Illinois Press, 1966), 81.
75. Link, *Wilson: Campaigns for Progressivism and Peace,* 111. Wilson, teasingly referring to Roosevelt, noted that "the only articulate voice" in the Republican Party "professes opinions and purposes at which the rest in private shiver and demur." Ibid., 107.
76. "Now and then," he wrote a friend, "the time comes when a man must hoist the black flag and sink or swim, without regard to what his fellows think, for the cause in which he with all his heart believes. In my judgment we are in a great world crisis. No other public man has ventured to tell the truth of Germany, of the pacifists, of the German-Americans, of Wilson. I have told it and shall tell it as strongly as I know how and without regard to its effect on me." Bishop, *Theodore Roosevelt and His Time,* 2:398–99. Even Lodge developed a "horrid suspicion" that most Americans were not with Roosevelt on the war. Widenor, *Lodge,* 248.
77. Bishop, *Theodore Roosevelt and His Time,* 2:398–99.

78. Link, *Wilson: Campaigns for Progressivism and Peace,* 3.
79. Harbaugh, *Power and Responsibility,* 485–486.
80. Wittke, *German-Americans and the World War,* 103.
81. Ibid., 93.
82. O'Leary would later be charged with attempting to blow up American shipyards. One of Hughes's biographers suggests he had no idea with whom he was meeting. Pusey, *Charles Evans Hughes,* 1:355.
83. "Nearly all" of them "were Republicans anyway," House noted. Seymour, *Intimate Papers,* 2:372; Wittke, *German-Americans and the World War,* 98; Child, *German-Americans in Politics,* 145–46.
84. Child, *German-Americans in Politics,* 140–41. Even to a less partisan observer like Lippmann, Hughes's campaigning "up and down the country declaring for an impartial neutrality in the orthodox pro-German sense" was enough to disqualify him for the presidency. Steel, *Walter Lippmann,* 106; Link, *Wilson: Campaigns for Progressivism and Peace,* 136.
85. A dramatic highlight of the campaign came in late September when the chairman of the Irish American America Truth Society, Jeremiah O'Leary, sent a telegram to the White House accusing Wilson of "truckling to the British Empire" and exercising a "dictatorship over Congress." The telegram's author was a well-known anti-British activist, and his organization was widely (and accurately) suspected of being funded by the German embassy. Wilson responded that "I would feel deeply mortified to have you or anybody like you vote for me," and, he continued, "since you have access to many disloyal Americans, and I have not, I will ask you to convey this message to them." Child, *German-Americans in Politics,* 148–49.
86. Thus U.S. senator Stone of Missouri, campaigning in St. Louis, could denounce Hughes as "an 'anti-German Welshman,'" some German-language Democratic newspapers, like the St. Louis *Amerika,* could justify sticking with Wilson, and even some lifelong Republican German Americans could vote for Wilson—all because Hughes would not distance himself from Roosevelt. Child, *German-Americans in Politics,* 147; DeWitt, *Degrees of Allegiance,* 46. George Sylvester Viereck, editor of the leading pro-German English-language publication in America, warned that "if Mr. Hughes is defeated, he owes his defeat to the Colonel." Child, *German-Americans in Politics,* 151.
87. Link, *Wilson: Campaigns for Progressivism and Peace,* 187, 151.
88. "Roosevelt Bitterly Attacks Wilson," *New York Times,* Nov. 4, 1916; Osgood, *Ideals and Self-Interest,* 150–51.
89. Pringle, *Life and Times of William Howard Taft,* 2:899.
90. Pusey, *Charles Evans Hughes,* 1:364.
91. Widenor, *Lodge,* 248.
92. Harbaugh, *Power and Responsibility,* 495.
93. Wilson would have lost the election had he not won in Ohio, a state with a sizable German American population, where the governor was Republican Warren G. Harding, and which had gone Republican in every election save one going back to 1856. The one exception was 1912, when Taft and Roosevelt split the Republican vote. The German-language press in the state believed that Roosevelt's campaign trip through the state had cost the Republicans German American votes, and Hughes did underperform in places like Cincinnati. Child, *German-Americans in Politics,* 151. Wilson also performed better than usual in Missouri, including in heavily German American St. Louis. DeWitt, *Degrees of Allegiance,* 47. In the end the German American vote, which ought to have been overwhelmingly Republican and might have handed Hughes a narrow victory, proved sufficiently split that it

played no decisive role in the final electoral tally. As one historian has observed, Wilson's slogan, "He kept us out of war," was probably as "irresistible to many German-Americans as it was to millions of other voters, particularly in the Middle and Far West." Wittke, *German-Americans and the World War,* 110–11.

94. Harbaugh, *Power and Responsibility,* 495.

Chapter Seven: The Path to War

1. Heaton, *Cobb of "The World,"* 268–70; Link, *Wilson: Campaigns for Progressivism and Peace,* 399.
2. The note, thought to be drafted by Wilhelm himself, said Germany would soon be "forced to regain the freedom of action" with regard to submarine warfare that it had "reserved to itself" in the Sussex Pledge of May 4. Seymour, *Intimate Papers,* 2:336.
3. As early as June he had confided to Tumulty that he feared war with Germany was becoming "inevitable." Tumulty, *Wilson As I Know Him,* 159; Pusey, *Charles Evans Hughes,* 1:356.
4. Link, *Wilson: Campaigns for Progressivism and Peace,* 139–40.
5. Pusey, *Charles Evans Hughes,* 1:356.
6. The idea was "to force you before the election to act, knowing if you are defeated nothing can be done by anyone for many months to come. They do not want to take the chance." Link, *Wilson: Campaigns for Progressivism and Peace,* 174.
7. Cooper, *Woodrow Wilson,* 352.
8. Grey dared not even mention the House memorandum to the French. He feared the French would see it as a sign "that we were weakening" and it therefore might "undermine their confidence in our determination to support them." Grey, *Twenty-Five Years,* 2:128–31. However, when the French ambassador in London, Paul Cambon, learned about it, he also saw it as a political maneuver: "Fundamentally, I think that this Colonel House has come simply to ask that the English and French press spare his President so as not to embarrass him when he is opening his campaign for the presidential election." Link, *Wilson: Confusions and Crises,* 139n106.
9. Grey, *Twenty-Five Years,* 133-34, 132. Some historians have also made the mistake of taking the German offers seriously. See Philip Zelikow, *The Road Less Traveled: The Secret Battle to End the Great War, 1916–1917* (PublicAffairs, 2021). Bethmann's offer of "conditional restoration" of Belgium in practice meant substantial German involvement in Belgium, militarily, to ensure that the British did not turn Belgium into a bulwark against Germany, and economically, to ensure that Germany enjoyed at least equal commercial and industrial benefits from Belgium as France. This was not an offer to restore Belgium in its full sovereign independence. Similarly, Bethmann offered to cede only "some of the territory of Alsace and Lorraine," taken by Germany in 1871, and then only in exchange for significant parts of the mineral-rich French region of Briey-Longwy, which the Germans had conquered in the present war. This would not have been acceptable to France or to Britain. Even Wilson believed that Alsace and Lorraine should be restored to France in their entirety, and he would not have supported ratifying German conquests of new parts of France. This was one reason the German leaders did not want Wilson to be the mediator but only the convener of peace talks, from which he would immediately withdraw. That was also not what Wilson had in mind.
10. Link, *Wilson: Confusions and Crises,* 118.
11. Ibid.
12. The difficulty, as Foreign Secretary Jagow wrote to Ambassador Bernstorff in

Washington, was that Wilson's "instincts" were "all favorable to the English point of view." If a peace conference were held, he would likely insist that any agreement include a return to the status quo ante in Europe, and "particularly with regard to Belgium." This was "unacceptable" to Germany, however, and since Wilson saw himself as "Lord Protector" of right and justice, Germany's refusal to accept his terms could "induce him to go over openly into the camp of our enemies." Link, *Wilson: Campaigns for Progressivism and Peace,* 31–32.

13. Zelikow cites as a "watershed moment" Bethmann's Aug. 18, 1916, telegram to the German ambassador in Washington, in which the German chancellor writes that Berlin would be "happy to accept a mediation by the President to start peace negotiations among the belligerents." Zelikow, *The Road Less Traveled,* 111. The Germans were very clear that they did not want Wilson involved in the peace talks once launched. Zelikow argues that Wilson would have been involved anyway, but if the Germans could reject Wilson's participation in the talks, they were unlikely to feel compelled to bend to his preferences when he was absent from the conference table. See Link, *Wilson: Campaigns for Progressivism and Peace,* chap. 1 passim.

14. Speaking before Wilson, Lodge told the assembled dignitaries that he supported their efforts to promote a league of nations. "Voluntary arbitration" had only limited utility in the modern world, he argued, and "the next step" was "to put force behind international peace." That might not solve the problem, but it could "be solved in no other." David Mervin, "Henry Cabot Lodge and the League of Nations," *Journal of American Studies* 4, no. 2 (February 1971): 202.

15. Ironically, although he considered the speech "the most important I shall ever be called upon to make," he had given the league idea so little thought that as he pre-pared his address, he had to ask House to remind him exactly what he and Grey had in mind. Link, *Wilson: Campaigns for Progressivism and Peace,* 23–26.

16. House warned Grey that Americans were beginning to think that Britain and France were more interested in punishing Germany than in agreeing to terms of peace that "neutral opinion would consider just." Link, *Wilson: Campaigns for Progressivism and Peace,* 18–19. The United States did not wish to force the Allies to do "something for which they are not ready," House told Grey, but if talks did not begin soon, the public would demand that the administration "assert our unde-niable rights against the Allies with the same insistence we have used towards the Central Powers." Ibid., 21–22.

17. Ibid., 16.

18. House had, in fact, employed a bit of legerdemain to try to bring the two men together. With Grey he negotiated a memorandum which stated that if Wilson invited the belligerents to a peace conference and the Germans refused to attend or proved intransigent in talks, "the United States would probably enter the war against Germany." He privately assured Grey that despite the hedged wording the purpose of the agreement was to get the United States into the war. Even though this was Grey's great object, however, he was noncommittal. He suspected that House was playing games and did not really have Wilson on board. The British government at that time was not interested in American mediation. Grey therefore refused to be pinned down by House. But that did not stop House from returning to Washington and telling Wilson that he had an "agreement" with Grey. Nor did he tell the president about his assurance to Grey that the United States would enter the war if peace talks failed. Wilson therefore believed that Grey had already agreed to accept mediation in return for the assurance that the United States would join a postwar league. Wilson made clear, however, that he would make this commit-ment only if he could simultaneously announce his intention of calling a "confer-

ence to discuss peace." This, of course, was not at all the quid pro quo Grey was asking for, or which House had offered him in London. House's game was now fully exposed: He had told Grey the purpose of the memorandum was to bring the United States into the war. Indeed, House wrote in his diary that his plan all along was to get the United States into the war. Link, *Wilson: Confusions and Crises,* 103. But to Wilson he said that the purpose of the memorandum was to keep the United States out of the war. Spring Rice immediately discerned that the president had "no intention whatever of entering the European arena as a belligerent" and assumed, along with the rest of the British government, that he only wanted to "appear before the country as the great pacificator" in time for the election. Grey, *Twenty-Five Years,* 126–29. Arthur S. Link, *Woodrow Wilson and the Progressive Era, 1910–1917* (Harper and Bros., 1954), 199; Link, *Wilson: Confusions and Crises,* 114. Grey and his colleagues therefore dismissed House's proposal as "humbug . . . a mere maneouvre of American politics." C. M. Mason, "Anglo-American Relations: Mediation and 'Permanent Peace,'" in F. H. Hinsley, ed., *British Foreign Policy Under Sir Edward Grey* (Cambridge University Press, 2008), 479, 477; May, *World War and American Isolation,* 358–59. House persuaded Wilson that the "only inducement" he could offer Britain to accept peace talks, other than promising to enter the war, which he would not do, was to agree to join a league. Flattering the president's ego, he said Wilson was "destined" to play this "noblest part that had ever come to a son of man." Link, *Wilson: Confusions and Crises,* 106. Wilson had House inform Grey that he was now willing to commit the United States to "joining with the other Powers in a convention looking to the maintenance of peace after the war." That convention would "bind the signatory Powers to side against any nation" that refused to settle a dispute peacefully. Link, *Wilson: Campaigns for Progressivism and Peace,* 19. When he read through the memorandum, however, he inserted a second "probably" in the text, right before the offer to leave the conference as a belligerent if Germany was unreasonable. American involvement should not appear "inevitable," he told House. It would depend on circumstances. May, *World War and American Isolation,* 352; Link, *Wilson: Campaigns for Progressivism and Peace,* 17.

19.   Link, *Wilson: Campaigns for Progressivism and Peace,* 23.
20.   For months, House complained, Grey had been telling him that the "solution of the problem of international well-being depended upon the United States being willing to take her part in world affairs." Now that Wilson had agreed, Grey "halts, stammers and questions." Link, *Wilson: Campaigns for Progressivism and Peace,* 20.
21.   Ibid., 24.
22.   Ibid., 21.
23.   The Europeans were plagued by mutual suspicion, by "conjectures about what this Government and that Government was going to do," by alliances and secret understandings, all producing a "complex web of intrigue and spying" that had inevitably entangled all of them "in its meshes." "Wilson Decries Trade War Fear," *New York Times,* Oct. 27, 1916.
24.   Even as late as December 1915 Wilson had privately remarked that he was "heart and soul for the Allies" and insisted that "no decent man, knowing the situation and Germany, could be anything else." Seymour, *Intimate Papers,* 2:50; Baker, *Woodrow Wilson: Life and Letters,* 5:376.
25.   Money was funneled to Ireland by the Irish revolutionary organization Clan-na-Gael, based in New York. David Brundage, *Irish Nationalists in America: The Politics of Exile, 1798–1998* (Oxford University Press, 2016), 138. The leader of Clan-na-Gael called it "the greatest deed done in Ireland in 100 years," and there-

after money poured in from enthusiastic backers of the Irish cause in the United States. Carroll. "America and the 1916 Rising," in *1916: The Long Revolution,* ed. Doherty and Keogh, 129; Brundage, *Irish Nationalists,* 146. When the leader of the rising proclaimed the very short-lived Irish Provisional Republic in Dublin, he offered special thanks to Ireland's "exiled children in America." Robert Schmuhl, *Ireland's Exiled Children: America and the Easter Rising* (Oxford University Press, 2016), 1.

26. Spring Rice reported that the Irish Americans had become permanent and bitter enemies: "They have blood in their eyes when they look our way." Schmuhl, *Ireland's Exiled Children,* 86.

27. Link, *Wilson: Campaigns for Progressivism and Peace,* 136–37.

28. Ibid., 136.

29. "British-American Irritation," *New Republic,* Dec. 9, 1916, 137-38.

30. Link, *Wilson: Campaigns for Progressivism and Peace,* 109; Gwynn, *Letters and Friendships,* 2:355–56.

31. Link, *Wilson: Campaigns for Progressivism and Peace,* 28; May, *World War and American Isolation,* 359.

32. Link, *Wilson: Campaigns for Progressivism and Peace,* 72–73.

33. Ibid., 78–79.

34. Grey in a friendly way expressed his apprehension to House that Wilson might offer to mediate, not on his own initiative but "at the request, or at least at the suggestion of the German Government." Page memorandum of conversation with Grey, July 27, 1916. *Foreign Relations of the United States, 1916, War Supp. I,* 42.

35. Gerard to Lansing, Sept. 26, 1916, ibid., 55.

36. See Daniel Larsen, "The First Intelligence Prime Minister: David Lloyd George (1916–1922)," https://www.gov.uk/government/uploads/system/uploads/attachment_data/file/80179/Lloyd-George-as-PM.pdf.

37. "Lloyd George Calls All Peace Talks Unfriendly," *New York Times,* Sept. 29, 1916.

38. Roy W. Howard, "Lloyd George Says: 'We Will Fight Germany to a Knockout'," UP, Sept 28, 1916. On the coverage in the United States, see Beard, *Newsmaker: Roy W. Howard,* 41. Page reported from London that Lloyd George's comments represented a "restrained expression of governmental and public opinion." Page to Lansing, October 11, 1916, *Foreign Relations of the United States Diplomatic Papers, 1916 War Supp. I,* ed. Joseph V. Fuller, et al. (Government Printing Office, 1929), Document 73.

39. Link, *Wilson: Campaigns for Progressivism and Peace,* 178–79.

40. In fact, even if Wilson did nothing, a sour mood among the American public might have the same effect. As Keynes put it, "Any feeling of irritation or lack of sympathy with this country or with its policy in the minds of the American public . . . would render it exceedingly difficult, if not impossible," to raise the funds on which the British war effort depended. Grey added that while it was true that the more money Americans lent to Britain the more interest they had in Britain's success, American investors might decide their money would be safer if peace came quickly. Link, *Wilson: Campaigns for Progressivism and Peace,* 179–81.

41. Ibid., 205–6.

42. Officials at the newly established Federal Reserve wanted to issue a warning against extending further short-term loans. Their concerns had nothing to do with the war or British behavior. They just worried that the more Americans lent to Britain, the more they would feel pressure to keep lending to prop up the British economy, to the point where the United States as a whole might become too heavily invested. Understanding the sensitivity of the question, they sent a draft of their proposed

warning to the president. Wilson might have said nothing or simply given verbal approval. Instead, he wrote and signed a letter urging the Federal Reserve to make the warning stronger and to offer "explicit advice" instead of "mere caution." His letter was not made public, but Spring Rice and other British officials soon learned that the president was behind the Federal Reserve's action—as he intended. Link, *Wilson: Campaigns for Progressivism and Peace,* 200–202.

43. Seymour, *Intimate Papers,* 2:390–91.

44. When he read the draft on Nov. 27, "strangely enough," the president had "fallen again into the same error of saying something which would have made the Allies frantic with rage. I have called his attention to this time after time, and yet in almost every instance where he speaks of the war he offends in the same way."House, *Intimate Papers,* 2:390–94. Once again, he feared, Wilson would "give further impetus to the belief that he does not yet understand what the Allies are fighting for." Ibid., 2:405.

45. Sterling Kernek, "The British Government's Reactions to President Wilson's 'Peace' Note of December 1916," *Historical Journal* 13, no. 4 (December 1970): 742, 729, 740, 728.

46. Steel, *Walter Lippmann,* 108.

47. Grey, *Twenty-Five Years,* 2:134.

48. These included, in the east, establishment of a kingdom of Poland wrested from Russian domination and brought under German influence, and annexation of Russia's Baltic provinces of Courland (western Latvia) and Lithuania. In the west, "guarantees in Belgium" or the annexation of Liège, annexation of Luxembourg and the French territories of Briey and Longwy, boundary adjustments in Alsace and Lorraine, and war indemnities. Link, *Wilson: Campaigns for Progressivism and Peace,* 210–11.

49. May, *World War and American Isolation,* 365. When Lippmann asked Wilson if he intended to support the German proposal, the president "looked pained." Steel, *Walter Lippmann,* 108.

50. A week later, even after France and Russia had denounced Bethmann's proposal, he wrote a friend that "we are just now . . . holding our breath for fear the overtures of the Central Powers with regard to peace will meet with a rebuff instead of an acceptance." Link, *Woodrow Wilson and the Progressive Era,* 260; Steel, *Walter Lippmann,* 108.

51. Link, *Wilson: Campaigns for Progressivism and Peace,* 217–18.

52. "Is the President's Note Pro-German? One Reason Why the Allies Think It Is." *The Outlook,* Jan. 10, 1917, 17.

53. Page reported from London that the substance of the note was far less offensive than the "remarks accompanying his suggestion," which were being interpreted "as placing the Allies and the Central Powers on the same level." Seymour, *Intimate Papers,* 2:406–07.

54. As Link notes, the reaction of American commentators "accurately reflected the commentator's attitude toward the war." Link, *Woodrow Wilson and the Progressive Era,* 261.

55. "The President's Note to the Powers: A Poll of the Press," *The Outlook,* Jan. 10, 1917, 17.

56. Osgood, *Ideals and Self-Interest,* 150.

57. Tucker, *Woodrow Wilson and the Great War,* 34–35.

58. "The Story of the War: Germany Replies to President Wilson," *The Outlook,* Jan. 10, 1917, 9.

59. Kernek, "British Government's Reactions," 732–33.

60. Ibid., 727–28.
61. Note here that it was the Allies, not Wilson, who suggested the breakup of Austria-Hungary and the self-determination of these various populations.
62. Link, *Wilson: Campaigns for Progressivism and Peace,* 233–38.
63. Seymour, *Intimate Papers,* 2:406.
64. Link, *Woodrow Wilson and the Progressive Era,* 262–63.
65. Link, *Wilson: Campaigns for Progressivism and Peace,* 234.
66. House, *Intimate Papers,* 2:412.
67. "Comment of Today's Newspapers on the President's Address," *New York Times,* Jan. 23, 1917.
68. J. W. Schulte, Nordholt, *Woodrow Wilson: A Life for World Peace,* trans. Herbert H. Rowen (University of California Press, 1990), 210.
69. See, for instance, "International Security," *New Republic,* Nov. 11, 1916, 35–37, and, by contrast, "A White Peace and Its Consequences," *New Republic,* Dec. 2, 1916, 168–70.
70. Wilson had worked hard, and successfully, to woo the editors during the campaign, especially Lippmann. After the election he remained keenly interested in what its editors had to say about all matters, foreign and domestic. The young journalist had visited Wilson at Shadow Lawn to offer campaign advice in September, and both he and Croly throughout the fall and winter months met frequently with House at the colonel's New York apartment. Wilson had specifically invited Lippmann to pass on his ideas, "either directly or in editorial expression." Steel, *Walter Lippmann,* 109; Link, *Wilson: Campaigns for Progressivism and Peace,* 93.
71. Even the Slavic peoples of the region—even the Serbians—had been "captivated, if not conquered, by the demonstration of German power" and by "the incontestable superiority of German methods." They could not help but "accept German leadership." "A White Peace and Its Consequences," *New Republic,* Dec. 16, 1916; "Twenty-Nine Months of War," *New Republic,* Dec. 23, 1916.
72. "A White Peace and its Consequences," *New Republic,* Dec. 16, 1916.
73. "Peace Without Victory," *New Republic,* Dec. 23, 1916; "The Note as Americanism," *New Republic,* Dec. 30, 1916.
74. Wilson wrote to Croly after the speech to report that in preparing it he had read the editorial and that it had served to "clarify and strengthen" his own thinking, which had been along the same lines. Levy, *Herbert Croly,* 232. Lippmann would later claim that he and Croly were "horrified" that Wilson had appropriated the phrase and employed it "in a sense we had never intended." See Walter Lippmann, "Notes for a Biography," *New Republic,* July 16, 1930. This was not Croly's response, however. He was thrilled that the *New Republic* had exerted such influence. Levy, *Herbert Croly,* 232. For some reason, Ronald Steel, Lippmann's biographer, asserts that Lippmann believed, and worked to persuade his fellow editors, that the German offer "had to be turned down" and that it was in the "Peace Without Victory" article that he "laid out his argument" against accepting it. Given the explicit recommendation in the article that the Allies should accept Bethmann's offer, this is hard to credit. Steel, *Walter Lippmann,* 109–110.
75. Woodrow Wilson, "Peace Without Victory," speech, Washington, D.C., Jan. 22, 1917 (The University of Michigan, http://www-personal.umd.umich.edu/~ppennock /doc-Wilsonpeace.htm); Link, *Wilson: Campaigns for Progressivism and Peace,* 238, 273. Cited in Gale, *Americanism,* 20.
76. Cited in Gale, *Americanism,* 20. In light of Wilson's later reputation as the quintessential moralist, this criticism, coming from the quintessential French realist, was ironic, but it was a view commonly shared by critics on both sides of the Atlantic.

Roosevelt and Lodge, also often described by historians as "realists," excoriated the president for his moral indifference and his failure to see clearly that the war in Europe was a struggle between good and evil.

77. Cooper, *Vanity of Power*, 136.
78. Ibid., 143.
79. Link, *Wilson: Campaigns for Progressivism and Peace*, 247.
80. Chickering, *Imperial Germany and the Great War*, 91–92.
81. That Bethmann himself had helped engineer the replacement of Falkenhayn by Hindenburg was ironic, given that the duo of Hindenberg and Ludendorff proved far more formidable than the former army chief of staff.
82. Link, *Wilson: Campaigns for Progressivism and Peace*, 244–46, 288–89.
83. May, *World War and American Isolation*, 414.
84. Birnbaum, *Peace Moves and U-Boat Warfare*, 321; Link, *Wilson: Campaigns for Progressivism and Peace*, 245–46.
85. Birnbaum, *Peace Moves and U-Boat Warfare*, 338.
86. A Social Democratic newspaper, possibly reflecting the chancellor's views, put great stock in both Wilson's determination to bring about a peace and his likely impartiality as a mediator. Birnbaum, *Peace Moves and U-Boat Warfare*, 274–75, 297.
87. Ibid, 330–31.
88. Ibid., 59–60 (translation on 346–47); H. E. Goemans and Mark Fey, "Risky but Rational: War as an Institutionally Induced Gamble," *Journal of Politics* 71, no. 1 (January 2009): 46.
89. Link, *Wilson: Campaigns for Progressivism and Peace*, 242.
90. May, *World War and American Isolation*, 229.
91. Link, *Wilson: Campaigns for Progressivism and Peace*, 244.
92. Gerard to Lansing, January 21, 1917, encl. in Lansing to Wilson, January 23, 1917, in Link et al., *The Papers of Woodrow Wilson*, 40 (1916–1917), 552–53.

Chapter Eight: America Declares War

1. Although he had hoped to do so by arming American ships, this had proved "impractical" and "ineffectual" and was likely to produce only what it was meant to prevent, "to draw us into the war without either the rights or the effectiveness of belligerents." Wilson in his address explained the problem at greater length: "Because submarines are in effect outlaws when used as the German submarines have been used against merchant shipping, it is impossible to defend ships against their attacks as the law of nations has assumed that merchantmen would defend themselves against privateers or cruisers, visible craft giving chase upon the open sea. It is common prudence in such circumstances, grim necessity indeed, to endeavour to destroy them before they have shown their own intention. They must be dealt with upon sight, if dealt with at all. The German Government denies the right of neutrals to use arms at all within the areas of the sea which it has proscribed, even in the defense of rights which no modern publicist has ever before questioned their right to defend. The intimation is conveyed that the armed guards which we have placed on our merchant ships will be treated as beyond the pale of law and subject to be dealt with as pirates would be. Armed neutrality is ineffectual enough at best; in such circumstances and in the face of such pretensions it is worse than ineffectual . . ." Woodrow Wilson, "Address to Congress Requesting a Declaration of War Against Germany," Washington, D.C., April 2, 1917 (University of Virginia, Miller Center, https://millercenter.org/the-presidency/presidential-speeches/april-2-1917-address-congress-requesting-declaration-war).

2. Link, *Wilson: Campaigns for Progressivism and Peace,* 296.
3. Ibid., 293–94.
4. Gwynn, *Letters and Friendships,* 2:376. Wilson was not the only one shocked that the Gemans would announce the return to unrestricted submarine warfare just as the American president was "pushing the question of peace to the front." For the views of the diplomat and Republican Henry White at the time, see Allan Nevins, *Henry White: Thirty Years of American Diplomacy* (Harper & Brothers, 1930), 336–37.
5. Link, *Wilson: Campaigns for Progressivism and Peace,* 291.
6. Ibid., 294.
7. Referring to Japan and its efforts to control China, Wilson argued that if "in order to keep the white race or part of it strong to meet the yellow race," it was necessary for the United States to stay out of the war, then he was prepared to submit to "any imputation of weakness or cowardice." One cabinet member commented that "this was a novel and unexpected angle." Link, *Wilson: Campaigns for Progressivism and Peace,* 291, 296.
8. Ibid., 294.
9. Ibid., 299.
10. Ibid., 300–301.
11. Ibid., 309.
12. Ibid., 324.
13. Gwynn, *Letters and Friendships,* 2:376, 381–83.
14. Cooper, *Vanity of Power,* 168.
15. Ibid., 174; Link, *Wilson: Campaigns for Progressivism and Peace,* 305–6.
16. Cooper, *Vanity of Power,* 174.
17. Wilson acknowledged to a French visitor that many in the West favored "peace at any price." Link, *Wilson: Campaigns for Progressivism and Peace,* 340.
18. Thomas Boghardt, *The Zimmermann Telegram: Intelligence, Diplomacy, and America's Entry into World War I* (Naval Institute Press, 2012), 161. Spring Rice explained the difference largely as a matter of economics and geography. The West had no "pecuniary or other interests in the war." In California, the only foreign nation that excited "fear or dislike" was Japan. Gwynn, *Letters and Friendships,* 2:381–83.
19. Link, *Wilson: Campaigns for Progressivism and Peace,* 307–8.
20. "The merchant marine of the United States," the *Washington Post* reported, had been "terrorized and driven from the seas." Boghardt, *Zimmermann Telegram,* 133.
21. Link, *Wilson: Campaigns for Progressivism and Peace,* 313.
22. The idea of an armed neutrality had been most fully elaborated in a widely read article by a Columbia history professor, Carlton Hayes. In it, Hayes argued that the United States had no interests at stake in the European war and no interest in the victory of either side. An Allied victory would do nothing to advance American neutral rights but would only strengthen British domination of the seas. Wilson had been given the article by House and, after reading it, passed it on to Lansing, and Hayes's influence was evident in Wilson's speech.
23. "Text of President Wilson's Address to Congress," *New York Times,* Feb. 27, 1917.
24. See the *New Republic,* "Justification," Feb. 10, 1917; "America's Part in the War," Feb. 10, 1917; "The Defense of the Atlantic World," Feb. 17, 1917; "A History of These Months," Feb. 19, 1917.
25. Lippmann also appealed to Wilson to lead the way. The "mass of the people" were "silently waiting for leadership," he insisted, and would "rejoice at being members

of a nation which rose after long and just patience to answer so deliberate an enemy of western civilization." *New Republic,* Feb. 17, 1917.

26. Jane Addams recorded that the "president's mood was stern and far from the scholar's detachment as he told us of recent disclosures of German machinations in Mexico and announced the impossibility of any form of adjudication." Boghardt, *Zimmermann Telegram,* 139–40.

27. Gwynn, *Letters and Friendships,* 2:383.

28. Lansing thought the telegram had "resulted in unifying public sentiment . . . against Germany" and in "putting the people solidly behind the government and in making war inevitable." The argument that the telegram did not have an appreciable effect on public opinion is laid out in Boghardt, *Zimmermann Telegram,* 159–80.

29. Ibid., 149–51.

30. Wittke, *German-Americans and the World War,* 118–19.

31. Ibid., 123.

32. Boghardt, *Zimmermann Telegram,* 159–80.

33. Gwynn, *Letters and Friendships,* 2:387.

34. The first was the freighter *Vigilancia,* carrying goods from New York to Le Havre. The ship was flying an American flag and was torpedoed on March 16 as it steamed past the British coast. Fifteen crew members died, along with six American passengers. Two more ships were sunk over the next two days, the *City of Memphis* and the *Illinois,* both on their way back from Europe. Although there were no deaths, their sinking showed that German submarines were targeting all ships, regardless of nationality, regardless of what direction they were traveling in, and regardless of what they might or might not be carrying. One tanker was sunk while traveling westbound from England, flying two American flags and with "U. S. A." printed in large letters on its hull. Byron Farwell, *Over There: The United States in the Great War, 1917–1918* (W. W. Norton, 2000), 33.

35. Before the war, many, including Roosevelt, had regarded Germany as a bulwark against the Slav menace. This was one reason why, even after the war had begun, some Americans, including Wilson, believed the most desirable outcome would be a draw. House early in the war had warned that if the Allies won, it would mean "the domination of Russia on the continent of Europe," a concern that Wilson shared, as did Roosevelt. Seymour, *Intimate Papers,* 1:285; Baker, *Woodrow Wilson: Life and Letters,* 5:64–65. Lippmann's case for a "peace without victory" was premised in part on concern that crushing German power would leave Russia too powerful for the rest of Europe to contain. This was also one reason for Roosevelt's ambivalence during the first months of the war. It was not immediately clear to him that a Russian victory was to be preferred to a German victory.

36. Levy, *Herbert Croly,* 231.

37. Link, *Wilson: Campaigns for Progressivism and Peace,* 395.

38. Christopher Lasch, the *American Liberals and the Russian Revolution* (McGraw-Hill, 1972), 23. Even the *Nation,* whose editor, Oswald Garrison Villard, was a leading opponent of war, believed that "the uprising of the Russian people" had "clarified . . . the moral issue" at stake. Lasch, *American Liberals and the Russian Revolution,* 29.

39. N. Gordon Levin, *Woodrow Wilson and World Politics: America's Response to War and Revolution* (Oxford University Press, 1968), 42.

40. Lansing, reflecting on Daniels's "pacifist tendencies and personal devotion to Mr. Bryan," wondered whether "he spoke with conviction or because he lacked strength of mind to stand out against the united opinion of colleagues." A full account of

the cabinet meeting can be found in Link, *Wilson: Campaigns for Progressivism and Peace,* 402–5.

41. Gwynn, *Letters and Friendships,* 2:387, 389. News leaks suggested that Wilson had made that decision as a result of the cabinet meeting, and this was no doubt what Wilson wanted everyone to believe. More likely he had made his decision before the meeting. He knew what the consensus among his advisers would be. Spring Rice, noting that Wilson was described in the newspapers as "having been influenced by the firm attitude of the members," hinted that the truth might be somewhat different. It seemed clear that "Mr. Wilson wished it to be known that the responsibility for such a step was shared by his official advisers."

42. Harbaugh, *Power and Responsibility,* 497.

43. Link, *Wilson: Campaigns for Progressivism and Peace,* 5:398–400.

44. Ibid., 5:399.

45. Ibid., 5:408–9; "Cabinet, Holding That War Exists, Urges Wilson to Summon Congress; Union League Calls for Action," *New York Times,* March, 21, 1917; "Has Plan to Call a Million Men," ibid., March 22, 1917; "Navy Needs 27,000 More Men," ibid., March 23, 1917; "Cabinet Weighs War Plan," ibid., March 24, 1917.

46. Link, *Wilson: Campaigns for Progressivism and Peace,* 416–18; There were fewer signs of enthusiastic support in the South and Southwest. William Howard Taft returned from a speaking tour reporting that he found "not one ounce of anti-war spirit" but also no "rampant jingoism." The people of the South and Southwest, he said, simply felt that war was "inevitable" and they were willing "to go into it to defend our rights." *New York Times,* April 3, 1917.

47. "Would Strike at Once," *New York Times,* March 21, 1917; "Cabinet Weighs War Plans," *New York Times,* March 24, 1917.

48. Thompson, *Woodrow Wilson,* 152.

49. Link, *Wilson: Campaigns for Progressivism and Peace,* 418.

50. Ibid., 422–29; "Lodge Knocks Down Pacifist Assailant," *New York Times,* April 3, 1917.

51. Link, *Wilson: Campaigns for Progressivism and Peace,* 416–17. One of the "Apostles," Jordan insisted that Wall Street was "running this thing" and had manipulated "Uncle Sam" into endorsing "billions of European bonds" and throwing money with "Morgan & Company into the bottomless pit of war." Perhaps the Germans had "behaved like sin," he said. That was "the nature of war." But the "intolerance and tyranny" with which Americans were being "pushed into war" were far worse than the "riotous methods which threw the Kaiser off his feet and brought on the crash of 1914." Link, *Wilson: Campaigns for Progressivism and Peace,* 418.

52. Ibid., 422–23; "President Calls for War Declaration, Stronger Navy, New Army of 500,000 Men, Full Co-operation with Germany's Foes," *New York Times,* April 3, 1917.

53. Woodrow Wilson, "Address to Congress Requesting a Declaration of War Against Germany," Washington, D.C., April 2, 1917 (University of Virginia, Miller Center, https://millercenter.org/the-presidency/presidential-speeches/april-2-1917-address -congress-requesting-declaration-war).

54. Link, *Wilson: Campaigns for Progressivism and Peace,* 423, 426; *New York Times,* April 3, 1917.

55. Gwynn, *Letters and Friendships,* 2:389.

56. Link, *Wilson: Campaigns for Progressivism and Peace,* 423–26; "President Calls for War Declaration, Stronger Navy, New Army of 500,000 Men, Full Co-operation With Germany's Foes," *New York Times,* April 3, 1917.

57. He certainly did not mean that it was America's task to spread democracy where it didn't already exist or was not already struggling to come into being.

58. Steel, *Walter Lippmann,* 112–13.

59. "Debate Lasted 16½ Hours,"*New York Times,* April 7, 1917.

60. David M. Kennedy, *Over Here: The First World War and American Society* (Oxford University Press, 2004), 23.

61. Ibid., 21.

62. Ibid.

63. "Debate Lasted 16½ Hours," *New York Times,* April 6, 1917.

64. Wilson was sufficiently troubled by this line of argument that he asked Page to convey to Lloyd George after the vote that offering the Irish "substantial self-government" would make it much easier for the United States to work closely with Britain in the war. Schmuhl, *Ireland's Exiled Children,* 93–94.

65. Kennedy, *Over Here,* 21–22.

66. Even Kitchin's hometown newspaper denounced him, charging that no more than five percent of his constituents agreed with his stance. "Stone and Kitchin Under Party Fire," *The New York Times*, April 7, 1917. "God of our Fathers," Congressman Heflin from Alabama exclaimed, "how long will there be divided loyalty in this country, how long?" "Debate Lasted 16½ Hours," *New York Times*, April 6, 1917.

67. The fifty-seven-year-old William Jennings Bryan requested to be made a private in the armed forces: "Gladly would I have given my life to save my country from war, but now that my country has gone to war, gladly will I give my life to aid it." "Bryan Asks the President to Enroll Him as a Private,"*New York Times,* April 7, 1917.

68. "Germans Here Quick to Back President," *New York Times,* April 7, 1917. German American organizations across the country began advising their members to remove German flags and pictures of German military leaders from their meeting rooms, and German-language papers warned readers to "silence hot-heads who might, by their unpatriotic utterings, throw the shame of doubt upon all German-Americans." Wittke, *German-Americans and the World War,* 130.

69. Americans in their first century and a quarter of existence had never given their unanimous approval for war. Many had opposed the War of 1812—the New England states even contemplated secession—and many in the North had opposed going to war with the South in 1861. Probably the war that came closest to enjoying unanimous support had been the war with Spain.

70. Gilbert, *Churchill and America,* 60.

71. Nevins, *Henry White,* 338.

72. Gilbert, *Churchill and America,* 61.

73. Ibid., 62.

74. Robert Lansing, *War Memoirs of Robert Lansing, Secretary of State* (Bobbs-Merrill, 1935), 18–19.

75. Gwynn, *Letters and Friendships,* 2:391–92.

76. Thompson, *Woodrow Wilson,* 148.

77. Ross Gregory, *The Origins of American Intervention in the First World War* (W. W. Norton, 1971), 135.

78. Doeneke, *Nothing Less Than War,* 283.

79. Gregory, *Origins of American Intervention,* 135.

80. *New York Times,* April 6, 1917.

81. Kennedy, *Rise of Anglo-German Antagonism,* 467–68.

82. J. Lee Thompson, *Never Call Retreat: Theodore Roosevelt," the Great War* (Palguave Macmillan, 2014), 28–29; Roosevelt, "The World War: Its Tragedies and Its Lessons," *Outlook,* Sept. 23, 1914, "Utopia or Hell," *The Independent* 81, Jan. 4, 1915.

83. Pusey, *Hughes,* 368–370.
84. Stimson and Bundy, *On Active Service,* 89.
85. Steel, *Walter Lippmann,* 110–12.
86. "Peace Without Victory," *New Republic,* Dec. 23, 1916.

Chapter Nine: America and the "War to End All Wars"

1. Zieger, *America's Great War,* 56.
2. Thompson, *Woodrow Wilson,* 153.
3. Ibid., 155.
4. Zieger, *America's Great War,* 113.
5. Ibid., 58.
6. Ibid., 114
7. Richard W. Van Alstyne, "Private American Loans to the Allies, 1914–1916," *Pacific Historical Review* 2, no. 2 (June 1933): 180.
8. "House Passes $7,000,000,000 War Loan; Not a Vote Recorded Against It: Wilson to Send Commission to Russia," *New York Times,* April 15, 1917.
9. As Pershing later recalled, "We were literally beggars as to every important weapon, except the rifle." Zieger, *America's Great War,* 93.
10. Gilbert, *First World War,* 341–42, 349, 372.
11. Thompson, *Woodrow Wilson,* 162.
12. This prompted a leading Democrat to condemn him as "the most potent agent the Kaiser has in America." Seward W. Livermore, *Politics Is Adjourned: Woodrow Wilson and the War Congress, 1916–1918* (Wesleyan University Press, 1966), 66, 64, 76–77, 38, 84, 101, 91–93, 67; "Roosevelt Starts for Washington," *New York Times,* Jan.22, 1918; "Roosevelt Sees Capital Leaders," ibid., Jan. 22, 1918.
13. Cooper, *Woodrow Wilson,* 391; Livermore, *Politics Is Adjourned,* 62–63.
14. Zieger, *America's Great War,* 68.
15. "The Crisis in Our Preparations for the War," *New York Times,* Jan. 22, 1918."
16. Cooper, *Woodrow Wilson,* 427.
17. Zieger, *America's Great War,* 58.
18. Cooper, *Woodrow Wilson,* 393; Livermore, *Politics Is Adjourned,* 17–18, 20–31.
19. Livermore, *Politics Is Adjourned,* 58–59, 61.
20. Zieger, *America's Great War,* 77; over $280 billion in 2017 dollars.
21. Cooper, *Woodrow Wilson,* 392.
22. Lodge speech, *New York Times,* Aug. 24, 1918.
23. Livermore, *Politics Is Adjourned,* 118.
24. Ibid.
25. Ibid., 120.
26. Ibid., 165–67.
27. Ibid., 145. Fitzgerald was future president John F. Kennedy's grandfather.
28. Ibid., 122, 138; Cooper, *Woodrow Wilson,* 437.
29. Zieger, *America's Great War,* 78.
30. "Berger Indicted for Conspiracy," *New York Times,* March 10, 1918.
31. Kennedy, *Over Here,* 58.
32. Ibid., 59.
33. Alan Axelrod, *Selling the Great War: The Making of American Propaganda* (St. Martin's Press, 2009), 143, 130, 145.
34. Kennedy, *Over Here,* 54.
35. "36 German Agents Off to Oglethorpe," *New York Times,* Jan. 20, 1918; "Seize Warship Spy in Navy Yard Here," ibid., Jan. 21, 1918.

36. Kennedy, *Over Here,* 44.

37. Harbaugh, *Power and Responsibility,* 497.

38. Gilbert, *First World War,* 333–34.

39. Ibid., 348, 350.

40. Ibid., 389. Prime Minister Lloyd George called it a "useless waste of life."

41. Arno J. Mayer, *Political Origins of the New Diplomacy, 1917–1918* (Yale University Press, 1959), 234, 269.

42. Ibid., 112.

43. Ibid.,114.

44. Chickering, *Imperial Germany and the Great War,* 160–61.

45. Adam Hochschild, *To End All Wars: A Story of Loyalty and Rebellion, 1914–1918* (Mariner Books, 2012), 302.

46. Mayer, *Political Origins of the New Diplomacy,* 32; Gilbert, *First World War,* 384.

47. "British War Aims," statement by David Lloyd George, Jan. 5, 1918, reprinted in the *New York Times,* "Lloyd George Restates British War Aims," *New York Times,* Jan. 6, 1918.

48. Nevins, *Henry White,* 345–46; as the American ambassador in Paris put it about the French Left, they had "confidence in his motives." Levin, *Woodrow Wilson and World Politics,* 56.

49. Lasch, *American Liberals and the Russian Revolution,* 37.

50. Thompson, *Woodrow Wilson,* 166; Mayer, *Political Origins of the New Diplomacy,* 323, 334, 340.

51. In later speeches he would make plain that what he sought was a "decisive victory." "President Wilson's Labor Day Message," *New York Times,* Sept. 2, 1918; Klaus Schwabe, *Woodrow Wilson, Revolutionary Germany, and Peacemaking, 1918–1919: Missionary Diplomacy and the Realities of Power,* trans. Rita Kimber and Robert Kimber (University of North Carolina Press, 1985), 20.

52. Thompson, *Woodrow Wilson,* 160.

53. Nevins, *Henry White,* 344–45. Wilson even denied American socialists passports to go to the Bolshevik-inspired socialist peace conference in Stockholm. They would only do "a deal of mischief," he explained, and he was unmoved when the conference organizers insisted they were only pursuing the idea of a "peace without victory." Mayer, *Political Origins of the New Diplomacy,* 226.

54. Thompson, *Woodrow Wilson,* 157.

55. Schwabe, *Woodrow Wilson, Revolutionary Germany,* 33, 24.

56. Zieger, *America's Great War,* 163.

57. David Stevenson, *French War Aims Against Germany, 1914–1919* (Oxford University Press, 1982), 101.

Chapter Ten: The Great War Ends

1. Gilbert, *First World War,* 398.

2. Ibid., 401.

3. John W. Wheeler-Bennett, *Brest-Litovsk: The Forgotten Peace, March 1918* (W. W. Norton, 1971), v.

4. He was disappointed by the German liberals and socialists, for they largely acquiesced in the ratification of the treaty. Chickering, *Imperial Germany and the Great War,* 165; Wheeler-Bennett, *Brest-Litovsk,* 365.

5. Wilson speech at the opening of the third Liberty Loan campaign, delivered in the Fifth Regiment Armory, Baltimore, April 6, 1918 (The American Presidency Project, https://www.presidency.vesb.edu/node/206655).

6. Gilbert, *First World War,* 385, 387, 406, 427, 435.

7. Thompson, *Woodrow Wilson,* 170.

8. Gilbert, *First World War,* 408.

9. Ibid., 420, 435.

10. Ibid., 420–21.

11. Ibid., 415.

12. Ibid., 416.

13. See Chickering, *Imperial Germany and the Great War,* 178.

14. Zieger, *America's Great War,* 97, 106.

15. Cooper, *Woodrow Wilson,* 437.

16. Zieger, *America's Great War,* 96.

17. Gilbert, *First World War,* 444.

18. Zieger, *America's Great War,* 98.

19. Ibid.

20. "The Draft Proclamation," *New York Times,* Sept. 2, 1918.

21. Gilbert, *First World War,* 451–52.

22. Ibid., 458; and see Zieger, *America's Great War,* 114.

23. Gilbert, *First World War,* 451–52.

24. Zieger, *America's Great War,* 114. See also Hagan, *This People's Navy,* 255–56. As Admiral Jellicoe commented, the convoy system could not have operated without the American contribution.

25. Historians estimate that between 750,000 and 1,000,000 soldiers avoided battle in these ways in 1918. Chickering, *Imperial Germany and the Great War,* 184.

26. Wheeler-Bennett, *Brest-Litovsk,* 368–69; Gilbert, *First World War,* 466–68.

27. David Stevenson, *The First World War and International Politics* (Oxford University Press, 1988), 224.

28. Schwabe, *Woodrow Wilson, Revolutionary Germany,* 33.

29. Ibid., 38.

30. He did express concern that the peace would not be stable if the Allies enjoyed "too much success." Cooper, *Woodrow Wilson,* 444.

31. Garraty, *Lodge,* 341; Schwabe, *Woodrow Wilson, Revolutionary Germany,* 51.

32. "Senate Condemns New Peace Pleas," *New York Times,* Oct. 8, 1918; Schwabe, *Woodrow Wilson, Revolutionary Germany,* 65; Livermore, *Politics Is Adjourned,* 218.

33. Schwabe, *Woodrow Wilson, Revolutionary Germany,* 65; Livermore, *Politics Is Adjourned,* 218.

34. The office of chancellor was made subservient to the Reichstag on key matters. The kaiser's powers were substantially curtailed, including his role as commander in chief. The government also promised substantial reforms to the notoriously undemocratic Prussian voting laws, and there was even talk of forcing the kaiser to abdicate. As one socialist minister put it, if the kaiser was gone the Allies would have nothing left to fight but "German democracy" and therefore this offered the best chance for lenient terms. Schwabe, *Woodrow Wilson, Revolutionary Germany,* 99, 105.

35. Ibid., 108.

36. Ibid., 118, 120, 63.

37. Eric D. Weitz, *Weimar Germany: Promise and Tragedy* (Princeton University Press, 2007), 18.

38. Thompson, *Woodrow Wilson,* 176.

39. Gilbert, *First World War,* 486.

40. Arthur Walworth, *America's Moment, 1918: American Diplomacy at the End of World War I* (W. W. Norton, 1977), 44.

41. Gilbert, *First World War,* 486; Wilson and his advisers also strongly suspected the general was playing to the Republican opposition and had his eyes on the presidency. Walworth, *America's Moment,* 44.

42. MacMillan, *Paris 1919,* 158.

43. General Haig believed the war could drag on well into 1919. Gilbert, *First World War,* 480, 482.

44. Walworth, *America's Moment,* 53.

45. Gilbert, *First World War,* 498, 500, 503.

46. MacMillan, *Paris 1919,* 159.

47. Cooper, *Woodrow Wilson,* 451.

48. David Blackbourn, *History of Germany, 1780–1918,* 364, 362; Preston, *Higher Form,* 50; Jeff Lipkes, *Rehearsals: The German Army in Belgium, August 1914* (The Brabant Press, 2014), 533.

49. The historian Niall Ferguson has suggested a victorious Germany "might have created a version of the European Union, eight decades ahead of schedule." Ferguson, *The Pity of War: Explaining World War I* (Penguin Press, 1998), 458.

50. Lipkes, *Rehearsals,* 546–47.

51. Chickering, *Imperial Germany and the Great War,* 84; Lipkes, *Rehearsals,* 546–47.

52. Lipkes, *Rehearsals,* 548.

53. Strachan, *First World War,* 270.

54. Lipkes, *Rehearsals,* 532.

55. Chickering, *Imperial Germany and the Great War,* 86.

56. Ibid., 84.

57. The reference to a "German India" is by historian Hans Delbruck, whose 1915 essay "Bismarck's Erbe" is quoted in "The New German Empire," *The Round Table,* March 1917, 8; the second quotation is also from that essay in *The Round Table,* same page.

58. Chickering, *Imperial Germany and the Great War,* 86–87.

59. Darwin, *Unfinished Empire,* 332.

60. Jan Willem Honig, "Totalitarianism and Realism: Hans Morgenthau's German Years," in Benjamin Frankel, ed., *Roots of Realism* (Frank Cass, 1996), 294–95.

61. Wilson reply to the Vatican, Aug. 22, 1917. Lawrence E. Gelfand, *The Inquiry: American Preparations for Peace, 1917–1919* (Yale University Press, 1963), 22.

62. Quoted in Osgood, *Ideals and Self-Interest,* 151.

Chapter Eleven: America and the European Peace

1. Peter Yearwood, *Guarantee of Peace: The League of Nations in British Policy, 1914–1925* (Oxford University Press, 2009), 60.

2. Adam Tooze, *The Deluge: The Great War, America and the Remaking of the Global Order, 1916–1931* (Viking, 2014), 10.

3. Ralph Haswell Lutz and William Z. Foster, The *German Revolution: Writings on the Failed Communist Rebellion in 1918–1919* (Red and Black Publishers, 2011 [1922]), 135–38.

4. George W. Egerton, *Great Britain and the Creation of the League of Nations: Strategy, Politics, and International Organization, 1914–1919* (University of North Carolina Press, 1978), 158.

5. Tooze, *The Deluge,* 5.

6. The British looked to wriggle out of their wartime agreements, seeking full control of Palestine and Mesopotamia, for instance, contrary to the Sykes-Picot agreement negotiated in 1916. They also wanted to push the French out of Somaliland and the Portuguese out of parts of East Africa. Erik Goldstein, *Winning the Peace, British Diplomatic Strategy, Peace Planning, and the Paris Peace Conference 1916–1920* (Clarendon Press, 1991), 16–17.

7. Jason Tomes, *Balfour and Foreign Policy: The International Thought of a Conservative Statesman* (Cambridge University Press, 1997), 155–56.

8. Goldstein, *Winning the Peace,* 270, 273–74.

9. Robert Tombs and Isabelle Toombs, *That Sweet Enemy: The French and the British from the Sun King to the Present* (Knopf, 2006), 506.

10. Jere Clemens King, *Foch Versus Clemenceau: France and German Dismemberment, 1918–1919:* (Harvard University Press, 1960), 44.

11. MacMillan, *Paris 1919,* 23.

12. This had been "the supreme object of our existence, the dream so often cherished." Tombs and Tombs, *That Sweet Enemy,* 515.

13. David Stevenson, "French War Aims and Peace Planning," in *The Treaty of Versailles: A Reassessment After 75 Years,* ed. Manfred F. Boemeke, Gerald D. Feldman, and Elisabeh Glaser (Washington, D.C., and Cambridge: German Historical Institute and Cambridge University Press, 1998), 100–101; Tombs and Tombs, *That Sweet Enemy,* 515.

14. Zara Steiner, *The Lights That Failed: European International History, 1919–1933* (Oxford University Press, 2005), 30. British officials frequently expressed apprehensions about French territorial and imperial ambitions. Intelligence officials warned that France in a future war might be more dangerous than a rearmed Germany. That was why they not only opposed French annexation of Luxembourg, the Saar, and the Rhineland but preferred giving Luxembourg to Belgium instead, which would act as a check on France as well as on Germany. P. A. Reynolds, *British Foreign Policy in the Inter-War Years* (Greenwood Press, 1974), 7; William Roger Louis, *British Strategy in the Far East, 1919–1939* (Clarendon Press, 1971), 101; Goldstein, *Winning the Peace,* 231–32. Lord Curzon, thinking perhaps more of the imperial competition, worried that "the great Power from which we have most to fear in the future is France." Yearwood, *Guarantee of Peace,* 91.

15. P. M. H. Bell, *France and Britain, 1900–1940: Entente and Estrangement* (Longman, 1996), 118.

16. Ibid.

17. Yearwood, *Guarantee of Peace,* 127. Goldstein, *Winning the Peace,* 191.

18. Bell, *France and Britain,* 118.

19. Yearwood, *Guarantee of Peace,* 127.

20. Bell, *France and Britain,* 111.

21. King, *Foch Versus Clemenceau,* 45; Steiner, *Lights That Failed,* 30–31.

22. Many Britons believed that "Britain was great by virtue of its empire alone," that this was its true source of wealth and power. All attention paid to the continent was an unfortunate diversion. Steiner, *Lights That Failed,* 27–29.

23. The financial writer Edgar Crammond in 1919: "There has been nothing approaching this destruction of life and wealth in the history of the world . . . this stupendous conflict has produced the greatest economic revolution of which we have any record." Dan P. Silverman, *Reconstructing Europe After the Great War* (Harvard University Press, 1982), 13–14.

24. Yearwood, *Guarantee of Peace,* 138.

25. Ibid., 94.

26. Ibid., 75. Notably, Cecil was contrasting the "British" point of view with that of the "Continental" nations, obviously drawing no distinction between the Germans and the French.

27. Tomes, *Balfour and Foreign Policy,* 189; Yearwood, *Guarantee of Peace,* 60.

28. Steiner, *Lights That Failed,* 34; Yearwood, *Guarantee of Peace,* 22.

29. MacMillan, *Paris 1919,* 32.

30. Stevenson, *French War Aims Against Germany,* 148, 164.

31. See Mark Ellis Swartzburg, "The Call for America: German-American Relations and the European Crisis, 1921–1924/25" (PhD diss., University of North Carolina, 2005), 63.

32. See Geir Lundestad, *The United States and Western Europe since 1945.* Tooze, in *The Deluge,* makes much of American hegemony and the resentment it caused among such figures as Hitler and Mussolini. He is less attentive to the countervailing views of many Germans, at least during the Weimar period, that the United States was Germany's only hope in a hostile world.

33. Only Roosevelt had even left the country, to visit the Panama Canal. Critics asked how Wilson could fulfill his duties from abroad, and Republicans demanded that he relinquish his powers the moment he left American shores. But the criticism did not just come from political opponents. Whether it was wise for Wilson to attend the talks himself was another question, which scholars have long debated.

34. In Britain, the treaty-making power resided entirely with the Crown, advised by his or her responsible ministers. Parliament had no role at all. See Robert B. Stewart, "Treaty-Making Procedure in the United Kingdom," *American Political Science Review* 32, no. 4 (August 1938): 655–69. In France, although the Parliament theoretically had the power to reject a treaty, there was very little chance of Clemenceau's treaty being rejected.

35. The Union Sacrée in France, and in Britain, after 1916, Lloyd George's coalition of Conservatives and Liberals. This did not mean there were no power struggles. Lloyd George usurped Asquith as prime minister at the end of 1916; in France there was constant carping between Clemenceau and Poincaré. In both countries there were numerous cabinet shuffles, as well as the occasional dissenting voices in Parliament.

36. Quoted in David Lawrence, *The True Story of Woodrow Wilson* (George H. Doran, 1924), 236.

37. Former Republican senator Albert Beveridge wrote Roosevelt during the campaign that Wilson had "hoisted the motley flag of internationalism," and "thank God" that he had. "That makes the issue, does it not? Straight Americanism for us." Roosevelt responded that "Americanism" would indeed be the issue "which we shall have to force against Wilson." W. Stull Holt, *Treaties Defeated by the Senate: A Study of the Struggle Between President and Senate over the Conduct of Foreign Relations* (Johns Hopkins Press, 1933), 252; Livermore, *Politics Is Adjourned,* 212.

38. Knock, *To End All Wars,* 49; "Roosevelt Demands the Speed Up of War," *New York Times,* Aug. 27, 1918.

39. Livermore, *Politics Is Adjourned,* 215–16.

40. Senator Pittman afterwards attributed the loss to Republicans' success in convincing the public that Wilson was trying to negotiate a "compromise peace with Germany." Betty Glad, *Key Pittman. The Tragedy of a Senate Insider* (Columbia University Press, 1986), 62.

41. Widenor, *Lodge,* 301; Holt, *Treaties Defeated,* 252.

42. Widenor, *Lodge,* 301.

43. Livermore, *Politics Is Adjourned,* 214.

44. Harold I. Nelson, *Land and Power: British and Allied Policy on Germany's Frontier, 1916–19* (Newton Abbot, 1971), 140.

45. Although Republicans expressed outrage, the move was hardly unprecedented. William McKinley did the same in 1898, asking the public to return a Republican Congress so as not to repudiate the ongoing negotiations with Spain after the war. McKinley differed from Wilson chiefly in that his appeal was successful.

46. Opposition parties usually picked up seats in the sixth year of a president's two terms, and 1918 was no exception. Republican gains and Democratic losses in 1918 were normal for a midterm election in a president's second term. The Republicans picked up 24 seats in the House and 6 seats in the Senate, which was smaller than the twentieth-century average. By way of comparison, Franklin Roosevelt lost 71 seats in the House in 1938, Dwight Eisenhower lost 47 seats in 1958, and Lyndon Johnson lost 47 seats in 1966. *Washington Times,* Jan. 21, 2006. See also Cooper, *Woodrow Wilson,* 447.

47. See Roosevelt op-ed in the *Kansas City Star,* Nov. 26, 1918. Republicans also excoriated Wilson for not naming a leading Republican to accompany him to Paris, which may have seemed reasonable in the American context. But no one would have dreamed of insisting that Lloyd George and Clemenceau bring a political opponent along with them.

48. *Kansas City Star,* Nov. 26, 1918.

49. Indeed, international agreements had been defeated so frequently in recent years that some questioned whether the constitutional powers given to the Senate were compatible with an active foreign policy. As one frustrated congressman had put it years earlier, watching another in a series of treaties go down, "We cannot enter into international agreements and at the same time maintain intact in every respect what is called sovereign power or senatorial prerogative." Kuehl, *Seeking World Order,* 142.

50. Bartlett, *League to Enforce Peace,* 105.

51. Garraty, *Lodge,* 347.

52. Nevins, *Henry White,* 361.

53. Ibid., 353–55. Lodge sent word in the form of a memorandum to Henry White, who did not pass it on to the Allies. However, Lodge delivered the same message through other channels, including the two embassies in Washington.

54. Yearwood, *Guarantee of Peace,* 123. Throughout December and January the French press reported constantly on the opposition Wilson faced at home. G. Bernard Noble, *Policies and Opinions at Paris, 1919* (MacMillan, 1935), 82.

55. Robert K. Murray, *The Harding Era: Warren G. Harding and His Administration* (University of Minnesota Press, 1969), 360.

56. Gelfand, *Inquiry,* 315. In addition to young, smart journalists with no international experience or training, like Walter Lippmann, or young lawyers like David Hunter Miller, they were "an aggregation of ancient historians, archaeologists, medievalists," and other scholars of largely irrelevant subjects. The Inquiry's chief, House's brother-in-law, Sidney Mezes, was a philosopher of religion. This does not mean they failed to produce respectable advice. See Gelfand, *Inquiry,* and Erick Goldstein, *Winning the Peace,* passim.; on the Inquiry, see 99–100. Nor can it be said that the "wrong" people were chosen. The study of international relations had not yet found a place in American academia. There were a few diplomatic historians, almost none of whom specialized in the twentieth century, and there were others who studied international law. But the major universities offered no courses in world affairs, much less in area studies. See Gelfand, *Inquiry,* 35–36. As Gelfand observes, there was "a heritage of ignorance which the United States found difficult

to overcome in its new role as a great power." Ibid., 48. It should have been no sur-prise that Wilson did not rely on these advisers as much as they believed he should have. The truth was, they were just as overwhelmed by the enormity of the crisis as he was.

57. Nevins, *Henry White,* 398, 410.

58. Ibid., 357.

59. Ibid., 389.

60. "Col. Theodore Roosevelt Writes on What America Should Learn from the War," *New York Times,* Sept. 27, 1914.

61. Theodore Roosevelt, "The International Posse Comitatus," *New York Times,* Nov. 8, 1914; *New York Times,* Oct. 4, 11, 18, Nov. 1, 1914; Kuehl, *Seeking World Order,* 178; Roosevelt, "The World War: Its Tragedies and Its Lessons," *Outlook,* Sept. 23, 1914.

62. Grey, *Twenty-Five Years,* 2:147–48; Roosevelt, "The International Posse Comita-tus," *New York Times,* Nov. 8, 1914. In the winter of 1914 Roosevelt included Ger-many as one of the "great powers of civilization" that had to be part of any league. Germany had legitimate fears of its neighbors, just as its neighbors had legitimate fears of Germany, and any peace that did not address those fears would "at some future day . . . bring about the repetition of this same awful tragedy." "Theodore Roosevelt on Ultimate Causes of the War," *New York Times,* Oct. 11, 1914; Roose-velt, *New York Times,* Sept. 27, 1914; "Theodore Roosevelt Writes on Helping the Cause of Peace," *New York Times,* Oct. 18, 1914.

63. George Harvey, "Europe at Armageddon," *North American Review* 200, no. 3 (Sep-tember 1914): 322; Link, *Wilson: Struggle for Neutrality,* 11.

64. Theodore Roosevelt, "The World War: Its Tragedies and Its Lessons," *Outlook,* Sept. 23, 1914; Roosevelt, *New York Times,* Sept. 27, 1914.

65. Garraty, *Lodge,* 349n. Lodge's prewar conception of the United States as a power "in the finer sense" had included the conviction that it should be "drawn into no alliances defensive or offensive . . . with any nation anywhere." Lodge, "The Mon-roe Doctrine and Morocco," *Harper's Weekly,* March 10, 1906.

66. Jessup, *Elihu Root,* 2:313–14.

67. Bartlett, *League to Enforce Peace,* 19–26; Kuehl, *Seeking World Order,*189.

68. Woodrow Wilson, "Opening the Campaign for the Fourth Liberty Loan," New York, September 27, 1918, *Foreign Relations of the United States, 1918,* supple-ment 1, *The World War,* vol. 1; Woodrow Wilson, "A World League for Peace," Jan. 22, 1917 (University of Virginia Miller Center, https://millercenter.org/the-presidency/presidential-speeches/january-22-1917-world-league-peace-speech).

69. Roosevelt, "The International Posse Comitatus," *New York Times,* Nov. 8, 1914.

70. Widenor, *Lodge,* 134.

71. Martin David Dubin, "Elihu Root and the Advocacy of a League of Nations, 1914–1917," *Western Political Quarterly* 19, no. 3 (September 1966): 440–45. Kuehl, *Seeking World Order,* 116, 113, 107.

72. Kuehl, *Seeking World Order,* 74.

73. Dubin, "Elihu Root," 440–45.

74. Kuehl, *Seeking World Order,* 171.

75. Jessup, *Elihu Root,* 2:373. See also Stephen Wertheim, "The League That Wasn't: American Designs for a Legalist-Sanctionist League of Nations and the Intellec-tual Origins of International Organization, 1914–1920," *Diplomatic History* 35, no. 5 (November 2011). They "would fight if at that time they were convinced that they ought to, and they would not fight if at that time they were convinced that they ought not to." Jessup, *Elihu Root,* 2:378.

76. "Miles Fears Great War." *New York Times,* Aug. 3, 1914.
77. As the historian Warren Kuehl has observed, the league Wilson had in mind on the eve of the Paris conference would not have included a "rigid guarantee." There is also the account of Isaiah Bowman, who listened and took notes as Wilson described his thinking on board the *George Washington.* They are reprinted in David Hunter Miller, *The Drafting of the Covenant,* Vol. 1 (G. P. Putnam's Sons, 1928), 41–44, fns 1 and 2. According to Bowman, Wilson spoke only of economic measures in response to a state "guilty of wrongdoing." Knock, *To End All Wars,* 149–50, 153; Nevins, *Henry White,* 359; Kuehl, *Seeking World Order,* 227, 256.
78. Cooper, *Vanity of Power,* 136.
79. Ibid., 143.
80. At Paris, the American delegation was alarmed at the positions the French were taking, which, as Henry White put it, indicated "an intention to assume the position in Europe and elsewhere of which Germany has been deprived by the war." For anyone not in Paris and in close touch with representatives of the French people, White wrote Lodge, it was "impossible to comprehend" France's "extraordinary obsession" with the possibility of a renewed German attack in a few years. It seemed the entire French population was "shell-shocked." Nevins, *Henry White,* 403, 412, 379.
81. As another member of the delegation, David Hunter Miller, wrote to Root, it didn't really matter whether these fears of Germany were "right or wrong." Miller, *Covenant,* I, 300–301.
82. The war debts would have to be repaid, and he would "not agree to any program that even looks like inter-Allied control of our economic resources after peace." Yearwood, *Guarantee of Peace,* 92.
83. Seymour, *Intimate Papers,* 1:300–81.
84. Walter A. McDougall, *France's Rhineland Policy, 1914–1924: The Last Bid for a Balance of Power in Europe* (Princeton University Press, 2016), 70–72, 88.
85. Miller, *Covenant,* 1, 300–301.
86. Nevins, *Henry White,* 415.
87. Had the United States kept out of the war, he wrote Lodge, "then there would have been a German peace in the spring or early summer of 1918." But instead, the United States had thrown its weight into the scales and changed the balance in Europe, "and no one advocated more earnestly our doing so than you." Nevins, *Henry White,* 397, 474. "It was our coming into the war that decided the issue," David Miller wrote Root. "We have financed and fed the Allies, and we shall have to continue to finance and to feed Europe. . . . The mere hint of the withdrawal by America . . . would see the fall of every government in Europe without exception, and a revolution in every country of Europe with one possible exception." Miller, *Covenant,* 1:45–46.
88. "The League of Nations was a product of British wartime diplomacy." Yearwood, *Guarantee of Peace,* 7.
89. Yearwood, *Guarantee of Peace,* 95; Steiner, *Lights That Failed,* 28. Lloyd George had pledged to support it in his election campaign and believed the public demanded it.
90. Yearwood, *Guarantee of Peace,* 124.
91. Clemenceau called Wilson "the inspired prophet" and once remarked of the Fourteen Points, "The Good Lord only had ten."
92. See letter from White to Lodge, Nov. 13, 1919, in Nevins, *Henry White,* 472.
93. Noble, *Policies and Opinions at Paris, 1919,* 88.
94. Ibid., 220.

95. Ibid., 88.
96. Miller, *Covenant,* 2:242–43. As the American general and delegation member Tasker Bliss later recalled, what the French had in mind was an international force of between "2,000,000 to 4,000,000 men" that would be available to come to France's aid at the first sign of aggression, some immediately and the rest "as rapidly as transportation can get them there." Bliss, "The Problem of Disarmament," in Edward M. House, *What Really Happened at Paris: The Story of the Peace Conference, 1918–1919* (Charles Scribner's Sons, 1921), 376.
97. Miller, *Covenant,* 1:295.
98. Noble, *Policies and Opinions at Paris, 1919,* 141.
99. Miller, *Covenant,* 1:209 (italics in original).
100. Noble, *Policies and Opinions at Paris, 1919,* 116.
101. Miller, *Covenant,* 1:169.
102. Ibid., I:170.
103. A "double veto," as the historian Lloyd Ambrosius has called it. Lloyd E. Ambrosius, "Woodrow Wilson, Alliances, and the League of Nations," *Journal of the Gilded Age and Progressive Era* 5, no. 2 (April 2006): 150. The latter course might put it in breach of the treaty, but as David Hunter Miller pointed out, that was the case with many treaties the United States had signed over the course of its existence—including its very first treaty with France. The United States had not honored its agreement to come to France's defense when France and Britain went to war. As Miller put it, Congress could "declare war and thus fulfill the treaty obligation, but it would also be within the power of Congress to refuse to declare war and thus breach the treaty obligation." Miller, *Covenant,* 1:27.
104. John Milton Cooper, Jr., *Breaking the Heart of the World: Woodrow Wilson and the Fight for the League of Nations* (Cambridge University Press), 2001, 155. Wilson went on to say that "a moral obligation is of course superior to a legal obligation, and . . . has a greater binding force," but still one has "the right to exercise one's judgment as to whether it is indeed incumbent upon one in those circumstances to do that thing." In a legal obligation, there was no "element of judgment." Herbert F. Margulies, *The Mild Reservationists and the League of Nations Controversy in the Senate* (University of Missouri Press, 1989), 74–75. David Hunter Miller had made this point, as well. See Miller, *Covenant,* 1:27. The Article 5 commitment in the NATO treaty was arguably more specifically binding than Article 10, but even that still left it to national governments, and in the United States, the Congress, to decide whether to go to war in any given circumstance. Miller, *Covenant,* 1:32.
105. As the journalist David Lawrence described the irony, "in Paris it was Woodrow Wilson who was fighting almost the entire Allied group in constituting a League of Nations which would not be an interference with the sovereignty of any signatory power but an advisory body through which all the nations could act independently or jointly if they desired. In the Senate, however, the League proposal was hailed as a supergovernment and a surrender of American sovereignty." Lawrence, *True Story,* 266.
106. Noble, *Policies and Opinions at Paris, 1919,* 116; Knock, *To End All Wars,* 222.
107. The United States, he explained, "had nothing to gain from the League of Nations." It could "let European affairs go and take care of her own." Even Britain, he warned, "while vitally interested in continental affairs," could also "stand apart" if it chose. Miller, *Covenant,* 1:216; Knock, *To End All Wars,* 222.
108. Ray Stannard Baker, who was at Wilson's side in Paris and then wrote a sympa-

thetic history of the talks, depicted the negotiations as a simple struggle between light and darkness, the light of Wilson's hopeful view of a new dawn for mankind versus the darkness of Clemenceau's insistence on remaining mired in the horrors of the past.

109. *Le Temps* opined that "it is on the banks of the Rhine that the fate of all of us will be determined if war should some day break out again." Noble, *Policies and Opinions at Paris, 1919,* 220.

110. As Keith L. Nelson observes, "Clemenceau's obstinacy, Lloyd George's anxiety, Europe's desperation, and America's impatience—must have intensified the president's desire to break the impasse." Keith L. Nelson, *Victors Divided: America and the Allies in Germany, 1918–1923* (University of California Press, 1975), 78–79.

111. Ibid., 81–83.

112. Robert Lansing, *The Peace Negotiations: A Personal Narrative* (Houghton Mifflin, 1921), 181.

113. Lansing, who opposed even the ambiguous commitment in Article 10, noted that the proposed "triple defensive alliance" went "even further in the assurance of affirmative action" by the United States and was therefore sure to be "laughed at and rejected." Lansing, *Peace Negotiations,* 178–80. General Bliss thought it "scandalous" that Wilson "did not make it clear" to the French "that neither he nor the Senate nor the people of the USA would form an Alliance with France." Stephen A. Schuker, "The Rhineland Question: West European Security at the Paris Peace Conference of 1919," in *Treaty of Versailles,* ed. Manfred F. Boemeke et al., 298–300.

114. King, *Foch Versus Clemenceau,* 48; Also see Bell: "Even in June 1919 it was unlikely that the American Senate would accept the treaty of guarantee. Foch said so openly. Lloyd George knew it, and it seems plain that the French knew that he knew it. The proposed guarantee thus appeared a mere trick." Bell, *France and Britain,* 121.

115. House agreed it was "practically promising only what we promise to do in the League of Nations." Schuker, "Rhineland Question," in *Treaty of Versailles,* ed. Manfred F. Boemeke et al., 299–300.

116. Some in France, like Tardieu, would later claim that the security treaties alone made it possible for Clemenceau eventually to agree to the overall peace settlement. This seems an exaggeration, designed to highlight the betrayal that the French felt and which justified their subsequent course with Germany. Antony Lentin, "'Une aberration inexplicable'? Clemenceau and the Abortive Anglo-French Guarantee Treaty of 1919," *Diplomacy & Statecraft* 8, no. 2 (July 1997): 30. French officials knew that the treaties did not solve the problem that France would face Germany alone until the Anglo-Saxons arrived. It was a "temporal" rather than a "spatial" guarantee, and France needed both. King, *Foch Versus Clemenceau,* 46–47.

117. Stevenson, *French War Aims,* 171–72. As McDougall puts it, Clemenceau's only choice was to "stand alone on the Rhine against a vengeful Germany, or rely on distant allies." McDougall, *France's Rhineland Policy,* 60.

118. As one of Clemenceau's advisers put it, "No Treaties of Guarantee, no evacuation in 1935." André Tardieu, *The Truth About the Treaty* (Bobbs-Merrill, 1921), 212.

119. McDougall, *France's Rhineland Policy,* 38.

120. MacMillan, *Paris 1919,* 172.

121. McDougall, *France's Rhineland Policy,* 57

122. Most of the French public was still counting on some separation of the Rhineland

from Germany, and the military remained adamant. As the commander of the two French armies on the Rhine put it, "One promises alliances, but like all human things, alliances are fragile." They could never substitute for a "material barrier." McDougall, *France's Rhineland Policy,* 58.

123. Ibid., 70.
124. Nevins, *Henry White,* 435.
125. McDougall, *France's Rhineland Policy,* 59, 70. David Robin Watson, *Clemenceau: A Political Biography* (Eyre Methuen, 1977), 362. Clemenceau was admittedly seventy years old when he retired, but he was still vigorous and had hoped to serve as president before such hopes were dashed.
126. Gordon Martel, "A Comment," in *Treaty of Versailles,* ed. Manfred F. Boemeke et al., 617n6.
127. Yearwood, *Guarantee of Peace,* 135.
128. Martel, "A Comment," in *Treaty of Versailles,* ed. Manfred F. Boemeke et al., 627.
129. William R. Keylor's description of Lippmann, Bullitt, and Keynes as "embittered, angry young men . . . who had briefly glimpsed the promised land . . . only to see it recede from view as the grim realities of national interest, power, and politics inconveniently intruded into the negotiations" is not entirely unfair. William R. Keylor, "Versailles and International Diplomacy," in *Treaty of Versailles,* ed. Manfred F. Boemeke et al., 505.
130. There were some "unsatisfactory settlements" that would not survive scrutiny by "a strictly impartial judge."
131. MacMillan, *Paris 1919,* 97.
132. Cooper, *Breaking the Heart,* 47; Antony Lentin, *Lloyd George, Woodrow Wilson and the Guilt of Germany: An Essay in the Pre-History of Appeasement* (Louisiana State University Press, 1985), 70.
133. Cooper, *Woodrow Wilson,* 498: "Wilson regarded the League as more important than the specific terms of the treaty."
134. Levin, *Woodrow Wilson and World Politics,* 159–60.
135. Levin, *Woodrow Wilson and World Politics,* 160.
136. Count Ulrich von Brockdorff-Rantzau, "Comments of the German Leaders on the Draft of the Treaty of Versailles," speech, May 7, 1919 (The British National Archives, https://www.nationalarchives.gov.uk/education/greatwar/tran script/g5cs1s3t.htm). They seemed to have "no idea of what other nations felt." MacMillan, *Paris 1919,* 161.
137. Levin, *Woodrow Wilson and World Politics,* 157.
138. Sally Marks, "Smoke and Mirrors: In Smoke-Filled Rooms and the Galerie des Glaces," in *Treaty of Versailles,* ed. Manfred F. Boemeke et al., 360. As Marks observes, "As time would conclusively demonstrate, under the Versailles treaty Germany remained the continent's greatest power, especially economically. As French leaders recognized, its predominance would only increase when the various temporary bonds of Versailles dissolved."
139. The new, independent Poland, did, however, provide a buffer between Germany and whatever threat the new Bolshevik Russia might pose. Gerhard L. Weinberg, "The Defeat of Germany in 1918 and the European Balance of Power," *Central European History* 2, no. 3 (September 1969): 253–54.
140. Keylor, "Versailles and International Diplomacy," in *Treaty of Versailles,* ed. Manfred F. Boemeke et al., 492–93. As the historian Zara Steiner has observed, the terms of the Versailles Treaty were "neither unduly nor unprecedentedly harsh. Germany was left intact. Its basic unity was preserved, as was its ability not just

to sustain itself but to recover much of its former economic status." Steiner, *Lights That Failed*, 54.

141. Costigliola, *Awkward Dominion*, 29.

Chapter Twelve: Wilson and the League Fight

1. Wilson address in Los Angeles, Sept. 20, 1919, *The Messages and Papers of Woodrow Wilson* (Review of Reviews Corp., 1924), 2:1033.
2. Lawrence, *True Story*, 268.
3. "Washington Hails Treaty," *New York Times*, May 8, 1919.
4. Bartlett, *League to Enforce Peace*, 137.
5. Ibid., 131.
6. "Hays Declares He's 'For a League,'" *New York Times*, June 27, 1919.
7. Claude G. Bowers, *Beveridge and the Progressive Era* (Riverside Press, 1932), 506.
8. Cooper, *Breaking the Heart*, 103.
9. Denna Frank Fleming, *The United States and World Organization, 1920–1933* (Columbia University Press, 1938), 24n.
10. Bartlett, *League to Enforce Peace*, 131. Hiram Johnson, who along with Borah led the battle of the "irreconcilables," privately remarked in mid-June: "I don't like the look of things." Cooper, *Breaking the Heart*, 102.
11. Lansing, *Peace Negotiations*, 188. Although Lansing's relations with Wilson by this point had broken down entirely, and the president would soon ask him to step down, he "personally believed that that would be the result."
12. As the anti-League Philander Knox chuckled to a friend, "When you hear of the membership of the committee on foreign relations you will be satisfied that the league of nations is going to have the time of its life when it is officially submitted." Cooper, *Breaking the Heart*, 95. Borah was a holdover, along with Brandegee, Knox, and Albert Fall. Lodge added Borah's partner, Hiram Johnson, as well as Warren Harding, Senator Harry S. New of Indiana, and the newly elected George H. Moses of New Hampshire, who had already made his anti-League stance known. Pro-League Republicans passed over included Frank Kellogg, the future secretary of state, who enjoyed seniority over Moses. Margulies, *Mild Reservationists*, 32.
13. The committee also heard spokesmen for Albania, Czechoslovakia, Egypt, Estonia, Greece, Hungary, India, Japan, Latvia, Lithuania, Persia, Ukraine, and Yugoslavia.
14. Cooper, *Breaking the Heart*, 99. Years later, Lippmann regretted his actions. "If I had to do it all over again," he wrote in 1930, "I would take the other side; we supplied the Battalion of Death with too much ammunition." Lippmann, "Notes for a Biography," *New Republic*, July 16, 1930.
15. Cooper, *Breaking the Heart*, 170–71. Lansing had long ago lost Wilson's confidence and legitimately felt slighted throughout his tenure as secretary.
16. Lodge knew that "the fate of the Democratic party in the Northern States" heavily depended on the Irish American vote, and Democrats did indeed fear the Irish Americans would abandon the party over the League. Creel warned that every German American was "eager to take advantage of the opportunity to embarrass our relations with Great Britain." Wilson would later place significant blame for his problems with the League on both the German Americans and "the foolish Irish. Would to God they might all have gone back home." Nevins, *Henry White*, 430–31, 454–56; Cooper, *Breaking the Heart*, 139; Brundage, *Irish Nationalists*, 155; Schmuhl, *Ireland's Exiled Children*, 105, 115.
17. Cooper, *Breaking the Heart*, 104, 100.

18. Margulies, *Mild Reservationists,* 68.
19. Cooper, *Breaking the Heart,* 104, 100.
20. Bowers, *Beveridge,* 503–4.
21. Lippmann chortled at how the likes of Lodge and Beveridge had "turned into a band of 'little Americans'" warning about European contamination. Steel, *Walter Lippmann,* 156.
22. *Congressional Record,* Senate, Feb. 28, 1919, 4522.
23. Miller, *Covenant,* I: 31–32.
24. Mark Sullivan, *Our Times: The United States, 1900–1925,* vol. 6, *The Twenties* (Charles Scribner's Sons, 1930), 163.
25. Ibid., 6:170.
26. Steel, *Walter Lippmann,* 156.
27. Sullivan, *Our Times,* 6:170 71.
28. After the armistice American troops spent months in Europe waiting to be shipped back, bivouacked in the homes of the French, whom they grew not to like, and of the Germans, whom they grew to like quite a bit. Slogans like "Lafayette, we are still here!" expressed the impatience of the troops waiting to get home. When they returned, their feeling about the war, and about Europe, was "Never Again!" Sullivan, *Our Times,* 6:114–15; Burl Noggle, *Into the Twenties: The United States from Armistice to Normalcy* (University of Illinois Press, 1974), 16.
29. The war had produced few celebrated heroes—Sergeants Alvin York and Dan Daly were among the more prominent. No presidential candidates had emerged as Roosevelt and Dewey had from the "splendid little war" of 1898.
30. Bartlett, *League to Enforce Peace,* 161. Lodge had experience with this strategy: During the Taft presidency he had defeated an arbitration treaty by attaching amendments he knew Taft would not accept. Fleming, *United States and World Organization,* 24.
31. Margulies, *Mild Reservationists,* 55–56.
32. The British and French had promised Japan it could keep Shantung as the price for entering the war in 1914. The British could never betray Australia, Canada, and its other dominions by denying them a vote in the less important League assembly.
33. Margulies, *Mild Reservationists,* 85 (italics added).
34. Ibid., 86, 84; Jessup, *Elihu Root,* 2:404.
35. Mervin, "Henry Cabot Lodge and the League of Nations," 206. The real issue, Lodge later noted, "was a simple one . . . We were determined that there should be no obligation of any kind left under Article 10." Lodge even admitted that advocates of the League went "pretty far in offering exceptions to the obligation." But the problem was "they kept the obligation alive." Cooper, *Breaking the Heart,* 308. The purpose of his reservation was to establish in the legal record that "under no circumstances must there be any legal or moral obligation upon the United States" to do anything—to go to war, to send troops abroad, or to engage in economic boycotts. Lodge, *The Senate and the League of Nations,* 1925), 202, 173–74.
36. Miller, *Covenant,* I, 371–72. Taft spoke of "the truculence, selfishness, partisanship, and personal spite" of certain Republican Senators. Bartlett, *League to Enforce Peace,* 160.
37. That Lodge's actions with regard to the League were driven by political rather than foreign policy considerations even his sympathetic biographer acknowledges. According to Widenor, Lodge might well have "swallowed the League had he seen therein the means of securing a Republican victory" in 1920. But as it happened, most agreed that the way to defeat Wilson was to defeat his league. Widenor, *Lodge,* 309. "Many of the men who should have been among the strongest supporters of

the League of Nations," Stimson recalled, had since 1914 become "bitter enemies of Woodrow Wilson." Stimson and Bundy, *On Active Service,* 101.

38. Jessup, *Elihu Root,* 2:404. Root himself played a controversial role. At the end of March, he had written a public letter to Hays stating that while he had doubts about the League, and especially Article 10, the United States nevertheless had a "duty" to help bring peace and stability to Europe. Article 10 was "an agreement to do that." Root letter to Hays, March 29, 1919. Published by Republican National Committee on March 31. Jessup, *Elihu Root,* 2:392–93. Pro-League Republicans like Taft and Root's protégé, Henry Stimson, assumed Root would support the League once Wilson made the necessary modifications. And if Root lent his support, pro-League Republicans predicted, "the Senate would be compelled to ratify the Covenant." Bartlett, *League to Enforce Peace,* 135. In June, however, Lodge appealed to Root for help, and at the end of the month Root sat down with Lodge, Knox, and Brandegee to draft a new letter. Jessup, *Elihu Root,* 2:399–401. In it, Root reversed himself. Now he claimed that Wilson had failed to "limit the vast and incalculable obligation" of Article 10, which he criticized as "an independent and indefinite alliance for preservation of the status quo." Insisting that the article was not an "essential or even an appropriate part" of a league, he said it should be eliminated entirely. Jessup, *Elihu Root,* 2:399–401; Bartlett, *League to Enforce Peace,* 139. It was clear from Root's notes that the letter was as much the work of the senators as of Root. When the letter became public, Taft howled at the "glaring inconsistency" between the new letter and the one Root had written back in March, particularly his "indefensible" turnabout on Article 10. He and other League supporters outside the Senate charged Root with surrendering to Lodge and Knox, who were bent on "getting back at Wilson." Bartlett, *League to Enforce Peace,* 141–42. In the Senate, however, pro-League Republicans quickly rallied around Root's "reservations." The result was a dramatic shift in the balance of power on the League question. Lodge exulted that Root's new letter "was more disastrous to the League than any statement that has been made by anyone." Lloyd E. Ambrosius, *Woodrow Wilson and the American Diplomatic Tradition: The Treaty Fight in Perspective* (Cambridge University Press, 1987), 150.

39. Margulies, *Mild Reservationists,* 88.

40. Widenor, *Lodge,* 331–32.

41. Louis A. R. Yates, *United States and French Security, 1917–1921: A Study in American Diplomatic History* (Twayne, 1957), 119–20. This despite the fact that five members of the committee—Lodge, Brandegee, Knox, Fall, and Moses—were irreconcilables who claimed to support the security guarantee. As Ambrosius notes, with seven Democrats on the committee, even two of these five "would have sufficed to report the French security treaty to the Senate." And yet it never happened. Lloyd E. Ambrosius, *Wilsonianism: Woodrow Wilson and His Legacy in American Foreign Relations* (Palgrave Macmillan, 2002), 95. Lodge later admitted that he never had any intention of bringing the French security treaty to a vote, if only because he did "not think there was the slightest chance that the Senate would ever have voted to accept it." In his 1925 account of the League fight, he wrote, "The treaty . . . was never taken up and never reported out." Lodge, *Senate and the League,* 154–56. It would have been quite useless to do so, even if the committee had favored it, for irreconcilables like Borah, Johnson, and George Norris had already publicly attacked it, with Borah calling it an Anglo-French-American "alliance for war." Yates, *United States and French Security,* 131fn71.

42. Schuker, "Rhineland Question," in *Treaty of Versailles,* ed. Manfred F. Boemeke et al., 310. Some historians have argued that Lodge and other Republicans had been perfectly willing to approve the French security treaty in lieu of the League.

According to Schuker, "Internationalist Republicans like Root, Taft, and Lodge were fully prepared to undertake specific and limited responsibilities consonant with the national interest, even though they repudiated the idea of making an open-ended commitment to the League. Schuker, "Rhineland Question," 310. Osgood suggests that "Lodge, George Harvey, and a number of other Realists approved of the specific entanglement embodied in the French Security Treaty." Osgood, *Ideals and Self-Interest,* 301. According to this reading, their disagreement with Wilson was therefore doctrinal, concerning "the proper scope of American commitments." Lodge was prepared to take on some obligations "to prevent future wars," but was "on guard against the tendency of idealists to promise more than was practicable." Walworth, *America's Moment,* 110; Widenor, *Lodge,* 331. For the most succinct version of this argument, see Lloyd E. Ambrosius, "Wilson, the Republicans, and French Security after World War I," *Journal of American History* 59, no. 2 (September 1972): 341–52. Some historians have even claimed that Wilson killed the French treaty, with some mistakenly asserting that he never even submitted it to Congress. See Lentin, "'Une aberration inexplicable'?," 31–49. The evidence doesn't support these conclusions. It was certainly true that Wilson did not want to submit the treaty and would have preferred if it had just been forgotten. He presented the Versailles Treaty before the Senate on July 10 and at the same time declared that "I shall presently have occasion to lay before you a special treaty with France whose object is the temporary protection of France from unprovoked aggression by the power with whom this treaty has been negotiated. Its terms link it with this treaty. I take the liberty, however, of reserving it, because of its importance, for special explication on another occasion." Quoted in Yates, *United States and French Security,* 118. However, Lodge insisted on its immediate submission, and the clamor became so loud that Wilson was forced to place the French security treaty before the Senate, which he did on July 29, 1919. As Yates records, "Lodge had asked the Senate on July 29, 1919, to receive the message and the treaty in open executive session. He also made a request that the injunction of secrecy be removed from the treaty. When the senator from California, James D. Phelan, inquired whether Lodge intended to consider and to act upon the treaty at that time, the reply was 'I want to have the message read and then to have it take the usual course required by the rule.' Lodge then asked that the treaty be formally referred to the committee. There was no official consideration of the aid agreement." Yates, *United States and French Security,* 119–20. William R. Keylor finds the treaty's death "mysterious." William R. Keylor, "The Rise and Demise of the Franco-American Guarantee Pact, 1919–1921," *Proceedings of the Annual Meeting of the Western Society for French History* 15: 367–77. It is "mysterious" only because, although Lodge claimed to support it, he then allowed it to languish in committee, which was a better indication of his real intentions. Had Lodge wished to take up the treaty at that point, or at any point over the next two years, he could have. He and the irreconcilables controlled the committee and the voting procedures in the full Senate. But he did not, and he later explained why: he believed, as had Lansing, House, Miller, White, Bliss, Wilson, Lloyd George, and probably Clemenceau, that such a treaty could never pass the Senate. According to the State Department's files, the treaty was submitted on July 29, 1919. It was "not considered by the Senate" and was "returned to the Secretary of State by resolution of the Senate, February 12, 1935." The treaty remains in the file "Unperfected Treaties H-9": "Assistance to France in the event of unprovoked aggression by Germany—Agreement between the United States and France, signed at Versailles, June 28, 1919," *Foreign Relations of the United States Diplomatic Papers, 1919, The Paris Peace Conference, 1919,* vol. 13, ed. Joseph V. Fuller et al., (Government Printing Office, 1947), File 185.8/11. https://history.state.gov/historicaldocuments/frus1919Parisv13/ch27.

43. Quoted in Lawrence, *True Story,* 276.

44. Wilson address in Los Angeles, Sept. 20; 1919, *Messages and papers,* 2:1,033. Robert Osgood and others have argued that Wilson never made the case based on national interest. These statements by Wilson would seem to come pretty close.

45. Ross A. Kennedy, *Will to Believe* (Kent State University Press, 2009), 194.

46. Margulies, *Mild Reservationists,* 172.

47. Ibid., 236.

48. Both quoted in ibid, 183.

49. Cooper, *Breaking the Heart,* 321. The letter caused a bit of a sensation in the United States because it appeared to contradict Wilson's claim that Lodge's reservations were unacceptable to the Allies. Lodge thought Grey's virtual endorsement of his reservations was "splendid." Margulies, *Mild Reservationists,* 217; Widenor, *Lodge,* 346.

50. Herbert Hoover, *The Ordeal of Woodrow Wilson* (McGraw-Hill, 1958), 281.

51. Ibid., 284.

52. "If Europe desires such an alliance or league with a power of this kind, so be it," Lodge declared. But the United States should have none of it. Cooper, *Breaking the Heart,* 134–35.

53. Ibid., 227.

54. Jessup, *Elihu Root,* 2:412.

55. Herbert Hoover, then charged with the task of feeding a starving postwar Europe, privately warned that the treaty and some kind of league were necessary to provide "a guiding hand" to bring "stability" to the continent. Costigliola, *Awkward Dominion,* 33, 30–31.

56. Jessup, *Elihu Root,* 2:408–9.

57. Ibid., 2:410.

58. Widenor, *Lodge,* 309.

59. Bartlett, *League to Enforce Peace,* 184.

60. Widenor, *Lodge,* 334; Margulies, *Mild Reservationists,* 207–8.

61. Even when Knox, an irreconcilable, proposed declaring merely that a threat to the "freedom and peace of Europe" would be of "grave concern" to the United States, and that Americans should be "prepared when the necessity arises to render every service, as we did in 1917, for the defense of civilization," Borah made Lodge veto that, too. Bartlett, *League to Enforce Peace,* 184; Cooper, *Breaking the Heart,* 382.

62. The "scene changes fast in Europe," he told Root, and so it was better not to suggest any commitments at all. Jessup, *Elihu Root,* 2:410.

63. Stimson and others had supported Leonard Wood, the old Rough Rider friend of Roosevelt, who supported League membership. Wood led in the early balloting at the convention, but when he became stuck in a deadlock with another candidate, Republican leaders picked Harding. Sullivan, *Our Times,* 6:60–61; Stimson and Bundy, *On Active Service,* 104–5; John Chalmers Vinson, *The Parchment Peace: The United States and the Washington Conference, 1921–1922* (University of Georgia Press, 1955), 41.

64. Jessup, *Elihu Root,* 2:412; Cooper, *Breaking the Heart,* 393. Taft went so far as to claim that "the only possible hope of making progress toward a league of nations to secure peace" was by electing Harding. Lawrence, *True Story,* 304.

65. One of the leaders of the irreconcilables, Senator Hiram Johnson, ridiculed their letter as a "rank misinterpretation" of the candidate's true position. Cooper, *Breaking the Heart,* 389; Bartlett, *League to Enforce Peace,* 198.

66. Bartlett, *League to Enforce Peace,* 183.

67. Ibid., 186.

68. Sullivan, *Our Times,* 6:128.

69. Ibid., 6:111n.

70. Ibid., 6:117–18.

71. The victory in the recent war played no role in the campaign. Cox noted that if "a man from Mars were to depend on the Republican platform . . . he would not find a syllable telling him that the war had been won and that America had saved the world." Ibid., 6:111, 17.

72. The Democrats did not disavow the League, but they did not support it with any great enthusiasm. Cox declared that the "first duty of the new administration" would be "the ratification of the treaty," and his vice presidential candidate, Franklin Delano Roosevelt, gave full-throated support for the League. But no one saw it as a winning issue. Ibid., 6:117.

73. The irreconcilables "had just won a tremendous victory over the Executive and they intended to keep the control of foreign policy in their own hands." Jessup, *Elihu Root,* 2:414.

74. Robert James Maddox, *William E. Borah and American Foreign Policy* (Louisiana State University Press, 1969), 99; Murray, *Harding Era,* 137.

75. Lawrence, *True Story,* 306.

76. In the nine presidential contests between 1896 and 1932, Wilson's were the only Democratic victories.

77. On this point, see Cooper, *Breaking the Heart,* 246.

78. This was despite Harding's assurance that joining the Court would not mean sneaking into the League "by the side door, or the back door or the cellar door." Lodge himself worked to kill American membership in the World Court throughout the remainder of his time in the Senate. Warren F. Kuehl and Lynne K. Dunn, *Keeping the Covenant, American Internationalists and the League of Nations* (Kent State University Press, 1997), 111, 114.

79. As Robert Osgood noted, "A large majority of the Senate and probably of the nation at large wanted to participate in an international organization of some kind, which, under certain conditions, would commit the United States in advance to join with other nations in coercing an aggressor." Osgood, *Ideals and Self-Interest,* 293.

80. Henry Kissinger, *Diplomacy* (Simon & Schuster, 1994), 244.

81. As McDougall notes, "The Treaty of Versailles cannot be shown to be deleterious, for it was never 'tried.'" McDougall, *France's Rhineland Policy,* 361.

82. It is worth noting that American officials certainly learned this lesson when they worked to build a new world order after the Second World War. A key element of that postwar settlement would be the continued presence of American troops on European soil, which provided the French, British, and others sufficient security to permit the economic revival of Germany. It helped, of course, that Germany at the end of the second was defeated, occupied, and dismembered. But the idea that German economic recovery was essential to European economic recovery, and that this would be possible only if the United States provided everyone security, had taken deep root.

83. MacMillan, *Paris 1919,* 493–94.

Chapter Thirteen: A Return to "Normalcy"?

1. Glad, *Charles Evans Hughes,* 213.

2. Like so much else in American history, the main revisionist accounts of the 1920s

occurred in the shadow of the Vietnam War. Republican policies looked better at least insofar as they managed to stay out of war. Those most committed to economic explanations for American foreign policy also found the 1920s to be something of a heyday in the use of economic and financial tools, until it all fell apart.

3. Roosevelt, "The International Posse Comitatus," *New York Times,* Nov. 8, 1914.

4. Sean Dennis Cashman, *America in the Twenties and Thirties: The Olympian Age of Franklin Delano Roosevelt* (New York University Press, 1989), 42, 496; William E. Leuchtenburg, *The Perils of Prosperity, 1914–32* (University of Chicago Press, 1958), 178–79, 194, 138.

5. Selig Adler, The *Isolationist Impulse: Its Twentieth-Century Reaction* (Collier Books, 1961), 58, 60.

6. As Robert Osgood notes, "One gets the distinct impression that revisionists were as much concerned with their own guilt in bringing about this failure as with the guilt of the belligerents, for there runs through their writings an unmistakable thread of confession and self-deprecation, concealed only by the eager acceptance of some scapegoat, be it Woodrow Wilson, propaganda, European statesmen, or the war profiteers." Osgood, *Ideals and Self-Interest,* 318.

7. Rochester, *American Liberal Disillusionment,* 104.

8. Peter Novick, *That Noble Dream: The "Objectivity Question" and the American Historical Profession* (Cambridge University Press, 1988), 208. Osgood, *Ideals and Self-Interest,* 317. The editors of the *New Republic* demanded that American diplomatic archives be opened to reveal who was "responsible for promulgating the idea that the war was a great 'crusade to defend civilization.'" Selig Adler, "The War Guilt Question and American Disillusionment, 1918–1928," *Journal of Modern History* 23, no. 1 (March 1951): 26.

9. As Barnes later put it, "I thought that Woodrow Wilson really meant his golden, glowing words. I thought he was in a position to know what I couldn't know, and would take the obvious steps to protect us from diplomatic perfidy." Rochester, *American Liberal Disillusionment,* 91–92. Bullitt in his resignation letter wrote bitterly of how he had "trusted confidently and implicitly" in Wilson's leadership. William G. Chrystal, "Reinhold Niebuhr and the First World War," *Journal of Presbyterian History* 55, no. 3 (Fall 1977): 293, 295; Martel, "A Comment," in *Treaty of Versailles,* ed. Manfred F. Boemeke et al., 617.

10. Rochester, *American Liberal Disillusionment,* 92. Some historical revision regarding the origins and meaning of the war was inevitable. During the nineteen months of U.S. participation, the public had been presented, and largely accepted, a fairly black-and-white picture of the contending forces in Europe: Militarist Germany had been the villain, and the democratic Allies were the innocent victims. Nothing in international politics is ever that simple, and it was only a matter of time before a more complex picture emerged. While some American historians who sifted through the mountain of documents still concluded that Germany bore primary responsibility for the war—and Beard warned against attempts "to white-wash" Germany's role—almost all agreed that the new picture also contained shades of gray. Adler, "War-Guilt Question," 1, 4.

11. Adler, "War-Guilt Question," 5.

12. The German strategy was inaugurated even before the peace terms had been settled. The German secretary for foreign affairs, Paul von Hintze, calculated that even if peace terms were harsh, the Fourteen Points provided "a platform for Germany's future foreign policy, which would demand a revision of the peace treaty." Klaus Schwabe, "Germany's Peace Aims and the Domestic and International Constraints," in *The Treaty of Versailles,* ed. Manfred F. Boemeke et al., 41.

13. Thomas C. Kennedy, "Charles A. Beard in Midpassage," *The Historian* 30, no. 2 (1968): 179–98.
14. Warren I. Cohen, *American Revisionists: The Lessons of Intervention in World War One* (University of Chicago Press, 1967), 57.
15. Osgood, *Ideals and Self-Interest,* 317.
16. Charles F. Howlett, *Troubled Philosopher: John Dewey and the Struggle for World Peace* (Kennikat Press, 1977), 41; Adler, "War-Guilt Question," 27; Adler, *Isolationist Impulse,* 61.
17. Adler, "War-Guilt Question," 28.
18. Joan Hoff Wilson, *American Business and Foreign Policy: 1920–1933* (University of Kentucky Press, 1971), 14.
19. Ibid., 14.
20. Ibid., 103.
21. Costigliola, *Awkward Dominion,* 63.
22. Wilson, *American Business and Foreign Policy,* 24, 28.
23. Charles DeBenedetti, *Origins of the Modern American Peace Movement, 1915 1929* (KTO Press, 1978), 173.
24. The prominent pacifist Frederick J. Libby, quoted in ibid., 88, 102.
25. Robert H. Ferrell, *Peace in Their Time: The Origins of the Kellogg-Briand Pact* (Franklin Classics, 2018), 13–14. For a comprehensive accounting of these groups, see DeBenedetti, *Origins of the Modern American Peace Movement.* An incomplete list would include the American Peace Society and its influential branch, the New York Peace Society, which had been around since the nineteenth century, as well as the Carnegie Endowment for International Peace, founded in 1910. During and after the war a bounty of new organizations joined them. Jane Addams helped found the Geneva-based Women's International League for Peace and Freedom, whose American executive was the Hull House veteran and peace activist Dorothy Detzer. Addams also helped found the Fellowship of Reconciliation, along with the socialist leaders A. J. Muste and Norman Thomas. Carnegie died in 1919, but before his death he established the Church Peace Union. Other new Christian pacifist organizations included the World Alliance for International Friendship Through the Churches, and the American Friends Service Committee. Other women's organizations included the Woman's Peace Union of the Western Hemisphere and the League of Women Voters, which became actively involved in peace efforts. Former suffragists like Carrie Chapman Catt became leaders of the American peace movement. The pacifist Frederick J. Libby established the National Council for the Prevention of War in 1922. The Council on Foreign Relations was established by New York businessmen and internationalists in 1921. The Foreign Policy Association grew out of the League of Free Nations Association. A Woodrow Wilson Foundation was established and awarded prizes for the best essays on international peace. The American Association for International Cooperation aimed at awakening popular interest in "a World Peace System based upon an expanding international law of peace which bans offensive war as a crime." The League of Nations Non-Partisan Association established branches in every state and hundreds of cities and towns, and, together with the Church Peace Union, sponsored more than two thousand meetings.
26. Kuehl and Dunn, *Keeping the Covenant,* 56–57.
27. Ibid., 110.
28. Sondra Herman, Manfred Jonas, Robert A. Divine, Walter LaFeber, Richard D. McKinzie, and Theodore A. Wilson, "Internationalism as a Current in the Peace Movement: A Symposium," *American Studies* 13, no. 1 (1972): 190.

29. Kuehl and Dunn, *Keeping the Covenant,* 56.
30. DeBenedetti, *Origins of the Modern American Peace Movement,* 27–28.
31. Ibid., 143, 147.
32. Ibid., 111.
33. Ibid., 159.
34. Cashman, *America in the Twenties and Thirties,* 45–46
35. Hiram Wesley Evans, "The Klan's Fight for Americanism," *North American Review* 223, no. 830 (March–May 1926): 59.
36. Cashman, *America in the Twenties and Thirties,* 514. France and other European countries responded with retaliatory tariffs against American goods. In the end, farmers wound up losing more than $300 million annually. Americans had to learn all over again the lesson of the Great War, that although the United States was more self-sufficient than any other nation in the world, its economy was still intertwined with those of Europe. Fully 11 percent of agricultural produce had been shipped to Europe during the war. When this fell by almost 60 percent between 1920 and 1922, the consequences for American farmers were severe. The American reaction, raising tariffs, was not the best remedy. Melvyn P. Leffler, *Elusive Quest: America's Pursuit of European Stability and French Security, 1919–1933* (University of North Carolina Press, 2009), 41–42.
37. As Evans explained the true meaning of the Klan's unprecedented popularity, "We are a protest movement protesting against being robbed." Evans, "Klan's Fight for Americanism," 51.
38. Ibid., 59, 35.
39. Maddox, *William E. Borah,* 99, 168; Murray, *Harding Era,* 137.
40. Among other reasons, both signed Root's letter during the campaign promising some form of association with a League. Joan Hoff Wilson, *Herbert Hoover: Forgotten Progressive* (Little, Brown, 1975), 173.
41. Maddox, *William E. Borah,* 99; Murray, *Harding Era,* 137.
42. Maddox, *William E. Borah,* 123.
43. Kuehl and Dunn, *Keeping the Covenant,* 23.
44. Glad, *Charles Evans Hughes,* 174.
45. Ibid., 212–13.
46. Costigliola, *Awkward Dominion,* 77.
47. Thus entering Europe, as one newspaper put it, "by the back door." Pusey, *Charles Evans Hughes,* 2:587.
48. Jeffrey J. Matthews, *Alanson B. Houghton: Ambassador of the New Era* (SR Books, 2004), 62.
49. As the British government noted, "The existence of this mass of external indebtedness . . . lay like a dead weight upon the credit of continental Europe, and made reconstruction even slower and more painful than it needed to be." Robert Self, *Britain, America and the War Debt Controversy: The Economic Diplomacy of an Unspecial Relationship, 1917–45* (Routledge, 2006), 25.
50. Melvyn Leffler, "The Origins of Republican War Debt Policy, 1921–1923: A Case Study in the Applicability of the Open Door Interpretation," *The Journal of American History* 59, no. 3 (Dec. 1972): 585–601.
51. Self, *Britain, America, War Debt,* 38, 26.
52. David M. Kennedy, *Freedom from Fear: The American People in Depression and War, 1929–1945* (Oxford University Press, 1999), 59.
53. Kennedy, *Over Here,* 113.
54. Melvyn Leffler, "The Origins of Republican War Debt Policy," 585–601.
55. As one British observer in the U.S. noted, "People here regard themselves as groan-

ing under a load of taxes mainly incurred in the interests of foreign people, and are in no mood to be generous." Self, *Britain, America, War Debt,* 29.

56. Hiram Johnson feared it was but a "prelude to the return of the Versailles Treaty . . . minus the League of Nations." Self, *Britain, America, War Debt,* 34.

57. In the final agreement reached in June 1923, Britain pledged to pay $4.6 billion, which was the entire amount of the original loan plus unpaid accrued interest from April 1919 to December 1922. Self, *Britain, America, War Debt,* 31, 51–52.

58. Ibid., 54. Walter Lippmann, *Men of Destiny* (Routledge, 2003), 194.

59. Britain's Balfour objected to treating the war debt as "no more than an ordinary commercial dealing between traders who borrow and capitalists who lend." R. J. Q. Adams, *Balfour: The Last Grandee* (Thistle Publishing, 2013), 352.

60. To be sure, some Americans, like Walter Lippmann, derided the notion that "if we armed Frenchmen to hold the line while the Americans were drilling in camp, the grandsons of the Frenchmen must pay in addition to the lives lost and the wounds suffered the price plus interest on their guns." Lippmann, *Men of Destiny,* 192–93.

61. Murray, *Harding Era,* 125.

62. Glad, *Charles Evans Hughes,* 213.

63. Henry T. Allen, *My Rhineland Journal* (Houghton Mifflin Company, 1923),107. The "unofficial" American representative was Pierrepont B. Noyes.

64. Among the best accounts of French thinking in this period is McDougall, *France's Rhineland Policy.*

65. Gilbert, *Churchill and America,* 92, 95.

66. In the fall of 1919 Clemenceau declared that if the Senate rejected "the two treaties," France would "make new arrangements concerning the Rhine." McDougall, *France's Rhineland Policy,* 89.

67. Allen, *My Rhineland Journal,* 101, 505.

68. Brendan Simms, *Hitler: A Global Biography* (Basic Books, 2019), 39.

69. The Reparations Commission's interim settlement in the spring of 1921 called for payments of between $600 million and $800 million annually—which was roughly 5 percent of Germany's GDP at the time. A debate has long raged over whether this was beyond Germany's capacity to pay. For many years, beginning with Keynes, the conventional wisdom held that the sums demanded by the Allies were impossibly exorbitant and could only have been paid by bankrupting Germany. In recent decades, however, the consensus has swung in the other direction, with many historians arguing that the reparations bill was not unreasonable. The Germans could have paid but simply refused.

70. This "root-and-branch hostility to reparations" meant that attempts either to pay or to compromise with France and Britain were condemned as "a sell-out." Detlev J. K. Peukert, *The Weimar Republic: The Crisis of Classical Modernity* (Hill and Wang, 1992), 54.

71. Costigliola, *Awkward Dominion,* 78.

72. Peukert, *Weimar Republic,* 73.

73. Ibid., 6.

74. Ibid., 62–63.

75. Hans Mommsen, *The Rise and Fall of Weimar Democracy* (Propyläen Verlag, 1989), 117.

76. Self, *Britain, America, War Debt,* 41; Tomes, *Balfour,* 190.

77. The American ambassador in London reported that the British were keenly aware of the "frightful possibilities." Charles DeBenedetti, "Borah and the Kellogg-Briand Pact," *Pacific Northwest Quarterly* 63, no. 1 (January 1972): 22–29.

78. Leffler, *Elusive Quest,* 114–15.

79. David D. Burks, "The United States and the Geneva Protocol of 1924: 'A New Holy Alliance'?," *American Historical Review* 64, no. 4 (July 1959): 891–905.

80. Howard C. Payne, Raymond Callahan, and Edward M. Bennett, *As the Storm Clouds Gathered: European Perceptions of American Foreign Policy in the 1930s* (Regina Books, 1979), 6, 13.

81. Ronald Hyam, *Britain's Declining Empire: The Road to Decolonization, 1918–1968* (Cambridge University Press, 2007), 34.

82. Allen, *My Rhineland Journal*, 203.

83. Lloyd George insisted that "the settlement of the international difficulties in which the world is still involved would be materially assisted by the co-operation of the United States." "The President of the Allied Conference (Lloyd George) to the Government of the United States," *Foreign Relations of the United States Diplomatic Papers, 1921,* vol. 1, ed. Joseph V. Fuller et al., (Government Printing Office, 1936), Document 18; Sally Marks, "The Myths of Reparations," *Central European History*, 11, no. 3 (1978): 242–4.

84. Allen, *My Rhineland Journal,* 202. The German ambassador in Washington pleaded with Hughes that "the situation was so critical and there was so much distrust that there was no Power but the United States that could command confidence and bring about a solution." "Memorandum by the Secretary of State of a Conversation with the German Ambassador (Wiedfeldt), October 9, 1922," *Foreign Relations of the United States Diplomatic Papers, 1922,* vol. 2, ed. Joseph V. Fuller et al., (Government Printing Office, 1938), Document 132.

85. Nelson, *Victors Divided,* 238–39.

86. Pusey, *Charles Evans Hughes,* 2:581.

87. Swartzburg, "The Call for America: German-American Relations and the European Crisis, 1921–1924/25," 232.

88. "The Ambassador in France (Herrick) to the Secretary of State, October 14, 1922," *Foreign Relations of the United States Diplomatic Papers, 1922,* vol. 2, ed. Joseph V. Fuller et al. (Government Printing Office, 1938), Document 135.

89. Allen, *My Rhineland Journal,* 409.

90. "The Ambassador in Germany (Houghton) to the Secretary of State, October 23, 1922," *Foreign Relations of the United States Diplomatic Papers, 1922,* vol. 2, ed. Joseph V. Fuller et al. (Government Printing Office, 1938), Document 138.

91. Bruce Kent, *The Spoils of War: The Politics, Economics, and Diplomacy of Reparations, 1918–1932* (Clarendon Press, 1992), 198.

92. Leffler, *Elusive Quest,* 76.

93. Glad, *Charles Evans Hughes,* 22; Leffler, *Elusive Quest,* 82.

94. Swartzburg, "The Call for America: German-American Relations and the European Crisis, 1921–1924/25," 183–84; *FRUS,* vol. 2, 169.

95. Charles S. Maier, *Recasting Bourgeois Europe: Stabilization in France, Germany, and Italy in the Decade After World War I* (Princeton University Press, 1975), 290.

96. Swartzburg, "The Call for America: German-American Relations and the European Crisis, 1921–1924/25," 201.

97. Allen, *My Rhineland Journal,* 409.

98. Hughes speech before American Historical Society, December 29; quoted in Swartzburg, "The Call for America: German-American Relations and the European Crisis, 1921–1924/25," 206.

99. Leffler, *Elusive Quest,* 72.

100. French officials even used American disapproval to resist popular pressures at home for more aggressive policies in the Rhineland. Nelson, *Victors Divided,* 199–200.

101. Ibid., 189.

102. Ibid., 176–77.
103. Harding by then was warning that there would be "a bad mess all the time in Europe if it were not for the mollifying and harmonizing influences which are wielded by" Allen and the occupying forces in Coblenz. Nelson, *Victors Divided,* 189–90, 184–85.
104. Ibid., 184–85.
105. Hughes complained that the United States was being "told to whistle for our money." Nelson, *Victors Divided,* 185–97. Allen attributed the decision to "the attitude of the Irreconcilables at home and the failure of the Allies to give us satisfaction." Allen, *My Rhineland Journal,* 330, 335–36.
106. Allen, *My Rhineland Journal,* 336, 340.
107. Nelson, *Victors Divided,* 234.
108. "Sharp Debate Over Troops," *New York Times,* Jan. 7, 1923.
109. Nelson, *Victors Divided,* 246–47.
110. Matthews, *Alanson B. Houghton,* 75–76.

Chapter Fourteen: The Collapse of Europe and the Rise of Hitler

1. Jon Jacobson, *Locarno Diplomacy: Germany and the West, 1925–1929* (Princeton University Press, 2016), 193–94.
2. Matthews, *Alanson B. Houghton,* 75–76.
3. As McDougall notes, "A policy of apparent submission would have substantiated for many the Rightist thesis that the Republic was a regime of traitors, unable to defend Germany against foreign and domestic foes." McDougall, *France's Rhineland Policy,* 270.
4. Ian Kershaw, *Hitler, 1889–1936: Hubris* (W. W. Norton, 1999), 191.
5. Fox, *Reinhold Niebuhr,* 78–79.
6. Liaquat Ahamed, *Lords of Finance: The Bankers Who Broke the World* (Penguin Press, 2009), 121.
7. Richard J. Evans, *The Coming of the Third Reich* (Penguin Press, 2005), 186.
8. McDougall, *France's Rhineland Policy,* 290.
9. Simms, *Hitler: A Global Biography,* 58.
10. Ibid., 58. New recruits came from all segments of society and, for the first time, from regions beyond the stronghold of Bavaria. See Kershaw, *Hitler, 1889–1936,* 189–90; Peukert, *Weimar Republic,* 73–74.
11. Simms, *Hitler,* 58–69.
12. McDougall, *France's Rhineland Policy,* 269.
13. Matthews, *Alanson B. Houghton,* 75–76.
14. Ibid., 76. Houghton died three months before Pearl Harbor.
15. Acheson letter to David Acheson May 4, 1936, in David S. McLellan and David C. Acheson, eds., *Among Friends: Personal Letters of Dean Acheson* (Dodd, Mead, 1980), 27–28. Acheson, like most Americans, held the French entirely responsible. A British official who served as private secretary to a series of chancellors of the Exchequer in the 1920s regarded the occupation of the Ruhr as "the most effective and direct cause of Hitler" and believed that "but for this there would have been no Second World War." P. J. Grigg, *Prejudice and Judgement* (Jonathan Cape, 1994),160, quoted in Charles P. Kindleberger, *The World in Depression, 1929–1939* (University of California Press, 1973), 20.
16. Costigliola, *Awkward Dominion,* 114.
17. Allen, *My Rhineland Journal,* 500–501.
18. Robert Sorbel, *Coolidge, An American Enigma* (Regnery, 1998), 339.

19. Robert H. Ferrell, *The Presidency of Calvin Coolidge* (University Press of Kansas, 1998), 145. Sorbel, *Coolidge,* 339.
20. McDougall, *France's Rhineland Policy,* 345.
21. Leffler, *Elusive Quest,* 107.
22. Keynes, "The Progress of the Dawes Plan," *New Republic,* Sept. 29, 1926, quoted in Ahamed, *Lords of Finance,* 216.
23. Pusey, *Charles Evans Hughes,* 2:591.
24. Costigliola, *Awkward Dominion,* 123.
25. Leffler, *Elusive Quest,* 100.
26. Stephen A. Schuker, *The End of French Predominance in Europe: The Financial Crisis of 1924 and the Adoption of the Dawes Plan* (University of North Carolina Press, 1976), 294.
27. Jonas, *United States and Germany,* 170–71.
28. Schuker, *End of French Predominance,* 317.
29. Leffler, *Elusive Quest,* 106.
30. McDougall, *France's Rhineland Policy,* 12.
31. Schuker, *End of French Predominance,* 316. Dawes himself was a Francophile who had supported the French occupation of the Ruhr and personally believed the continued presence of French troops in the Rhineland was the best safeguard against another war. Leffler, *Elusive Quest,* 97.
32. Allen, *My Rhineland Journal,* 546, 548.
33. Leffler, *Elusive Quest,* 36
34. Quoted in Ahamed, *Lords of Finance,* 215.
35. Jacobson, *Locarno Diplomacy,* 43.
36. Leffler, *Elusive Quest,* 116.
37. Jacobson, *Locarno Diplomacy,* 5, 165. As Leffler notes, American "financial pressure" was "among the important considerations impelling the leaders of both nations to reconcile their differences and come to terms with one another." Leffler, *Elusive Quest,* 117.
38. Jacobson, *Locarno Diplomacy,* 23–24.
39. Ibid., 377.
40. As one official put it, the situations that might require British action were "so remote and contingent that we are not likely in fact ever to be called upon to intervene." Ibid., 37.
41. Correlli Barnett, *The Collapse of British Power* (Prometheus Books, 1986), 329–30; Michael L. Dockerill, *British Establishment Perspectives on France, 1936–1940* (Palgrave Macmillan, 1999), 4.
42. Sally Marks, *Illusion of Peace: International Relations in Europe, 1918–1933* (Palgrave Macmillan, 2003), 79.
43. Michael Brecher, *The World of Protracted Conflicts* (Lexington Books, 2016), 204.
44. Costigliola, *Awkward Dominion,* 126.
45. As the historian Melvyn P. Leffler has put it, whether the alterations in the postwar status quo "would constitute a threat to France's well-being would depend upon the extent to which the expansionist, militarist, and nationalist strains latent in German culture and society would be submerged by the evolution of a prosperous, interdependent, capitalist order among European nations, bound together by technocratic elites sharing corporatist values and a common fear of Bolshevism." Leffler, *Elusive Quest,* 118.
46. Marks, *Illusion of Peace,* 72.
47. Benjamin Carter Hett, *The Death of Democracy: Hitler's Rise to Power and the Downfall of the Weimar Republic* (Henry Holt, 2018), 59–60. Many historians

certainly believe that Stresemann's "aim of restoring Germany to the status of a great power was always counter-balanced by a commitment to international links and obligations." Peukert, *Weimar Republic,* 206; Mommsen, *Weimar Democracy,* 214–15.

48. Leffler, *Elusive Quest,* 164–65.
49. Jacobson, *Locarno Diplomacy,* 42, 231, 65.
50. Ibid., 59, 147–48.
51. "Although the Reichstag quickly ratified [the Dawes Plan], the rancorous protests from every wing of German politics against the 'burdens' of the settlement ought to have left little doubt about the prospects of appeasing even a 'democratic' Germany." McDougall, *France's Rhineland Policy,* 368–69.
52. The French were under particular pressure to get a deal because by the terms of an agreement struck with the United States, if parliament did not ratify the Mellon-Bérenger agreement before August 1929, the French treasury would have to pay the United States a lump sum of $400 million. The bill was for purchases of weapons and materiel in 1919 and was to come due in ten years. If the Mellon-Bérenger agreement was ratified first, the $400 million would be rolled into the overall debt settlement. If the agreement was not ratified, France would have to make the payment. Jacobson, *Locarno Diplomacy,* 160.
53. Leffler, *Elusive Quest,* 235.
54. Their goal was "making money, not policy." William C. McNeil, *American Money and the Weimar Republic: Economics and Politics on the Eve of the Great Depression* (Columbia University Press, 1986), 279.
55. Costigliola, *Awkward Dominion,* 124–25.
56. McNeil, *American Money and the Weimar Republic,* 183–84.
57. As McNeil explains, "The two men were allied in pursuing the same policy with the ironic difference that they expected precisely the opposite results." Ibid., 176.
58. By cutting off access to foreign lending, Gilbert hoped, as one German Finance Ministry official put it, "to force in this indirect way, a reduction in our entire budget and financial behavior." Ibid., 174–75.
59. Ibid.
60. Ibid., 183.
61. Mommsen, *Weimar Democracy,* 276.
62. Some historians argue that the American bull market by itself drove Germany into recession. See Hett, *Death of Democracy,* 86.
63. Evans, *Coming of the Third Reich,* 234.
64. McNeil, *American Money and the Weimar Republic;* 271; Ahamed, *Lords of Finance,* 325.
65. Evans, *Coming of the Third Reich,* 235.
66. Leffler, *Elusive Quest,* 173, 178.
67. The amounts during those last twenty-two years matched almost exactly what the Allies would owe Washington. Ahamed, *Lords of Finance,* 332; Jacobson, *Locarno Diplomacy,* 272. The Young Plan allotted funds to cover "outpayments," which were really war debt payments to the United States.
68. McNeil, *American Money and the Weimar Republic,* 234; Leffler, *Elusive Quest,* 185.
69. Ahamed, *Lords of Finance,* 337.
70. Jacobson, *Locarno Diplomacy,* 193–94.
71. Ibid., 245–46.
72. Ibid., 214.
73. Mary Fulbrook, *A History of Germany, 1918–2020: The Divided Nation* (Wiley-Blackwell, 2021), 40.

74. Ibid., 41.
75. Mommsen, *Weimar Democracy,* 169.
76. Ibid., 215.
77. Marks, *Illusion of Peace,* 72.
78. Evans, *Coming of the Third Reich,* 250–51.
79. Bernard V. Burke, *Ambassador Frederic Sackett and the Collapse of the Weimar Republic, 1930–1933* (Cambridge University Press, 2003), 79.
80. Ibid., 79.
81. Fulbrook, *History of Germany,* 42. Mommsen, *Weimar Democracy,* 316–17.
82. Marks, *Illusion of Peace,* 121 (italics added).
83. Adolf Hitler, quoted in Simms, *Hitler: A Global Biography,* 97. As Joseph Goebbels put it, if Germany was to regain its independence, it would have to gain control of the "necessary space, natural forces and natural resources for its material life." Hett, *Death of Democracy,* 109, 114.
84. Hett, *Death of Democracy,* 90, 92.
85. Walter Lippmann, looking back on the Hoover presidency, suggested that Hoover had "never believed in America as global power with military and political commitments in every continent. He was an isolationist and, insofar as his beliefs could be reconciled with his duties as president and commander in chief, he was a conscientious objector." Steel, *Walter Lippmann and the American Century,* 287.
86. Leffler, *Elusive Quest,* 229.
87. Ibid., 196.
88. Ibid., 248.
89. See, for instance, ibid., 233.
90. Ibid., 228.
91. Burke, *Sackett,* 83. "For Sackett and his fellow diplomats, American national interests in Germany were economic and the most dangerous threat to those interests lay in the possibility of repudiation of debt." Ibid., 96.
92. Ibid., 92.
93. Ibid., 93.
94. Stimson would continue to believe for years to come that the most powerful anti-Weimar force in 1931 was the communists. Stimson and Bundy, *On Active Service,* 157, 271; Burke, *Sackett,* 110, 158.
95. Burke, *Sackett,* 101.
96. Ibid., 113, 303.
97. He hoped thereby to "wrest the leadership of the movement for a Greater Germany from Hitler and win additional support from the nationalistic Right." Ibid., 126.
98. Kennedy, *Freedom from Fear,* 71.
99. Burke, *Sackett,* 129.
100. Kennedy, *Freedom from Fear,* 70.
101. Jacobson, *Locarno Diplomacy,* 346–47.
102. Hett, *Death of Democracy,* 123.
103. Burke, *Sackett,* 151. "The Hoover Moratorium was of little help to the Germans. It provided relief for only a matter of days, but worse than that, it constituted a serious political problem for the chancellor. Not only did he fail to win much political credit for the moratorium, which after all was a gift from the Americans, but any further move in the direction of ending reparations was forestalled by the year-long holiday in intergovernmental debts."
104. Evans, *Coming of the Third Reich,* 293–95.
105. "The Ambassador in Germany (Sackett) to the Secretary of State," March 9, 1933, *FRUS 1933,* vol. 2, document 151: 206–9.

106. Allen, *My Rhineland Journal,* 548–49.
107. Wilson, *American Business and Foreign Policy,* 145–46.
108. Allen, *My Rhineland Journal,* 265.
109. Ibid., 483.
110. Kellogg was widely regarded as a weak secretary of state, but he did manage to win the Nobel Peace Prize for his part in the Pact of Paris.
111. Costigliola, *Awkward Dominion,* 80.
112. Some historians have argued that at least part of the American response, or lack thereof, was due to their belief that the risks to American interests were not "great enough to justify political embroilments." See Leffler, *Elusive Quest,* 228. That is certainly what they said, but it is clear that officials were responding to what they regarded as political reality, not to an assessment of relative interests. They adjusted their calculation of interests to meet what they believed Congress and the American public were willing to do in defense of those interests.
113. Men like Hoover, Hughes, and Stimson had favored ratification of the Versailles Treaty, if in modified form, because they feared the consequences of a breakdown of the peace. Even an irreconcilable like Knox had proposed a "new American doctrine," stating that a threat to the "freedom and peace of Europe" would be of "grave concern" to the United States and that Americans needed to be "prepared when the necessity arises to render every service, as we did in 1917, for the defense of civilization." Bartlett, *League to Enforce Peace,* 184; Cooper, *Breaking the Heart,* 382. As secretary of state, Hughes understood that American prosperity depended on "the economic settlements which may be made in Europe" and that the Americans were "vitally interested" in the reparation settlement. Costigliola, *Awkward Dominion,* 59. During and just after the war Lodge had regarded it as vital to establish "physical guarantees" against the possibility of a revival of German power and German desire for revenge. He had declared that Americans could not "escape doing our part in aiding the people to whom we have helped give freedom and independence" by helping "erect the barriers" that were essential to prevent the outbreak of another war." Along with Root he had professed to support a guarantee of French security to ensure the peace of Europe and because France was "our barrier and outpost." It was only later that he and others decided that the United States did not have sufficient interests in Europe even to require official American attendance at international conferences. A number of historians have argued that had Lodge, Root, and Roosevelt "been in actual control of American foreign policy" in 1919, they would have "constructed an alternative to the Wilsonian settlement . . . on a different philosophical foundation" but with the United States still as "a guarantor of the European settlement." Lodge's actions in the 1920s, when it was possible to construct an alternative policy, raise doubts about this assessment. Widenor, *Lodge,* 286, 297, 305, 319, 325, 332.
114. Schuker, *End of French Predominance,* 343.
115. Adam Tooze, *The Wages of Destruction* (Penguin Books, 2006), 30. And see the discussion of this point on 30–33.

Chapter Fifteen: Toward a New Order in Asia

1. Makino Shinken, quoted in Pyle, *Japan Rising,* 153.
2. Winston Churchill, *The World Crisis,* vol. 4, *The Aftermath, 1918–1922,* 315–16; Tooze, *The Deluge,* 4.
3. DeBenedetti, *Origins of the Modern American Peace Movement,* 61.
4. Howlett, *Troubled Philosopher,* 89, 85.

5. Levinson, like Dewey, had supported the war, Wilson, and the League, but had been disillusioned by the Versailles Treaty and had turned against the "European League." Howlett, *Troubled Philosopher,* 81; DeBenedetti, *Origins of the Modern American Peace Movement,* 61.

6. Howlett, *Troubled Philosopher,* 80.

7. DeBenedetti, *Origins of the Modern American Peace Movement,* 133, 147.

8. Ibid., 134.

9. Ibid., 126.

10. Ibid., 32; Ferrell, *Peace in Their Time,* 81; Charles G. Cleaver, "Frank B. Kellogg's View of History and Progress," *Minnesota History* 35, no. 4 (December 1956): 157–66.

11. Kuehl and Dunn, *Keeping the Covenant,* 186.

12. Ibid., 188.

13. Ibid.

14. DeBenedetti, *Origins of the Modern American Peace Movement,* 191.

15. Ibid., 193.

16. Ibid., 161.

17. Harold Josephson, "Outlawing War: Internationalism and the Pact of Paris," *Diplomatic History* 3, no. 4 (1979): 377–90.

18. Ferrell, *Peace in Their Time,* 106–7.

19. Ibid., 81, 141.

20. Ibid., 75.

21. Costigliola, *Awkward Dominion,* 190.

22. As DeBenedetti notes, "By the time that Borah had finished his work, the marks of political purposelessness had been indelibly impressed upon the antiwar negotiations." *Origins of the Modern American Peace Movement,* 191.

23. Ferrell, *Peace in Their Time,* 227, 236–37.

24. German newspaper editorial quoted in Maynard Moser, *Jacob Gould Schurman: Scholar, Political Activist and Ambassador of Good Will, 1892–1942* (Ayer Co., 1981), 167.

25. Shotwell, although he had been outmaneuvered by Borah and the "outlawrists," preferred to regard the treaty as a "door that opens to the League as well as to Arbitration and the Court." Josephson, "Outlawing War," 377–90.

26. Ibid.

27. Ferrell, *Peace in Their Time,* 205–6.

28. Norman A. Graebner, "Hoover, Roosevelt, and the Japanese," in *Pearl Harbor as History: Japanese-American Relations, 1931–1941,* ed. Dorothy Borg and Shumpei Okamoto (Columbia University Press, 1973), 27.

29. Louise Young, *Japan's Total Empire: Manchuria and the Culture of Wartime Imperialism* (University of California Press, 1998), 23.

30. As the historian Akira Iriye describes the system, there was an effort "to maintain an equilibrium by means of a series of alliances, ententes, and agreements designed to affirm their mutual spheres of influence and to harmonize the interests of as many imperialists as possible." Akira Iriye, *After Imperialism: An Inner History of American–East Asian Relations* (Atheneum, 1969), 6.

31. Walter LaFeber, *The Clash: U.S.-Japanese Relations Throughout History* (W. W. Norton, 1998), 87; Marius B. Jansen, *The Making of Modern Japan* (Belknap Press of Harvard University Press, 2000), 450.

32. As Churchill, then First Lord of the Admiralty, later put it, "Our last look round the oceans before the fateful signal left us . . . in no immediate anxiety about the

Pacific." Russell H. Fifield, *Woodrow Wilson and the Far East: The Diplomacy of the Shantung Question* (Archon Books, 1952), 14.

33. Ikuhiko Hata, "Continental Expansion, 1905–1941," in *Cambridge History of Japan*, vol. 6, *The Twentieth Century* (Cambridge University Press, 1989), 279; Iriye, *After Imperialism*, 7; Ian Nish, *Japanese Foreign Policy, 1869–1942: Kasumigaseki to Miyakezaka* (Routledge and Kegan Paul, 1977), 95.

34. David C. Evans and Mark R. Peattie, *Kaigun: Strategy, Tactics, and Technology in the Imperial Japanese Navy, 1887–1941* (Naval Institute Press, 1997), 192; Sadao Asada, "Japanese Admirals and the Politics of Naval Limitation: Kato Tomosaburo vs Kato Kanji," in Gerald Jordan, ed., *Naval Warfare in the Twentieth Century 1900–1945: Essays in Honour of Arthur Marder* (Crane Russak, 1977), 146. Even before the war, Roosevelt's naval program had already made the U.S. Navy the second-largest in the world, with 41 major warships to Japan's 26. In the decade since, the United States had completed 16 new capital ships while Japan had strained to build an additional 14. Evans and Peattie, *Kaigun,* 147, 153.

35. Erik Goldstein, "The Evolution of British Diplomatic Strategy for the Washington Conference," in *The Washington Conference, 1921–22: Naval Rivalry, East Asian Stability and the Road to Pearl Harbor,* eds. Erik Goldstein and John H. Maurer (F. Cass, 1994), 11, 15, 13; Sadao Asada, "From Washington to London: The Imperial Japanese Navy and the Politics of Arms Limitation, 1921–1930," *Diplomacy & Statecraft* 4, no. 3 (1993): 153, 148, 151. The Finance Ministry warned senior naval officers that Japan's financial position was "fast becoming hopeless" and that whether Japan would face ruin or not was "entirely up to you Navy people." Asada, "Japanese Admirals and the Politics of Naval Limitation," 147.

36. Akira Iriye, "The Failure of Economic Expansionism: 1918–1931," in *Japan in Crisis: Essays on Taisho Democracy,* eds. Bernard S. Silberman and H. D. Harootunian (University of Michigan Press, 1999), 242.

37. Chihiro Hosoya, "Britain and the United States in Japan's View of the International System, 1919–1937," in *Anglo-Japanese Alienation, 1919–1952: Papers of the Anglo-Japanese Conference on the History of the Second World War,* ed. Ian Nish (Cambridge University Press, 2010), 4–5; Pyle, *Japan Rising,* 153.

38. Iriye, "Failure of Economic Expansionism," 245, 241.

39. As one put it, "The time for Japan to take new initiatives has passed. . . . Now is the time for us to consolidate what we have and protect the position of the Japanese Empire." Hosoya, "Britain and the United States," 6.

40. Asada, "From Washington to London," 153.

41. The Taisho era begins in 1912 with the death of the Meiji Emperor; he was succeeded by his son, who would later be known as the Taisho Emperor. For a discussion of how Japanese perceptions of international trends shaped domestic politics as well as foreign policy, see Kenneth B. Pyle, "Profound Forces in the Making of Modern Japan," *Journal of Japanese Studies* 32, no. 2 (Summer 2006): 393–418. According to Pyle, "Japan's conservative elite not only revised its foreign policies, it sanctioned a newly proclaimed democratic politics at home that would accord with the new international norms."

42. Jansen, *Making of Modern Japan,* 499; see also Pyle, *Japan Rising,* 151: "The effect of the external environment on domestic politics in the Taisho period was most markedly evident in the new practice of appointing the head of one of the political parties in the Diet as prime minister."

43. Pyle, *Japan Rising,* 150–51.

44. Iriye, "Failure of Economic Expansionism," 239. The Taisho period begins with the

accession to the throne of a Taisho Emperor in 1912. However, the era of "Taisho Democracy" roughly speaking begins after the war. Pyle, *Japan Rising,* 151–52.

45. Iriye, "Failure of Economic Expansionism," 239.

46. Ian Nish, *Japanese Foreign Policy in the Interwar Period* (Praeger, 2002), 47.

47. Marius B. Jansen, *Japan and China: From War to Peace, 1894–1972* (Rand McNally, 1975), 322.

48. Ibid., 360.

49. John W. Dower, *Empire and Aftermath: Yoshida Shigeru and the Japanese Experience, 1878–1954* (Harvard University Press, 1988), 46–47.

50. Hosoya, "Britain and the United States," 4–5.

51. Neu, *Troubled Encounter,* 108–9.

52. Braisted, *United States Navy in the Pacific,* 498–99.

53. Iriye, *After Imperialism,* 14.

54. Ibid., 14; Fifield, *Woodrow Wilson and the Far East,* 231–32.

55. Ian Nish, "Japan in Britain's View of the International System, 1919–1937," in Nish, *Anglo-Japanese Alienation, 1919–1952,* 31.

56. The Japanese and British both valued their alliance and, rather than scrapping it, had proposed including the United States in a tripartite pact. This was unacceptable to the Americans, of course. The new Four Power agreement was the furthest thing from an alliance, requiring only consultation in the event of crises, and although Borah attacked it as a new "League," Lodge assured everyone the agreement was "harmless." The signatories of the Nine Power Treaty were the United States, Britain, Japan, France, Italy, Belgium, the Netherlands, Portugal, and China.

57. Glad, *Charles Evans Hughes,* 158; Lodge, Congressional Record, vol. 51, part 4, March 2–22, 1922, 3551–3552.

58. Murray, *Harding Era,* 156; Arthur Waldron, ed., *How the Peace Was Lost: The 1935 Memorandum "Developments Affecting American Policy in the Far East,"* (Hoover Institution Press, 1992), 63–64; Harold Hance Sprout and Margaret Tuttle Sprout, *Toward a New Order of Sea Power: American Naval Policy and the World Scene, 1918–1922* (Princeton University Press, 1946), 255–57.

59. Iriye, *After Imperialism,* 26.

60. William L. Neumann, "Franklin D. Roosevelt and Japan, 1913–1933," *Pacific Historical Review* 22, no. 2 (1953): 150.

61. Ian Nish, *Japanese Foreign Policy, 1869–1942,* 141. Japanese naval planners had insisted that Japan's tonnage could be no less than 70 percent of America's. Many Japanese felt dishonored by the second-class status of the 5–5–3 ratio—"Rolls Royce, Rolls Royce, Ford," as some complained. Sprout and Sprout, *Toward a New Order of Sea Power,* 155–57.

62. One Japanese historian writes that the general public attitude was "one of nostalgia, tinged with regret." Hosoya, "Britain and the United States," 7–8. The head of the army's delegation to Washington recorded that the conference was "an attempt to oppress the non-Anglo-Saxon races . . . by the two English-speaking countries" and that Japan had been the victim of "crafty British diplomacy." Ibid., 8.

63. Nish, *Japanese Foreign Policy, 1869–1942,* 142.

64. Waldron, *How the Peace Was Lost,* 19.

65. Ibid., 51.

66. As Nish observes, "It is doubtful whether in the hasty, secret preparation of the conference there was enough time, or indeed organization, to set the hopes of the participants as high as the achievement of a 'system.' Nor was there in the proceedings of the conference much awareness that they were devising a carefully balanced structure. . . . There was no sign of a master plan." Nish, *Japanese Foreign Policy,*

1869–1942, 141. He also notes that there was little evidence that the British were conscious of the existence of a 'Washington system.'" Nish, "Japan in Britain's View," 31.

67. Murray, *Harding Era,* 156. Edmund S. K. Fung, "The Sino-British Rapprochement, 1927–1931," *Modern Asian Studies* 17, no. 1 (1983): 81–83; W. G. Beasley, *Japanese Imperialism, 1894–1945* (Clarendon Press, 1991), 167–68.

68. "Most of the rights of sovereignty that China had been forced to surrender during the previous 80 years remained unretrieved." Warren I. Cohen, *America's Response to China: A History of Sino-American Relations* (Columbia University Press, 1990), 105–6.

69. William Appleman Williams, "China and Japan: A Challenge and a Choice of the Nineteen Twenties," *Pacific Historical Review* 26, no. 3 (August 1957): 270.

70. Waldron, *How the Peace Was Lost,* 63–64. Hughes in January 1922 to Schurman: "Various American expressions of sympathy with an academic position may have misled the Chinese." Williams, "China and Japan," 266.

71. This was certainly the policy of the British, who adopted a posture of "masterly inactivity" while waiting for a Chinese government to emerge and stabilize the situation. Fung, "Sino-British Rapprochement," 82.

72. Iriye, *After Imperialism,* 28.

73. Williams, "China and Japan," 270.

74. Fung, "Sino-British Rapprochement," 80–81.

75. Russell D. Buhite, *Nelson T. Johnson and American Policy Toward China, 1925–1941* (Michigan State University Press, 1968), 20–21; Dorothy Borg, *American Policy and the Chinese Revolution, 1925–1928* (Octagon Books, 1968), 138.

76. Williams, "China and Japan," 273–74. He and other American diplomats also proposed negotiating with the Beijing government in the hopes of preempting the more extreme demands of the Communists and the Kuomintang. Iriye, *After Imperialism,* 45.

77. Waldron, *How the Peace Was Lost,* 42.

78. Iriye, *After Imperialism,* 45.

79. Buhite, *Nelson T. Johnson,* 23–24.

80. Williams, "China and Japan," 274. Beasley, *Japanese Imperialism,* 172. As Foreign Secretary Austen Chamberlain explained, the British were "a nation of shopkeepers" whose only desire was "to keep our shops open" and therefore sought only a "strong, united, independent, orderly, and prosperous China," with which to trade. Fung, "Sino-British Rapprochement," 86.

81. Nish, *Japanese Foreign Policy, 1869–1942,* 155–57.

82. Waldron, *How the Peace Was Lost,* 43.

83. MacMurray was indeed attacked in the press as "America's gunboat minister." Ibid., 22.

84. Williams, "China and Japan," 273.

85. Waldron, *How the Peace Was Lost,* 85. A survey of editorial opinion across the country revealed a widespread feeling that the United States should go its own way in China. Borg, *American Policy and the Chinese Revolution, 1925–1928,* 323–25.

86. Williams, "China and Japan," 275; Borg, *American Policy and the Chinese Revolution, 1925–1928,* 303, 323.

87. Borg, *American Policy and the Chinese Revolution,* 321.

88. Waldron, *How the Peace Was Lost,* 110.

89. Ibid., 80–81, 110n.

90. America's pro-Chinese policy, complained Consul General Yada Shichitaro at Shanghai in the summer of 1928, "will obtain the Chinese people's gratitude for the

United States and be likely to turn them to disliking and cursing us." Iriye, "Failure of Economic Expansionism," 262–63.

91. He regretted to inform the British government that the United States was "not in a position to associate itself with the action which His Majesty's Government is taking in this matter." Buhite, *Nelson T. Johnson,* 29.

92. Borg, *American Policy and the Chinese Revolution,* 290–95.

93. Ibid., 326.

94. Nish, "Japan in Britain's View," 31–32, 36.

95. By comparison, under 6 percent of Britain's overseas investment was in China, and American investments were under 2 percent of U.S. foreign investments worldwide. Christopher Thorne, *The Limits of Foreign Policy: The West, the League, and the Far Eastern Crisis, 1931–1933* (Putnam, 1973), 51, 32.

96. Armin Rappaport, *Henry L. Stimson and Japan, 1931–33* (University of Chicago Press, 1963), 11; Young, *Japan's Total Empire,* 31–32, 22.

97. Shidehara even rejected a British offer to send a joint force to protect the foreign concessions in Shanghai, for instance, because he did not want anti-foreign sentiment aroused against Japan. Hosoya, "Britain and the United States," 11.

98. Iriye, *After Imperialism,* 46.

99. Dower, *Empire and Aftermath,* 179, 82.

100. Nish, *Japanese Foreign Policy, 1869–1942,* 158–60.

101. Iriye, *After Imperialism,* 186, 127.

102. Fung, "Nationalist Foreign Policy, 1928–1937," in Pong and Fung, *Ideal and Reality: Social and Political Change in Modern China, 1860–1949* (University Press of America, 1985), 197–98.

103. Waldron, *How the Peace Was Lost,* 118–19; Hosoya, "Britain and the United States," 14.

104. As the historian Arthur Waldron has commented, Uchida's "shift from support of internationalism to unilateralism may be connected with his experiences during this trip, which convinced him of the Western Powers' lack of concern for Japan's position." Ibid., 110n.

Chapter Sixteen: The Manchurian Crisis

1. Justus D. Doenecke, *When the Wicked Rise: American Opinion-Makers and the Manchurian Crisis of 1931–1933* (Associated University Presses, 1984), 51.

2. As MacMurray later observed, the Japanese were far more "concerned about us than we are about them." Michael A. Barnhart, "Driven by Domestics: American Relations with Japan and Korea, 1900–1945," in Warren I. Cohen, ed., *Pacific Passage* (Columbia University Press, 1996), 199.

3. Thorne, *Limits of Foreign Policy,* 53.

4. From 1922 to 1930, Japanese sales of silk fabric in the United States fell from $18 million to about $3 million. Figures from Lei (Sandy) Ye, "U.S. Trade Policy and the Pacific Rim, from Fordney-McCumber to the Trade Expansion Act of 1962: A Political-Economic Analysis," undergraduate honors thesis, Stanford University, May 11, 2007.

5. Kato Shuichi, "Taisho Democracy as the Pre-Stage for Japanese Militarism," in *Japan in Crisis: Essays on Taisho Democracy,* eds. Bernard S. Silberman and H. D. Harootunian (University of Michigan Press, 1999), 227; Iriye, *After Imperialism,* 279.

6. Iriye, *After Imperialism,* 279; Thorne, *Limits of Foreign Policy,* 52. Throughout the 1920s "perceptions of deflation, depression, and economic crisis" colored the pub-

lic's view of everything, including the democratic government and its relations with the West. Jansen, *Making of Modern Japan,* 532–33.

7. Iriye, "Failure of Economic Expansionism," 264–65.

8. Beasley, *Japanese Imperialism,* 175.

9. That this view dominated in military circles was shown by the fact that, as early as 1923, Japan's national defense policy had designated the United States as the main enemy and warned that "a clash" was "inevitable." Asada, "Japanese Admirals and the Politics of Naval Limitation," 159. Dower warns against the "categorical dichotomies frequently read into this decade of Japanese history: military versus civilian; ultranationalist versus internationalist, Tanaka diplomacy versus Shidehara diplomacy; Asia clique versus Anglo-American clique." Dower, *Empire and Aftermath,* 57–58. Where they disagreed was in the means of accomplishing it, preferring "economic diplomacy," financial influence, and cooperation to the exercise of raw power and "territorial expansion." Nish, *Japanese Foreign Policy, 1869–1942,* 155.

10. Pyle, *Japan Rising,* 178–79.

11. Evans and Peattie, *Kaigun,* 200.

12. Pyle, *Japan Rising,* 175; Jansen, *Making of Modern Japan,* 519; Ikuhiko Hata, "Continental Expansion, 1905–1941," in *Cambridge History of Japan,* vol. 6, 283.

13. Prince Fumimaro Konoe, quoted in Pyle, *Japan Rising,* 176. A senior army official, on his deathbed in 1922, had an aide draw a red line around Siberia, India, Southeast Asia, Australia, and New Zealand, and declared, "That all belongs to Japan." Jansen, *Japan and China,* 345.

14. As Pyle notes, Japan's victories had shown that "the hierarchy of prestige in the world rested, above all, on the exercise of military power." Pyle, *Japan Rising,* 113–14, 118.

15. For instance, Junnosuke Inouye, the governor of the Bank of Japan and sometime finance minister, and the MIT-educated head of the Mitsui zaibatsu, Baron Takuma Don. Ron Chernow, *The House of Morgan: An American Banking Dynasty and the Rise of Modern Finance* (Grove Press, 1990), 246.

16. Pyle, *Japan Rising,* 175; Jansen, *Making of Modern Japan,* 533.

17. It was a standard critique that the liberal leaders lacked sufficient "enthusiasm for expansion." Sadako Nakamura Ogata, *Defiance in Manchuria: Making of Japanese Foreign Policy, 1931–32* (University of California Press, 1964), 28, 30.

18. James Buckley Crowley, *Japan's Quest for Autonomy: National Security and Foreign Policy, 1930–1938* (Princeton University Press, 2016), 290.

19. Ibid., 208.

20. Ibid., 398.

21. Jansen, *Japan and China,* 343.

22. As the historian Marius B. Jansen explains, the Manchurian incident was "less an act of insubordination than it was an acceleration of plans the high command had approved in the proper manner." Ibid., 347.

23. *New York Herald Tribune,* March 27, 1932, quoted in Rappaport, *Henry L. Stimson and Japan, 1931–33,* 25.

24. Doenecke, *When the Wicked Rise,* 23.

25. As Justus D. Doenecke observes, "In the first few months of the crisis, most elements of opinion backed an administration thus far united in its caution." *When the Wicked Rise,* 45–46.

26. As one top State Department official put it just before the intervention, "If Manchuria is destined to become part of Japan, I do not see why that should necessarily embroil us." Cohen, *America's Response to China,* 125.

27. Rappaport, *Henry L. Stimson and Japan,* 66.
28. Doenecke, *When the Wicked Rise,* 38–40. Rappaport, *Henry L. Stimson and Japan,* 38.
29. Richard N. Current, *Secretary Stimson: A Study in Statecraft* (Rutgers University Press, 1954), 79.
30. James C. Thomson, Jr., "The Role of the Department of State," in *Pearl Harbor as History: Japanese-American Relations, 1931–1941,* eds. Dorothy Borg and Shumpei Okamoto (Columbia University Press, 1973), 92.
31. The various treaties that Japan had signed, including the Kellogg Pact and the Nine-Power Treaty, were the new "scraps of paper." State Department officials called Japan "a Pacific Germany." Doenecke, *When the Wicked Rise,* 53–54, 58.
32. Barabra W. Tuchman, *Stillwell and the American Experience in China: 1911–45* (Bantam Books, 1989), 172.
33. Rappaport, *Henry L. Stimson and Japan,* 80; Norman A. Graebner, "Hoover, Roosevelt, and the Japanese," in *Pearl Harbor as History: Japanese-American Relations, 1931–1941,* eds. Dorothy Borg and Shumpei Okamoto (Columbia University Press, 1973), 27.
34. The Republican congressman Hamilton Fish insisted that the United States had been "a Santa Claus long enough for all the foreign nations," and the government had "no mandate to preserve the lives of missionaries or business men who do not come out of the battle zone." Doenecke, *When the Wicked Rise,* 56. As Doenecke notes, "Despite an almost universal sense of outrage, the Shanghai crisis made many Americans extremely cautious." Ibid., 54.
35. Will Rogers, "Mr. Rogers Is Pessimistic on the Manchurian Muddle," *New York Times,* Dec. 17, 1931.
36. Doenecke, *When the Wicked Rise,* 81.
37. Ibid.
38. Ibid., 84.
39. Ibid., 88.
40. Steel, *Walter Lippmann and the American Century,* 328–29.
41. Thomson, "Role of the Department of State," 93.
42. Doenecke, *When the Wicked Rise,* 43.
43. Ibid., 47.
44. Ibid., 31, 45, 59, 64, 89.
45. Rappaport, *Henry L. Stimson and Japan,* 115.
46. Doenecke, *When the Wicked Rise,* 49, 59.
47. Hoover worried that collaboration with the League would lead the French to demand a new security guarantee. Rappaport, *Henry L. Stimson and Japan,* 68.
48. Dorothy Borg, *The United States and the Far Eastern Crisis of 1933–1938: From the Manchurian Incident Through the Initial Stage of the Undeclared Sino-Japanese War* (Harvard University Press, 1964), 4; Rappaport, *Henry L. Stimson and Japan,* 49.
49. On the one occasion during the crisis when Stimson did allow an American official to attend a League Council meeting, Borah lashed him for ignoring the public will, and Stimson immediately pulled the official out. Current, *Secretary Stimson,* 73; Rappaport, *Henry L. Stimson and Japan,* 52.
50. Williams, "China and Japan," 278.
51. Current, *Secretary Stimson,* 73; Borg, *United States and the Far Eastern Crisis,* 2. Hoover thought the United States was already out too far. In November he told Castle that he wanted "to get completely out of the League connection" and complained that it would "have been wise, politically, to make Stimson keep out." Graebner, "Hoover, Roosevelt, and the Japanese," 27.

52. The fifteen capital ships stationed in the Asian theater had to protect British holdings and trade and could not be deployed in a conflict with Japan. Nish, "Japan in Britain's View," 37.
53. Ibid., 40. Louis, *British Strategy in the Far East*, 190.
54. Current, *Secretary Stimson*, 98; Rappaport, *Henry L. Stimson and Japan*, 166; Louis, *British Strategy in the Far East*, 189.
55. Doenecke, *When the Wicked Rise*, 51.
56. Evans and Peattie, *Kaigun*, 353, 586.
57. The Washington Treaty had called for a 60 percent ratio, but by 1932 Japanese battleship tonnage was 80 percent of American tonnage. Evans and Peattie, *Kaigun*, 237.
58. Rappaport, *Henry L. Stimson and Japan*, 65; Evans and Peattie, *Kaigun*, 199. "From a naval perspective, a system of international control over naval armaments had proved to be a most effective way to safeguard the empire." Crowley, *Japan's Quest for Autonomy*, 30–31.
59. One civilian leader argued that America's "agreement or disagreement" need no longer "be of great concern" to Japan. Dower, *Empire and Aftermath*, 74.
60. Current, *Secretary Stimson*, 97.
61. Rappaport, *Henry L. Stimson and Japan*, 116.
62. Ibid., 34.
63. Current, *Secretary Stimson*, 103.
64. Rappaport, *Henry L. Stimson and Japan*, 116.
65. Ibid., 120; Current, *Secretary Stimson*, 103.
66. Rappaport, *Henry L. Stimson and Japan*, 121n.
67. Waldo H. Heinrichs, Jr., "The Role of the United States Navy," in *Pearl Harbor as History: Japanese-American Relations, 1931–1941*, eds. Dorothy Borg and Shumpei Okamoto (Columbia University Press, 1973), 207.
68. Current, *Secretary Stimson*, 104.
69. Americans would fight to defend the "Continental United States," but neither America's "obligations, nor our own interests, nor our dignity" required going to war over China. Rappaport, *Henry L. Stimson and Japan*, 117, 36. Current, *Secretary Stimson*, 95.
70. As one official summarized his thinking, "Why should we build our navy up to London Treaty limits when it will have nothing to do after we have built it? . . . No wars are on now and no war is in sight." Alexander DeConde, "Herbert Hoover and Foreign Policy: A Retrospective Assessment," in *U.S. Senate, Herbert Hoover Reassessed: Essays Commemorating the Fiftieth Anniversary of the Inauguration of Our Thirty-First President* (University Press of the Pacific, 2002), 322.
71. Thomson,"The Role of the Department of State," 85.
72. "Nanking Will Invoke Kellogg Peace Pact, Neal Fighting Feared," *New York Times*, Sept. 21, 1931; Sara R. Smith, *The Manchurian Crisis, 1931–1932: A Tragedy in International Relations* (Columbia University Press, 1948), 28.
73. Nish, *Japanese Foreign Policy, 1869–1942*, 181.
74. Thorne, *Limits of Foreign Policy*, 61.
75. In Ogata's view, Stimson's initial "soft-pedaling was interpreted by Kwantung Army leaders as an invitation to resort to even more drastic measures in defiance of the government" in the belief that they could do so "without risking the chance of a major war." Ogata, *Defiance in Manchuria*, 73. Shidehara later complained that it was the endless succession of Stimson's notes that had caused him the greatest problems, for each note had played into the military's hands by bringing forth a nationalist, anti-American public reaction. "The tone and frequency of official

notes" produced feelings in Japan that were "exactly what their military leaders wanted." Elting E. Morison, *Turmoil and Tradition: A Study of the Life and Times of Henry L. Stimson* (Houghton Mifflin, 1960), 331.

76. See, for instance, Smith, *Manchurian Crisis,* 34.
77. Pyle, *Japan Rising,* 188.
78. John Huizenga, "Yosuke Matsuoka and the Japanese-German Alliance," in Gordon A. Craig and Felix Gilbert, eds., *The Diplomats, 1919–1939,* vol. 2, *The Thirties* (Atheneum 41B, 1963), 617. As the historian Ian Nish put it, "They were proud that at long last they were not hanging on to the coat-tails of the world but considering their national self-interest and casting only a sideways glance at foreign views." Nish, *Japanese Foreign Policy, 1869–1942,* 199.
79. MacMurray, *How the Peace Was Lost,* 43.
80. Ibid., 54, 126.

Chapter Seventeen: The Fascist Challenge

1. Franklin Delano Roosevelt to Elihu Root in *F.D.R.: His Personal Letters, 1928–1945,* ed. Elliott Roosevelt, 2 vols. (Duell, Sloan, and Pearce, 1952), 1:451–52.
2. As Doenecke observes, "public attention to the Far East virtually disappeared." Doenecke, *When the Wicked Rise,* 62–63.
3. Graebner, "Hoover, Roosevelt, and the Japanese," 31.
4. Josephson, "Outlawing War," 383–84.
5. Graebner, "Hoover, Roosevelt, and the Japanese," 31.
6. Doenecke, *When the Wicked Rise,* 111.
7. Ibid.
8. Lionel Trilling, "Freud and Literature," in *The Liberal Imagination: Essays on Literature and Society* (Viking Press, 1950), 56.
9. As the historian Ian Kershaw has observed, "The calming of international relations from the mid-1920s onwards had been brought about by democratic governments. As long as they survived, there were fair prospects for peace in Europe." Ian Kershaw, *To Hell and Back: Europe 1914–1949* (Viking, 2015), 183.
10. Patricia Knight, *Mussolini and Fascism* (Routledge, 2003), 86. For example, he acquired control of Fiume peacefully in an agreement with Yugoslavia. The glaring exception was his forceful occupation of the Greek island of Corfu in 1923. He was "always keenly sensitive to shifts in American opinion" and employed a newspaper clipping bureau to keep track of American press commentary. John P. Diggins, *Mussolini and Fascism: The View from America* (Princeton University Press, 1972), 49.
11. Simms, *Hitler: A Global Biography,* 156.
12. By way of explaining to Hitler why he was so "misrepresented, so misunderstood" in the United States, Hearst pointed to the "very large and influential and respected element in the United States who are very resentful of the treatment of their fellows in Germany." Simms, *Hitler: A Global Biography,* 233.
13. Ibid., 163, 180, 192, 230–31.
14. Robert O. Paxton, *The Anatomy of Fascism* (Vintage Books, 2005), 25.
15. What constituted governing legitimacy had been different in 1820, and had the war ended in a stalemate with Germany in control of *Mitteleuropa,* it is unlikely that so many nations would have adopted democracy as their form of government.
16. Edwin J. James, "Our World Power and Moral Influence," *International Digest* 1 (October 1930): 21–24, excerpted in Norman A. Graebner, ed., *Ideas and Diplo-*

macy: Readings in the Intellectual Tradition of American Foreign Policy (Oxford University Press, 1964), 549.

17. Michael R. Godley, "Lessons from an Italian Connection," in Pong and Fung, *Ideal and Reality,* 101. These did not have to be new resentments. As Robert Paxton notes, as a political and social phenomenon, fascism represented a backlash against "the dominant liberal faith in individual liberty, reason, natural human harmony, and progress" that had come to hold sway over much of Europe since the late nineteenth century. Paxton, *Anatomy of Fascism,* 32.

18. Nicholas Farrell, *Mussolini* (Sharpe Books, 2018), 157.

19. Paxton, *Anatomy of Fascism,* 80.

20. MacGregor Knox, "Fascism: Ideology, Foreign Policy, and War," in Adrian Lyttelton, ed., *Liberal and Fascist Italy* (Oxford University Press, 2002), 113, 121.

21. MacGregor Knox, "Expansionist Zeal, Fighting Power, and Staying Power in the Italian and German Dictatorships," in Richard Bessel, ed., *Fascist Italy and Nazi Germany: Comparisons and Contrasts* (Cambridge University Press, 1996), 114.

22. Gerhard L. Weinberg, *Hitler's Foreign Policy: The Road to World War II, 1933–1939* (Enigma, 2005), 44.

23. Max Lerner, *Ideas Are Weapons; The History and Uses of Ideas* (Viking Press, 1939), 501.

24. Michael R. Godley, "Lessons from an Italian Connection," in Pong and Fung, *Ideal and Reality,* 101.

25. Diggins, *Mussolini and Fascism,* 88–93.

26. Knox, "Fascism: Ideology, Foreign Policy, and War," 113.

27. Paxton, *Anatomy of Fascism,* 55.

28. Godley, "Lessons from an Italian Connection," 101.

29. Knox, "Fascism: Ideology, Foreign Policy, and War," 111, 116.

30. Ibid., 113.

31. Weinberg, *Hitler's Foreign Policy,* 64.

32. Knox, "Fascism: Ideology, Foreign Policy, and War," 122.

33. Ibid., 112.

34. As the historian A. J. P. Taylor, among others, has pointed out.

35. Kershaw, *To Hell and Back,* 179.

36. Simms, *Hitler: A Global Biography,* 149.

37. Weinberg, *Hitler's Foreign Policy,* 47.

38. Ernst L. Presseisen, *Germany and Japan: A Study in Totalitarian Diplomacy, 1933–1941* (Howard Fertig, 1969), 47.

39. The pacts and alliances they would form among themselves over the course of the decade could rightly be described as "hollow" and without more than an appearance of real cooperation. Weinberg, *Hitler's Foreign Policy,* 132–37.

40. The Nazis were even willing to set aside their aversion to the "yellow" race. After all, the "unity of the white race . . . was buried at Versailles." Presseisen, *Germany and Japan,* 40.

41. Ambassador Joseph Grew, quoted in ibid., 75.

42. Alfred Rosenberg, quoted in ibid., 7.

43. Pyle, *Japan Rising,* 191.

44. Huizenga, "Yosuke Matsuoka and the Japanese-German Alliance," 2:618.

45. Timothy Snyder, *Bloodlands: Europe Between Hitler and Stalin* (Basic Books, 2010), 17.

46. Weinberg, *Hitler's Foreign Policy,* 35; Simms, *Hitler: A Global Biography,* 236.

47. Knox, "Fascism: Ideology, Foreign Policy, and War," 126–27.

48. Ibid., 128.
49. Yosuke Matsuoka, quoted in Presseisen, *Germany and Japan,* 32.
50. Issimarou Foujita, quoted in Presseisen, *Germany and Japan,* 73.
51. Stephen Kotkin, *Stalin: Waiting for Hitler, 1929–1941* (Penguin Press, 2017), 355.

Chapter Eighteen: Franklin D. Roosevelt: Isolationist

1. Franklin Delano Roosevelt to Elihu Root in Elliott Roosevelt, ed., *F.D.R.: His Personal Letters, 1928–1945,* 1:451–52.
2. Although he was also an early advocate of American intervention in Europe after 1914 and a critic, like his cousin Theodore, of Wilson's neutrality policy. He was known to have exclaimed, "We've got to get into this war." Susan Dunn, *1940: FDR, Willkie, Lindbergh, Hitler—the Election amid the Storm* (Yale University Press, 2013), 22.
3. In his 1920 campaign for the vice presidency, he declared that Americans could "either shut our eyes," build "an impregnable wall of costly armaments," and attempt to be a "hermit nation," as the "Orient used to live," or they could open their eyes and recognize the complexity of a "modern civilization" in which their lives were now so "interwoven" with the lives of peoples in other nations that "intimate foreign relations" had become "impossible to avoid." The League might be flawed, but it was a "practical solution of a practical situation," and through it the United States could join with other nations and "throw our moral force and potential power into the scale of peace." Franklin Delano Roosevelt, "Acceptance of V.P. Nomination," speech, Hyde Park, N.Y., Aug. 9, 1920 (Franklin D. Roosevelt Presidential Library & Museum, Master Speech File, Box 2, Speech File 131 http://www.fdrlibrary.marist.edu/_resources/images/msf/msf00133).
4. Norman H. Davis, "American Foreign Policy: A Democratic View," *Foreign Affairs* 3 (September 1924): 22–34.
5. David K. Adams, "The Concept of Parallel Action: FDR's Internationalism in a Decade of Isolationism," in *From Theodore Roosevelt to FDR: Internationalism and Isolationism in American Foreign Policy,* ed. Daniela Rossini (Ryburn Publishing, Keele University Press, 1995), 116, 122, 113; William R. Rock, *Chamberlain and Roosevelt: British Foreign Policy and the United States, 1937–1940* (Ohio State University, 1989), 203.
6. Franklin Delano Roosevelt, "Messages to Heads of State Participating in the World Economic Conference and the World Disarmament Conferences," speech, May 16, 1933 (Franklin D. Roosevelt Presidential Library & Museum, Master Speech File, Box 15, Speech File 631 http://www.fdrlibrary.marist.edu/_resources/images/msf/msf00649).
7. Robert Dallek, *Franklin D. Roosevelt and American Foreign Policy, 1932–1945* (Oxford University Press, 1979), 54.
8. Franklin Delano Roosevelt, "Message to London Economic Conference," speech, July 3, 1933 (Franklin D. Roosevelt Presidential Library & Museum, Master Speech File, Box 15, Speech File 640 http://www.fdrlibrary.marist.edu/_resources/images/msf/msf00659).
9. Dallek, *Franklin D. Roosevelt and American Foreign Policy,* 67, 69.
10. Zara Steiner, *The Triumph of the Dark: European International History, 1933–1939* (Oxford University Press, 2011), 37–38.
11. Steel, *Walter Lippmann and the American Century,* 306.
12. Steiner, *Triumph of the Dark,* 37–38.
13. The embassy noted that Roosevelt, in order to pass his domestic programs, needed

the support of precisely those progressive senators who stood firm against any deeper U.S. involvement in Europe and that his influence would be diminished "if he pressed them vigorously on a foreign question." Adams, "Concept of Parallel Action," 116, 122, 113; Rock, *Chamberlain and Roosevelt,* 203.

14. Nasaw, *The Chief,* 453–54. Hearst had opposed America's entry into the war in 1917, to the point of being charged with pro-German sympathies, and then had led the assault against the League. As a Democrat he blamed Wilson for the party's crushing defeat in 1920, as well as the subsequent twelve years of Republican rule. He was determined to prevent another "Wilsonian" from grabbing the party's nomination in 1932. Hearst did not believe Roosevelt and thought that he remained "at heart an internationalist," but the publisher grudgingly supported his candidacy. Roosevelt was not the only former Wilsonian who had to disavow his earlier beliefs. Newton D. Baker, who had served as Wilson's secretary of war, had been a staunch proponent of the League, but he also hoped for the Democratic nomination in 1932 and declared (in a statement written by Walter Lippmann) that nothing was "to be gained by an exaggerated interest in the machinery of peace." Steel, *Walter Lippmann and the American Century,* 293.

15. Frank Freidel, *Franklin D. Roosevelt,* vol. 4, *Launching the New Deal* (Little, Brown, 1973), 103.

16. Franklin Delano Roosevelt, "Inaugural Address," Washington, D.C., March 4, 1933 (Franklin D. Roosevelt Presidential Library & Museum, Master Speech File, Box 13, Speech File 610 http://www.fdrlibrary.marist.edu/_resources/images/msf/msf00628).

17. Steel, *Walter Lippmann and the American Century,* 285–86.

18. Arthur M. Schlesinger, Jr., *The Age of Roosevelt,* vol. 3, *The Politics of Upheaval* (Riverside Press, 1960), 646.

19. Fox, *Reinhold Niebuhr,* 170.

20. Senior State Department officials also had a generally favorable view of the Italian ruler, at least until the war with Ethiopia. Under Secretary of State William Castle saw much good in Mussolini's efforts. Secretaries of State Frank Kellogg and Henry Stimson were annoyed by the complaints of Americans whom Kellogg referred to as "communists, socialists, and anarchists." Diggins, *Mussolini and Fascism,* 267. The year before the market crash the *Saturday Evening Post,* with almost three million subscribers, serialized Mussolini's autobiography, ghostwritten by a former American ambassador to Italy, Richard Washburn Child, a conservative Harding appointee who spent a decade promoting the virtues of Italian fascism in the United States. Mussolini won plaudits from William Randolph Hearst for his "enlightened administration." Ibid., 28, 48.

21. Ibid., 26, 37–38.

22. Ibid., 283. As the *Washington Post* put it in 1926, the Italian people "needed a leader, and having found him they gladly confer power upon him." Ibid., 59.

23. Peter Carlson, "Encounter: Will Rogers Befriends Benito Mussolini," HistoryNet, August 2016. John Diggins notes that Cole Porter's famous 1934 song included the lyric "You're the tops—you're Mussolini." The lyric was later removed. Diggins, *Mussolini and Fascism,* 287.

24. Weinberg, *Hitler's Foreign Policy,* 151; "Future of Hitler Declared at Stake," *New York Times,* July 1, 1934, 7. The following year the popular columnist Dorothy Thompson and others published a collection of essays entitled *Nazism: An Assault on Civilization.* Michaela Hoenicke Moore, *Know Your Enemy: The American Debate on Nazism, 1933–1945* (Cambridge University Press, 2009), 41.

25. Steel, *Walter Lippmann and the American Century,* 331. He went on to observe that

all people were capable of good and evil. You couldn't judge the French by the Terror, Protestantism by the Klan, Catholics by the Inquisition, or "the Jews by their parvenus."

26. Moore, *Know Your Enemy,* 72.
27. Much of the initial decline had little to do with the new government's policies, but this did not diminish the perception of the Nazis' success. See Arthur van Riel and Arthur Schram, "Weimar Economic Decline, Nazi Economic Recovery, and the Stabilization of Political Dictatorship," *Journal of Economic History* 53, no. 1 (March 1993): 97. Numbers are seasonally adjusted.
28. Moore, *Know Your Enemy,* 66.
29. James T. Patterson, *Mr. Republican: A Biography of Robert A. Taft* (Houghton Mifflin Company, 1972), 245–46.
30. Moore, *Know Your Enemy,* 61–62.
31. Dallek, *Franklin D. Roosevelt and American Foreign Policy,* 142; Kenneth S. Davis, *FDR: Into the Storm, 1937–1940* (Random House, 1993), 15–16.
32. The lay Catholic journal *Commonweal* appreciated fascism's "thorough-going opposition to what is termed liberalism," which the editors described as an "attempt to push back the forces of human nature." Diggins, *Mussolini and Fascism,* 182, 187, 192.
33. Francine Du Plessix Gray, "The Journalist and the Dictator," *New York Times,* June 24, 1990.
34. Schlesinger, *Politics of Upheaval,* 182–83. Edmund Wilson, the literary critic, viewed Stalin's regime as "designed to make exploitation impossible." Steel, *Walter Lippmann and the American Century,* 325.
35. Diggins, *Mussolini and Fascism,* 264, 223.
36. Quoted in Robert H. Ferrell, *American Diplomacy in the Great Depression: Hoover-Stimson Foreign Policy, 1929–1933* (Yale University Press, 1957), 1.
37. Steel, *Walter Lippmann and the American Century,* 280. Rochester, *American Liberal Disillusionment,* 100, 121–22.
38. Osgood, *Ideals and Self-Interest,* 381–83.
39. The "essential logic of the New Deal," observed Max Lerner, was "increasingly the naked fist of a capitalist state." I. F. Stone warned, "Mr. Roosevelt intends to move toward fascism." Schlesinger, *Politics of Upheaval,* 175–76.
40. Fox, *Reinhold Niebuhr,* 142.
41. As Edmund Wilson put it, "Marx showed how people's theories of society and economics—no matter how well-reasoned or sober—have a way of turning out to be a defense of their class position and financial interests." Scott Stossel, "The Other Edmund Wilson," *American Prospect,* Nov. 17, 2001.
42. Schlesinger, *Politics of Upheaval,* 176.
43. Thomas C. Kennedy, *Charles A. Beard and American Foreign Policy* (University Press of Florida, 1975), 58, 73. Eric F. Goldman, *Rendezvous with Destiny: A History of Modern American Reform* (Ivan R. Dee, 2001), 378.
44. Howlett, *Troubled Philosopher,* 140–41.
45. Ibid.
46. Patterson, *Mr. Republican,* 217.
47. Ibid., 200–201.
48. Wayne S. Cole, *Roosevelt & the Isolationists, 1932–45* (University of Nebraska Press, 1983), 145–49.
49. Ibid., 141–42.
50. Cohen, *American Revisionists,* 162.
51. Ibid., 139.

52. The argument in Millis's *Road to War* was that defense of traditional neutral rights
     had made the United States "a silent partner of the Entente." Millis wrote of those
     "Frenzied Years of 1914–17 when . . . a peace-loving democracy, muddled but
     excited, misinformed and whipped to frenzy, embarked upon its greatest foreign
     war." "Read it and blush!" read the jacket copy. "Read it and beware!" Walter Mil-
     lis, *Road to War—America, 1914–1917* (Houghton Mifflin, 1935); Osgood, *Ideals
     and Self-Interest,* 368.
53. Diggins, *Mussolini and Fascism,* 328.
54. Joseph Lash, *The Campus Strike Against War* (Student League for Industrial
     Democracy, 1935), 5.
55. Cole, *Roosevelt & the Isolationists,* 167–69.
56. Roosevelt and Hull wanted discretionary authority to embargo shipments of arms
     and munitions to Italy and Ethiopia. Senate Foreign Relations Committee chair-
     man Key Pittman warned that Roosevelt was "riding for a fall" if he insisted on
     "designating the aggressor in accordance with the wishes of the League of Nations."
     Ibid., 174.
57. Robert A. Divine, *The Illusion of Neutrality* (University of Chicago Press, 1962),
     115.
58. Cole, *Roosevelt & the Isolationists,* 169.
59. Ronald H. Carpenter, *Father Charles E. Coughlin: Surrogate Spokesman for the
     Disaffected* (Greenwood Press, 1998), 167.
60. As the British ambassador observed, Roosevelt always "had his eye on his future
     influence over Senators for support on domestic questions, and the manner in
     which that influence might be impaired if he pressed them vigorously on a foreign
     question." Cole, *Roosevelt & the Isolationists,* 124.
61. William Allen White wrote to Harold Ickes in 1935, "Roosevelt can't win next year
     without the progressive Republican votes of the Middle West from Ohio to the
     Coast, but particularly the Mississippi Basin north of Tennessee." Cole, *Roosevelt
     & the Isolationists,* 189.
62. Franklin Delano Roosevelt, "President's Address at Woodrow Wilson Founda-
     tion," speech, Washington, D.C., Dec. 28, 1933 (Franklin D. Roosevelt Presidential
     Library & Museum, Master Speech File, Box 16, Speech File 671 http://www.fdrli-
     brary.marist.edu/_resources/images/msf/msf00691).
63. Franklin Delano Roosevelt to Henry L. Stimson in Elliott Roosevelt, ed., *F.D.R.:
     His Personal Letters, 1928–1945,* 1:450.
64. Dallek, *Franklin D. Roosevelt and American Foreign Policy,* 96–97.
65. Arthur Krock, "In Washington: Neutrality Legislation Is Victory for Both Sides,"
     New York Times, Feb. 19, 1936.
66. Diggins, *Mussolini and Fascism,* 109, 304–5.
67. As Dallek notes, "His interest at this time in helping that government preserve
     Spain from Fascist rule was either small or nonexistent." Dallek, *Franklin D. Roo-
     sevelt and American Foreign Policy,* 96–127.
68. Franklin Delano Roosevelt, "Message to Congress on the State of Union," speech,
     Jan. 4, 1935 (Franklin D. Roosevelt Presidential Library & Museum, Master
     Speech File, Box 24, Speech File 834 http://www.fdrlibrary.marist.edu/_resources
     /images/msf/msf00858).
69. Franklin Delano Roosevelt, "Message to Congress on the State of Union," speech,
     Jan. 3, 1936 (Franklin D. Roosevelt Presidential Library & Museum, Master
     Speech File, Box 24, Speech File 834 http://www.fdrlibrary.marist.edu/_resources
     /images/msf/msf00858).
70. He railed against the authors of the Neutrality Act, who seemed "willing to see

a city burn down just so long as their own houses remain standing in the ruins." Franklin Delano Roosevelt to Edward M. House in Elliott Roosevelt, ed., *F.D.R.: His Personal Letters, 1928–1945,* 506–7; Divine, *Illusion of Neutrality,* 119–20.

71. Franklin Delano Roosevelot to Elihu Root in ibid., 451–52.
72. Despite the U.S. ambassador's view that it was the victim of "an international fascist conspiracy" to destroy democracy. Dallek, *Franklin D. Roosevelt and American Foreign Policy,* 131.
73. Borg, *United States and the Far Eastern Crisis,* 88.
74. Joseph Grew, *Ten Years in Japan* (Simon & Schuster, 1944), 91–94.
75. Borg, *United States and the Far Eastern Crisis,* 35.
76. Ibid., 116–17.
77. *Foreign Relations of the United States, 1935, The Far East,* vol. 3, ed. John G. Reid, Louis E. Gates, and Ralph R. Goodwin (Government Printing Office, 1953), Document 836.
78. Vinson-Trammell Bill of 1934, Pub. L., No. 136, 73rd Congress, Session 2 (1934); Five Power-Treaty, Aug. 17, 1923, 43 Stat. 1655, Treaty Series 671; Treaty for the Limitation and Reduction of Naval Armaments, March 26, 1936, 50 Stat. 1936, Treaty Series 919.
79. Borg, *United States and the Far Eastern Crisis,* 110.
80. Dallek, *Franklin D. Roosevelt and American Foreign Policy, 101.*
81. Ibid., 76.
82. It was in these years that the myth was born about Roosevelt's supposedly central role in the decision to defeat the Spanish in the Philippines. The scholar Julius W. Pratt published his seminal article on the "Large Policy" of 1898 in 1932: see *Journal of American History* 19, no. 2 (September 1932): 219–42.
83. "In academic circles a generation trained to look for economic motives in all governmental action explained the policy of the United States as primarily an effort to promote American trade and get profits for American bankers." Dana Gardner Munro, *The United States and the Caribbean Republics, 1921–1933* (Princeton University Press, 1973), 14.
84. Cole, *Roosevelt & the Isolationists,* 358.
85. Munro, *United States and the Caribbean Republics,* 15.
86. Ibid., 215.
87. Cole, *Roosevelt & the Isolationists,* 358.
88. Munro, *United States and the Caribbean Republics,* 381–83.
89. Cole, *Roosevelt & the Isolationists,* 179–80.
90. Cole, *Roosevelt & the Isolationists,* 199. Stimson was bitter. "The Republicans, in coming out against the World Court and cooperation with the League as well as in their attack on reciprocal treaties, pretty effectively stopped my mouth from speech making. If the foreign issues had been the only ones in the campaign, I should have voted the other way." Ibid., 205.
91. Cordell Hull, *The Memoirs of Cordell Hull* (Macmillan, 1948), 475–79.
92. The speech was drafted by William Bullitt and geared specifically to appeal to Senator Nye. Ickes believed Nye's endorsement "would go a long way toward assuring [Roosevelt's] reelection." Cole, *Roosevelt & the Isolationists,* 200. Franklin Delano Roosevelt, "I have seen war," speech, Chautauqua, N.Y., Aug. 14, 1936. (Franklin D. Roosevelt Presidential Library & Museum, Master Speech File, Box 26, Speech File 889 http://www.fdrlibrary.marist.edu/_resources/images/msf/msf00913).
93. Franklin Delano Roosevelt, "I have seen war," speech, Chautauqua, N.Y., Aug. 14, 1936. The Democratic Party platform also promised "to guard against being drawn,

by political commitments, international banking or private trading, into any war which may develop anywhere." Cohen, *American Revisionists,* 180.

94. Franklin Delano Roosevelt, "I have seen war," speech, Chautauqua, N.Y., Aug. 14, 1936. The Democratic platform in 1936 took the same tack, calling for the United States to "observe a true neutrality in the disputes of others . . . to work for peace and to take the profits out of war; to guard against being drawn, by political commitments, international banking or private trading, into any war which may develop anywhere. Dallek, *Franklin D. Roosevelt and American Foreign Policy,* 129.

95. Franklin Delano Roosevelt to William E. Dodd in Elliott Roosevelt, ed., *F.D.R.: His Personal Letters, 1928–1945,* 605–6. In his nomination acceptance speech at the Democratic convention, he said, "It is not alone a war against want and destitution and economic demoralization. It is more than that: it is a war for the survival of democracy. We are fighting to save a great and precious form of government for ourselves and for the world." Franklin Delano Roosevelt, "Address of the President on the Occasion of his Acceptance of the Unanimous Nomination of the Democratic Party," Philadelphia, June 27, 1936 (Franklin D. Roosevelt Presidential Library & Museum, Master Speech File, Box 25, Speech File 879 http://www.fdrlibrary.marist.edu/_resources/images/msf/msf00902).

96. Schlesinger, *Politics of Upheaval,* 655.

97. Franklin Delano Roosevelt to William E. Dodd in Elliott Roosevelt, ed., *F.D.R.: His Personal Letters, 1928–1945,* 648–49.

98. Schlesinger, *Politics of Upheaval,* 656.

99. Dallek, *Franklin D. Roosevelt and American Foreign Policy,* 134.

100. Angus Maddison, *2001 The World Economy: A Millennial Perspective* (Paris: Organization of Economic Cooperation and Development, 2001) 126–27.

101. Frederick W. Marks, *Wind over Sand: The Diplomacy of Franklin Roosevelt* (University of Georgia Press, 1988), 149.

Chapter Nineteen: The United States and Appeasement

1. Franklin D. Roosevelt to Roger B. Merriman, quoted in David Reynolds, *From Munich to Pearl Harbor: Roosevelt's America and the Origins of the Second World War* (Ivan R. Dee, 2001), 44.

2. Rock, *Chamberlain and Roosevelt,* 254; Anne Orde, *The Eclipse of Great Britain: The United States and British Imperial Decline, 1895–1956* (Red Globe Press, 1996), 104.

3. Cole, *Roosevelt & the Isolationists,* 221, 207.

4. "By 1937, the administration thought it futile and tactically unwise even to propose draft legislation of its own." Cole, *Roosevelt & the Isolationists,* 230. Hull wrote in his memoirs, "I felt that Congress was determined on neutrality legislation of an inflexible nature, and our arguments in favor of flexible neutrality legislation that would leave the widest possible discretion to the Executive would have little effect. Where we could, we obtained slight modifications more in conformity with our ideas." Ibid., 231; Hull, *The Memoirs of Cordell Hull* 508.

5. "The Ambassador in Spain (Bowers), Then in France, to the Secretary of State March 16, 1937," *Foreign Relations of the United States Diplomatic Papers, 1937,* general, vol. 1, ed. Matilda F. Axton et al. (Government Printing Office, 1954), Document 159.

6. Adam Hochschild, *Spain in Our Hearts: Americans in the Spanish Civil War, 1936–1939* (Houghton Mifflin Harcourt, 2016), 23.

7. Adam Hochschild notes that, from mid-1936 to early 1939, the *New York Times* ran more than 1,000 front-page headlines about the war. Ibid., xvi.

8. As Adam Hochschild writes, "If there was a prototypical volunteer, he was a New Yorker, a Communist, an immigrant or the son of immigrants, a trade unionist, and a member of a group that has almost vanished from the United States today, working-class Jews." Ibid., 100.

9. Williamson Murray, *The Change in the European Balance of Power, 1938–1939: The Path to Ruin* (Princeton University Press, 1984), 134. Apparently, these progressives did not regard supporting the Spanish government as contradicting their otherwise blanket opposition to American overseas meddling, especially in Europe. In Britain, too, the Labour Party and others on the left simultaneously demanded support for the Loyalists while strenuously opposing even minimal efforts at British rearmament.

10. Hochschild, *Spain in Our Hearts,* 63–64.

11. Ibid., 171.

12. Roosevelt's close adviser Harold Ickes favored lifting the embargo against the Spanish Republic, but he knew that Roosevelt's concern about the Catholic vote would be decisive. Cole, *Roosevelt & the Isolationists,* 234–35.

13. Hochschild, *Spain in Our Hearts,* 172.

14. Cole, *Roosevelt & the Isolationists,* 236. The official was J. Pierrepont Moffat, then head of the State Department's Western European Division.

15. Ibid., 224–25.

16. Ibid., 235.

17. The crisis was sparked by a series of events that became known as the Marco Polo Bridge incident. After the invasion of Manchuria and the establishment of Manchukuo as part of the Japanese Empire, the Japanese had stationed thousands of troops in the new North China demilitarized zone, along the railways between Beijing and Tientsin. This produced occasional clashes between the Japanese and Chinese forces in the area. When a Japanese soldier went missing on the night of July 7, the local Japanese commander demanded that his troops be allowed to enter the town and search for him. The Chinese side refused, and by the time the lost Japanese soldier found his way back to his unit, the situation had escalated. When Chiang Kai-shek rejected Japanese demands for an apology and other measures, the Japanese launched attacks across a vast area of northern China. See S. C. M. Paine, *The Wars for Asia, 1911–1949* (Cambridge University Press, 2012), 128–31.

18. Crowley, *Japan's Quest for Autonomy,* 353–54.

19. *Foreign Relations of the United States Diplomatic Papers, 1937, The Far East,* vol. 3, eds. Matilda F. Axton et al. (Government Printing Office, 1954), Document 545; Borg, *United States and the Far Eastern Crisis,* 310–11.

20. "The Secretary of State to the Ambassador in Japan (Grew), July 29, 1937," *Foreign Relations of the United States Diplomatic Papers, 1937, The Far East,* vol. 3, eds. Matilda F. Axton et al. (Government Printing Office, 1954), Document 312.

21. Jonathan G. Utley, *Going to War with Japan, 1937–1941* (Fordham University Press, 2005), 25.

22. Robert Post, "Americans Are Told to Quit China by Roosevelt, but Troops Remain," *New York Times,* Sept. 6, 1937; Borg, *United States and the Far Eastern Crisis,* 324–25. This was evidence of how little Roosevelt was affected by his family's missionary (and opium-smuggling) background prior to 1939.

23. Dallek, *Franklin D. Roosevelt and American Foreign Policy,* 77.

24. George Messersmith, then serving as assistant secretary of state for Europe, believed Japan had invaded China "as a result of understandings with Germany."

C. A. MacDonald, *The United States, Britain and Appeasement, 1936–1939* (St. Martin's Press, 1981), 61. I have come across no evidence to support this, except in the indirect sense that the Japanese may have felt emboldened by Germany's defiance of the democracies.

25. Steel, *Walter Lippmann and the American Century,* 340–41.

26. Hull told Grew that the Japanese needed to be told, if only privately, that their actions were "destroying the world's good will" and setting Japan up for a "potential ostracism which it would take many, many years of benevolent endeavor on her part to liquidate." *Foreign Relations of the United States Diplomatic Papers, 1937, The Far East,* vol. 3, eds. Matilda F. Axton et al., Document 570.

27. MacDonald, *The United States, Britain and Appeasement,* 37.

28. Franklin D. Roosevelt Press Conference #381, Executive Offices of the White House, July 13, 1937. (Franklin D. Roosevelt Presidential Library & Museum, 378–381 http://www.fdrlibrary.marist.edu/_resources/images/pc/pc0050.pdf).

29. Henry Morgenthau, Jr., "The Diaries of Henry Morgenthau, Jr.," Monday, Sept. 20, 1937, 50–52 (Franklin D. Roosevelt Presidential Library & Museum, Master Volume 89 http://www.fdrlibrary.marist.edu/_resources/images/morg/md0117.pdf).

30. Elliott Roosevelt, ed., *F.D.R.: His Personal Letters, 1928–1945,* 2 vols. (Duell, Sloan and Pearce, 1952), 1:699-701.

31. Franklin Delano Roosevelt to Benito Mussolini in ibid, 1:699-701.

32. Dallek, *Franklin D. Roosevelt and American Foreign Policy,* 144.

33. Ickes understood that the plan aimed at "keeping out of war ourselves" while preventing future wars from occurring. Borg, *United States and the Far Eastern Crisis,* 379.

34. Sumner Welles, *A Time for Decision* (Harper & Brothers, 1944), 56–57.

35. Hull, *Memoirs of Cordell Hull,* 547–49.

36. Ibid., 536.

37. Ibid., 544.

38. Franklin Delano Roosevelt, "Outerlink Bridge Dedication—'Quarantine,'" speech, Oct. 5, 1937 (Franklin D. Roosevelt Presidential Library & Museum, Master Speech File, Box 35, Speech File 1093 http://www.fdrlibrary.marist.edu/_resources/images/msf/msf01127).

39. Quoting from the bestselling 1933 novel *Lost Horizon,* the movie version of which had just been released, he warned of an approaching time "when men, exultant in the technique of homicide, will rage so hotly over the world that every precious thing will be in danger, every book and picture and harmony, every treasure garnered through two millenniums, the small, the delicate, the defenseless—all will be lost or wrecked or utterly destroyed." The movie version, directed by Frank Capra, was released a month before Roosevelt's speech. Franklin Delano Roosevelt, "Outerlink Bridge Dedication—'Quarantine,'" Oct. 5, 1937 (Franklin D. Roosevelt Presidential Library & Museum, Master Speech File, Box 35, Speech File 1093 http://www.fdrlibrary.marist.edu/_resources/images/msf/msf01127).

40. J. Pierrepont Moffat, quoted in Dallek, *Franklin D. Roosevelt and American Foreign Policy,* 151. After the speech Roosevelt remarked to his personal secretary, "Well, it's done now. It was something that needed saying." Davis, *FDR: Into the Storm,* 132.

41. Kennedy, *Charles A. Beard and American Foreign Policy,* 87.

42. Davis, *FDR: Into the Storm,* 133; Dunn, *1940,* 24. Historians have generally concluded that the public response was, on the whole, favorable. See William E. Leuchtenburg, *Franklin D. Roosevelt and the New Deal, 1932–1940* (Harper Torchbooks, 1963), 226–27; Dallek, *Franklin D. Roosevelt and American Foreign Policy,*

150–51. Roosevelt may not have been wrong, however, to regard the behavior of leading Democrats in Congress as a surer indication of the political realities.

43. Franklin D. Roosevelt, quoted in Leuchtenburg, *Franklin D. Roosevelt and the New Deal,* 226.

44. Davis, *FDR: Into the Storm,* 133–34; Leuchtenburg, *Franklin D. Roosevelt and the New Deal,* 226–27.

45. Davis, *FDR: Into the Storm,* 133–34.

46. Crowley, *Japan's Quest for Autonomy,* 359.

47. "You hear of nothing but rape," one German observer reported. Rana Mitter, *Forgotten Ally: China's World War II, 1937–1945* (Houghton Mifflin Harcourt, 2013), 135.

48. Ibid., 136.

49. Ibid., 142. According to Paine, it was indeed Japanese strategy, and not just in Nanking, to "brutalize [. . . .] occupied populations to undermine their will to resist." Paine, *Wars for Asia,* 137.

50. Mitter, *Forgotten Ally,* 142.

51. Roosevelt contemplated a naval blockade cutting off Japan's access to raw materials, believing that would be sufficient to curb Japanese behavior. Utley, *Going to War with Japan,* 28–30.

52. Franklin Delano Roosevelt to Rhoda Hinkley in Elliott Roosevelt, ed., *F.D.R.: His Personal Letters, 1928–1945,* 733–34.

53. As Friedländer notes, whereas in *Mein Kampf* and its sequel, *Hitlers Zweites Buch,* Hitler writes of America as a "new force which threatens to upset the existing balance of power among nations," "his writings dating from the depression years express only scorn for America." Saul Friedländer, *Prelude to Downfall: Hitler and the United States, 1939–1941* (Alfred A. Knopf, 1965), 4. See also Ernst Hansfstaengl, *Unheard Witness* (J. B. Lippincott, 1957), 197, 234.

54. Adolf Hitler, quoted in Gerhard L. Weinberg, "Hitler's Image of the United States," *American Historical Review* 69, no. 4 (July 1964): 1013. According to Weinberg, the Neutrality Act may even have "encouraged Hitler to start World War II by assuring him that none of his prospective enemies would be able to secure supplies from across the Atlantic even by purchase."

55. Kershaw, *To Hell and Back,* 589.

56. Hans Dieckhoff, quoted in Davis, *FDR: Into the Storm,* 136.

57. Weinberg, "Hitler's Image of the United States," 1012. Mussolini agreed that the Americans would not fight and that their role would be negligible if they did. Denis Mack Smith, *Mussolini's Roman Empire* (Viking Press, 1976), 245.

58. Rock, *Chamberlain and Roosevelt,* 47, 254–55.

59. MacDonald, *United States, Britain and Appeasement,* 18, 43, 57.

60. Borg, *United States and the Far Eastern Crisis,* 495–503; Bradford Lee, *Britain and the Sino-Japanese War, 1937–1939: A Study in the Dilemmas of British Decline* (Stanford University Press, 1973), chap. 3, esp. 63–70.

61. Borg, *United States and the Far Eastern Crisis,* 415.

62. Ibid., 415–16.

63. "The Ambassador in the United Kingdom (Bingham) to the Secretary of State, October 28, 1936; "The Ambassador in Japan (Grew) to the Secretary of State, January 25, 1937; "Memorandum from the Files of President Roosevelt's Secretary; "The Chairman of the American Delegation (Davis) to the Secretary of State, November 2, 1937," *Foreign Relations of the United States Diplomatic Papers, 1937, The Far East,* vol. 4, eds. Matilda F. Axton et al. (Government Printing Office, 1954), Documents 126, 94,158.

64. "The Acting Secretary of State to the Ambassador in France (Bullitt), November 9, 1937," ibid., Document 178.

65. "Memorandum from the Files of President Roosevelt's Secretary," ibid., Document 94. Hull declared that Washington would not "assume the role of mentor to the League or accept a responsibility which initially lies with and belongs to the League." "The Secretary of State to the Minister in Switzerland (Wilson), at Geneva, March 31, 1922," *Foreign Relations of the United States Diplomatic Papers, 1933, The Far East,* vol. 3, eds. John G. Reid et al. (Government Printing Office, 1949), Document 273.

66. David Reynolds, *The Creation of the Anglo-American Alliance, 1937–1941: A Study in Competitive Co-operation* (University of North Carolina Press, 1982), 33.

67. Borg, *United States and the Far Eastern Crisis,* 421.

68. MacDonald, *The United States, Britain and Appeasement,* 19.

69. Howard C. Payne, "French Security and American Policy in the 1930s," in Payne et al., *As the Storm Clouds Gathered,* 32.

70. Rock, *Chamberlain and Roosevelt,* 254; Orde, *Eclipse,* 104. Baldwin later commented that he had gotten "to loathe Americans so much" that he could not stand meeting with them. MacDonald, *United States, Britain and Appeasement,* 20. As one British official put it, Roosevelt's speech amounted to saying "Open your mouth and shut your eyes and see what I will give you," and observed that this was "not quite a fair attitude for one country to take to another in matters involving the possibility of war." Reynolds, *Creation of the Anglo-American Alliance,* 36.

71. Adam B. Ulam, *Expansion & Coexistence: The History of Soviet Foreign Policy, 1917–67* (Frederick A. Praeger, 1968), 217.

72. Ibid., 212–13.

73. Ibid., 214.

74. Ibid., 214–15. This assessment was reflected in Stalin's "show trials" in the coming years. While the various "Trotskyists" and other alleged regime opponents were accused of spying for Britain, France, and other foreign, "capitalist" governments, none was accused of being an American spy. As the historian Adam Ulam explains, the United States could not be taken seriously as a dangerous or capable foe of anyone. Ibid., 240.

75. Max Beloff, *The Foreign Policy of Soviet Russia, 1929–1941,* vol. 2 (Oxford University Press, 1949), 125.

76. Rock, *Chamberlain and Roosevelt,* 9.

77. Chamberlain and other conservatives were not about to throw their lot in with Moscow, both for ideological reasons and because Stalin was then still in the process of purging the ranks of his senior officers and hardly seemed ready for a war.

78. Rock, *Chamberlain and Roosevelt,* 70, 83.

79. Ibid., 69–70. As the historian Robert A. Divine has observed, "American isolation had become the handmaiden of European appeasement." Divine, *The Reluctant Belligerent: American Entry into World War II* (John Wiley and Sons, 1965), 55; Kennedy, *Freedom from Fear,* 418–19. Understanding the role of the United States in shaping British appeasement policy provides support to those historians who have argued that appeasement was "a rational response to the very difficult position" in which the British found themselves in the mid-to-late 1930s. See Peter Neville, *Hitler and Appeasement: The British Attempt to Prevent the Second World War* (Hambledon Continuum, 2006), xi.

80. Rock, *Chamberlain and Roosevelt,* 8–9.

81. Arnold A. Offner, *American Appeasement: United States Foreign Policy and Germany, 1933–1938* (Belknap Press of Harvard University Press, 1969), 230.

82. Murray, *Change in the European Balance of Power,* 136.

83. Ibid.

84. Adolf Hitler, *Mein Kampf* (Houghton Mifflin, 1999), 3. Stresemann and successive Weimar governments had made tentative gestures toward union. In fact, it was Germany's declaration of a customs union with Austria in 1931, and the resulting French-inspired bank failures, that had helped produce the global depression.

85. Murray, *Change in the European Balance of Power,* 166.

86. "If we can avoid another violent coup in Czechoslovakia, which ought to be feasible," Chamberlain believed, "it may be possible for Europe to settle down again, and some day for us to start peace talks with the Germans." Steiner, *Triumph of the Dark,* 557.

87. Ibid., 563.

88. Murray, *Change in the European Balance of Power,* 151–55.

89. Steiner, *Triumph of the Dark,* 573.

90. The "Schnellplan" included production of medium-range bombers and naval vessels, both intended for combat with the British. Steiner, *Triumph of the Dark,* 574.

91. Murray, *Change in the European Balance of Power,* 253.

92. Steiner, *Triumph of the Dark,* 554.

93. Murray, *Change in the European Balance of Power,* 157–59.

94. Ibid., 158–59.

95. Steiner, *Triumph of the Dark,* 558–59.

96. Ibid., 565.

97. Ibid., 567.

98. Leuchtenburg, *Franklin D. Roosevelt and the New Deal,* 285, 285n.

99. Steiner, *Triumph of the Dark,* 633. Roosevelt also regarded the prime minister as a "slippery" member of the "Bank of England crowd" who sought "peace at any price" and were just looking out for their financial interests—a British version of the Republican "economic royalists" he was struggling with at home. Callum A. MacDonald, "The United States, Appeasement and the Open Door," in Wolfgang J. Mommsen and Lothar Kettenacker, eds., *The Fascist Challenge* (Routledge, 1983), 73, 401. Franklin Delano Roosevelt to Roger B. Merriman, quoted in Reynolds, *From Munich to Pearl Harbor,* 44.

100. Franklin Delano Roosevelt to Winston Churchill, quoted in ibid., 39.

101. Marks, *Wind over Sand,* 142.

102. Franklin Delano Roosevelt, Address at Queen's University, speech, Kingston, Ontario, Canada, Aug. 18, 1938 (Franklin D. Roosevelt Presidential Library & Museum, Master Speech File, Box 41, Speech File 1168 http://www.fdrlibrary .marist.edu/_resources/images/msf/msf01205).

103. Hull, *Memoirs of Cordell Hull,* 587.

104. Cole, *Roosevelt & the Isolationists,* 286.

105. MacDonald, *United States, Britain and Appeasement,* 86.

106. Murray, *Change in the European Balance of Power,* 198.

107. MacDonald, *United States, Britain and Appeasement,* 86.

108. Ibid., 88. Perhaps they agreed with Borah that "it was natural" for Hitler to seize it since Austria was "really a German state" that had been "crippled" by the Versailles agreement. Cole, *Roosevelt & the Isolationists,* 278.

109. Kennedy was "obsessed with the communist danger" and believed that the only consequence of a war with Hitler would be the domination of central Europe by the Soviet Union. "Selling out a small nation" and giving Hitler another "triumph," he insisted, was preferable to "an Asiatic despotism established on the

fields of the dead." MacDonald, *United States, Britain and Appeasement,* 87. He wrote to Hull that while it was "entirely honorable to urge another nation to go to war if one is prepared to go to war at once on the side of that nation," there was "nothing more dishonorable than to urge another nation to go to war if one is determined not to go to war on the side of that nation." Cole, *Roosevelt & the Isolationists,* 284.

110. Dallek, *Franklin D. Roosevelt and American Foreign Policy,* 164–66.

111. Ibid., 164–66; Sir R. Lindsay (Washington) to Viscount Halifax in *The Diaries of Henry Morgenthau Jr.* (Monday, September 20, 1938): 627–29 (Franklin D. Roosevelt Presidential Library & Museum, Master Volume 141 http://www.fdrlibrary .marist.edu/_resources/images/morg/md0187.pdf).

112. Steel, *Walter Lippmann and the American Century,* 371.

113. Murray, *Change in the European Balance of Power,* 364, 176, 263.

114. Tooze, *Wages of Destruction,* 255, 269; Steiner, *Triumph of the Dark,* 575.

115. Tooze, *Wages of Destruction,* 271–73.

116. Steiner, *Triumph of the Dark,* 576.

117. Murray, *Change in the European Balance of Power,* 205.

118. Ibid., 264.

119. Steiner, *Triumph of the Dark,* 578.

120. Ibid., 577.

121. Murray, *Change in the European Balance of Power,* 267.

122. Ibid., 265, 269.

123. Ibid., 265.

124. Ibid., 274.

125. Members of Chamberlain's own cabinet, such as Anthony Eden, as well as several top officials in the Foreign Office, knew this was a misreading of Hitler, as of course did some members of the opposition, like Winston Churchill. Oher skeptics included prominent French, Soviet, and American officials, including Roosevelt. As Murray observes of Chamberlain, "Having pursued a course that revealed the nature of Nazi policy, he refused to recognize that reality." Ibid., 214.

126. Ibid., 206.

127. Wayne S. Cole, "American Appeasement," in David F. Schmitz and Richard D. Challener, *Appeasement in Europe: A Reassessment of U.S. Policies* (Praeger, 1990), 6.

Chapter Twenty: *Kristallnacht* and Its Effect on American Policy

1. Ian Kershaw, *Hitler, 1936–1945: Nemesis* (W. W. Norton, 2000), 5.

2. Lewis Mumford, *Men Must Act* (Harcourt, Brace, 1939), 6.

3. Kershaw, *Hitler 1936–1945,* 135.

4. Ibid., 134.

5. Ronnie S. Landau, *The Nazi Holocaust* (I. B. Tauris, 2006),137.

6. As the organ of Heinrich Himmler's SS put it in October, "The Jews living in Germany and Italy are the hostages which fate has placed in our hands so that we can defend ourselves effectively against the attacks of world Jewry." Kershaw, *Hitler, 1936–1945,* 135, 151.

7. Ibid., 138–43.

8. "The Jew . . . agitates for war all over the world," Goering said in July 1938, and four months later Goebbels told the foreign press that it was "World Jewry" that had suffered a defeat at Munich and in response had "instigated" a new campaign

to destroy Germany. Tooze, *Wages of Destruction,* 280–83; "No Regret Voiced," *New York Times,* Nov. 12, 1938.

9. Richard Breitman and Allan J. Lichtman, *FDR and the Jews* (Belknap Press of Harvard University Press, 2013), 120.

10. See, for instance, the *New York Times* reporting beginning on Nov. 12, 1938. According to a Gallup poll in December, Americans regarded *Kristallnacht* and the Munich settlement as the two "most interesting" news stories of a year full of interesting stories. Moore, *Know Your Enemy,* 45.

11. Hans-Heinrich Dieckhoff to Carl Friedrich Freiherr von Weizsäcker, quoted in Friedländer, *Prelude to Downfall,* 8.

12. The American ambassador to Berlin, recalled to Washington by Roosevelt, found on his return a "blaze of hatred" that had to be "seen to be believed." Press Conference #500, Executive Offices of the White House, Nov. 15, 1938; Franklin Delano Roosevelt, Press Conference #500, Executive Office of the White House, Nov. 15, 1938 (Franklin D. Roosevelt Presidential Library & Museum, 491-496, http://www .fdrlibrary.marist.edu/_resources/images/pc/pc0071.pdf).

13. James V. Compton, *The Swastika and the Eagle* (Houghton Mifflin, 1967), 59.

14. Ibid., 57, 60.

15. In a 1934 article, "Shall We Seek World Peace or the Peace of America?," he wrote, "There is very little that can be done to stop an international war," and whatever could be done should be done by the Europeans. Paul Merkley, *Reinhold Niebuhr* (McGill–Queen's University Press, 1975), 131.

16. Alan Brinkley, *The End of Reform: New Deal Liberalism in Recession and War* (Alfred A. Knopf, 1995), 29; Leuchtenburg, *Franklin D. Roosevelt and the New Deal,* 249.

17. "Liberals no longer had effective control of Congress." New Deal reforms were over. Brinkley, *End of Reform,* 102–3.

18. Lerner, *Ideas Are Weapons,* 13–14. Robert Jackson warned that "certain groups of big business have now seized upon a recession in our prosperity to 'liquidate the New Deal' and to throw off all governmental interference with their incorporated initiative." Brinkley, *End of Reform,* 57.

19. The "first principle of sound American statesmanship," Mumford insisted, was refusal to cooperate with "the exploiting classes in England and France" in their appeasement of the fascists. Mumford, *Men Must Act,* 87. Lerner, *Ideas Are Weapons,* 16; Mumford, *Men Must Act,* 89; Lerner, *Ideas Are Weapons,* 9. Niebuhr agreed that it was "perfectly clear that the British Tories will not accept the German challenge until imperial interests are directly imperiled. When that happens they will fight for 'democracy' and not before." Merkley, *Reinhold Niebuhr,* 141–42.

20. Among the peculiar qualities of this letter was that among the signers were John Dewey, Charles A. Beard, and Oswald Garrison Villard, all unwavering opponents of American overseas intervention. The Spanish Civil War, however, had always been an exception for such liberals. "President Urged to Aid Loyalists," *New York Times,* Nov. 11, 1938.

21. Leo P. Ribuffo, *The Old Christian Right: The Protestant Far Right from the Great Depression to the Cold War* (Temple University Press, 1983), 181.

22. Patterson, *Mr. Republican,* 245–46. Although he spoke in the language of "interests," even a sympathetic biographer notes that his "instinctive anti-communism showed that he was more of a moralist about international relations than his cool objections to messianism suggested." Ibid., 249. Lindbergh declared, "I would a hundred times rather see my country ally herself with England, or even with Germany with all her faults, than the cruelty, the Godlessness, and the barbarism that

exists in Soviet Russia." Justus D. Doenecke, *Storm on the Horizon: The Challenge to American Intervention, 1939–1941* (Rowman & Littlefield, 2003), 218–19.

23. Ribuffo, *Old Christian Right,* 15.

24. Elizabeth Dilling, for instance, became famous for naming all the suspected "reds" in the Roosevelt administration and in society at large. She also wrote a book called *The Octopus,* warning of the Jewish threat to America. Christine K. Erickson, " 'I Have Not Had One Fact Disproven': Elizabeth Dilling's Crusade Against Communism in the 1930s," *Journal of American Studies* 36, no. 3, part 1 (December 2002): 473, 489.

25. The driving force behind the institution of the Hays Code governing the content of films was Catholics opposed to the "Hollywood lasciviousness," among other things, which they blamed on Jewish writers, directors, and studio heads. Ribuffo, *Old Christian Right,* 11–13. The powerful head of the Production Code Administration, Joseph Ignatius Breen, was a devout Catholic who had once referred to Jews as "the scum of the earth." Gregory D. Black, *Hollywood Censored: Morality Codes, Catholics, and the Movies* (Cambridge University Press, 1994), 70, 170.

26. Moore, *Know Your Enemy,* 72–73.

27. In 1940 the bulletin of the American Jewish Congress reported that "at no time in American history has anti-Semitism been as strong as it is today." Leonard Dinnerstein, *Anti-Semitism in America* (Oxford University Press, 1994), 123.

28. Pelley traced all of America's problems to the Jews, including the New Deal, which in his eyes represented "the political penetration of a predominantly Christian country and Christian government, by predatory, megalomaniacal Israelites and their agents." Ibid., 112.

29. Although not previously known for being especially hostile to Jews, Coughlin was clearly irked by the overwhelmingly sympathetic treatment they received. On Coughlin's late turn to anti-Semitism, see Alan Brinkley, *Voices of Protest: Huey Long, Father Coughlin, the Great Depression* (Ramdom House, 1982), 272–73.

30. Although the Jews were a tiny fraction of the American population, he observed, they were a "closely woven," "powerful minority," "endowed with an aggressiveness and initiative" which had "carried their sons to the pinnacle of success in journalism, in radio, in finance, in all the sciences and arts." With those "facilities at their disposal," it was no surprise that the story of their fellow Jews' persecution was "so well" and "so thoroughly" told. Father Charles E. Coughlin, "Persecution—Jewish and Christian," radio broadcast, Nov. 20, 1938.

31. Moore, *Know Your Enemy,* 73fn107.

32. Maria Mazzenga, "Condemning the Nazis' 'Kristallnacht': Father Maurice Sheehy, the National Catholic Welfare Conference, and the Dissent of Father Charles Coughlin," *U.S. Catholic Historian* 26, no. 4 (2008): 71–87.

33. Dinnerstein, *Anti-Semitism in America,* 114.

34. Essays on the Jewish "World Program" drew heavily on the tsarist-era anti-Semitic forged document, "The Protocols of the Elders of Zion." The volumes treated such subjects as "The Historic Basis of Jewish Imperialism," "The Scope of Jewish Dictatorship in the U.S.," "Jew Trade Links with World Revolutionaries," and "Will Jewish Zionism Bring Armageddon?"

35. Jews had supposedly formed a "solid ring" around Woodrow Wilson; Jewish "Copper Kings" had profited from the war; and Bernard Baruch, Wilson's chairman of the War Industries Board, had been the "Jewish high governor of the United States." It was no great leap of imagination to believe that Jews were conspiring to bring the United States into another European war. Over the course of the next decade, Ford had several hundred thousand copies of *The International Jew* distrib-

uted, winning the praise of J. P. Morgan and other establishment figures. Ribuffo, *Old Christian Right,* 11–13. There is evidence that Ford's publications influenced not only American but German anti-Semites—Germans revered Ford as the epitome of modern American industrial prowess. Ford was the only American whom Hitler mentioned by name in *Mein Kampf.*

36. Nye, "War Propaganda," Vital Speeches, Sept. 15, 1941, 720–21, quoted in Bill Kauffman, *America First!, Its History, Culture, and Politics* (Prometheus Books, 1995) 86–87.

37. As one prominent Catholic noted, his "utterances stiffened the backs of all those who in one way or another were friendly to Hitler and Mussolini." Dinnerstein, *Anti-Semitism in America,* 119.

38. Ibid., 121.

39. Ibid., 111.

40. More vituperative in his hostility than Coughlin, Winrod he denied opposing Jews "as a race or as a religion" but pled guilty to opposing the "coterie of international Jewish bankers ruling the Gentile world by the power of gold," as well as the power of "international Jewish Communism." He believed that the Great Depression was the work of Satan and that Roosevelt was a "devil" linked to the international Jewish conspiracy, and, like many American conservatives, he believed that Hitler was trying to save Europe from a communist takeover. In Sinclair Lewis's novel *It Can't Happen Here* (1935), a character modeled on Winrod becomes the fascist leader of the United States.

41. The Protestant minister Gerald L. K. Smith, a popular orator and onetime lieutenant of Louisiana governor Huey Long, also spoke to audiences across the country about the threat posed by Jews and their links to communism. Ribuffo, *Old Christian Right,* 121–22.

42. Joe Allen, "It Can't Happen Here?" *International Socialist Review* 87 (January 2013).

43. In Chicago two weeks later, 3,000 protesters stormed another Bund meeting while outside the hall four veterans of the Abraham Lincoln Brigade carrying both American and Spanish Republican flags led the crowd in singing the Internationale. Ibid.

44. Ibid. There was little doubt that the overwhelmingly Irish Catholic New York police force was more in sympathy with those inside the Garden than with the "revolutionaries" outside—more than 400 members of the force belonged to the Christian Front. Dinnerstein, *Anti-Semitism in America,* 121–22.

45. Johnson admitted to his son that he would not say such things in public, because "everybody" was afraid of "offending the Jews." Cole, *Roosevelt & the Isolationists,* 308.

46. Lindbergh expressed sympathy for the Jews' plight and did not blame them for "looking out for what they believe to be their own interests," but Americans also had to "look out for ours." Ribuffo, *Old Christian Right,* 185; Charles Lindbergh, "Des Moines Speech," Sept. 11, 1941. Nye also excused the Jews for their "un-American" views and for losing sight "of what some Americans might call the first interests of America." Quoted in Bill Kauffman, *America First!,* 86–87.

47. Gerald L. K. Smith received financial and other assistance from Ford and other business titans and worked closely with the Republican governor of Ohio, New York congressman Hamilton Fish, and House Republican leader Joseph W. Martin. He enjoyed a "cordial alliance" with Senator Arthur Vandenberg. Ribuffo, *Old Christian Right,* 245.

48. Moore, *Know Your Enemy,* 58. In a column addressed to "a Jewish Friend," she insisted that this was not just a "Jewish crisis," it was "a human crisis." Ibid., 55, 55n, 58.

49. As Cole notes, "Circumstances abroad in 1938–39, however, did provide the president and his party with politically advantageous alternatives at a time when his domestic New Deal program was becoming a serious liability." Cole, *Roosevelt & the Isolationists,* 291.

50. Ibid., 294–95.

51. Roger Daniels, *Franklin D. Roosevelt,* vol. 2, *The War Years, 1939–1945* (University of Illinois Press, 2016), 1.

52. Cole, *Roosevelt & the Isolationists,* 296.

53. Franklin D. Roosevelt, "Message to Congress—The State of the Union," speech, Washington, D.C., Jan. 4, 1939 (Franklin D. Roosevelt Presidential Library & Museum, Master Speech File, Box 43, Speech File 1191B http://www.fdrlibrary .marist.edu/_resources/images/msf/msf01229).

54. Cole, *Roosevelt & the Isolationists,* 304–05; Dallek, *Franklin D. Roosevelt and American Foreign Policy,* 181.

55. Leuchtenburg, *Franklin D. Roosevelt and the New Deal,* 287.

56. Dallek, *Franklin D. Roosevelt and American Foreign Policy,* 180.

57. Hans L. Trefousse, *Germany and American Neutrality, 1939–1941* (Bookman Associates, 1951), 20.

58. Ibid., 20.

59. Ibid., 21.

60. "The Ambassador in France (Bullitt) to the Secretary of State, April 8, 1939," *Foreign Relations of the United States Diplomatic Papers, 1939,* vol. 1, eds. Matilda F. Axton et al. (Government Printing Office, 1956), Document 109.

61. Cole, *Roosevelt & the Isolationists,* 305–06.

62. Ibid., 305 06.

63. Franklin Delano Roosevelt, "Pan American Day Address," speech, April 14, 1939; Franklin D. Roosevelt, "Pan American Day Address," April 14, 1939 (Franklin D. Roosevelt Presidential Library & Museum, Master Speech File, Box 45, Speech File 1215 http://www.fdrlibrary.marist.edu/_resources/images/msf/msf01254).

64. Rock, *Chamberlain and Roosevelt,* 184–85.

65. Hull, *Memoirs of Cordell Hull,* 641–43.

66. Dallek, *Franklin D. Roosevelt and American Foreign Policy,* 183.

67. Rock, *Chamberlain and Roosevelt,* 186.

68. When a furious Cordell Hull invited Borah to read the cables he was receiving from Europe, Borah said he didn't trust State Department reporting: "I have my own sources of information." Hull, *Memoirs of Cordell Hull,* 649–51.

69. Dunn, *1940,* 33.

70. Francis O. Wilcox, "American Government and Politics: The Neutrality Fight in Congress, 1939," *American Political Science Review* 33, no. 5 (October 1939): 823.

71. Charles A. Beard, "We're Blundering into War," *American Mercury,* April 1939, 388–99; C. Hartley Grattan, "No More Excursions! The Defense of Democracy Begins at Home," *Harper's Magazine,* April 1939, 457–65. In the same issue of *Harper's,* Oswald Garrison Villard, posing the question of why Americans believed they were in danger, answered that the "only explanation is that from this field reason has fled." Villard agreed that Roosevelt might get the United States into a war because he "now realizes that the New Deal is stopped." Oswald Garrison Villard, "Wanted: A Sane Defense Policy," *Harper's Magazine,* April 1939, 449–56.

72. Wilcox, "American Government and Politics," 823fn60.
73. Dallek, *Franklin D. Roosevelt and American Foreign Policy,* 187. For a full accounting of the meeting, see Hull, *Memoirs of Cordell Hull,* 641–53.
74. Cole, *Roosevelt & the Isolationists,* 317.
75. Ibid., 315.

Chapter Twenty-One: Blitzkrieg and America's "Great Debate"

1. Whether the latest defeat of neutrality revision spurred Hitler to move quickly against Poland is doubtful, but it certainly relieved any concerns he may have had about the United States and the effect American policy might have on stiffening British spines. As Ribbentrop put it, the "setbacks which Roosevelt's policy had recently suffered in the House of Representatives and in the Senate again threw light on America's doubtful attitude, and Britain was probably hoping for too much if she counted with absolute certainty on the cooperation of the United States in the event of a conflict." Up until the day he invaded Poland, Hitler expected that the British would do nothing, and this assumption was based in part his belief that Americans would not involve themselves, even indirectly. Friedländer, *Prelude to Downfall,* 21–23.
2. Dallek, *Franklin D. Roosevelt and American Foreign Policy,* 197.
3. Handwritten bedside note on the German invasion of Poland (Sept. 1, 1939) (http://www.fdrlibrary.marist.edu/archives/pdfs/docsworldwar.pdf); Charles Edison to Franklin Delano Roosevelt in Elliott Roosevelt, ed., *F.D.R.: His Personal Letters, 1928–1945,* 915–17.
4. Franklin Delano Roosevelt, Press Conference #575, Executive Office of the White House, Sept. 1, 1939 (Franklin D. Roosevelt Presidential Library & Museum, 578-584 http://www.fdrlibrary.marist.edu/_resources/images/pc/pc0086.pdf).
5. Franklin D. Roosevelt "War in Europe," Fireside Chat #14, Sept. 3, 1939 (Franklin D. Roosevelt Presidential Library & Museum, Master Speech File, Box 47, Speech File 1240 http://www.fdrlibrary.marist.edu/archives/collections/franklin/index.php?p=collections/findingaid&id=582).
6. Reynolds, *From Munich to Pearl Harbor,* 45.
7. Ibid., 43–44.
8. Franklin Delano Roosevelt, "On the Arsenal of Democracy," Fireside Chat #16, Dec. 29, 1940 (Franklin D. Roosevelt Presidential Library & Museum, Master Speech File, Box 58, Speech File 1351A http://www.fdrlibrary.marist.edu/_resources/images/msf/msf01403).
9. Franklin D. Roosevelt, "Message to Congress, State of the Union Address," Jan. 3, 1940 (Franklin D. Roosevelt Presidential Library & Museum, Master Speech File, Box 49, Speech File 1262 http://www.fdrlibrary.marist.edu/_resources/images/msf/msf01301).
10. Franklin Delano Roosevelt, "Speech at the University of Virginia," June 10, 1940 (Franklin D. Roosevelt Presidential Library & Museum, Master Speech File, Box 52, Speech File 1285 http://www.fdrlibrary.marist.edu/_resources/images/msf/msf01330).
11. Ibid.
12. Welles, *Time for Decision,* 119–20.
13. "Congress Gives Ovation as He Requests Arms to Smash Invader, 'Must Face Reality,'" *New York Times,* May 16, 1940.
14. Daniels, *Franklin D. Roosevelt,* 2:73.
15. Franklin Delano Roosevelt, "On the Arsenal of Democracy," Fireside Chat #16,

Dec. 29, 1940 (Franklin D. Roosevelt Presidential Library & Museum, Master Speech File, Box 58, Speech File 1351A http://www.fdrlibrary.marist.edu/_resources /images/msf/msf01403).

16. Dallek, *Franklin D. Roosevelt and American Foreign Policy,* 243.

17. Viscount Halifax Lord Lothian, quoted in *The Diaries of Henry Morgenthau, Jr.,* June 17, 1940, 588–589 (Franklin D. Roosevelt Presidential Library & Museum, Master Volume 273 http://www.fdrlibrary.marist.edu/_resources/images/morg/md0366 .pdf; http://www.fdrlibrary.marist.edu/_resources/images/morg/md0367.pdf).

18. William Langer and S. Everett Gleason, *The Challenge to Isolation, 1937–1940: The World Crisis of 1937–1940* (Harper & Brothers, 1952), 568–69; Franklin Delano Roosevelt miscellany in Elliot Roosevelt, ed., *F.D.R.: His Personal Letters, 1928–1945,* 1050–52.

19. Winston Churchill to Franklin Delano Roosevelt in *Roosevelt and Churchill: Their Secret Wartime Correspondence,* eds. Francis L. Loewenheim, Harold D. Langley, and Manfred Jonas (E. P. Dutton, 1975), 106–9.

20. Dunn, *1940,* 181.

21. Franklin Delano Roosevelt, "Formally Opening 1940 Campaign," Philadelphia, Oct. 23, 1940 (Franklin D. Roosevelt Presidential Library & Museum, Master Speech File, Box 54, Speech File 1320, http://www.fdrlibrary.marist.edu/_resources /images/msf/msf01366); Franklin Delano Roosevelt to Robert S. Allen in *F.D.R.: His Personal Letters, 1928–1945,* 1073–74.

22. Franklin Delano Roosevelt, "Campaign Address at Boston, Massachusetts," Boston, Oct. 30, 1940 (Franklin D. Roosevelt Presidential Library & Museum, Master Speech File, Box 55, Speech File 1330A http://www.fdrlibrary.marist.edu /_resources/images/msf/msf01378).

23. James Ramsay Montagu Butler, *Lord Lothian (Philip Kerr)* (Macmillan, 1960), 307.

24. Franklin Delano Roosevelt, Press Conference #702, Executive Office of the White House, Dec. 17, 1940 (Franklin D. Roosevelt Presidential Library & Museum, 698-705 http://www.fdrlibrary.marist.edu/_resources/images/pc/pc0111.pdf); "H.R. 1776 A Bill Further to promote the defense of the United States and for other purposes," (Lend-Lease Bill) dated January 10, 1941, https://www.visitthecapitol.gov/exhibitions /artifact/hr-1776-bill-further-promote-defense-united-states-january-10-1941#:~: text=H.R.-,1776%2C%20A%20Bill%20further%20to%20promote%20the%20 defense%20of%20the,strapped%20nations%20like%20Great%20Britain.

25. See Alexander DeConde, "The South and Isolationism," *Journal of Southern History* 24, no. 3 (August 1958): 341–42.

26. Ibid., 332.

27. Goldman, *Rendezvous with Destiny,* 381.

28. Rochester, *American Liberal Disillusionment,* 148, 168n.

29. As Andrew Preston notes, "German brutality against Jews and Christians particularly moved him. Niebuhr decided that the democracies—Britain and France—might be tainted by imperialism and imperfect democracy, but they were infinitely better than the totalitarian alternatives of fascism, communism, and Nazism." Preston, *Sword of the Spirit,* 306. See also William C. Inboden, "The Prophetic Conflict: Reinhold Niebuhr, Christian Realism, and World War II," *Diplomatic History* 38, no. 1 (January 2014): 49–82. That it was Munich and *Kristallnacht* that turned him around was clear from the timing of his shift. In a 1934 article, "Shall We Seek World Peace or the Peace of America?," he had written that there was "very little that can be done to stop an international war" and that whatever could be done should be done by the Europeans. In early 1938 he was still arguing against the "billion dollar defense budget of the Roosevelt administration," which

he described as the "worst piece of militarism in modern history." Merkley, *Reinhold Niebuhr,* 131, 142.

30. Rochester, *American Liberal Disillusionment,* 81.
31. Goldman, *Rendezvous with Destiny,* 382–83.
32. Henry Luce, "The American Century," *Life,* Feb. 17, 1941.
33. Steel, *Walter Lippmann and the American Century,* 389–90.
34. Rochester, *American Liberal Disillusionment,* 147.
35. David McCullough, *Truman* (Simon & Schuster, 1992), 234. Two years earlier Truman had voted for the strictest version of the Neutrality Act.
36. Reinhold Niebuhr, *Love and Justice: Selections from the Shorter Writings,* ed. D. B. Robertson (Westminster, John Knox Press, 1992), 202–3.
37. Sumner Welles, quoted in Robert A. Divine, *Second Chance: The Triumph of Internationalism in America During World War II* (Atheneum, 1967), 45.
38. Walter Lippmann, "The Atlantic and America," *Life,* April 7, 1941, 87–88. In this article, Lippmann argued that "for their physical security, for the continuation of the free way of life," Americans had to ensure that "the other shore of the Atlantic" would in the future always be under the control of "friendly and trustworthy powers." This fundamental truth, Lippmann argued, which Wilson had understood and acted upon, had been forgotten or deliberately buried in the intervening two decades.
39. Andrew Johnstone, *Against Immediate Evil: American Internationalists and the Four Freedoms on the Eve of World War II* (Cornell University Press, 2014), 5.
40. Ibid., 77.
41. The majority of German Americans, who normally voted Democratic, turned against Roosevelt in both 1940 and 1944. Howard W. Allen, "Isolationism and German-Americans," *Journal of the Illinois State Historical Society* 57, no. 2 (Summer 1964): 143, 149. As one historian has observed, "By far the strongest common characteristic of the isolationist-voting counties" in the United States was "the residence there of ethnic groups with a pro-German or anti-British bias." Samuel Lubell, *The Future of American Politics* (Doubleday, 1956), 145.
42. Republican critics referred disparagingly to Roosevelt's "New Deal foreign policy." Two weeks before Pearl Harbor, the former State Department official William Castle observed to one of the heads of the America First Committee that the United States was being led into war by "New Dealers who see in the war an opportunity to promote their socialist theories." Letter from Castle to Stuart, Nov. 22, 1941, in Justus D. Doenecke, ed., *In Danger Undaunted: The Anti-Interventionist Movement of 1940–1941 as Revealed in the Papers of the America First Committee* (Hoover Institution Press, 1990), 443.
43. Patterson, *Mr. Republican,* 217.
44. The fact that America First worked incessantly to avoid the taint of anti-Semitism reflected the reality that many of its followers were among the more virulent anti-Semites. Although America First is often thought of as representing midwestern middle America or as a populist protest against "elite" foreign policy, America First was itself an elite organization. The seeds of the movement were sown at Yale, the leaders of the movement were corporate heads and advertising executives almost entirely of Protestant Anglo-Saxon backgrounds, and their young followers included such blue bloods as Kingman Brewster and Gore Vidal. As American elites often do, they claimed to be speaking for "real" Americans, but there was little to distinguish the "elites" of America First from the "elites" of the Century Group, which favored early intervention in the war—except their worldview.

45. Ellen Nore, *Charles A. Beard: An Intellectual Biography* (Southern Illinois University Press, 1983), 179. The quotation is from Beard's 1939 book, *Giddy Minds and Foreign Quarrels: An Estimate of American Foreign Policy* (Macmillan, 1937).

46. Hugh R. Wilson, *Diplomat Between Wars* (Longmans, Green and Co., 1941), 269, 283. It was not only the United States that suffered from this proclivity, according to Wilson. He believed that attacks on Nazism in the League of Nations Assembly when Goebbels came for the first time "prepared the ground for Germany's eventual withdrawal from the League and . . . this man of high intelligence was, by this experience, converted into an implacable enemy of the institution." Ibid., 291.

47. Cole, *Roosevelt & the Isolationists*, 507.

48. Grattan, "No More Excursions!," 457–65.

49. George Eliot Fielding, in Osgood, *Ideals and Self-Interest*, 394. On the emergence of this "new realism," see ibid., 391–96.

50. In the weeks following the Munich conference in the fall of 1938, for example, one of the country's best-known military analysts, George Fielding Eliot, concluded, after "a detailed consideration of America's strategic position and military requirements," that American security was not in danger from any European power so long as the United States maintained an adequate navy. Eliot took a similar view of the Asian situation, noting that, given the balance of forces, "a Japanese attack on Hawaii" was a "strategical impossibility." Edward Mead Earle, review of *The Ramparts We Watch: A Study of the Problems of American National Defense* by George Fielding Eliot, in *Political Science Quarterly* 54, no. 1 (March 1939): 98–100.

51. Nicholas J. Spykman, "Geography and Foreign Policy I," *American Political Science Review* 32, no. 1 (February 1938): 29. Nicholas J. Spykman, "Geography and Foreign Policy II," *American Political Science Review* 32, no. 2 (April 1938): 212–13, 222, 233, 226. In 1942, after the attack on Pearl Harbor and the declaration of war by Germany, Spykman wrote, "We, like the British, dream idle dreams of detachment in peace time because there is a little water between us and our neighbors." Nicholas J. Spykman, *America's Strategy in World Politics: The United States and the Balance of Power* (Routledge, 2007), 128. Charles Lindbergh, widely regarded as the world's leading expert on aviation, insisted that, contrary to Roosevelt's warnings, there could be "no invasion by foreign aircraft," nor would any foreign navy "dare to approach within bombing range of our coasts." Dunn, *1940*, 46.

52. "Under fire from bomb and gun, soldiers and heavy equipment would have to be transshipped to small boats from the transports anchored offshore. Then the small boats would have to make a landing through the surf. Once on the hostile beach, the enemy would have to struggle to get their tanks and field pieces off ramp-bowed landing boats onto the beach under shells and machine-gun fire, their only support, their carrier-based aviation and the guns of their warships." Baldwin, *United We Stand: Defense of the Western Hemisphere* (Whittlesey House, McGraw Hill, 1941), 78–79. This, of course, would turn out to be a very good description of the D-Day landing.

53. Clarence Wunderlin, Jr., ed., *The Papers of Robert A. Taft, 1939–1944*, 2 vols. (Kent State University Press, 2001), 2:57.

54. After the Japanese attack on Pearl Harbor in December 1941, it would become an axiom of "realist" foreign policy that, in the words of Robert E. Osgood, "the domination of either Europe or Asia by a hostile and aggressive power would be a disaster for America's hemispheric security." Osgood, *Ideals and Self-Interest*, 411. Roosevelt believed it—as early as February 1939 he warned a group of congressmen that "as soon as one nation dominates Europe, that nation will be able to turn

to the world sphere." Quoted in Stetson Conn and Byron Fairchild, *The Western Hemisphere: Framework of Hemisphere Defense*, vol. 1 (U.S. Army, 1960), 6–8.

55. Lindbergh argued that "regardless of which side" won, "peaceful relationships between America and the countries of Europe" would continue. Dunn, *1940,* 46–47. Taft did not "understand why . . . we could not trade as well with Germany as with England." Ibid., 75–76.

56. Howard K. Beale, *Some Fallacies of the Interventionist View* (Washington, DC, 1941), 7.

57. Breitman and Lichtman, *FDR and the Jews,* 121.

58. Robert A. Taft, in Nancy Schonmaker and Doris Fielding Reid, eds., *We Testify* (Smith and Durrell, 1941), 216–17; Patterson, *Mr. Republican,* 197. The idea that the American people lacked the capacity to play a helpful role was a common realist theme. As Hugh Wilson put it, "Those who believe that the United States should have been on the League argue about the influence we could exert, as if the United States were unanimously in favor of acceptance of responsibility abroad. If we were such people, if we had even a large majority in favor of continuing and persistent effort in world affairs, and if we were willing to accept the risk involved, then, I think, I should have been in favor of our membership. We might then have exerted a genuinely useful influence. But until we become such people, I doubt whether we can collaborate effectively and usefully in any such organization." For that reason he had concluded, even as late as 1941, that "on the whole it was better for Europe and ourselves that we stayed out." Wilson, *Diplomat Between Wars,* 334–35; Moore, *Know Your Enemy,* 65.

59. Doenecke, *Storm on the Horizon,* 241–42. As Baldwin put it, "Somehow, in some way, armies must be put on the Continent," yet the same factors that made it impossible for Germany or any other nation to attack the United States would make it impossible for the United States to attack Germany on the European continent. Baldwin, *United We Stand!,* 47.

60. Instead, he charged, they "always dodge the question of where and how and with what weapons we are going to conquer Hitler." Beale, *Some Fallacies,* 220.

61. In Europe, the core "realist" policy of the 1930s was appeasement. As Neville Chamberlain put it in 1936, "What we require is to divest our diplomacy of cant metaphysics and the jargon of collective security, and to begin talking . . . in the terms of Realpolitik." John Bew, *Realpolitik: A History* (Oxford University Press, 2015), 173. In one of the seminal works of realism, *The Twenty Years' Crisis,* published in 1939, the British diplomat and intellectual E. H. Carr defended Chamberlain's "realist" policies, including the Munich settlement. Jonathan Haslam, *The Vices of Integrity: E. H. Carr 1892–1982* (Verso, 1999), 60, 79. The "change in the European equilibrium of forces" made it "inevitable that Czechoslovakia should lose part of its territory and eventually her independence." Lucian M. Ashworth, "Did the Realist-Idealist Great Debate Really Happen? A Revisionist History of International Relations,"*International Relations* 16, no. 1 (April 2002): 41.

62. Czechoslovakia was, "after all, a central European state," and its "fortunes must in the long run lie with—and not against—the dominant forces in this area." The Munich settlement had at least left "the heart of the country . . . physically intact," Kennan observed at the time, but he apparently did not change his view after Hitler seized the rest of Czechoslovakia a few months later. George F. Kennan, *From Prague After Munich: Diplomatic Papers, 1938–1940* (Princeton University Press, 1968), 4–5.

63. Steel, *Walter Lippmann and the American Century,* 375.

64. Dunn, *1940,* 55.

65. Justus D. Doenecke, *The Battle Against Intervention, 1939–1941* (Krieger, 1997), 15.
66. Moore, *Know Your Enemy,* 65–66.
67. Robert G. Kaufman, "E.H. Carr, Winston Churchill, Reinhold Niebuhr, and Us: The Case for Principled, Prudential, Democratic Realism," in Frankel, ed., *Roots of Realism,* 320.
68. Rochester, *American Liberal Disillusionment,* 114.
69. Kennedy, *Charles A. Beard and American Foreign Policy,* 95. Although more famous for his economic explanation of history, Beard was certainly a realist in his approach to foreign policy. As one biographer notes, Beard's book *The Idea of the National Interest,* published in 1934, was "a sophisticated study that was a precursor to the post–World War II 'realist' school of diplomacy." Kennedy, *Charles A. Beard and American Foreign Policy,* 165.
70. Robert A. Taft, quoted in Patterson, *Mr. Republican,* 245.
71. Ibid., 243.
72. Taft, in *We Testify,* 216–17; Baldwin, *United We Stand!,* 47. Congressman Hamilton Fish blasted those who wanted to "police the world with American blood and treasure." Dunn, *1940,* 58.
73. Doenecke, *Battle Against Intervention,* 25.
74. Ibid. The Germans, Beale argued, would probably regard "Anglo-American 'policing'" much as Germany's victims in Europe now regarded German occupation. Beale did not want an "Anglo-American world imperialism" to replace "a German imperialism." He did not want the United States to "dominate the world." Beale, *Some Fallacies,* 2–3. A decade later, with the Cold War in full swing and American forces deployed all across the globe, Taft was not the only anti-interventionist to reflect that had the United States stayed out of the war and even allowed Hitler to triumph, Americans could not "be any worse off than we are today." Patterson, *Mr. Republican,* 248. Howard K. Beale, in his 1956 biography, also wrote from the perspective that American policies, which he traced back to the first president Roosevelt, had not led to a "better world" but to "the present desperate state of international relations." Beale, *Theodore Roosevelt,* vii.
75. Patterson, *Mr. Republican,* 240.
76. Moore, *Know Your Enemy,* 66 (italics added).
77. Patterson, *Mr. Republican,* 243; Rock, *Chamberlain and Roosevelt,* 186.
78. Cole, *America First,* 32, 91, 30.
79. Ibid., 46.
80. Ibid., 50.
81. Harry Elmer Barnes, "Europe's War and America's Democracy," *Virginia Quarterly Review* 16, no. 4 (Autumn 1940): 558.
82. "If the President intends to involve us in this war," said the Republican Thomas Dewey, "he should say so openly." Daniels, *Franklin D. Roosevelt,* 2:69.
83. Cole, *Roosevelt & the Isolationists,* 468.
84. He made a point of noting to advisers who questioned him that if some other nation attacked the United States, it would not be a "foreign war." Dunn, *1940,* 229.
85. His confidant Harry Hopkins told the British that the president was "a believer in bombing as the only means of gaining a victory." Reynolds, *From Munich to Pearl Harbor,* 153.
86. Doenecke, *Storm on the Horizon,* 244.
87. Cole, *America First,* 165.
88. Ibid., 63.
89. As Wayne Cole observes, Roosevelt "sought Congressional authorization only for those measures for which he could reasonably anticipate the support of a majority

in Congress and in the nation. He could be relied upon to choose no grounds which would give the noninterventionists a serious chance to defeat him. . . . Despite the America First Committee's efforts, the foreign policy debate in 1941 was conducted primarily upon grounds chosen by the President—not simply on the issue of war or peace." Cole, *America First,* 65–67.

90. On the closest ballot, New Englanders voted 73–11 against Taft, while delegates from New York, New Jersey, Maryland, and Delaware voted 121–12. Patterson, *Mr. Republican,* 230.

91. Dunn, *1940,* 257.

92. Roosevelt is often credited with greater political skill in both following and molding public opinion than Wilson showed when he failed to win support for the Versailles Treaty and League of Nations. Although Roosevelt was certainly a more skilled politician, however, he also benefited from a much more favorable political situation.

93. Dunn, *1940,* 265.

Chapter Twenty-Two: Accelerating Toward War

1. Franklin D. Roosevelt, "Maintaining Freedom of the Seas," Fireside Chat #18, Sept.11, 1941 (Franklin D. Roosevelt Presidential Library & Museum, Master Speech File, Box 63, Speech File 1401 http://www.fdrlibrary.marist.edu/_resources /images/msf/msfb0004).

2. Admiral Isoroku Yamamoto, quoted in Pyle, *Japan Rising,* 204.

3. Adolf Hitler, quoted in Compton, *Swastika and the Eagle,* 17.

4. Dallek, *Franklin D. Roosevelt and American Foreign Policy,* 260–64.

5. Ibid.

6. Winston Churchill to Franklin D. Roosevelt in Franklin Delano Roosevelt and Winston Churchill, *Roosevelt and Churchill: Their Secret Wartime Correspondence,* ed. Francis L. Loewenheim et al. (E. P. Dutton, 1975), 132–46; Winston S. Churchill, *The Second World War,* vol. 3, *The Grand Alliance* (Houghton Mifflin, 1950), 101–10, 218–37; Franklin Delano Roosevelt to Winston Churchill in Elliott Roosevelt, ed., *F.D.R.: His Personal Letters, 1928–1945,* 1148–50.

7. Franklin Delano Roosevelt, "On an Unlimited National Emergency," Washington, D.C., May 27, 1941 (Franklin D. Roosevelt Presidential Library & Museum, Master Speech File, Box 60, Speech File 1368A http://www.fdrlibrary.marist.edu /_resources/images/msf/msf01426).

8. Ibid.

9. "The Atlantic Charter," Declaration of Principles issued by the President of the United States and the Prime Minister of the United Kingdom, (Aug. 14, 1941), https://www.nato.int/cps/en/natohq/official_texts_16912.htm; Report by Winston Churchill to War Cabinet, August 19, 1941, CAB 65/19, WM 84 (41), pp. 104–106 http://filestore.nationalarchives.gov.uk/pdfs/large/cab-65-19.pdf.

10. Dallek, *Franklin D. Roosevelt and American Foreign Policy,* 289.

11. Ibid., 286–87.

12. Franklin D. Roosevelt, "Maintaining Freedom of the Seas," Fireside Chat #18, Sept. 11, 1941 (Franklin D. Roosevelt Presidential Library & Museum, Master Speech File, Box 63, Speech File 1401 http://www.fdrlibrary.marist.edu/_resources /images/msf/msfb0004).

13. Ibid.

14. Dallek, *Franklin D. Roosevelt and American Foreign Policy,* 288.

15. *The Public Papers and Addresses of Franklin D. Roosevelt,* 1941 vol., *The Call to Battle Stations,* compiled by Samuel I. Rosenman (New York: Harper, 1950), 438–444, 487–490; Dallek, *Franklin D. Roosevelt and American Foreign Policy,* 291–92.
16. Adolf Hitler, quoted in Compton, *Swastika and the Eagle,* 9–10.
17. Friedländer, *Prelude to Downfall,* 4.
18. As his longtime associate Ernst "Putzi" Hanfstaengl put it, America had "simply been banished from his mind." Compton, *Swastika and the Eagle,* 7–10.
19. Ibid., 5.
20. Ibid., 31.
21. Adolf Hitler, quoted in ibid., 17.
22. Friedländer, *Prelude to Downfall,* 22–23.
23. Hull, *Memoirs of Cordell Hull,* 647–48; Joachim von Ribbentrop, quoted in Friedländer, *Prelude to Downfall,* 22.
24. Ibid., 15–26.
25. Kershaw, *Hitler, 1936–1945,* 178; Friedländer, *Prelude to Downfall,* 15–17.
26. Carl Friedrich von Weizsäcker to Joachim von Ribbentrop, quoted in Friedländer, *Prelude to Downfall,* 35–36.
27. Adolf Hitler, quoted in ibid., 86.
28. Ibid., 43.
29. Hans-Heinrich Dieckhoff, quoted in ibid., 36.
30. Hans-Heinrich Dieckhoff, quoted in ibid., 169.
31. Adolf Hitler to General Alfred Jodl, quoted in ibid., 171.
32. Ibid., 56–58. As the historian Adam Tooze notes, Germany's strategic dilemma in the summer of 1940 was not merely to defeat Britain but "to neutralize Britain before America could intervene decisively on its side. Unleashing the U-boats against the Anglo-American umbilical cord was certainly the most direct approach to this problem. But it was not quick-acting and it was the strategy that bore the highest risk of bringing down upon Germany the full weight of American power." Tooze, *Wages of Destruction,* 400.
33. Holger H. Herwig, "Miscalculated Risks: The German Declaration of War Against the United States, 1917 and 1940," *Naval War College Review* 39, no. 4 (Autumn 1986): 91.
34. Joachim von Ribbentrop to Benito Mussolini, quoted in Friedländer, *Prelude to Downfall,* 88–89.
35. Ibid., 22, 83, 267–68.
36. Adolf Hitler to Benito Mussolini, quoted in ibid., 134.
37. As one Japanese scholar has noted, many Japanese "were confused by a dual and simultaneous capacity of the United States to embrace both realism and idealism." Masato Kimura, "The Zakai's Perception of and Orientation Towards the United States in the 1930s," in *Tumultuous Decade: Empire, Society, and Diplomacy in 1930s Japan,* ed. Masato Kimura and Tosh Minohara (University of Toronto Press, 2013), 5–7, 14.
38. Ibid., 9.
39. Pyle, *Japan Rising,* 191
40. Beasley, *Japanese Imperialism,* 175.
41. Miles Fletcher, "Intellectuals and Fascism in Early Showa Japan," *Journal of Asian Studies* 39, no. 1 (November 1979): 62.
42. Beasley, *Japanese Imperialism,* 175.
43. In 1932, the prime minister was assassinated in an attempted coup ostensibly aimed at "restoring" power to the emperor. In 1936, another coup attempt by young offi-

cers aimed at "restoring direct imperial rule" also failed. In both cases senior military officials put down the rebellions, but in the process expanded their control of the government and gradually dismantled the democratic system.

44. Fletcher, "Intellectuals and Fascism in Early Showa Japan," 39.

45. In 1937, a power shuffle briefly brought an unusually moderate government to power, with a foreign minister who rejected the idea of "a pugnacious foreign policy" and insisted that if Japan walked "the open path straightforwardly," pursued a "fair policy" toward the Chinese, negotiated with Chiang Kai-shek on the basis of equality, gave up trying to detach the northern provinces from the rest of China, and respected the "open door," it could acquire all it needed without a conflict with the United States. The government fell after four months. Crowley, *Japan's Quest for Autonomy*, 316–18.

46. "'Co-prosperity,' signifying an exclusive and unequal economic partnership between China and Japan, became the slogan of the decade." Beasley, *Japanese Imperialism*, 175.

47. Ibid., 175–76.

48. For a discussion of the three principal "factions" in Japan at this time, see Hattori, "Japan's Diplomatic Gamble for Autonomy: Rethinking Matsuoka Yosuke's Diplomacy," in *Tumultuous Decade*, eds. Masato Kimura and Tosh Minohara, 216.

49. Pyle, *Japan Rising*, 191.

50. As the strategy document put it, "to secure command of the Western Pacific," it would be necessary to pursue "a consistent policy of overseas expansion." The new strategy was encapsulated in the phrase "Defend in the north, advance to the south." Crowley, *Japan's Quest for Autonomy*, 286, 290.

51. Akira Iriye, *The Origins of the Second World War in Asia and the Pacific* (Longman, 1987), 38.

52. Kenneth Colegrove, "The New Order in East Asia," *Far Eastern Quarterly* 1, no. 1 (November 1941): 6.

53. As Iriye put it, the pact "signaled Japan's readiness to associate itself with revisionist powers in Europe. . . . Japan was definitely alienating itself from the Washington powers." Iriye, *Origins of the Second World War*, 35.

54. Crowley, *Japan's Quest for Autonomy*, 305.

55. Eighty percent of Japan's oil and gasoline, 60 percent of its machine tools, over 90 percent of its copper, and 75 percent of its scrap iron all had to be purchased from the Americans. Pyle, *Japan Rising*, 201–2.

56. Katsu H. Young, "The Nomonhan Incident: Imperial Japan and the Soviet Union," *Monumenta Nipponica* 22, no. 1/2 (1967): 95–96.

57. Chihiro Hosoya, "Miscalculations in Deterrent Policy: Japanese-U.S. Relations, 1938–1941," *Journal of Peace Research* 5, no. 2 (1968): 100.

58. Dower, *Empire and Aftermath*, 118–19.

59. Ibid., 129.

60. "The Ambassador in Japan (Grew) to the Secretary of State, December 18, 1939," *Foreign Relations of the United States Diplomatic Papers, 1939, The Far East*, vol. 3, eds. Matilda F. Axton et al. (Government Printing Office, 1955), Document 582.

61. Hosoya, "Miscalculations in Deterrent Policy," 102–3.

62. Cohen, *America's Response to China*, 132.

63. Utley, *Going to War with Japan*, 33 (emphasis added).

64. Later critics of Roosevelt's policies would accuse the administration of an absurd and uniquely American "legalism" in citing the defunct treaty. But, of course, American insistence that Tokyo abide by the principles of the Washington treaty was just an excuse for making no concessions.

65. Michael A. Barnhart, *Japan Prepares for Total War: The Search for Economic Security, 1919–1941* (Cornell University Press, 1987), 268–71.

66. Hattori, "Japan's Diplomatic Gamble for Autonomy: Rethinking Matsuoka Yosuke's Diplomacy," in *Tumultuous Decade*, eds. Masato Kimura and Tosh Minohara, 220.

67. Borg, *The United States and the Far Eastern Crisis*, 250–51.

68. Hosoya, "Miscalculations in Deterrent Policy," 97–115 fn33–35.

69. Friedländer, *Prelude to Downfall*, 48–49.

70. Hosoya, "Miscalculations in Deterrent Policy," 106.

71. Barnhart, *Japan Prepares for Total War*, 176–78.

72. Dallek, *Franklin D. Roosevelt and American Foreign Policy*, 274–75.

73. See Iriye, *Across the Pacific*, 195; and Utley: "Japan understood that the United States did not like what it was doing, but it also knew the United States had no intention of doing anything about it." Utley, *Going to War with Japan*, 35.

74. Hotta, *Japan 1941*, 240.

75. Pyle, *Japan Rising*, 204.

76. Hotta, *Japan 1941*, 175.

77. Ibid., 148.

78. "The Ambassador in Japan (Grew) to the Secretary of State, December 27, 1935," *Foreign Relations of the United States Diplomatic Papers, 1935, The Far East*, vol. 3, eds. John G. Reid et al. (Government Printing Office, 1953), Document 825.

79. Hotta, *Japan 1941*, 167.

80. Hotta describes the Yamato spirit as "a supposedly inborn trait that made the Japanese a unique, resilient, disciplined, and hardworking people." Ibid., 168.

81. Barnhart, *Japan Prepares for Total War*, 167.

82. This strategy was easier for both services to agree to in any case because there was something in it for everyone. The army would conduct the move into Indochina and would therefore be allocated the additional resources necessary for that operation. The navy would prepare for the war that might eventuate with the United States, garnering its share of the available resources for that purpose, even as it hoped that no such war would come. And assuming that the United States was not provoked into war, the result would serve everyone's purpose. The compromise nevertheless only papered over the differences between the two services. The army was interested in moving ahead quickly and continued to favor a military alliance with Germany, even at the risk of angering the Americans. For the navy, the number one objective, after ensuring its share of the budget and securing Japan's access to vital resources, remained avoiding war with the United States.

83. Presseisen, *Germany and Japan*, 242–43.

84. Hull, *Memoirs of Cordell Hull*, 895–97.

85. "The Ambassador in Japan (Grew) to the Secretary of State, July 7, 1940," *Foreign Relations of the United States Diplomatic Papers, 1940, The Far East*, vol. 4, eds. John G. Reid et al. (Government Printing Office, 1955), Document 57.

86. Barnhart, *Japan Prepares for Total War*, 158–59; Iriye, *Origins of the Second World War*, 102.

87. Hotta, *Japan 1941*, 54, 129.

88. The government led by former navy minister Mitsumasa Yonai, appointed by Emperor Hirohito in January 1940, had continued the previous Abe government's attempts at a rapprochement with the British and Americans, despite the toughening of China policy, and Yonai, representing the navy's perspective, still opposed an alliance with Germany. Iriye, *Origins of the Second World War*, 116.

89. The new foreign minister was Yosuke Matsuoka, and General Hideki Tojo became

minister of war. All three leaders of the new government were fervent advocates of military alliance with Germany as critical to Japan's future strength and independence.

90. Hotta, *Japan 1941*, 54.
91. Iriye, *Origins of the Second World War*, 116.
92. Hotta, *Japan 1941*, 54.
93. Presseisen, *Germany and Japan*, 242–43.
94. Barnhart, *Japan Prepares for Total War*, 162.
95. "The Ambassador in Japan (Grew) to the Secretary of State, September 5, 1940," *Foreign Relations of the United States Diplomatic Papers, 1940, The Far East*, vol. 4, eds. John G. Reid et al. (Government Printing Office, 1955), Document 1085.
96. Ibid.
97. "The Ambassador in Japan (Grew) to the Secretary of State, September 12, 1940," *Foreign Relations of the United States Diplomatic Papers, 1940, The Far East*, vol. 4, eds. John G. Reid et al. (Government Printing Office, 1955), Document 646.
98. Hotta, *Japan 1941*, 27.
99. Barnhart, *Japan Prepares for Total War*, 219; Hosoya, "Miscalculations in Deterrent Policy," 110.

Chapter Twenty-Three: The United States Enters the War

1. Churchill, *Second World War*, 3:606–8.
2. Barnhart, *Japan Prepares for Total War*, 227.
3. *Foreign Relations of the United States Diplomatic Papers, 1941*, vol. 1, *General, The Soviet Union*, ed. Matilda F. Axton et al. (Government Printing Office, 1959), Document 369.
4. Dallek, *Franklin D. Roosevelt and American Foreign Policy*, 278–79, 294–98.
5. Franklin Delano Roosevelt to Ickes in ibid., 273–74.
6. Barnhart, *Japan Prepares for Total War*, 215.
7. Ibid., 224–25.
8. Hotta, *Japan 1941*, 132–33; Barnhart, *Japan Prepares for Total War*, 168, 224.
9. Hotta, *Japan 1941*, 130–31.
10. Barnhart, *Japan Prepares for Total War*, 212.
11. Ibid., 226–28.
12. Ibid. The Japanese were forced to apply for all purchases on a case-by-case basis, and on a case-by-case basis U.S. officials found reasons to turn them down.
13. Much has been made of the possibility that Roosevelt may not have been fully aware as he departed for his meeting with Churchill just how completely Acheson and his colleagues were going to tighten the screws. In fact, there is no clear evidence that he was uninformed and, even if he was, no reason to believe he disapproved once he learned what was happening. According to Heinrichs, Under Secretary of State Sumner Welles, Roosevelt's closest confidant at the State Department, did know what was happening and was in frequent communication with the president throughout. See Waldo Heinrichs, *Threshold of War: Franklin D. Roosevelt and American Entry into World War II* (Oxford University Press, 1990), 177. Heinrichs goes into great detail regarding the available documentation on this question in a lengthy footnote. See ibid., fn246–47. Acheson's most thorough biographer, Robert L. Beisner, writes that Acheson had Welles's "implicit support" and Roosevelt "looked the other way." See Robert L. Beisner, *Dean Acheson: A Life in the Cold War* (Oxford University Press, 2006), 15. The argument that Acheson acted contrary to Roosevelt's wishes is most virulently put forth by Utley, who charges

Acheson with arrogance, deception, and recklessness. See Utley, *Going to War with Japan,* 154–56. A more measured conclusion is by Dallek, who argues that while Roosevelt did not know how stringently the freeze was being applied, he nevertheless accepted the full embargo when he learned about it. This was, Dallek argues, "one expression of his growing belief that only a firm policy would have an impact on Japan." See Dallek, *Franklin D. Roosevelt and American Foreign Policy,* 275. As a domestic political matter, there were increasing oil shortages in the United States, especially in the East, and people were starting to ask why Japan should get oil when Americans were going without. Ibid.

14. Heinrichs, *Threshold of War,* 123. As Heinrichs notes, the administration had been holding off, but "once Japan's purpose in Indochina became evident in July, the sentiment for oil sanctions became overpowering." Heinrichs, *Threshold of War,* 133.

15. As Barnhart notes, "The decision to freeze Japanese assets was taken in conjunction with other steps designed rigorously to limit Japan's ability to stockpile materials for a forceful advance to the south. These steps were taken in the firm belief that Japan was commencing such an advance and that nothing the United States did or failed to do would shake Tokyo's resolve." Barnhart, *Japan Prepares for Total War,* 264.

16. Heinrichs, *Threshold of War,* 141–42. Dallek, *Franklin D. Roosevelt and American Foreign Policy,* 305. Barnhart observes, "It must be remembered that Washington did not believe it had anything to lose by maintaining the freeze, even after Hull and Roosevelt realized the freeze had hardened into a de facto total embargo . . . all the talk in Washington was of progressively tightening, not loosening, the freeze." Barnhart, *Japan Prepares for Total War,* 264.

17. Nomura came away with "no room for doubt . . . that the President hopes that matters will take a turn for the better." Hull, *Memoirs of Cordell Hull,* 1016–21; "The Secretary of State to the Ambassador in Japan (Grew), August 18, 1941," *Foreign Relations of the United States Diplomatic Papers, 1941, The Far East,* vol. 4, eds. John G. Reid et al. (Government Printing Office, 1956), Document 266.

18. Heinrichs, *Threshold of War,* 75–76.

19. Hull, *Memoirs of Cordell Hull,* 1016–27; Joint Committee on the Investigation of the Pearl Harbor Attack, part 17 (Washington, D.C.: United States Congress, June 1946) 2794-95, S. Con. Res 27, 39th Congress, http://www.ibiblio.org/pha/congress /Vol40.pdf.

20. Hotta, *Japan 1941,* 252.

21. Barnhart, *Japan Prepares for Total War,* 238–39. Contrary to a common view, the embargo did not cause the war with Japan. The Japanese had already determined to make their move for the East Indies oil and other acquisitions in Southeast Asia. The mere fact that the United States could cut off Japan's access to oil and other resources whenever it chose had been the motivating factor for the "total war" officers going back to the 1920s. It was the dependence itself that was intolerable. Japanese leaders knew the "noose" would always be around their neck, whether Roosevelt tugged on it or not, and it was to relieve themselves of this dangerous vulnerability that the Japanese had embarked on the southern strategy in the first place. That Roosevelt finally did what the Japanese always assumed he would do was not the determining factor that led to war. Nor did the oil embargo by itself lead the Japanese to pursue a southern rather than a northern course. That decision, too, had already been made. The surprising success of Soviet resistance in the fall of 1941 had made Russia a less inviting target. Japanese leaders were leaning heavily toward the "southern strategy" before Acheson made it clear they would not be able to get any more oil. What the embargo did do,

however, was speed up the timetable, which was the opposite of what Roosevelt intended.

22. Hotta, *Japan 1941,* 152.

23. Ibid., 152.

24. In early August the government had Nomura transmit a proposed settlement that would keep Japanese troops in China, even after an end to the Sino-Japanese conflict. Chiang Kai-shek would have to recognize Manchukuo officially as no longer part of China. Outside powers would have to end all support for the Chinese and cease their "interference" with Japan's efforts to reach an accord with China. Japanese troops would also not withdraw from Indochina until after the China "incident" was settled, and then the United States would have to recognize Japan's "special status" in Indochina. The Americans and the British could not build additional bases in East Asia nor strengthen existing forces. In return the Japanese would promise not to use Indochina as a base for attack against any countries except China and would guarantee the "neutrality" of the Philippines. As for the Tripartite Pact, the Japanese reserved the right to interpret their obligations as they saw fit. They would not agree to Hull's request that they disavow any intention of attacking the United States if Washington did not declare war on Germany. Hull, *Memoirs of Cordell Hull,* 1028–33.

25. Dallek, *Franklin D. Roosevelt and American Foreign Policy,* 302–3.

26. Nish, *Japanese Foreign Policy, 1869–1942,* 220.

27. Hans-Heinrich Dieckhoff, quoted in Friedländer, *Prelude to Downfall,* 236.

28. Eugen Ott to Hans-Heinrich Dieckhoff, quoted in ibid., 273–74.

29. Gerhard L. Weinberg, *A World at Arms: A Global History of World War II* (Cambridge University Press, 2005), 250–51.

30. Adolf Hitler to Admiral Erich Raeder, quoted in Friedländer, *Prelude to Downfall,* 255.

31. Admiral Erich Raeder, quoted in ibid, 258.

32. J. F. C. Fuller, *The Second World War, 1939–1945: A Strategical and Tactical History* (Duell, Sloan and Pearce, 1949), 117.

33. Friedländer, *Prelude to Downfall,* 202.

34. Ibid., 171.

35. Ibid., 33.

36. Joachim von Ribbentrop to Eugen Ott, quoted in Friedländer, *Prelude to Downfall,* 277–78.

37. Joachim von Ribbentrop to Ambassador Hiroshi Oshima, quoted in ibid., 198.

38. Eugen Ott, quoted in Friedländer, *Prelude to Downfall,* 278–79.

39. Weinberg, *World at Arms,* 250–51.

40. According to Iriye: "Historians have debated whether the summit conference [between Roosevelt and Konoe], had it materialized, would have achieved anything significant and prevented a Japanese-American war. It seems highly unlikely." Iriye, *Origins of the Second World War,* 166. Barnhart concurs: "The requirement that Konoe adhere to the terms of the 4 August liaison conference virtually ensured that a summit, had one been held, would have failed." Barnhart, *Japan Prepares for Total War,* 242.

41. The problem was not one of "misunderstanding." The United States understood "quite well Japan's fundamental foreign policy"; it simply did not accept it. J. Davidann, *Cultural Diplomacy in U.S.-Japanese Relations, 1919–1941* (Palgrave Macmillan, 2016), 207.

42. Barnhart, *Japan Prepares for Total War,* 236.

43. Heinrichs, *Threshold of War,* 183.
44. Ibid., 183.
45. Joint Committee on the Investigation of the Pearl Harbor Attack, part I (Washington, D.C.: United States Congress, June 1946), pp. 260–61, S. Con. Res 27, 39th Congress.
46. Halifax reported to Churchill that "the President had a good deal to say about the great effect that their planting some heavy bombers at the Philippines was expected to have upon the Japs." Halifax to Churchill, Oct. 11, 1941, quoted in Dallek, *Franklin D. Roosevelt and American Foreign Policy,* 303.
47. Heinrichs, *Threshold of War,* 195, 196, 176.
48. Joint Committee on the Investigation of the Pearl Harbor Attack, part 14 (United States Congress, June 1946), pp. 1061–65, S. Con. Res. 27; Roosevelt to Churchill in Roosevelt and Churchill, *Roosevelt and Churchill,* 163–64.
49. Heinrichs, *Threshold of War,* 183.
50. Iriye, *Origins of the Second World War,* 126.
51. Hotta, *Japan 1941.* 105–06.
52. Ibid., 197.
53. Ibid., 191.
54. Ibid., 198.
55. Ibid., 194.
56. Apparently, most people did survive the jump off the famous platform of the Buddhist temple in eastern Kyoto. So it was not quite tantamount to committing suicide.
57. Hotta, *Japan 1941,* 201.
58. Cole, *Roosevelt & the Isolationists,* 498–99.
59. Dallek, *Franklin D. Roosevelt and American Foreign Policy,* 307.
60. Barnhart, *Japan Prepares for Total War,* 250.
61. John T. Kuehn, "The War in the Pacific, 1941–1945," in John Ferris and Evan Mawdsley, eds., *The Cambridge History of the Second World War,* vol. 1, *Fighting the War* (Cambridge University Press, 2015), 424; Kennedy, *Freedom from Fear,* 520–27.
62. Eleanor Roosevelt, *This I Remember* (Harper and Brothers, 1949), 235–36.
63. Churchill, *Second World War,* 606–8.
64. Halifax to Churchill, December 9, 1941, quoted in Dallek, *Franklin D. Roosevelt and American Foreign Policy,* 311–12.

Conclusion

1. Weinberg, *World at Arms,* 317–19.
2. Ibid., 319–20.
3. Pyle, *Japan Rising,* 205.
4. John A. Thompson, *A Sense of Power: The Roots of America's Global Role* (Cornell University Press, 2015), 195.
5. Ibid., 195.
6. Ibid., 196–97.
7. Ibid., 197. Partly this was due to dramatic improvements in American worker productivity.
8. Herwig,"Miscalculated Risks," 97.
9. Jesse H. Stiller, *George Messersmith, Diplomat of Democracy* (University of North Carolina Press, 1987), 80.

10. Churchill made this comment in 1935. William Manchester, *The Last Lion: Winston Spencer Churchill,* vol. 2, *Alone, 1932–1940* (Little, Brown, 1988), 140.

11. Although the America First Committee shut its offices the day after Pearl Harbor, and the anti-interventionists went silent, most never stopped believing that their "principles were right." Cole, *Roosevelt & the Isolationists,* 503–5.

12. Ibid.

13. Mumford, *Men Must Act,* 74–75, 95. It has been a common assumption ever since the Cold War that Nazism did not pose the same kind of global strategic threat that Communism posed. See, for instance, Bruce M. Russett, *No Clear and Present Danger: A Skeptical View of the United States Entry into World War II* (Routledge, 1997), 43. This would have made no sense to 1930s liberals, who did not regard communism as much of a threat at all but certainly regarded fascism as a global threat.

14. Franklin Delano Roosevelt, "Speech at the University of Virginia," June 10, 1940 (Franklin D. Roosevelt Presidential Library & Museum, Master Speech File, Box 52, Speech File 1285 http://www.fdrlibrary.marist.edu/_resources/images/msf/msf01330).

15. Thompson, *Sense of Power,* 158.

16. Gerhard L. Weinberg, *Visions of Victory: The Hopes of Eight World War II Leaders* (Cambridge University Press, 2005), 17–20.

17. Kershaw, *Hitler, 1936–1945,* 462.

18. Weinberg, *Visions of Victory,* 32, 33.

19. See Thompson, *Sense of Power,* for a fine discussion of this issue.

20. For the argument that such ambitions were the motivating factor behind American policy in this period, see Stephen Wertheim, *Tomorrow, the World: The Birth of U.S. Global Supremacy* (Harvard University Press, 2020), 51, 63.

21. Thompson, *Sense of Power,* 146.

22. "In 1920 Russia appeared so weak that the Polish Republic, itself less than two years old, decided that this was the time to invade. . . . When the Soviets marched westward they suffered a crushing defeat outside Warsaw." Tooze, *The Deluge,* 21.

23. Manchester, *Last Lion,* 2:140.

BIBLIOGRAPHY

GDP of U.S. and other major powers

(in billions of 2022 dollars)

	U.S.	UK	France	Germany	Japan
1914	1,018,672	483,934	286,332	431,337	148,260
1919	1,278,031	483,456	232,086	334,031	214,584
1929	1,798,593	536,238	414,241	559,490	253,420
1941	2,344,157	769,504	279,553	855,762	451,049
1945	3,508,513	740,276	217,909	645,185	237,829

Data from Angus Maddison Statistics on World Population, GDP and Per Capita GDP, 1-2008 AD https://web.archive.org/web/20211102093357fw_/http://www.ggdc.net/maddison/Historical_Statistics/vertical-file_02-2010.xls

Adams, C. F. *Works of John Adams.* 10 vols. Little, Brown, 1856.

Adams, Henry., *The Education of Henry Adams.* Houghton Mifflin Company, 1918.

Adams, R. J. Q. *Balfour: The Last Grandee.* Thistle Publishing, 2013.

———. *British Politics and Foreign Policy in the Age of Appeasement, 1935–39.* Macmillan, 1993.

Adler, Selig. *The Isolationist Impulse: Its Twentieth Century Reaction.* Collier Books, 1961.

———. *The Uncertain Giant, 1921–1941.* Macmillan, 1965.

———. "The War-Guilt Question and American Disillusionment, 1918–1928." *Journal of Modern History* 23, no. 1 (March 1951): 1–28.

Ahamed, Liaquat. *Lords of Finance: The Bankers Who Broke the World.* Penguin Press, 2009.

Allen, Frederick Lewis. *Only Yesterday: An Informal History of the 1920s.* Open Road Media, 2015.

Allen, Henry T. *My Rhineland Journal.* Houghton Mifflin Company, 1923.

Allen, Howard W. "Isolationism and German-Americans." *Journal of Illinois State Historical Society* 57, no. 2 (Summer 1964): 143–49.

Allen, Joe. "It Can't Happen Here? Confronting the Fascist Threat in the United States in the 1930s." *International Socialist Review* 87 (Jan. 2013).

Alter, Peter. *The German Question and Europe: A History.* Arnold, 2000.

Ambrosius, Lloyd E. "Wilson, the Republicans, and French Security After World War I." *Journal of American History* 59, no. 2 (Sept. 1972): 341–52.

———. *Wilsonian Statecraft: Theory and Practice of Liberal Internationalism During World War I.* SR Books, 1991.

———. *Wilsonianism: Woodrow Wilson and His Legacy in American Foreign Relations.* Palgrave Macmillan, 2002.

———. "Woodrow Wilson, Alliances, and the League of Nations." *Journal of the Gilded Age and Progressive Era* 5, no. 2 (Apr. 2006): 139–65.

———. *Woodrow Wilson and the American Diplomatic Tradition: The Treaty Fight in Perspective.* Cambridge University Press, 1987.

Angell, Norman. *The Great Illusion: A Study of the Relation of Military Power in Nations to Their Economic and Social Advantage.* G. P. Putnam's Sons, 1910.

Arendt, Hannah. *The Origins of Totalitarianism.* Harcourt, Brace, 1951.

Armstrong, Hamilton Fish. *Peace and Counter-Peace: From Wilson to Hitler.* Harper & Row, 1971.

Arnett, Alex Mathews. *Claude Kitchin and the Wilson War Policies.* Little, Brown, 1937.

Asada, Sadao. "From Washington to London: The Imperial Japanese Navy and the Politics of Naval Limitation, 1921–1930." *Diplomacy and Statecraft* 4, no. 3 (1993): 147–91.

Ashby, LeRoy. *William Jennings Bryan: Champion of Democracy.* Twayne Publishers, 1987.

Ashworth, Lucian M. "Did the Realist-Idealist Debate Really Happen? A Revisionist History of International Relations." *International Relations* 16, no. 1 (2002): 33–51.

Atkinson, Rick. *An Army at Dawn: The War in North Africa, 1942–1943.* Henry Holt, 2002.

Axelrod, Alan. *Selling the Great War: The Making of American Propaganda.* St. Martin's Press, 2009.

Bagby, Wesley. *The Road to Normalcy: The Presidential Campaign and Election of 1920.* Princeton University Press, 1950.

Bailey, Thomas A. *America Faces Russia: Russian-American Relations from Early Times to Our Day.* Cornell University Press, 1950.

———. *Wilson and the Peacemakers.* Macmillan, 1947.

———. *Woodrow Wilson and the Great Betrayal.* Macmillan, 1945.

———. *Woodrow Wilson and the Lost Peace.* Macmillan, 1944.

Baker, Ray Stannard. *Woodrow Wilson and World Settlement.* Doubleday, Page, 1922.

———. *Woodrow Wilson: Life and Letters*, 8 vols. Doubleday, 1931–1946.

Baker, Ray Stannard, and William E. Dodd, eds. *The Public Papers of Woodrow Wilson.* Vol. 5/6, *War and Peace.* Harper & Brothers, 1925.

Balakian, Peter. *The Burning Tigris: The Armenian Genocide and America's Response.* Harper, 2003.

Balderston, Theo. *Economics and Politics in the Weimar Republic.* Cambridge University Press, 2002.

Baldwin, Hanson Weightman. *United We Stand!: Defense of the Western Hemisphere.* Whittlesey House, McGraw Hill, 1941.

Balfour, Michael. *The Kaiser and His Times.* Houghton Mifflin, 1964.

Barnes, Harry Elmer. "Europe's War and America's Democracy." *Virginia Quarterly Review* 16, no. 4 (Autumn 1940): 552–62.

———. *History and Social Intelligence.* Alfred A. Knopf, 1926.

Barnett, Correlli. *The Collapse of British Power.* Prometheus Books, 1986.

Barnhart, Michael. *Japan Prepares for Total War: The Search for Economic Security, 1919–1941.* Cornell University Press, 1987.

Barron, Gloria J. *Leadership in Crisis: FDR and the Path to Intervention.* Kennikat Press, 1973.

Barrow, Clyde. *More Than a Historian: The Political and Economic Thought of Charles A. Beard.* Routledge, 2017.

Bartlett, Ruhl Jacob. *The League to Enforce Peace.* University of North Carolina Press, 1944.

Bassett, John Spencer. *Expansion and Reform, 1889–1926.* Hassell Street Press, 2021.

Baumgart, Winfried. *Imperialism: The Idea and Reality of British and French Colonial Expansion, 1880–1914.* Oxford University Press, 1982.

Beale, Howard K., ed. *Charles A. Beard.* University of Kentucky Press, 1954.

———. *Theodore Roosevelt and the Rise of America to World Power.* Johns Hopkins University Press, 1956.

———. *Theodore Roosevelt and the Rise of America to World Power.* Collier, 1962.

Beard, Charles A. *American Foreign Policy, 1932–1940: A Study in Responsibilities.* Archon Books, 1968.

———. *Contemporary American History, 1877–1913 (1914).* Kessinger Publishing, 2010.

———. *The Devil Theory of War: An Inquiry into the Nature of History and the Possibility of Keeping Out of War.* Praeger, 1969.

———. *Giddy Minds and Foreign Quarrels.* Macmillan, 1937.

Beard, Charles A., and Mary Ritter Beard. *The Rise of American Civilization.* Macmillan, 1927.

Beasley, W. G. *Japanese Imperialism, 1894–1945.* Clarendon Press, 1991.

Becker, William H. *The Dynamics of Business-Government Relations: Industry and Exports, 1893–1921.* University of Chicago Press, 1981.

Beisner, Robert L., ed. *American Foreign Relations Since 1600: A Guide to the Literature.* ABC-CLIO, 2003.

———. *Dean Acheson: A Life in the Cold War.* Oxford University Press, 2006.

———. *From the Old Diplomacy to the New: 1865–1900.* Wiley-Blackwell, 1986.

———. *Twelve Against Empire: The Anti-Imperialists, 1898–1900.* McGraw-Hill, 1968.

Bell, David A. *The First Total War: Napoleon's Europe and the Birth of Warfare as We Know It.* Houghton Mifflin, 2007.

Bell, P. M. H. *France and Britain, 1900–1940: Entente and Estrangement.* Longman, 1996.

Bell, Peter. *Chamberlain, Germany, and Japan, 1933–4.* St. Martin's Press, 1996.

Beloff, Max. *Britain's Liberal Empire, 1897–1921.* Palgrave Macmillan, 1987.

———. *The Foreign Policy of Soviet Russia, 1929–1941.* Oxford University Press, 1949.

Bender, Thomas. *A Nation Among Nations: America's Place in World History.* Hill and Wang, 2006.

Benjamin, Jules R. *The United States and the Origins of the Cuban Revolution: An Empire of Liberty in an Age of National Liberation.* Princeton University Press, 1990.

Berg, A. Scott. *Wilson.* Putnam, 2013.

———, ed. *World War I and America: Told by the Americans Who Lived It.* Library of America, 2017.

Berger, Henry. *A William Appleman Williams Reader: Selections from His Major Historical Writings.* Ivan R. Dee, 1992.

Berghahn, Volker R. *Germany and the Approach of War in 1914.* Bedford St. Martins, 1993.

———. *Imperial Germany, 1871–1918: Economy, Society, Culture and Politics.* Berghahn Books, 2005.

Bernard, Philippe, and Henri Dubief. *The Decline of the Third Republic, 1914–1938.* Translated by Thony Forster. Cambridge University Press, 1988.

Bessel, Richard, ed. *Fascist Italy and Nazi Germany: Comparisons and Contrasts.* Cambridge University Press, 1996.

————. *Germany After the First World War.* Clarendon Press, 1993.

Best, Gary Dean. *To Free a People: American Jewish Leaders and the Jewish Problem in Eastern Europe, 1890–1914.* Greenwood Press, 1982.

Beveridge, Albert J. *The Russian Advance.* Harper & Brothers, 1903.

Birnbaum, Karl E. *Peace Moves and U-Boat Warfare: A Study in Imperial Germany's Policy Towards the United States, April 18, 1916–January 9, 1917.* Archon Books, 1970.

Bishop, Joseph Bucklin. *Theodore Roosevelt and His Time: Shown in His Own Letters.* 2 vols. Charles Scribner's Sons, 1920.

Black, Conrad. *Franklin Delano Roosevelt: Champion of Freedom.* PublicAffairs, 2003.

Black, Gregory D. *Hollywood Censored: Morality Codes, Catholics, and the Movies.* Cambridge University Press, 1994.

Blackbourn, David. *History of Germany, 1780–1918: The Long Nineteenth Century* Blackwell, 2002.

Blackbourn, David, and Geoff Eley. *The Peculiarities of German History: Bourgeois Society and Politics in Nineteenth-Century Germany.* Oxford University Press, 1984.

Blum, John Morton. *Joe Tumulty and the Wilson Era.* Shoe String Press, 1969.

————. *Roosevelt and Morgenthau.* Houghton Mifflin, 1970.

————. *The Republican Roosevelt.* Harvard University Press, 1954.

Boemeke, Manfred F., Gerald D. Feldman, and Elisabeth Glaser, eds. *The Treaty of Versailles: A Reassessment After 75 Years.* German Historical Institute and Cambridge University Press, 1998.

Bohlen, Charles E. *Witness to History, 1929–1969.* W. W. Norton, 1973.

Bond, Jon R., and Richard Fleisher. *The President in the Legislative Arena.* University of Chicago Press, 1990.

Borg, Dorothy. *American Policy and the Chinese Revolution, 1925–1928.* Octagon Books, 1968.

————. *The United States and the Far Eastern Crisis of 1933–1938: From the Manchurian Incident Through the Initial Stage of the Undeclared Sino-Japanese War.* Harvard University Press, 1964.

Borg, Dorothy, and Shumpei Okamoto, eds. *Pearl Harbor as History: Japanese-American Relations, 1931–1941.* Columbia University Press, 1973.

Bosworth, R. J. B. *Mussolini.* Arnold, 2002.

Bourgeois, Emile. *History of Modern France, 1815–1913.* Palala Press, 2015.

Bourne, Kenneth. *Britain and the Balance of Power in North America, 1815–1908.* University of California Press, 2020.

Bourne, Randolph Silliman. *War and the Intellectuals: Essays, 1915–1919.* Harper & Row, 1964.

Bowers, Claude G. *Beveridge and the Progressive Era.* Riverside Press, 1932.

Bracher, Karl Dietrich. *The German Dictatorship: The Origins, Structure, and Effects of National Socialism.* Praeger Publishers, 1970.

Braeman, John. *Albert J. Beveridge: American Nationalist.* University of Chicago Press, 1971.

Braisted, William Reynolds. *The United States Navy in the Pacific, 1897–1909.* University of Texas Press, 1958.

Brandenburg, Erich. *From Bismarck to the World War: A History of German Foreign Policy, 1870–1914.* Translated by Annie Elizabeth Adams. Howard Fertig, 1997. First published 1927 by Oxford University Press.

Brands, H. W. *American Colossus: The Triumph of Capitalism, 1865–1900.* Anchor, 2011.

————. *Bound to Empire: The United States and the Philippines.* Oxford University Press, 1992.

———. *T.R.: The Last Romantic.* Basic Books, 1998.

———. *Woodrow Wilson.* Times Books, 2003.

Breitman, Richard, and Allan J. Lichtman. *FDR and the Jews.* Belknap Press of Harvard University Press, 2013.

Bridge, F. R. *From Sadowa to Sarajevo: The Foreign Policy of Austria-Hungary, 1.* Routledge and Kegan Paul, 1972.

Brinkley, Alan. *The End of Reform: New Deal Liberalism in Recession and War.* Alfred A. Knopf, 1995.

———. *Voices of Protest: Huey Long, Father Coughlin, & the Great Depression.* Random House, 1982.

Brodsky, Alyn. *Grover Cleveland: A Study in Character.* Truman Talley Books, 2000.

Brundage, David. *Irish Nationalists in America: The Politics of Exile, 1798–1998.* Oxford University Press, 2016.

Bryce, James. *The American Commonwealth: The National Government.* MacMillan and Co., 1891.

Buehrig, Edward H. *Woodrow Wilson and the Balance of Power.* Indiana University Press, 1955.

Buhite, Russell D. *Nelson T. Johnson and American Policy Toward China, 1925–1941.* Michigan State University Press, 1968.

Buhle, Paul M., and Edward Rice-Maximin. *William Appleman Williams: The Tragedy of Empire.* Routledge, 1995.

Bullitt, William C. *The Great Globe Itself: A Preface to World Affairs.* Charles Scribner's Sons, 1946.

Burks, David D. "The United States and the Geneva Protocol of 1924: 'A New Holy Alliance'?" *American Historical Review* 64, no. 4 (July 1959): 891–905.

Burton, David H. *Taft, Wilson, and World Order.* Associated University Presses, 2003.

———. *Theodore Roosevelt, American Politician: An Assessment.* Fairleigh Dickinson University Press, 1997.

———. *William Howard Taft: Confident Peacemaker.* St. Joseph's University Press, 2004.

Bury, J. P. T. *France, 1814–1940.* Routledge, 2003.

Butler, James Ramsay Montagu. *Lord Lothian (Philip Kerr).* Macmillan, 1960.

Butler, Susan. *Roosevelt and Stalin: Portrait of a Partnership.* Vintage, 2016.

Cain, P. J., and A. G. Hopkins. *British Imperialism, 1688–2000.* Longman, 2001.

Calhoun, Charles W. *Gilded Age Cato: The Life of Walter Q. Gresham.* University Press of Kentucky, 1988.

Calhoun, Frederick S. *Power and Principle: Armed Intervention in Wilsonian Foreign Policy.* Kent State University Press, 1986.

———. *Uses of Force and Wilsonian Foreign Policy.* Kent State University Press, 1993.

Calleo, David P. *The German Problem Reconsidered: Germany and the World Order, 1870 to the Present.* Cambridge University Press, 1978.

Cameron, Nigel. *Barbarians and Mandarins: Thirteen Centuries of Western Travelers in China.* University of Chicago Press, 1976.

Campbell, A. E. *America Comes of Age: The Era of Theodore Roosevelt.* American Heritage Press, 1971.

———. *Great Britain and the United States, 1895–1903.* Longmans, 1960.

Campbell, Charles S., Jr. *Anglo-American Understanding, 1898–1903.* Johns Hopkins University Press, 1957.

———. *The Transformation of American Foreign Relations, 1865–1900.* Harper & Row, 1976.

Cantril, Hadley. "America Faces the War: A Study in Public Opinion." *Public Opinion Quarterly* 4, no. 3 (September 1940): 387–407.

Caquet, P. E. *The Bell of Treason: The 1938 Munich Agreement in Czechoslovakia.* Profile Books, 2018.

Carpenter, Ronald H. *Father Charles E. Coughlin: Surrogate Spokesman for the Disaffected.* Greenwood Press, 1998.

Carr, Edward Hallett. *The Twenty Years' Crisis, 1919–1939: An Introduction to the Study of International Relations.* Perennial, 2001.

Carter, John. *Conquest—America's Painless Imperialism.* Harcourt, Brace, 1929.

Carter, Purvis M. *Congressional and Public Reaction to Wilson's Caribbean Policy, 1913–1917.* Vantage Press, 1977.

Case, Josephine Young, and Everett Needham Case. *Owen D. Young and American Enterprise: A Biography.* David R. Godine, 1986.

Casey, Steven. *Cautious Crusade: Franklin D. Roosevelt, American Public Opinion, and the War Against Nazi Germany.* Cambridge University Press, 2001.

Cashman, Sean Dennis. *America in the Age of the Titans: The Progressive Era and World War I.* New York University Press, 1988.

———. *America in the Gilded Age: From the Death of Lincoln to the Rise of Theodore Roosevelt.* New York University Press, 1993.

———. *America in the Twenties and Thirties: The Olympian Age of Franklin Delano Roosevelt.* New York University Press, 1989.

Castle, Alfred L. *Diplomatic Realism: William R. Castle, Jr., and American Foreign Policy, 1919–1953.* University of Hawaii Press, 1998.

Charmley, John. *Chamberlain and the Lost Peace.* Hodder & Stoughton, 1989.

———. *Splendid Isolation? Britain, the Balance of Power, and the Origins of the First World War.* Hodder & Stoughton, 1999.

Chernow, Ron. *The House of Morgan: An American Banking Dynasty and the Rise of Modern Finance.* Atlantic Monthly Press, 1990.

Cherny, Robert W. *A Righteous Cause: The Life of William Jennings Bryan.* University of Oklahoma Press, 1994.

Chickering, Roger. *Imperial Germany and the Great War, 1914–1918.* Cambridge University Press, 2004.

Chickering, Roger, et al., eds. *A World at Total War: Global Conflict and the Politics of Destruction, 1937–1945.* Cambridge University Press, 2013.

Child, Clifton James. *The German-Americans in Politics, 1914–1917.* University of Wisconsin Press, 1939.

Chrystal, William G. "Reinhold Niebuhr and the First World War." *Journal of Presbyterian History* 55, no. 3 (Fall 1977): 285–98.

Churchill, Winston. *The Second World War.* Vol. 1, *The Gathering Storm.* Houghton Mifflin, 1948.

———. *The Second World War.* Vol. 3, *The Grand Alliance.* Houghton Mifflin, 1950.

———. *The World Crisis.* 5 vols. Charles Scribner's Sons, 1923–1931.

Clark, Christopher M. *The Sleepwalkers: How Europe Went to War in 1914.* Harper, 2013.

Cleaver, Charles G. "Frank B. Kellogg's View of History and Progress." *Minnesota History* 35, no. 4 (December 1956): 157–66.

Clements, Kendrick A. *William Jennings Bryan: Missionary Isolationist.* University of Tennessee Press, 1983.

———. "Woodrow Wilson and World War I." *Presidential Studies Quarterly* 34, no. 1 (March 2004): 62–82.

———. *Woodrow Wilson, World Statesman.* Twayne, 1987.

Cline, Howard Francis. *The United States and Mexico.* Harvard University Press, 1967.

Clymer, Kenton J. *John Hay: The Gentleman as Diplomat.* University of Michigan Press, 1975.

Cohen, Warren I. *American Revisionists: The Lessons of Intervention in World War One.* University of Chicago Press, 1967.

———. *America's Response to China: A History of Sino-American Relations.* Columbia University Press, 1990.

———. *Empire Without Tears: America's Foreign Relations, 1921–1933.* Alfred A. Knopf, 1987.

———. *The New Cambridge History of American Foreign Relations: Challenges to American Primacy, 1945 to the Present.* Cambridge University Press, 2015.

———, ed. *Pacific Passage.* Columbia University Press, 1996.

Cohrs, Patrick O. *The Unfinished Peace After World War I: America, Britain and the Stabilisation of Europe, 1919–1932.* Cambridge University Press, 2006.

Cole, Wayne S. *America First: The Battle Against Intervention, 1940–1941.* Octagon Books, 1971.

———. *Charles A. Lindbergh and the Battle Against American Intervention in World War II.* Harcourt Brace Jovanovich, 1974.

———. *An Interpretive History of American Foreign Relations.* Dorsey Press, 1974.

———. *Roosevelt & the Isolationists, 1932–45.* University of Nebraska Press, 1983.

———. *Senator Gerald P. Nye and American Foreign Relations.* University of Minnesota Press, 1962.

Colegrove, Kenneth. "The New Order in East Asia." *Far Eastern Quarterly* 1, no. 1 (November 1941): 5–24.

Coletta, Paolo E. *The Presidency of William Howard Taft.* University Press of Kansas, 1973.

———, ed. *Threshold to American Internationalism: Essays on the Foreign Policies of William McKinley.* Exposition Press, 1970.

———. *William Jennings Bryan.* 3 vols. University of Nebraska Press, 1964–1969.

Collin, Richard H., ed. *Theodore Roosevelt and Reform Politics.* Heath, 1972.

———. *Theodore Roosevelt, Culture, Diplomacy, and Expansion: A New View of American Imperialism.* Louisiana State University Press, 1985.

———. *Theodore Roosevelt's Caribbean: The Panama Canal, the Monroe Doctrine, and the Latin American Context.* Louisiana State University Press, 1990.

Collins, Doreen. *Aspects of British Politics, 1904–1919.* Elsevier, 1965.

Combs, Jerald A. *American Diplomatic History: Two Centuries of Changing Interpretations.* University of California Press, 1983.

Compton, James V. *The Swastika and the Eagle: Hitler, the United States, and the Origins of World War II.* Houghton Mifflin, 1967.

Conn, Stetson, and Byron Fairchild. *The Framework of Hemisphere Defense.* U.S. Army, 1960.

Conquest, Robert. *The Great Terror: Stalin's Purge of the Thirties.* Macmillan, 1968.

Coogan, John W. *The End of Neutrality: The United States, Britain, and Maritime Rights, 1899–1915.* Cornell University Press, 1981.

Coolidge, Archibald Cary. *The United States as a World Power.* Macmillan, 1908.

Cooper, John Milton, Jr. *Breaking the Heart of the World: Woodrow Wilson and the Fight for the League of Nations.* Cambridge University Press, 2001.

———. *The Vanity of Power: American Isolationism and the First World War, 1914–1917.* Greenwood Press, 1969.

———. *The Warrior and the Priest: Woodrow Wilson and Theodore Roosevelt.* Belknap Press of Harvard University Press, 1983.

———. *Woodrow Wilson: A Biography.* Alfred A. Knopf, 2009.

Cooper, Sandi E. *Patriotic Pacifism: Waging War on War in Europe, 1815–1914.* Oxford University Press, 1991.

Cordery, Stacy A. *Theodore Roosevelt: In the Vanguard of the Modern.* Wadsworth, 2002.

Costigliola, Frank. *Awkward Dominion: American Political, Economic, and Cultural Relations with Europe, 1919–1933.* Cornell University Press, 1984.

———. *Roosevelt's Lost Alliances: How Personal Politics Helped Start the Cold War.* Princeton University Press, 2012.

Costigliola, Frank, and Michael J. Hogan, eds. *America in the World: The Historiography of American Foreign Relations Since 1941.* Cambridge University Press, 2013.

Couvares, Francis G., et al. *Interpretations of American History: Patterns & Perspectives: Through Reconstruction.* Bedford/St. Martin's, 2008.

Craig, Gordon A. *Germany, 1866–1945.* Oxford University Press, 1980.

Craig, Gordon A., and Felix Gilbert, eds. *The Diplomats, 1919–1939.* Vol. 2, *The Thirties.* Atheneum 41B, 1963.

Craig, Gordon A., and Francis L. Loewenheim, eds. *The Diplomats, 1939–1979.* Princeton University Press, 1994.

Crane, Daniel, and Thomas A. Breslin. *An Ordinary Relationship: American Opposition to the Republican Revolution in China.* University Press of Florida, 1986.

Crichton, Judy. *America 1900: The Turning Point.* Holt Paperbacks, 2000.

Crowley, James Buckley. *Japan's Quest for Autonomy: National Security and Foreign Policy, 1930–1938.* Princeton University Press, 2016.

Current, Richard N. *Secretary Stimson: A Study in Statecraft.* Rutgers University Press, 1954.

Curti, Merle. *American Philanthropy Abroad: A History.* Rutgers University Press, 1963.

———. *Peace or War: The American Struggle, 1636–1936.* Angell Press, 2007.

Dallek, Robert. *Franklin D. Roosevelt and American Foreign Policy, 1932–1945.* Oxford University Press, 1979.

———. *Harry S. Truman.* The American Presidents Series, edited by Arthur M. Schlesinger, Jr., and Sean Wilentz. Times Books, 2008.

Dalton, Kathleen. *Theodore Roosevelt: A Strenuous Life.* Alfred A. Knopf, 2002.

Daniels, Roger. *Franklin D. Roosevelt.* Vol. 1, *Road to the New Deal, 1882–1939.* University of Illinois Press, 2015.

———. *Franklin D. Roosevelt.* Vol. 2, *The War Years, 1939–1945.* University of Illinois Press, 2016.

Darby, Phillip. *Three Faces of Imperialism: British and American Approaches to Asia and Africa, 1870–1970.* Yale University Press, 1987.

Daughton, J. P. *An Empire Divided: Religion, Republicanism and the Making of French Colonialism, 1880–1914.* Oxford University Press, 2006.

Davidann, Jon Thares. *Cultural Diplomacy in U.S.-Japanese Relations, 1919–1941.* Palgrave MacMillan, 2007.

Davies, Joseph E. *Mission to Moscow.* Garden City Publishing, 1943.

Davis, Joseph S. *The World Between the Wars, 1919–1939: An Economist's View.* Johns Hopkins University Press, 1975.

Davis, Kenneth S. *FDR: Into the Storm 1937–1940: A History.* Random House, 1993.

Davis, Norman H. "American Foreign Policy: A Democratic View." *Foreign Affairs,* September 1924.

Davis, Richard Harding. *Soldiers of Fortune.* Broadview Press, 2006.

Dawes, Charles G. *A Journal of Reparations.* Macmillan, 1939.

———. *Notes as Vice President, 1928–1929.* Little, Brown, 1935.

Dawley, Alan. *Changing the World: American Progressives in War and Revolution.* Princeton University Press, 2005.

DeBenedetti, Charles. "Borah and the Kellogg-Briand Pact." *Pacific Northwest Quarterly* 63, no. 1 (January 1972): 22–29.

———. *Origins of the Modern American Peace Movement, 1915–1929.* KTO Press, 1978.

———. *The Peace Reform in American History.* Indiana University Press, 1984.

DeConde, Alexander. *Ethnicity, Race, and American Foreign Policy: A History.* University Press of New England, 1992.

———. *A History of American Foreign Policy.* Scribner, 1963.

———. "The South and Isolationism." *Journal of Southern History* 24, no. 3 (August 1958): 332–46.

de Grazia, Victoria. *Irresistible Empire: America's Advance Through Twentieth-Century Europe.* Belknap Press of Harvard University Press, 2005.

De Santis, Vincent P. *The Shaping of Modern America, 1877–1916.* Allyn and Bacon, 1973.

Dehio, Ludwig. *Germany and World Politics in the Twentieth Century.* Chatto & Windus, 1959.

Dennett, Tyler. *Roosevelt and the Russo-Japanese War.* Doubleday, Page, 1925.

Dennis, Alfred L. P. *Adventures in American Diplomacy, 1896–1906.* Dutton, 1928.

Department of State. *Foreign Relations of the United States, 1915.* Vol. 2, 1928.

———. *Foreign Relations of the United States, 1918.* Vol. 1, 1930.

———. *Foreign Relations of the United States, 1919.* Vol. 13, 1947.

———. *Foreign Relations of the United States, 1921.* Vol. 1, 1936.

———. *Foreign Relations of the United States, 1922.* Vol. 2, 1938.

———. *Foreign Relations of the United States, 1933.* Vol. 3, 1949.

———. *Foreign Relations of the United States, 1935.* Vol. 3, 1953.

———. *Foreign Relations of the United States, 1937.* Vol. 3, 1954.

———. *Foreign Relations of the United States, 1940.* Vol. 4, 1955.

———. *Foreign Relations of the United States, 1941.* Vol. 1, 1959.

———. *Foreign Relations of the United States, 1941.* Vol. 4, 1956.

Department of the Army. *Correspondence Relating to the War with Spain Including the Insurrection in the Philippine Islands and the China Relief Expedition.* Government Printing Office, 1902.

Deutscher, Isaac. *The Prophet Armed: Trotsky, 1879–1921.* Oxford University Press, 1954.

Devine, Michael J. *John W. Foster: Politics and Diplomacy in the Imperial Era, 1873–1917.* Ohio University Press, 1981.

Devlin, Patrick. *Too Proud to Fight: Woodrow Wilson's Neutrality.* Oxford University Press, 1974.

DeWitt, Petra. *Degrees of Allegiance: Harassment and Loyalty in Missouri's German-American Community During World War I.* Ohio University Press, 2012.

Diggins, John P. *Max Weber: Politics and the Spirit of Tragedy.* Basic Books, 1996.

———. *Mussolini and Fascism: The View from America.* Princeton University Press, 1972.

———. *The Rise and Fall of the American Left.* W. W. Norton, 1992.

Diner, Steven J. *A Very Different Age: Americans of the Progressive Era.* Macmillan, 1998.

Dingman, Roger. *Power in the Pacific: The Origins of Naval Arms Limitation, 1914–1922.* University of Chicago Press, 1976.

Dinnerstein, Leonard. *Anti-Semitism in America.* Oxford University Press, 1994.

Divine, Robert A. *Foreign Policy and U.S. Presidential Elections, 1952–1960.* New Viewpoints, 1974.

———. *The Illusion of Neutrality.* University of Chicago Press, 1962.

———. *Second Chance: The Triumph of Internationalism in America During World War II.* Atheneum, 1967.

Dobson, John M. *America's Ascent: The United States Becomes a Great Power, 1880–1914*. Northern Illinois University Press, 1978.

———. *Reticent Expansionism: The Foreign Policy of William McKinley*. Duquesne University Press, 1988.

Doenecke, Justus D. *The Battle Against Intervention, 1939–1941*. Krieger, 1997.

———, ed. *In Danger Undaunted: The Anti-Interventionist Movement of 1940–1941 As Revealed in the Papers of the America First Committee*. Hoover Institution Press, 1990.

———. *Nothing Less Than War: A New History of America's Entry into World War I*. University Press of Kentucky, 2011.

———. *Storm on the Horizon: The Challenge to American Intervention, 1939–1941*. Rowman & Littlefield, 2003.

———. *When the Wicked Rise: American Opinion-Makers and the Manchurian Crisis of 1931–1933*. Associated University Presses, 1984.

Doenecke, Justus D., and John E. Wilz. *From Isolation to War, 1931–1941*. Wiley-Blackwell, 2015.

Doerr, Paul W. *British Foreign Policy, 1919–1939*. Manchester University Press, 1998.

Doerries, Reinhard. *Imperial Challenge: Ambassador Count Bernstorff and German-American Relations, 1908–1917*. University of North Carolina Press, 1989.

Doherty, Gabriel, and Dermot Keogh, eds. *1916: The Long Revolution*. Mercier Press, 2008.

Domínguez, José. *Cuba: Order and Revolution*. Belknap Press of Harvard University Press, 1978.

Dorwart, Jeffrey M. *The Pigtail War: American Involvement in the Sino-Japanese War of 1894–1895*. University of Massachusetts Press, 1975.

Dower, John W. *Empire and Aftermath: Yoshida Shigeru and the Japanese Experience, 1878–1954*. Harvard University Press, 1988.

———. *Japan in War and Peace: Selected Essays*. The New Press, 1995.

Drake, Richard. *The Education of an Anti-imperialist: Robert La Follette and U.S. Expansion*. University of Wisconsin Press, 2013.

Dubin, Martin David. "Elihu Root and the Advocacy of a League of Nations, 1914–1917." *Western Political Quarterly* 19, no. 3 (September 1966): 439–55.

Dulles, Foster Rhea. *America's Rise to World Power, 1898–1954*. Harper & Brothers, 1955.

Dunn, Dennis J. *Caught Between Roosevelt & Stalin: America's Ambassadors to Moscow*. University Press of Kentucky, 1998.

Dunn, Susan. *1940: FDR, Willkie, Lindbergh, Hitler—the Election amid the Storm*. Yale University Press, 2013.

Duroselle, Jean-Baptiste. *France and the Nazi Threat: The Collapse of French Diplomacy, 1932–1939*. Translated by Catherine E. Dop and Robert L. Miller. Enigma Books, 2004.

Dyer, Thomas G. *Theodore Roosevelt and the Idea of Race*. Louisiana State University Press, 1980.

Earle, Edward Mead. "Review of 'The Ramparts We Watch: A Study of the Problems of American National Defense.'" *Political Science Quarterly* 54, no. 1 (March 1939): 98–100.

———. *Turkey, the Great Powers, and the Bagdad Railway: A Study in Imperialism*. Russell & Russell, 1966.

Egerton, George W. *Great Britain and the Creation of the League of Nations: Strategy, Politics, and International Organization, 1914–1919*. University of North Carolina Press, 1978.

Eggert, Gerald G. *Richard Olney: Evolution of a Statesman*. Penn State University Press, 1991.

Einstein, Lewis. *A Diplomat Looks Back.* Edited by Lawrence E. Gelfand. Yale University Press, 1968.

———. *A Prophecy of the War, 1913–1914.* Sagwan Press, 2015.

Eliot, George Fielding. *The Ramparts We Watch: A Study of the Problems of American National Defense.* Reynal & Hitchcock, 1938.

Ellis, L. Ethan. *Republican Foreign Policy, 1921–1933.* Rutgers University Press, 1968.

Engerman, Stanley, and Robert E. Gallman, eds. *The Cambridge Economic History of the United States.* 3 vols. Cambridge University Press, 1996–2000.

Erickson, Christine K. "'I Have Not Had One Fact Disproven': Elizabeth Dilling's Crusade Against Communism in the 1930s." Part 1. *Journal of American Studies* 36, no. 3 (December 2002): 473–89.

Esthus, Raymond A. *Double Eagle and Rising Sun: The Russians and Japanese at Portsmouth in 1905.* Duke University Press, 1988.

———. *Theodore Roosevelt and the International Rivalries.* Ginn-Blaisdell, 1970.

———. *Theodore Roosevelt and Japan.* University of Washington Press, 1966.

Etkind, Alexander. *Roads Not Taken: An Intellectual Biography of William C. Bullitt.* University of Pittsburgh Press, 2017.

Evans, David C., and Mark R. Peattie. *Kaigun: Strategy, Tactics, and Technology in the Imperial Japanese Navy, 1887–1941.* Naval Institute Press, 1997.

Evans, Hiram Wesley. "The Klan's Fight for Americanism." *North American Review* 223, no. 830 (May 1962): 33–63.

Evans, Richard J. *The Pursuit of Power: Europe, 1815–1914.* Viking, 2016.

———. *The Coming of the Third Reich.* Penguin Press, 2005.

———. *The Third Reich in History and Memory.* Little, Brown, 2015.

Eyck, Erich. *A History of the Weimar Republic.* Vol. 1, *From the Collapse of the Empire to Hindenburg's Election.* Translated by Harlan P. Hanson and Robert G. L. Waite. Harvard University Press, 1962.

———. *A History of the Weimar Republic.* Vol. 2, *From the Locarno Conference to Hitler's Seizure of Power.* Translated by Harlan P. Hanson and Robert G. L. Waite. Harvard University Press, 1962.

Farber, David R. *The Rise and Fall of Modern American Conservatism: A Short History.* Princeton University Press, 2010.

Farnham, Barbara Rearden. *Roosevelt and the Munich Crisis: A Study of Political Decision-Making.* Princeton University Press, 2000.

Farwell, Byron. *Over There: The United States in the Great War, 1917–1918.* W. W. Norton, 2000.

Feilitzsch, Heribert von. *The Secret War on the United States in 1915: A Tale of Sabotage, Labor Unrest, and Border Troubles.* Henselstone Verlag, 2015.

Feis, Herbert. *Europe: The World's Banker, 1870–1914.* W. W. Norton, 1965.

———. *The Road to Pearl Harbor: The Coming of the War Between the United States and Japan.* Princeton University Press, 1950.

Ferguson, Niall. *The House of Rothschild.* Viking, 1998.

———. *The Pity of War.* Penguin Press, 1998.

Ferrell, Robert H. *American Diplomacy in the Great Depression: Hoover-Stimson Foreign Policy, 1929–1933.* Yale University Press, 1957.

———. *Peace in Their Time: The Origins of the Kellogg-Briand Pact.* Franklin Classics, 2018. First published in 1952 by Yale University Press.

———. *The Presidency of Calvin Coolidge.* University Press of Kansas, 1998.

———. *Woodrow Wilson & World War I, 1917–1921.* Harper & Row, 1985.

Field, James A., Jr. "American Imperialism: The Worst Chapter in Almost Any Book." *The American Historical Review* 83, no. 3 (June 1978): 644–68.

Fieldhouse, D. K. *The Colonial Empires: A Comparative Survey from the Eighteenth Century*. Delacorte Press, 1967.

————. *Economics and Empire, 1830–1914*. Weidenfeld and Nicolson, 1973.

Fifield, Russell H. *Woodrow Wilson and the Far East: The Diplomacy of the Shantung Question*. Crowell, 1952.

Fischer, Fritz. *Germany's Aims in the First World War*. W. W. Norton, 1968.

Fischer, Klaus P. *Hitler & America*. University of Pennsylvania Press, 2011.

————. *Nazi Germany: A New History*. Continuum, 1995.

Fish, Carl Russell. *American Diplomacy*. Henry Holt, 1938.

Fish, Hamilton. *FDR: The Other Side of the Coin; How We Were Tricked into World War II*. Vantage Press, 1976.

Fitzgerald, John. *Awakening China: Politics, Culture, and Class in the Nationalist Revolution*. Stanford University Press, 1998.

Fleming, Denna Frank. *The United States and the League of Nations, 1918–1920*. G. P. Putnam's Sons, 1932.

————. *The United States and World Organization, 1920–1933*. Columbia University Press, 1938.

Fleming, Thomas J. *The Illusion of Victory: America in World War I*. Basic Books, 2003.

————. *The New Dealers' War: Franklin D. Roosevelt and the War Within World War II*. Basic Books, 2001.

Fletcher, Miles. "Intellectuals and Fascism in Early Showa Japan." *Journal of Asian Studies* 39, no. 1 (Nov. 1979): 39–63.

Flood, Charles Bracelen. *Hitler: The Path to Power*. Houghton Mifflin, 1989.

Foner, Philip Sheldon. *The Spanish-Cuban-American War and the Birth of American Imperialism, 1895–1902*. Monthly Review Press, 1972.

Forcey, Charles. *The Crossroads of Liberalism: Croly, Weyl, Lippmann and the Progressive Era, 1900–1925*. Oxford University Press, 1961.

Foster, John F. *A Century of American Diplomacy: Being a Brief Review of the Foreign Relations of the United States, 1776–1876*. Forgotten Books, 2017.

Fox, Richard Wightman. *Reinhold Niebuhr*. Cornell University Press, 1996.

Freeman, Joseph, and Scott Nearing. *Dollar Diplomacy: A Study in American Imperialism*. Literary Licensing, 2011.

Freidel, Frank. *Franklin D. Roosevelt*. 4 vols. Little, Brown, 1952–1973.

————. *Franklin D. Roosevelt: A Rendezvous with Destiny*. Little, Brown, 1990.

Friedberg, Aaron L. *The Weary Titan: Britain and the Experience of Relative Decline, 1895–1905*. Princeton University Press, 2010.

Friedländer, Saul. *Prelude to Downfall: Hitler and the United States, 1939–1941*. Alfred A. Knopf, 1965.

Fritz, Stephen. *The First Soldier: Hitler as Military Leader*. Yale University Press, 2018.

Fromkin, David. *A Peace to End All Peace: The Fall of the Ottoman Empire and the Creation of the Modern Middle East*. Henry Holt, 1989.

Frothingham, Thomas. *The Naval History of the World War: The Stress of Sea Power, 1915–1916*. Harvard University Press, 1925.

————. *The Naval History of the World War: United States in the War, 1917–1918*. Harvard University Press, 1927.

Fulbrook, Mary. *A History of Germany, 1918–2020: The Divided Nation*. Wiley-Blackwell, 2021.

Fung, Edmund S. K. *The Intellectual Foundations of Chinese Modernity: Cultural and Political Thought in the Republican Era*. Cambridge University Press, 2010.

————. "The Sino-British Rapprochement, 1927–1931." *Modern Asian Studies* 17, no. 1 (1983): 79–105.

Gabaccia, Donna R. *Foreign Relations: American Immigration in Global Perspective.* Princeton University Press, 2015.

Gaddis, John Lewis. *George F. Kennan: An American Life.* Penguin Press, 2011.

Gardner, Lloyd C. *Imperial America: American Foreign Policy Since 1898.* Harcourt Brace Jovanovich, 1976.

———, ed. *Redefining the Past: Essays in Diplomatic History in Honor of William Appleman Williams.* Oregon State University Press, 1986.

———. *Safe for Democracy: The Anglo-American Response to Revolution, 1913–1923.* Oxford University Press, 1984.

Gardner, Lloyd C., Walter F. LaFeber, and Thomas J. McCormick. *Creation of the American Empire.* Vol. 1, *U.S. Diplomatic History to 1901.* Rand McNally & Co., 1976.

Garraty, John A. *Henry Cabot Lodge: A Biography.* Alfred A. Knopf, 1953.

Gatzke, Hans W. *Germany's Drive to the West: A Study of Germany's Western War Aims During the First World War.* Johns Hopkins University Press, 1963.

———. *European Diplomacy Between Two Wars, 1919–1939.* Quadrangle Books, 1972.

———. *Stresemann and the Rearmament of Germany.* Literary Licensing, 2012.

Gay, Peter. *Weimar Culture: The Outsider as Insider.* Harper & Row, 1970.

Gelfand, Lawrence Emerson. *Essays on the History of American Foreign Relations.* Holt, Rinehart and Winston, 1971.

Gellately, Robert. *Lenin, Stalin, and Hitler: The Age of Social Catastrophe.* Alfred A. Knopf, 2007.

Gellman, Irwin F. *Roosevelt and Batista: Good Neighbor Diplomacy in Cuba, 1933–1945.* University of New Mexico Press, 1973.

Gerstle, Gary. *American Crucible: Race and Nation in the Twentieth Century.* Princeton University Press, 2017.

Gilbert, Martin. *Churchill and America.* Free Press, 2005.

———. *The First World War: A Complete History.* Holt, 2004.

———. *Winston S. Churchill: The Challenge of War, 1914–1916.* Houghton Mifflin Harcourt, 1971.

Gilbert, Martin, and Richard Gott. *The Appeasers.* Phoenix, 2000.

Gilderhus, Mark T. *Diplomacy and Revolution: U.S.-Mexican Relations Under Wilson and Carranza.* University of Arizona Press, 1977.

———. *Pan American Visions: Woodrow Wilson in the Western Hemisphere, 1913–1921.* University of Arizona Press, 1986.

Ginger, Ray. *Altgeld's America: The Lincoln Ideal Versus Changing Realities.* Quadrangle Books, 1965.

———. *The Bending Crisis: A Biography of Eugene V. Debs.* Rutgers University Press, 1947.

Glad, Betty. *Charles Evans Hughes and the Illusions of Innocence: A Study in American Diplomacy.* University of Illinois Press, 1966.

———. *Key Pittman: The Tragedy of a Senate Insider.* Columbia University Press, 1986.

Glad, Paul W. *McKinley, Bryan, and the People.* J. B. Lippincott, 1964.

———. *The Trumpet Soundeth: William Jennings Bryan and His Democracy, 1896–1912.* University of Nebraska Press, 1960.

Goemans, H. E., and Mark Fey. "Risky but Rational: War as an Institutionally Induced Gamble." *Journal of Politics* 71, no. 1 (January 2009): 35–54.

Goldstein, Erik. *The First World War Peace Settlements, 1919–1925.* Longman, 2002.

———. *Winning the Peace: British Diplomatic Strategy, Peace Planning, and the Paris Peace Conference, 1916–1920.* Clarendon Press, 1991.

Goldstein, Erik, and John H. Maurer, eds. *The Washington Conference, 1921–22: Naval Rivalry, East Asian Stability and the Road to Pearl Harbor.* F. Cass, 1994.

Gollwitzer, Heinz. *Europe in the Age of Imperialism, 1880–1914.* Edited by Geoffrey Barraclough. W. W. Norton, 1979.

Goodman, Grant Kohn. *Imperial Japan and Asia: A Reassessment.* Columbia University Press, 1967.

Gordon, Linda. *The Second Coming of the KKK: The Ku Klux Klan of the 1920s and the American Political Tradition.* Liveright, 2017.

Gordon, Peter Eli, and John P. McCormick, eds. *Weimar Thought: A Contested Legacy.* Princeton University Press, 2013.

Gould, Lewis L. *The Presidency of Theodore Roosevelt.* University Press of Kansas, 1991.

———. *The Presidency of William McKinley.* Regents Press of Kansas, 1980.

———. *The Progressive Era.* Syracuse University Press, 1974.

———. *The Spanish-American War and President McKinley.* University Press of Kansas, 1982.

Gould, Lewis L., and Courtney Q. Shah. *America in the Progressive Era, 1890–1917.* Routledge, 2021.

Graebner, Norman A. "Hoover, Roosevelt, and the Japanese." In *Pearl Harbor as History: Japanese-American Relations 1931–1941,* edited by Dorothy Borg and Shumpei Okamoto, 25–52. Columbia University Press, 1973.

———. *Ideas and Diplomacy: Readings in the Intellectual Tradition of American Foreign Policy.* Oxford University Press, 1964.

———. *Traditions and Values: American Diplomacy, 1865–1945.* University Press of America, 1985.

Graebner, Norman A., and Edward M. Bennett, eds. *The Versailles Treaty and Its Legacy: The Failure of the Wilsonian Vision.* Cambridge University Press, 2011.

Grattan, C. Hartley. "No More Excursions! The Defense of Democracy Begins at Home." *Harper's Magazine,* April 1939, 457–65.

Green, Michael. *By More than Providence: Grand Strategy and American Power in the Asia Pacific Since 1783.* Columbia University Press, 2017.

Gregory, Ross. *The Origins of American Intervention in the First World War.* W. W. Norton, 1971.

Grenville, John A. S. *Lord Salisbury and Foreign Policy: The Close of the Nineteenth Century.* Athlone Press, 1970.

Grenville, John A. S., and George Berkeley Young. *Politics, Strategy, and American Diplomacy: Studies in Foreign Policy, 1873–1917.* Yale University Press, 1966.

Grew, Joseph C. *Ten Years in Japan.* Simon & Schuster, 1944.

———. *Turbulent Era: A Diplomatic Record of Forty Years, 1904–1945.* Houghton Mifflin, 1952.

Grey of Fallodon, Viscount [Edward]. *Twenty-Five Years, 1892–1916.* 2 vols. Frederick A. Stokes, 1925.

Griswold, Alfred Whitney. *The Far Eastern Policy of the United States.* Yale University Press, 1938.

Gwynn, Stephen, ed. *The Letters and Friendships of Sir Cecil Spring Rice.* 2 vols. Houghton Mifflin, 1929.

Haberman, Arthur. *1930: Europe in the Shadow of the Beast.* Wilfrid Laurier University Press, 2018.

Hagan, Kenneth J. *This People's Navy: The Making of American Sea Power.* Free Press, 1991.

Hahn, Peter L., and Mary Ann Heiss, eds. *Empire and Revolution: The United States and the Third World Since 1945.* Ohio State University Press, 2017.

Hale, Oron J. *The Great Illusion, 1900–1914.* Harper & Row, 1971.

Haley, P. Edward. *Revolution and Intervention: The Diplomacy of Taft and Wilson with Mexico, 1910–1917.* MIT Press, 1970.

Halle, Louis J. *American Foreign Policy: Theory and Reality.* G. Allen & Unwin, 1960.

———. *Dream and Reality: Aspects of American Foreign Policy.* Greenwood Press, 1973.

Hamilton, Alexander. *Camillus.* In vol. 5, *The Works of Alexander Hamilton,* edited by Henry Cabot Lodge. J. F. Trow, 1850.

Hamilton, Richard F. *President McKinley, War and Empire: President McKinley and America's New Empire.* Routledge, 2007.

Hamilton, Richard F., and Holger H. Herwig. *Decisions for War, 1914–1917.* Cambridge University Press, 2004.

Hampton, Mary N. *The Wilsonian Impulse: U.S. Foreign Policy, the Alliance, and German Unification.* Praeger, 1996.

Hanebrink, Paul. *A Specter Haunting Europe: The Myth of Judeo-Bolshevism.* Belknap Press of Harvard University Press, 2018.

Hanfstaengl, Ernst. *Unheard Witness.* J. B. Lippincott, 1957.

Harbaugh, William Henry. *Lawyer's Lawyer: The Life of John W. Davis.* Oxford University Press, 1973.

———. *Power and Responsibility: The Life and Times of Theodore Roosevelt.* Octagon Books, 1975.

Hardach, Karl. *The Political Economy of Germany in the Twentieth Century.* University of California Press, 1980.

Harrington, Fred Harvey. "Literary Aspects of American Anti-Imperialism, 1898–1902." *New England Quarterly* 10, no. 4 (December 1937): 650–67.

Hart, Bradley W. *Hitler's American Friends: The Third Reich's Supporters in the United States.* Thomas Dunne Books, 2018.

Hart, Liddell. *The Defence of Britain: England in September 1939.* Random House, 1939.

Haslam, Jonathan. *The Spectre of War: International Communism and the Origins of World War II.* Princeton University Press, 2021.

Hastings, Max. *Catastrophe 1914: Europe Goes to War.* Alfred A. Knopf, 2013.

Hathaway, Oona A., and Scott Shapiro. *The Internationalists: How a Radical Plan to Outlaw War Remade the World.* Simon & Schuster, 2017.

Hawley, Josh. *Theodore Roosevelt: Preacher of Righteousness.* Yale University Press, 2008.

Hays, Samuel P. *The Response to Industrialism, 1885–1914.* University of Chicago Press, 1957.

Heald, Morrell. *Culture and Diplomacy: The American Experience.* Praeger, 1977.

Healy, David F. *Drive to Hegemony: The United States in the Caribbean, 1898–1917.* University of Wisconsin Press, 1988.

———. *Gunboat Diplomacy in the Wilson Era: The U.S. Navy in Haiti, 1915–1916.* University of Wisconsin Press, 1976.

———. *The United States in Cuba, 1898–1902: Generals, Politicians, and the Search for Policy.* University of Wisconsin Press, 1963.

———. *US Expansionism: The Imperialist Urge in the 1890s.* University of Wisconsin Press, 1970.

Heaton, John L. *Cobb of "The World": A Leader in Liberalism* F. P. Dutton, 1924.

Heinrichs, Waldo H., Jr. "The Role of the United States Navy." In *Pearl Harbor as History: Japanese-American Relations, 1931–1941,* edited by Dorothy Borg and Shumpei Okamoto. Columbia University Press, 1973.

———. *Threshold of War: Franklin D. Roosevelt and American Entry into World War II.* Oxford University Press, 1988.

Heinrichs, Waldo H., Marc Gallicchio, and Jonathan G. Utley, eds. *Diplomacy and Force: America's Road to War, 1931–1941.* Imprint Publications, 1996.

Henig, Ruth B. *Versailles and After, 1919–1933.* Methuen, 1984.

Herbert Hoover Reassessed: Essays Commemorating the Fiftieth Anniversary of the Inauguration of Our Thirty-First President. Collected and with a foreword by Mark O. Hatfield. Introduction by Arthur S. Link. University Press of the Pacific, 2002.

Herman, Arthur. *Freedom's Forge.* Random House, 2012.

———. *1917: Lenin, Wilson, and the Birth of the New World Disorder.* Harper, 2017.

Herman, Sondra R. *Eleven Against War.* Hoover Institution Press, 1969.

Herman, Sondra, Manfred Jonas, Robert A. Divine, Walter LaFeber, Richard D. McKinzie, and Theodore A. Wilson. "Internationalism as a Current in the Peace Movement: A Symposium." *American Studies* 13, no. 1 (Spring 1972): 189–209.

Herring, George C. *From Colony to Superpower: U.S. Foreign Relations Since 1776.* Oxford University Press, 2011.

Herrmann, David G. *The Arming of Europe and the Making of the First World War.* Princeton University Press, 1997.

Hertzberg, Arthur. *The Jews in America: Four Centuries of an Uneasy Encounter: A History.* Simon & Schuster, 1980.

Herwig, Holger H. "Miscalculated Risks: The German Declaration of War Against the United States, 1917 and 1940." *Naval War College Review* 39, no. 4 (Autumn 1986): 88–100.

Higham, John. *Strangers in the Land: Patterns of American Nativism, 1860–1925.* Rutgers University Press, 2002.

Hildebrand, Klaus. *The Foreign Policy of the Third Reich.* Translated by Anthony Fothergill. University of California Press, 1973.

Hill, Howard C. *Roosevelt and the Caribbean.* Hunt Press, 2008.

Hillgruber, Andreas. *Germany and the Two World Wars.* Translated by William C. Kirby. Harvard University Press, 1982.

Hinsley, F. H. *British Foreign Policy Under Sir Edward Grey.* Cambridge University Press, 2008.

Hitchman, James H. *Leonard Wood and Cuban Independence, 1898–1902.* Springer, 1971.

Hitler, Adolf. *Hitler's Second Book: The Unpublished Sequel to Mein Kampf.* Edited by Gerhard L. Weinberg. Enigma Books, 2006.

———. *Mein Kampf.* 1925; Houghton Mifflin, 1999.

Hobsbawm, Eric. *The Age of Empire: 1875–1914.* Vintage, 1989.

Hobson, John Atkinson. *Imperialism: A Study.* Hassell Street Press, 2021.

Hochschild, Adam. *Spain in Our Hearts: Americans in the Spanish Civil War, 1936–1939.* Houghton Mifflin Harcourt, 2016.

———. *To End All Wars.* Mariner Books, 2012.

Hodgson, Godfrey. *The Colonel: The Life and Wars of Henry Stimson, 1867–1950.* Alfred A. Knopf, 1990.

———. *Woodrow Wilson's Right Hand: The Life of Colonel Edward M. House.* Yale University Press, 2006.

Hofstadter, Richard. *The Age of Reform from Bryan to F.D.R.* Alfred A. Knopf, 1955.

———. *The American Political Tradition: And the Men Who Made It.* Vintage, 1989.

———. *The Paranoid Style in American Politics and Other Essays.* Harvard University Press, 1996.

———. *Social Darwinism in American Thought.* Beacon Press, 1992.

Hofstadter, Richard, and Warren Chappell. *The Progressive Historians: Turner, Beard, Parrington.* Alfred A. Knopf, 1968.

Hogan, Michael J., ed. *The Ambiguous Legacy: U.S. Foreign Relations in the "American Century."* Cambridge University Press, 1999.

Hogan, Michael J., and Thomas G. Paterson, eds. *Explaining the History of American Foreign Relations.* Cambridge University Press, 2004.

Hoganson, Kristin L. *Fighting for American Manhood: How Gender Politics Provoked the Spanish-American and Philippine-American Wars.* Yale University Press, 1998.

Holbo, Paul S. "The Convergence of Moods and the Cuban-Bond 'Conspiracy' of 1898." *Journal of American History* 55, no. 1 (June 1968): 54–72.

Holland, James. *The Rise of Germany, 1939–1941.* Vol. 1 of *The War in the West.* Atlantic Monthly Press, 2015.

Hollingsworth, Rogers. *The Whirligig of Politics.* University of Chicago Press, 1963.

Holmes, James R. *Theodore Roosevelt and World Order: Police Power in International Relations.* Potomac Books, 2006.

Holt, James. *Congressional Insurgents and the Party System, 1909–1916.* Harvard University Press, 1967.

Holt, W. Stull. *Treaties Defeated by the Senate: A Study of the Struggle Between President and Senate over the Conduct of Foreign Relations.* Johns Hopkins Press, 1933.

Hoover, Herbert. *The Ordeal of Woodrow Wilson.* McGraw-Hill, 1958.

Horne, John, and Alan Kramer. *German Atrocities 1914: A History of Denial.* Yale University Press, 2009.

Hosoya, Chihiro. "Miscalculations in Deterrent Policy: Japanese-U.S. Relations, 1938–1941." *Journal of Peace Research* 5, no. 2 (1968): 97–115.

Hotta, Eri. *Japan 1941: Countdown to Infamy.* Alfred A. Knopf, 2013.

House, Edward Mandell. *The Intimate Papers of Colonel House.* Edited by Charles Seymour. 4 vols. Houghton Mifflin, 1926–1928.

———. *What Really Happened at Paris: The Story of the Peace Conference, 1918–1919.* Charles Scribner's Sons, 1921.

Howard, Christopher H. D. *Splendid Isolation: A Study of Ideas Concerning Britain's International Position and Foreign Policy During the Later Years of the Third Marquis of Salisbury.* Macmillan, 1967.

Howard, Michael. *The Continental Commitment: The Dilemma of British Defence Policy in the Era of the Two World Wars.* Ashfield Press, 1989.

Howlett, Charles F. *Troubled Philosopher: John Dewey and the Struggle for World Peace.* Kennikat Press, 1977.

Hoyer, Katja. *Blood and Iron: The Rise and Fall of the German Empire, 1871–1918.* History Press, 2021.

Hull, Cordell. *The Memoirs of Cordell Hull.* Macmillan, 1948.

Hull, Isabel V. *Absolute Destruction: Military Culture and the Practices of War in Imperial Germany.* Cornell University Press, 2005.

Hunt, Michael H. *Crises in U.S. Foreign Policy: An International History Reader.* Yale University Press, 1996.

———. *Ideology and U.S. Foreign Policy.* Yale University Press, 2009.

———. *The Making of a Special Relationship: The United States and China to 1914.* Columbia University Press, 1983.

Hyam, Ronald. *Britain's Declining Empire: The Road to Decolonisation, 1918–1968.* Cambridge University Press, 2007.

———. *Britain's Imperial Century, 1815–1914: A Study of Empire and Expansion.* Palgrave Macmillan, 2016.

Immerwahr, Daniel. *How to Hide an Empire: A History of the Greater United States.* Farrar, Straus and Giroux, 2019.

Inboden, William C. "The Prophetic Conflict: Reinhold Niebuhr, Christian Realism, and World War II." *Diplomatic History* 38, no. 1 (January 2014): 49–82.

Ingram, Edward. *The British Empire as a World Power: Ten Studies.* Routledge, 2001.

Iriye, Akira. *Across the Pacific: An Inner History of American–East Asian Relations.* Harcourt, Brace & World, 1967.

———. *After Imperialism: The Search for a New Order in the Far East, 1921–1931.* Harvard University Press, 1965.

———. *The Cambridge History of American Foreign Relations: The Globalizing of America, 1913–1945.* Cambridge University Press, 1993.

———. *China and Japan in the Global Setting.* Harvard University Press, 1998.

———. *Cultural Internationalism and World Order.* Johns Hopkins University Press, 1997.

———. *From Nationalism to Internationalism: US Foreign Policy to 1914.* Routledge and Kegan Paul, 1977.

———, ed. *Mutual Images: Essays in American-Japanese Relations.* Harvard University Press, 1975.

———. *The Origins of the Second World War in Asia and the Pacific.* Longman, 1987.

———. *Pacific Estrangement: Japanese and American Expansion, 1897–1911.* Harvard University Press, 1972.

Israel, Jerry. *Progressivism and the Open Door: America and China, 1905–1921.* University of Pittsburgh Press, 1971.

Jackson, J. Hampden. *Clemenceau and the Third Republic.* English Universities Press, 1965.

Jackson, Julian. *The Politics of Depression in France, 1932–1936.* Cambridge University Press, 1985.

———. *The Popular Front in France: Defending Democracy, 1934–1938.* Cambridge University Press, 1988.

Jacobson, Jon. *Locarno Diplomacy: Germany and the West, 1925–1929.* Princeton University Press, 2016.

Jacobson, Matthew Frye. *Barbarian Virtues: The United States Encounters Foreign Peoples at Home and Abroad, 1876–1917.* Hill and Wang, 2001.

James, D. Clayton, and Anne Sharp Wells. *America and the Great War: 1914–1920.* Wiley-Blackwell, 1997.

James, Lawrence. *The Rise and Fall of the British Empire.* St. Martin's Press, 1996.

James, William. *The Moral Equivalent of War, and Other Essays: And Selections from Some Problems of Philosophy.* Edited by John Roth. Harper & Row, 1971.

Jansen, Marius B. *Japan and China: From War to Peace, 1894–1972.* Rand McNally, 1975.

———. *The Making of Modern Japan.* Belknap Press of Harvard University Press, 2000.

Jeansonne, Glenn. *Gerald L. K. Smith: Minister of Hate.* Louisiana State University Press, 1997.

Jeffers, H. Paul. *Colonel Roosevelt: Theodore Roosevelt Goes to War, 1897–1898.* Wiley, 1996.

Jenkins, Roy. *Churchill: A Biography.* Farrar, Straus, Giroux, 2001.

Jessup, Philip C. *Elihu Root.* 2 vols. Dodd, Mead, 1938.

Johnson, Robert David. *The Peace Progressives and American Foreign Relations.* Harvard University Press, 1995.

Johnstone, Andrew. *Against Immediate Evil: American Internationalists and the Four Freedoms on the Eve of World War II.* Cornell University Press, 2014.

Jonas, Manfred. *Isolationism in America, 1935–1941.* Cornell University Press, 1966.

———. *The United States and Germany: A Diplomatic History.* Cornell University Press, 1984.

Jones, Kenneth Paul, ed. *U.S. Diplomats in Europe, 1919–1941*. ABC-Clio, 1981.

Jones, Larry Eugene. *German Liberalism and the Dissolution of the Weimar Party System, 1918–1933*. University of North Carolina Press, 2011.

Jones, Seth G. *In the Graveyard of Empires: America's War in Afghanistan*. W. W. Norton, 2009.

Jordan, David Starr. *America's Conquest of Europe*. Wentworth Press, 2019.

Josephson, Harold. "Outlawing War: Internationalism and the Pact of Paris." *Diplomatic History* 3, no. 4 (Fall 1979): 377–90.

Judd, Denis. *Balfour and the British Empire: A Study in Imperial Evolution, 1874–1932*. Macmillan, 1968.

Kagan, Robert. *Dangerous Nation: America's Foreign Policy from Its Earliest Days to the Dawn of the Twentieth Century*. Vintage Books, 2006.

Kantrowitz, Stephen. *Ben Tillman and the Reconstruction of White Supremacy*. University of North Carolina Press, 2000.

Kaplan, Amy, and Donald E. Pease, eds. *Cultures of United States Imperialism*. Duke University Press, 1994.

Kaplan, Edward S. *American Trade Policy, 1923–1995*. Greenwood Press, 1996.

Kaplan, Edward S., and Thomas W. Ryley. *Prelude to Trade Wars: American Tariff Policy, 1890–1922*. Greenwood Press, 1994.

Karnow, Stanley. *In Our Image: America's Empire in the Philippines*. Random House, 1989.

Kauffman, Bill. *America First! Its History, Culture, and Politics*. Prometheus Books, 1995.

Kaufman, Burton. *Washington's Farewell Address: The View from the 20th Century*. Quadrangle Books, 1969.

Kaufman, Robert Gordon. *Arms Control During the Pre-Nuclear Era: The United States and Naval Limitation Between the Two World Wars*. Columbia University Press, 1990.

Kazin, Michael. *A Godly Hero: The Life of William Jennings Bryan*. Anchor, 2007.

———. *War Against War: The American Fight for Peace, 1914–1918*. Simon & Schuster, 2018.

Keane, John. *The Life and Death of Democracy*. W. W. Norton, 2009.

Keene, Jennifer D. *The United States and the First World War*. Longman, 2000.

Kennan, George F. *American Diplomacy, 1900–1950*. Mentor Books, 1970.

———. *From Prague After Munich: Diplomatic Papers, 1938–1940*. Princeton University Press, 1968.

———. *Memoirs: 1925–1950*. Little, Brown, 1967.

———. *Russia and the West Under Lenin and Stalin*. Little, Brown, 1961.

———. *Russia Leaves the War: The Americans in Petrograd and the Bolshevik Revolution*. Princeton University Press, 1956.

Kennedy, David M. *Freedom from Fear: The American People in Depression and War, 1929–1945*. Oxford University Press, 1999.

———. *Over Here: The First World War and American Society*. Oxford University Press, 2004.

Kennedy, David M., and Lizabeth Cohen. *The American Pageant: A History of the American People*. Cengage Learning, 2018.

Kennedy, Paul M. *The Rise and Fall of British Naval Mastery*. Scribner, 1976.

———. *The Rise and Fall of the Great Powers: Economic Change and Military Conflict From 1500–2000*. Random House, 1987.

———. *The Rise of the Anglo-German Antagonism, 1860–1914*. Allen & Unwin, 1980.

Kershaw, Ian. *Hitler, 1889–1936: Hubris*. W. W. Norton, 1999.

———. *Hitler, 1936–45: Nemesis*. W. W. Norton, 2000.

————. *The "Hitler Myth": Image and Reality in the Third Reich.* Oxford University Press, 2001.

————. *The Nazi Dictatorship: Problems and Perspectives of Interpretation.* E. Arnold, 1985.

————. *To Hell and Back: Europe, 1914–1949.* Viking, 2015.

Keylor, William R. "The Rise and Demise of the Franco-American Guarantee Pact, 1919–1921." *Proceedings of the Annual Meeting of the Western Society for French History* 15 (1987): 367–77.

Keynes, John Maynard. *The Economic Consequences of the Peace.* Skyhorse, 2016.

Kimball, Warren F. *The Juggler: Franklin Roosevelt as Wartime Statesman.* Princeton University Press, 1991.

Kimura, Masato, and Tosh Minohara, eds. *Tumultuous Decade: Empire, Society, and Diplomacy in 1930s Japan.* University of Toronto Press, 2013.

Kindleberger, Charles P. *The World in Depression, 1929–1939.* University of California Press, 1973.

King, Jere Clemens. *Foch Versus Clemenceau: France and German Dismemberment, 1918– 1919.* Harvard University Press, 1960.

Kirshner, Jonathan. *Appeasing Bankers: Financial Caution on the Road to War.* Princeton University Press, 2007.

Kissinger, Henry. *Diplomacy.* Simon & Schuster, 1994.

Kitchen, Martin. *Europe Between the Wars: A Political History.* Longman, 1988.

Kneer, Warren G. *Great Britain and the Caribbean, 1901–1913: A Study in Anglo-American Relations.* Michigan State University Press, 1975.

Knock, Thomas J. *The Rise of a Prairie Statesman: The Life and Times of George McGovern.* Princeton University Press, 2016.

————. *To End All Wars: Woodrow Wilson and the Quest for a New World Order.* Oxford University Press, 1992.

————. *To End All Wars: Woodrow Wilson and the Quest for a New World Order.* New edition. Princeton University Press, 2019.

Koenig, Louis W. *Bryan: A Political Biography of William Jennings Bryan.* Putnam, 1971.

Kohn, Hans. *American Nationalism: An Interpretative Essay.* Macmillan, 1957.

Kolb, Eberhard. *The Weimar Republic.* Translated by P. S. Falla. Unwin Hyman, 1988.

Kotkin, Stephen. *Stalin: Paradoxes of Power, 1878–1928.* Penguin Books, 2015.

————. *Stalin: Waiting for Hitler, 1929–1941.* Penguin Press, 2017.

Kraut, Alan M. *The Huddled Masses: The Immigrant in American Society, 1880–1921.* Harlan Davidson, 1982.

Krauze, Enrique. *Mexico: Biography of Power.* Harper, 1997.

Kuehl, Warren F., *Seeking World Order: United States and International Organization to 1920.* Vanderbilt University Press, 1969.

Kuehl, Warren F., and Lynne Dunn. *Keeping the Covenant: American Internationalists and the League of Nations, 1920–1939.* Kent State University Press, 1997.

LaFeber, Walter. *The Cambridge History of American Foreign Relations: The American Search for Opportunity, 1865–1913.* Cambridge University Press, 1995.

————. *The Clash: U.S.-Japanese Relations Throughout History.* W. W. Norton, 1998.

————. *Inevitable Revolutions: The U.S. in Central America.* W. W. Norton, 1983.

————. *The New Empire: An Interpretation of American Expansion, 1860–1898.* Cornell University Press, 1963.

Lane, Jack C. *Armed Progressive: General Leonard Wood.* Bison Books, 2009.

Langer, William L. *The Diplomacy of Imperialism, 1890–1902.* Alfred A. Knopf, 1935.

————. *The Undeclared War, 1940–1941: The World Crisis and American Foreign Policy.* Harper & Brothers, 1953.

Langer, William L., and S. Everett Gleason. *The Challenge to Isolation: The World Crisis of 1937–1940*. Harper & Brothers, 1952.

Langley, Lester D. *America and the Americas: The United States in the Western Hemisphere*. University of Georgia Press, 2010.

———. *The United States and the Caribbean in the Twentieth Century*. University of Georgia Press, 1982.

Lansing, Robert. *The Peace Negotiations: A Personal Narrative*. Houghton Mifflin, 1921.

———. *War Memoirs of Robert Lansing, Secretary of State*. Bobbs-Merrill, 1935.

Laqueur, Walter, and George L. Mosse. *International Fascism, 1920–1945*. Harper, 1966.

Large, David Clay. *Between Two Fires: Europe's Path in the 1930s*. W. W. Norton, 1991.

Larrabee, Eric. *Commander in Chief: Franklin Delano Roosevelt, His Lieutenants and Their War*. HarperCollins, 1987.

Larson, Erik. *Dead Wake: The Last Crossing of the Lusitania*. Crown Publishers, 2015.

Lasch, Christopher. *The American Liberals and the Russian Revolution*. McGraw-Hill, 1972.

Lash, Joseph. *The Campus Strike Against War*. Student League for Industrial Democracy, 1935.

Latané, John Holladay. *America as a World Power, 1897–1907*. Harper & Brothers, 1907.

Lautenschlager, Karl. "The Submarine in Naval Warfare, 1901–2001." *International Security* 11, no. 3 (Winter 1987): 94–140.

Lawrence, David. *The True Story of Woodrow Wilson*. George H. Doran, 1924.

Lee, Stephen J. *European Dictatorships, 1918–1945*. 3rd ed. Routledge, 2008.

Leffler, Melvyn P. *Elusive Quest: America's Pursuit of European Stability and French Security, 1919–1933*. 1979; University of North Carolina Press, 2009.

———. "The Origins of Republican War Debt Policy, 1921–1923: A Case Study in the Applicability of the Open Door Interpretation." *Journal of American History* 59, no. 3 (December 1972): 585–601.

———. *A Preponderance of Power: National Security, the Truman Administration, and the Cold War*. Stanford University Press, 1992.

———. *Safeguarding Democratic Capitalism: U.S. Foreign Policy and National Security, 1920–2015*. Princeton University Press, 2017.

Lentin, Antony. *Guilt at Versailles: Lloyd George and the Pre-History of Appeasement*. Methuen, 1984.

———. *Lloyd George, Woodrow Wilson and the Guilt of Germany: An Essay in the Pre-History of Appeasement*. Louisiana State University Press, 1985.

———. "'Une aberration inexplicable'? Clemenceau and the Abortive Anglo-French Guarantee Treaty of 1919." *Diplomacy and Statecraft* 8, no. 2 (July 1997): 31–49.

Leonard, Thomas M. *United States–Latin American Relations, 1850–1903*. The University of Alabama Press, 1999.

Leopold, Richard W. *Elihu Root and the Conservative Tradition*. Edited by Oscar Handlin. Little, Brown, 1954.

Lerner, Max. *Ideas Are Weapons: The History and Uses of Ideas*. Viking Press, 1939.

———. *Ideas for the Ice Age: Studies in a Revolutionary Era*. Routledge, 1992.

Leuchtenburg, William E. *Franklin D. Roosevelt and the New Deal, 1932–1940*. Harper Torchbooks, 1963.

———. *The Perils of Prosperity, 1914–32*. University of Chicago Press, 1958.

Levering, Ralph B. *American Opinion and the Russian Alliance, 1939–1945*. University of North Carolina Press, 1976.

Levin, Norman Gordon. *Woodrow Wilson and World Politics: America's Response to War and Revolution*. Oxford University Press, 1968.

Levine, Lawrence W., and Cornelia R. Levine. *The People and the President: America's Conversation with FDR.* Beacon Press, 2002.

Levy, David W. *Herbert Croly of the New Republic: The Life and Thought of an American Progressive.* Princeton University Press, 2016.

Lewis, David Levering. *The Improbable Wendell Willkie: The Businessman Who Saved the Republican Party and His Country and Conceived a New World Order.* Liveright, 2018.

Lewis, W. Arthur. "International Competition in Manufacturers." *The American Economic Review* 47, no. 2 (1957): 578–87.

Lincoln, W. Bruce. *In War's Dark Shadow: The Russians Before the Great War.* Northern Illinois University Press, 2003.

Linderman, Gerald F. *The Mirror of War: American Society and the Spanish-American War.* University of Michigan Press, 1974.

Link, Arthur S. *The Higher Realism of Woodrow Wilson, and Other Essays.* Vanderbilt University Press, 1971.

———. *Wilson.* 5 vols. Princeton University Press, 1947–1965.

———. *Wilson the Diplomatist: A Look at His Major Foreign Policies.* Johns Hopkins Press, 1957.

———, ed. *Woodrow Wilson and a Revolutionary World, 1913–1921.* University of North Carolina Press, 1982.

———. *Woodrow Wilson and the Progressive Era, 1910–1917.* Harper & Row, 1963.

———. *Woodrow Wilson: Revolution, War, and Peace.* AHM Publishers, 1979.

———. et al., eds. *The Papers of Woodrow Wilson.* 69 vols. Princeton University Press, 1966–1994.

Linn, Brian McAllister. *Guardians of Empire: The U.S. Army and the Pacific, 1902–1940.* University of North Carolina Press, 1997.

———. *The Philippine War, 1899–1902.* University Press of Kansas, 2000.

———. *The U.S. Army and Counterinsurgency in the Philippine War, 1899–1902.* University of North Carolina Press, 1989.

Lipkes, Jeff. *Rehearsals: The German Army in Belgium, August 1914.* Leuven University Press, 2008.

Lippmann, Walter. *Drift and Mastery: An Attempt to Diagnose the Current Unrest.* Andesite Press, 2015.

———, ed. *Men of Destiny.* Routledge, 2003.

———. *Stakes of Diplomacy.* Henry Holt, 1915.

———. *The Stakes of Diplomacy.* H. Holt and Company, 1917.

Livermore, Seward W. *Politics Is Adjourned: Woodrow Wilson and the War Congress, 1916–1918.* Wesleyan University Press, 1966.

Loades, Judith, ed. *The Life and Times of David Lloyd George.* Headstart History, 1991.

Lodge, Henry Cabot. *The Senate and the League of Nations.* Charles Scribner's Sons, 1925.

———. *War Addresses.* Houghton Mifflin Company, 1917.

Looze, Helene Johnson. *Alexander Hamilton and the British Orientation of American Foreign Policy, 1783–1803.* Mouton, 1969.

Louis, William Roger. *British Strategy in the Far East, 1919–1939.* Clarendon Press, 1971.

———. *Ends of British Imperialism: The Scramble for Empire, Suez, and Decolonization.* I.B. Tauris, 2007.

Lowe, C. J. *The Reluctant Imperialists: British Foreign Policy, 1878–1902.* Routledge and Kegan Paul, 1967.

Lowe, C. J., and M. L. Dockrill. *The Mirage of Power: British Foreign Policy, 1902–14.* Routledge and Kegan Paul, 1972.

———. *The Mirage of Power: British Foreign Policy, 1914–22.* Routledge and Kegan Paul, 1972.

Lowe, John. *The Great Powers, Imperialism, and the German Problem, 1865–1925.* Routledge, 1994.

Luce, Henry. "The American Century." *Life,* February 17, 1941.

Lukacs, John. *The Hitler of History.* Alfred A. Knopf, 1997.

———. *The Last European War, September 1939–December 1941.* Anchor Press, 1976.

Lundestad, Geir. *The American "Empire" and Other Studies of US Foreign Policy in a Comparative Perspective.* Oxford University Press, 1991.

———. *"Empire" by Integration: The United States and European Integration, 1945–1997.* Oxford University Press, 1998.

Lutz, Ralph Haswell. *Fall of the German Empire, 1914–1918.* Stanford University Press, 1932.

———. *The German Revolution, 1918–1919.* Stanford University Publications, 1922.

Lyttelton, Adrian, ed. *Liberal and Fascist Italy.* Oxford University Press, 2002.

Macaulay, Neill. *The Sandino Affair.* Quadrangle Books, 1967.

MacDonald, C. A. *The United States, Britain and Appeasement, 1936–1939.* St. Martin's Press, 1981.

MacKay, Ruddock F. *Balfour: Intellectual Statesman.* Oxford University Press, 1985.

MacMillan, Margaret. *Paris 1919: Six Months That Changed the World.* Random House, 2003.

———. *The War That Ended Peace: The Road to 1914.* Random House, 2013.

MacMurray, John Van Antwerp. *How the Peace Was Lost: The 1935 Memorandum "Developments Affecting American Policy in the Far East."* Edited and with an introduction by Arthur Waldron. Hoover Institution Press, 1992.

Maddox, Robert James. *William E. Borah and American Foreign Policy.* Louisiana State University Press, 1969.

Mahan, Alfred Thayer. *Mahan on Naval Warfare.* Dover Publications, 2011.

Maier, Charles S. *Recasting Bourgeois Europe: Stabilization in France, Germany, and Italy in the Decade After World War I.* Princeton University Press, 1975.

Mamatey, Victor S. *The United States and East Central Europe, 1914–1918: A Study in Wilsonian Diplomacy and Propaganda.* Princeton University Press, 1957.

Manchester, William. *The Last Lion: Winston Spencer Churchill.* Vol. 2, *Alone, 1932–1940.* Little, Brown, 1988.

———. *The Last Lion: Winston Spencer Churchill.* Vol. 1, *Visions of Glory, 1874–1932.* Little, Brown, 1983.

Manela, Erez. *The Wilsonian Moment: Self-Determination and the International Origins of Anticolonial Nationalism.* Oxford University Press, 2007.

Margulies, Herbert F. *The Mild Reservationists and the League of Nations Controversy in the Senate.* University of Missouri Press, 1989.

Marks, Frederick W. *Velvet on Iron: The Diplomacy of Theodore Roosevelt.* University of Nebraska Press, 1979.

———. *Wind over Sand: The Diplomacy of Franklin Roosevelt.* University of Georgia Press, 1988.

Marks, Sally. *The Illusion of Peace: International Relations in Europe, 1918–1933.* Palgrave Macmillan, 2003.

Martel, Gordon, ed. *American Foreign Relations Reconsidered, 1890–1993.* Routledge, 1994.

———. *Origins of the First World War.* Routledge, 2016.

———, ed. *The Origins of the Second World War Reconsidered: The A. J. P. Taylor Debate After Twenty-Five Years.* Allen & Unwin, 1986.

Martin, Benjamin F. *France and the Après Guerre, 1918–1924: Illusions and Disillusionment.* Louisiana State University Press, 1999.

Masamichi, Rōyama. *Foreign Policy of Japan: 1914–1939.* Greenwood Press, 1973.

Matthews, Jeffrey J. *Alanson B. Houghton: Ambassador of the New Era.* Rowman & Littlefield, 2004.

Maurice, Frederick. *Haldane, 1856–1915: The Life of Viscount Haldane of Cloan, K.T., O.M.* Faber and Faber, 1937.

May, Ernest R. *American Imperialism: A Speculative Essay.* Atheneum, 1968.

———. *Imperial Democracy: The Emergence of America as a Great Power.* Harcourt, Brace & World, 1961.

———. *Strange Victory: Hitler's Conquest of France.* Hill and Wang, 2000.

———. *The World War and American Isolation, 1914–1917.* Quadrangle Books, 1966.

May, Ernest R., and John King Fairbank, eds. *America's China Trade in Historical Perspective: The Chinese and American Performance.* Harvard University Press, 1986.

May, Ernest R., and James C. Thomson Jr., eds. *American–East Asian Relations: A Survey.* Harvard University Press, 1972.

May, Henry. *The End of American Innocence: A Study of the First Years of Our Own Time, 1912–1917.* Columbia University Press, 1994.

Mayeur, Jean-Marie, and Madeleine Rebérioux. *The Third Republic from Its Origins to the Great War, 1871–1914.* Translated by J. R. Foster. Cambridge University Press, 1984.

Maynard, William Barksdale. *Woodrow Wilson: Princeton to the Presidency.* Yale University Press, 2008.

Mayo, Marlene J., ed. *The Emergence of Imperial Japan: Self-Defense or Calculated Aggression?* Heath, 1970.

Mazower, Mark. *Hitler's Empire: How the Nazis Ruled Europe.* Penguin Press, 2008.

Mazzenga, Maria. "Condemning the Nazis' Kristallnacht: Father Maurice Sheehy, the National Catholic Welfare Conference, and the Dissent of Father Charles Coughlin." *U.S. Catholic Historian* 26, no. 4 (Fall 2008): 71–87.

McCormick, Thomas J. *China Market: America's Quest for Informal Empire, 1893–1901.* Quadrangle Books, 1967.

McCullough, David. *The Path Between the Seas: The Creation of the Panama Canal, 1870–1914.* Simon & Schuster, 1977.

———. *Truman.* Simon & Schuster, 1992.

McDonough, Frank, ed. *The Origins of the Second World War: An International Perspective.* Continuum, 2011.

McDougall, Walter A. *France's Rhineland Policy, 1914–1924: The Last Bid for a Balance of Power in Europe.* Princeton University Press, 1978.

McKercher, B. J. C. *Transition of Power: Britain's Loss of Global Pre-eminence to the United States, 1930–1945.* Cambridge University Press, 1999.

McLellan, David S., and David C. Acheson, eds. *Among Friends: Personal Letters of Dean Acheson.* Dodd, Mead, 1980.

McMeekin, Sean. *July 1914: Countdown to War.* Basic Books, 2013.

———. *The Russian Origins of the First World War.* Belknap Press of Harvard University Press, 2011.

———. *The Russian Revolution: A New History.* Basic Books, 2017.

McNeil, William C. *American Money and the Weimar Republic: Economics and Politics on the Eve of the Great Depression.* Series: The Political Economy of International Change. Columbia University Press, 1986.

Meacham, Jon. *Franklin and Winston: An Intimate Portrait of an Epic Friendship.* Random House, 2004.

Meijer, Hendrik. *Arthur Vandenberg: The Man in the Middle of the American Century.* University of Chicago Press, 2017.

Meiser, Jeffrey W. *Power and Restraint: The Rise of the United States, 1898–1941.* Georgetown University Press, 2015.

Merkley, Paul. *Reinhold Niebuhr.* McGill–Queen's University Press, 1975.

Merrill, Horace Samuel, and Marion Galbraith Merrill. *The Republican Command: 1897–1913.* University Press of Kentucky, 1971.

Mervin, David. "Henry Cabot Lodge and the League of Nations." *Journal of American Studies* 4, no. 2 (February 1971): 201–14.

Meyer, G. J. *A World Undone: The Story of the Great War, 1914 to 1918.* Delacorte Press, 2006.

Meyer, Milton W. *Japan: A Concise History.* Rowman & Littlefield, 2009.

Miller, David Hunter. *The Drafting of the Covenant.* 2 vols. G.P. Putnam's Sons, 1928.

Miller, Kenneth E. *From Progressive to New Dealer: Frederic C. Howe and American Liberalism.* Penn State University Press, 2010.

Miller, Stuart Creighton. *Benevolent Assimilation: The American Conquest of the Philippines, 1899–1903.* Yale University Press, 1984.

Millett, Allan R., and Williamson Murray, eds. *Military Effectiveness: The Interwar Period.* Cambridge University Press, 2010.

Millis, Walter. *The Martial Spirit: A Study of Our War with Spain.* Viking Press, 1965.

———. *Road to War: America, 1914–1917.* Houghton Mifflin, 1935.

Minger, Ralph Eldin. *William Howard Taft and United States Foreign Policy: The Apprenticeship Years, 1990–1908.* University of Illinois Press, 1975.

Mitchener, Kris James, and Marc Weidenmier. "Empire, Public Goods, and the Roosevelt Corollary." *Journal of Economic History* 65, no. 3 (September 2005): 658–92.

Mitter, Ranna. *Forgotten Ally: China's World War II, 1937–1945.* Houghton Mifflin Harcourt, 2013.

Mombauer, Annika. *The Origins of the First World War: Controversies and Consensus.* Longman, 2002.

———, ed. *The Origins of the First World War: Diplomatic and Military Documents.* Manchester University Press, 2013.

Mommsen, Wolfgang J. *Imperial Germany, 1867–1918: Politics, Culture, and Society in an Authoritarian State.* Bloomsbury Academic, 2009.

Monger, George W. *The End of Isolation: British Foreign Policy, 1900–1907.* T. Nelson, 1963.

Moore, Colin D. *American Imperialism and the State, 1893–1921.* Cambridge University Press, 2017.

Moore, Michaela Hoenicke. *Know Your Enemy: The American Debate on Nazism, 1933–1945.* Cambridge University Press, 2009.

Morgan, H. Wayne. *America's Road to Empire: The War with Spain and Overseas Expansion.* John Wiley & Sons, 1965.

———. *Eugene V. Debs: Socialist for President.* Greenwood Press, 1973.

———. *From Hayes to McKinley: National Party Politics, 1877–1896.* Syracuse University Press, 1969.

———. *William McKinley and His America.* Syracuse University Press, 1963.

Morgenthau, Henry. *Ambassador Morgenthau's Story.* Franklin Classics, 2018.

Morgenthau, Henry, Jr. "The Diaries of Henry Morgenthau, Jr." Franklin D. Roosevelt Presidential Library and Museum, Diaries of Henry Morgenthau, 1933.

Morison, Elting E. *Turmoil and Tradition: A Study of the Life and Times of Henry L. Stimson.* Houghton Mifflin, 1960.

Bibliography

Morley, James William, ed. *The Fateful Choice: Japan's Advance into Southeast Asia, 1939–1941: Selected Translations from Taiheiyō Sensō e No Michi, Kaisen Gaikō Shi.* Columbia University Press, 1980.

———, ed. *Japan's Foreign Policy, 1868–1941: A Research Guide.* Columbia University Press, 1974.

Morris, Edmund. *Colonel Roosevelt.* Random House, 2010.

———. *The Rise of Theodore Roosevelt.* Coward, McCann & Geoghegan, 1979.

———. *Theodore Rex.* Random House, 2001.

Moser, Maynard. *Jacob Gould Schurman: Scholar, Political Activist, and Ambassador of Good Will.* Arno Press, 1982.

Mowat, Charles Loch. *Britain Between the Wars, 1918–1940.* Methuen, 1972.

Mowry, George E. *The Era of Theodore Roosevelt and the Birth of Modern America, 1900–1912.* Harper & Row, 1958.

Mulligan, William. *The Origins of the First World War.* Cambridge University Press, 2010.

Mumford, Lewis. *Men Must Act.* Harcourt, Brace, 1939.

Munro, Dana Gardner. *Intervention and Dollar Diplomacy in the Caribbean, 1900–1921.* Princeton University Press, 2016.

———. *The United States and the Caribbean Republics, 1921–1933.* Princeton University Press, 1973.

Murray, Robert K. *The Harding Era: Warren G. Harding and His Administration.* University of Minnesota Press, 1969.

———. *The Politics of Normalcy: Governmental Theory and Practice in the Harding-Coolidge Era.* W. W. Norton, 1973.

———. *Red Scare: A Study in National Hysteria, 1919–1920.* McGraw-Hill, 1964.

Murray, Williamson. *The Change in the European Balance of Power, 1938–1939: The Path to Ruin.* Princeton University Press, 1984.

Murray, Williamson, and Allan R. Millett. *A War to Be Won: Fighting the Second World War.* Harvard University Press, 2001.

Musicant, Ivan. *Empire by Default: The Spanish-American War and the Dawn of the American Century.* Henry Holt, 1998.

Myers, Ramon Hawley, and Mark R. Peattie, eds. *The Japanese Colonial Empire, 1895–1945.* Princeton University Press, 1984.

Nagorski, Andrew. *1941: The Year Germany Lost the War.* Simon & Schuster, 2019.

Nasaw, David. *Andrew Carnegie.* Penguin Press, 2006.

———. *The Chief: The Life of William Randolph Hearst.* Mariner Books, 2001.

Nash, George H., ed. *The Crusade Years, 1933–1955: Herbert Hoover's Lost Memoir of the New Deal Era and Its Aftermath.* Hoover Institution Press, 2013.

———. *The Life of Herbert Hoover: The Humanitarian, 1914–1917.* W. W. Norton, 1988.

Nash, Roderick. *The Nervous Generation: American Thought, 1917–1930.* Elephant Paperbacks, 1990.

Nau, Henry R. *Conservative Internationalism: Armed Diplomacy Under Jefferson, Polk, Truman, and Reagan.* Princeton University Press, 2015.

Neiberg, Michael S. *Dance of the Furies: Europe and the Outbreak of World War I.* Belknap Press of Harvard University Press, 2011.

Nelson, Harold I. *Land and Power: British and Allied Policy on Germany's Frontier, 1916–19.* Routledge and Kegan Paul, 1963.

Nelson, Keith L. *Victors Divided: America and the Allies in Germany, 1918–1923.* University of California Press, 1975.

Neu, Charles E. *The Troubled Encounter: The United States and Japan.* Wiley, 1975.

Neville, Peter. *Hitler and Appeasement: The British Attempt to Prevent the Second World War.* Hambledon Continuum, 2006.

Nevins, Allan. *Henry White: Thirty Years of American Diplomacy.* Harper & Brothers, 1930.

Nicolson, Harold. *Diplomacy.* Institute for the Study of Diplomacy, 1988. First published in 1939 by Thornton Butterworth.

———. *Peacemaking 1919.* Houghton Mifflin, 1933.

Niebuhr, Reinhold. *The Essential Reinhold Niebuhr: Selected Essays and Addresses.* Edited and introduced by Robert McAfee Brown. Yale University Press, 1987.

———. *The Irony of American History.* Scribner, 1962.

———. *Love and Justice: Selections from the Shorter Writings of Reinhold Niebuhr.* Edited by D. B. Robertson. Westminster John Knox Press, 1992.

———. *The Structure of Nations and Empires: A Study of the Recurring Patterns and Problems of the Political Order in Relation to the Unique Problems of the Nuclear Age.* Scribner, 1959.

Ninkovich, Frank. *The Global Republic: America's Inadvertent Rise to World Power.* University of Chicago Press, 2014.

———. "Theodore Roosevelt: Civilization as Ideology." *Diplomatic History* 10, no. 3 (Summer 1986): 221–45.

———. *The United States and Imperialism.* Blackwell, 2001.

———. *The Wilsonian Century: U.S. Foreign Policy Since 1900.* University of Chicago Press, 1999.

Nish, Ian, ed. *Anglo-Japanese Alienation, 1919–1952: Papers of the Anglo-Japanese Conference on the History of the Second World War.* Cambridge University Press, 2010.

———. *The Anglo-Japanese Alliance: The Diplomacy of Two Island Empires, 1984–1907.* Bloomsbury Academic, 2013.

———. *Japanese Foreign Policy, 1869–1942: Kasumigaseki to Miyakezaka.* Routledge and Kegan Paul, 1977.

———. *The Origins of the Russo-Japanese War.* Longman, 1985.

Noble, David W. *The Paradox of Progressive Thought.* University of Minnesota Press, 1958.

Noble, G. Bernard. *Policies and Opinions at Paris, 1919.* The MacMillan Company, 1935.

Noggle, Burl. *Into the Twenties: The United States from Armistice to Normalcy.* University of Illinois Press, 1974.

Nolan, Mary. *The Transatlantic Century: Europe and America, 1890–2010.* Cambridge University Press, 2012.

Nordholt, J. W. Schulte. *Woodrow Wilson: A Life for World Peace.* Translated by Herbert H. Rowen. University of California Press, 1990.

Nore, Ellen. *Charles A. Beard: An Intellectual Biography.* Southern Illinois University Press, 1983.

Northedge, F. S. *The Troubled Giant: Britain Among the Great Powers, 1916–1939.* Praeger, 1967.

Notter, Harley A. *The Origins of the Foreign Policy of Woodrow Wilson.* Johns Hopkins Press, 1937.

Novick, Peter. *That Noble Dream: The "Objectivity Question" and the American Historical Profession.* Cambridge University Press, 1988.

Noyes, Pierrepont. *While Europe Waits for Peace: Describing the Progress of Economic and Political Demoralization in Europe During the Year of American Hesitation.* Macmillan, 1921.

Nugent, Walter T. K. *The Tolerant Populists: Kansas, Populism and Nativism.* University of Chicago Press, 1968.

O'Connor, Richard. *The German-Americans: An Informal History.* Little, Brown, 1968.

Offner, Arnold A. *American Appeasement: United States Foreign Policy and Germany, 1933–1938.* Belknap Press of Harvard University Press, 1969.

———. *The Origins of the Second World War: American Foreign Policy and World Politics, 1917–1941.* Praeger, 1975.

Offner, John L. *An Unwanted War: The Diplomacy of the United States and Spain over Cuba, 1895–1989.* University of North Carolina Press, 1992.

Olcott, Charles. *The Life of William McKinley.* Houghton Mifflin, 1916.

Olson, Lynne. *Those Angry Days: Roosevelt, Lindbergh, and America's Fight over World War II, 1939–1941.* Random House, 2013.

Orde, Anne. *The Eclipse of Great Britain: The United States and British Imperial Decline, 1895–1956.* Red Globe Press, 1996.

———. *Great Britain and International Security, 1920–1926.* Royal Historical Society, 1978.

Osborne, Thomas J. *Empire Can Wait: American Opposition to Hawaiian Annexation, 1893–1898.* Kent State University Press, 1981.

Osgood, Robert Endicott. *Ideals and Self-Interest in America's Foreign Relations: The Great Transformation of the Twentieth Century.* University of Chicago Press, 1953.

Overy, R. J. *The Inter-War Crisis 1919–1939.* Longman, 1994.

———. *The Twilight Years: The Paradox of Britain Between the Wars.* Viking, 2009.

Pagden, Anthony. *Lords of All the World: Ideologies of Empire in Spain, Britain and France, c. 1500—c. 1800.* Yale University Press, 1998.

Paine, S. C. M. *The Japanese Empire: Grand Strategy from the Meiji Restoration to the Pacific War.* Cambridge University Press, 2017.

———. *The Wars for Asia, 1911–1949.* Cambridge University Press, 2012.

Pakenham, Thomas. *The Scramble for Africa: White Man's Conquest of the Dark Continent from 1876 to 1912.* Random House, 1991.

Parker, Robert. *Chamberlain and Appeasement: British Policy and the Coming of the Second World War.* Red Globe Press, 1993.

Parrini, Carl P. *Heir to Empire: United States Economic Diplomacy, 1916–1923.* University of Pittsburgh Press, 1969.

Paterson, J. Garry, et al. *American Foreign Policy: A History Since 1900.* D. C. Heath, 1977.

Patterson, David S. *Toward a Warless World: The Travail of the American Peace Movement, 1887–1914.* Indiana University Press, 1976.

Patterson, James T. *America in the Twentieth Century: A History.* Cengage Learning, 1999.

———. *Mr. Republican: A Biography of Robert A. Taft.* Houghton Mifflin, 1972.

Paxton, Robert O. *The Anatomy of Fascism.* Vintage Books, 2005.

Payne, Howard C., Raymond Callahan, and Edward M. Bennett. *As the Storm Clouds Gathered: European Perceptions of American Foreign Policy in the 1930s.* Regina Books, 1979.

Peck, Harry Thurston. *Twenty Years of the Republic, 1885–1905.* Dodd, Mead & Company, 1929.

Pedersen, Susan. *The Guardians: The League of Nations and the Crisis of Empire.* Oxford University Press, 2015.

Pérez, Louis A., Jr. *Cuba: Between Reform and Revolution.* Oxford University Press, 1988.

———. *Cuba Between Empires, 1878–1902.* University of Pittsburgh Press, 1983.

.———. "Incurring a Debt of Gratitude: 1898 and the Moral Sources of United States Hegemony in Cuba." *American Historical Review* 104 (April 1999): 356–98.

———. *The War of 1898: The United States and Cuba in History and Historiography.* University of North Carolina Press, 1998.

Perkins, Bradford. *The Creation of a Republican Empire, 1776–1865.* Vol. 1 of *The Cambridge History of American Foreign Relations.* Cambridge University Press, 1993.

———. *The Great Rapprochement: England and the United States, 1895–1914.* Atheneum, 1968.

Perkins, Dexter. *Charles Evans Hughes and American Democratic Statesmanship.* Little, Brown, 1956.

Perkins, Whitney T. *Constraint of Empire: The United States and Caribbean Interventions.* Praeger, 1981.

———. *Denial of Empire: The United States and Its Dependencies.* A. W. Sythoff/Leyden, 1962.

Peukert, Detlev J. K. *Inside Nazi Germany: Conformity, Opposition, and Racism in Everyday Life.* Yale University Press, 1987.

———. *The Weimar Republic: The Crisis of Classical Modernity.* Hill and Wang, 1992.

Phelps, Edith M. *Selected Articles on a League of Nations.* Palala Press, 2015.

Phillips, Kevin. *William McKinley.* Times Books, 2003.

Pietrusza, David. *1932: The Rise of Hitler and FDR; Two Tales of Politics, Betrayal, and Unlikely Destiny.* Lyons Press, 2015.

———. *TR's Last War, Theodore Roosevelt, the Great War, and a Journey of Triumph and Tragedy.* Lyons Press, 2018.

Pipes, Richard. *The Russian Revolution.* Alfred A. Knopf, 1990.

Plesur, Milton. *America's Outward Thrust: Approaches to Foreign Affairs, 1865–1890.* Northern Illinois University Press, 1971.

———. *Creating an American Empire, 1865–1914.* Pitman, 1971.

Pletcher, David M. *The Diplomacy of Trade and Investment: American Economic Expansion in the Hemisphere, 1865–1900.* University of Missouri Press, 1998.

Plummer, Brenda Gayle. *Rising Wind: Black Americans and U.S. Foreign Affairs, 1935–1960.* University of North Carolina Press, 1996.

Pogue, Forrest C. *George C. Marshall: Statesman, 1945–1959.* Viking, 1987.

Polonsky, Antony. *The Little Dictators: The History of Eastern Europe Since 1918.* Routledge and Kegan Paul, 1975.

Ponomarev, Valeri Nikolaevich. *Imperial Russian Foreign Policy.* Edited by Hugh Ragsdale. Cambridge University Press, 1993.

Poole, DeWitt Clinton. *An American Diplomat in Bolshevik Russia.* Edited by Lorraine M. Lees and William S. Rodner. University of Wisconsin Press, 2015.

Posner, Richard A., ed. *The Essential Holmes: Selections from the Letters, Speeches, Judicial Opinions, and Other Writings of Oliver Wendell Holmes, Jr.* University of Chicago Press, 1992.

Pratt, Julius W. *America and World Leadership, 1900–1921.* Collier-Macmillan, 1970.

———. *Expansionists of 1898: The Acquisition of Hawaii and the Spanish Islands.* Literary Licensing, 2012. First published in 1936 by the Johns Hopkins Press.

———. "The 'Large Policy' of 1898." *The Mississippi Valley Historical Review* 19, no. 2, (Sept. 1932): 219–42.

Pratt, Julius W., Vincent P. De Santis, and Joseph M. Siracusa. *A History of United States Foreign Policy.* 4th ed. Prentice-Hall, 1980.

Presseisen, Ernst L. *Germany and Japan: A Study in Totalitarian Diplomacy, 1933–1941.* Howard Fertig, 1969.

Preston, Andrew. *Sword of the Spirit, Shield of Faith: Religion in American War and Diplomacy.* Alfred A. Knopf, 2012.

Preston, Diana. *Lusitania: An Epic Tragedy.* Walker Books, 2002.

Preston, Paul, and Anne L. Mackenzie, eds. *The Republic Besieged: Civil War in Spain, 1936–1939.* Edinburgh University Press, 1996.

Pribram, Alfred Francis. *England and the International Policy of the European Great Powers, 1871–1914.* Frank Cass & Co., 1966.

Pringle, Henry F. *The Life and Times of William Howard Taft.* 2 vols. Archon Books, 1964.

———. *Theodore Roosevelt: A Biography.* Harcourt, Brace, 1931.

Pusey, Merlo J. *Charles Evans Hughes.* 2 vols. MacMillan, 1951.

Pyle, Kenneth B. *Japan Rising: The Resurgence of Japanese Power and Purpose.* Public Affairs, 2007.

———. "Profound Forces in the Making of Modern Japan." *Journal of Japanese Studies* 32, no. 2 (Summer 2006): 393–418.

Quinn, Frederick. *The French Overseas Empire.* Praeger, 2000.

Rappaport, Armin. *Henry L. Stimson and Japan, 1931–33.* University of Chicago Press, 1963.

Rappleye, Charles. *Herbert Hoover in the White House: The Ordeal of the Presidency.* Simon & Schuster, 2016.

Ratner, Sidney, James H. Soltow, and Richard Sylla. *The Evolution of the American Economy: Growth, Welfare and Decision Making.* Basic Books, 1980.

Reischauer, Edwin. *The Japanese.* Belknap Press of Harvard University Press, 1977.

Retallack, James, ed. *Imperial Germany, 1871–1918.* Oxford University Press, 2008.

Reynolds, David. *Britannia Overruled: British Policy and World Power in the Twentieth Century.* Routledge, 2014.

———. *The Creation of the Anglo-American Alliance, 1937–1941: A Study in Competitive Co-operation.* University of North Carolina Press, 1982.

———. *From Munich to Pearl Harbor: Roosevelt's America and the Origins of the Second World War.* Ivan R. Dee, 2001.

———. "Rethinking Anglo-American Relations." *International Affairs (Royal Institute of International Affairs 1944–)* 65, no. 1 (Winter, 1988–1989): 89–111.

Reynolds, P. A. *British Foreign Policy in the Inter-War Years.* Greenwood Press, 1974.

Rhodes, James Ford. *The McKinley and Roosevelt Administrations.* Macmillan, 1922.

Ribuffo, Leo P. *The Old Christian Right: The Protestant Far Right from the Great Depression to the Cold War.* Temple University Press, 1983.

Rich, Norman. *Great Power Diplomacy: 1814–1914.* McGraw-Hill, 1991.

———. *Hitler's War Aims: The Establishment of the New Order.* W. W. Norton, 1974.

———. *Hitler's War Aims: Ideology, the Nazi State and the Course of Expansion.* W. W. Norton, 1973.

Rippy, Fred J. *America and the Strife of Europe.* University of Chicago Press, 1938.

Ritter, Gerhard. *The Sword and the Scepter: The Problem of Militarism in Germany.* Vol. 2, *The European Powers and the Wilhelmian Empire, 1890–1914.* University of Miami Press, 1969.

Robbins, Keith. *The First World War.* Oxford University Press, 1984.

Roberts, Andrew. *Churchill: Walking with Destiny.* Viking, 2018.

Robinson, Ronald, John Gallagher, and Alice Denny. *Africa and the Victorians: The Official Mind of Imperialism.* 2nd ed. Palgrave Macmillan, 1978.

Rochester, Stuart. *American Liberal Disillusionment in the Wake of World War I.* Penn State University Press, 1991.

Rock, William R. *Chamberlain and Roosevelt: British Foreign Policy and the United States, 1937–1940.* Ohio State University, 1989.

Rodgers, Daniel T. *Atlantic Crossings: Social Politics in a Progressive Age.* Harvard University Press, 2000.

Roosevelt, Elliott, ed. *F.D.R.: His Personal Letters, 1928–1945.* 2 vols. Duell, Sloan, and Pearce, 1952.

Roosevelt, Franklin Delano, and Winston Churchill. *Roosevelt and Churchill: Their Secret Wartime Correspondence.* Edited by Francis L. Loewenheim, Harold D. Langley, and Manfred Jonas. E. P. Dutton, 1975.

Roosevelt, Theodore. *Fear God and Take Your Own Part.* Cornell University Library, 2009.

Roosevelt, Theodore, and William Griffith. *Roosevelt: His Life Meaning and Messages.* Current Literature Publishing, 1919.

Roosevelt, Theodore, and Henry Cabot Lodge. *Selections from the Correspondence of Theodore Roosevelt and Henry Cabot Lodge, 1884–1918.* 2 vols. Scribner's, 1925.

Rosen, Jeffrey. *William Howard Taft.* Henry Holt, 2018.

Rosenberg, Emily S. *Financial Missionaries to the World: The Politics and Culture of Dollar Diplomacy, 1900–1930.* Duke University Press, 2004.

———. *Spreading the American Dream.* Hill and Wang, 1982.

Ross, Graham. *The Great Powers and the Decline of the European States System, 1914–1945.* Longman, 1983.

Rossini, Daniela, ed. *From Theodore Roosevelt to FDR: Internationalism and Isolationism in American Foreign Policy.* Ryburn Publishing, Keele University Press, 1995.

Rossiter, Clinton. *Marxism: The View from America.* Harcourt, Brace, 1960.

Rossiter, Clinton, and James Lare, eds. *The Essential Lippmann: A Political Philosophy for Liberal Democracy.* Harvard University Press, 1982.

Rostow, Nicholas. *Anglo-French Relations, 1934–36.* Palgrave Macmillan, 1984.

Roth, Joseph. *What I Saw: Reports from Berlin, 1920–1933.* Translated by Michael Hofmann. W. W. Norton, 2003.

Rozwenc, Edwin C., and Kenneth Lindfors. *The United States and the New Imperialism.* Heath, 1968.

Ruoff, Kenneth J. *Imperial Japan at Its Zenith: The Wartime Celebration of the Empire's 2,600th Anniversary.* Cornell University Press, 2010.

Ruotsila, Markku. *The Origins of Christian Anti-Internationalism: Conservative Evangelicals and the League of Nations.* Georgetown University Press, 2007.

Russett, Bruce M. *No Clear and Present Danger: A Skeptical View of the United States Entry into World War II.* Routledge, 1997.

Rystad, Göran. *Ambiguous Imperialism: American Foreign Policy and Domestic Politics at the Turn of the Century.* Esselte Studium, 1975.

Safford, Jeffrey J. *Wilsonian Maritime Diplomacy, 1913–1921.* Rutgers University Press, 1978.

Sands, Kathleen M. *America's Religious Wars: The Embattled Heart of Our Public Life.* Yale University Press, 2019.

Scally, Robert James. *The Origins of the Lloyd George Coalition: The Politics of Social Imperialism, 1900–1918.* Princeton University Press, 2016.

Schild, Georg M. *Between Ideology and Realpolitik: Woodrow Wilson and the Russian Revolution, 1917–1921.* Praeger, 1995.

Schlesinger, Arthur Meier. *Political and Social Growth of the United States, 1852–1933.* Macmillan, 1937.

Schlesinger, Arthur M., Jr. *The Age of Roosevelt.* Vol. 2, *The Coming of the New Deal, 1933–1935.* Mariner Books, 2003.

———. *The Age of Roosevelt.* Vol. 1, *The Crisis of the Old Order, 1919–1933.* Mariner Books, 2003.

———. *The Age of Roosevelt.* Vol. 3, *The Politics of Upheaval.* Riverside Press, 1960.

Schmitt, Bernadotte Everly. *The Origins of the First World War.* Routledge and Kegan Paul, 1958.

Schmitt, Karl Michael. *Mexico and the United States, 1821–1973: Conflict and Coexistence.* John Wiley & Sons, 1974.

Schmitz, David F. *Henry L. Stimson: The First Wise Man.* Rowman & Littlefield, 2000.

———. *The Triumph of Internationalism: FDR and a World in Crisis, 1933–1941.* Potomac Books, 2007.

Schmuhl, Robert. *Ireland's Exiled Children: America and the Easter Rising.* Oxford University Press, 2016.

Scholes, Walter Vinton, and Marie V. Scholes. *The Foreign Policies of the Taft Administration.* University of Missouri Press, 1970.

Schonberger, Howard B. *Transportation to the Seaboard: The Communication Revolution and American Foreign Policy, 1860–1900.* Greenwood Publishing, 1971.

Schoonover, Thomas David. *Uncle Sam's War of 1898 and the Origins of Globalization.* University Press of Kentucky, 2003.

———. *The United States in Central America, 1860–1911: Episodes of Social Imperialism and Imperial Rivalry in the World System.* Duke University Press, 1991.

Schorske, Carl E. *German Social Democracy, 1905–1917: The Development of the Great Schism.* Harvard University Press, 1983.

Schriftgiesser, Karl. *The Gentleman from Massachusetts: Henry Cabot Lodge.* Little, Brown, 1944.

Schröder, Hans-Jürgen. *Confrontation and Cooperation: Germany and the United States in the Era of World War I, 1900–24.* Berg Publishers, 1993.

Schroeder, Paul W. *The Axis Alliance and Japanese American Relations, 1941.* Cornell University Press, 1961.

Schuker, Stephen A. *End of French Predominance in Europe: The Financial Crisis of 1924 and the Adoption of the Dawes Plan.* University of North Carolina Press, 1976.

Schulz, Gerhard. *Revolutions and Peace Treaties, 1917–1920.* Routledge, 1967.

Schwabe, Klaus. *Woodrow Wilson, Revolutionary Germany, and Peacemaking, 1918–1919: Missionary Diplomacy and the Realities of Power.* Translated by Rita Kimber and Robert Kimber. University of North Carolina Press, 1985.

Scott, James Brown. "The Central American Peace Conference of 1907." *American Journal of International Law* 2, no. 1 (January 1908): 121–43.

Seaman, L. C. B. *From Vienna to Versailles.* Routledge, 1990.

Self, Robert. *Britain, America and the War Debt Controversy: The Economic Diplomacy of an Unspecial Relationship, 1917–45.* Routledge, 2006.

Semmel, Bernard. *Imperialism and Social Reform: English Social-Imperial Thought, 1895–1914.* Gregg Revivals, 1983.

Service, Robert. *Lenin: A Biography.* Belknap Press of Harvard University Press, 2000.

Seton-Watson, Hugh. *The Russian Empire, 1801–1917.* Clarendon Press, 1967.

Seward, Frederick William. *Reminiscences of a War-Time Statesman and Diplomat, 1830–1915.* Wentworth, 2019.

Sharp, Alan. *The Versailles Settlement: Peacemaking in Paris.* St. Martin's Press, 1991.

Shewmaker, Kenneth E. *Americans and Chinese Communists, 1927–1945: A Persuading Encounter.* Cornell University Press, 1971.

Shippee, Lester Burrell. "Germany and the Spanish-American War." *American Historical Review* 30, no. 4 (July 1925): 754–77.

Shlaes, Amity. *Coolidge.* Harper, 2013.

Shotwell, James T. *The Autobiography of James T. Shotwell.* Bobbs-Merrill, 1961.

Silberman, Bernard S., and H. D. Harootunian, eds. *Japan in Crisis: Essays on Taishō Democracy.* University of Michigan Press, 1999.

Silverman, Dan P. *Reconstructing Europe After the Great War.* Harvard University Press, 1982.

Simms, Brendan. *Hitler: A Global Biography.* Basic Books, 2019.

Simms, Brendan, and Charlie Laderman. *Hitler's American Gamble: Pearl Harbor and Germany's March to Global War.* Basic Books, 2021.

Simonds, Frank H. *The ABC of War Debts and the Seven Popular Delusions About Them.* Harper & Brothers, 1933.

———. *American Foreign Policy in the Post-War Years.* Johns Hopkins Press, 1935.

———. *Can America Stay at Home?* Harper & Brothers, 1932.

———. *History of the World War.* Doubleday, Page, 1919.

———. *How Europe Made Peace Without America.* William Heinemann and Doubleday, Page, 1927.

Simonds, Frank H., and Brooks Emeny. *The Great Powers in World Politics: International Relations and Economic Nationalism.* American Book Company, 1935.

———. *The Price of Peace: The Challenge of Economic Nationalism.* Harper & Brothers, 1935.

Siracusa, Joseph M. *New Left Diplomatic Histories and Historians: The American Revisionists.* Kennikat Press, 1973.

Skidelsky, Robert Jacob Alexander. *John Maynard Keynes: Fighting for Freedom, 1937–1946.* Penguin Books, 2002.

Sklar, Martin J. *The Corporate Reconstruction of American Capitalism, 1890–1916: The Market, the Law, and Politics.* Cambridge University Press, 1988.

———. *The United States as a Developing Country: Studies in U.S. History in the Progressive Era and the 1920s.* Cambridge University Press, 1992.

Small, Melvin. *Democracy and Diplomacy: The Impact of Domestic Politics in U.S. Foreign Policy, 1789–1994.* Johns Hopkins University Press, 1995.

Smith, Daniel Malloy. *The Great Departure: The United States and World War I, 1914–1920.* J. Wiley, 1965.

Smith, Denis Mack. *Mussolini's Roman Empire.* Viking Press, 1976.

Smith, Ephraim K. "'A Question from Which We Could Not Escape': William McKinley and the Decision to Acquire the Philippine Islands." *Diplomatic History* 9, no. 4 (Fall 1985): 363–75.

Smith, Helmut Walser, *The Continuities of German History.* Cambridge University Press, 2008.

———. ed. *Protestants, Catholics and Jews in Germany, 1800–1914.* Berg Publishers, 2001.

Smith, Jean Edward. *FDR.* Random House, 2007.

Smith, Leonard V., Stéphane Audoin-Rouzeau, and Annette Becker. *France and the Great War.* Cambridge University Press, 2003.

Smith, Patrick. *Japan: A Reinterpretation.* Random House, 1999.

Smith, Sara R. *The Manchurian Crisis, 1931–1932: A Tragedy in International Relations.* Columbia University Press, 1948.

Smith, Tony. *The Pattern of Imperialism: The United States, Great Britain, and the Late-Industrializing World Since 1815.* Cambridge University Press, 1981.

Smuts, Jan Christian. *The League of Nations: A Practical Suggestion.* Hodder and Stoughton, 1918.

Snyder, Timothy. *Black Earth: The Holocaust as History and Warning.* Tim Duggan Books, 2016.

———. *Bloodlands: Europe Between Hitler and Stalin.* Basic Books, 2010.

Sobel, Robert. *Coolidge, An American Enigma.* Regnery Publishing, 1998.

Sprout, Harold Hance, and Margaret Tuttle Sprout. *The Rise of American Naval Power, 1776–1918.* Naval Institute Press, 1980.

————. *Toward a New Order of Sea Power: American Naval Policy and the World Scene, 1918–1922.* Greenwood Press, 1943.

Spykman, Nicholas J. *America's Strategy in World Politics: The United States and the Balance of Power.* Routledge, 2007.

————. "Geography and Foreign Policy I." *American Political Science Review* 32, no. 1 (February 1938): 28–50.

————. "Geography and Foreign Policy II." *American Political Science Review* 32, no. 2 (April 1938): 213–36.

Stead, W. T. *The Americanization of the World; or, The Trend of the Twentieth Century.* Andesite Press, 2017. First published in 1901 by H. Markley.

Stedman, Andrew David. *Alternatives to Appeasement: Neville Chamberlain and Hitler's Germany.* I.B. Tauris, 2011.

Steel, Ronald. *Walter Lippmann and the American Century.* Little, Brown, 1980.

Steiner, Zara. *The Lights That Failed: European International History, 1919–1933.* Oxford University Press, 2005.

————. *The Triumph of the Dark: European International History, 1933–1939.* Oxford University Press, 2011.

Steiner, Zara, and Keith Neilson. *Britain and the Origins of the First World War.* Red Globe Press, 2003.

Sternhell, Zeev. *The Birth of Fascist Ideology.* Translated by David Maisel. Princeton University Press, 1995.

Stevenson, David. *The First World War and International Politics.* Oxford University Press, 1988.

————. *French War Aims Against Germany, 1914–1919.* Oxford University Press, 1982.

Stewart, Robert B. "Treaty-Making Procedure in the United Kingdom." *American Political Science Review* 32, no. 4 (August 1938): 655–69.

Stid, Daniel D. *The President as Statesman: Woodrow Wilson and the Constitution.* University Press of Kansas, 1998.

Stiller, Jesse H. *George S. Messersmith, Diplomat of Democracy.* University of North Carolina Press, 1987.

Stimson, Henry L. *American Policy in Nicaragua: The Lasting Legacy.* Markus Wiener, 1991.

Stimson, Henry L., and McGeorge Bundy. *On Active Service in Peace & War.* Harper & Brothers, 1947.

Stoler, Mark A. *Allies in War: Britain and America Against the Axis Powers, 1940–1945.* Hodder Arnold, 2005.

Stone, Ralph A. *The Irreconcilables: The Fight Against the League of Nations.* University Press of Kentucky, 1970.

————, ed. *Wilson and the League of Nations: Why America's Rejection?* Holt, Rinehart and Winston, 1957.

Stossel, Scott. "The Other Edmund Wilson." *The American Prospect,* November 2001.

Strachan, Hew. *The First World War.* Viking, 2003.

Strong, Josiah. *Our Country: Its Possible Future and Its Present Crisis.* Baker & Taylor, 1885.

————. *The United States and the Future of the Anglo-Saxon Race.* Saxon and Co., 1889.

Strouse, Jean. *Morgan: American Financier.* Random House, 1999.

Stürmer, Michael. *The German Empire.* Weidenfeld & Nicolson, 2000.

Sullivan, Mark. *Our Times: The United States, 1900–1925.* 6 vols. Charles Scribner's Sons, 1926–1935.

Sun, Youli. *China and the Origins of the Pacific War, 1931–41.* Palgrave Macmillan, 1993.

Tansill, Charles Callan. *Back Door to War: The Roosevelt Foreign Policy 1933–1941.* Henry Regnery, 1952.

———. *The Foreign Policy of Thomas F. Bayard, 1885–1897.* Fordham University Press, 1940.

Tardieu, André. *The Truth About the Treaty.* Bobbs-Merrill, 1921.

Taylor, A. J. P. *English History, 1914–1945.* Oxford University Press, 1978.

———. *A History of the First World War.* Berkley Publishing, 1963.

———. *The Origins of the Second World War.* Hamilton, 1961.

———. *The Struggle for Mastery in Europe, 1848–1918.* Clarendon Press, 1954.

Taylor, Edmond. *The Fall of the Dynasties: The Collapse of the Old Order, 1905–1922.* Doubleday, 1963.

Thayer, William Roscoe, and John Hay. *The Life and Letters of John Hay.* 2 vols. Houghton Mifflin, 1915.

Thelen, David P. *Robert M. La Follette and the Insurgent Spirit.* Little, Brown, 1976.

Thomas, Evan. *The War Lovers: Roosevelt, Lodge, Hearst, and Rush to Empire, 1898.* Little, Brown & Co., 2010.

Thomas, Martin. *The French Colonial Mind.* Vol. 1, *Mental Maps of Empire and Colonial Encounters.* University of Nebraska Press, 2011.

———. *The French Colonial Mind.* Vol. 2, *Violence, Military Encounters, and Colonialism.* University of Nebraska Press, 2011.

Thompson, J. *Never Call Retreat: Theodore Roosevelt and the Great War.* Palgrave Macmillan, 2014.

Thompson, John A. *Reformers and War: American Progressive Publicists and the First World War.* Cambridge University Press, 1987.

———. *A Sense of Power: The Roots of America's Global Role.* Cornell University Press, 2015.

———. *Woodrow Wilson.* Longman, 2002.

Thompson, John M. *Russia, Bolshevism, and the Versailles Peace.* Princeton University Press, 2016.

Thomson, James C., Jr. "The Role of the Department of State." In *Pearl Harbor as History: Japanese-American Relations, 1931–1941,* edited by Dorothy Borg and Shumpei Okamoto. Columbia University Press, 1973.

Thomson, James C., Jr., Peter W. Stanley, and John Curtis Perry. *Sentimental Imperialists: The American Experience in East Asia.* Harper & Row, 1981.

Thorne, Christopher. *Allies of a Kind: The United States, Britain and the War Against Japan, 1941–1945.* Oxford University Press, 1978.

———. *The Approach of War, 1938–1939.* St. Martin's Press, 1967.

———. *The Limits of Foreign Policy: The West, the League, and the Far Eastern Crisis, 1931–1933.* Putnam, 1973.

Thornton, A. P. *The Imperial Idea and Its Enemies: A Study in British Power.* Macmillan, 1959.

Thorsen, Niels. *The Political Thought of Woodrow Wilson, 1875–1910.* Princeton University Press, 1988.

Tilchin, William N. *Theodore Roosevelt and the British Empire: A Study in Presidential Statecraft.* St. Martin's Press, 1997.

Tillman, Seth P. *Anglo-American Relations at the Paris Peace Conference of 1919.* Princeton University Press, 2016.

Toland, John. *The Rising Sun: The Decline and Fall of the Japanese Empire, 1936–1945.* Random House, 1970.

Tomes, Jason. *Balfour and Foreign Policy: The International Thought of a Conservative Statesman.* Cambridge University Press, 1997.

Tompkins, E. Berkeley. *Anti-Imperialism in the United States: The Great Debate, 1890–1920.* University of Pennsylvania Press, 1970.

Tooze, Adam. *The Deluge: The Great War, America and the Remaking of the Global Order, 1916–1931.* Viking, 2014.

———. *The Wages of Destruction: The Making and Breaking of the Nazi Economy.* Viking, 2007.

Trani, Eugene P., and David L. Wilson. *The Presidency of Warren G. Harding.* Regents Press of Kansas, 1977.

Trask, David F. *The United States in the Supreme War Council: American War Aims and Inter-Allied Strategy, 1917–1918.* Wesleyan University Press, 1961.

———. *The War with Spain in 1898.* Macmillan, 1981.

Trefousse, Hans L. *Germany and America: Essays on Problems of International Relations and Immigration.* Columbia University Press, 1980.

———. *Germany and American Neutrality, 1939–1941.* Octagon Books, 1969.

Trilling, Lionel. *The Liberal Imagination: Essays on Literature and Society.* Viking Press, 1950.

Tuchman, Barbara W. *The Zimmermann Telegram.* Viking Press, 1958.

Tucker, Robert W. *Woodrow Wilson and the Great War: Reconsidering America's Neutrality, 1914–1917.* University of Virginia Press, 2007.

Tumulty, Joseph P. *Woodrow Wilson As I Know Him.* HardPress Publishing, 2012.

Turner, Henry Ashby, Jr. *Stresemann and the Politics of the Weimar Republic.* Princeton University Press, 1963.

Ulam, Adam B. *Expansion & Coexistence: The History of Soviet Foreign Policy, 1917–67.* Praeger, 1968.

Ullman, Richard Henry. *Anglo-Soviet Relations, 1917–1921.* Vol. 1, *Intervention and the War.* Princeton University Press, 2019.

Ullrich, Volker. *Eight Days in May: The Final Collapse of the Third Reich.* Translated by Jefferson S. Chase. Liveright, 2021.

Unger, Nancy C. *Fighting Bob La Follette: The Righteous Reformer.* University of North Carolina Press, 2003.

Utley, Jonathan G. *Going to War with Japan, 1937–1941.* Fordham University Press, 2005.

Van Alstyne, Richard W. *American Crisis Diplomacy: The Quest for Collective Security, 1918–1952.* Stanford University Press, 1952.

———. "Private American Loans to the Allies, 1914–1916." *Pacific Historical Review* 2, no. 2 (June 1933): 180–93.

———. *The Rising American Empire.* Oxford University Press, 1960.

van Riel, Arthur, and Arthur Schram. "Weimar Economic Decline, Nazi Economic Recovery, and the Stabilization of Political Dictatorship." *Journal of Economic History* 53, no. 2 (March 1993): 71–105.

Varg, Paul A. *America, from Client State to World Power: Six Major Transitions in United States Foreign Relations.* University of Oklahoma Press, 1990.

———. *The Making of a Myth: The United States and China, 1897–1912.* Greenwood Press, 1980.

Veblen, Thorstein. *Imperial Germany and the Industrial Revolution.* Franklin Classics, 2018.

Verhey, Jeffrey. *The Spirit of 1914: Militarism, Myth and Mobilization in Germany.* Cambridge University Press, 2000.

Villard, Oswald Garrison. *Fighting Years: Memoirs of a Liberal Editor.* Harcourt, Brace and Company, 1939.

———. "Wanted: A Sane Defense Policy." *Harper's Magazine,* April 1939.

Vinson, John Chalmers. *The Parchment Peace: The United States and the Washington Conference, 1921–1922.* University of Georgia Press, 1955.

———. *Referendum for Isolation: Defeat of Article Ten of the League of Nations Covenant.* University of Georgia Press, 1961.

———. *William Borah and the Outlawry of War.* University of Georgia Press, 1957.

Von Eschen, Penny M. *Race Against Empire: Black Americans and Anticolonialism, 1937–1957.* Cornell University Press, 1997.

Von Feilitzsch, Heribert. *The Secret War Council: The German Fight Against the Entente in America in 1914.* Henselstone Verlag, 2015.

Walker, William O. *Opium and Foreign Policy: The Anglo-American Search for Order in Asia, 1912–1954.* University of North Carolina Press, 2011.

Wall, Joseph Frazier. *Andrew Carnegie.* University of Pittsburgh Press, 1989.

Wallace, Max. *The American Axis: Henry Ford, Charles Lindbergh, and the Rise of the Third Reich.* St. Martin's Press, 2003.

Walton, Gary M., and Hugh Rockoff. *History of the American Economy.* Cengage Learning, 2013.

Walworth, Arthur. *America's Moment, 1918: American Diplomacy at the End of World War I.* W. W. Norton, 1977.

———. *Wilson and His Peacemakers: American Diplomacy at the Paris Peace Conference, 1919.* W. W. Norton, 1986.

Ward, Adolphus William, and George Peabody Gooch, eds. *The Cambridge History of British Foreign Policy, 1783–1919.* 3 vols. Cambridge University Press, 2011.

Ward, Geoffrey C., and Dayton Duncan. *Mark Twain.* New York, 2001.

Ward, Robert D. "The Origin and Activities of the National Security League, 1914–1919." *Mississippi Valley Historical Review* 47, no. 1 (June 1960): 51–65.

Warren, Cohen. *New Frontiers in American–East Asian Relations.* Columbia University Press, 1983.

Warth, Robert D. *The Allies and the Russian Revolution.* Duke University Press, 1954.

Watts, Stephen. *The People's Tycoon: Henry Ford and the American Century.* Alfred A. Knopf, 2005.

Wehler, Hans-Ulrich. *The German Empire, 1871–1918.* Translated by Kim Traynor. Berg Publishers, 1985.

Weigley, Russell F. *A Great Civil War: A Military and Political History, 1861–1865.* Indiana University Press, 2004.

———. *History of the United States Army.* B. T. Batsford, 1968.

Weinberg, Gerhard L. "The Defeat of Germany in 1918 and the European Balance of Power." *Central European History* 2, no. 3 (September 1969): 248–60.

———. *The Foreign Policy of Hitler's Germany: Diplomatic Revolution in Europe, 1933–36.* University of Chicago Press, 1970.

———. *The Foreign Policy of Hitler's Germany: Starting World War II, 1937–1939.* University of Chicago Press, 1980.

———. *Hitler's Foreign Policy: The Road to World War II, 1933–1939.* Enigma, 2005.

———. "Hitler's Image of the United States." *American Historical Review* 69, no. 4 (July 1964): 1006–21.

———. *Visions of Victory: The Hopes of Eight World War II Leaders.* Cambridge University Press, 2005.

———. *A World at Arms: A Global History of World War II.* Cambridge University Press, 2005.

Weitz, Eric D. *Weimar Germany: Promise and Tragedy.* Princeton University Press, 2007.

Welch, Richard E. *The Presidencies of Grover Cleveland.* University Press of Kansas, 1988.

———. *Response to Imperialism: The United States and the Philippine-American War, 1899–1902.* University of North Carolina Press, 1979.

Welles, Sumner. *The Time for Decision.* Harper & Brothers, 1944.

Wells, H. G. *The Shape of Things to Come.* Macmillan, 1933.

———. *The War That Will End War.* Duffield & Company, 1914.

Wertheim, Stephen. "The League That Wasn't: American Designs for a Legalist-Sanctionist League of Nations and the Intellectual Origins of International Organization, 1914–1920." *Diplomatic History* 35, no. 5 (November 2011): 797–836.

Wesseling, H. L. *The European Colonial Empires, 1815–1919.* Translated by Diane Webb. Pearson/Longman, 2004.

Weyl, Walter E. *American World Policies.* Forgotten Books, 2018.

Wheeler, Gerald E. *Prelude to Pearl Harbor: The United States Navy and the Far East, 1921–1931.* Literary Licensing, 2012.

Wheeler-Bennett, John W. *Brest-Litovsk: The Forgotten Peace, March 1918.* W. W. Norton, 1971.

Whitaker, Arthur Preston. *The Western Hemisphere Idea: Its Rise and Decline.* Cornell University Press, 1954.

White, Donald Wallace, and Donald Jerry White. *The American Century: The Rise and Decline of the United States as a World Power.* Yale University Press, 1996.

Whyte, Kenneth. *Hoover: An Extraordinary Life in Extraordinary Times.* Alfred A. Knopf, 2017.

Widenor, William C. *Henry Cabot Lodge and the Search for an American Foreign Policy.* University of California Press, 1980.

Wiebe, Robert H. *The Search for Order, 1877–1920.* Hill and Wang, 1967.

Wilcox, Francis O. "American Government and Politics: The Neutrality Fight in Congress, 1939." *American Political Science Review,* vol. 33, no. 5 (October 1939): 811–25.

Williams, R. Hal. *Years of Decision: American Politics in the 1890s.* Waveland Press, 1978.

Williams, William Appleman. "China and Japan: A Challenge and a Choice of the Nineteen Twenties." *Pacific Historical Review* 26, no. 3 (August 1956): 259–79.

———. *The Roots of the Modern American Empire: A Study of the Growth and Shaping of Social Consciousness in a Marketplace Society.* Random House, 1969.

———. *The Tragedy of American Diplomacy.* World Publishing, 1959.

Williamson, David G. *The Age of the Dictators: A Study of the European Dictatorships, 1918–53.* Pearson/Longman, 2007.

Wilson, Ann Marie. "In the Name of God, Civilization, and Humanity: The United States and the Armenian Massacres of the 1890s." *Le Mouvement Social.* 2, no. 227 (2009).

Wilson, Hugh R. *Diplomat Between Wars.* Longmans, Green, 1941.

Wilson, Joan Hoff. *American Business and Foreign Policy: 1920–1933.* University of Kentucky Press, 1971.

———. *Herbert Hoover: Forgotten Progressive.* Little, Brown, 1975.

Winkler, Heinrich August. *The Age of Catastrophe: A History of the West, 1914–1945.* Translated by Stewart Spencer. Yale University Press, 2015.

———. *Germany.* Vol. 2, *The Long Road West 1933–1990,* translated by Alexander J. Sager. Oxford University Press, 2006.

———. *Germany.* Vol. 1, *The Long Road West, 1789–1933,* translated by Alexander J. Sager. Oxford University Press, 2006.

Winter, J. M., and Antoine Prost. *The Great War in History: Debates and Controversies, 1914 to the Present.* Cambridge University Press, 2005.

Wohl, Robert. *The Generation of 1914.* Harvard University Press, 1979.

Wolfers, Arnold. *Britain and France Between Two Wars: Conflicting Strategies of Peace from Versailles to WWII.* W. W. Norton, 1968.

———. *Discord and Collaboration: Essays on International Politics.* Johns Hopkins University Press, 1979.

Wortman, Marc. *1941: Fighting the Shadow War; A Divided America in a World at War.* Atlantic Monthly Press, 2016.

Wright, Gordon. *The Ordeal of Total War, 1939–1945.* Harper & Row, 1968.

Wunderlin, Clarence, Jr., ed. *The Papers of Robert A. Taft.* Vol. 1, *1889–1938.* Kent State University Press, 2001.

———, ed. *The Papers of Robert A. Taft.* Vol. 2, *1939–1944.* Kent State University Press, 2001.

Wynn, Neil A. *From Progressivism to Prosperity: World War I and American Society.* Holmes & Meier, 1987.

Yagami, Kazuo. *Konoe Fumimaro and the Failure of Peace in Japan, 1937–1941: A Critical Appraisal of the Three-Time Prime Minister.* McFarland, 2006.

Yates, Louis A. R. *United States and French Security, 1917–1921: A Study in American Diplomatic History.* Twayne, 1957.

Young, Katsu H. "The Nomonhan Incident: Imperial Japan and the Soviet Union." *Monumenta Nipponica* 22, no. 1/2 (1968): 82–102.

Young, Louise. *Japan's Total Empire: Manchuria and the Culture of Wartime Imperialism.* University of California Press, 1998.

Young, Marilyn Blatt. *The Rhetoric of Empire: American China Policy, 1895–1901.* Harvard University Press, 1968.

Young, Robert J. *France and the Origins of the Second World War.* St. Martin's Press, 1996.

Zabriskie, Edward H. *American-Russian Rivalry in the Far East: A Study in Diplomacy and Power Politics, 1895–1914.* University of Pennsylvania Press, 2021.

Zakaria, Fareed. *From Wealth to Power: The Unusual Origins of America's World Role.* Princeton University Press, 1999.

Zelikow, Philip. *The Road Less Traveled: The Secret Battle to End the Great War, 1916–1917.* PublicAffairs, 2021.

———. "Why Did America Cross the Pacific? Reconstructing the U.S. Decision to Take the Philippines, 1898–99." *Texas National Security Review* 1, no. 1 (November 2017): 36–67.

Zelikow, Philip D., and Condoleezza Rice. *Germany Unified and Europe Transformed: A Study in Statecraft.* Harvard University Press, 1997.

Zieger, Robert H. *America's Great War: World War I and the American Experience.* Rowman & Littlefield, 2000.

Zimmermann, Warren. *First Great Triumph: How Five Americans Made Their Country a World Power.* Farrar, Straus and Giroux, 2002.

Zuckerman, Larry. *The Rape of Belgium: The Untold Story of World War I.* New York University Press, 2004.

INDEX

Abbott, Lyman, 30, 39
Abdul Hamid II, 24
Abe, Nobuyuki, 430–32, 589n88
Abraham Lincoln Brigade, 365, 578n43
Acheson, Dean, 283, 442, 549n15, 590n13, 591n21
Adams, Brook, 33
Adams, Henry, 471n9, 493n34
Adams, John, 27
Adams, John Quincy, 28, 37
Addams, Jane, 143, 329, 510n23, 523n26, 545n25
Afghanistan, 91
Africa, 32, 63, 64, 68, 86, 87, 90–92, 247, 313, 377, 418, 456
Afrika Korps, 418
Aguinaldo, Emilio, 47, 53–55, 58, 61
Aiken, George, 412
Albania, 396
Albert, Heinrich F., 135
Albert Papers, 135–38
Albert I of Belgium, 31, 100–102, 507n69
Aldrich, Nelson, 475n23
Alexander I of Russia, 463
Algeciras, 93
Algeria, 63
Allen, Henry T., 271, 276–79, 287–88, 302
Allen, William V., 475n14
alliance system, 230–31, 236, 237, 381
    as basis of World War I, 230, 264
    League of Nations and, 230, 231, 236
Allison, William, 475n23
Alsace, 153, 164, 201, 204, 211, 215, 222–24, 291, 515n9
Amau doctrine, 357
Ambrosius, Lloyd, 535n103

America First Committee, 412–13, 452, 582n42, 582n44, 586n89
American Bar Association, 268
American exceptionalism, 254
American Expeditionary Force, 196, 453
American Federation of Labor, 203
American Red Cross, 34, 35
American Revolution, 25, 28, 90
anarchists, 248
Andrew Jackson Veterans Democratic Club, 394
Anglo-Saxons, 26, 27, 32, 48, 89, 90, 103, 106, 107, 129, 134, 221, 225, 295, 406, 407, 582n44
Anschluss (German annexation of Austria), 291, 299–300, 378–80, 382, 388, 422, 430
Anti-Comintern Pact, 358, 429, 437
Antwerp, 131
appeasement, 376
    Chamberlain's Munich agreement, 376–85, 387, 390, 411, 428, 430, 445, 460, 584nn61, 62
    with Japan, 431, 445
Arabic, SS, 126, 127, 138, 507n42
arbitration, 33–34, 72, 86, 97, 98, 125, 150, 232, 233, 249, 266, 289 306–7, 516n14
aristocracies, 24–25
Arizona, USS, 52
Armenian genocide, 34–35, 38, 39, 132, 474n7
arms industry, 353–54, 393, 407
Army, U.S., 23, 81, 456
    Cuba occupied by, 43
    Native Americans and, 23

A NOTE ON THE TYPE

The text of this book was set in a typeface called Times New Roman, designed by Stanley Morison (1889–1967) for *The Times* (London) and first introduced by that newspaper in 1932.

Composed by North Market Street Graphics,
Lancaster, Pennsylvania

Printed and bound by Berryville Graphics,
Berryville, Virginia

Designed by Michael Collica